Praise for **thepurplebook**®

"The Bible of online shopping guides." —*Kirkus Reviews*

"Shopaholics, rejoice! Like the Yellow Pages—but, well, purple—this book is witty and comprehensive." —*Boston Herald*

"A Google for shoppers....The sleekly designed book brims with helpful cross-references and hints for getting the most out of an online shopping experience." —*Publishers Weekly*

"A well-planned guidebook, much like the popular dining directories compiled by Zagat—only bigger." —*Los Angeles Times*

"A consumer haven." —*Bookreporter.com*

D1264736

thepurplebook®

the definitive guide to exceptional online shopping

2007 edition

WARNER BOOKS

NEW YORK BOSTON

thepurplebook®

Editor-in-chief & Founder
Hillary Mendelsohn

Co-Founder
Lawrence Butler

Author
Ian Anderson

Art Director
Jerome Curchod

Technology Director
Christian Giangreco

Copyright © 2007 by **thepurplebook** LLC
All rights reserved. Except as permitted under the U.S. Copyright Act of 1976, no part of this publication may be reproduced, distributed, or transmitted in any form or by any means, or stored in a database or retrieval system, without the prior written permission of the publisher.

thepurplebook is a registered trademark of **thepurplebook** LLC

Warner Books

Hachette Book Group USA
1271 Avenue of the Americas, New York, NY 10020
Visit our Web site at www.HachetteBookGroupUSA.com.

Printed in the United States of America

First Edition: February 2007
10 9 8 7 6 5 4 3 2 1

Warner Books and the "W" logo are trademarks of Time Warner Inc. or an affiliated company. Used under license by Hachette Book Group USA, which is not affiliated with Time Warner Inc.

ISBN-10 0-446-69703-6
ISBN-13 978-0-446-69703-3

Cover and interior design by Jerome Curchod

This book is dedicated to the following people, who continue to support, encourage, inspire and tolerate me:

Michael—thank you for your love, thoughtfulness, enthusiasm, ideas and patience;
to my kids—I couldn't live without your love, laughter and great big hugs;
and to my Mom and Dad—thank you for always being there to cheer me on, help me out, and lift me up.

The love of my family is my greatest treasure and my most precious gift.

*

Over the past six years, I have assembled a special group of people that have become my team. Together we have turned a good idea into a great business! I appreciate them all for their individual gifts:

Larry—for neverending confidence, support, ideas and guidance;
Ian—for your exceptional talent, beautifully written words, humor, loyal dedication and kindred spirit;
Jerome—for your inspired visual sensibility;
Christian—for your technical prowess.

This wouldn't be any fun without you. I count on your talent, your gifts and most of all your friendship.

I am truly grateful to have you all in my world.

acknowledgments

With sincere gratitude and appreciation, I would like to thank the following people for their effort and dedication to make this book happen:

The Hachette Book Group USA
Jamie Raab and Harvey-Jane Kowal, thank you for your energy, your ideas and your support.
Natalie Kaire – Thank you for making the day-to-day process work so beautifully, you are a joy to work with.
Rebecca Isenberg, Elly Weisenberg, Margaret Wolf, Anna Maria Piluso, Brigid Pearson and the rest, your efforts are appreciated.

A special thank you to Luke Janklow and Bennet Ashley for keeping the dream real and finding us a wonderful new home.

To the newer members of the team, Kimberly Murray, Eric Philipson and Jeffrey Lim, thank you for all of your energy, talent and enthusiasm!

thepurplebook

TABLE OF CONTENTS

foreword

This has been a big year for us at thepurplebook. We have grown quite a bit, thanks to your interest and enthusiastic support. What began as frustrating encounter with a search engine six years ago, has become a powerful niche industry, informing and enticing those of you who want to know where to find the best shopping online. From our first edition ,released in October of 2003, to this, our fifth book, we have come a long way. With your help, we have successfully established **thepurplebook** as the go to source for the very best shopping the internet has to offer. The treasure hunt for exceptional sites is an endeavor I truly enjoy; the only hard part is that bookstore shelves have weight limits, so I can't always include every terrific site I find. The good news is, you can find all of the sites listed in previous books, along with some great new ones that didn't fit this edition, on our newly launched website **www.thepurplebook.com**.

In addition to the website, expansion has included our first specialty book: **thepurplebook baby**. This handy book covers maternity, baby and toddler needs, packed with great boutiques, specialty shops, necessities and fabulous gifts to outfit Baby or Mommy. Next up is our second specialty book, **thepurplebook wedding**, due in Spring 2007. You can count on more specialty books from us in the months and years to come.

TV came looking for **thepurplebook** this past year. ABC's *20/20* did a feature story on us, as did the *Today Show*, and there were lots of interviews on news programming across the country. Other unique and unanticipated opportunities in the past couple of years include writing the "Hot Sites" feature for *InStyle Magazine*, contributing to *Practical eCommerce*, some corporate consulting, and tons of print and media interviews. We've definitely been getting the word out, and big business has come a courtin'. But we think keeping our information objective and consistent is the key to earning and keeping your confidence and loyalty. Having the opportunity of a front-row seat to watch the fastest-growing retail sector connect with the needs and demands of people all over the globe has been fascinating and enlightening.

And somehow, every year, there are more new and interesting sites to look at. We have now researched well over 50,000 sites—thank goodness for high-speed connections! You can live almost anywhere and have access to almost everything at any time of the day or night. Shopping online is about convenience, access and discovery, and that is what we have aimed to deliver, and hopefully we've made it enjoyable along the way.

Feedback from readers and retailers has been invaluable, entertaining, insightful and encouraging. You have helped us to refine the book, turned us on to sites we hadn't come across (yes, there are a few we haven't seen), and turned us off to a few sites that were listed erroneously, and have been summarily removed from our books. We want to sincerely thank those of you who have contributed to make this the best edition yet, and encourage more of you to let us know what you think at **www.thepurplebook.com**. Happy Shopping!

Sincerely,

Hillary Mendelsohn
Editor In Chief

thepurplebook:
introduction

How do you improve on a good thing? This is a question we're constantly asked ourselves as we've delved deeper into this, our fourth edition of **thepurplebook**. See, the world wide web keeps growing, keeps getting better. Even after years of exploration we're constantly amazed at the riches we keep stumbling across, at the golden opportunities we're still uncovering. Improving on a good thing takes a lot of people, and a lot of hard work, and it's happening out there, every day, in cyberspace. In some ways, this magnificent growth makes it easy for us to improve each edition. In other ways, though, it makes it quite hard.

We started out on a mission to guide consumers to the internet's best shopping locations and, over time, deciding which sites were worthy became increasingly difficult. The continuing expansion of the world of e-commerce has forced us to make some tough decisions with each edition we publish, and we've had to let go of a few worthy sites each year, replacing them with something bigger, better or more distinctive. This isn't to say we don't still appreciate what they do, but there's only so much room on our pages.

Our solution has been to remove the big, famous, nationally known franchise site listings from the chapter pages of our book, and place them in easy-access lists following the introduction of each section. Likewise, we have used this space to list stellar sites that specialize in a single product or two, but not enough selection to compete with bigger stores. The result is a book filled with a slew of new family-run businesses, independent web enterprises and quirky, off-the-beaten-path shops that few of us would likely find without a little nudge in the right direction. When you add it all up we've come close to recommending 2,000 sites in this edition. As for the thousands of terrific sites we didn't mention... you can always search for them at **www.thepurplebook.com.**

>> thepurplebook REQUIREMENTS & STANDARDS

Finding just any online retailer is easy. Finding the good ones—that takes a bit of work. We've scoured search engines, message boards, magazines and web directories in search of great sites, and received recommendations from our readers and friends. Tens of thousands of web sites promised the best prices and the greatest selections, but we took a close look at each one, and held them up to the following list of requirements:

• **SECURE TRANSACTIONS** •Each site must offer a secure credit card transaction that can be completed in a single session. This means we disqualified any sites that only accept fax orders, email inquiries, payments over the phone or PayPal transactions. These methods of payment are both less secure and less reliable than those for sites operating encrypted commerce engines.

• **CUSTOMER SERVICE NUMBER** •Every site in **thepurplebook** must provide a working customer service number. Finding this number is not always easy, and in some cases we've had to play detective to get them, but we've included one with each site listed in this book, because we've found that a lack of direct contact with a service representative can ruin an otherwise satisfactory shopping experience.

• **OPEN BROWSING** •No site will be listed in **thepurplebook** that requires consumers to enter credit card numbers or other personal data before viewing its full catalog of products. Such sites usually intend to sell a customer's personal information for profit.

If an e-tailor met these requirements, we then subjected it to our own rigorous set of standards, scrutinizing each aspect of the site: Is it easy to use? Does it have a good selection? Are the prices good? Will it download in a reasonable amount of time? We whittled down the selection to include only the finest catalogs, the most beautiful web designs, the best bargains and that occasional ingenious purveyor of a product or service of such unique charm that we couldn't possibly leave it out. Our final tally includes brick-and-mortar stores that have established a viable online presence, manufacturers who have done the same, internet juggernauts that have managed to survive the dot-com backlash and small businesses, often individuals working out of their bedrooms, who've embraced the virtual marketplace in their pursuit of the American dream. It's a pretty good bunch, capable of fulfilling nearly any online shopping need you may have, and possibly turning you on to something new.

>> thepurplebook ONLINE SHOPPING FUNDAMENTALS

Make a habit of using these tips and precautions, and your online shopping experience will be easy, convenient, fruitful and, above all, safe.

• **USE ONE CREDIT CARD** • Dedicate a single credit card for all of your online purchases. This makes it especially easy to spot fraudulent and/or unauthorized charges.

• **PRINT A COPY** • To document your online purchases, print a copy of both your order page (before you click the Submit button) and your order confirmation (receipt) to save for your records.

• **SAVE ALL CORRESPONDENCE** • Online retailers should email a confirmation of your order and/or shipping information. Save these emails until you are fully satisfied with your purchase, as you may need to refer to this information if problems arise.

• **PROTECT YOURSELF AGAINST IDENTITY THEFT** • Never give out credit card numbers or any personal information via email. Emails are not secure, and identity thieves commonly pose as customer service representatives in order to acquire your payment information. Only submit personal data through a secure, encrypted web site.

• **REPORT FRAUD IMMEDIATELY** • If you suspect fraud or other mistakes, notify your credit card company and/or the Federal Trade Commission (877-382-4357) immediately, because identity thieves will not waste any time abusing your information.

• **USE THE CUSTOMER SERVICE NUMBER** • **thepurplebook** has provided a customer service phone number for every shopping site listed in the book. Do not hesitate to use them. If you have any question not addressed by the web site, speak to a customer service representative before placing an order (you may need to call during normal business hours).

• **USE THE COMMENTS BOX** • Most online order forms offer a comments box for special requests or any questions you may have. This will be the surest way of contacting the actual humans in charge of fulfilling your order, so that they can properly address your needs.

• **READ THE WEB SITE'S POLICIES** • Before you make a purchase, take note of the web site's return and exchange policies, as well as shipping, privacy and security, because once you place your order, you've agreed to their terms and conditions. The FAQ (Frequently Asked Questions) section of a web site often proves a good source of information.

• **AVOID UNWANTED SOLICITATIONS** • When entering your billing and email address, a lot of shopping sites will ask if you're interested in receiving catalogs and/or advertising materials from them and other sites. In most cases, the answer defaults to "Yes," and you'll need to actively change this answer to "No" if you hope to avoid junk mail and spam.

• **REPORT BAD BUSINESS PRACTICES** • If you do have a bad experience with an online retailer, make a report with the Better Business Bureau, at www.BBB.org.

 GENERAL INFORMATION & RESOURCES

These sites offer handy tools to help you with all your online shopping activities.

About.com	Encyclopedic resource of information and links
DIYnet.com	Instructional resource
eHow.com	Instructional resource
NetLingo.com	Glossary of internet terms
OnlineConverters.com	Measurements conversion
OAndA.com	Currency converter
WhatsItWorthToYou.com	Online appraisals

 BUSINESS & PRODUCT INFORMATION

The following sites may help you make wiser shopping decisions.

BBB.org	Better Business Bureau site
ConsumerReports.org	Consumer product information and reviews
CPSC.gov	Consumer Product Safety Commission
Recalls.gov	Consumer product recall information

 PERSONAL INFORMATION & SAFETY

The following URLs may help protect you from identity theft.

Consumer.gov/idtheft	Identity theft information and resources
Equifax.com	Obtain your credit report
Experian.com	Obtain your credit report
TransUnion.com	Obtain your credit report

 HELPFUL SERVICES

Here are some sites we've found handy in a variety of ways.

1800GotJunk.com	Junk removal
CreditCardGuide.org	Credit card information and service comparison
ExcessAccess.org	Donation of goods matches needs of nonprofits
MyUS.com	Forward packages to overseas address
ShopForDSL.com	Compare local internet service providers
USGlobalMail.com	Forward packages to overseas address

WHAT YOU CAN EXPECT...

We have assembled all of these sites into a single collection, indexed and split up into several categories to correspond with the nation's most common shopping needs, as follows:

ART & COLLECTIBLES

Whether you want to bid on the original masterworks of the century, poster your dorm room or add to your collection of kitsch, we have the online tools to help dress your surroundings in any mode, medium or era, across all price ranges.

CRAFTS & HOBBIES

Our newest category guides you to all manner of creative, educational and recreational activities, including domestic crafts, science experiments, artistic creation, musical performance, building models and more.

ENTERTAINMENT

Whatever your tastes, we have a listing for just the sort of music, movie or book you may want to find, whether you're seeking old (records, print, video) or new (CD, eBook, DVD) formats. Or, if you prefer a less passive pastime, you can find plenty of puzzles and games, as well as tickets to live performances/events.

EPICUREAN

Named for the sensuous embrace of luxurious living, this section features stores dedicated to grocery items, gourmet foods, vintage wines and fine cigars. While there's an obvious disparity between listings for health food and tobacco products, we have to figure that it all balances out.

GADGETS & ELECTRONICS

Improving life from the outside in, this category includes computer hardware and software, along with a lengthy list of electronics for your home or pocket, whether your aim is to enjoy music or to hold conversations over great distances. Then there are the whimsical, nonelectric devices that can accomplish stuff bare hands just never could.

HEALTH & BEAUTY

All the convenience of a corner drugstore, and all the glamour of a high-priced salon; in this section, you will find the pills, dressings and ointments it takes to keep your body healthy, as well as all the cosmetics, cleansers and fragrances you favor to keep yourself looking and feeling beautiful.

HOME & GARDEN

From home improvement to making your garden grow, this section comes complete with listings to help furnish any room in the house or landscape your grounds with flowers, latticework or even bodies of water.

LIFESTYLES & MEGASTORES

These are stores that don't fit the mold. Any of them might offer everything you want to buy in a single location. Some cater to a specific lifestyle or interest you may have, while others have simply assembled an eclectic array of merchandise. Either way, the benefits of these shops include wide selections and the optimization of shipping charges.

MATERNITY

Between special equipment and expert advice, the primary focus of this section is the comfort and health of parent and child. On the other hand, a thorough selection of fashionable clothing will help show off the radiance of impending motherhood during the nine months of changes. You'll have to see the Epicurean section to satisfy any odd food cravings, though.

MEN'S APPAREL

Clothes for any event, style or day of the week make for easy browsing with this list of man-friendly stores. If the appropriate dress involves a tie, no problem. If jeans are better suited to the activity, find them here. Whether the aim is to impress a woman, satisfy the boss or wile away the days in comfort, you can find your threads in the best way possible: fast.

MINORS (0-18)

From infants to teenagers, this section caters to children, whether you're doing the shopping for them or they're picking things out themselves. Toy stores will most likely be at the top of their lists, while parents might prefer the clothes or educational opportunities, any of which span a range of prices and interests.

PETS

For the animals with the greatest owners, these sites cover all the basics, like food and hygiene, and even manage to include a lot of indulgences, ranging from toys to furniture and even some clothing. A healthy, happy pet is a cinch, whether it walks, flies, crawls, swims or trots.

SENIORS

The tools and products found in this section address the lifestyle changes typically faced by those over the age of fifty-five. Most prominently featured are items that promote independent living, whether by combating the symptoms of a particular physical ailment or by increasing access to the world of technology.

SHOES & ACCESSORIES

True style includes every part of the body, from head to toe. With that in mind, this section offers everything from hats to shoes, alongside some jewelry, watches and eyewear, with handbags and wallets to stow it all in. Whatever the accoutrements, men and women alike will find some great ones here.

SPORTS & OUTDOORS

Physical lifestyles get more active with less effort thanks to these online shops devoted to home gyms, athletic equipment and outdoor gear. Whether you intend to trounce the competition, camp high up in the stratosphere or pursue your own body's limits, these listings will help.

STATIONERY & GIFTS

The Stationery portions of this section feature anything from personalized letterheads to invitations and greeting cards, while the Gifts that are offered include standards like flowers, baskets and confections, with a few innovative ideas thrown in for those tough-to-shop-for special occasions.

TRAVEL

Get out of town. Better yet, do it with ease and comfort. Here you can find several different means of booking flights, car rentals, hotel rooms and any other kind of accommodation you might require on your travels. Better still, outfit yourself with the right clothes, luggage and other gear, to make getting there nearly as fine as being there.

WOMEN'S APPAREL

Your wardrobe just got better. In this section, you will find an extensive selection of shops, featuring every layer of clothing between the world and your skin. Whether you're looking for lingerie, swimwear, outerwear or a killer evening gown, here you can easily find the best designers and/or the greatest bargains.

CHARITY

Have you got something to give? Here are some fine ways to devote yourself to the betterment of the planet, whether you're improving peoples' lives or saving the environment. If nothing else, in this section you'll discover that helping out is easier and more effective today than ever before.

HOW TO USE thepurplebook

While we've made every effort to be discriminating, the number of web sites listed in this book does exceed 1,600. Though these comprise a mere fraction of the tens of thousands of sites we viewed, we're well aware that it's a lot to handle. With this in mind, we've split the book into nineteen categories, and designed a system to make individual sites and products easier to locate. If you're looking for a good place to shop or find a gift, for example, you can browse the alphabetical site listings. If you have something more specific in mind, you can search one of our several indexes for products, companies or key words.

BROWSING

Within each category, **thepurplebook** site listings are arranged alphabetically by URL and presented along with a five-or-six-sentence review that should give you a general idea of what to expect from the site before ever logging on. Alongside these reviews, you will find icons that evaluate the site's service, selection and usability, as well as a list of key words describing the store's product selection.

Using the icons and key words, you can browse each category to find specific product types, or to locate stores that offer services like gift wrapping or overnight delivery. See the sample site listing below, and the descriptions on the following pages, for further details.

SAMPLE SITE LISTING

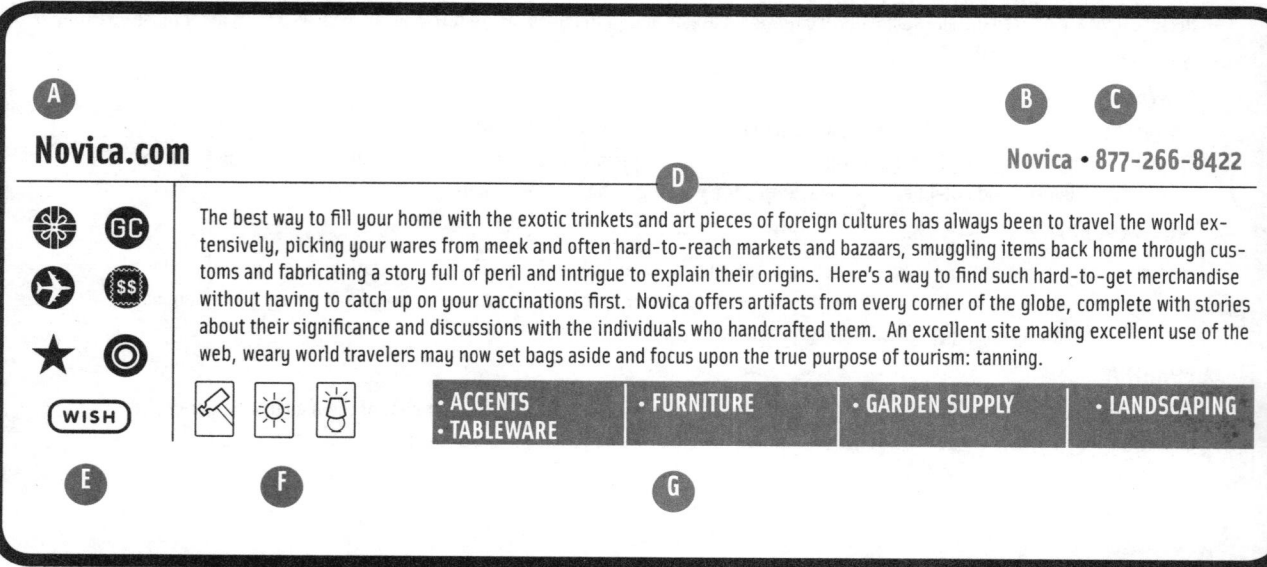

✳ UNDERSTANDING THE SITE LISTINGS

Ⓐ URL
Each site in this book has been listed alphabetically by its URL (internet address). We've left out the standard **http://www.** that precedes each domain name and extension. In other words, to visit Novica.com, go to the address bar in your browser and type in **http://www.Novica.com**.

Ⓑ COMPANY NAME
The company name often does not differ from the site's URL, especially in the case of exclusively online entities. Occasionally, though, a more familiar name may turn up here.

Ⓒ CUSTOMER SERVICE NUMBERS
We've listed each company's customer service phone number along with its site entry (some sites like to hide them). This should help if you can't log on to the site for some reason, or if you cannot easily find the number listed there. Oftentimes when things go wrong, using the web site's human support staff is more productive than sending emails.

Ⓓ REVIEW
These reviews are intended to offer some insight into the breadth and scope of the web site at hand, but more often than not have deteriorated into base humor and wry observation. This is wholly to be blamed on the writer, who admittedly does not often know a good thing when he sees it.

Ⓔ UNIVERSAL ICONS
The set of round Universal Icons found throughout the book depict some of the particulars about each store that may come in handy when deciding where to shop: shipping costs, overnight shipping, gift certificates, gift wrapping, user-friendliness, a star to indicate whether a site is exceptionally useful or unique and the word *Wish,* to designate sites offering wish lists or gift registries (see pages 20-21).

Ⓕ SECTION ICONS
The rectangular Section Icons specific to each chapter have been included to help you distinguish between specific types of stores commonly housed in each category. For example, an icon in the Shoes & Accessories section will pinpoint the shoe stores, whereas one in the Epicurean section will highlight gourmet foods.

Ⓖ KEY WORDS
At the bottom of each site listing, you will find a list of Key Words that offer general descriptions of the types of products available from that store. A quick scan of these words should give you a rough idea of whether a store has what you seek.

UNDERSTANDING THE ICONS

SHIPPING COSTS

A huge consideration when shopping online is the cost of shipping and handling. High fees can turn what seemed like a great deal into a waste of cash, whereas a cheap shipping policy can mean the difference between competitive prices.

 Free, Incentivized or Flat Rate Shipping – Sites marked by this icon either cover shipping costs, reduce the cost of shipping if you spend more or charge a single, preset amount to cover shipment of your entire order, regardless of cost or weight.

 Standard Shipping Rates – Sites covered by this icon either charge the same weight-based amount for shipping as determined by the carrier (usually UPS, FedEx, Airborne Express or the US Postal Service), or compute comparable rates based on the value of the purchase.

 Exorbitant or Unknown Shipping & Handling Fees – Sites tagged with this icon either charge excessive handling fees designed to pad their profit margins or do not inform you of an order's shipping charges until after a credit card has been used to make the purchase. A third category of these sites simply ship very large, heavy items that require special companies or even individual trucks, usually at great expense.

OVERNIGHT SHIPPING

 When you see this icon, the site in question offers the option of overnight shipping or next day delivery, in most cases at an extra charge, and often not on weekends. Bear in mind that sites usually have an early-afternoon or morning deadline for one-day delivery, and that time zones may consequently play a big role in your last-minute purchases.

GIFT CERTIFICATES

 This icon only appears when gift certificates are available for purchase, in either electronic or paper form. Electronic gift certificates will be sent to the recipient's email address, and therefore make excellent last-second gifts.

GIFT WRAPPING

 We offer an entire section of sites boasting great gift ideas, but really just about any site in this book has the perfect gift for somebody. Any site will also send your order in a plain brown box. Some will wrap it up a bit nicer (usually at an extra charge). Such sites are noted by this icon.

USER-FRIENDLINESS

Product selection is the most important aspect to building an online store, but presentation is often what sells, and if using a site to make a purchase is just too much work it may not be worth it. We've ranked each site's performance with the following three icons:

 These sites have gone the distance to make sure that you can find the products you need without hassle and order them with minimal difficulty, either through fancy web design or plain common sense. Or the site only has a handful of products to begin with and everything may be viewed or purchased on one page. Either way, we wish all the sites qualified for this rank, but very few did.

 Savvy web shoppers are used to the industry standard—a left-side menu of options, with a few more general choices thrown across the top of the page for good measure. Such sites warrant no complaints, as everything you need is laid out logically so that browsing and buying is easy on the mind, and only hard on the mouse-clicking finger.

 In some cases, these sites involve dramatic and failed attempts to create the virtual world's best new shopping technique. On the other end of the spectrum are the web designers who simply weren't up to the task. In between, we have the online shopkeepers who apparently didn't care, and scattered their products haphazardly across cyberspace for hackers to trip over. Whatever the case, these sites are often impossible to load, browse and/or order from. Ironically, these aberrations wouldn't have made the cut except that they're offering some of the best the web has to offer.

thepurplebook RECOMMENDS

 If you see this star next to a site you know that we found some reason to favor it over the rest. Either it stands out among its field of competitors with excellent offerings and design, or it stands alone by offering something unique and/or innovative to the realm of e-commerce.

WISH LISTS & REGISTRIES

 Our newest Icon will clue you in to sites offering wish lists, gift registries and bridal registries. These will allow you to browse and save all the products you want so that your friends and loved ones may browse your selection at their leisure and buy you the perfect gift every time. This is particularly useful when buying for children.

USING THE INDEXES

These indexes will help you track down specific products, stores and sites of interest in the most efficient manner.

KEY WORD INDEXES
Located in the introduction to each section you will find a key word index that can help you locate which stores carry particular types of products within that category.

PRODUCT INDEX (PAGE 614)
At the end of the book you will find a detailed listing of products and the corresponding names of sites that carry them. Note that this is not necessarily a comprehensive list, and that you will be able to find some of these products on sites not mentioned in the index. By the same token, using the key word indexes within each section, you are bound to find some products we missed. (Please note that, when using this index, general terms will refer to sites that carry an abundant variety of products, while specific terms will clue you in to dedicated and exemplary selections. For example, a site indexed to the word "accents (for the home)" will offer a great assortment of vases, throw pillows and room dividers. However, a site indexed to the term "accents, room dividers" may only be presumed to offer a decent variety of dividers, but won't necessarily offer vases or throw pillows).

BRAND NAME & COMPANY INDEX (PAGE 657)
This list of brand and company names, located at the end of the book, is simply meant to help you locate web sites for companies that may not otherwise be readily familiar.

URL INDEX (PAGE 673)
Also located at the end of the book, this index simply lists each of the site URLs in alphabetical order, regardless of category.

FIND ONLY WHAT YOU NEED... AND LET US KNOW WHAT YOU LIKE

We at **thepurplebook** are always looking for ways to improve this book directly, and welcome all constructive criticism, suggestions and ideas to help us do so. If you would like to submit a comment, look for the Suggest A Site or Contact Us links on our web site, www.thepurplebook.com. Or, fill out and submit the feedback form in the back of this book. Thank you, and happy shopping!

NOTES:

_____

_____

_____

_____

_____

_____

_____

_____

_____

_____

_____

_____

_____

_____

_____

_____

_____

_____

_____

_____

_____

NOTES:

_____

_____

_____

_____

_____

_____

_____

_____

_____

_____

_____

_____

_____

_____

_____

_____

_____

_____

Art & Collectibles

It's not often that shopping doubles as an enlightening pursuit, but for this first section of our book we've found many sites that prove as culturally enriching as they are convenient. After all, how many museums would you have to visit to view the same number of artworks you can see online in a single afternoon? Better yet, you're not subjected to anybody else's views of what fine art should be. Whether you're buying an original Picasso or a reproduction of dogs playing poker, when you shop online, there's nobody around to second-guess.

Of course, more than paintings can be found on the web sites featured in this section. We discovered a very healthy selection of sculpture, photography, posters and prints created by emerging artists, old masters and traditional craftsmen. Pottery, woodcarvings and other cultural artifacts may return less on your investment, but they're no less lovely, and in many cases purchasing them may even support a few starving artisans. If you're searching for artifacts that have already withstood the test of time, take a look at our bevy of online antique shops, which offer endless selections of beautiful relics, without forcing us to drive down endless backcountry roads. On the opposite end of the spectrum you'll find stores favoring kitsch and other pop culture collectibles that chronicle the times in stamp, coin, crystal, autograph and action figure form. Turns out, collecting art and collectibles can be a pretty indulgent pursuit, but there's a reason they call it enrichment.

TIPS ON BUYING ART & COLLECTIBLES ONLINE

These suggestions should help prevent your cultural purchases from offending the senses.

• **COLOR DISCREPANCIES** • Differences in monitor settings and digital image compression in most cases mean that the image you see online of a painting, print or poster may not match up precisely to the actual colors of the item. Usually, this difference is trivial.

• **CERTIFY AUTHENTICITY** • Original artwork, antiques, collectibles and memorabilia can be a very large investment. Online, as in person, it is very important that you receive a valid certificate of authenticity with your purchase. Make sure the online seller guarantees such certification before you make your purchase, and definitely make a phone call if you are uncertain.

• **CHECK FRAMING OPTIONS & COSTS** • In some cases, you may anticipate paying a lot for a specific item, and will be ready to make your online purchase. However, some merchants may include default framing options that run up the price of the work. When buying framed artwork, be sure you're not paying more for the frame than you are for the art itself.

• **SHIPPING INSURANCE** • As with any valuable long-distance purchase, you'll want to be sure your merchandise is insured during transit. This section in particular includes many fragile and/or one-of-a-kind pieces, and it's a safe bet to be covered in case your order shows up in pieces. When in doubt, call before ordering.

• **SHIPPING WEIGHTS & COSTS** • Heavy frames, bulky materials and odd sizes can significantly drive up the cost of shipping art items. Before you agree to a purchase, take note of the shipping methods and rates offered by the vendor, so you won't find too big a surprise on your credit card bill.

• **REMEMBER WHY YOU BUY** • Impulse buys are easy to make online, but if you're going to relish your art purchase, most of the time you'll want to take a moment to consider whether you're buying something because you appreciate its artistic sensibilities, or whether you simply think it will look cool filling an empty spot in your home. More important, you might want to take measurements to make sure the artwork in question will actually fit in that spot.

• **KNOW YOUR PRINTS** • The definition of the word *print* can be pretty vague, as it's commonly used to refer to lithographs, glicées, silk-screens, computer reproductions and more. When ordering a print, be sure to take note of its production technique.

• **CARE FOR YOUR INVESTMENTS** • Your original piece of art will quite likely increase in value over time (presuming you select wisely), so you'll want to stay well versed on preservation techniques and supplies for whichever medium you've decided to invest in. You may also want to take a moment to learn more about the artist, as spreading his or her name and story might help boost the value of your purchase.

SITES THAT MAY COME IN HANDY

The following URLs may be useful when you wish to trade in art, antiques or collectibles.

AntiqueAppraisals.ne	Antique appraisals online (detailed)
AntiqueCC.comt	Antique and collector pricing guides
ArtAntiqueDealersLeague.com	Locate art and antique dealers
ArtCyclopedia.com	Locate art museums and collections
ArtFact.com	Art auction catalogs and results
ArtMarketResearch.com	Art market valuations
ArtNet.com	Art gallery directory and news
AskArt.com	Information about American artists
ASOPA.com	Locate a portrait artist
AXA-Art.com	Art and collectibles insurance
Directiques.com	Locate art and antique dealers
Kovels.com	Antique and collectibles price guide
Linns.com	Collectible stamp resource
NAADAA.org	National Antique and Art Dealers Association of America
NAWCC.org	Clock and watch collectors resource
PCGS.com	Collectible coin price guide
WhatsItWorthToYou.com	Antique appraisals online (general)

MUSEUM GIFT SHOPS & GALLERY SITES

These sites represent international museums and their respective gift shops.

AMNH.org
ArtInstituteShop.org
AsiaSociety.org
BrooklynArt.org
FolkArtMuseum.org
Frick.org
Getty.edu
Guggenheim.org
Louvre.fr
MetMuseum.org
MFA.org

MOCA.org
MoMAStore.org
NeueGallerie.org
NGA.gov
NYBGShopInTheGarden.org
SalvadorDaliMuseum.org
SFMoMA.org
Smithsonianstore.com
WarholStore.com
Whitney.org

*For in-depth reviews of these sites and more, check out **www.thepurplebook.com**.

SECTION ICON LEGEND

Use the following guide to understand the rectangular icons that appear throughout this section.

ANTIQUES

Either we're getting older, or antiques are getting newer. Regardless, whenever technology passes an object by, it becomes antiquated, the irony being that its value may rise. We found sites offering a wider range of antique objects and furniture than we can list here. Suffice it to say, if it's out there, it's online.

COLLECTIBLES

Their value may be monetary, sentimental, decorative, based in hobby or invested against the future. The objects denoted by this symbol may be stamps, coins, baseball cards, collector's plates, porcelain figurines or any variety of similar items people see fit to collect.

ORIGINAL ARTWORK

This icon is meant to distinguish those sites that offer artworks that have actually been crafted by their creators, as opposed to prints, reproductions, replicas, posters or artifacts created in kind along an assembly line.

POSTERS & PRINTS

The affordable way to fill your walls with the flat images that stir your fancy, posters include photos of athletes and movie stars as well as replicas of famous paintings, pinup girls and sleek automobiles. Prints usually fare a little better; at least, they tend to feature a higher-quality paper...

 **LIST OF KEY WORDS**

The following words represent the types of items typically found on the sites listed in this section. You will find them listed in the orange strip at the bottom of each entry, as appropriate.

ARTIFACTS	Cultural objects ranging from fossils, maps and pottery to religious, political and military items.
BOOKS & MEDIA	Books, audio recordings, video and software pertaining to art history, antiques, artifacts and collectibles.
COLLECTING	Hobbies such as collectible stamps, coins, baseball cards and comic books, etc.
DECORATIVE	Art and collectibles that are created more to accent living space than as an act of self-expression.
EMERGING ART	Original art created by unknown and/or obscure contemporary artists.
KITSCH	Items adhering to popular culture; things like cartoon lunchboxes, promotional movie items, refrigerator magnets and old advertisements. This stuff is often as gaudy as it sounds, and often quite remarkable.
LIMITED ED.	Prints and posters produced in limited editions or limited numbers.
MASTER ARTISTS	The work of acclaimed and historically relevant artists, in original art, reproduction or print form.
MEMORABILIA	Collectible items focusing on cultural/historical figures or events, usually in the world of politics, sports or entertainment, including autographs and commemorative merchandise.
PAINTINGS	Original paintings or painted reproductions by celebrated or unknown artists.
PHOTOGRAPHY	Artistic and/or documentary prints by famed or obscure photographers, either in limited or mass edition.
POSTERS	Usually low-quality replications of popular and/or licensed images from art, sports, graphic design or entertainment.
PRINTS	Higher quality, printed reproductions of rare and/or popular images, often in limited edition.
REPRODUCTIONS	Artistic pieces replicating well-known original artwork, whether painting or sculpture, usually using the same medium, often by hand.
SCULPTURE	Three-dimensional artistic designs made from a variety of materials, whether in replica form or made by the original artists.

KEY WORD INDEX

Use the followings lists to locate online retailers that sell the art and collectibles you seek.

ARTIFACTS

AncientArt.co.uk
AntiqNet.com
BathAntiquesOnline.com
Biddingtons.com
Chisholm-Poster.com
CollectorsPrints.com
CondeNastArt.com
DoWahDiddy.com
HeritagePhotographs.com
JosephMarc.com
MaxillaAndMandible.com
OldPrintShop.com
PopHouse.com
RauAntiques.com
RubyLane.com

BOOKS & MEDIA

AnselAdams.com
ArtRepublic.com
Biddingtons.com
Guild.com
OldPrintShop.com
PhotoEye.com
PopHouse.com
TIAS.com

COLLECTING

Automates-Anciens.com
BathAntiquesOnline.com
CoinWire.com
CollectableDieCast.com
CollectiblesToday.com
DavidHall.com
EntertainmentEarth.com
FranklinMint.com
JamesMcCusker.com
JosephMarc.com
KenmoreStamps.com
KidRobot.com
LilliputMotorCompany.com
RauAntiques.com
RubyLane.com
StampFinder.com

COLLECTING (cont.)

Steuben.com
TIAS.com
UpperDeckStore.com
USMint.gov

DECORATIVE

AllPosters.com
AntiqNet.com
ArtSelect.com
BareWalls.com
BathAntiquesOnline.com
CollectiblesToday.com
CollectorsPrints.com
CondeNastArt.com
DoWahDiddy.com
Guild.com
MD-Canvas.com
PopHouse.com
RauAntiques.com
RubyLane.com
Statue.com
Steuben.com
Tapestries-Inc.com
TheMaskStore.com
TIAS.com
WallKandy.com
Yokodana.com

EMERGING ART

Art4Sale.com
Biddingtons.com
DeviantArt.com
EyeStorm.com
Guild.com
MixedGreens.com
NextMonet.com
OnlineGalleryArt.com
PacePrints.com
PaintingsDirect.com
PhotoEye.com
PicassoMio.com

KITSCH

AllPosters.com
AntiqNet.com
Art.com
Automates-Anciens.com
BareWalls.com
BathAntiquesOnline.com
Cartoon-Factory.com
ClassicPhotos.com
CollectiblesToday.com
CollectorsPrints.com
DoWahDiddy.com
EntertainmentEarth.com
FranklinMint.com
KidRobot.com
LilliputMotorCompany.com
PopHouse.com
PosterGroup.com
RubyLane.com
TIAS.com

LIMITED ED.

ArtRock.com
Automates-Anciens.com
Biddingtons.com
Cartoon-Factory.com
EntertainmentEarth.com
ESGallery.com
EyeStorm.com
FranklinMint.com
GlobalGallery.com
JosephMarc.com
KidRobot.com
MovieGoods.com
OnlineGalleryArt.com
PhotoEye.com
PicassoMio.com
PosterGroup.com
Tapestries-Inc.com
TIAS.com
Yaneff.com

MASTER ARTISTS

AllPosters.com
AnselAdams.com
Art4Sale.com
ArtOnCanvas.com
BareWalls.com
BasilStreet.com
EyeStorm.com
GlobalGallery.com
MastersCollection.com
OceansBridge.com
OnlineGalleryArt.com
PacePrints.com
PicassoMio.com
RauAntiques.com
Yaneff.com

MEMORABILIA

ArtRock.com
AutographsForSale.com
BathAntiquesOnline.com
Cartoon-Factory.com
ClassicPhotos.com
CollectorsPrints.com
CondeNastArt.com
DoWahDiddy.com
FranklinMint.com
GraphicExpectations.com
JosephMarc.com
OldPrintShop.com
OnlineSports.com
RoslynHerman.com
RubyLane.com
TIAS.com
UpperDeckStore.com

PAINTINGS

Art4Sale.com
ArtOnCanvas.com
ArtSelect.com
BasilStreet.com
Biddingtons.com
Cartoon-Factory.com
EyeStorm.com
Guild.com
MastersCollection.com
MixedGreens.com
NextMonet.com
OceansBridge.com
OnlineGalleryArt.com
PaintingsDirect.com
PicassoMio.com
RauAntiques.com

PHOTOGRAPHY

AmericanPostcardArt.com
AnselAdams.com
Art.com
Biddingtons.com
ClassicPhotos.com
CondeNastArt.com
DeviantArt.com
EyeStorm.com
GlobalGallery.com
Guild.com
HeritagePhotographs.com
MixedGreens.com
NextMonet.com
OnlineGalleryArt.com
PhotoEye.com
PicassoMio.com
WallKandy.com

POSTERS

AllPosters.com
AmericanPostcardArt.com
Art.com
ArtRepublic.com
ArtRock.com
ArtSelect.com
BareWalls.com
Chisholm-Poster.com
CondeNastArt.com
GlobalGallery.com
GraphicExpectations.com
HeritagePhotographs.com
MovieGoods.com
MPAGallery.com
PopHouse.com
PosterGroup.com
Yaneff.com

PRINTS

AmericanPostcardArt.com
Art.com
ArtSelect.com
Biddingtons.com
CollectorsPrints.com
CondeNastArt.com
DeviantArt.com
ESGallery.com
EyeStorm.com
GlobalGallery.com
HeritagePhotographs.com
MD-Canvas.com
NextMonet.com
OldPrintShop.com
OnlineGalleryArt.com
PacePrints.com
PhotoEye.com
PicassoMio.com

REPRODUCTIONS

ArtOnCanvas.com
ArtSelect.com
Automates-Anciens.com
BareWalls.com
BasilStreet.com
CollectableDieCast.com
GlobalGallery.com
LilliputMotorCompany.com
MastersCollection.com
MaxillaAndMandible.com
MovieGoods.com
OceansBridge.com
Statue.com

SCULPTURE

Biddingtons.com
Guild.com
MaxillaAndMandible.com
MixedGreens.com
NextMonet.com
OnlineGalleryArt.com
PicassoMio.com
RauAntiques.com
Statue.com

AllPosters.com

AllPosters.com · 888-654-0143

Somewhere between wallpaper and paintings there are posters. You can't find a less expensive way to fill your walls with the indelible images of great artists, and this specialty retailer knows how to make it easy for you to find them. Of course, it's not all high-culture here, as there're plenty of movie posters, celebrity glamour shots and spectacular athletic moments captured on film, each equally easy to locate. Finally, there are harder-to-categorize images, such as pictures of unicorns or a baby playing the drums; and yet somehow even these may be found without difficulty.

| ·DECORATIVE | ·KITSCH | ·MASTER ARTISTS | ·POSTERS |

AmericanPostcardArt.com

AmericanPostcardArt.com · 941-954-3124

"With topics ranging from Art Nouveau Pigeons to the Zodiac," this vintage prints retailer boasts over 80,000 images culled from a half-century's worth of postcards, and not all of them American. Visit the International section to see what sort of images people in Cuba, Sri Lanka or Japan send each other, or browse by People, Places or Things for a wide variety of early 20th-century depictions of Bathing Beauties, Amusement Parks, Drive-Thru Trees and endless charming topics. Browsing is thoroughly entertaining and all images are available in several sizes on canvas, watercolor paper or as glossy photo prints. You rarely see such charming decorative art at so reasonable a price.

| ·PHOTOGRAPHY | ·POSTERS | ·PRINTS | |

AncientArt.co.uk

Ancient Art Online · 44-208-882-1509

New stuff is all right, but this intriguing site makes a case that old is better. With a selection ranging from Roman coins and Greek swords to the handwritten pages of a medieval Bible, we mean really old. Going back a little further, you can also find Egyptian beads and Chinese pottery dating from the Ming, Yuan, Han or Tang dynasties. And if that makes you wonder just how ancient these artifacts get, look to the Fossils category, where you'll find such desirable dinosaur items as eggs, bones and dung—all right, so not all of this stuff is expressly beautiful, but it's never less than fascinating.

| ·ARTIFACTS | | | |

AnselAdams.com

The Ansel Adams Gallery · 888-361-7622

Even in the unlikely event that the name doesn't ring a bell, you're undoubtedly familiar with at least one of the images captured by this most prolific landscape photographer. Adams gained fame taking beautiful pictures of natural sites such as Yosemite National Park and Alaska's Mt. McKinley. Likewise, all the photographers featured in this shop offer landscape portraits in natural settings, here in the form of posters, calendars and original photography. The only way to get a better glimpse of the beautiful world around us is to go out and take a look for yourself.

| ·PHOTOGRAPHY | ·BOOKS & MEDIA | ·MASTER ARTISTS | |

888-959-1605 · AntiqNet.com

AntiqNet.com

As years go by, the definition of "antique" continually expands to include items from more and more eras past. It's therefore not surprising that more antiques stores exist than anyone would care to count. AntiqNet strives to bring thousands of these stores together on the web so that antiques hunters can track down rare items in one easy place. They've mostly succeeded, but not without problems. First, with over 5,000 vendors contributing every imaginable kind of item, finding what you want could take a while. Secondly, many of these wares are not actually available for online purchase, meaning all these antiques have been brought together in one difficult place.

| ·DECORATIVE | ·ARTIFACTS | ·KITSCH | | |

800-952-5592 · Art.com

Art.com

What do you get from the art site with the easiest to remember name? For starters, over 100,000 posters, prints and photographs bearing some quite memorable images rendered by some of this and every century's greatest, all at quite competitive prices. Oh yeah, several of these are actually posters and 8x10 glossy photos celebrating top sports figures, pop stars, actors and less easily categorized personalities (Einstein, anyone?). Does the inclusion of these alternatives to wallpapering a teenager's bedroom besmirch the good name of "Art"? We can only hope.

| ·PHOTOGRAPHY | ·KITSCH | ·POSTERS | ·PRINTS | |

561-630-5050 · Swahn Galleries

Art4Sale.com

The Swahn Gallery, operating out of North Palm Beach, Florida, boasts a 12,000-square-foot showroom to house the many paintings passing through its collection, but for those of us far from America's Southeast, this online arm of the fine art dealer will suffice. With perpetual auctions taking places and consigned collections for sale, the eclectic assortment of art here can be confusing to sort through, and many visits to the site may prove disappointing. Rest assured, though, there is plenty of amazing stuff housed within these pages, and whatever your taste, a little perseverance will make all the difference in finding that enviable gem by one of the world's best known or up-and-coming artists.

| ·PAINTINGS | ·EMERGING ART | ·MASTER ARTISTS | |  |

314-436-1118 · ARTonCANVAS.com

ArtOnCanvas.com

Specializing in "Museum Framed Fine Art Reproductions On Canvas," this site's offerings are a bit limited, and not exactly unique. However, there may be no better way to find a decoratively framed, replica oil painting at so reasonable a price. Masterworks by the likes of Raphael, Michelangelo and Boticelli are digitally transferred onto canvas, then hand-coated "with a subtle crackle finish... which reflects the patina of the original." You'll also find a wealth of Impressionist and contemporary pieces, enough to turn your home into a replica museum. Since each reproduction is printed and framed to order, you may opt to shrink or enlarge the artwork as needed to fit your available wall space... not exactly pleasing to the purist, but handy for the interior decorator.

| ·PAINTINGS | ·MASTER ARTISTS | ·REPRODUCTIONS | | |

ArtRepublic.com

Archer Publications · 011-44-1273-724829

"Free Delivery Worldwide" makes this UK site an especially great find for those of us with transatlantic tastes. Granted, these are posters we're talking about—not exactly the hardest products to find in domestic web shops. Also, the prices list in pounds sterling, which doesn't exactly translate well against the American dollar these days (as the site's currency converter will tell). Still, in many cases these guys do offer a selection of art posters slightly larger, if not more sophisticated, than those seen on any of the massive retailers this side of the pond, so keep it in mind when you have trouble finding that particular poster.

·BOOKS & MEDIA	·POSTERS		

ArtRock.com

ArtRock Online · 415-777-5736

The rock poster has become an iconic art form all its own, and just happens to be this site's specialty. A constantly changing selection proves a constantly reliable source for classic posters commemorating concerts by legend like the Beatles, Led Zeppelin and Jimi Hendrix. Lest you think the art form archaic, a Modern Rock section proves the genre alive and well, with colorful, design-savvy and/or psychedelic limited editions hyping the likes of the Beastie Boys, White Stripes and even the late, great Wesley Willis. Your walls will never be boring again.

·MEMORABILIA	·LIMITED ED.	·POSTERS	

ArtSelect.com

Art Select · 888-686-4254

When we purchase art, more often than not our selection is based on the way we personally respond to the subject and style of the piece. On this site it's sometimes more about how the artwork relates to your interior decorating. In addition to Artists, Subjects and Art Styles, you may browse this selection of paper prints and canvas reproductions by Colors, which organizes the selection of classic images and masterpieces into their predominant tones and shades. Try on a variety of frames, and you may quickly find the perfect addition to any room in the house.

·PAINTINGS ·PRINTS	·DECORATIVE	·POSTERS	·REPRODUCTIONS

AutographsForSale.com

AutographsForSale.com · 858-571-2754

Half the fun of getting an autograph is actually asking the famous actress, athlete, musician or astronaut to sign your picture, books, sports equipment or body part. However, crossing paths with your favorite celebrities can be tough, so collectors will enjoy this site that offers signatures from famous folk across the popular spectrum. Their thoroughly categorized collection doesn't include any body parts, but you can find signed baseballs, magazine covers, compact discs and plenty else.

·MEMORABILIA			

011-33-142-2291 · Galerie Le Sévrien

Automates-Anciens.com

It's as difficult to explain this "androids, automatons and artificial animals" site as it is to use. Multilingual ordering requires you to enter items manually, which can be tricky because they often defy description. The key to understanding is to begin with the most common product: music boxes. With complex inner mechanics, these beautiful and expensive boxes loop up to 144 notes of music. As it turns out, the same quaint European technology has been applied to automated dolls and figures that enact repeating scenes, dances and/or musics of their own, similar to cuckoo clock mimes. The selection is deep enough to represent the entirety of human imagination, and any of these objects will certainly become the most valuable piece of any toy collection.

·KITSCH	·COLLECTING	·LIMITED ED.	·REPRODUCTIONS

877-227-3925 · BareWalls.com

BareWalls.com

Like a tabula rasa, bare walls offer us an unlimited realm of options, space to fill. That seems to be the general idea here, anyway, as this art print and poster seller is set up to provide you with options upon options, which lead to, you guessed it, more options. It starts when you browse for an image by Style, Artist or Subject. A long list of categories as general as Still Life and as particular as Smoking will each in turn show a long list of subcategories that will lead you to a collection of images to peruse. Once you select a piece, though, the choosing doesn't stop; rather, you then have several framing options and in some instances the choice to have the print transferred to canvas, and then to (if you want) have brush strokes added by hand.

·DECORATIVE ·REPRODUCTIONS	·KITSCH	·MASTER ARTISTS	·POSTERS

800-525-9661 · Basil Street Gallery

BasilStreet.com

Representing the Basil Street Gallery of London, this snooty-sounding dealer offers "framed oil replicas on canvas." In other words, you'll find some of the greatest paintings history has to offer for mere hundreds of dollars; they just happen to be painted by a machine or an art student rather than by the original artist. It may be unoriginal, but it turns out to be a great shop to visit if you've come to realize you'll never likely own a real Vermeer, Kandinsky or Magritte but would still like to see one on your wall.

·PAINTINGS	·MASTER ARTISTS	·REPRODUCTIONS	

011-44-1225-311061 · Bath Antiques Online

BathAntiquesOnline.com

Boasting "the finest antiques and collectables from the West of England," this superstore promises "hand-picked items… to suit every taste and budget." Unfortunately, finding these splendid items requires more reading than a Tolstoy novel. Don't be distracted by the Google ads; it's the alphabetical menu of products you'll want to browse. Even the left-hand menu of "Latest Items," though the half-finished descriptions will entice, only lead you away from your objective. Should you lose patience, this site's version of a Wish List includes an email form wherein you make a specific request to the shop's experienced buyers, then simply sit back and wait for them to contact you. Not a bad alternative given the difficult nature of this otherwise great site.

·DECORATIVE ·COLLECTING	·ARTIFACTS	·KITSCH	·MEMORABILIA

Biddingtons.com

Though it sounds like something from *The Simpsons*, this New York fine art dealer actually offers a pretty brilliant assortment of contemporary artwork across all mediums. It just doesn't do it well. The cluttered, unfriendly site seems to give the impression that the average shopper isn't good enough to browse the great works contained within. However, either by direct purchase or auction those with patience may view a solid collection of paintings, photographs, sculpture and prints covering modern abstract movements, realism, surrealism and pop art. Most of the artists represented have already established themselves in a museum or gallery, so at the very least you know this marketable artwork may be more than just pretty, but a sound investment as well.

·PAINTINGS ·BOOKS & MEDIA	·ARTIFACTS ·EMERGING ART	·PHOTOGRAPHY ·LIMITED ED.	·SCULPTURE ·PRINTS

Cartoon-Factory.com

Animation fans will get an anvil-size kick out of this "Largest Selection of Animation Cels on the Internet." Like a snapshot from your favorite cartoon, each of these original production cels, hand-painted images and giclées cover popular characters from Disney, Hanna-Barbera, Warner Bros. and The Cartoon Network, as well as cult favorites such as *Ren & Stimpy*, *Beavis & Butthead* and *The Simpsons*. Browsing begins by studio, and like a cat chasing a clever mouse, gets clumsier as it goes. But artwork like this is worth more than just the chase.

·PAINTINGS	·KITSCH	·MEMORABILIA	·LIMITED ED.

Chisholm-Poster.com

We've long been fond of this vintage and international poster specialist based in New York, and have been thrilled to see its user-friendliness improve over the years. Although not all of their incredible images are available for purchase, viewing the various film, ad and political posters is more fun than ever, either by decade, designer, topic or nation of origin. We're partial to the Russian propaganda of the mid-20th-century, but with more than 18,000 amazing posters in this very well rounded catalog, we'd recommend getting comfortable and spending a few hours looking at everything.

·ARTIFACTS	·POSTERS		

ClassicPhotos.com

Whether it's Muhammad Ali standing over a knocked-out Sonny Liston, the Beatles performing on *The Ed Sullivan Show*, Sophia Loren glaring at the cleavage of Jayne Mansfield or the Wright brothers taking flight at Kitty Hawk, the 20th century was punctuated by a great variety of memorable images. This site offers a good deal of these memorable pictures, with black-and-white 8x10s arranged by Celebrity, Sports or the catch-all General Interest category. Browsing here can provide a lot of nostalgic fun, except that you have to open each photo on a separate page; then, you already know what most of these pics look like.

·PHOTOGRAPHY	·KITSCH	·MEMORABILIA	

877-415-4435 · CoinWire.com

CoinWire.com

What this coin dealer lacks in pictures, it makes up for in variety. Unlike most of the online US coin dealers we've found, this one features foreign coins and currency, for starters, and plenty of options in domestic mint to make it worth your while. Browsing is slow, though not necessarily difficult. Still, some of these coins do cost a pretty penny, and the lack of pictures will make it tough to be sure about the quality of the collectible. In other words, you may want to call to make sure the penny you're buying really is pretty.

·COLLECTING

626-282-2154 · CollectibleDiecast.com

CollectableDieCast.com

Some of the greatest cars ever made may be purchased from this site... in miniature form. The die-cast models represent pretty much every major manufacturer, both toy and auto, and include special edition machines and cars as memorable as Steve Mc-Queen's 1956 Jaguar XKSS, or the Mustang driven by James Bond in *Diamonds Are Forever*. You'll also find a few fun extra touches like replacement rims, mechanic action figures and diorama display cases, but the best part is that nobody can accuse your car collection of damaging the environment.

·COLLECTING   ·REPRODUCTIONS

877-268-6638 · CollectiblesToday.com

CollectiblesToday.com

Giving the word *collectible* a serious workout, this massive store has the capacity to fill every shelf in your home with the assorted offerings of Bradford, Hamilton, Ashton Drake, Van Hygan & Smythe, Thomas Kinkade and numerous other manufactured collectible brands. The various plates, music boxes, angels and other ornaments make for a dizzying selection, and the site's many featured shops and browsing techniques don't always help. Fortunately, you can't summon a single page here without stumbling into adorable, precious, memorable and/or delightful pieces for any odd collection you keep.

·DECORATIVE   ·KITSCH   ·COLLECTING

011-44-207-253-1337 · CollectorsPrints.com

CollectorsPrints.com

With "over 20,000 genuine antique prints available at any one time," this vintage art site is your escape from the abstract textures and geometries of modern graphic design. These simple, cartoonish and/or realistic sketches, ads and magazine pages offer nostalgic renditions of the people and places of the early 20th century. Although these prints are guaranteed authentic, you won't find any scandalous prices here, as even French Erotica from the 1930s doesn't usually cost more than a hundred dollars. Whether you search this selection with traditional or ironic tastes, you'll find a terrific variety and a lovely online window into the pre-computer era.

·DECORATIVE   ·ARTIFACTS   ·KITSCH   ·MEMORABILIA
·PRINTS

CondeNastArt.com
Condé Nast Art · 888-728-4021

The prolific Condé Nast magazine publisher has found a great way to recycle its remarkable cover art from the first half of the 20th-century: offering framed and mounted prints through this intriguing web site. After all, it's not like these unique, artist-commissioned works have a place on today's gaudy and glossy magazine racks. In fact, this selection of *Vanity Fair*, *House & Garden* and *Vogue* covers seem positively classy by comparison, which makes them perfect for use decorative wall art or, if you prefer, as sets of note cards. Either way, these lovely photos and illustrations deliver sophistication with a cultural context that makes them all the more memorable.

·DECORATIVE ·POSTERS	·ARTIFACTS ·PRINTS	·PHOTOGRAPHY	·MEMORABILIA

DavidHall.com
David Hall Rare Coins · 800-759-7575

If you're interested in seeing a retailer charge thousands of dollars for a single penny, you should check out this dealer of rare and memorable coins. It sounds like a bad investment, but it turns out these are "gem quality coins," which means that they're worth significantly more than nickels and dimes, despite anything the coins themselves may profess. Many of these items lack an image, but those that are pictured are done so with great detail. Probably the most reputable dealer online; serious collectors should look here first.

·COLLECTING			

DeviantArt.com
deviantART · 877-433-8278

Don't expect to log on to this site and find a lot of disturbing images of an adult nature—that's not necessarily what they mean by "deviant." Then again, you might expect to find some such pieces, because this is one of the great advances of the internet: a community of online artists. Individuals upload their photography, digital art and writing for viewing and critiques, and in the Shop some are made available for printing, whether in standard formats or on mugs, magnets, coasters and calendars. The result is a populist art gallery and print shop that removes the influence of the "art world" and allows you to directly interact with vibrant, daring and original work from around the world. In a word: brilliant.

·PHOTOGRAPHY	·EMERGING ART	·PRINTS	

DoWahDiddy.com
Do Wah Diddy · 928-632-5458

Pop culture has a virtual home here, which you can see by following the Merchandise link. You will actually see the category menu laid out in the floor diagram of a house, where links to The Funroom, Attic, Dad's Den and Mom's Boudoir prove almost as enticing as the items within, and these pop culture collectibles are as kitschy as they come. On any given visit, you may find a 50s-era Fallout Shelter sign, old pin-up calendars, fuzzy dice and a dashboard hula dancer. Of course, the site would not be complete without special sections devoted to Elvis, Marilyn Monroe and Bettie Page, just like no home is complete without a leopard print toilet seat cover.

·DECORATIVE	·ARTIFACTS	·KITSCH	·MEMORABILIA

818-255-0095 · Entertainment Earth

EntertainmentEarth.com

Probably the most bizarre range of collectibles you're likely to come across in this life is action figures, which sort of qualify as dolls, but are maybe a little more masculine. This shop seems devoted to the things, particularly those that are too good to be considered toys. These plastic, molded figurines are akin to comic book art in their flair for style and detail, and in fact you'll find several comic book characters brought to three-dimensional life here. Of course, there's also plenty of *Star Wars*, *GI Joe*, *The Simpsons* and *Lord of the Rings* figures, and loads of anime characters, but there are hundreds of action figures available and the joy of this shop is in discovering the unexpected.

| ·KITSCH | ·COLLECTING | ·LIMITED ED. | | |

703-706-0025 · Elizabeth Stone Gallery

ESGallery.com

Unless you're deeply immersed in the world of picture books, you are probably going to have a difficult time browsing the site put up by this purveyor of children's book illustrations. The whimsical, lovely and occasionally brilliant images are arranged strictly by artist, and if an artist's name has an asterisk beside it, the shop offers no items for sale online. Nevertheless, the limited-edition prints, culled from a variety of popular youth titles, are usually worth the time it takes to shop, especially when you do find the work of an artist you recognize, such as Lucy Cousins or the inimitable Dr. Seuss.

| ·LIMITED ED. | ·PRINTS | | |  |

866-393-4278 · Eyestorm

EyeStorm.com

Keeping abreast of current trends in art from vantage points in New York City as well as the UK, this site features newly discovered emerging artists as well as established masters such as Andy Warhol, David Hockney and Helmut Newton. An excellent search feature allows you to sort items by price range, subject and medium as well as by artist, although simply browsing is always a pleasure. Brief artist bios explain what the artist is up to and why he or she is receiving recognition, as if you couldn't tell just by viewing the beautifully rendered images. Fine work.

| ·PAINTINGS ·LIMITED ED. | ·PHOTOGRAPHY ·PRINTS | ·EMERGING ART | ·MASTER ARTISTS | |

877-843-6468 · The Franklin Mint

FranklinMint.com

What better way to sell collectible items than to make them yourself? Model cars, Fabergé eggs, special edition plates, celebrity dolls and commemorative tankards mark some of the not-so-standard fare offered by this world-leading collectibles manufacturer. Look close and you'll find die-cast metal and porcelain objects thematically linked to race cars, princesses, dragons, patriotism and Harley-Davidson motorcycles. Somebody had to make this stuff; we're just glad they made a web site for our convenience.

| ·KITSCH | ·MEMORABILIA | ·COLLECTING | ·LIMITED ED. |  |

GlobalGallery.com

Global Gallery · 888-456-2254

On the surface, this site seems like just another art poster shop, and in some ways, it is. However, this one offers something most of the others don't: canvas prints. This means that, for a very reasonable price, you may opt to have some of your favorite paintings by the likes of Chagall, Van Gogh, Lichtenstein and Picasso printed onto canvas, stretched onto a frame and ready to hang. Much cheaper than a hand-painted reproduction, but much sturdier and better looking than a poster, it's hard to go wrong when you have thousands of affordable masterpieces at your disposal.

·PHOTOGRAPHY ·REPRODUCTIONS	·MASTER ARTISTS ·PRINTS	·LIMITED ED.	·POSTERS

GraphicExpectations.com

Graphic Expectations · 818-780-5353

Movie posters aren't that difficult to find, not even those from foreign countries. But where most movie poster sites end, this one is just getting started. Film festival posters, Broadway show posters, music album posters and other similar cultural marketing fare dominate the unique and very cosmopolitan selection, along with some French bus stop ads. Browsing by category takes a little while, but proves a lot of fun, but you should put aside any expectations, because this one's bound to surprise you.

·MEMORABILIA	·POSTERS		

Guild.com

Guild.com · 877-344-8453

This "source of the finest artists and their work" has a great selection of original art pieces from an extensive list of contemporary artists you may not know offhand, but whose work could easily invigorate your environment. The great thing is, this stuff isn't limited to paintings, or even photography. All manner of visual representation has a place here, whether of wood, metal, plaster or any other physical form. Ranging from lovely to edgy, this site provides a great way to decorate your surroundings while making an investment in the future of art.

·PAINTINGS ·BOOKS & MEDIA	·DECORATIVE ·EMERGING ART	·PHOTOGRAPHY	·SCULPTURE

HeritagePhotographs.com

Heritage Photographs · 603-456-2159

The key to appreciating this site is to remember that photography has been around for a long, long time. Hence, when you see the category Women Of The 80's And 90's, it's referring to the 1880's and 1890's. These vintage photographs date as far back as the Civil War, and only as recent as World War 2. Between wars you'll find plenty of Americana, including pony carts, steam locomotives and vintage automobiles. You'll also find some early fashion photos, pictures of houses and portraits of everyday people, as well as singular folk like Abraham Lincoln. Sure, these people never dreamt their immortal images would be available for purchase over something called the internet, but if they did, they'd surely be glad to know the photos were available in poster sizes.

·ARTIFACTS	·PHOTOGRAPHY	·POSTERS	·PRINTS

800-852-0076 · James T. McCusker

JamesMcCusker.com

First day covers are the sorts of stamps collected by serious philatelists, and given the difficulty of using this specialty site, we'd only recommend avid collectors try to shop here. Many sets and individual cachets are available at intermittent auctions, but if you find the Online Cover Shopping link you can try the Power Search Menu, selecting from lists of Scott numbers, cachet-makers and stamp topics to find some very particular items for sale at prices ranging from a couple bucks to hundreds of dollars. If it sounds confusing, well, it is to us too. If it doesn't, then you've just found a great site to improve your collection.

·COLLECTING

215-932-7485 · JosephMarc

JosephMarc.com

Noticing that, in the antiques market, "online auctions tend to require a leap of faith," the founders of this Antiques and Collectibles Showcase aimed to provide a place where buyers and sellers alike could trade valued pieces securely, without artificially driving up the price. The result is a lovely selection of multicultural art, antiques and collectible items that you may regard with some semblance of trust, especially if you remain well versed with each dealer's Seller's Policy, and remember to contact them with any important questions you may have about a product's appraisal history and condition.

·ARTIFACTS ·MEMORABILIA ·COLLECTING ·LIMITED ED.

800-225-5059 · Kenmore Stamp Co.

KenmoreStamps.com

Stamp collectors will find a great source of foreign and domestic postage on this specialty site devoted to philately. Easily browsed US Stamp subcategories include First Day Covers, Confederate States, Commemorative Sheets and Errors, while the Foreign Stamps category offers stamp samplings of the British Empire, Zeppelin Flight Covers and Asia. Best of all, it's uncharacteristically easy to use; whereas most stamp sites make you research and suffer a bit before finding what you need, here even the fledgling collector should come away happy.

·COLLECTING

212-777-7735 · KidRobot

KidRobot.com

"Devoted to bringing you the best in urban vinyl action figures," the attraction of this site may be lost on a lot of people. But, if a child lives in your house, or in your soul, the collectible characters found here in abundance might just provide one of the more entertaining shopping experiences you'll find this year. Indeed, the quirky, creative appeal of these limited edition designer toys make Beanie Babies look flaccid and boring. Like their bean-filled predecessors, though, many of these rare items will probably appreciate in value, but in the meantime will only be appreciated by the young and funky at heart.

·KITSCH ·COLLECTING ·LIMITED ED.

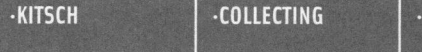

LilliputMotorCompany.com

Lilliput · 800-846-8697

Collectors couldn't ask for a better source of classic toys than this alluring specialty shop. Steam toys, wind-up toys, rare dolls, die-cast models, miniatures and immaculately made game sets head up a selection guaranteed to electrify the young at heart, whether you intend to play with them or place them on shelves to be admired. The only real problem we could find with this constantly improving site is the lack of a gift wrap feature; given how many of these products make the perfect present for the whimsical adult or precocious child, it proves an excellent place to shop for gifts.

	·KITSCH	·COLLECTING	·REPRODUCTIONS	

MastersCollection.com

The Masters' Collection · 800-222-6827

Considering the the prices of fine art, most of us would never dream of hanging a Monet, Renoir, Michelangelo or Degas painting on our wall. However, thanks to this hand-painted reproduction specialist, we can afford to enjoy such luxuries in our waking lives. Some of the great paintings of the ages have been painstakingly replicated by trained artists, reducing the cost of multi-million-dollar images to mere hundreds of bucks. This is the rare situation where it makes more sense to browse by Artist than Category, although if you don't have a master painter in mind, selecting among such sections as Impressionist, Portraits and Surrealists is almost easy enough to be accomplished in your sleep.

	·PAINTINGS	·MASTER ARTISTS	·REPRODUCTIONS	

MaxillaAndMandible.com

Maxilla & Mandible · 212-724-6173

Poorly designed and difficult to use, you get the feeling this unique site was designed in some antiquated or even prehistoric era, which could explain why it houses such a terrific assortment of dinosaur fossils, animal skulls, ostrich eggs and preserved butterflies. Ordering these authentic and reproduction artifacts can be a real pain, but seeing as the result is a piece of natural history you may display on your shelves, we wouldn't skip it for the world.

	·ARTIFACTS	·SCULPTURE	·REPRODUCTIONS	

MD-Canvas.com

m-dc · 888-345-0870

The "MD" here stands for "modern digital," which refers to the process in which this small but appealing selection of decorative prints are transferred onto canvas. The canvas is then stretched onto a wooden frame, thus arriving "ready to hang." The end result is an artistic piece of contemporary graphic design that has all the heft and staying power of a traditional painting. Follow the Gallery link to view the available images, and while the page will probably take a very long time to load, assuming it does you'll be able to decide quickly if there's anything here for you.

	·DECORATIVE	·PRINTS		

866-647-3367 · Mixed Greens

MixedGreens.com

Though this very modern online dealer only features a limited number of artists, each of them offers fashionable and aesthetically appealing original work representative of contemporary times. You might find the bubble photos of Julianne Schwartz, the socio-critical acrylic yarn portraits of Rob Conger or medicine cabinet prints of Coke Wisdom O'Neal. These emerging artists are relatively high profile, and when all the aforementioned works sell out, we're sure they'll be replaced by next years up-and-comers.

·PAINTINGS	·PHOTOGRAPHY	·SCULPTURE	·EMERGING ART	

866-279-2403 · Movie Goods

MovieGoods.com

Film buffs may ultimately prefer good movies, but for the purposes of home and office decoration this, "the single largest online movie poster art product inventory anywhere," proves particularly satisfying. Aside from new and recent releases, these guys offer a healthy selection of vintage posters, either in reproductions/replica, or occasionally original, form. Browsing is a lot easier if you have particular films in mind, though the categorical separation of movies by genre, actor, director or year should get you closer to what you like.

·LIMITED ED.	·POSTERS	·REPRODUCTIONS		

212-223-1009 · Motion Picture Arts Gallery

MPAGallery.com

There's not a lot of cachet in displaying current movie posters in your home; slick, glossy and commercial, most of these movies have yet to prove themselves over time. However, put up a vintage movie poster and you certainly demonstrate some class. Better yet, if the poster's in French, you get to display some international flair. This site will help you find a poster from as early in film history as 1900, in a variety of genres and from more than a dozen countries in addition to domestic releases. You can search by size, title, actors/actresses and director to ensure that your movie posters will be the envy of every film buff.

·POSTERS				

888-914-5050 · NextMonet.com

NextMonet.com

Claiming to offer "one of the largest collections of original artwork available for purchase anywhere in the world," this art dealer out of Florida could probably get away with just tossing a lot uninspiring sculptures, paintings, photographs and prints online and trolling for profits. However, a juried selection process ensures that a "panel of art specialists" appreciates the merits of each artist's work, meaning the selection you'll find here may be one of the best in contemporary art, not just the biggest. At the very least, an hour spent on this site is a fine way to spend an afternoon.

·PAINTINGS ·PRINTS	·PHOTOGRAPHY	·SCULPTURE	·EMERGING ART	

OceansBridge.com

Ocean's Bridge Group Ltd. · 800-206-3749

Chances are, you've never commissioned an artist to paint your portrait. Well, along comes the internet to change that! This site features a wide range of hand-painted reproductions of the great masterpieces of art history, each at a great price. But for a little more personal attention, you merely need to email a digital photograph, and a trained artist will transfer the image into a painting. Whether it's a copy of the Mona Lisa, or a hand-painted family portrait, this unique web retailer could very well provide the best gift you ever give.

·PAINTINGS	·MASTER ARTISTS	·REPRODUCTIONS	

OldPrintShop.com

The Old Print Shop · 212-683-3950

On the internet, describing a shop as old usually means it's been in business for maybe a decade. Not this one. Founded in 1898, it started dealing in 19th-century prints when they were still contemporary. Now online, it offers photos, prints and antique maps dating back up to two hundred years and more. These relics of the past captured the nation's political, natural and cultural events as they were happening, and all the while this New York art dealer has been sharing them with collectors who favor classic styles and traditional techniques that have fallen by the wayside as technology progresses. Rest assured, though, the only computer-aided imagery to be seen in this Old Print Shop is the handiwork of its web designer.

·ARTIFACTS	·BOOKS & MEDIA	·MEMORABILIA	·PRINTS

OnlineGalleryArt.com

Gallery Art Online · 305-932-6166

We might not recommend this hard-to-use site at all, except that when you take the time to dig deep into its collection you'll find a treasure trove of great art. Contemporary masters and emerging talents alike are featured among the many, many product categories, which turn usually describe the visual or sculptural medium, such as Acrylic, Animation Cell, Bas-Relief, Bronze, Collage, Engraved Lithograph, Silk Screen and other mixed varieties. While this may occasionally lead you to something perfect, your best bet might be to search one of your favorite modern artists: you'll be surprised how many may turn up.

·PAINTINGS ·MASTER ARTISTS	·PHOTOGRAPHY ·LIMITED ED.	·SCULPTURE ·PRINTS	·EMERGING ART

OnlineSports.com

OnlineSports.com · 800-856-2638

This site may just offer the widest price range discrepancy ever seen in the online sale of basketballs. See, you can buy a ball here for a measly five bucks. Or you can buy one autographed by Michael Jordan, and suddenly the price shoots up to nearly $2000. A poorly constructed sporting goods store, the strength of this site really lies in its Memorabilia section, which is full of autographed and commemorative items ranging from photographs and trading cards to jerseys and batting gloves. It's still a terrible site to shop from, but hardcore sports fans might just find a valuable new addition to their collections.

·MEMORABILIA			

877-440-7223 · **Pace Editions**

PacePrints.com

If you're uncertain about the difference between a poster and a print, this proves an excellent site to find out, as it does a great job of distinguishing between the two. More importantly, it also does a great job of demonstrating just how beautiful and evocative a fine art print can be, offering an incredible selection covering a wide range of techniques and styles. Browsing begins with the Artist link, which reveals an alphabetical listing of mostly unfamiliar names (although luminaries such as Claes Oldenburg, Ed Ruscha, Roy Lichtenstein and Kate Shepherd may also be found). To get a good feel for each artist, we suggest finding the Selected Images section, which allows you to view some brilliant samples on a single page.

·EMERGING ART	·MASTER ARTISTS	·PRINTS	

212-504-8151 · **PaintingsDirect.com**

PaintingsDirect.com

One problem particular to shopping for art online is that the world is filled with contemporary artists we've never heard of, so locating a piece that suits our needs can require a lot of research and a lot of digging through artwork that's not quite right. This dealer of modern paintings has found a way to skirt this issue by thoroughly organizing each of its 10,000 or so products so that you may perform complex searches for specific Subjects, Styles, Techniques, Size and Price Range. You may even pinpoint dominant colors and browse artists based on the current status of their reputations. There may be no ideal way to browse 10,000 paintings, but if you use this site properly, you won't have to.

·PAINTINGS	·EMERGING ART		

800-227-6941 · **Photo-Eye Gallery**

PhotoEye.com

Specializing in artistic photography, this online art dealer offers three different shopping arenas and a Magazine link. First up are the Galleries, which offer a deep and splendid variety of photographs, prints of which may usually be purchased unmatted and unframed. The Bookstore, of course, caters more to coffee table collectors, with art books featuring specific artists or themes, including some signed and first editions. Thirdly, the Auctions category offers an uneven smattering of everything, with new lots constantly added, and which give you the impression at least that you're really chasing down hard-to-come-by titles. None of these shopping areas may be perfect, but they all offer captivating, beautiful and/or moving images to look at.

·PHOTOGRAPHY ·PRINTS	·BOOKS & MEDIA	·EMERGING ART	·LIMITED ED.

877-212-5879 · **PicassoMio**

PicassoMio.com

This site's "juried selection of thousands of one-of-a-kind and limited edition artworks...is sourced from over a thousand artists and art dealers, across Europe, Americas and worldwide." Such sweeping scope gives them bragging rights to a snootiness their competitors just can't match. It also fills the site with untold pages of material, so much that search and browsing techniques can't always keep up. Though it gives you a good idea of what styles and techniques have come to pass in the art world, gems are hard to find unless you have the patience to pursue them.

·PAINTINGS ·MASTER ARTISTS	·PHOTOGRAPHY ·LIMITED ED.	·SCULPTURE ·PRINTS	·EMERGING ART

PopHouse.com

House Pop-Culture Artifacts · 888-515-2327

This kitschy retailer has a mad and hilarious assortment of either timeless or dated materials, depending on your point of view. With merchandise ranging in subject from Jesus to Ronald Reagan, with a dab of Fat Albert in between, you can be sure that these lunchboxes, trading cards, wobble-head dolls and salt'n'pepper shakers will have you shaking your head and/or clicking furiously at the Add to Cart button. In search of a Madonna action figure? Look no further. Just be aware that there's more than one product per category—keep an eye out for links at the bottom of the page.

	·DECORATIVE ·POSTERS	·ARTIFACTS	·BOOKS & MEDIA	·KITSCH

PosterGroup.com

The Ross Group · 866-897-1525

You probably wouldn't put many of today's advertising posters on your wall, and we're guessing they felt much the same way in early 20th-century Europe. Nevertheless, some of those posters did survive the age and we can now clearly appreciate the craftsmanship displayed by early commercial artists in what was truly a burgeoning young art form. The charming illustrated images here promoted such delights as food, drink, operas, circuses, movies, travel opportunities and military service in much more intriguing ways than we're used to today. Then, who's to say collectors in Europe won't be hanging the bikini and beer of our liquor stores on their walls someday?

	·KITSCH	·LIMITED ED.	·POSTERS	

RauAntiques.com

M.S. Rau Antiques · 800-544-9440

For nearly a century, this fine antiques dealer has taken up residence in New Orleans' French Quarter, and it's still here to be "the most comprehensive antiques site on the web." While it may not boast the largest, or even the most varied selection of antique furniture, jewelry, art and cultural artifacts, it's quite probable this is the best site of its kind. The key here is that it's "fine antiques," meaning that these wares are incredibly valuable (read: expensive), and brilliant to see. For starters, you won't find better canes, clocks or music boxes anywhere, and there are more than a dozen other categories to consider.

	·PAINTINGS ·COLLECTING	·DECORATIVE ·MASTER ARTISTS	·ARTIFACTS	·SCULPTURE

RoslynHerman.com

Roslyn Herman & Co. · 718-846-3496

Offering "Authentic Celebrity Apparel," which means that all of this stuff was at one time owned by somebody famous, the site's wares include certificates of authenticity to prove it. Thus you may find items like Charlie Chaplin's cuff links, Cary Grant's wallet, a fur worn by Bette Davis and one of Joan Crawford's pillboxes (no wire hangers, though). Consisting mostly of jewelry and other fashion accessories, it may cause you to question many of these legends' sense of style, but then again, in many cases that's exactly why these items are intriguing to begin with.

	·MEMORABILIA			

415-864-4563 · Ruby Lane

RubyLane.com

Ruby Lane has gathered hundreds of small antique and collector's shops together under one massive web site, allowing you a single point of access to an incredible wealth of memorabilia, artwork, furniture, jewelry and kitsch from points international. While the prospect of finding a single, unique item in the mix of thousands might seem terrifying, the proprietors of this site have actually done a terrific job over the years organizing and arranging all these products into sortable sections; if you filter by sub-category and price range you may just narrow down your selection to a couple dozen or so. Even if you have to look through 500 items, though, the amazing opportunity to find the exact sort of rare item you want makes the whole hunt worthwhile.

·DECORATIVE ·COLLECTING	·ARTIFACTS	·KITSCH	·MEMORABILIA	

954-581-2751 · Stamp Finder

StampFinder.com

You must really be devoted to philately to put yourself through this one, or at least know what it is. That's because this site operates exclusively for the stamp collector, whether a collection is strictly domestic or includes postage from all over the planet. The irony of some of these stamps is that they don't cover current postal rates, and wouldn't get a letter to its destination, but here they sell for sometimes exponentially more than the cost to send a first-class flat. A complicated and thorough search feature holds this site together, but as it turns out, photos are miserably lacking. Know what you're here for going in, or put it off.

·COLLECTING				

877-675-2634 · Statue.com

Statue.com

If you've been wondering where you can pick up a lovely marble statue for your lawn or entrance hall, now you have an answer. While slow to load and at times convoluted, there's no denying this site's massive selection, which includes classic reproductions along the lines of Michelangelo's *David* and the Venus de Milo, as well as a slew of cherubs (plus fountains). You may also find the busts of famous people (Beethoven for example) and plenty representing the native cultures of Africa and the Americas. Be sure to keep an eye on the shipping costs of these heavy items.

·DECORATIVE	·SCULPTURE	·REPRODUCTIONS		

800-424-4240 · Steuben Glass

Steuben.com

Having spent nearly 100 years "at the forefront of glass design," it's little surprise that Steuben offers a variety of exquisite creations, whether sculpted from molten crystal or cut from cooled glass. They have beautiful bowls, vases, candleholders and hand coolers (holdovers from the 17th/18th centuries), plus a list of miscellaneous products ranging from paperweights to clocks. These dazzling wares prove ironic: who'd have thought one could spend so much time looking at something you can actually see through?

·DECORATIVE	·COLLECTING			

Tapestries-Inc.com

Operating out of Northern California, this company imports fine hanging tapestries are from Belgium, France and Italy, the sort that will make your home feel like a European castle. Most of the tapestries are actually reproductions of classic palace and museum pieces that date back as far as the 12th century, and range in size from small to too big for most walls. Most of the images hand-woven into these lengths of cloth represent medieval and pastoral images, including Arthurian myths, legendary gardens and royal coats of arms. You'll have to buy a throne elsewhere.

| | ·DECORATIVE | ·ARTIFACTS | ·LIMITED ED. | ·REPRODUCTIONS |

TheMaskStore.com

Masks used to be a big part of theatrical entertainment, whether it was Greek tragedies or tribal African dance. Nowadays, in this country at least, masks tend to be useful only one day out of the year, and even then they're not convincing. However, the beautiful and intricate masks you'll find here resemble nothing you're likely to see on any trick-or-treaters. Here you'll find the elaborate masks of classical theater, cultural masks and some that serve no historical purpose but do look amazing hanging from your walls. Leave it to this site to make even Zorro seem boring.

| | ·DECORATIVE | ·ARTIFACTS | ·REPRODUCTIONS |

TIAS.com

When you enter this site, you enter perhaps the most massive, daunting conglomeration of collectibles, antiques and artifacts ever assembled in modern times. Seriously, there have been empires that have plundered less booty than you may find in these pages. Unfortunately, 99 percent will hold absolutely no interest to you. But that last 1 percent...that's the kicker, and the key to the enjoyment of this one is being able to find it. Of course, it will take a while. You need to click from category to subcategory to sub-subcategory, and in some cases to sub-sub-sub-category. Then, you might just see that single desirable object you will probably find nowhere else in the free world.

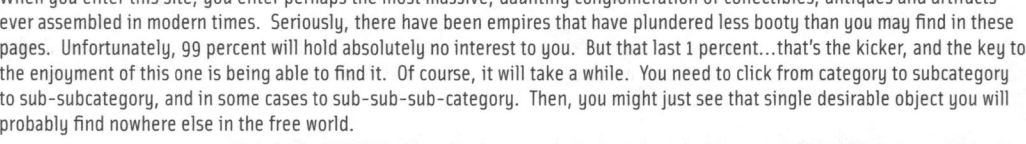

| | ·DECORATIVE ·MEMORABILIA | ·ARTIFACTS ·COLLECTING | ·BOOKS & MEDIA ·LIMITED ED. | ·KITSCH |

UpperDeckStore.com

The signatures of the greatest athletes on the planet don't come easy or cheap. Actually, wait a second—they do come easy, as evidenced by this shop, which features autographed photos and souvenirs owing to the likes of Tiger Woods, Randy Johnson, Jerry Rice and Michael Jordan. "Expensive" is the word, though, especially given the number of legendary figures here (like Larry Bird, Hank Aaron, Jim Brown, Jack Nicklaus and Julius Erving). Hey, if it was this easy to find and cheap as well, what would be the point?

| | ·MEMORABILIA | ·COLLECTING | | |

800-872-6468 · **The United States Mint**　　　　　**USMint.gov**

Interested in buying some money? Why not go straight to the source? Here you may find commemorative coins, first-edition coins, uncut currency and plenty of money-related memorabilia, such as coin jewelry, collectors' spoons and our favorite, the Mixed Quarters Bag (you never know what you're going to get!). In typical government fashion, they manage to charge you more than the actual money is worth as legal tender, but many of us will be surprised to find that the site is well designed, attractive to view and surprisingly efficient.

·COLLECTING				

866-995-2639 · **Wall Kandy**　　　　　**WallKandy.com**

If you'd like to use your wall space as a window to other times and places, this site offers a unique little selection of photographs depicting popular global destinations. Hence, you can easily browse photos taken of places such as Paris, New York, Venice, Prague and Rio. Click on Search By Theme to see Beaches, Cafes, Countryscapes and Night Scenes, or go to Search By Decor for Modern, Romantic and Traditional options. Any way you look, you'll find decorative visions of the world at large, all attainable from your desk chair.

·DECORATIVE	·PHOTOGRAPHY			

888-304-7843 · **Yaneff International Gallery**　　　　　**Yaneff.com**

A splendid glimpse into some of the origins of graphic design, this site offers century-old posters and magazine covers by some of the best and earliest artists who embraced the forms. You'll find posters by Toulouse-Lautrec depicting the cancan dancers of the Moulin Rouge, as well as self-designed posters advertising gallery showings for Pablo Picasso and Marc Chagall. We can pretty much guarantee that, wherever your life takes you, you'll never find a wider variety of images depicting women in petticoats.

·MASTER ARTISTS	·LIMITED ED.	·POSTERS	·REPRODUCTIONS	

610-987-9720 · **Yoko Trading**　　　　　**Yokodana.com**

The image "antiquing" conjures is usually that of long drives through the New England countryside to find quaint, cluttered shops run by white-haired, eccentric locals. This is only because a Sunday drive to Japan is out of the question. Fortunately this shop offers an incredible wealth of prewar Japanese items, ranging from bamboo umbrellas to decorative prints, with a lot of amazing vintage kimonos and fabrics in between. The great drawback is that you have to manually enter catalog numbers into the order form, assuming you can find it. If all else fails, go to the Site Map, then click on Order Form (Web Site Secure SSL ordering). It's a hassle, but worth it.

·DECORATIVE				

NOTES:

_____
_____
_____
_____
_____
_____
_____
_____
_____
_____
_____
_____
_____
_____
_____
_____
_____
_____
_____
_____
_____

Crafts
& Hobbies

In our first couple of years publishing **thepurplebook**, we received a lot of feedback from enthusiastic hobbyists asking that we include their favorite crafts stores in our listings. Well, it took a lot of research, but now we're very excited to add this new section to our book, and it's a big one. Not just because there are a lot of crafts retailers out there, but because they cover a huge number of activities that may start out as a way to kill time, but may soon become a passion. Either way, they're all better than watching television.

In the pursuit of creativity we discovered art supplies, musical instruments, model trains, telescopes and knitting supplies on sale by more terrific sites than we could know what to do with. After all, we had to leave room for the scrapbooking, jewelry-making and dressmaking products, which happen to be spread across a menagerie of sites too diverse to leave out. Neither could we refrain from including all the mosaic tiles, candle wax, soap-making materials, basketry supplies, seashells, beads, leather tools, ribbons, stickers, glues and other general crafts necessities we've seen, nor neglect sites dealing in baking, magic tricks, juggling, radio-controlled toys, amateur radio, robotics and rocketry. There is something here to inspire every creative spirit, from novice to expert, whether you are musically inclined, scientifically fascinated, artistically talented, aesthetically challenged or just plain crafty. We couldn't have kept it small if we wanted to.

TIPS ON BUYING CRAFTS & HOBBIES PRODUCTS ONLINE

These suggestions may help you plan and achieve your vision.

• **ORDER WHAT YOU NEED** • It would be incredibly frustrating to run out of a craft project's raw materials before it's finished, especially if you're using yarns, fabrics or other limited-issue designs that may soon be discontinued. Make sure to buy enough to finish what you started (leftovers can always be incorporated into your next project).

• **BATTERIES NOT INCLUDED** • When ordering craft sets or science kits, take note of which items are included in the set, and which must be purchased separately. This holds especially true if you're buying a gift.

• **PLAN YOUR TIME WISELY** • Handmade gifts are both personal and memorable. If you intend to make a gift, be sure to order the materials with plenty of time for delivery as well as assembly.

• **KNOW YOUR LIMITS** • With many hobbies and crafts, inexperience just leads to ill-fitting sweaters and bad music. Some of the materials and activities found on this group of sites can be a bit dangerous. Take caution, and please refrain from ordering materials exceeding your comfortable skill level, especially when you're involving children.

SITES THAT MAY COME IN HANDY

The following URLs may be useful when planning your next project.

AllCrafts.net	Craft projects and patterns
AmericanQuilter.com	Quilting resource
CandleTech.com	Candle- and soap-making guide
ClayTimes.com	Ceramics tips and instruction
CookingSchools.com	Locate a cooking school
HobbyRetailer.com	Find local hobby shops
HyperScale.com	Aviation and military model resource
LearnToKnit.com	Knitting tips and instruction
Make-Stuff.com	Craft projects and instructions
ModelTrainsGuide.com	Resource for model train enthusiasts
MTNA.org	Find a music instructor
MusicStaff.com	Find a music instructor
Trains.com	Resource for model train enthusiasts
VogueKnitting.com	Resource for knitting enthusiasts

SECTION ICON LEGEND

Use the following guide to understand the rectangular icons that appear throughout this section.

CREATIVE HOBBIES

Creativity may be explored in many different ways, but this icon represents shops offering art supplies, musical instruments, home crafts kits and any performance art.

DOMESTIC & HANDMADE CRAFTS

If you enjoy making things by hand, this icon will guide you to web shops offering tools, patterns and materials for all kinds of needlework, dressmaking, scrapbooking, jewelry making, baking, candy making and more.

MODELS & MACHINES

The mechanically inclined may want to watch out for this icon, which denotes shops catering to modeling, electric train, radio-controlled vehicle and robot-building enthusiasts.

EDUCATIONAL HOBBIES

Whether the subject is educational, explorative or simply fun, this icon will point out the more fascinating aspects of science, history, culture and nature. These shops carry telescopes, microscopes, chemistry sets, rocket kits, ant farms, dinosaur models and many more intriguing tools, experiments and guides.

LIST OF KEY WORDS

The following words represent the types of items typically found on the sites listed in this section. You will find them listed in the orange strip at the bottom of each entry, as appropriate.

ART SUPPLIES	Whether your preferred medium is paint, clay, stone, pencil, charcoal, wood, metal, photography, mosaic tiles or a conglomeration of techniques, you'll find plenty to work with on these art sites.
CRAFTS	General craft kits, tools and raw materials abound on the web, and the stores noted by this key word offer plenty to help stretch your creative muscles.
DRESSMAKING	Homemade clothing is easily within reach if you browse the patterns, sewing machines, fabrics, fasteners and other decorative adornments carried by these sites.
FOOD HOBBIES	General food preparation is well covered in our Epicurean section, but this collection of sites can help you with special baking projects, candy making, home brewing and other treats you can make from scratch.
INSTRUCTION	The novice hobbyist should keep an eye out for this key word, which will clue you in to sites offering patterns, kits and instructional materials for any of the activities featured in this section.
JEWELRY-MAKING	There's a surprising amount of jewelry-making tools and materials online, so making your own accessories can be easy if you follow this key word.
MODELS & TRAINS	Models, miniature machinery and radio-controlled devices are well covered by web retailers. Find them with this key word.
MUSIC	Whether you're making sweet sounds or cranking out the squeaks and squeals of the novice musician, these sites should help, with terrific new and vintage instrument selections, instructional materials and sheet music.
NEEDLEWORK	Knitting, quilting, crocheting, quilling and needlepoint are just some of the needle-and-thread hobbies covered by dozens and dozens of great sites.
PERFORMANCE	if you thrive in front of a crowd, we found a few sites catering to the needs of magicians, thespians, jugglers and other performers.
SCIENCE HOBBIES	As complicated as rocketry or as simple as looking at the stars, this key word represents a great variety of science and nature disciplines, the sites in question offering kits, books, tools and experiments to teach us all about the world.
SCRAPBOOKING	Scrapbooking has grown to become one of the most popular crafts over the past decade, and a terrific wealth of sites have sprung up to offer scrapbooks, paper, rubber stamps, stickers and other adornments for personalized documentation projects.

 **KEY WORD INDEX**

Use the followings lists to locate online retailers that sell the craft and hobby items you seek.

ART SUPPLIES

ArchivalSuppliers.com
ArtSuppliesOnline.com
BobRoss.com
ContinentalClay.com
CraftsEtc.com
DarkLilac.com
DickBlick.com
Herrschners.com
HobbyLinc.com
LightImpressionsDirect.com
Michaels.com
MisterArt.com
MosaicMercantile.com
Sculpt.com
ShopTheArtStore.com

CRAFTS

AddictedToRubberStamps.com
ArtSuppliesOnline.com
CandylandCrafts.com
CraftsEtc.com
DarkLilac.com
DharmaTrading.com
DickBlick.com
EdinburghImports.com
FactoryDirectCraft.com
FloralTrims.com
FlowerDepotStore.com
Herrschners.com
LorAnnOils.com
Martingale-Pub.com
Michaels.com
MisterArt.com
MJTrim.com
MoonGlowCandles.com
MosaicMercantile.com
QuilledCreations.com
Quilling.com
SeaShellCity.com
Seashells.com
SewTrue.com
ShipwreckBeads.com
ShopTheArtStore.com

CRAFTS (cont.)

TallPoppyCraft.com
TandyLeather.com
VanguardCrafts.com
WildPonyBaskets.com
ZarinFabrics.com

DRESSMAKING

DharmaTrading.com
Fabric.com
Greenberg-Hammer.com
HancockFabrics.com
Herrschners.com
McCall.com
MJTrim.com
NancysNotions.com
SewTrue.com
TandyLeather.com
TheSewingPlace.com

FOOD HOBBIES

CandylandCrafts.com
CreativeCutters.com
FactoryDirectCraft.com
Herrschners.com
KitchenKrafts.com
LorAnnOils.com

INTRUCTION

Abra4Magic.com
AmericanMusical.com
ArtSuppliesOnline.com
BobRoss.com
DarkLilac.com
DaytonaMagic.com
DharmaTrading.com
DickBlick.com
EdinburghImports.com
Fabric.com
GuitarTrader.com
HancockFabrics.com
Herrschners.com
HomeSpunSamplar.com
JenniferKnits.com
KnitWitts.com
LionBrand.com
LorAnnOils.com
Martingale-Pub.com
MaterialGirlsQuilts.com
McCall.com
MoonGlowCandles.com
MorehouseFarm.com
MusiciansStorehouse.com
NewYorkKnits.com
PurlSoho.com
QuilledCreations.com
Quilt-In-A-Day.com
RobotKitsDirect.com
ScientificsOnline.com
SheetMusicCatalog.com
SheetMusicPlus.com
ShopTheArtStore.com
SublimeStitching.com
SwakKnit.com
TallPoppyCraft.com
TheSewingPlace.com
TheTrickery.com
VanguardCrafts.com
WildPonyBaskets.com
WoolStock.com

JEWELRY-MAKING

AuntiesBeads.com
BruceFrankBeads.com
CraftsEtc.com
Herrschners.com
JewelrySupply.com
Michaels.com
ShipwreckBeads.com
TrollBeads.com

MODELS & TRAINS

1stPlaceHobbies.com
eHobbies.com
HobbyLinc.com
HobbyTron.net
HorizonHobby.com
Miniatures.com
RobotKitsDirect.com
RobotStore.com

MUSIC

AmericanMusical.com
BrooksMays.com
Elderly.com
GuitarTrader.com
Music123.com
MusiciansFriend.com
MusiciansStorehouse.com
SamAsh.com
SheetMusicCatalog.com
SheetMusicPlus.com

NEEDLEWORK

CraftsEtc.com
DarkLilac.com
EhrmanTapestry.com
eQuilter.com
Fabric.com
FabricsToDyeFor.com
HancockFabrics.com
Herrschners.com
HomeSpunSamplar.com
JenniferKnits.com
KnitWitts.com
LionBrand.com
Martingale-Pub.com
MaterialGirlsQuilts.com
Michaels.com
MorehouseFarm.com
NancysNotions.com
NeedlePointHeaven.com
NewYorkKnits.com
PurlSoho.com
Quilt-In-A-Day.com
QuiltHome.com
SublimeStitching.com
SwakKnit.com
TallPoppyCraft.com
WoolStock.com

PERFORMANCE

Abra4Magic.com
DaytonaMagic.com
HobbyTron.net
TheTrickery.com

SCIENCE HOBBIES

Binoculars.com
BuyTelescopes.com
eHobbies.com
HobbyLinc.com
HobbyTron.net
HorizonHobby.com
RobotKitsDirect.com
RobotStore.com
ScienceCompany.com
ScientificsOnline.com
SciPlus.com
ScopeCity.com

SCRAPBOOKING

AddictedToRubberStamps.com
ArchivalSuppliers.com
ArtSuppliesOnline.com
AScrappersDream.com
DickBlick.com
eSticker.com
GetScrappy.com
Herrschners.com
LightImpressionsDirect.com
Michaels.com
MisterArt.com
MostlyHearts.com
PaperAddict.com
PebblesInMyPocket.com
QuilledCreations.com
Quilling.com
RockyMountainHobbies.com
RubberBaby.com
Scrapbook.com
ScrappinCorners.com
ShopSei.com
StickerPlanet.com

1stPlaceHobbies.com

First Place Hobbies · 260-827-0765

Model train enthusiasts get a great first place to stop with this all-things-loco shop. It all starts, of course, with the trains, and you'll find an almost too large selection of freight and passenger cars, along with plenty of modern and retro locomotives, and no shortage of cabooses. But the site does delve deeper, offering much in the way of scaled-down architecture and scenery to fill in the world between the tracks (also available in massive quantities). Circus and military sections head up a host of miniature decorations like cars, people, utility poles and foliage that bring this classic hobby to life.

·MODELS & TRAINS				

Abra4Magic.com

Abracadabra Magic · 732-805-0200

For a performing art that relies so heavily on presentation, magic sure doesn't seem to inspire great-looking sites. But for all this shop's basic web design, it certainly offers an exquisitely savvy selection of card tricks, street magic, mentalism and plenty more involving ropes, rings and handkerchiefs. Browsing options include sections for beginners and children of differing age groups, as well as larger, more advanced tricks for the experienced prestidigitator. Browsing the vast number of items may take a while, but at least all the pointing and clicking will keep those fingers limber!

·PERFORMANCE	·INSTRUCTION			

AddictedToRubberStamps.com

Addicted To Rubber Stamps · 800-913-2877

Click on the Ideas link of this rubber stamp specialist and then scroll down the page to view the various categories of stamps available. Animals, People, Gardens, Celestials, World Themes and Occasions will lead you to illustrated images to spice up your scrapbook and/or other crafts projects, but it's under Collaging that you'll find the most handy selections, including Alphabets, Backgrounds, Frames and Patterns. Look under Accessories to find a wealth of colorful ink pads, papers, stickers, adhesives and embellishments. Somewhere here there might even be our stamp of approval.

·CRAFTS	·SCRAPBOOKING			

AmericanMusical.com

American Musical Supply · 800-458-4076

Probably the most comprehensive selection of instruments online, this music superstore covers a startling range of manufacturers but, more impressively, offers a great variety of models and styles within each brand, whether acoustic, electric or electronic. As a result, browsing here could take a while, but not in a bad way. While special edition and custom models may run a bit high, standard instrument prices actually prove to be quite reasonable for an online retailer, and while you might be able to talk a live salesperson into a better bargain at a brick-and-mortar store, the benefit of shopping here is that you don't have to talk to a salesperson at all.

·MUSIC	·INSTRUCTION			

800-628-1912 · University Products

ArchivalSuppliers.com

Whatever your paper passion, it can be conserved, presented, stored and preserved with a little help from this site. And by little, we mean a lot. This selection will quite likely exceed both your expectations and awareness of archival technology, and if it weren't for some pretty thorough organization (which is, of course, to be expected), we wouldn't know what to make of half these products. Fortunately, these boxes, sleeves, adhesives, scrapbooks and shelves are well suited to mount, bind and display your favorite photos, cards, coins, bills or other precious collectibles.

·ART SUPPLIES | ·SCRAPBOOKING | | |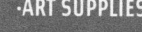

800-967-7367 · Penco Graphic Supply

ArtSuppliesOnline.com

Playing out like a inverted study in perspective, this site appears to be a modestly stocked art shop. However, take a closer look and you'll discover the catalog to be much deeper and wider that its surface suggests. Follow the Browse Our Catalog link to get a better look at the offerings of this art supply superstore. While a dull layout may try your attention span, the bevy of kid's crafts and instructional materials illustrate the shop's friendliness toward young and novice artists, not to mention anyone buying gifts for the creative type. But experts and professionals will find plenty to take advantage of as well, beginning with quality products, and ending with great prices.

·ART SUPPLIES | ·CRAFTS | ·SCRAPBOOKING | ·INSTRUCTION |

602-765-1580 · A Scrapper's Dream

AScrappersDream.com

Finally, a scrapbooking site that actually seems to have been designed by scrapbookers. However, this shop's appeal goes beyond its great looks—you'll find a terrific selection of stylish albums and cardstock, and in particular a fantastic assortment of embellishments, up to and including ribbons, metal charms and rubber stamps. The products here tend to favor sophisticated tastes, so if you're trying to assemble a cutesy baby book, you may want to shop elsewhere. However, we'd suggest taking a look around here, regardless, because this stuff may be good enough to change your mind.

·SCRAPBOOKING | | | |

866-262-3237 · Auntie's Beads

AuntiesBeads.com

The word *beads* does not effectively describe the full selection of this jewelry-making site, which offers all manner of baubles for your handmade accessories. Extensive varieties of chains, clasps, pendants and charms will be found on these well-organized pages, as well as tools, glue and other crafty supplies. But it will be the beads and baubles that occupy most of your time here, whether Austrian crystal, Czech glass, pearls or gemstones. There's no word as to just who Auntie is, but she should be commended.

·JEWELRY-MAKING | | | |

Binoculars.com

For optics devices as far as the eye can see, check out this specialty shop that betters your view of the world and beyond. The Binoculars selection might only compare unfavorably to the Digital Binoculars category, whereas there's no short supply of laser sightings, night vision goggles and opera glasses, whether or not you plan to use them for some nefarious activity. Not least, though, is a fantastically extensive catalog of telescopes, which may be used for the typical activities in addition to astronomy. There's too much to simply browse here, so you'll want to use the Advanced Search to narrow it down by intended use, special features and price range.

 ·SCIENCE HOBBIES

BobRoss.com

If you or someone you know is interested in painting but shy about getting started, public television painting guru Bob Ross has a way to help you to it. Although Ross passed on several years ago, his television show and "wet-on-wet technique" continue to inspire budding artists by taking away creative anxiety and instilling a sense of structure into the composition of the artwork. Thus, simple methods result in surprisingly detailed final products, and more importantly, everybody has fun in the process. On this site, you'll find preassembled kits that include all the tools and colors you'll need to create specific portraits and landscapes. Even in death, Mr. Ross may prove the best art teacher you've ever had.

  ·ART SUPPLIES   ·INSTRUCTION

BrooksMays.com

Specializing in school band equipment for more than a century, this musical instrument specialist provides a convenient place to shop for kid-size strings, brass and wind instruments online. Though established well before electric music was the norm, let alone electronic, the company has done a good job keeping up with the times, sourcing gear from some of the better-known techno-manufacturers as well as powered instruments and amplifiers. If your child is just learning, however, you might want to start him on something a little quieter. Your neighbors will appreciate it.

  ·MUSIC

BruceFrankBeads.com

Who is Bruce Frank? Well, he's an "antique collector by nature" who runs a bead and ethnographic arts gallery in New York as he is "captivated by the intense artistry and skill" these little threaded baubles possess. To be sure, he knows his stuff, so if you scroll to the Online Store link at the bottom of the page, you'll find an exquisite little catalog of beaded jewelry, things like necklaces and eyeglass chains, as well as strings of semiprecious stones. The coup de grace, though, is his unparalleled selection of glass beads. Each more beautiful than the last, they're likely to make his obsession your own.

 ·JEWELRY-MAKING

360-588-9000 · Anacortes Telescope & Wild Bird

BuyTelescopes.com

A multitiered focus makes this site worth a visit whether you're looking at birds, the universe or anything you'd like to capture on film. A wide range of binoculars will suit your bird-watching needs as well as long-distance sporting events. The Photo & Video section is highlighted by a variety of lenses, whether fisheye, wide angle or zoom. But it's clearly the telescopes and accessories selection that's built to please here, as the Astronomy section is uniquely set up to satisfy both beginners and knowledgeable enthusiasts, with simple and high-quality scopes, and even mini observatories for the particularly devoted (and well to do).

·SCIENCE HOBBIES			

908-685-0410 · Candyland Crafts

CandylandCrafts.com

If you want to take a hand in satiating your own sweet tooth, take a good look at this candy-making and cake-decorating specialist. You'll find plenty of delicious ingredients, such as caramel, creamy centers and edible glitter, plus a wide selection of molds and tins to shape your baked good and confections to suit a variety of themes, whether it's characters like Scooby Doo and Spider Man, free-domain fun such as trains and butterflies, or more elegant/traditional shapes. You may complete your presentation with a slew of packaging supplies, though be warned: it may be hard not to eat the finished product right away.

·CRAFTS	·FOOD HOBBIES		

800-432-2529 · Continental Clay Company

ContinentalClay.com

Getting your hands dirty may never be more fun than when you throw your own pottery. Everything you need to get your ceramics habit on may be found through this site, beginning with a tremendous variety of clays and continuing through glazes, sculpting tools and even kilns. Of course, you'll be needing a wheel, and the site offers plenty, including portable and kick styles, as well as a great variety of motorized models. Obviously, most of this stuff is very heavy, and despite the best efforts of the site to keep delivery costs down, even standard shipping rates are going to sting a little.

·ART SUPPLIES			

800-888-0321 · Crafts Etc!

CraftsEtc.com

Boasting "Over 20,000 Items at Discount Prices," one gets the feeling that this "Etc." is covering a lot of ground. Well, between art supplies, needlework, jewelry-making gear and materials for making mosaics, leather, wood and glass goods, that feeling definitely pans out. Although the site proves somewhat scattered, the ambitious crafter should find plenty to work with, and probably more than you bargained for. However, along with the site's broad range comes a slight lack of focus; if you've got something very specific in mind, you might want to look to a specialty shop.

·NEEDLEWORK	·ART SUPPLIES	·CRAFTS	·JEWELRY-MAKING

CreativeCutters.com

If you're still baking cakes in rectangular tins, you're totally square. To add a few more interesting shapes to your life, begin by logging on to this baking specialist, which offers cookie cutters and candy molds in addition to cake tins, each in a wide range of shapes, and we're talking more than just the bundt variety. Even better, you'll find airbrush tools, incredible colors and plenty else to make you next cake the best-looking thing that ever came out of your oven.

·FOOD HOBBIES

DarkLilac.com

If you've never viewed yourself as a particularly crafty person, but would like to get started or even just set something aside for a rainy day, this easy-to-use site with a wide focus offers a broad sampling of projects that can get you started with a variety of needlework activities, paint by numbers, children's crafts and more. Most of these are fairly simple, providing detailed instruction, but the shop's Beginner, Intermediate and Advanced ratings should prove useful if you discover yourself to be especially inept at one creative task or another.

·NEEDLEWORK ·ART SUPPLIES ·CRAFTS ·INSTRUCTION

DaytonaMagic.com

Magicians use distraction to get away with their sleights of hand, but don't be distracted by the paltry looks of this magic trick retailer. Behind the horrid façade lies one of the biggest collections of specially designed tricks ranging from the simple to the sublime. Beginning and experienced illusionists can benefit greatly from the site, but only if they follow the Search Engine Web Site link, then click on the Search By Category button. It's puzzling how far the shop's proprietors will make you go in order to find their card, coin, fire, rope and escapist tricks (to name just a few), but seeing as your audience will be just as stymied by your performance, we can't complain.

·PERFORMANCE ·INSTRUCTION

DharmaTrading.com

This site describes its wares as "Textile Craft Supplies & Clothing Blanks," which turns out to be a lot more fun than it sounds. The Clothing Blanks consist of t-shirts, pants, dresses, swimsuits, socks, scarves and other apparel/accessory items that consist of basic designs and a single uniform color (usually white), although you may also buy fabric by the yard. The Textile Craft Supplies are the paints, dyes, wax and tools needed to tie-dye, marble, stamp, transfer and/or batik your own patterns and images onto the clothes. The possibilities are endless, even if the fabric selections are finite. Still, with linens, rayons, hemps and silks in addition to basic cotton, there are enough materials to fill dozens of lively wardrobes.

·CRAFTS ·DRESSMAKING ·INSTRUCTION

800-723-2787 · Dick Blick

DickBlick.com

With a name somehow synonymous with art supplies, Dick Blick stores have been catering to the creative community for nearly a century. Now they bring their experience, expertise and customer-service philosophy to the web with this incredibly well-stocked site. As you begin to sift through the painting, pottery, sculpture, scrapbooking, archival, mosaic, silkscreening and crafts supplies, lengthy subcategory menus might make you feel like you're getting in over your head. But, no fear; when it comes to the products, you'll find a great representation of colors, detailed images and even the occasional shopping guide. These guys clearly know what they're doing.

·ART SUPPLIES	·CRAFTS	·SCRAPBOOKING	·INSTRUCTION

800-334-6274 · Edinburgh Imports

EdinburghImports.com

You might already be aware of the site that allows you to custom build a teddy bear to order. But, truth is, even choosing your own particular stuffed animal and costume can be a tad limiting. Here, on the other hand, you'll find all the raw materials you need to make your own bear. There are fabrics such as mohair, wool and alpaca, along with a lengthy list of patterns for stuffed bears, dogs, cats, horses and bunnies. Ultimately, you should probably start simple, but once you've got the hang of it, you can relish the thought that you've put a personalized touch on a classic toy, and for slightly less money than it would have cost to buy one readymade.

·CRAFTS	·INSTRUCTION		

877-346-2243 · The Hobby Hub

eHobbies.com

If you've been wading through all the sewing, scrapbooking, jewelry-making and domestic crafts sites and wondering what sort of Hobbies section this is, you may just be looking for this site. With electric trains, die-cast cars, radio-controlled toys and model kits, there's a decidedly more masculine leaning to this site's interpretation of hobbies. The rest of the selection focuses on educational and recreational science hobbies, with stuff as cool as rocket sets, as classic as ant farms and as out of this world as telescopes. Little boys will appreciate this site at whatever age, but we're guessing some little girls might like it too.

·MODELS & TRAINS	·SCIENCE HOBBIES		

888-826-8600 · Ehrman Tapestry

EhrmanTapestry.com

Practicing needlework on a canvas can be fun and rewarding... but only to a point. If you're ready to move on, this needlepoint specialist offers some decidedly more interesting mediums for the craft. Namely, you'll find kits designed to make decorative throw pillows, seat cushions and wall tapestries. The end results may or may not prove more functional than traditional samplers, as it were, but these projects will at the very least require a little more effort and focus, ultimately offering a greater degree of satisfaction.

·NEEDLEWORK			

Elderly.com

If you want the aesthetic appeal of your guitar to include its looks as well as sound, this string specialist will give you plenty to choose from. An incredibly comprehensive list of brands only tells half the tale, as the selection of stylish new guitars, banjos and ukuleles is trumped by the extraordinary assortment of vintage instruments. It may take a few tries to acclimate to the site's navigational structure, but the payoff is worthwhile, as you'll often find as many as nine detailed images of each item, offering close inspection of fretboards, headstocks, bodies and bridges. If you think this sounds good, you have got to take a look.

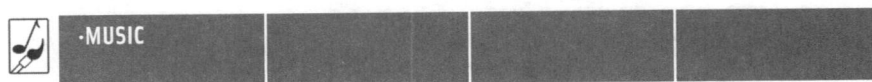
·MUSIC

eQuilter.com

Here's a must-see site for anyone who thinks quilting fabrics are boring. Sure, checks and plaids are overdone, and we could go twenty years without seeing another floral print, but visit this shop and you'll get plenty of modern takes on these traditional patterns that could change your mind. Better yet, there are hundreds of innovative and even outrageous fabrics here that are at the very least tough to ignore. Begin by following the eQuilter Store link, then start clicking through the poorly sorted pages until you've found more great fabrics than you could possibly need.

·NEEDLEWORK

eSticker.com

How much fun may be had with self-adhesive bits of paper? Visit this site to find out. With stickers covering a broad range of topics, you'll find plenty of materials for your scrapbooking and other crafts projects. Licensed stickers depicting characters from Disney, Nickelodeon, Warner Brothers and Marvel Comics are easily browsed, as are Holidays and Sports themes. Meanwhile, a section devoted to temporary tattoos may not help your scrapbook directly, but they can make for some great photo-ops.

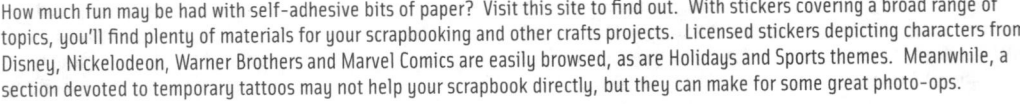

·SCRAPBOOKING

Fabric.com

Although this fabric specialist didn't use much creativity in coming up with its site name, the creative freedom it offers quilters, dressmakers and upholsterers is stunning. A quick glance at its menus turns up terrific varieties of corduroy, silk, flannel, faux fur, terrycloth, wool, velvet, velour and denim—and that's just in the Apparel & Fashion section; you'll find more in the Quilting and Home Decor pages. If the abundance of options leaves you lacking for inspiration, check out the tremendous assortment of patterns to see just what sort of homemade outfits you could be getting yourself into.

·NEEDLEWORK ·DRESSMAKING ·INSTRUCTION

401-348-0779 · Fabrics To Dye For

FabricsToDyeFor.com

Quilting gets a little easier and a lot better looking for the novice thanks to the hand-painted cotton designs offered by this site. The lovely quilt tops include floral patterns and pretty landscapes, as well as a few funky designs that will keep your hands busy as you fuse or stitch ornate designs around your choice of filler material. Understanding how the site works can take some time, and determining which supplies come with which designs and/or kits can be confusing as well. The process itself should be easy, however, and if you do it right these beautiful patterns will also keep you warm at night.

·NEEDLEWORK

800-252-5223 · Factory Direct Craft Supply

FactoryDirectCraft.com

Is it coincidence that the largest overall crafts selection online seems to be the most difficult-to-browse crafts selection? Probably not, but there's little excuse for the mess made of this utterly confusing site. However, wallow if you will among these pages, for the wealth of raw materials is unparalleled, whether your craft medium is metal, wood, paper, clay, glass, wax, fabric, foliage or something altogether edible. Order enough of these items and shipping is free; just try not to mix up which is which.

·CRAFTS   ·FOOD HOBBIES

800-589-1199 · FloralTrims.com

FloralTrims.com

When it comes to floral arrangements, the thousand varieties of flowers provided by nature and your favorite online nursery are usually all you'll need to put together something beautiful. But that's not to say you can't embellish with butterflies, birds or pink flamingos. This niche retailer is exclusively devoted to these faux natural decorative flourishes, offering many animal shapes made of feather, fabric, plastic or stone. How many uses can you find for these products?

·CRAFTS

877-780-2099 · Flower Depot Store

FlowerDepotStore.com

For a wealth of dried flowers and other floral arrangement supplies, it's tough to do better than this Kansas-based site. Along with all the tools and supplies you'll need to set, glue and/or preserve your standard arrangements, you'll find plenty of wreaths and bases to lend a bit of variety to your decorating projects. As for the flowers, stalwarts like hydrangeas, peonies, roses, larkspur and eucalyptus are well complemented by selections of ferns, pods, berries and lavender, delivering a wide range of colors and textures to dress any room of the house.

·CRAFTS

GetScrappy.com

Get Scrappy · 604-530-7677

A word of caution about this scrapbook embellishments shop: it's quite easy to get carried away. A wealth of categories includes Adhesives, Charms, Card Stock, Fiber & Ribbon, Cork, Stamping, Stickers, Paper and Transparencies, and even the ones that sound boring turn out to be surprisingly fun to browse. If there is one drawback to the site, it's a dearth of albums available, but in a way we understand. After all, when you have such charming functional adornments as heart-shaped brads and ghost-shaped eyelets, any album is bound to seem boring by comparison.

·SCRAPBOOKING

Greenberg-Hammer.com

Greenberg & Hammer · 800-955-5135

With an incredibly thorough selection of dressmaking tools and accessories, this site gives us a whole new appreciation for fashion designers. It's not always immediately clear just how much can go into the creation of any garment, but here more expected components like buttons, sewing needles and fabric dyes are enhanced by less obvious items along the lines of Piping, Bust Pads, Grommets, Elastic, Skirt Forms and Snaps. You'll find categories filled with each of these items and plenty more to give your homemade apparel a more professional touch.

·DRESSMAKING

GuitarTrader.com

Guitar Trader · 888-424-8482

If you're going to buy a guitar online, don't put the purchase through until you've checked this site first. While its selection of acoustic, electric, bass and left-handed guitars doesn't necessarily measure up to those of other music shops, its prices invariably do, even if the refurbished Scratch & Dent section doesn't offer anything special. All of the most popular and/or respected brands are represented, and you'll also find a healthy supply of amps, effects processors and recording equipment to help you achieve rock immortality.

·MUSIC   ·INSTRUCTION

HancockFabrics.com

Hancock Fabrics · 877-322-7427

Making your own clothing and quilts requires a steady hand, but if the final product is really going to be good you'll need to work with great raw materials. That's exactly why you'll want to check out the fantastic selection of fabrics that fill this national retailer's site. Actually, with the sewing notions, instructional guides and patterns here, you may be able to redecorate your home with just a needle and thread, as a good deal of these textiles are strong enough for furniture and accents. Still, it's easy to forget this while browsing the Fine Fashion fabrics.

·NEEDLEWORK   ·DRESSMAKING   ·INSTRUCTION

800-441-0838 · Herrschners

Herrschners.com

Seemingly designed to suit this section, this multifaceted site covers a full range of home projects, needlework and paper crafts. Within each category you'll find a wide, if not deep selection, including plenty of instructional materials, making this a terrific place to shop if you want to try out a new hobby or plan some daily activities for children. With a little help from this shop you can embroider a quilt, put together a scrapbook, make your own candy, paint by numbers or knit a scarf, and that's just during a slow week.

·NEEDLEWORK ·SCRAPBOOKING	·ART SUPPLIES ·DRESSMAKING	·CRAFTS ·FOOD HOBBIES	·JEWELRY-MAKING ·INSTRUCTION	

706-654-0176 · HobbyLinc.com

HobbyLinc.com

Attention to detail is the hallmark of the model builder, so any site catering to such a hobbyist should offer exquisite detail as well as a broad selection. This site offers both, with an incredible array of wood, metal and plastic model kits featuring ships, cars, planes, trains and more. You'll also find plenty of tools to help you work with the tiniest of parts, along with airbrush and acrylic paints for those finishing touches. If you prefer a bit of motion in your miniature machines, there are also decent selections of radio-controlled toys, electric trains and slot cars, as well as science kits covering everything from rockets and telescopes to chemicals and crystals. It's an excellent place to shop for an enthusiastic child, or for yourself, if you want to feel like a kid again.

·ART SUPPLIES	·MODELS & TRAINS	·SCIENCE HOBBIES		

801-434-7664 · HobbyTron.net

HobbyTron.net

Dabbling hobbyists could keep themselves entertained for decades with this multipurpose, one-stop fun shop. Which isn't to say that a dedicated enthusiast won't particularly enjoy the selections of remote-controlled vehicles, amateur radio transmitters, rockets, models and magic tricks, along with kits devoted to robots, electronics and other fields of science. Some of these items are purely educational, some recreational, and most exist somewhere in between, but whether you're a beginner or devotee, there's little doubt this site will feed your hobby habit.

·MODELS & TRAINS	·SCIENCE HOBBIES	·PERFORMANCE		

401-732-2131 · Homespun Samplar

HomeSpunSamplar.com

Not just a quaint wall decoration, a sampler can be a great means of practice for the sewing aficionado. This site delivers a complete sampler selection, including stamped linens, threads, a variety of blank linens and complete learner's kits that offer everything you need and guide you through every step of the process. You'll also find charts to follow for very simple alphabet primers, intermediate holiday scenes and on up to some complex illustrated tapestries. In no time at all you'll be forging your own designs, and then move on… maybe to embroidery.

·NEEDLEWORK	·INSTRUCTION			

HorizonHobby.com

Horizon Hobby · 800-338-4639

Radio-control hobbyists are not likely to find a better-equipped shop than this, offline or on. With thousands of RC airplanes, cars, boats and helicopters, you'll find working models and kits, as well as replacement parts and upgrades for just about all of them. You'll also find electric train parts and sets, a huge variety of die-cast models, slot cars and a number of working rockets in case you want to launch a hamster into space. Whether you're new to these toys or already an enthusiast, this shop will soon become one of your favorites.

 ·MODELS & TRAINS   ·SCIENCE HOBBIES

JenniferKnits.com

Jennifer Knits · 310-471-8733

Located just between the posh Los Angeles neighborhoods of Brentwood and Bel Air, it's little wonder this upscale yarn shop's brick-and-mortar store attracts a famous clientele. These celebrity knitting enthusiasts are probably attracted to the extensive selection of fine cashmere and silk skeins available here. Or maybe they prefer the tidy assortment of fashionable and sexy sweater, wrap and scarf patterns. Famous or not, we're betting you'll love everything about this site, right up to the surprisingly stylish knitting needles and entirely useful online lessons.

 ·NEEDLEWORK   ·INSTRUCTION

JewelrySupply.com

Jewelry Supply · 916-780-9610

We all know that making your own jewelry is easier on the pocketbook than buying it. Now, thanks to this shop we realize that it can be just as easy on the eyes. That would be due in part to the incredible variety of beads, baubles, chains, settings, clasps and charms you'll find within these pages. But that's only half the story. Just as important is the extensive selection of tools that ensure you can string, polish, solder, glue, cast and shape even the smallest of trinkets to your liking. And in case you're worried about missing out on the jewelry store boxes, you'll find those here too.

 ·JEWELRY-MAKING

KitchenKrafts.com

Kitchen Krafts · 800-776-0575

For dedicated bakers and fruit confectionists, this site offers tools and ingredients for cake decorating, candy making and canning. You'll find selections of cake pans, candy molds and cookie cutters with ease; the problem is that you must click all the way through to the item before you can get a look at it. However, the myriad products here range from the simple to the sublime and, with the help of the site's many tips, a bit of perseverance will pay off almost as much as some homemade marzipan will at your next bake sale.

 ·FOOD HOBBIES

877-877-5648 · Knit Witts Yarns & Patterns

KnitWitts.com

A fine garment begins with a great pattern and fine materials. Both are available from this top-tier knitting and yarn shop that forsakes a broad selection in favor of quality. From Shetland Wools and faux Chinchilla to Mohair and Alpaca Lace, you'll find soft, fuzzy and or stylish materials here for variety of projects including sweaters, shawls and socks. At this point, only your talent with a set of knitting needles can prevent your next project from becoming superior-quality, highly fashionable garb.

| ·NEEDLEWORK | ·INSTRUCTION | | |  |

800-828-6216 · Light Impressions

LightImpressionsDirect.com

Avid photographers may never run out of images to capture, however, they might just run out of space to store them. Not with this archival supply specialist that offers a wide range of storage options for pictures, slides and negatives—and that's just for the shots you want to tuck away from view. An extensive array of presentation items include mounting and framing materials, protective sleeves and a variety of scrapbooks and photo albums will ensure longevity for those pictures you wish to show off as well as preserve.

| ·ART SUPPLIES | ·SCRAPBOOKING | | | |

212-243-8995 · Lion Brand Yarn Company

LionBrand.com

A lot of knitting shops will carry a greater variety of yarns than does this specialty manufacturer, but few offer a selection so intriguing. Branded styles such as Moonlight Mohair, Magic Stripes, Glitterspun and Festive Fur are impossible not to explore, while Cotton, Lamé, Suede and Chenille options offer everything you'd expect and more. If it wasn't enough that the site makes something so simple as wool seem suddenly exciting, it also offers free downloadable patterns, so you can very inexpensively put these great materials to task.

| ·NEEDLEWORK | ·INSTRUCTION | | |  |

888-456-7266 · LorAnn Oils

LorAnnOils.com

What do soap and candy have in common? Probably little more than this site. However, both are so well represented that they'll be forever in our minds connected. Of course, it's not that this site sells soap and candy; rather, it sells the tools and ingredients necessary for you to make your own. And not mediocre stuff, either, but gourmet candy and gift-quality soaps. Molds for soap include geometric, floral and animal shapes, while the candy molds come in... slightly different geometric, floral and animal shapes. No word on whether they're interchangeable.

| ·CRAFTS | ·FOOD HOBBIES | ·INSTRUCTION | |  |

Martingale-Pub.com

Martingale & Company · 800-426-3126

Crafts supplies will only get you so far on their own—at some point you'll need a few tips on how to hook that rug or pad your quilt. This small but useful site offers instructional books for a variety of crafts projects, including an intro to knitting, painting techniques and how to make your own paper. The books make great gifts for crafty friends, or will teach you how to make a great gift for the less crafty people in your life. Hobbyists in doubt should shop here first, then check out other shops in this section to find the materials you need to proceed.

	·NEEDLEWORK	·CRAFTS	·INSTRUCTION	

MaterialGirlsQuilts.com

Material Girls Quilters' Emporium · 918-747-7525

Despite the name, quilt makers of both genders will adore this unique and well-stocked fabric shop out of Tulsa, Oklahoma. In fact, if more men haven't taken up the hobby, they just haven't seen how simple and rewarding it can be. One good look at this site should change that, as the fabric selection is wide and varied enough to please all tastes, whether a guy favors traditional floral patterns, cutesy illustrations or something vibrantly funky. Okay, so maybe most of the happy quilters shopping here will be female, but we're predicting they will be very, very happy.

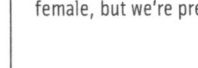

	·NEEDLEWORK	·INSTRUCTION		

McCall.com

McCall Pattern Company · 800-766-3619

If you happen to have some skills with a sewing machine, this site offers a tremendous opportunity for you to boost the quality of your wardrobe without busting your bank account. With hundreds of dress, blouse, pants and skirt patterns at your disposal, you become privy to the designs of some fantastic designer apparel, some of which you may recognize, and probably all of which will look great on you (assuming you make them right). Materials are not available here, but since this lack allows you to track down the fabrics and patterns you like best, we figure this is a good thing.

	·DRESSMAKING	·INSTRUCTION		

Michaels.com

Michaels Stores · 800-642-4235

This crafty individual's one-stop shop covers a wide range of products, including those necessary for scrapbooking, painting, knitting, jewelry-making and plenty of domestic and family projects that don't fall easily into one category or another. Seasonal items make the site a great place to shop for bits and pieces to be applied to your holiday decorations, while a Weddings category provides inexpensive solutions to ceremony and reception decor, as well as invitations. While there's a lot here to see, finding it won't always be easy, so you'll need to be as adept at shopping for crafts as you are putting them together.

	·NEEDLEWORK ·SCRAPBOOKING	·ART SUPPLIES	·CRAFTS	·JEWELRY-MAKING

800-223-7171 · Benamy International

We're going to hazard a guess that anyone familiar with the Hobby Builders Supply catalog is a big fan of dollhouses. Well, here's the web version of the catalog, with all the miniature dollhouse furniture and decorative accents it's offered for the past three decades. If you're a fan of dollhouses and have never seen the catalog, make haste to log on to this lovely site devoted to the most intricately detailed little objects, where you'll find just about anything imaginable, from mini bar furniture (and ashtrays) to tiny (decorative only) home theater equipment.

| ·MODELS & TRAINS | | | | |

866-672-7811 · MisterArt.com

Like marketable art, some sites get by being expensive but pretty, while others thrive by being functional and affordable. This site represents the latter. The art shop's layout may not be great to look at, but with these prices we'll gladly wade through the many pages of "The World's Largest Online Discount Art & Crafts Supply Store" for markers, canvas, textile paints, archival supplies, clays, sculpting tools, mosaic items, papier-mâché, candle making materials and airbrushes. Your hands may be busy for a while.

| ·ART SUPPLIES | ·CRAFTS | ·SCRAPBOOKING | | |

800-965-8746 · M&J Trimming

If you've sewn yourself the perfect outfit, only to discover that it's missing that special something, this site ought to help. Replete with fashionable trim options, ranging from lace, fur and fringe to braids, rhinestones and ribbons, the materials here should offer just the right decorative panache to your newly assembled wardrobe. You'll also find buttons, buckles, clasps and other closures, along with a selection of handles, in case your designer instincts veer toward handbags as well. To that end, what you do with these sartorial components is up to you; there are probably a million projects that would benefit from this specialty shop's touch of flair.

| ·CRAFTS | ·DRESSMAKING | | |  |

866-477-1408 · Moon Glow

Scented candles and soap are popular gifts, in part because they're beautiful and functional, but mostly because they require little thought or effort, making the act of choosing a gift tremendously easy for the giver. This site offers a way to give these products as gifts, but still offer a touching sentiment—by making them yourself. A full complement of soy-based ingredients enable you to craft soap and candles in a variety of shapes, colors and scents. If you're not enthralled by any of the numerous molds available, you may opt to make cream, lotion or shower gels, with an assortment of reusable containers as well. Buying these products off the shelf may be easier, but they'll never be so well received.

| ·CRAFTS | ·INSTRUCTION | | | |

MorehouseFarm.com

If you're relatively new to knitting, this merino wool specialist can get you started with several stylish kits to help you make a variety of sweaters, scarves, shawls and hats. If you can already knit your own designs in your sleep, you'll still appreciate the quality and selection of yarns, available in several weights, in a wide array of natural and variegated colors. This Hudson River Valley farm aspires to "grow the finest wool in this country," and they may well have succeeded. Making the finest wool clothes and accessories is up to you.

 ·NEEDLEWORK ·INSTRUCTION

MosaicMercantile.com

Piecing together a great site must have come naturally to the proprietors of this mosaic specialty shop. To begin with, they offer a spectacular selection of proprietary Tile & Tesserae, including mini, metallic and assorted color tiles, as well as beach glass, pebbles and opalescents. But these materials aren't enough to make a mosaic alone, so the site provides nippers, adhesives and other tools to fit and grout your tesserae into place, whether you have your own unique project in mind, or wish to follow one of the forms or kits also available here. With a little help from this site, the truly ambitious may even refloor parts of their home.

  ·ART SUPPLIES ·CRAFTS

MostlyHearts.com

Rubber stamps may be both the easiest and most fun way to embellish your scrapbook, dress up a personal note or print your return address on an envelope. Regardless, this site's been designed to meet your rubber-stamping needs. Primarily, you'll find a bevy of fun mini images as well as greetings and more general messages of universal appeal. Browsing can take a while but proves entertaining, and though it may be the least fun part of your shopping experience here, sifting through the available variety of inks may just be the most rewarding part of your visit, because (as we can attest) sometimes black ink is just boring.

 ·SCRAPBOOKING

Music123.com

Getting the band together will be the hard part if you visit this musical superstore, which offers just about every kind of instrument, as well as sheet music, lighting, recording and PA gear. Nearly every conceivable brand is also represented, whether in strings, woodwinds, percussion or brass, and you'll even find a healthy selection of DJ equipment for the modern music enthusiast. The site's design handles this vast selection fairly well, so while getting around may take a bit of time, it won't be very difficult. On thing sure is easy, though: spending lots and lots of money. You will find some good bargain instruments, but the truly great ones rarely come cheap.

 ·MUSIC

800-391-8762 · Musician's Friend

MusiciansFriend.com

Every age, level and style of musician will want to become better acquainted with this musician's superstore, which caters equally well to rock bands, DJs, producers and high school orchestras, whether you're strictly acoustic or dabble in the electronic realm. Brand, category and price filters will easily locate your desired range of products from a selection of thousands, and a handy comparison feature will help you narrow it down from there. Once you realize just how easy this one is, you'll want to pick up a new instrument.

·MUSIC

866-458-8687 · Musiciansstorehouse.com

MusiciansStorehouse.com

Experienced musicians may take exception to the name of this site, as its wares prove somewhat less than professional grade. However, their loss is our gain, as the shop proves a fantastic place to buy your first instrument, especially with regard to price. Guitars head up the list, including specific categories for Left-Handed and Girl Guitars (usually pastel), while other stringed instruments like Mandolins, Banjos and Ukuleles also receive special treatment. Brass, Woodwinds and Percussion instruments are less thoroughly represented, though the benefit of a site like this isn't extensive selection; rather, it's a place where you may easily find reasonable solutions to your burgeoning instrument needs.

·MUSIC ·INSTRUCTION

800-245-5116 · Nancy's Notions

NancysNotions.com

Whatever your needle-and-thread need, this all-sewing-all-the-time site will probably answer it. After all, site founder Nancy Zieman hosts *Sewing With Nancy*, the longest-running sewing show on television, meaning that more than two decades' worth of needlework knowledge is represented in this catalog. Dozens of categories cover a slew of crafts, guiding you to dressmaking supplies, fabrics, patterns and trims, along with plenty of embroidery, quilting and knitting materials. Whether you follow the show or head in your own direction, you won't go wrong here.

·NEEDLEWORK ·DRESSMAKING

877-446-0704 · NeedlepointHeaven

NeedlePointHeaven.com

If keeping those hands occupied is your idea of heaven, this needlepoint specialist certainly will prove divine. Stocked full of colorful canvases, these products will guide your needle to create lovely images and patterns, ranging from storybook scenes to pet portraits. Categories such as Fruits & Flowers, Country At Heart and Decorator's Corner make finding samplers to suit your style a simple matter, and though you may need to scroll and hunt the page to view all the products and pages, rest assured there's plenty here to make both your hand and eyes happy.

·NEEDLEWORK

NewYorkKnits.com

New York Knits · 585-924-1950

New York is inarguably the US center of fashion, but did you know it's also a big knitting hub? Well, this upstate knit shop is actually closer to Canada than Manhattan, but it does seem to effortlessly bridge the gap between do-it-yourself clothes making and sophisticated style. A fine selection of yarns complements an outstanding assortment of patterns covering cool summer and hot winter garb for men, women and children. If you feel you've knitted enough scarves and blankets to last a lifetime, check out this excellent small business turned web seller and take your hobby to the next level.

 ·NEEDLEWORK · INSTRUCTION

PaperAddict.com

PaperAddict · 914-245-7706

Unless you're trying to write down somebody's phone number, a piece of paper is never hard to find. So why make a fuss about this site, which deals almost exclusively in sheets of paper? You'd almost have to see it to believe it. The incredible textures, colors and styles of paper here are unprecedented, with enough to keep you ravenously browsing for hours. It might just take you that long, as all these products are arranged by brand name, in a list that runs four times the length of the home page. But if you're jonesing for a very particular sort of page for your scrapbook or craft project, time spent shopping here will be worth it.

 ·SCRAPBOOKING

PebblesInMyPocket.com

Pebbles in my Pocket · 800-438-8153

If scrapbooking is a hobby but not a passion, this might be the site you want to shop from. While the selection of scrapbooking supplies is comparable to that of most standard sites, this one is unique in offering quick-and-easy thematic shopping for when you just want the right materials to record the right memories. Just pull down the Category menu and select Themes to view a list of easy to mix-and-match items for holiday, animal, seasonal and family-appropriate products that will let you get in, get out and get scrapbooking in time to create the next memorable moment.

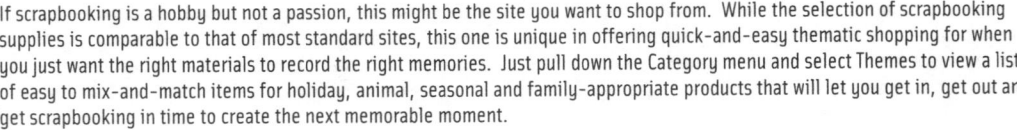

 ·SCRAPBOOKING

PurlSoho.com

Purl · 800-597-7875

In most cases, it's tough to make the case that shopping for yarn online will be easier than browsing in a brick-and-mortar store. With this site, we're willing to stake such a claim. This is due not only to the fantastic selection of yarns the shop has to offer, but also to the terrific organization that allows you to shop by Brand, by Weight/Gauge, By Fiber or by a combination of the three traits. As a result, you may easily narrow down the Wool, Bamboo, Cashmere, Alpaca, Angora, Mohair, Nylon and Silk yarns to find the best material for your particular project. To that end, the same organization carries over into a wide range of knitting and crochet patterns, so you may shop by garment, size or person to make anything from scarves and shawls to sweaters and even bikinis.

 ·NEEDLEWORK · INSTRUCTION

585-388-0706 · Quilled Creations

QuilledCreations.com

If you've ever expressed yourself by twisting pieces of paper into patterns or shapes, you may be pleased to discover there's a name for it: quilling. Useful when decorating scrapbook pages, or creating decorative home accents, quilling can technically be done with your fingers and any old scrap of paper. But why take such a sloppy approach when this site offers a vast array of colorful and textured papers, not to mention a batch of helpful dedicated tools? Take a look, and this one might just turn your nervous habit into a full-fledged hobby.

·CRAFTS	·SCRAPBOOKING	·INSTRUCTION		

417-725-8444 · Lake City Craft Co.

Quilling.com

Also known as paper filigree, quilling is a craft that involves coiling paper strips and piecing them together into various patterns and images. It's tough to explain, and may even be difficult to decipher from looking at photos, but rest assured this may be the ultimate in craft projects for fidgety hands. Here you'll find books, guides and kits, as well as the raw paper materials and tools to quill your own designs, then apply them to family craft, home decorating or scrapbooking projects.

·CRAFTS	·SCRAPBOOKING			

800-777-4852 · Quilt in a Day

Quilt-In-A-Day.com

You may of course dictate your own pace, but if you want to get going on a new quilting hobby, this is the place to start. With plenty of books, patterns and instructional media, you'll find the site a nice orientation into the quilting world. Same goes for the fabrics and other materials, which don't exist in great supply but do offer some time-tested looks. If you enjoy your initial attempts, you may quickly find yourself outgrowing this selection, but you'll never forget your first time.

·NEEDLEWORK	·INSTRUCTION			

877-684-9001 · Quilt Home

QuiltHome.com

If you only make one quilt this year, be sure to check this shop before deciding on a fabric. With hundreds to choose from, you'll find traditional floral designs, a broad range of textured solids and plenty of contemporary patterns you probably wouldn't expect. On top of that, a comprehensive quilting library includes tips on sewing and fabric care, as well as a helpful glossary of terms, should you feel the need to brush up on the lingo and impress your sewing circle. Chances are, if you visit this one, you'll make at least two or three quilts this year.

·NEEDLEWORK				

RobotKitsDirect.com

ScienceKits.com · 301-294-9729

Sure, the word *robot* brings you in to this site, but in truth you'll find all manner of science represented here, including chemistry, paleontology, environmental science, geology, astronomy and general electronics. Of course, there is some robotics fun to be had, and while none of these areas are comprehensively represented, the collection generally provides a good place to start, whether for children or for grown-ups who didn't get to nurture their science hobby urges at an early age. If you buy one of these kits for the family, please remember to share.

  ·MODELS & TRAINS · ·SCIENCE HOBBIES · ·INSTRUCTION

RobotStore.com

Mondo-tronics · 415-491-4600

It seems that everywhere you look these days there are some robots in need of a home. Check out this "Original Robot Site" to find one to call your own. The vast selection includes toy robots, robot pets, robot kits and, for the advanced user, robot components and parts that will help you design your own. This may just be the coolest hobby science has ever had to offer, and there's plenty here to get both novice robot owners and old hands into the act. Adopt one today.

  ·MODELS & TRAINS · ·SCIENCE HOBBIES

RockyMountainHobbies.com

Rocky Mountain Hobbies · 720-929-9596

If you're suffering from scrapbooker's block, this site offers two ways you might try to get over it. The first: take a look at The Gold Mine gallery for inspiration from other scrappers who're willing to share tips and ideas. The second: visit The General Store. This well-organized shop makes it easy for you to find a range of unique products that should kick start your scrapbooking heart. The paper selection is particularly impressive, but with dozens and dozens of available brand names, it's also large enough to be frightening. Be sure to use the Refine Results menu to guide you through the 2,000 brilliant paper designs, or you'll never get started on that next book.

 ·SCRAPBOOKING

RubberBaby.com

Rubber Baby Buggy Bumpers · 970-224-3499

Find the Product List link on this site to get started... not that it will make things very easy. However difficult to use, this site proves worthwhile simply by virtue of the bizarre and unexpected rubber stamps in its catalog. Among the designs we found were a map of Rome, an old-fashioned bathtub and an entire section devoted to Surrealist painter Rene Magritte. Given its propensity for slow loading and surprising images, this is not a site you'll want to take in all in one sitting; rather, come back to it every so often, and eventually you'll find something great.

 ·SCRAPBOOKING

800-472-6274 · Sam Ash Music Stores

SamAsh.com

Established in 1924, Sam Ash music is actually pretty close to being, as it claims, "The World's Favorite Music Store," boasting "over 70,000 square feet of gear in stock at all times." We're not sure exactly how many square feet a single guitar takes up, but the national retailer's online selection includes an incredible variety of musical instruments, performance gear and recording equipment across hundreds of brands and a broad range of prices. Offers of free shipping, interest-free payment plans and a lowest-price guarantee may not be enough to make this the planet's favorite, but might be enough to make it yours.

·MUSIC

800-372-6726 · The Science Company

ScienceCompany.com

When you're running short on microscope slides or potassium iodide, don't forget to take this site into account. Devoted to the pursuit of science, it's thoroughly stocked with chemicals, lab supplies, telescopes, microscopes, and water-quality instruments and meteorological equipment, so you can explore the physical world from the inside out, or vice versa. Plenty of beginner's science kits will also help kids get on the road to genius, but please keep in mind that many of the materials found here involve some pretty heavy science, so be sure to offer parental direction, unless of course, your child is already smarter than you.

·SCIENCE HOBBIES

800-728-6999 · Edmund Scientifics

ScientificsOnline.com

With a distinctly educational slant, this science hobby specialist offers a wealth of beginner-oriented materials disarming enough to win over even the least studious among us. Whether chemistry sets, anatomical models, rudimentary engines or microscopes, the products contained within this site demonstrate the principles of the physical world without ever becoming boring or mundane. Thus, understanding weather, the solar system, electricity and solar power becomes way more interesting than it might sound. Heck, here even rocks sound fun.

·SCIENCE HOBBIES ·INSTRUCTION

847-647-0011 · American Science & Surplus

SciPlus.com

Faced with the unenviable task of making electrophysical science seem fun, this site succeeds with great humor and educational aplomb. Categories like Communications & Electronics, Optics, Drives & Wheels, Lab Supplies, Militaria and Robot Parts may not turn up exactly what you'd expect, and frankly we don't know enough about science to contradict their categorization. However, browse these pages and you'll soon find yourself riveted to product descriptions describing Seismic Detectors, Solar Panels, Transistor Kits and Crystal Radios. Now did you ever think that would happen?

·SCIENCE HOBBIES

ScopeCity.com

Scope City · 800-235-3344

Whether you're enamored of the world around you, far above you, or invisible to your naked eye, this site offers some incredibly high-end solutions, and yes, they pretty much all involve lenses of some size. The telescopes are impressive, whether you're buying a new one outright or want to upgrade certain components of the one you've got. But the same quality and quantity applies to most of the categories here, including Binoculars, Microscopes and Night Vision. Particularly appealing is the Brass, Antique & Decorative section, which is great in looks, if small in scope.

·SCIENCE HOBBIES

Scrapbook.com

Scrapbook.com · 800-727-2726

We're always happy to see a memorable URL attached to a worthy web shop, and this site is certainly built to please. You simply will not find an easier-to-use online scrapbooking shop without sacrificing quality and selection. These guys ask you to sacrifice nothing, delivering a comprehensive selection of memorable albums, papers and embellishments, including plenty in the way of stickers and rubber stamps. Given that half of your scrapbooking success takes place while shopping for materials, visit this site to give yourself a huge head start.

·SCRAPBOOKING

ScrappinCorners.com

Scrappin' Corners · 817-563-1340

Most scrapbooking sites with this large a selection of card stock, embellishments, stickers, rubber stamps, ribbons, albums and myriad other materials would be incredibly difficult to use. This one, however, combines exquisitely thorough organization and helpful menu animation to make shopping for anything a satisfying breeze. Other, smaller shops may specialize in quirky or fancy materials, but if you're looking for simple, straightforward and affordable avenues to express yourself in scrapbook form, this is the shop you want.

·SCRAPBOOKING

Sculpt.com

The Compleat Sculptor · 800-972-8578

If you see shapes where others see formless rocks, you've probably got a sculptor inside that will definitely benefit from this site. Along with a terrific assortment of colorful stones, you'll find chisels, hammers, sanders, grinders and polishes to help coax them into your creative vision. But it's not all limited to rock work, as you'll find a comprehensive selection of casting materials, clays, wood-carving tools and then some, offering you a mastery over the physical realm in almost every conceivable form.

·ART SUPPLIES

888-743-5524 · Sea Shell City

SeaShellCity.com

This "largest seashell store on the shore" offers more than allusion to a tongue twister. Its assortment of shells is top notch, with more than three dozen categories of spiral shells alone. You'll also find deep selections of bivalves, sand dollars, starfish, sponges, urchins and blowfish, whether you intend them as raw materials for a crafts project or as aquarium decor. Finding this many types of shells for yourself would require hundreds of hours scouring hundreds of miles of coastline, and even then you'd have to be pretty lucky. If you're going to buy shells online, do it here.

·CRAFTS

239-472-1603 · Sanibel Seashell Industries

Seashells.com

However far you live from the ocean, its unique decorative charms are available to you thanks to this nautical specialist. Starfish, Sand Dollars and Sea Glass warrant their own categories, and actually prove easy to browse. However, it's obviously the seashell selection we're here for, and it will be well worth your time to sift through the Mini, Medium and Large shell pages to find the right clam shells, tritons, sundials, trochuses, nerites, hermit crab shells and conchs for your sea-oriented projects.

·CRAFTS

800-739-8783 · Sew True Zipper Company

SewTrue.com

If you'd like to hem your drapes, or even turn them into a dress, you'll need more than needle and thread. This site's smart selection of sewing machines will get you started, but it's all the little things that will get the job done. Things like fasteners, measuring tools, cutting tools, chalks and elastics will help you turns a formless piece of fabric into a custom-made frock, or will at least be enough to let you alter and repair the clothes you already have. Check out the Instructional Books section if you have any doubts.

·CRAFTS   ·DRESSMAKING

800-395-5471 · Sheet Music Catalog

SheetMusicCatalog.com

MP3 downloads are currently the most popular format for music, claiming the crown from CDs, which followed cassettes, 8-tracks and vinyl records, but this site offers what is arguably the first musical medium: the songbook. Way back before recording technology, if people wanted to listen to popular music in their own homes they had to play it themselves. A shop like this would have come in handy, offering the notation for decades' worth of popular songs and compositions, covering a great variety of instruments and styles. Stage lights, microphones and roadies sold separately.

·MUSIC   ·INSTRUCTION

SheetMusicPlus.com

Sheet Music Plus · 800-743-3868

When the endless self-amusement of jamming has lost its luster, take a look to this site for inspiration. More precisely, look here for an impressively comprehensive selection of sheet music for a full range of popular artists. However, regardless of the popularity of the performer or composer, odds are good the music will turn up here, whether the genre is rock, jazz, country, choral, new age, blues, showtunes or classical. Or, if you have a particular instrument in mind, you may browse by strings, woodwinds, brass and percussion, including such specific instruments as accordion, harmonica, mandolin and dulcimer. You can also find out what a dulcimer is.

·MUSIC	·INSTRUCTION		

ShipwreckBeads.com

Shipwreck Beads · 800-950-4232

We've seen a lot of things online, but nothing could prepare us for the simply awesome number of beads we found on this site. Czech Lamp Beads, Dichroic Art Glass, Peruvian Ceramic, Painted Porcelain, Swarovski Crystal, India Glass and Fiber Optics only account for some of the more exotic bead selections. Then there are the Gem Stone, Pearls, Precious Metal, Bone & Horn and Shell beads, along with standard wood, plastic, rubber, glass and duller metal varieties, each in plenty of shapes and colors. If you think that's all, you're ignoring the all-important beading tools, strings and clasps, necessary to any design, and even beading software, for the technologically ambitious jewelry designer.

·CRAFTS	·JEWELRY-MAKING		

ShopSEI.com

Sew Easy Industries · 800-333-3279

A scrapbook is only as good as its contents, and while most of those are up to you, there are a few things you can use to make them look better, and this site has most of them. Beginning with the albums and papers themselves, you'll find a bevy of colorful and funky designs that will right away give your book some flair. But the shop takes it a bit further, offering embellishments like stickers, ribbons, buttons and iron-ons, which may add a little context to your photos and clippings, or might just be fun to add into your memory-preserving project.

·SCRAPBOOKING			

ShopTheArtStore.com

The Art Store · 800-652-2225

It's not often a site's URL offers good advice, but in this case it might: if you're looking for a fine selection of art supplies, shopping the Art Store will serve you right. Check out the Product Catalog to see the extensive list of available supplies and materials, including Calligraphy Markers, Canvas & Materials, Mosaic Supplies, Origami Paper, Sketch Books and Watercolors. Of course, you'll find paints and brushes of all kinds, as well as clays and plenty of other sculptural materials. And, since we are shopping in the digital world, there's a complete Digital Art Supplies section that offers fonts, photos, images and backgrounds to make a graphic designer's work a little easier.

·ART SUPPLIES	·CRAFTS	·INSTRUCTION	

800-557-8678 · Sticker Planet

StickerPlanet.com

If you come to this site looking for stickers of all shape, size and purpose, you'll probably be disappointed. If, however, you are an ardent scrapbooker looking for a wide selection of self-adhesive graphics to adorn your collection of memorable moments, read on. While clumsily assembled, this site turns out to be pretty well organized and, once you've figured out how to navigate the very long category menu and its various subheadings, wading through the impressive amount of pastel alphabets and thematic illustrations should be worth your while.

·SCRAPBOOKING

512-922-1413 · Sublime Stitching

SublimeStitching.com

Embroidery has been called "the art of enriching a fabric with stitchery." Well, thanks to this site, it's and easy and affordable way to enrich your fabrics. You can easily get started on this needlework hobby with a few easy instructional patterns and kits available from the specialty shop, then practice on the selection of blank pillows, towels and bibs. Once you've grown accustomed to the ins and outs of the art form, you'll be able to personalize just about anything a needle can penetrate, at which point you probably won't even need the help of this sublime retailer anymore.

·NEEDLEWORK ·INSTRUCTION

405-282-8649 · Sealed With A Kiss

SwakKnit.com

Finding a particular type of yarn in this online knit shop may not be easy or even possible, but if you happen to be in the market for an appealing, quality yarn, this site makes it hard not to find one. Though you may only browse individual skeins by brand, even the unfamiliar names turn up quirky, colorful and extravagant yarns with names like Gossamer, Baby Monkey and Fizz. In most cases, the texture and hues of these snazzy finds are tough to predict, but if you'd like a little inspiration for your next knitting venture, try picking one of these yarns at random, and see what sort of project springs to mind.

·NEEDLEWORK ·INSTRUCTION

212-613-3166 · Tall Poppy Craft Products

TallPoppyCraft.com

This site offers a very particular craft that will prove incredibly entertaining and especially useful to the handy fashion maven. Specifically, it offers everything you need to design and make your own handbags. Sure, this book can point you to dozens of web shops offering beautiful and remarkable selections of this all-important ladies' accessory, but if you find the high cost of a designer tote discouraging, wade through the fabrics, handles, beads, buckles and tools available from this still-growing site and find all the inspiration you need to make a fashion statement truly your own.

·NEEDLEWORK ·CRAFTS ·INSTRUCTION

TandyLeather.com

Tandy Leather Company Direct · 888-890-1611

There are many things that can be made with leather, but a look at this site begs the question: what can't you make with leather? Certainly belts springs to mind as the easiest and most common project, and a devoted section can help you design a buckle as well. But the true power of this specialty shop is that it offers all the materials and knowledge you need to create whatever is your inspiration, whether you prefer to work with specific project kits or simply browse a variety of animal skins including deer, lamb, goat and rattlesnake. While we don't recommend designing your own leather raincoat, your only true limitations are the properties of physical science.

·CRAFTS	·DRESSMAKING		

TheSewingPlace.com

The Sewing Place · 800-587-3937

While this site specializes in "hard-to-find items for fashion sewists," including buttons, ribbons, elastic, zippers, shoulder pads and more, the truth is, one very important item is missing from this dressmaker's catalog: fabric. Neither will you find the actual tools necessary to piece together all of your homemade wardrobe's components. However, as a first step toward putting together your own outfits from scratch, this shop does offer a terrific selection of patterns for a wide variety of garments and styles, ranging from lingerie and sleepwear to dresses and accessories. You can always find your choice of fabric elsewhere, but come here for inspiration.

·DRESSMAKING	·INSTRUCTION		

TheTrickery.com

The Trickery · 973-657-0446

Probably the best magic shop on the web, this site makes great use of interactive technology to show off the wide and deep variety of tricks for sale, including detailed descriptions, top ten lists and customer reviews to help you track down the best illusions for your repertoire. While the site's clearly designed for intermediate and experienced prestidigitators, if you keep your eyes open you'll notice a link to a whole separate store designed for beginners, where the same ease of use will point you in the right direction so that, someday, you can add words like *the great* or even *the magnificent* to the end of your name.

·PERFORMANCE	·INSTRUCTION		

TrollBeads.com

Trollbeads · 011-453-393-6093

If your jewelry-making skills have run their course using standard materials, take a good look at the unique selection of baubles offered by this European bead specialist. These thematically shaped gold, silver and gemstone components are often inspired by mythology, fairy tales and nature, combining brilliant colors, vibrant patterns and the occasional funky caricature. Piece them together with the site's offering of chains, clasps and pendants, or incorporate them into your usual motifs; either way, you'll wind up with homemade jewels that feel entirely new.

·JEWELRY-MAKING			

800-662-7238 · **Vanguard Crafts**

If you're pursuing crafts activities without the aid of children, somebody's missing out. Of course, very detailed and advanced projects are the realm of adults, but if you've got some small hands helping out, there are some crafts kits here that will prove fun for kids and grown-ups alike. You'll find the obligatory paperweight projects, along with classic favorites such as the tissue box cover and recipe holder, but look under the Online Catalog and you'll see dozens of crafts categories, including raw materials as well as dedicated kits. In other words, some fun for everyone.

·CRAFTS ·INSTRUCTION

573-472-1960 · **Wild Pony Baskets**

Basket-weaving used to be a fairly common skill, but chances are most members of your family have never acquired it. Here's your chance to remedy that, as this site offers a distinctive variety of basket-weaving kits that will prove once and for all that the time-honored craft isn't just easy, but fun. What's more, the resulting baskets happen to be pretty fantastic, as well as useful. Once you've got the hang of weaving your own, come back for some raw materials and see what happens when you design your own....

·CRAFTS ·INSTRUCTION

410-517-1020 · **Woolstock Knit Shop**

With under one hundred different yarns available from this knitting specialist, you can bet they'd have to be pretty unusual to catch our attention. Such is the case, as these yarns are alternately furry, silky, soft and colorful, and often all of the above. Potentially more intriguing is the shop's peculiar devotion to zippers. There actually aren't a lot of these either, but they're so colorful and different that it'll be hard to imagine using buttons in your next sweater project. This knit shop's almost in a category all its own.

·NEEDLEWORK ·INSTRUCTION

212-925-6112 · **Harry Zarin Co.**

The "largest warehouse of discounted designer fabrics in New York City," Zarin has been offering crafty home decorators plenty to work with for seventy years, "stocked with thousands of bolts of upholstery and drapery fabrics" at reasonable prices. If anything, though, this web version of the shop is an improvement, as you may quickly and easily browse through all available patterns by fabric type or color. The same easy shopping goes for the drapery hardware, upholstery tools, curtain ties, trim and other materials necessary to design or refurbish your furniture and home accents when you've got more ingenuity than disposable income.

·CRAFTS

NOTES:

_____

_____

_____

_____

_____

_____

_____

_____

_____

_____

_____

_____

_____

_____

_____

_____

_____

_____

_____

_____

_____

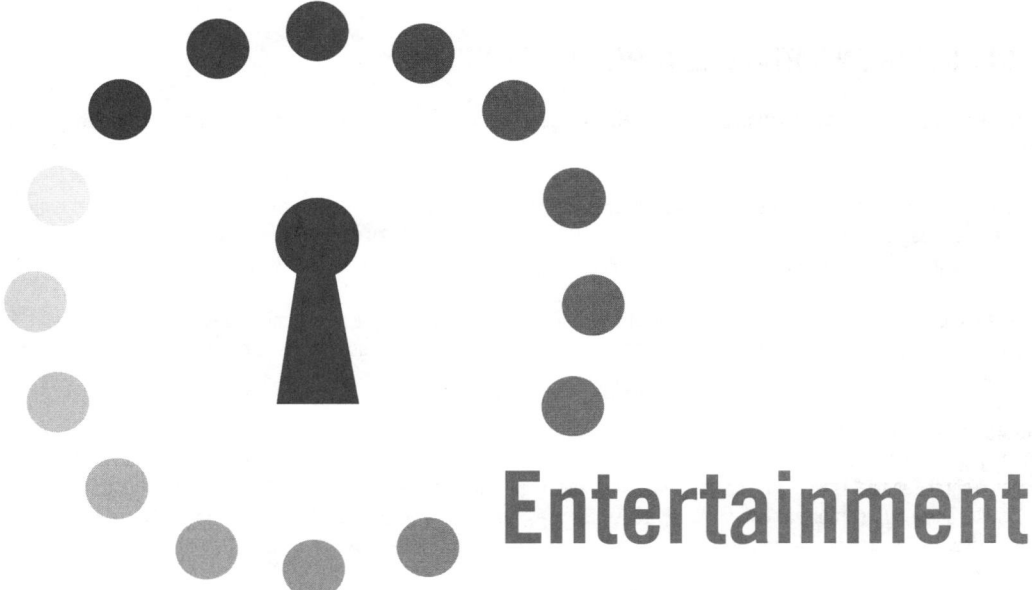

Entertainment

Chances are, if you've shopped online at all, you've bought a video, book or CD, if not for yourself then for someone else. It's also a safe bet that there are a couple of web sites you already know and trust for these purchases. After all, a DVD costs and plays the same wherever you pick it up, so why not settle for that tried-and-true megaseller of movies, books and music? The truth is you can, if you already know the name of every single flick, text and album you ever want to own. The standby supersites even offer sponsored recommendations, samples and customer reviews.

However, we'd like to refer the truly adventurous viewers, readers and listeners among us to a more eclectic assortment of sites, each devoted to particular genres, cultural affinities and/or tastes. Some represent a sampling of the smaller, independent shops that dot the less flashy neighborhoods of our hometowns. Others simply promote nostalgic or exotic alternatives to entertainment products with larger advertising budgets. We think they make a great complement to the mainstream retailers, as well as to the ticket brokers, board game specialists and videogame boutiques that round out our selection. If you're still shopping at the same web site you were ten years ago, odds are good you're missing out on a lot. This section has the potential to expand your horizons and provide fun in the process.

TIPS ON BUYING ENTERTAINMENT PRODUCTS ONLINE

These suggestions may prevent frustration and alleviate boredom when shopping online for entertainment products.

• **BUYING MUSIC** • In most cases the internet makes it possible to actually listen to a piece of music before you buy it. This is all but essential these days, as there's a lot of bad music out there. If you can't listen to an album on one site, you may want to look around— chances are, you can sample the music elsewhere.

• **DOWNLOAD WISELY** • Downloading music has just about become the norm, but with the RIAA aiming lawsuits at file sharers, it helps to know the score. Most downloading sites have limits on how the MP3s may be used, so remember to read the fine print before purchase, and check out WhatsTheDownload.com for current legal information.

• **BUYING MOVIES** • Seeing as you can rent a movie for a fraction of the cost, it rarely makes sense to purchase a film you haven't seen yet. If you decide to, however, take advantage of the consumer review areas posted on many sites, and try to view a trailer and/or clips from the movie as well, just so you know what you're getting into (see our Sites That May Come in Handy for assistance). Also, some DVD editions offer additional special features, so you may want to check out all editions that are available and at what prices before committing to one or the other.

• **BUYING USED AUDIO & VIDEO** • It's often possible to find a used copy of the videogame, CD, DVD, record, VHS or tape you are looking for. Sometimes it's the only version available of rare and out-of-print stuff. Before you buy, make sure the site offers a guarantee that the item will play.

• **BUYING TICKETS** • Event tickets will often be easier to purchase online than anywhere else (it's often the only way to avoid endless voicemail menus). However, keep an eye out for the excessive add-on fees sometimes charged for this service, and be sure to take note of whether the tickets will be mailed to you or made available at the Will Call window (usually you'll have a choice). Also, before buying tickets to seated events, you may want to take advantage of the services offered by SeatAdvisor.com (use the helpful sites on the next page) to see what sort of view you can expect from your seats.

• **BUYING TICKETS SECONDHAND** • Some sites offer tickets that other fans are unable to use, in which case you will be forced to trust that person's intentions. In these cases, take special notice of the site's policies with regard to fraud and delivery failures. When buying from a broker, be wary of the ticket source and look for guarantees as to authenticity. It's bad enough to lose a large sum of money, but worse if you're then left ticketless to an exciting event!

• **USE THE WEB FOR RESEARCH & RECOMMENDATIONS** • When it comes to buying games, movies, music and books these days, word of mouth is rapidly being replaced by word of blog. Many online shops, fan sites and web databases are filled with customer reviews, message board debates, song lyrics, actor bios, trivia, artist interviews and every other conceivable piece of information that might sway you one way or another in your entertainment choices. We've listed some on the next page, but there are thousands of useful sites out there waiting to expose you to something new.

>> SITES THAT MAY COME IN HANDY

The following URLs may be useful when you shop for entertainment products.

AllMusic.com	Research music genres, history, artists and news
BookReporter.com	Book reviews
BookSense.com	Locate local bookstores
Catalog.LOC.gov	Library of Congress site
CitySearch.com	Local club, event and restaurant guides
Drive-Ins.com	Locate drive-in theaters
GameSpot.com	Videogames information
ILoveLanguages.com	Online language resource
IMDB.com	Internet movie database
Kids-In-Mind.com	Rates and reviews films as appropriate for children
LibrarySpot.com	Locate and search libraries
LitteraScripta.com	Search for rare and out-of-print books
MovieFone.com	Local movie listings and times
MRQE.com	Search for movie reviews
OpenTable.com	Restaurant reservations
OurMedia.org	Digital media file sharing network
Pandora.com	Interactive music recommendations and radio
PlayBill.com	Theater news, reviews and information
SeatAdvisor.com	Preview event seating and venue information
SuperHeroHype.com	Comic book hero resource
TalkinBroadway.com	Theater news, reviews and information
TicketMaster.com	Tickets and event calendars
TheCelebrityCafe.com	News on movies, music, books and more
TrailersWorld.com	Movie trailers, past and present
UBL.com	Music artist information and audio samples
YouTube.com	Homemade digital film shorts

SECTION ICON LEGEND

Use the following guide to understand the rectangular icons that appear throughout this section.

AUDIO RECORDINGS

The mediums of music and spoken-word recordings have changed almost as often as the styles, and recently added to the list including vinyl, 8-track, cassette, CD and SACD are downloadable MP3s or AACs. Finding an 8-track cassette may prove difficult, but the rest should be easy.

FILM & VIDEO

As with music, home movie formats have changed over the years, and here you'll find a smattering of them all. Not just DVD and VHS, occasionally in these sites you'll also come across Video Disc and Beta cassettes. You won't just find films either, but also television shows, professional sports, performing arts and other recorded events.

GAMES

Games of chance, games of skill and games that let you put your brain on hold for hours at a time; if it can be played, this icon will indicate if it's for sale or rent in one of these shops. Board games, videogames and puzzles only scratch the surface.

THE WRITTEN WORD

Books are the most common items, but with this icon we include comic books, magazines, zines, individual articles, screenplays, audio books and downloadable eBooks, in addition to traditional fiction and nonfiction.

TICKETS

The ticket industry isn't always fair, and it's not always easy, but with the smattering of sites listed here, you should be able to get a decent ticket to any show or event you like… if you can afford it. Still, many of these sites will keep you informed of impending ticket sales and presales, so you can be ready when the time comes.

 **LIST OF KEY WORDS**

The following words represent the types of items typically found on the sites listed in this section. You will find them listed in the orange strip at the bottom of each entry, as appropriate.

AUDIO BOOKS	Audio recordings of written materials, either on cassette, CD or downloadable digital audio format.
BOOKS	Whether fiction, nonfiction, hard cover, paperback, children's books, poetry, art books, coffee table books or in digital format, this one's pretty self-explanatory.
COMICS	All comic books, graphic novels and newspaper comic collections.
DOWNLOADS	Any entertainment that can be downloaded, including audio books, music, video, gaming software and event tickets.
GAMES	All nonvideogames, including board games, rec room games, puzzles and party games.
HOW-TO	Books, audio, video and software media designed to teach and/or guide, including self-help, motivation, exercise and language instruction.
MOVIES & TV	All representations of film and television, whether videotape, DVD or movie tickets.
MUSIC	Recorded music in all formats and genres.
PERIODICALS	Perpetually published media, including newspapers and magazines.
RARE	Hard-to-find and/or limited edition publications and media, including autographed works, and first and special editions.
RENTALS	Indicates online shops that will rent media such as DVDs, audio books and videogames.
SHOWS & EVENTS	Tickets to and/or audio/video recordings of sporting events, music concerts or other live performances.
TEXTBOOKS	Printed academic materials, usually college-level textbooks.
USED	Retailers offering used media, including books, audio recordings, videos or videogames.
VIDEOGAMES	All electronic games, either handheld or for any number of popular gaming console or computer platforms.

KEY WORD INDEX

Use the followings lists to locate online retailers that sell the type of entertainment you seek.

AUDIO BOOKS

AbeBooks.com
AllBooks4Less.com
Amazon.com
Audible.com
AudioEditions.com
BarnesAndNoble.com
BooksFree.com
iTunes.com
Powells.com

BOOKS

AbeBooks.com
Alibris.com
AllBooks4Less.com
Amazon.com
AtomicBooks.com
BarnesAndNoble.com
BooksFree.com
eFollett.com
ElephantBooks.com
GEMM.com
LastGasp.com
Loompanics.com
Maggs.com
MultilingualBooks.com
OpampBooks.com
Powells.com
SamuelFrench.com
ShopPBS.org
Store.AETV.com
UbiBooks.com
VintageLibrary.com
Zooba.com

COMICS

AbeBooks.com
AtomicBooks.com
GEMM.com
LastGasp.com
NewKadia.com
Powells.com
VintageLibrary.com

DOWNLOADS

Audible.com
eClassical.com
eFollett.com
eMusic.com
Fandango.com
iTunes.com
MovieTickets.com
Music.MSN.com
Powells.com
UbiBooks.com

GAMES

AnyCraze.com
ArcadeGames.com
AreYouGame.com
BitsAndPieces.com
BoardGames.com
CasinoSupply.com
ChessForum.com
GameTablesUSA.com
HomeGameRoom.com
NewtsCards.com
PuzzleHouse.com
RecRooms.com
Spilsbury.com
TurnOffTheTV.com

HOW-TO

AbeBooks.com
Alibris.com
AllBooks4Less.com
Amazon.com
AtomicBooks.com
AudioEditions.com
BarnesAndNoble.com
LastGasp.com
MultilingualBooks.com
OpampBooks.com
Powells.com
Teach12.com

MOVIES & TV

AbeBooks.com
Alibris.com
AllBooks4Less.com
Amazon.com
AtomicBooks.com
AudioEditions.com
BarnesAndNoble.com
LastGasp.com
MultilingualBooks.com
OpampBooks.com
Powells.com
Teach12.com

MUSIC

Alibris.com
Amazon.com
BarnesAndNoble.com
BlackMarket.co.uk
ColonyMusic.com
DeepDiscountCD.com
Descarga.com
DjangoMusic.com
DVDPlanet.com
EBReggae.com
eClassical.com
eMusic.com
FatBeats.com
Footlight.com
GEMM.com
InterPunk.com
iTunes.com
KaraokeWH.com
Music.MSN.com
OtherMusic.com
ShopPBS.org
TicketWeb.com
TowerRecords.com

PERIODICALS

AtomicBooks.com
InterPunk.com
Magazines.com
NetMagazines.com

RARE

AbeBooks.com
Alibris.com
AtomicBooks.com
BarnesAndNoble.com
ElephantBooks.com
Footlight.com
GEMM.com
InterPunk.com
LastGasp.com
Maggs.com
MoviesUnlimited.com
NewKadia.com
OtherMusic.com
Powells.com
TowerRecords.com
VintageLibrary.com

RENTALS

BooksFree.com
NetFlix.com
RedOctane.com
RentAnime.com

SHOWS & EVENTS

Amazon.com
DVDPlanet.com
Footlight.com
MoviesUnlimited.com
NetFlix.com
RazorGator.com
SamuelFrench.com
ShopPBS.org
Store.AETV.com
StubHub.com
TeleCharge.com
TicketWeb.com

TEXTBOOKS

AbeBooks.com
Alibris.com
BarnesAndNoble.com
eFollett.com
ElephantBooks.com
MultilingualBooks.com
OpampBooks.com
Powells.com

USED

AbeBooks.com
Alibris.com
Amazon.com
CasinoSupply.com
DjangoMusic.com
EBGames.com
eFollett.com
ElephantBooks.com
GameStop.com
GEMM.com
Maggs.com
NetFlix.com
NewKadia.com
OpampBooks.com
Powells.com
RedOctane.com
TowerRecords.com
VintageLibrary.com

VIDEOGAMES

Amazon.com
ArcadeGames.com
DeepDiscountDVD.com
DjangoMusic.com
EBGames.com
GameStop.com
HomeGameRoom.com
RedOctane.com
Spilsbury.com

VINYL

BlackMarket.co.uk
DjangoMusic.com
EBReggae.com
FatBeats.com
Footlight.com
GEMM.com
InterPunk.com
OtherMusic.com
TowerRecords.com

AbeBooks.com

AbeBooks.com · 250-475-6013

While this "largest online marketplace for books" offers the tagline "Because You Read," what it really ought to mean is "because you collect." Possibly the best shop online for anybody building a distinguished home library, the site's incredible wealth of titles includes well-categorized Rare Books, First Edition Books and Signed Books across all genres. It's a particularly good spot to find out-of-print titles, and you may even specifically look for those still possessing a dust jacket. Casually browsing a selection that includes more than 800,000 poetry volumes alone may not be the best way to go about shopping here, but the knowledgeable reader should have no trouble finding anything at all.

·BOOKS ·TEXTBOOKS	·AUDIO BOOKS ·HOW-TO	·COMICS ·RARE	·USED

Alibris.com

Alibris · 877-254-2747

With "over 50 million used, new and out-of-print books," it's tough to imagine finding anything worthwhile on this enormous online bookstore. However, a few effective browsing techniques at least give the impression that you're discovering a great read around every corner. Of course, most of these first issues, signed copies and other rarities must be explicitly sought with the Advanced Search feature, and if you're a student trying to save money by shopping the comprehensive used-textbook selection, you may need the ISBN to ensure you're getting the proper edition for your class. None can deny, though, this is a first-rate bookseller for premium and discount shoppers alike.

·BOOKS ·TEXTBOOKS	·MUSIC ·HOW-TO	·MOVIES & TV ·RARE	·USED

AllBooks4Less.com

AllBooks4Less.com · 888-402-7323

While you may not find every hot best-selling title on this massive discount bookseller, it's a good bet you'll find a lot of public-domain works, including the plays of Shakespeare and most other enduring literature, at prices that can't be beat. But that doesn't begin to describe the entire selection, which features pages upon pages of relatively contemporary fiction, endless categories of nonfiction, poetry, cookbooks, self-help, study aids and how-to books. You may get lost in these pages, but you'll never go broke.

·BOOKS	·AUDIO BOOKS	·HOW-TO	

Amazon.com

Amazon.com · 800-201-7575

Even if you're one of the three people who have never shopped from Amazon, it may seem familiar, as the oft-imitated retail giant pretty much set the standard for e-commerce. Included among its incredibly thorough product details are music audio samples, book excerpts, videogame screen shots, consumer reviews, personalized recommendations and extensive cross-referencing between authors, directors, actors, musicians and similar items. Basically, it offers more helpful information than any traditional brick-and-mortar ever could, and the innovations keep on coming. The recent launch of a short fiction shop that enables readers to purchase individual stories further proves that this perennial web's best just keeps getting better.

·BOOKS ·AUDIO BOOKS	·MUSIC ·USED	·MOVIES & TV ·SHOWS & EVENTS	·VIDEOGAMES ·HOW-TO

866-269-2723 · AnyCraze.com

AnyCraze.com

If you or someone you love has gotten caught up in a card collecting game like Magic or Yu-Gi-Oh, this site can help you get hold of those rare and/or powerful cards you crave. To be honest, we don't know enough about the games themselves to understand how the search functions on this site work, but we take this as a good sign, because they appear to be very complex and thorough. We do know you can view spoilers, 5 Star cards or, if you're out for some fun, random selections. We also know that the best cards will cost the most money. Then again, with games like these, it seems buying more can actually make you a better player....

·GAMES				

877-956-0223 · Arcade Games

ArcadeGames.com

Today's videogames possess a sophistication scarcely dreamt of back in the heyday of the video arcade, but to many of us they're simply not as fun. This site keeps the 80s alive by offering many of the classic games that eased us into the modern push-button era: *Pac Man*, *Pole Position*, even the original *Star Wars* game and a host of pinball machines. These aren't discs or cartridges for your home console, but the full stand-up editions, complete down to the joysticks. Also available here are such savvy game tables as roulette wheels, blackjack stands and air hockey, in case you run out of quarters.

·GAMES	·VIDEOGAMES			

800-471-0641 · AreYouGame.com

AreYouGame.com

This "largest game and puzzle store on the planet" has such a huge selection that it not only includes all the standby favorites, but even sells stuff that nobody likes. Categories such as Brain Teasers, Magic and Dinosaurs make it easy to find great stuff for kids, or even fun-minded adults. If you're looking for games that are educational, no problem, but there're also plenty that require almost no brain cells at all. More or less, though, it's all about passing time in entertaining and social ways, without resorting to the word *video*.

·GAMES				

410-662-4444 · Atomic Books

AtomicBooks.com

The literary equivalent of a hip record shop, this indie Baltimore store turned Web retailer caters in equal parts to the forward-thinking, passionate and plain old freaky. While browsing the site is a convoluted and messy endeavor, somehow these guys make it easier to notice titles that commonly get tucked aside or even completely ignored by other bookstores, offering great descriptions when you find them. Thus, fringe philosophers, conspiracy theorists and knitting enthusiasts can find an outlet here alongside contemporary literati and underworld luminaries like Charles Bukowski. Particularly rich categories include Zines, Strange Science and Scams/Pranks/Revenge, but you'll have to visit in order to find your kink.

·BOOKS ·HOW-TO	·MOVIES & TV ·RARE	·PERIODICALS	·COMICS

Audible.com

Music downloads have gotten so much attention the past few years that other audio alternatives have been easily overlooked. Not by this site, which focuses on audio books, comedy, poetry, storytelling and self-help to be played on your computer, burned onto a CD or listened to on your MP3 player. You may even order monthly or annual subscriptions to popular radio shows from across the country, such as *Fresh Air*, *Charlie Rose*, *Car Talk* and *This American Life*. Of course, popular books make up the bulk of this catalog, complete with the key advantage to downloading music: a lower price.

 ·AUDIO BOOKS · ·DOWNLOADS

AudioEditions.com

Even if you don't consider yourself much of a reader, you may still find literary satisfaction through this site, provided you're a good listener. The focus here is books in an audio format, and on top of having a greater selection of audio titles than most online booksellers, this dedicated store also offers greater organization. Hence, if you particularly like a certain voice, you may browse for the reader of the audio book, as well as author, and filter your search for unabridged selections, or condensed versions (if you're in a hurry). Fiction and popular nonfiction titles are well balanced by poetry, instruction, original radio broadcasts and more than you could hear on a thousand road trips.

 ·AUDIO BOOKS · ·HOW-TO

BarnesAndNoble.com

You'd almost have to be agoraphobic not to be aware of this retail book-selling chain. Most of the nation's suburban malls and urban centers have one, and many of them include built-in coffee shops. So why should anyone shop from the web site? For one thing, you'll find professional and consumer reviews of the book you seek, as well as used copies and audio editions for most. Secondly, whereas most of their brick-and-mortar stores now offer music and video sales, very few of them offer this comprehensive a selection. The only drawback we see is that you'll have to make your own coffee.

·BOOKS · ·MUSIC · ·MOVIES & TV · ·AUDIO BOOKS
·TEXTBOOKS · ·HOW-TO · ·RARE

BitsAndPieces.com

Here's a fun site that's wholeheartedly devoted to...well, fun. That is, all the fun that may be had with puzzles and games. Puzzles make up the bulk of the offerings and, sorted by the number of bits and pieces (Under 1000, 1000 and 1500 Pieces and Up), their selection even includes Novelty Jigsaws and Jigsaw Accessories (these won't help you assemble it, but will enable you to preserve the finished product for posterity). A section devoted to Brainteasers will put your mind in a twist, but the most immediate fun may be had in the Puzzle Arcade, which features enough flash-based games to kill your workday.

 ·GAMES

011-44-207-437-047 · Black Market Music

BlackMarket.co.uk

This "most notorious dance record store in the UK" has "consistently been at the forefront of all genres of dance music" for twenty years now, which is amazing considering the styles of music represented still feel so new. House music, drum and bass, garage, dub and grime will be found in new releases and the occasional reissue, and though this music is strictly vinyl, most records are offered with great-quality MP3 samples so you can listen before you buy. It's no wonder this stalwart store has survived the ever-changing flavors of DJ culture.

$$$

| ·MUSIC | ·VINYL | | |  |

908-429-0202 · Boardgames.com

BoardGames.com

If you've ever wondered just how many different towns, movies, television shows, sports franchises, educational institutions, recreational activities and scenic vistas could be turned into Monopoly games, this is the place to look. Once you've settled on your favorite, however, you may wish to turn your attention to the rest of this specialty game shop's selection, which includes board games covering the gambit from classic to kitschy. Strategy games, card games, trivia games and party games abound; enough so you may never be bored again.

$$

| ·GAMES | | | | |

703-748-2390 · booksfree.com

BooksFree.com

If late fees and waiting lists have left you fed up with the local library, this site offers a comparable service that will allow you to always keep a good book on hand. Similar to the wildly popular and successful Netflix site, here you make yourself an online reading list, and your top choices are delivered, to be read at your convenience. Once you've hit The End—however long it takes—you drop the paperback or audiobook in a prepaid return envelope, and in a few short days the next title shows up in your mailbox. Unlike the library, this service isn't free, but you may be less likely to put off reading if you're paying for it.

GC

$

| ·BOOKS | ·AUDIO BOOKS | ·RENTALS | | |

800-789-2101 · Casino Supply Co.

CasinoSupply.com

There are many lures to Las Vegas, Atlantic City and other casino towns, but if you're mostly in it for the thrill of the game, take a look at this industry and consumer game supply site. You'll find professional-quality roulette wheels, craps tables and slot machines, as well as many small, inexpensive home models. The site's greatest appeal, however, may be to poker players. If you've caught on to the card game's recent surge in popularity, a little bit of shopping here could set up your regular poker night with some classy chips, cards, automatic shufflers and traditional green felt tables. You'll have to provide your own lounge act.

$$

| ·GAMES | ·USED | | | |

ChessForum.com
chessforum · 212-475-2369

If your chess game could use a boost, you might want to pick up one of the many sets available from this gaming specialist, which include pieces in stone, glass, wood and a variety of metals as well as plastic and resin. Many of the traditionally shaped pieces are beautiful in their own right, but if the zest of using keen stratagems and thinking ahead isn't doing it for you, perhaps one of the several themed sets will thrill you, whether your pieces are finely crafted Samurai or the gang and ghouls of Scooby Doo. Buy a full set, pick up one of the beautiful ebony boards or simply upgrade your cadre of pieces. It won't improve your game, but it should at least make you a more graceful loser.

 ·GAMES

ColonyMusic.com
Colony Music · 212-265-2050

Nothing says "wild party" better than karaoke, and what's wilder to sing along to than show tunes? Well, here is the spot where these two avant-garde musical formats come together into one happy-go-lucky retailer. Buy either the original cast recordings of your favorite Broadway musicals, or try your hand at a variety of popular favorites across genres, with nothing but a microphone, a musical sound track and your ability to read and sing simultaneously. Practically everything you need is here; just add liquor.

 ·MUSIC

DeepDiscountCD.com
DeepDiscountCD.com · 800-258-1995

There are enough shops online offering the "lowest" prices on CDs that we could fill an entire chapter of this book. As a matter of fact, we could point you to a site or two that list lower prices than the ones found here. However, this site offers a little something called Free Shipping, and that changes everything. When all is charged, shipped, said and done, this turns out to be the cheapest place to find most popular new CDs in one simple transaction, especially if you're just buying one or two at a time. For many a music junky, this may be your best bet short of selling out to music journalism.

 ·MUSIC

DeepDiscountDVD.com
DeepDiscountDVD.com · 800-264-5076

The avid video collector simply should not do without this site, which guarantees the "lowest total price" on an exhaustive selection of DVDs. What's the catch? With uncounted thousands of titles available, including plenty of foreign, anime and children's flicks, browsing is an absolutely miserable process, so you'll really need to know coming in exactly which film you want, and even which edition of the DVD you'd prefer. Of course, for the true film buff, this will never be asking too much.

 ·MOVIES & TV   ·VIDEOGAMES

800-377-2647 · Descarga.com

Descarga.com

This one's not a great site, but it sure is a great niche retailer, specializing in "Tropical Afro-Latin" music. After all, how can you fault such an upbeat, multicultural selection of music that stems from one island paradise or another? You simply can't. There are various search options available from this store (whose name, we're told, refers to the musical art of jamming), but if you don't have a particular artist or song in mind, the most fun can be had browsing in sections such as Cumbia Vallenato, Merengue Bachata and Latin Soul Boogaloo.

·MUSIC				

877-935-2646 · Djangos

DjangoMusic.com

From its humble beginnings as a neighborhood record store in Portland, OR, Django's has developed into somewhat of an internet juggernaut, linking together the inventory of roughly 300 independent music stores nationwide to offer a terrific assortment of new and used music, covering just about all known genres. You'll find extensive information about each artist or musical style, whether it's New Orleans Jazz, Dub Reggae, Cuban Pop or Rockabilly. As if this comprehensive musical prowess wasn't enough, the site also happens to be one of the best places anywhere to find used videos. Don't miss it.

·MUSIC ·USED	·MOVIES & TV	·VIDEOGAMES	·VINYL	

800-818-9693 · DVD Planet

DVDPlanet.com

DVDs are available all over the place, in a variety of editions at variable prices, so why would we want to shop from a site like this, which offers no visible appeal and throws titles at you in alphabetical order? Basically, it's the Power Search feature, which offers a thorough selection of filters that can narrow your results by available special features, MPAA ratings, audio formats, screen formats and available languages (including English overdubs on foreign-language films). Another benefit of this site is a growing selection of DVD-Audio titles, which incorporate surround-sound mixes to many popular albums and live-performance recordings.

·MUSIC	·MOVIES & TV	·SHOWS & EVENTS		

877-432-9675 · EB Games

EBGames.com

"EB" stands for "Electronics Boutique," and this selection makes you feel derelict for not having the highest-speed processor, top-end video card or latest, greatest gaming console platform. Then there are the special controllers, expansion packs and other obliquely necessary accessories, which up until moments ago seemed overindulgent. And let us not forget the games; games for Sega, Sony, Nintendo, Mac and PC, even a section of "Classic" titles for obsolete platforms. Everything here holds the promise that fun may be returned to lives we suddenly realize have become dreary.

·VIDEOGAMES	·USED			

EBReggae.com

Ernie B started out selling reggae records at San Francisco Bay Area flea markets, and slowly but surely become the go-to source for reggae and dancehall recordings for record stores and mail-order customers alike. The "world's largest catalog of reggae music" has only in recent years made the transition to the web, and while browsing may be difficult to the uninitiated, there's no denying this is a comprehensive selection. Die-hard fans will clean up; the rest of us can find gold browsing the Essential Picks and Best Selling searches.

·MUSIC	·VINYL		

eClassical.com

Once we got over the irony of purchasing some of the world's oldest musical compositions in technology's newest media format, we came to realize that classical music and MP3 downloads make a perfect marriage, especially on this splendidly easy-to-use site. A bevy of browsing options allow you to quickly find those special recordings of your favorite composers and pieces, performed by your favorite players, orchestras and conductors. For those of us a tad less knowledgeable of such things, the comprehensive specialty shop also offers browsing by featured instrument as well as a unique category called Moods and Special Events, which includes such headings as After a Divorce, Making Babies, Making Your Baby Smarter and Having a Hangover.

·MUSIC	·DOWNLOADS		

eFollett.com

Buying college textbooks used to involve wading through a crowded bookstore, standing in long lines and spending vast amounts of money on texts you might not ever get around to reading. No more, thanks to sites like this, which offer the reading lists for a growing list of national colleges and universities. Once you track down your school you have only to filter down your department, course number and section to view the list of required materials, available new or used for prices that leave plenty of room to buy beer—we mean pizza. Pizza for you and your study partners. Yes, that sounds right.

·BOOKS	·USED	·DOWNLOADS	·TEXTBOOKS

ElephantBooks.com

It's said elephants never forget, and as long as this site is around, its thousands of "out-of-print, rare and used books" won't be forgotten either. Follow the Browse By Category link to find dozens of organized sections including Rare Books, Signed Books, Illustrated Books, Miniature Books and Rhetoric, along with typical Fiction, Non-Fiction and Children's selections. Look further and you'll see subcategories as explicit as Fables, Correspondences, Fictional Biographies and Egyptology. With loads of first and forgotten editions, this could wind up being the last place you look for that tough-to-come-by book, unless you make it the first.

·BOOKS	·USED	·TEXTBOOKS	·RARE

858-777-7639 · eMusic

eMusic.com

If you're a heavy user of one of the many buck-per-song music download sites, you may want to consider switching over to this subscription-based MP3 specialist, which seems new sometimes, but has actually been around since 1998, lending credence to its claim to be the first shop of its kind. A flat monthly fee grants you access to a surprisingly large number of tracks from more than 600,000 available titles, many from a variety of independent labels and artists not readily available on the aforementioned competitors. Better yet, these files are available without restriction, making this the best music deal on the web.

·MUSIC	·DOWNLOADS			

800-326-3264 · Fandango

Fandango.com

Even though giant new movie multiplexes seem to pop up all over town as often as franchise coffeehouses, when you go to catch that hot new weekend blockbuster, odds are good the show you want to see is going to be sold out. That's where this site comes in. Instead of rushing over to the theater box office when it opens to stand in line, you may leisurely order your tickets (for a growing number of participating theaters), and be assured of a seat when the lights go down. From now on, you won't even need to show up in time for the previews.

·MOVIES & TV	·DOWNLOADS		

718-875-8191 · Fat Beats

FatBeats.com

Turntablists in Los Angeles and New York have been getting their vinyl grooves at Fat Beats stores for years, but only recently has the hip hop specialist crafted a web shop to service the growing nation of shoppers outside of these urban centers. While the site still isn't up to par with most slickly designed online music stores, it does get the job done when it comes to new and reissue hip hop and CDs, in particular those hailing from independent labels that too often get overlooked by mainstream culture. An ever-rotating selection and good written descriptions keep it real, but we suspect the dearth of audio samples may be an intentional means of keeping the best records in the hands of only the truly knowledgeable fans.

·MUSIC	·VINYL			

212-533-1572 · Footlight Records

Footlight.com

If show tunes get you going, and original cast recordings render you speechless, this is the site for you. Featuring a long list of audio and video gems related to live performance, this site celebrates the stage with rare and popular recordings, including spoken word, choral albums and a slew of jazz on vinyl thrown in for effect. You might find yourself easily distracted by an abundance of new and featured items, but just so you know, there's a whole lot of great songs hidden within these pages. We're going to go ahead and call it fabulous.

·MUSIC	·VINYL	·SHOWS & EVENTS	·RARE	

GameStop.com

Do you lead an active virtual life? Whatever your favorite platform, you'll find a thorough list of videogames and accessories on this specialty site, including some incredibly good deals on preowned titles. Keep tabs on the latest developments in console technology and future releases, or get your hands on the latest nifty controller to help you rule your MUD. With military pilots and surgeons currently using joysticks and video screens to perform vital tasks, no one can even claim you're wasting your time anymore.

	·VIDEOGAMES	·USED		

GameTablesUSA.com

If you've ever found yourself uttering the words "it's all in the wrist," there's a good chance you're going to like the selection of games featured here. These are the sort of toys that make your rec room complete, specifically: Foosball, Ping-Pong, billiards, air hockey and bumper pool tables. Considering the fact these games take up as much room as furniture, there's a surprising variety here, including outdoor models and combination tables that can be changed on a whim. Curbside delivery is included in the price, though you'll be responsible for the heavy lifting required to get the table inside, at which point it's important to remember: it's all in the legs.

	·GAMES			

GEMM.com

You can find the latest hit CDs at just about every online music shop you visit. Fortunately for people with more complex cravings, there's Global Electronic Music Marketplace, whose powerful search engine scours a worldwide collaboration of retailers, collectors, record labels, importers and artists (browsing is NOT recommended). The result will be an incredible list of titles matching your search in various formats, different editions, new or used and at prices you can compare on the spot. This is perfect for collectors, or anyone who's having trouble finding rare or out-of-print music. Note the links to the GEMM book and video sister sites that offer this amazing resource to suit all your entertainment needs.

	·BOOKS ·VINYL	·MUSIC ·USED	·MOVIES & TV ·RARE	·COMICS

HomeGameroom.com

While far from ideal, this pricey rec room game specialist has some very good things going for it—namely: Pac Man, Galaga and Space Invaders. These classic arcade games and several others may be purchased here in the traditional upright cabinets, providing nostalgic players with the ultimate in gameroom luxuries. Of course, shipping costs alone could pay for one of today's technologically superior home videogame consoles, but these machines definitely win points for style. Besides, you can optimize delivery fees by adding a jukebox, pinball machine, air hockey table, pool table or other gameroom standard to your order.

	·GAMES	·VIDEOGAMES		

571-434-1105 · Interpunk

InterPunk.com

Typically associated with outlandish hairstyles and boisterous antics, it may seem unlikely that punk rockers would create the ideal web model for independent music distribution. But that is the case with this site, which offers recordings of the "world's largest collection of small, mostly unknown punk bands." Homegrown punk, hardcore, emo and ska may be found on CD, vinyl and even cassette, and if you happen to be curious about what do-it-yourself musicians are doing in places like Malaysia, Luxembourg and Brazil, you'll find that too. Think what you will about the music, which is best known for pushing the boundaries of good taste; this is an excellent forum for indie artists and labels to sell their recordings, along with the requisite stickers, patches and zines.

·MUSIC	·PERIODICALS	·VINYL	·RARE

800-692-7753 · Apple iTunes

iTunes.com

Here's the service that taught the recording industry to embrace the download. For about a buck per song you can select individual, CD-quality MP3s from most contemporary recording artists, meaning you can buy tracks rather than entire albums, though albums give you more bang for your buck. You'll even find audio books, movie trailers and music videos. In order to play, you must download special software, which acts as a music library, player, store and distributor all in one. Services include music allowances for children, plenty of music samples and the inclusion of images for single tracks and albums, in case you thought you were going to miss cover art.

·MUSIC	·AUDIO BOOKS	·DOWNLOADS	

800-645-8401 · Karaoke Warehouse

KaraokeWH.com

Unleash your inner pop idol with the help of this karaoke specialist that carries all the equipment you'll need to get your sing-along party started. Most importantly, the site offers a wide range of karaoke CDGs, featuring plenty of pop, hip hop, rock, country and show tunes, easily searchable by song title or artist. Most of the music is marketed in loosely connected compilations that often include songs you've never heard of, but if you're willing to pay a premium you can design a custom CD covering only your handpicked favorites. Spotlight sold separately.

·MUSIC			

415-824-6636 · Last Gasp

LastGasp.com

Lovers of alternative press publications need look no further than this utterly original small press and bookstore out of the San Francisco Bay Area. Whether you're a devotee of underground comic books, fringe art, independent poetry, literary zines, pseudo-science, marginalized demographics or popular culture, you'll want to take time perusing these pages. If it all sounds a little weird, you definitely need to log on immediately to get a titillating glimpse into the world that exists just over the rainbow from mainstream publishing.

·BOOKS	·COMICS	·HOW-TO	·RARE

Loompanics.com

An air of danger looms over this site. Perhaps it's category headings like Heresy, Anarchism and Egoism, Prison and Head For The Hills. These feature books that touch both extreme ends of the ideological spectrum, books that possess and distribute knowledge that alternately makes you proud and terrified to be a human being. Self-sufficiency, financial trickery, forensics, locksmithing and sex guides are some of the least troubling topics to be found, whereas others make a great case for censorship. However, we live in a free society, and some of these books remind us that it's important to know why.

·BOOKS

Magazines.com

Sometimes it seems there are as many magazines out there as there are people, so it's fortunate to find a site like this, which makes it relatively easy to wade through thousands of titles to subscribe to that periodical that best suits you. An alphabetical search may help you find a specific title quickly, however your best bet for browsing is to Search by Category, which includes dozens of particular interests such as politics, sports, hobbies, health, fashion, entertainment, art, pets, comics and a variety of regional publications. All, of course, at an annual subscription well below cover price.

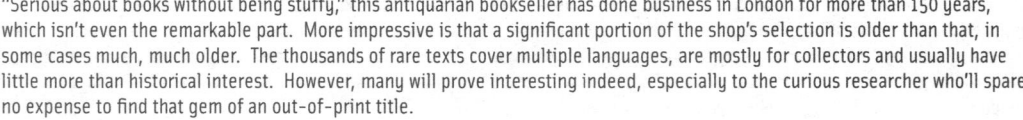

·PERIODICALS

Maggs.com

"Serious about books without being stuffy," this antiquarian bookseller has done business in London for more than 150 years, which isn't even the remarkable part. More impressive is that a significant portion of the shop's selection is older than that, in some cases much, much older. The thousands of rare texts cover multiple languages, are mostly for collectors and usually have little more than historical interest. However, many will prove interesting indeed, especially to the curious researcher who'll spare no expense to find that gem of an out-of-print title.

·BOOKS   ·USED   ·RARE

MoviesUnlimited.com

Although the quality of its graphic design is closer to *Tron* than it is *The Matrix*, most film buffs will have no trouble seeing through this site's basic exterior to appreciate the brilliantly simple browsing opportunities afforded by the DVD and VHS specialist. Whereas you may browse by Title, Actor, Director or Decade, the unique value of this shop will be found perusing the movie genres and subjects, each of which is expertly cultivated to allow maximum exposure to well-known, cultish and flat-out obscure titles related to such specific themes as Composer Biodramas, the Brat Pack and Rap Musicals. This site is what happens when fanatics get to feeling entrepreneurial.

·MOVIES & TV   ·SHOWS & EVENTS   ·RARE

888-440-8457 · MovieTickets.com

 **MovieTickets.com**

Built specifically with movie fanatics in mind, this site enables you to buy tickets ahead of time (with a very small service charge) to avoid long lines and sellouts, and gives you all the information you might want about the film, including trailers, release dates, ratings, running times, cast lists and synopses. Simply enter your zip code, and a list of participating nearby theaters will turn up, complete with showtimes and featured amenities (including wheelchair access, digital sound and stadium seating). Some even allow printable tickets, though most will be picked up at automated vendors at the theater. Good stuff assuming there's a participating theater near you.

| ·MOVIES & TV | ·DOWNLOADS | | |  |

800-218-2737 · Multilingual Books

MultilingualBooks.com

Whether you're looking to brush up on your high school language courses, or wish to broaden your horizons with a new one, this site offers instructional media encompassing more than 150 languages and dialects, including some dead ones (Latin), a made-up one (Esperanto) and roughly a dozen Native American tongues. Materials often involve much more than books, whether you opt for instructional CDs, DVDs or even software packages to help you gain proficiency in oral and aural communications. Just choose your language, place your order, then head over to our Travel section and book a trip to the non-English-speaking world.

| ·BOOKS | ·TEXTBOOKS | ·HOW-TO | | |

866-672-4551 · MSN Music

Music.MSN.com

If you haven't heard of Microsoft, chances are you're also unfamiliar with the word *internet*, or even *computer*. So, if you're reading this, we're sure you're well aware of the software behemoth. What you might not realize is that the company used its vast resources to tap into the music download market, with great results. With a selection as deep as its Apple rival, and its own batch of exclusive offerings, the real value of this site will be tested over time, with rumored technological advances that will change the way we download music. As of this writing, though, the site's just like the rest, only with higher audio quality and wider MP3 player compatibility—unless you want to listen to these tunes on something called an iPod. Maybe you've heard of it?

| ·MUSIC | ·DOWNLOADS | | |  |

888-638-3549 · Netflix

NetFlix.com

The lazy film buff's dream come true, this site set the standard for online video rentals, and has become one of the web's greatest success stories in the process. For a flat monthly fee you may rent up to three DVDs at a time, which you select from a list of titles numbering over 50,000. When you are finished viewing one, simply slide it into the accompanying postage-paid envelope and drop it in a mailbox. Another DVD will arrive in a couple of days. Though it would seem there's little room for improvement, rumors that the site will soon implement a movie download service can only make this one even better.

| ·MOVIES & TV | ·USED | ·RENTALS | ·SHOWS & EVENTS | |

NetMagazines.com

NetMagazines.com · 206-621-5354

Maybe you do all of your magazine reading in dentist offices, but if your thirst for in-depth news, cultural trends, entertainment reviews and provocative images goes beyond what you can squeeze into twenty minutes, you might be ready for a magazine sub-scription. They're easy to find here, though you may be surprised just how many periodicals cater to your interests. If your orders start adding up, you may want to try one of their package features, which offer discounts on certain selections when you buy in bulk. Then, just go to dental school and you'll be in business.

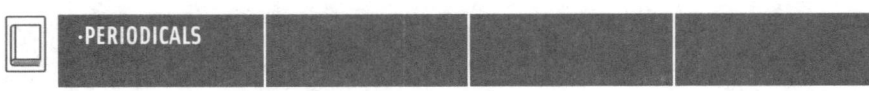

·PERIODICALS

NewKadia.com

NewKadia.com · 610-277-3000

Almost fanatically determined to provide "the web's best comic book store," the folks behind this site have done their research and pulled out the stops to provide an incredible selection, beautifully functional browsing and top-rate customer service. And they still have plans to make the shop better. Well, better is always good, but so far as we're concerned they've already reached their goal. The unique search function may take a moment to understand, but once you've got it you'll be able to sprint through a collection of popular and obscure titles numbering in the hundreds of thousands. More importantly, protective packaging ensures your order will never be damaged during shipping. Other web merchants take note: this is what the best looks like.

·COMICS ·USED ·RARE

NewtsCards.com

Newt's Playing Cards · 614-834-9350

You wouldn't think buying a pack of cards would require any difficult decision making, unless you've seen this site. Dozens, even hundreds of different deck varieties are available, and we're not just talking about pinochle sets. Included in the selection are decks for left-handers, novelty cards, low vision sets, cards in odd shapes, souvenirs and political packs, including the famous Iraqi Most Wanted deck. You'll also find magic trick cards, children's games, magnetic decks, poker chips and automatic shufflers. Playing cards online just doesn't stack up anymore.

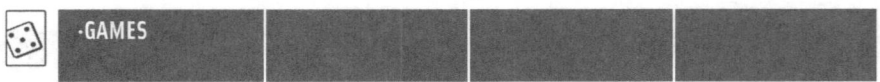

·GAMES

OpampBooks.com

Opamp Technical Books · 800-468-4322

Given that this site lists more than 600 books about the web, you'd think it would look a lot better than the jumbled mess of colors and words you'll find on the home page. With a site this big, though, nobody's got time to worry about aesthetics. Dozens of cat-egories lead to hundreds of subcategories, whereas the actual number of books is too high to count without a powerful computer. Covering the technical side of Business, Computers, Construction, Electronics, Engineering, Legal, Manufacturing, Mathematics, Medical, Sciences and the Entertainment Industry, this ugly site may be the most comprehensive source of industrial information online.

·BOOKS ·USED ·TEXTBOOKS ·HOW-TO

212-477-8150 · Other Music

OtherMusic.com

This online version of a decidedly hip New York City music store may be confusing at first, as the category names are weird and all seem to lead you nowhere. A little patience and exploration can prove quite valuable, though, and the About This Genre links will let you know just what may be found in categories named In, Out, Decadance, Groove and Psychedelia. All in all, it's definitely not the perfect musical shopping experience, but with this breadth of product, we feel the web would be lacking without it.

·MUSIC ·VINYL ·RARE

800-291-9676 · Powell's City of Books

Powells.com

Probably the only bookstore in the world that qualifies as a tourist attraction, this Portland, Oregon, retailer fills entire city blocks with books, covering over 100 subject areas, including rooms stacked high with rare and out-of-print volumes, comic books, audio books and enough used material to warrant a whole other store. This web site probably doesn't attract as many visitors each day as its downtown namesake, but with at least as many easily browsed titles to offer, it proves a fine destination in its own right.

·BOOKS ·DOWNLOADS ·AUDIO BOOKS ·TEXTBOOKS ·COMICS ·HOW-TO ·USED ·RARE

877-924-6895 · PuzzleHouse.com

PuzzleHouse.com

With "over 1,100 jigsaw puzzles" to choose from, it's a pretty safe bet this specialty puzzle retailer will be the only one you ever need. Ranging between 500 and 6,000 pieces, the vast selection of puzzle images are divided handily by size and then subject, but you'll definitely want to turn on the thumbnails feature to browse by pictures, many of which are artistic in nature. Other options include 3-D, Photomosaic, Wooden, Metallic and Glow In The Dark puzzles. In every case, the pieces add up to a great site.

·GAMES

800-852-7771 · RazorGator

RazorGator.com

When the search for tickets to that sold-out concert, play or sporting event becomes an act of desperation, there are a few things you can do: 1) Try to win tickets from your local radio station by being the 57th caller. 2) Engage in an all-out bidding war on eBay competing for the title of Ultimate Uberfan. 3) Go to the event with a wad of cash in pocket and present it to the shadiest character around in hopes he's a scalper. 4) Check out this site for potentially expensive but usually very desirable tickets available up to the last minute. Prices on 2) and 3) won't wind up being all that great, with the added concern of counterfeit tickets. Good luck with the radio station, but otherwise, this is your last, best bet.

·SHOWS & EVENTS

RecRooms.com

RecRooms Direct · 800-890-3010

You could turn that extra room in your house into a library, study or office, but where's the fun in that? This site will help turn it into the most (or at least second-most) fun room in the house, filled with game furniture, whether it be billiards, Foosball, Ping-Pong, shuffleboard or air hockey you prefer. You'll also find rec room essentials like dartboards and card tables, plus poker chips, pool cues, spare paddles and all other necessary accessories. If it's really important to you, go ahead and squeeze a desk and some bookshelves in the corner, just as long as they're out of the way of the action.

 ·GAMES

RedOctane.com

RedOctane · 888-737-8038

If you go through games as fast as you go through DVDs, you may want to check out this videogame specialist that offers a few affordable alternatives to buying every new game that comes out. Aside from a regular assortment of new and used games and accessories, the site offers a monthly rental service similar to that of NetFlix and other online video rental sites. Simply pay a monthly fee and receive two games in the mail. When you're finished with one, put it back in the mail and receive the next one a few days later. For those who can finish a game in just a few dedicated days, this site will enable you to win them all, with enough money left over to buy a book or something.

 ·VIDEOGAMES ·USED ·RENTALS

RentAnime.com

RentAnime · 888-692-6463

There are a variety of DVD rental sites out there these days where you may order your favorite classic films, indie flicks and movie blockbusters for unlimited rentals, and for most people that's all you'll need. But if you have a taste for anime, those regular on-line rental sites will be sorely lacking. This anime rental specialist operates much the same way, except it covers much more than the popular crossover features, delving into the old, the obscure, the Japanese TV hits and misses and even the kinky hentai titles that casual anime fans can conveniently ignore elsewhere.

 ·MOVIES & TV ·RENTALS

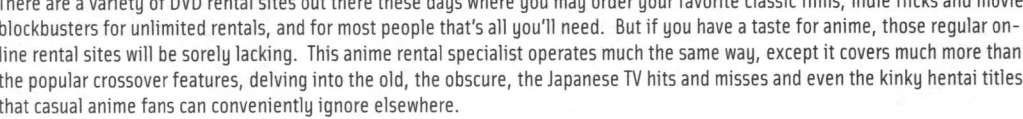

SamuelFrench.com

Samuel French · 212-206-899

Theater is so often considered an actor's medium that it's easy to forget some of the best writing history has seen was meant for the stage. The big guns—Shakespeare, Tennessee Williams, Arthur Miller and even Moliere—may usually be found in regular bookstores. But for the ardent fan of tragedies, comedies and musicals, finding the scripts and/or musical scores of the lengthy list of memorable theater would prove a nearly impossible task were it not for this terrific specialty site. You will find the classics here, but you'll also find more obscure one acts, ensemble pieces and monologues, whether you want a script for personal perusal or to stage your own production (in which case royalty fees may apply).

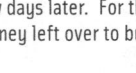 ·BOOKS ·SHOWS & EVENTS

800-531-4727 · PBS

ShopPBS.org

Public television may lack the showmanship and brand recognition of even the most obscure basic cable channels, but somewhere, deep down, you probably recognize its intrinsic value to the American broadcasting landscape. Despite the increasing frequency of federal budget cuts, that network of locally operated channels has managed to produce and/or broadcast some high quality television, including several British comedies, *Masterpiece Theatre*, all of Ken Burns's documentaries, the science show *NOVA* and the indispensable *Sesame Street*. All of these and more are available here on DVD, giving us reason to ponder: why haven't we been watching PBS more often?

·BOOKS	·MUSIC	·MOVIES & TV	·SHOWS & EVENTS

800-285-8619 · Spilsbury

Spilsbury.com

If your family is tired of the same old fun, this engaging selection of games, puzzles and activities can spur even the staunchest of couch potatoes into action. The oddball assortment of products is far-reaching enough to satisfy children and wacky adults as well as more sophisticated folk looking to bolster their rec rooms. Highlights include trampoline shoes, giant tennis balls and a glow-in-the-dark bocce set, along with nostalgic handheld videogames and gag gifts that never seem to get old. Basically, there's never a shortage of inspired board games and puzzles for those who think they've seen it all.

·GAMES	·VIDEOGAMES

888-423-1212 · A&E Television Networks

Store.AETV.com

Good television may be hard to come by these days, but if you take a good look at this site you'll be reminded that, every once in awhile, there's some great entertainment to be found between the commercial breaks. You'll find a litany of some of the best shows from home and aboard, primarily packaged in collectors' sets on DVD or VHS. Of course, given that the Arts & Entertainment channels are behind this store, the bulk of the selection features the network's superb original productions, including their famous Biographies, and a comprehensive list of extraordinarily compelling History Channel documentaries. You may spend hours just browsing the site; the shows could keep you busy for months at a time.

·BOOKS	·SHOWS & EVENTS

866-788-2482 · StubHub

StubHub.com

With a business model that may one day eradicate the presence of empty seats at concert and sporting events, this site offers a marketplace for people who won't make the show or game for whatever reason. Thus, sports team season-ticket holders can re-coup the cost of their seats on games they can't make, and those with extra concert tickets can sell them to desperate fans. Sort of like a cleaner, easier way to scalp tickets in advance (you'll need to order at least a few days ahead of time), once you get to know this site the words *Sold Out* will cease to have any meaning.

·SHOWS & EVENTS			

Teach12.com

Certain school experiences can never be replicated by any online retailer. However, if you're actually more interested in education than parties and casual dating, this site offers a flexible, affordable alternative to college enrollment. A wide variety of high school and university level lectures are available in audio and visual formats, covering topics in science, math and the humanities. You'll be exposed to some of the nation's top professors, learning at your own pace without fear of being called on during class.

·HOW-TO			

TeleCharge.com

To give you an idea how dominant this theater ticketing service is, even the mighty Ticketmaster defers to it when it comes to Broadway productions. Whether the show you want tickets to is actually on Broadway, Off Broadway or so far off Broadway that it's in another state, you'll find a long list of musicals, comedies, one-person shows and dramas here. Unfortunately, at this time most of the shows represented here do perform in New York or nearby cities such as Boston, Philadelphia and Washington, D.C. For other regional theater tickets we'd have to refer you back to that other dominant ticketing service.

·SHOWS & EVENTS			

TicketWeb.com

Of the few event-ticket retailers out there, this would be the one that you'd have to consider the underdog (in the unlikely event that you would view such things in the context of a competitive free market). You will come across some intriguing events here, including some you might never have known about if browsing elsewhere, and a few of them might even surprise you. You may browse by venue or search for a particular event, but your best bet is using the Search to narrow down a date and region to find out what's happening in the low-fee universe.

·MUSIC	·SHOWS & EVENTS		

TowerRecords.com

When a music superstore offers more than 50,000 titles in its Classical section alone, you know you're going to find something you want to buy. That's the case with this international franchise, which offers an incredibly comprehensive assortment of popular and world music covering every conceivable genre. As if that weren't enough, the shop also carries close to 50,000 DVD titles as well. With so much to choose from it would seem the only problem is finding anything, but with incredibly exhaustive organization and browsing techniques, this site actually makes it hard not to find what you want.

·MUSIC ·RARE	·MOVIES & TV	·VINYL	·USED

800-949-8688 · TURN OFF the TV.com

TurnOffTheTV.com

This site doesn't just ask you to turn off the boob tube, it offers a slew of alternative activities for you to pursue with your family and friends; namely, a terrific selection of games. Ranging from educational games and brainteasers to board and travel games, clicking through these many pages can be more of a drag than channel-surfing with your remote. However, it's worthwhile to browse this unique selection, in particular for some of the puzzling gift ideas.

·GAMES

011-31-5379-20-89 · Bookeen

UbiBooks.com

More and more often, reading is something we do while looking at a computer screen of some sort, and while this saves paper, it does little for our literary enrichment. This is no longer the case if you've been willing to embrace the world of eBooks, which allow you to download the printed word to your computer or a variety of handheld devices. This site offers a wealth of classic and popular contemporary texts covering five languages, delivering affordable, on-demand reading with instant gratification. If you haven't tried e-texts yet, a few minutes on this site may convince you they're worthwhile. Just take a few moments to read about the advantages.

·BOOKS   ·DOWNLOADS

623-551-5840 · The Vintage Library

VintageLibrary.com

This is not a slick site, neither is it glamorous, but then, neither is its subject matter. After all, this is a site devoted to pulp fiction. From hard-boiled detective novels to weird tales, monster stories, fan zines, westerns and sci-fi, this retailer has a surprising abundance of tattered paperbacks and comics, many long since out of print, most having to do with the legendary and/or fantastic. Some of these titles seem like they should cost more than they do, some less, but all are off the beaten path, touting the gritty charms of the likes of Mickey Spillane, Zorro and Girls of the Slime God. Cool stuff.

·BOOKS   ·COMICS   ·USED   ·RARE

866-228-7359 · zooba

Zooba.com

Your classic book-of-the-month club gets a welcome update with this ingenious member-driven site. The old system? Pay a monthly fee to receive a book somebody else wants you to read. The Zooba way? Less than ten dollars per month gets you the new hardcover title of your choosing (shipping included). You may select from an extensive list of new releases and best sellers, and if you have trouble picking just one, it's no big deal. You may purchase as many additional books as you like each month for only another ten bucks apiece. Whether you buy twelve books a year or fifty, this may be your best bet.

·BOOKS

NOTES:

_____
_____
_____
_____
_____
_____
_____
_____
_____
_____
_____
_____
_____
_____
_____
_____
_____
_____
_____

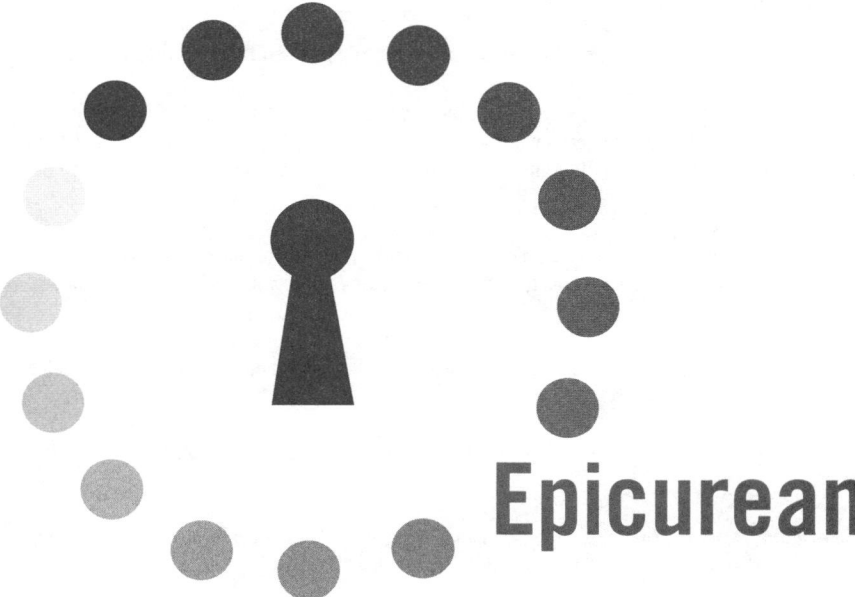

Epicurean

Admittedly, you can't satisfy an immediate craving by shopping online... yet. However, if you love to eat well, there's no better place than the internet to find a wealth of healthy and delicious foods. Gourmands will find plenty of prime grade meats, exotic game fowl, live lobster, caviar, foie gras and other delicacies. Those with special diets can stock up on organic produce, soy meat substitutes, low-carb products or health food. Anyone with a predilection for regional fares can easily track down Japanese candy, French wine, New England clam chowder, Kenyan coffee and mouthwatering Southern BBQ. And if you're perpetually in a hurry (or culinarily challenged), there's no shortage of prepared, heat-and-serve meals covering a broad range of budgets and tastes.

Perhaps the greatest benefits may be noticed, not by your tongue, but by the rest of your body. The web makes it incredibly easy to avoid the processed, pesticide-laced, hormone-infused and otherwise unhealthy fast food and supermarket sale items that have contributed to the epidemic obesity and malnourishment in our country. After all, everybody wants to eat better. That being said, temptation exists, and we can point you to an unworldly selection of chocolate, baked goods, ice cream and other sweet treats for those cravings doomed to return, not to mention a few cigars and dessert liqueurs to top them all off. You may wish to consult the Health & Beauty and Sports & Outdoors sections when you're through here.

TIPS ON BUYING EPICUREAN ITEMS ONLINE

These suggestions may keep your online food and drink purchases from leaving a bad taste in your mouth.

• **TAKE NOTE OF DELIVERY TIMES** • Most perishable items are delivered overnight with special packaging, and with good reason. Make sure somebody will be around to accept delivery, or you could have some expensive spoiled food on your hands. (Note: some items, such as chocolate, may melt during transit in the summer, and so require special considerations. Make sure the retailer knows this going in.)

• **SPECIAL EVENTS & CATERING** • When ordering a lot of food for a big event, it is best to order well ahead of time. Most retailers will plan to send the stuff on a specified date, but it's a good idea to use comments boxes and customer service phone numbers when ordering, to ensure punctual delivery.

• **FROZEN VS. FRESH MEAT & FISH** • When ordering meat and fish, make sure to note whether the product you're ordering is being sold fresh or frozen.

• **BE WARY OF FOOD ALLERGIES** • International food orders may include unlisted or differently named ingredients. If you suffer from food allergies, take note.

• **INSURE FINE WINES** • Simple rule: if it comes in a bottle, it can break during delivery. Make sure big investments are insured during transit, and know ahead of time whether your state allows the sale of wine via the internet.

SITES THAT MAY COME IN HANDY

The following URLs may be useful when you pursue epicurean pleasures.

CigarFriendly.com	Locate cigar-friendly establishments
CoffeeReview.com	Coffee buying guide
CookingSchools.com	Locate a cooking school in your area
Epicurious.com	Etiquette, food information and recipes
FoodSafety.gov	FDA food safety guidelines
FoodTV.com	The Food Network's recipes and resources
FreeTheGrapes.com	State-by-state alcohol shipping laws
Hire-A-Chef.com	Find a chef in your area
ItalianWineMerchant.com	Italian wine resource
Mixology.com	Cocktail recipes
Nal.USDA.gov/fnic	Nutritional information
Nat.UIUC.edu	Nutritional analysis tool
OnlineConversion.com	Measurements converter
TheFishList.org	A guide to sustainable fish consumption
TheGroceryGame.com	Tracks best current supermaket deals
WineAccess.com	Wine reviews and search
Wine-Searcher.com	Locate wine merchants

>> SITES WITH A SINGLE FOCUS

The following sites excel at selling one or two specific products.

BearCreekSmokeHouse.com	Smoked meats
CandyDirect.com	Bulk and novelty candy
CheeseExpress.com	Gourmet cheese
Cigar.com	Fine cigars
CollinStreetBakery.com	Holiday fruitcake
DiabeticFriendly.com	Sugar-free sweets
FatWitch.com	Brownies
FlyingNoodle.com	Pastas and sauces
FransChocolate.com	Gourmet chocolates
FudgeKitchens.com	Homemade fudge
GourmetGuides.com	Cookbooks
Graeters.com	Gourmet ice cream
HamIAm.com	Bacon and ham
HamptonPopcorn.com	Sweetened popcorn
HoneyBell.com	Citrus fruits
ILovePeanutButter.com	Gourmet peanut butters
JoesStoneCrab.com	Crabs and key lime pie
LittlePieCompany.com	Dessert pies
LiveLob.com	Lobster and fresh seafood
LouLousGarden.com	Jams and jellies
MoHatta.com	Hot sauces and condiments
OmahaSteaks.com	Steaks
OrientalPantry.com	Asian pantry items
Penzeys.com	Spices
Picnic-Baskets.com	Picnic baskets
PikePlaceFish.com	Fresh seafood
Plantin.com	Truffles and oils
SalsaExpress.com	Sauces and condiments
Seafoods.com	Fresh seafood
Sherry-Lehman.com	Wine
SmithfieldHams.com	Ham and turkey
SpecilaTeas.com	Teas
SquirrelBrand.com	Gourmet nuts
SunflowerFoodCompany.com	Snacks and nuts
TheOlivePress.com	Gourmet olive oils
TheWineClub.com	Fine wines
VermontGold.com	Maple products
VeryVera.com	Layer cakes

*For in-depth reviews of these sites and more, check out **www.thepurplebook.com**.

SECTION ICON LEGEND

Use the following guide to understand the rectangular icons that appear throughout this section.

ADULT VICES
If you're going to drink or smoke, this icon may at least point you toward some sites offering fine wines, good liquor and fine cigars. You may also come across some nice beer and pipe tobacco, along with some smoking accessories (no cigarettes, though).

GOURMET
We use this icon to cover a wide range of high-quality foods, from chocolates to fungi, including infused oils, caviar, exotic meats, cheeses, wines, coffees and all manner of ingredients.

PRE-PREPARED
These dishes don't necessarily arrive at your doorstep ready-to-eat, but they do require only a minimal effort, usually just the application of a little heat. Selections include plates of appetizers, gourmet meals, Chicago pizza and full clam bakes.

REGIONAL
This icon will guide you to some incredible food, whether it's from the American South, New England, Mexico or a variety of points abroad. We've found some great international grocers and specialty shops that will easily introduce a little excitement to your taste buds.

SPECIALTY STORE
As opposed to supermarkets, these shops usually devote themselves to one particular type of food item or ingredient, whether it be pasta, spices, salsas, meat, fish, baked goods or chocolate. As you might expect, these shops offer excellent selections of whatever it is they sell.

SUPERMARKET
We've included this icon to make it easier to find supermarket sites that stock a great variety of foods and flavors. Some of these are as basic as your local grocer, while others offer a glimpse of what supermarket shopping looks like in other countries.

 **LIST OF KEY WORDS**

The following words represent the types of items typically found on the sites listed in this section. You will find them listed in the orange strip at the bottom of each entry, as appropriate.

ALCOHOL	All alcoholic beverages, including wine, beer, spirits and liqueurs.
BAKED GOODS	Baked items, including breads, bagels, cakes, pies, cookies, brownies and pastries.
COFFEE/TEA	All coffees, teas, cocoas and other ingredients related to hot beverages.
CONDIMENTS	All sauces and dressings, including salsas, dressings, syrups, extracts, spreads, marinades, pasta sauces, BBQ sauces and powdered mixes.
DELICACIES	Gourmet items, such as charcuterie, pâté, caviar, fungi and cheeses.
HEAT & SERVE	Pre-prepared food items that need only be heated, not cooked, before consumption.
MEAT & FISH	Live, fresh, frozen, organic, cured and/or cooked meat and fish, including beef, pork, poultry, game, lamb, shellfish and seafood.
OILS & SPICES	Oils, vinegars, whole or ground spices, gourmet olive oils, infused oils and more.
PANTRY	Items typically to be found in a pantry, including canned goods, bulk grains, cooking mixes, pastas and baking ingredients.
PRODUCE	Fruits, nuts and vegetables, whether organic, fresh, frozen, dried, pickled or preserved.
RECIPES	Any shop that offers online recipes or cookbooks.
SNACKS	Basically a catchall for foodstuffs that aren't easily categorized, such as potato chips or trail mix.
SOFT DRINKS	Sodas, fruit juices or other nonalcoholic cold beverages.
SPECIAL DIETS	Sites that cater in whole or in part to low-fat, low-carb, sugar-free, vegetarian, macrobiotic and/or kosher diets.
SWEETS	Perhaps our most popular items, including chocolate, candy, cookies and other desserts.
TOBACCO	All cigars, chewing tobacco, pipe tobacco and smoking accessories.

KEY WORD INDEX

Use the followings lists to locate online retailers that sell the food and drink you seek.

ALCOHOL

AfricanHut.com
AGFerrari.com
BevMo.com
DiamondOrganics.com
FinestWine.com
Il-Vino.com
KAndL.com
LeVillage.com
PopsWine.com
QueenAnneWine.com
RussianFoods.com
WallyWine.com
WineLibrary.com

BAKED GOODS

AnaSuper.com
BakersCatalogue.com
BarneyGreenGrass.com
Bissingers.com
BittersweetPastriesDirect.com
BuyLebanese.com
CajunGrocer.com
DiamondOrganics.com
DivineDelights.com
Elenis.com
EliZabar.com
FerraraCafe.com
GermanDeli.com
GreenBeanz.com
Lepicerie.com
Polana.com
ProteinBakery.com
RussianFoods.com
StonewallKitchen.com
WikstromsGourmet.com
WmGreenbergDesserts.com
Zingermans.com

COFFEE & TEA

Adagio.com
AdrianasCaravan.com
BevMo.com
BuonItalia.com
ChefShop.com
ChefsWarehouse.com
Citarella.com
CoffeeAM.com
CoffeeTraders.com
DeanAndDeluca.com
DiBruno.com
iGourmet.com
iKoreaPlaza.com
ImportFoods.com
Kalustyans.com
Lepicerie.com
MarkTWendell.com
Rishi-Tea.com
ShopNatural.com

CONDIMENTS

AdrianasCaravan.com
AfricanHut.com
AGFerrari.com
AnaSuper.com
AsiaMex.com
AsianFoodGrocer.com
BakersCatalogue.com
BarneyGreenGrass.com
BuonItalia.com
BuyLebanese.com
CajunGrocer.com
ChefShop.com
ChefsWarehouse.com
Citarella.com
ClarksOutpost.com
CorkysBBQ.com
DeanAndDeluca.com
DiamondOrganics.com
DiBruno.com
Earthy.com
EthnicGrocer.com
FreshPasta.com
GermanDeli.com
GreenBeanz.com

CONDIMENTS (cont.)

HomeTownFavorites.com
iGourmet.com
iKoreaPlaza.com
ImportFoods.com
Kalustyans.com
Lepicerie.com
LeVillage.com
Melissas.com
MexGrocer.com
PacificRimGourmet.com
RussianFoods.com
SeaBear.com
ShopNatural.com
StonewallKitchen.com
Tienda.com
WikstromsGourmet.com
Zingermans.com

DELICACIES

AdrianasCaravan.com
AGFerrari.com
ALaZing.com
ArtisanalCheese.com
BarneyGreenGrass.com
BuonItalia.com
Cheese-Online.com
ChefShop.com
ChefsWarehouse.com
Citarella.com
ComtesseDuBarry.com
DArtagnan.com
DeanAndDeluca.com
DiamondOrganics.com
DiBruno.com
Earthy.com
iGourmet.com
Lepicerie.com
LeVillage.com
Melissas.com
MurraysCheese.com
Petrossian.com
TheFreshLobsterCompany.com
TsarNicoulai.com
WallyWine.com
WikstromsGourmet.com

HEAT & SERVE

ALaZing.com
AllenBrothers.com
AnaSuper.com
AppetizersToGo.com
ArtikoChef.com
CajunCrawfish.com
CajunGrocer.com
Citarella.com
ClamBakeCo.com
ClarksOutpost.com
ComtesseDuBarry.com
CorkysBBQ.com
CrabPlace.com
DiamondOrganics.com
EthnicGrocer.com
GourmetStation.com
HancockGourmetLobster.com
IpswichFishMarket.com
Kalustyans.com
KosherMeal.com
Polana.com
SeaBear.com
SmokeHouse.com
StonewallKitchen.com
TastesOfChicago.com
TheFreshLobsterCompany.com
VirginiaTraditions.com

MEAT & FISH

AfricanHut.com
AlaskanHarvest.com
ALaZing.com
AllenBrothers.com
AnaSuper.com
ApplegateFarms.com
AsiaMex.com
BarneyGreenGrass.com
Bissingers.com
BuonItalia.com
CajunCrawfish.com
CajunGrocer.com
CatalinaOP.com
ChefsWarehouse.com
Citarella.com
ClamBakeCo.com
ClarksOutpost.com

MEAT & FISH (cont.)

ComtesseDuBarry.com
CorkysBBQ.com
CrabPlace.com
DArtagnan.com
DeanAndDeluca.com
DiamondOrganics.com
DiBruno.com
EthnicGrocer.com
GermanDeli.com
HancockGourmetLobster.com
HeritageFoodsUSA.com
iGourmet.com
iKoreaPlaza.com
IpswichFishMarket.com
Kalustyans.com
LeVillage.com
Lobels.com
NimanRanch.com
Petrossian.com
Polana.com
RussianFoods.com
SeaBear.com
SmokeHouse.com
StonewallKitchen.com
TastesOfChicago.com
Tayeeb.com
TheFreshLobsterCompany.com
Tienda.com
TsarNicoulai.com
UptownPrime.com
VirginiaTraditions.com
WikstromsGourmet.com
Zingermans.com

OILS & SPICES

AdrianasCaravan.com
AfricanHut.com
AGFerrari.com
AmericanSpice.com
AnaSuper.com
AsiaMex.com
BuonItalia.com
BuyLebanese.com
CajunGrocer.com
ChefShop.com
ChefsWarehouse.com
Citarella.com
DeanAndDeluca.com
DiBruno.com
Earthy.com
EthnicGrocer.com
iGourmet.com
iKoreaPlaza.com

OILS & SPICES (cont.)

ImportFoods.com
Kalustyans.com
Lepicerie.com
LeVillage.com
Melissas.com
MexGrocer.com
PacificRimGourmet.com
Penzeys.com
RussianFoods.com
SBOlive.com
ShopNatural.com
StonewallKitchen.com
TheSpiceHouse.com
TheSpiceShop.co.uk
Tienda.com
Zingermans.com

PANTRY

AdrianasCaravan.com
AfricanHut.com
AGFerrari.com
AmericanSpice.com
AsiaMex.com
AsianFoodGrocer.com
BakersCatalogue.com
BuonItalia.com
BuyLebanese.com
CajunGrocer.com
ChefShop.com
ChefsWarehouse.com
Citarella.com
DeanAndDeluca.com
DiamondOrganics.com
DiBruno.com
Earthy.com
EthnicGrocer.com
FreshPasta.com
GermanDeli.com
GreenBeanz.com
HomeTownFavorites.com
iGourmet.com
iKoreaPlaza.com
ImportFoods.com
Kalustyans.com
Lepicerie.com
LeVillage.com
MexGrocer.com
PacificRimGourmet.com
ShopNatural.com
StonewallKitchen.com
Tayeeb.com
WikstromsGourmet.com
Zingermans.com

PRODUCE

AdrianasCaravan.com
AnaSuper.com
AsiaMex.com
AsianFoodGrocer.com
BuyLebanese.com
ChefsWarehouse.com
DArtagnan.com
DiamondOrganics.com
Earthy.com
EthnicGrocer.com
HadleyFruitOrchards.com
ImportFoods.com
Melissas.com
SBOlive.comHoneyBell.com
Melissas.com
OrientalPantry.com

RECIPES

AGFerrari.com
AlaskanHarvest.com
AllenBrothers.com
ApplegateFarms.com
AsianFoodGrocer.com
CajunCrawfish.com
CajunGrocer.com
ChefShop.com
ChocolateSource.com
DeanAndDeluca.com
Earthy.com
EthnicGrocer.com
GreenBeanz.com
iGourmet.com
ImportFoods.com
IpswichFishMarket.com
Kalustyans.com
LeVillage.com
Lobels.com
Melissas.com
MexGrocer.com
NimanRanch.com
PacificRimGourmet.com
RussianFoods.com
SeaBear.com
SmokeHouse.com
Stirrings.com
StonewallKitchen.com
Tayeeb.com
TheSpiceHouse.com
Tienda.com
VirginiaTraditions.com
WikstromsGourmet.com

SNACKS

AfricanHut.com
AnaSuper.com
AppetizersToGo.com
AsianFoodGrocer.com
BuyLebanese.com
EthnicGrocer.com
GermanDeli.com
GreenBeanz.com
HadleyFruitOrchards.com
HomeTownFavorites.com
MexGrocer.com
PacificRimGourmet.com
ShopNatural.com
Tienda.com
WikstromsGourmet.com

SOFT DRINKS

AfricanHut.com
AnaSuper.com
AsiaMex.com
AsianFoodGrocer.com
BuyLebanese.com
ChefsWarehouse.com
CoffeeAM.com
GermanDeli.com
GreenBeanz.com
iKoreaPlaza.com
LeVillage.com
MexGrocer.com
PacificRimGourmet.com
ShopNatural.com
SodaPopStop.com
Stirrings.com

SPECIAL DIETS

AmericanSpice.com
Bissingers.com
CajunGrocer.com
CandyWarehouse.com
ChocolateSource.com
FinestWine.com
GreenBeanz.com
KosherMeal.com
Melissas.com
NimanRanch.com
ProteinBakery.com

SWEETS

AGFerrari.com
ALaZing.com
AsianFoodGrocer.com
BakersCatalogue.com
BarneyGreenGrass.com
Bissingers.com
BittersweetPastriesDirect.com
BuonItalia.com
BuyLebanese.com
CandyWarehouse.com
CapoGiroGelato.com
ChefShop.com
ChocolateSource.com
ChocoSphere.com
Citarella.com
Compartes.com
ComtesseDuBarry.com
DeanAndDeluca.com
DebauveAndGallais.com
DivineDelights.com
Earthy.com
eCreamery.com
Elenis.com
FerraraCafe.com
GermanDeli.com
GreenBeanz.com
HadleyFruitOrchards.com
HomeTownFavorites.com
iGourmet.com
Lepicerie.com
MexGrocer.com
Petrossian.com
Polana.com
ProteinBakery.com
Route29Napa.com
RussianFoods.com
ShopNatural.com
StonewallKitchen.com
Tayeeb.com
Tienda.com
VosgesChocolate.com
WikstromsGourmet.com
Zingermans.com

TOBACCO

BevMo.com
CigarGold.com
JRCigars.com
QueenAnneWine.com
WallyWine.com

NOTES:

_____

_____

_____

_____

_____

_____

_____

_____

_____

_____

_____

_____

_____

_____

_____

_____

_____

_____

_____

Adagio.com

How slick is this niche tea retailer? Not only are its pages neatly organized and cleanly designed, but the people behind it have managed to do what we would have thought impossible: taken very clear and appealing photographs of tea leaves. Thus, not only can you read very detailed descriptions and histories of a wide variety of oolongs, rooibos, herbals, white, green and black teas, but you may even get a good idea of what they look like. It's hard to argue with such a demonstration of devotion and expertise. This is a great site.

·COFFEE/TEA			

AdrianasCaravan.com

It's not an easy thing to stock "Every Ingredient for Every Recipe You've Ever Read," so we're giving these guys big points for trying. Indeed, their selection of fungi, oils, vinegars, grains, spices, sauces, extracts, coffees and teas makes for tough shopping, as alphabetical listings don't usually help when you're browsing "culinary exotica." However, particularly with regard to spices, it proves an indispensable resource when recipes include ingredients you've probably never heard of, like Hawaj or Flageolet. Let your cookbook guide you through this one, or stick to ordering takeout.

·OILS & SPICES ·COFFEE/TEA	·DELICACIES ·PANTRY	·CONDIMENTS	·PRODUCE

AfricanHut.com

Have a taste for some bacon kips? How about some chakalaka and samp invicta? Okay, maybe you prefer to have your morning toast spread with a bit of fig jam? Chances are, if any of this sounds the least bit appetizing or even familiar, you've spent some time in South Africa. Once better known for its racial divisions than its beer, now we can order six-packs of Castle Lager and plenty of other regional grocery items from this store based in…Laguna Beach, California? Consider this one as evidence that the world is shrinking.

·MEAT & FISH ·SOFT DRINKS	·OILS & SPICES ·ALCOHOL	·CONDIMENTS ·PANTRY	·SNACKS

AGFerrari.com

You may have heard that Italian food is some of the best on the planet, and may in fact keep your pantry well stocked with pastas and sauces to support the notion. Chances are, though, you haven't tasted anything yet. The proprietor of this site "scours the Italian countryside several times a year in his relentless pursuit of the best that Italy has to offer," and the results are impossible to contend. Toss out everything you think you know about Italian cuisine and let this incredible site educate you on the difference between various northern and southern regions. Then buy the imported pastas, oils, truffles, sauces, olives and cured meats featured throughout these pages. Your taste buds will thank you.

·SWEETS ·CONDIMENTS	·OILS & SPICES ·ALCOHOL	·RECIPES ·PANTRY	·DELICACIES

888-824-4278 · Alaskan Harvest Seafood

AlaskanHarvest.com

Fresh Alaskan seafood and USDA prime meats highlight the selection of this Oregon web shop that guarantees "the most flavorful, freshest, firmest [seafood] you've ever eaten." Surf'n'turf has rarely been so attractive an option, with Angus tenderloins to match with swordfish, halibut, tuna, black cod, rockfish and wild salmon, either filleted or smoked. Of course, no northern Pacific selection would be complete without shellfish, and this one offers lobster, clams, oysters, shrimp, scallops and crab, all packaged so well you can practically smell the ocean when you open the box.

·MEAT & FISH	·RECIPES		

888-959-9464 · A La Zing

ALaZing.com

The top three easiest ways to eat a good meal are to go to a restaurant, hire a chef or go home to visit Mom. The fourth easiest may be found on this pre-prepared specialty site. A broad menu of gourmet and hearty home-style meals may be simply browsed and ordered, and upon arrival will usually involve no more than ten minutes of heating time. Chicken Cordon Bleu, Shrimp Fettucini Alfredo, BBQ Pulled Pork Sandwiches and Prime Rib are just a few of your entrée options, each complete with a nutritious variety of side dishes, any of which may be complemented by one of the company's delicious desserts. All you have to do is lift a finger.

·SWEETS	·MEAT & FISH	·DELICACIES	·HEAT & SERVE

877-548-7777 · Allen Brothers

AllenBrothers.com

These "purveyors of the finest meats" originate out of Chicago—a town that knows its meats. Hence, here you will find steaks, roasts, ground meats, pork, chicken, veal, game meats, seafood and jerky. While you might have reservations about eating meat that's been through the postal service, these cuts are frozen, vacuum-sealed and packed in dry ice to maintain a freshness you won't always find in the grocery store. More importantly, here you'll only find meats that rate in the top 2 percent of the nation: USDA Prime.

·MEAT & FISH	·RECIPES	·HEAT & SERVE	

888-502-8058 · The Great American Spice Co.

AmericanSpice.com

Fort Wayne, Indiana, definitely sounds like a place to look for Americana, but it wouldn't necessarily be the first place you'd think of when you hear the word *spice*. However, a visit to this Hoosier spice shop's web site might change your mind. Although you're likely to find deeper and more exotic assortments of spices elsewhere, rarely will you find them on a site so user-friendly as this, which also offers a comprehensive supply of dehydrated fruit, nuts, powdered dairy products, condiments, marinades, baking mixes and homespun candies. Best of all, prices are low, so you can start up with some spice and finish up with something sweet.

·OILS & SPICES	·SPECIAL DIETS	·PANTRY	

AnaSuper.com

Rarely are the differences and similarities between cultures so pronounced as when you compare grocery stores. This Japanese answer to the online supermarket teems with products so foreign to the American palate that they can't even be accurately translated. Hence, the Tsukemono and Okazu categories may perplex you, and we won't pretend to understand them any better, other than to say they seem predominately to offer pickled produce and pre-prepared meals (respectively). The meat, rice, fish, snacks, beverages, noodles and bakery items are easier to decipher, but still offer the thrill of the exotic in an easy-to-browse manner. *Sozo ijo no mono deshta!*

·MEAT & FISH ·SNACKS	·OILS & SPICES ·HEAT & SERVE	·BAKED GOODS ·SOFT DRINKS	·CONDIMENTS ·PRODUCE

AppetizersToGo.com

If you decide to cater your own party, you'll have to face down the many daunting tasks that cooking for large groups of people entails. This site can do a lot to ease your burden, though—at least part of it. The first part. With an extraordinary selection of appetizing heat-and-serve hors d'oeuvres to choose from, you can offer your guests a wide variety of dumplings, cheese puffs, stuffed mushrooms, mini quiches, buffalo wings, chicken fingers, crab cakes and rangoons. Prepare enough and you won't even need to worry about the main course.

·SNACKS	·HEAT & SERVE		

ApplegateFarms.com

If there's an organic deli in your neighborhood, you probably won't be all that interested in this site. But, seeing as most neighborhoods don't have an organic anything, we're guessing that the hormone-, nitrate-, gluten- and antibiotic-free lineup of sliced meats found here will thrill anybody looking to adhere to an all-natural diet. Better yet, the site claims its stock comes only from farms that raise their cows and fowl with plenty of space, fresh air and sunshine. In other words, get ready for a lifetime of healthy, guilt-free club sandwiches.

·MEAT & FISH	·RECIPES		

ArtikoChef.com

Cooking for one can be a drag. Heating and serving for one has been a staple food-preparation technique for bachelors and single women since before the term *bachelorette* even existed. However, unlike the classic TV dinner, the pre-prepared meals offered by this purveyor of frozen dinners are all-natural, nutritious and preservative free. Most of these complete meals or à la carte items could even be called gourmet, although you'd never believe it to look at the prices. Almost more affordable than picking out your single-serving ingredients at the market, they are without a doubt easier to make.

·HEAT & SERVE			

877-797-1200 · Artisanal Cheese

ArtisanalCheese.com

If you live in a world with only Cheddar, American, Swiss, Monterey Jack and Mozzarella, then you're missing out on a great, wide adventurous world of cheeses. This site takes you on a journey, passing through Brie, Gouda, Parmesan and Camembert, enabling you to explore rich, textured differences like Asiago, Gruyère, Lancashire, Pecorino and more. Search for cheeses from nearly a dozen countries in varying degrees of hardness or softness, from goats, cows, sheep or buffalo, and break free of the limitations of your local deli.

·DELICACIES			

636-272-2746 · Pacific Island Market

AsiaMex.com

Representing about fifty nations covering six continents, and a few islands beside, this multifaceted ethnic grocer can't promise you a comprehensive selection of any particular regional foodstuffs. However, individual ingredients and mixes abound, making this the perfect spot to plot a fusion of cultural cuisines, whether your tastes veer toward pan-Asian, African, Latin American, Caribbean and/or European. Shopping by country is only occasionally fruitful, but product categories ranging from Beans & Peas to Fish Sauce, Noodles and Soup turns up a global cornucopia of flavors.

·MEAT & FISH ·PRODUCE	·OILS & SPICES ·PANTRY	·CONDIMENTS	·SOFT DRINKS

888-482-2742 · Asian Food Grocer

AsianFoodGrocer.com

Here's a California-based Asian food specialist that makes convenience a priority, which is refreshing because, although we usually prefer to go to the source, Overseas grocery stores tend to be confusing to use. This one offers a good number of explicit categories to help you wade through an extensive selection of primarily Japanese and Korean snacks, noodles, sauces, sodas and candy. Colorful pictures, low prices and endless serving suggestions will keep you browsing, and though you'll come for the Pocky Sticks you'll probably leave with a whole lot more.

·SWEETS ·SOFT DRINKS	·RECIPES ·PRODUCE	·CONDIMENTS ·PANTRY	·SNACKS

800-827-6836 · The Baker's Catalogue

BakersCatalogue.com

Ladies and gentlemen, preheat your ovens. The products you will find on this site will raise dough in your kitchen, beginning with a fine assortment of ingredients and mixes that promise to make baking not just a pastime, but a source of delicious breads, cookies, cakes, pastries and pies. If the ingredients aren't enough, you'll find a good deal of bakeware, kitchen gadgets and small appliances, including bread machines, cookie molds and cake decorating tools. You'll have the whole neighborhood knocking down your door.

·SWEETS	·BAKED GOODS	·CONDIMENTS	·PANTRY

BarneyGreengrass.com

From one of the nation's most upscale department stores comes one of its most upscale food retailers. Part deli, part charcuterie, Barney's shoppers have long enjoyed Greengrass sandwiches, salads and breakfast dishes. Now, the restaurant offers a tidy feast of gourmet delicacies, New York bagels, pickles, side salads, smoked fish, freshwater fish and deli meats through this site, which doesn't exactly replicate the dining experience, but does meet every expectation you might have of Barney's quality.

·SWEETS ·CONDIMENTS	·MEAT & FISH	·BAKED GOODS	·DELICACIES

BevMo.com

If you can drink it, you stand a good chance at finding it here. This beverage (and more) site devotes nearly half its selection to wine, but no less impressive are its sections offering coffees, soft drinks, juices, sodas, liquors and beers. In fact, its beer selection is one of the best you'll ever see, with more than eight hundred domestics and imports, including regional favorites and a few hard-to-find foreign brews. Such a vice-laden shop would not be complete without a few tobacco products, and sure enough, you'll find plenty of cigars if you follow the & More link.

·TOBACCO	·COFFEE/TEA	·ALCOHOL	

Bissingers.com

We have to warn you: this site may induce uncontrollable drooling with talk of "luscious chocolate-covered fresh fruits, decadent truffles and hand-crafted chocolate confections." If you think that's bad, wait until you see the pictures of rich, smooth chocolate as it embraces a glistening strawberry, or molded perfectly around a candied pecan. You may find a moment's respite in the gourmet meats section, just so long as you don't stumble into the pies and cookies area…. It's probably best that those with weak wills refrain from viewing this one.

·SWEETS	·MEAT & FISH	·BAKED GOODS	·SPECIAL DIETS

BittersweetPastriesDirect.com

Perennial winners at the Summer International Fancy Food Show, the tarts offered by this specialty desserts company will make your tongue tingle. Flavors like Apple Crumb, Bourbon Pecan and Cabernet Pear are tantalizing enough to bust any diet, never mind the layer cakes, truffle cakes and cookies. Chocolate and fruit lovers alike will be hard-pressed to make a decision once they get a look at the site, but if you plan to order more than one of these perishable desserts, make sure you have company over or risk eating an entire cake in one sitting.

·SWEETS	·BAKED GOODS		

212-633-9090 · Buonitalia

BuonItalia.com

The great taste of Italy is never difficult to find, as the legendary Mediterranean cuisine is so popular in our country that even the most incompetent of bachelor chefs can usually whip up a decent pasta. You may be surprised, then, to find out this Italian food importer doesn't offer much in the way of pasta at all. Rather, it delivers a wide selection of fine cheeses, gourmet delicacies, condiments, smoked meats, pickled fish and of course olive oil. However, as the proprietors choose only "the very best individual product in every possible category," finding Italy's greatest tastes has rarely been easier.

·SWEETS ·CONDIMENTS	·MEAT & FISH ·COFFEE/TEA	·OILS & SPICES ·PANTRY	·DELICACIES

011-961-360-2405 · Buy Lebanese

BuyLebanese.com

Straight out of Beruit comes this Lebanese bakery and marketplace, which offers an excellent sampling of the country's culture, in particular its "taste and savour." Most familiar may be the site's Baklawa, Lebanese Bread and Baba Ghannouge, although excellent written descriptions of lesser-known items such as Borghol Khechen Asmar, Halawa bi Shokola and Kadami will tempt you to try something new. We're assured that these foods are made from all-natural ingredients, and may best be washed down with regional soft drinks like orange blossom water, for a truly authentic dining experience.

·SWEETS ·SNACKS	·OILS & SPICES ·SOFT DRINKS	·BAKED GOODS ·PRODUCE	·CONDIMENTS ·PANTRY

888-254-8626 · Moe's Cajun Crawfish

CajunCrawfish.com

The word *Cajun* is usually enough to start anyone drooling, and this crawfish specialist is well enough outfitted to satisfy any savory craving. Foremost, of course, is the live shellfish, available in quantities of up to sixty pounds, which almost sounds like an infestation. You may also opt for gulf shrimp, alligator filets, andouille, tur-duc-ken and a variety of other meats and fish. Of course, none of it would go down so well without an assortment of Cajun spices, condiments and BBQ rubs. When in doubt, stick to the heat-and-serve entrees and a king cake for dessert.

·MEAT & FISH	·RECIPES	·HEAT & SERVE	

888-272-9347 · CajunGrocer.com

CajunGrocer.com

Louisiana might just be the most creative region in the nation when it comes to culinary concoctions, and not just because they eat things like alligator burgers and crawfish pies. While Cajun and Creole dishes are primarily known for the sizzling spiciness, the more adventurous among us may take an interest in some of these more intriguing delicacies. There's much more to this site than gumbo and jambalaya, as evidenced by the tur-duc-ken, which is probably the most bizarre holiday tradition you'll ever encounter: a chicken smeared with crawfish dressing, stuffed in a shrimp-slathered duck and then crammed inside a turkey. When in doubt, just order a king cake.

·MEAT & FISH ·SPECIAL DIETS	·OILS & SPICES ·CONDIMENTS	·BAKED GOODS ·HEAT & SERVE	·RECIPES ·PANTRY

CandyWarehouse.com

If for some reason you're in need of 2,500 Pixy Stix, or some other insanely huge candy order, check out this candified version of a warehouse supermarket. You can shop by delicious category, or through more than sixty brands, ranging from popular candy-makers such as Nestle, Willy Wonka and Jolly Rancher to lesser-knowns such as Trolli, Candy Tech and Andy Wertz. There are even options here such as Sugar Free Candy, Low Carb Candy and Candy Jewelry & Fashion. The Gummy section alone is enough to give you a virtual head rush.

 ·SWEETS · ·SPECIAL DIETS

CapoGiroGelato.com

Ice cream is not an easy thing to market over the internet, and gelato is no different. This Philadelphia specialty shop does offer fresh selections of its gelatos and sorbets for sale online, but they don't make it easy. Some of the problems? You must order in bulk, usually meaning six or more, and in most cases the flavors are determined by availability. Ordering is also a cumbersome process, and then there's the fact they only ship on Tuesdays. It's a long way to go for some authentic cold treats, but it's still easier than going to Italy.

 ·SWEETS

CatalinaOP.com

Finding fresh fish is not a problem if you live near the coast, but go more than a couple hundred miles inland and you might run into some problems. This goes double for fish you don't plan to cook. Here's one of the few web sites brave enough to offer su-shi-quality fish for national delivery. Well stocked with fresh tuna, yellowtail, sea bass, sea urchin, shellfish and roe, the site's quick processing and overnight delivery can get the cooler-packed seafood to you within thirty hours of its capture. You can expect shipping costs to be high, but if the alternative is frozen fish sticks, it's probably worth it.

 ·MEAT & FISH

Cheese-Online.com

Welcome to the "fascinating world of traditional French cheeses," where names like Cheddar and Monterey Jack are rarely, if ever, uttered. The seasonal cheese source instead focuses on selections such as Bleu des Causses. Coeur de Touraine, Couronne Lochoise, Beaufort and Brebis du Lavort. Don't know what these are? No matter—detailed descriptions explain all about these cheeses: what region they come from; whether they're made from the milk of a cow, sheep or goat; and even which types of wines and entrees best complement their complex flavors and nuances. This site is indeed a cheese adventure you can pursue without ever boarding a plane.

  ·DELICACIES

877-337-2491 · Chefshop.com

ChefShop.com

Gourmet cooking is often less about the recipes you use or the culinary skills you possess than it is about the ingredients you begin with. Shopping from this high-quality pantry site won't necessarily make you a better chef, but it should still make your meals taste better. Category shopping will lead you to plenty of flavorful grains, spices, oils and condiments, as well as delicacies like olives, mushrooms, nuts and smoked fish. Or, you may shop by Pantry to browse items grouped into Spanish, French, Moroccan, Gluten Free, Kosher and other regional or dietary themes, in case you want to be a good organic gourmet cook, for example.

·SWEETS ·CONDIMENTS	·OILS & SPICES ·COFFEE/TEA	·RECIPES ·PANTRY	·DELICACIES

718-842-8700 · Dairyland U.S.A.

ChefsWarehouse.com

If you love to buy in bulk but don't think warehouse grocers live up to your high epicurean standards, check out this big purchase site from "one of the leading suppliers to most of the finest restaurants, hotels and caterers in New York City and up and down the East Coast." Twenty-five-pound bags of rice, fifty-pound bags of flour and twenty-pound orders of pasta might result in exorbitant shipping costs, no matter how great the variety is. However, with four-pound wheels of cheese, an eight-ounce tub of truffle butter and 125-gram tins of caviar should fit under the shop's ten-pound flat shipping rate. Truth is, though, you can find massive amounts of just about every imaginable food here, whether you're entertaining large groups or planning the end of the world.

·MEAT & FISH ·SOFT DRINKS	·OILS & SPICES ·PRODUCE	·DELICACIES ·COFFEE/TEA	·CONDIMENTS ·PANTRY

800-214-4926 · ChocolateSource.com

ChocolateSource.com

We don't know what we can say about this site that isn't already evident in its name, and we're guessing that the most zealous chocoholics skipped this review and went straight to the site anyway. For those still reading, we can tell you it's a more-than-worthwhile web stop, its categories filled with Dark Chocolate, Milk Chocolate, Sugar-Free Chocolate, Baking Chocolate, Bars, Marzipan and Cocoa covering all price ranges. You'd be hard-pressed to find any poor-quality chocolate here, as most of the featured brands are considered the best in the biz. Are you still with us?

·SWEETS	·RECIPES	·SPECIAL DIETS	

877-992-4626 · Chocosphere.com

ChocoSphere.com

When making chocolate becomes an artistic pursuit, it usually winds up being distributed by this high-end chocolatier. Immediately clear, however, is that the making of web sites is not considered an artistic pursuit at Chocosphere headquarters, as this interface offers little in the way of effort or imagination. While some of the most delectable, decadent chocolates in the world are easily within reach, the clumsy layout leads to less-than-ideal browsing. We forgive them, however, because we all love to get our fix, and in terms of chocolate selection, this one raises the bar.

·SWEETS			

CigarGold.com

If you're a true cigar aficionado, you will almost certainly be impressed by the dozens-long list of brands available from this online tobacconist. However, if you're a novice smoker or looking for that special-event stogie, you will not be confused or disappointed. A Cigars by Type menu will guide you to a fine, full selection of smokes based on their size. A better bet, though, will be the Cigar by Occasion browsing, which recommends good smokes for such important life milestones as a graduation, the birth of a child and the completion of a great meal.

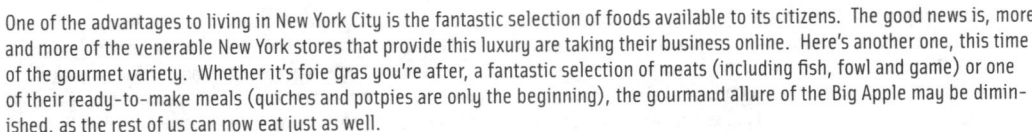

·TOBACCO

Citarella.com

One of the advantages to living in New York City is the fantastic selection of foods available to its citizens. The good news is, more and more of the venerable New York stores that provide this luxury are taking their business online. Here's another one, this time of the gourmet variety. Whether it's foie gras you're after, a fantastic selection of meats (including fish, fowl and game) or one of their ready-to-make meals (quiches and potpies are only the beginning), the gourmand allure of the Big Apple may be diminished, as the rest of us can now eat just as well.

·SWEETS ·CONDIMENTS | ·MEAT & FISH ·HEAT & SERVE | ·OILS & SPICES ·COFFEE/TEA | ·DELICACIES ·PANTRY

ClamBakeCo.com

When it's time for a good old-fashioned clambake, you can do no better than to visit this newfangled specialty retailer. What's a clambake? Well, as these guys have it, it's a shindig that involves steamed lobster, mussels, vegetables, Portuguese sausage and, of course, clams. Yes, it sounds like a lot to prepare, but that's the great thing about this site: they send you a prepacked steamer pot, loaded with ingredients. You simply add water, put the pot over a flame and twenty minutes (or so) later you have a full-fledged clambake for as many people as you want. It couldn't be easier, and you get to keep the pot.

·MEAT & FISH | ·HEAT & SERVE

ClarksOutpost.com

Follow the About Us link on this site and you may not learn a lot about the Texas BBQ joint that operates this site, but you'll learn a lot about the smoked brisket, turkey, ribs and ham that makes the restaurant one of the best of its kind on the planet. Indeed, if you can make it through this page without drooling you have more willpower than we do, and even if you can refrain from ordering the mouthwatering meats, the barbecue sauce alone will give you reason to come back for more.

·MEAT & FISH | ·CONDIMENTS | ·HEAT & SERVE

800-803-7774 · CoffeeAM.com

CoffeeAM.com

There's a lot more than just coffee to this site, although there doesn't need to be. Hundreds of coffee roasts are available, regular and decaf, organic and flavored, from dozens of countries of origin. Each whole-bean coffee is available in a single-pound bag, promised to be "fresh roasted the day it ships." Everything else the site has to offer would seem like an afterthought, except that it's all similarly well represented and enticing. Whether you prefer the teas, chais, bubble teas, frappes, fruit smoothies or gourmet sweets, this one's great any time of day.

| ·SOFT DRINKS | ·COFFEE/TEA | | |  |

800-345-5282 · Montana Coffee Traders

CoffeeTraders.com

It's a phenomenon of recent years that purchasing coffee has become an ethical act for Americans, even a form of activism. This coffee specialist should satisfy the more globally and ecologically aware caffeine addicts, offering a rich assortment of coffee beans produced using sustainable agriculture and purchased from free trade farms. Thus, the conscientious coffee consumer can rest assured these fine brews have been grown "in harmony with the rain forest," and that your dollars spent will actually support the hard-working folk who help kick-start your morning.

| ·COFFEE/TEA | | | |  |

800-213-6485 · Compartes

Compartes.com

Sometimes a piece of candy comes along that puts the kinds of flavored plastic and machine-made confections you find in grocery lines and movie theater concessions to shame. This site offers just that type of candy. With toffees, chocolate-covered fruit, fruits stuffed with nuts, assorted confections, marzipan and fudge, this site may be scattered by web standards, but they have clearly got things organized in their kitchens. This is a sure winner for candy connoisseurs who're not impressed by fluorescent colors and flashy packaging.

| ·SWEETS | | | |  |

011-33-562-67-9812 · Comtesse du Barry

ComtesseDuBarry.com

For nearly a hundred years this French family business has served high-quality foie gras to the most demanding of customers, but its selection of gourmet dishes has expanded so much in that time that pâté is almost the last thing you notice. Instead, this champion of French gastronomy offers heat-and-serve meals that outdo anything most of us could ever prepare on our own, ranging from coq au vin and scallop flan to duck breast ravioli and chocolate soufflé. In time you'll want to try them all.

| ·SWEETS | ·MEAT & FISH | ·DELICACIES | ·HEAT & SERVE | |

CorkysBBQ.com

By reputation some of the South's best barbecue, this Memphis mainstay offers the sauce that makes it famous through an un-complicated site guaranteed to set your cursor on fire, and probably your taste buds as well. The true advantage of Corky's is that they'll send you a batch of their hand-pulled, slow-cooked ribs, packaged frozen and ready to heat, with extra sauce included, of course. You can also procure a small variety of pork, or a whole turkey, and anybody expecting more has clearly not experienced the mouthwatering simplicity of this authentic BBQ specialist.

·MEAT & FISH	·CONDIMENTS	·HEAT & SERVE	

CrabPlace.com

The best reason anybody has to visit Maryland is the fresh crabs. Well, thanks to this Terrapin State shop that delivers live crabs to anywhere in the nation, there's no longer any good reason to stop when driving between Washington, D.C. and Philadelphia. Of course, once you've shopped here a few times you will have developed a taste for the site's variety of Atlantic shellfish, which also includes snow crab, softshell crab, gulf shrimp. Maine lobster tails, crab cakes, Chesapeake oysters and of course clam chowder; and you'll plan a trip out there really soon.

·MEAT & FISH	·HEAT & SERVE		

DArtagnan.com

If you can walk into a local butcher and find partridge, pheasant, squab, ostrich, rabbit, goat and wild boar, you won't need this site. If you already have a local purveyor of truffles, cured meats, gourmet oils and foie gras, then the delicacies offered by this New Jersey-based, French-inspired shop may fail to impress. You might be interested to know, however, that this first-class natural and organic market supplies many of the nation's "top restaurants, hotels, retailers, cruise ships and airlines" with impressive and hard-to-find fare, and unless you live in Paris, we doubt you'll find anything like this in your neighborhood.

·MEAT & FISH	·DELICACIES	·PRODUCE	

DeanAndDeluca.com

In nearly thirty years, this SoHo-based retailer has become nearly synonymous with epicurean delights, and the high-quality edibles found here will not let you down. Meats, cheese, grains, sauces, fish, herbs and assorted fungi are just a sampling of what's available in their Fine Foods section, and most of the items are good enough to offer as gifts. Neatly laid out and elegantly presented, the only problem we can find on this site is the cost. But hey, if they can get away with charging this much it's got to be good.

·SWEETS ·DELICACIES	·MEAT & FISH ·CONDIMENTS	·OILS & SPICES ·COFFEE/TEA	·RECIPES ·PANTRY

212-734-8880 · Debauve & Gallais

DebauveAndGallais.com

"Purveyor to French kings and a must for all true connoisseurs," this Parisian chocolatier has been making some of the world's finest confections for more than two centuries, and though once a "closely guarded" national treasure, this web site allows us relatively easy access to the ultraindulgent treats. Boasting startling percentages of cocoa, there aren't enough of the extravagant chocolate bars, tablets and assorted bonbons to make shopping difficult, but if you don't keep your eyes open viewing the site you might miss out on something that would make any chocolate purist drool.

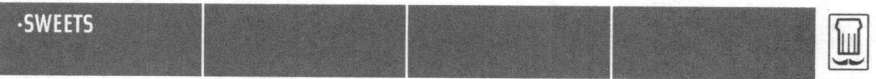

·SWEETS

888-674-2642 · Diamond Organics

DiamondOrganics.com

Taking the natural-grocery concept to a new level, this fantastic shop offers nothing less than organic fruits and vegetables, available seasonally and delivered fresh. Still, you may want to eat this stuff quick, as your produce will not be tainted by synthetic preservatives, fertilizers or pesticides. Additional sections such as Soy Dairy, Mushrooms, Macrobiotics and Herbs should entice health-food lovers and gourmet connoisseurs alike, though we're not exactly sure what segment of the population will be drawn to the Edible Flowers category.

·MEAT & FISH ·HEAT & SERVE	·BAKED GOODS ·PRODUCE	·DELICACIES ·ALCOHOL	·CONDIMENTS ·PANTRY

888-322-4337 · Di Bruno Bros.

DiBruno.com

When we think of Italian food, it's not uncommon to think of meat, cheese and olive oil. However, this Italian specialty foods site offers something considerably better than pepperoni pizza. Here you'll find an incredibly comprehensive list of fine international cheeses along with the best charcuterie selection online. Gourmet oils, vinegars and edible delicacies are also well represented, all on a very clean and easy-to-use site that's good enough to change your perception of Italian cuisine altogether.

·MEAT & FISH ·COFFEE/TEA	·OILS & SPICES ·PANTRY	·DELICACIES	·CONDIMENTS

800-443-2836 · Divine Delights

DivineDelights.com

Cakes are known to be fattening, but if you shrink a cake down to morsel size, what's to stop you from indulging? Not much, especially if you're shopping from this site, which specializes in petit fours. The only problem you may encounter is that these petit fours are so reasonably priced and delicious looking that it might be hard to stop yourself from eating two, four, eight or an entire thirty-six-cake package. Next time around you might try one of their several different flavors, and you may wish to exercise between orders.

·SWEETS	·BAKED GOODS		

Earthy.com

Offering "specialty produce, fine hand-crafted cheese, aged balsamic vinegar, exotic spices and hard-to-find ingredients to the professional chef and the at-home culinary artist," this high-quality food source will have no trouble appealing to the demanding gourmand. While the list of fresh delicacies runs long, its specialty is wild harvested items, mushrooms and truffles in particular, and while the shop's browsing options have improved dramatically over the years, many of its items are only available in season, so you'll have to get used to the Out of Stock notice, and return frequently to satisfy your most refined cravings.

·SWEETS ·CONDIMENTS	·OILS & SPICES ·PRODUCE	·RECIPES ·PANTRY	·DELICACIES

eCreamery.com

Thirty-odd flavors? That's nothing. This fantastic ice cream site lets you custom create your own flavors from a batch of dozens of varieties and toppings. Begin by deciding whether you prefer a gelato, standard or premium ice cream. Then you get to choose from an array of distinctive flavors that would easily stand on their own, including rare tastes like cucumber, cantaloupe, tamarind, nutmeg and avocado. Next add sprinkles, nuts, candies and chunks as you like to add some texture. Finally, you may give this new ice cream flavor a name, and hope it tastes delicious. If not, the choices will still be limitless on your next visit.

·SWEETS			

Elenis.com

Brownies, Candies, Cookies and Cupcakes. That's what you'll find in the Sweet Shop section of this site, and what else would you need to know? How about the fact these sweets are "made with the finest all-natural ingredients?" Or that the cupcakes offer "hand-iced shapes and whimsical designs?" Any way you look at it, if you view the site you're bound to come away with some sweet, delicious desserts from this "homespun" bakery out of New York's Chelsea neighborhood.

·SWEETS	·BAKED GOODS		

EliZabar.com

We've been hearing that sliced bread is one of the great inventions of the modern era for so long that we have trouble thinking otherwise. But consider, for a moment, the bread loaves offered from this New York City bakery. Rye, sourdough and brioche selections make a great case for slicing your own, and those are only a scant few of the bakery's offerings. There are also croissants, rugelach, babkas, brownies and a great assortment of cookies. It just goes to show that online commerce is the greatest thing since....

·BAKED GOODS			

847-640-9570 · EthnicGrocer.com

EthnicGrocer.com

If you're sick of American food already, you may take delight in this international-themed online grocer. Shop By Product will turn up interesting categories like Sweet Spreads and Edible Wrappings, alongside the staple foods of several cultures. These you'll notice when you Shop By Country, a long list of which includes India, Japan, Turkey, the Philippines, Vietnam, Korea, Thailand, Mexico, Poland and several other European nations. You may become perplexed by some of the unusual items to be found inside, but a list of recipes and featured cookbooks should have you preparing the exotic dishes you long for in no time. Take that, meat-loaf and mashed potatoes.

·MEAT & FISH ·SNACKS	·OILS & SPICES ·HEAT & SERVE	·RECIPES ·PRODUCE	·CONDIMENTS ·PANTRY

212-226-6150 · Ferrara Cafe

FerraraCafe.com

Because making your own cannolis can be a delicate and time-consuming process, you may simply want to log on to this site, which represents a long-established New York City cafe that specializes in Italian baked goods. We should warn you, though, that once exposed you'll very likely be coming back soon for a cheesecake, tiramisu, pannetone alto, petit fours and cookies; even the biscotti is surprisingly tempting. If you do want to give your own cannolis a hand, however, these guys are kind enough to offer a recipe here.

·SWEETS	·BAKED GOODS

877-572-0305 · FinestWine.com

FinestWine.com

Any Frenchman will tell you, and many wine connoisseurs agree, that the finest wines come from France. The prices on this site certainly don't call that into dispute, as even the Low-Priced Wines section charges upward of a thousand dollars a bottle. Truth is, these are pedigreed bottles of wine, highly rated and with classy-sounding names, and generally intended for special occasions. To that end, the site also offers fine champagnes and cognac, as well as several kosher selections; although not every category on this site is quite fully stocked—that would be too easy.

·SPECIAL DIETS	·ALCOHOL		

800-747-2782 · Florentyna's Fresh Pasta Factory

FreshPasta.com

It used to be, only restaurants were privy to the fine fresh pastas created by this Los Angeles-based pasta factory. Thanks to a simple but effective online presence, retail customers can take advantage of what is among the best pasta selections available anywhere. Selections such as Tomato Fettucini and Tricolor Fusilli provide for beautiful presentation, but the real value of the shop is seen in the Ravioli and Stuffed section, which includes pastas filled with smoked salmon, grilled vegetables, wild mushrooms, lobster and much more. The only way to do better is to make your own.

·CONDIMENTS	·PANTRY		

GermanDeli.com

The Meats section of this Dallas, Texas, area German grocer is reason enough for you to pay a visit, offering all the liverwurst, sauerkraut, fleischkäse, schinken, kassler and sausage you can manage in a single year. However, with more than twenty-five-hundred items in stock, you'll find plenty more in these virtual aisles, including a wide assortment of breads, sweets, condiments and grains. Sadly, you won't find any varieties of German beer here, but otherwise your own authentic Oktoberfest is merely a home delivery away.

| ·SWEETS | ·MEAT & FISH | ·BAKED GOODS | ·CONDIMENTS |
| ·SNACKS | ·SOFT DRINKS | ·PANTRY | |

GourmetStation.com

Any food site that offers categories like Parisian, Tuscan, Cajun and Fusion is bound to get our attention. That this one offers them in the form of heat-and-serve meals makes them simply mouthwatering. Elegant presentation and slick design make the gourmet specialist a delight to browse, but most of the credit has to go with the meals offered within each cuisine's section: rack of lamb, bayou catfish, eggplant ravioli and seared coconut salmon are just a few of the entrees that may be ordered à la carte or as full-course meals along with a variety of complementary sides, soups, artisan breads, desserts and postprandial beverages.

| ·HEAT & SERVE | | | |

GreenBeanz.com

With the low-carb snacks, desserts, condiments and beverages found here, you'll find you may still get your fill of candy bars, protein shakes, salad dressings, cookies and tortilla chips, without overloading on those dastardly sugars and starches. More importantly, an assortment of pancake, bread and muffin mixes can return the joy of baked goods to your breakfast and lunch. If the low-carb diet craze is still thriving in your home, this is a site you'll want to bookmark.

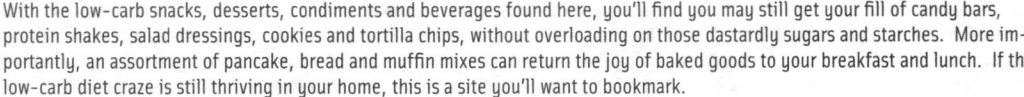

| ·SWEETS | ·BAKED GOODS | ·RECIPES | ·SPECIAL DIETS |
| ·CONDIMENTS | ·SNACKS | ·SOFT DRINKS | ·PANTRY |

HadleyFruitOrchards.com

Everybody gets the urge to snack; it's what we do with that urge that affects our cholesterol and our waistlines. As crazy as it may sound, this site offers a fine assortment of snacks that are somehow healthy and delicious at the same time. We're talking about dried fruits and nuts. Sure, there'll be times you choose chocolate-dipped apricots over the regular kind, or the candied Jordan almonds instead of the unsalted, roasted variety, but you'll still come much closer to a healthy lifestyle than if you grab a bag of corn chips.

| ·SWEETS | ·SNACKS | ·PRODUCE | |

800-552-0142 · Hancock Gourmet Lobster Co.

HancockGourmetLobster.com

This homegrown business hails from a small fishing town on the coast of Maine, which has given the lobster specialist a clear advantage when it comes to developing the perfect recipes for a variety of shellfish entrees and appetizers, including potpies, dips, rolls, cakes, stews and chowders. Here, we can all take advantage of the family's expertise, ordering gourmet heat-and-serve lobster, crab, scallop and mussel dishes with ease. Still think you can do better? Try following the Live Lobsters link, and take a crack at them.

·MEAT & FISH	·HEAT & SERVE		

734-213-7653 · Heritage Foods USA

HeritageFoodsUSA.com

It's always gratifying when you come across a meat-and-poultry seller that adheres to much higher standards than the USDA, and particularly so with this group, which "exists to promote genetic diversity, small family farms, and a fully traceable food supply." What this means is that the meat aggregator buys only from farms using natural, sustainable methods, to the point that you can trace the origins and lineage of the livestock and even view some of the turkeys via web cam. It also means availability is limited both by quantity and season, so you must often preorder if you hope to get a hold of some of the best-tasting, most trusted meat in the nation.

·MEAT & FISH			

888-694-2656 · Hometown Favorites

HomeTownFavorites.com

Assembling a catalog of "Old-Time Favorites and Regionally Exclusive Foods," this site has definitely done something right. This is the kind of stuff city folk find "quaint" in rural areas, or that rural folk are surprised not to find in major metropolises. Or, it may just be stuff that has been around seemingly forever, but for some reason or another is tough to track down wherever you live. This proves to be an excellent manifestation of the internet, allowing us to stock up on those foodstuffs we've grown to miss, such as Mallowmars, Moxie soda or Booberry cereal. You're almost guaranteed to find delight in some of this stuff, whatever town you call home.

·SWEETS	·CONDIMENTS	·SNACKS	·PANTRY

877-446-8763 · iGourmet.com

iGourmet.com

Trying to figure out what all the fuss is about stinky cheeses and pâté? Wondering why anybody in his right mind would put escargot in his mouth? This site goes into tremendous detail when describing its gourmet food items, offering delectable photos, recipes, serving tips and links to complimentary or related items. Still a bit uncertain what you're getting yourself into? In that case they offer resources such as the iGourmet Library and Encyclopedia of Cheese, each of which will let you know (among other things) why you should like these foods. Thus, this excellent and comprehensive purveyor of palatable pleasures leaves you with the most unusual of sensations: an educated appetite.

·SWEETS ·DELICACIES	·MEAT & FISH ·CONDIMENTS	·OILS & SPICES ·COFFEE/TEA	·RECIPES ·PANTRY

iKoreaPlaza.com

In all probability the only web shop with entire sections devoted to both kimchi and ramen, this site is always authentic, all the time, right down to the gummies. Actually based in Oakland, California, it nevertheless has replicated the Korean grocery experience with products like Ilhua Chunyeon Cider, Yamasa Kamaboko, Shirakiku Fish Sausage and Pyongyang Naengmyun. We don't really know what this stuff is, but as always we really enjoy the fact that it's out there, and available to us over the internet.

·MEAT & FISH ·COFFEE/TEA	·OILS & SPICES ·PANTRY	·CONDIMENTS	·SOFT DRINKS

Il-Vino.com

If you are going to appreciate this incredible European wine-and-liquor resource, all of the following must be true. 1) You must be patient enough to wade through the difficult user interface to search the more than 13,000 items available. 2) You must be wealthy enough to shrug off the high costs of these bottles as well as the exorbitant international shipping fees. And, 3) You must possess enough knowledge and interest in wines, scotches and liqueurs to truly appreciate this massive, heady selection and just why it is so valuable. Casual drinkers will want to stay away; devoted collectors will never want to leave.

·ALCOHOL			

ImportFoods.com

If you get excited by the word *import*, you may be doubly excited to know this one refers to grocery items straight from Thailand. Of course, the top of your shopping list here might include curry pastes, rice noodles, jasmine rice, a variety of spicy sauces and coffee. But even more enticing may be the small selection of fresh vegetables, including lemongrass, Thai chiles and betel leaves. Helping you round out the list is a Shop As You Learn Recipes section, which features over a hundred Thai dishes and handily makes all the ingredients and tools needed to make each one available for purchase.

·OILS & SPICES ·COFFEE/TEA	·RECIPES ·PANTRY	·CONDIMENTS	·PRODUCE

IpswichFishMarket.com

If you're a fan of New England seafood, this fish market site will get it to you fresh; so fresh in fact that sometimes it's up to you to kill it. You'll find salmon, sea bass, haddock and scallops, but the real reasons to visit the Massachusetts-based shop are the live lobsters, clambake sets and of course, the clam chowder. While the site can be a little confusing at first, there's a big payoff in that you get to eat like a New Englander without having to deal with any cold, rain or wind.

·MEAT & FISH	·RECIPES	·CONDIMENTS	·HEAT & SERVE

888-574-3576 · JRCigars.com

JRCigars.com

If you're going to buy tobacco, you might as well buy it from people in a position to know what they're talking about. No, not Cubans: North Carolinians. From deep in tobacco country, JR Cigars offers a wide selection of stogies, both Hand Made and Machine Rolled, including dozens of domestic and Latin American brands. Or, if you're on a tight budget, you might just check out the JR Alternatives brand, which mimic fine cigars much in the same way generic medications do name-brand prescriptions. Either way, this homegrown tobacconist proves an affordable way to satisfy your smoker's thirst.

·TOBACCO

800-352-3451 · Kalustyan's

Kalustyans.com

Originally an Indian foods market, this New York grocery now offers "Foods of Nations," including a list of dozens of countries representing every inhabitable continent. The resulting selection, of course, is enormous, and you can probably find at least one sampling of any culinary product you seek (but more likely dozens). Given the massive nature of this superstore's catalog, it's hard to hold below-standard page design against it, and the truth of the matter is, if the shop actually included photos for each of its products, it would only slow you down. Still, browsing is a daunting process, so be sure to have a very explicit grocery list ready when you visit.

·MEAT & FISH	·OILS & SPICES	·RECIPES	·CONDIMENTS
·HEAT & SERVE	·COFFEE/TEA	·PANTRY	

877-559-4637 · K&L Wine Merchants

KAndL.com

If you don't like to order a bottle of wine without first learning a little about it, check out this very well-stocked wine specialist, which offers fairly thorough organization of imports and domestics to go along with decent browsing options. The true benefit, though, is that each listing is accompanied by a brief but detailed review of the bottle in question, with more comprehensive information available on the product page, so you may never have to stab blindly to find the right wine for the right occasion again. Better yet, they offer the same service for single-malt scotch enthusiasts.

·ALCOHOL

718-756-7500 · Koshermeal.com

KosherMeal.com

All of the pre-prepared meals listed on this site are "certified kosher and halal, and many… are all-natural, wheat free and gluten free," which is pretty handy, presuming you can figure out this horrible web site. We'll go ahead and take it for granted that this Beverly hills catering company is better suited to design healthy and delicious meals than pretty web pages, but once you make it through the animated opening sequence, follow the Order Now link, and then follow another Order Now link to view your options, which are neither numerous nor difficult to prepare. Ultimately, it proves a great way to keep kosher even when you travel.

·SPECIAL DIETS	·HEAT & SERVE		

Lepicerie.com

Pronounced "lepisri," this French term for what we call a general store implies a thorough collection of necessities. In this case, it's the items necessary for fine cooking and baking. With the goal "to provide chefs and bakers at home with the best ingredients and products that are only available to chefs and restaurants," the New York City shop covers a lot of ground that general stores leave out, including various nut pastes, ready-to-bake croissants, gourmet pastas and oil extracts. Figure out what to do with all this stuff and you'll be eating well indeed.

·SWEETS ·CONDIMENTS	·OILS & SPICES ·COFFEE/TEA	·BAKED GOODS ·PANTRY	·DELICACIES

LeVillage.com

Is there any better gourmet than French gourmet? If you think not, you'll probably enjoy this specialty site that caters to would-be nouveau and/or haute cuisine chefs. Maybe you want some raviolis stuffed with pheasant, rabbit or wild boar. Perhaps you just want the meat of these wild game creatures. It's simple enough to find all this among the pâtés, truffles, coffees, confections and pastries you'd expect from any French store. Oh yeah, if you're crazy enough to eat escargots, you can find them here as well. Just don't kid yourself: they're still snails.

·MEAT & FISH ·CONDIMENTS	·OILS & SPICES ·SOFT DRINKS	·RECIPES ·ALCOHOL	·DELICACIES ·PANTRY

Lobels.com

One term is all it will take to draw you to this purveyor of Northeast-raised meat: *USDA Prime*, which refers only to the top 2 percent of beef produced in America. But a couple of other phrases will probably make this New York City butcher shop your favorite. The first is *High Prime*, which means this site sells only the top 2 percent of beef certified USDA prime, which is of course the best you can buy. The other is *All-Natural*, as all of the beef, lamb, poultry and pork on this site was raised organically, on vegetarian diets, without artificial hormones or antibiotics. There's less than a 1 percent chance you'll find better meat anywhere.

·MEAT & FISH	·RECIPES		

MarkTWendell.com

Boasting more than five dozen varieties, this Concord, Massachusetts, specialty shop "has been providing fine teas to tea connoisseurs since 1904." While its internet presence leaves something to be desired, ultimately the site manages to offer one of the web's best tea assortments complete with detailed histories of black, white, green, oolong iced and Hu-Kwa teas as well as herbal tisanes, along with brewing tips and a healthy assortment of teapots appropriate to each flavor or your personal taste.

·COFFEE/TEA			

800-588-0151 · Melissa's

Melissas.com

The local farmers' market has become an increasingly valuable and popular place to buy fresh produce, however, even your regional growers will concede that the selection is limited. "With over 800 items available at any given time," this Los Angeles-based produce specialist "imports and distributes exotic fresh fruits and vegetables from around the globe." Without question this is one of the largest assortments of staple, seasonal, organic and exotic produce you will ever come across, along with excellent selections of dried fruits, fungi, nuts, meat substitutes and bulk grains. Speedy shipping ensures freshness, and an incredibly huge assortment of recipes ensures you know what to do with it all.

·OILS & SPICES ·CONDIMENTS	·RECIPES ·PRODUCE	·SPECIAL DIETS ·PANTRY	·DELICACIES	

877-463-9476 · MexGrocer.com

MexGrocer.com

No more flying down to Mexico for horchata; now you can simply order it online, courtesy of this retailer of nonperishable items from south of the border. It's not that we can't find an abundance of Mexican food just about everywhere we look in this country, it's just that the odds of it being authentic drop dramatically the farther north you go. Based in San Diego, these guys are about as close to the real thing as many of us are going to get. Sure, there's nothing wrong with the hard shells, ground beef, cheese and lettuce of "gringo tacos," but once you get a taste for the real thing you will never go back.

·SWEETS ·SNACKS	·OILS & SPICES ·SOFT DRINKS	·RECIPES ·PANTRY	·CONDIMENTS	

888-692-4339 · Murray's Online

MurraysCheese.com

These guys won't just sell you a wheel or wedge of cheese, they'll tell you how it was made, what it was made of, what type of wine best complements its flavor, how its flavor is defined, how its consistency is defined, how to serve it, how to store it and generally how it is you might like to eat it. Well, this may all be appreciated, as long as it doesn't get in the way of convenient shopping. As it turns out, it doesn't; the cheeses are easily organized by country of origin and listed with pictures and descriptions so that you can simply follow your craving to checkout.

·DELICACIES				

510-808-0340 · Niman Ranch

NimanRanch.com

If you're looking for proof that humanely raised livestock can yield incredible meats, look no further than this sustainable farming advocate's site. Sourcing its meats from "over 300 independent family farmers," as well as its own original Northern California ranch, Niman offers beef, pork and lamb that promises to adhere to strict guidelines, meaning they "never use growth-promoting antibiotics or hormones," nor feed the livestock with any animal byproducts. Sure, it all sounds great but how do you know it tastes good? Hundreds of the best restaurants in the country serve only Niman Ranch meats.

·MEAT & FISH	·RECIPES	·SPECIAL DIETS		

PacificRimGourmet.com

i-Clipse · 800-910-9657

The Pacific ocean covers more than 30 percent of the Earth's surface, so you can imagine that a grocery store devoted to the Pacific Rim has a lot of ground to cover. You'd be right, and this site makes a valiant attempt, offering cookbooks, kitchen items and foodstuffs pertaining to a long list of nations ranging from Bali, Bangladesh, Japan, Korea, Singapore and the Philippines to Mexico, Australia and the West Coast of the United States. The store doesn't stock as many products as it could, but offers just enough to give you authentic tastes of a very big and diverse planet.

·OILS & SPICES ·SOFT DRINKS	·RECIPES ·PANTRY	·CONDIMENTS	·SNACKS

Penzeys.com

Penzeys Spices · 800-741-7787

Usually, we like to see pictures of anything we want to buy online. However, when it comes to this spice site, we've discovered that words are better. After all, when you look at spices, you generally see some sort of leaves or ground powder, and aside from the occasional difference in color, they'd be tough to tell apart by sight. Instead, this site offers lists of several dozen spices, next to which you'll find a quick description, either explaining the flavor of each particular spice or listing dishes that contain it. A glance at each individual product page takes it further, offering histories and recommending recipes. Nice to see a spice site that so deftly avoids being bland.

·OILS & SPICES			

Petrossian.com

Petrossian Paris · 800-828-9241

     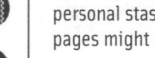

Slickly designed, and quite easy to operate, this site's destined to become a favorite of the online gourmand, allowing you to glide effortlessly through fine selections of caviar, foie gras, truffles and smoked fish, as well as gourmet coffees and sweets. All items are of exceeding quality (and price), available in varied serving quantities, whether enough to serve at your next fete, or merely a personal stash to fulfill those high-class cravings. Were the connoisseurs of such indulgent items inclined to drool, a look at these pages might make it happen.

·SWEETS	·MEAT & FISH	·DELICACIES	

Polana.com

Polana · 888-765-2621

Whether you were introduced to Polish cooking through your family heritage, or simply have been lucky enough to happen across the incredibly satisfying tastes of kielbasa, pierogi and golabki in your lifetime, this specialty shop is sure to make your mouth water. If you're new to the delicious breads, sausages, sweets and various stuffed food concoctions, here's your chance to become better acquainted, either by browsing the site's collection of recipes or by sticking to the appetizing assortment of heat-and-serve dishes designed to permanently win you over to the Eastern European cuisine.

·SWEETS	·MEAT & FISH	·BAKED GOODS	·HEAT & SERVE

516-431-0025 · Pop's Wine & Spirits

PopsWine.com

How many ways are there to categorize wines? This Long Island, New York, wine and liquor store has figured out dozens of ways to help guide you through its thousands of bottles. It may not be enough. While you will have no trouble sifting through Japanese wines or California Rieslings, poring through the hundreds of available Italian wines and California Cabernets will be so arduous you'll have really earned a drink by the time you're finished. You should only really attempt it if you know exactly what you're looking for, or if you stick to the equally impressive but significantly less daunting Spirits selection.

·ALCOHOL				

888-459-6652 · The Protein Bakery

ProteinBakery.com

Even your typical health nut has a sweet tooth, which is why the stricter than average dieter might appreciate this baked goods specialist that offers cookies and brownies that are wheat free, high in fiber and, yes, packed with a protein punch. Focusing "on taste and indulgence in addition to nutritional balance," the all-natural, vegetarian bakery may sound like a buzzkill to the indulgent gourmand, but featuring items like the Wicked Mint Brownie and Double Chocolate White Chip Cookie, we're willing to give these sweet treats the benefit of the doubt.

·SWEETS	·BAKED GOODS	·SPECIAL DIETS		

201-692-1555 · Queen Anne Wine & Spirit Emporium

QueenAnneWine.com

Just across the Hudson River from Manhattan, this North Jersey wine-and-liquor shop has been operating for more than twenty years as a labor of love, and proprietor Kevin Roche "is an impassioned mentor, and ardent scholar of the fine art of wine appreciation," tasting thousands of wines every year. The vast majority of them never turn up on his store's shelves or the web site, meaning novice enthusiasts can be certain every bottle here has made the cut. The same high standards are extended to single-malt scotches, kosher spirits and a not so standard selection of cigars, vodkas, cognacs, brandies and tequilas, making this an online liquor store you'll still remember in the morning.

·TOBACCO	·ALCOHOL			

866-747-4483 · Rishi Tea

Rishi-Tea.com

While this may not be the most complete tea site, or even the easiest to browse, it is the most helpful. It does offer a rich and varied selection, covering black, green, white, red, oolong, pu-erh, organic and caffeine-free herbal teas. But, more importantly, it tells you about these teas: where they came from, how best to brew them and how they express themselves. Truly, when most of us are faced with a choice of more than a hundred teas, we usually just guess. Thanks to this site, we no longer have to.

Route29Napa.com

Caramel, licorice, toffee and cotton candy aren't usually what kids think of today when they think of candy. Come to think of it, they haven't been for a long time. But this "old-fashioned confectionary company" out of Napa, California, doesn't dwell on the present, preferring instead to make high-quality treats that will taste good to kids of any age. That being said, if the thought of Chewy Peps and Nut Rolls aren't enough to attract your sweet tooth to the site, maybe the lure of chocolate-covered potato chips will.

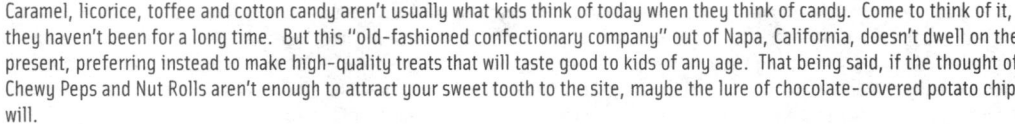

·SWEETS			

RussianFoods.com

The Cold War may have left us with a limited understanding of Russian cuisine, but the Information Age is here to reverse the trend. Specifically, this Russian supermarket site out of New York can teach us all about the many joys of Georgian wine, pickled vegetables, Russian baked goods and seafood from the other side of the planet. The labels may use the Cyrillic alphabet, but helpful descriptions should explain away any confusion, while the opinions of other customers should help you decide just which of these mysterious foreign foodstuffs are worth a try.

·SWEETS ·RECIPES	·MEAT & FISH ·CONDIMENTS	·OILS & SPICES ·ALCOHOL	·BAKED GOODS

SBOlive.com

With over five thousand trees, this Santa Barbara family farm "boasts more specialty olives than any other olive company," making this a fantastic place to get your diverse olive fix. The selection of black and green olives include sun-dried, low-sodium, hand-picked, pitted and organic varieties, and even a few imported options. Others are stuffed with almonds, cheeses and chipotle, while oils are infused with rosemary, garlic and chili peppers. As if all the olive love wasn't enough, there are some tasty sounding pasta sauces, salad dressings, salsas and other pickled vegetables to keep your palate feeling alive.

·OILS & SPICES	·PRODUCE		

SeaBear.com

We've seen a lot of online smokehouses offering mouthwatering selections of pork, poultry and beef, but none have demonstrated such a succulent devotion to seafood as this one. The Washington state specialist delivers ready-to-heat and ready-to-eat varieties of salmon, shellfish and ahi tuna, as well as some belly-warming chowders, fish-friendly condiments and delectable appetizers. You can do almost nothing to most of this seafood and it will still taste great, but the site's kind enough to offer a host of intriguing recipes that will keep you coming back for more.

·MEAT & FISH	·RECIPES	·CONDIMENTS	·HEAT & SERVE

520-884-0745 · Shop Natural

ShopNatural.com

As "your trusted online source for natural and organic products," this web shop offers more than 6,000 products for those sensitive to the ecological problems caused by chemicals and mass production. Most of these items will be found in the Grocery section, where a simple layout doesn't immediately reveal the fact that each product page includes a written description, ingredients list and nutritional information, so shoppers can rest easy knowing their orders satisfy their own ethical and dietary restrictions, whether buying in small proportions or in bulk.

·SWEETS ·SOFT DRINKS	·OILS & SPICES ·COFFEE/TEA	·CONDIMENTS ·PANTRY	·SNACKS

800-624-5426 · Burgers' Smokehouse

SmokeHouse.com

These guys have been curing meats since back when doing so was actually necessary. The full name is Burgers' Smokehouse, but don't start to think that beef is the only thing these guys have to offer. Actually, their selection is the most extensive we've seen, including categories stocked full of Veal, Game Birds, Buffalo, Catfish and the somewhat enigmatic and disturbing Jowl (described as "more flavorful and less expensive" than bacon). All of this in addition to your carnivorous mainstays, and even some heat-and-serve omelets—it's enough to give a vegetarian nightmares.

·MEAT & FISH	·RECIPES	·HEAT & SERVE	

323-255-7115 · Soda Pop Stop

SodaPopStop.com

Not all soft drink companies advertise during the Super Bowl; in fact, the best soda pops usually go unnoticed by consumers and retailers alike. Not so on this terrific beverage site, which offers soft drink equivalents of beer microbrews. With categories dedicated to colas, root beers, cream sodas, ginger ales and even sarsaparillas, you'll find it tremendously easy to discover a surprising range of top-quality drinks, complete with brief descriptions and ingredients lists, so you can see exactly what goes into these superior sodas.

·SOFT DRINKS			

508-324-9800 · Stirrings

Stirrings.com

Behind the tagline "better ingredients make better cocktails," this site doesn't actually try to sell you liquor. Instead, the soft drink brands offers "super premium cocktail mixers," for such drinks as apple martinis, cosmopolitans, mojitos, bloody marys, lemon drops and margaritas. Specially concocted to complement your favorite alcoholic beverages, the mixers may be matched with an array of rimmers, sodas and essences. Of course, the site would not be complete without a bevy of cocktail recipes—put it all together and you've got a great excuse for a party.

·RECIPES	·SOFT DRINKS		

StonewallKitchen.com Stonewall Kitchen · 800-207-5267

This shop started out as a vinegar-and-preserves table at a Maine farmers' market, and in less than fifteen years has expanded to become one of the most reliable purveyors of quality foods online. Though the selection is small by most market standards, the relishes, syrups, chutneys, jams and dressings are alone worth a visit. In the meantime, a fantastic assortment of baking mixes, breakfasts, appetizers and pre-prepared meals will give you something fantastic to garnish with these New England-style gourmet condiments.

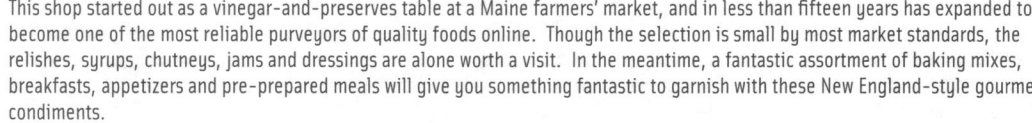

·SWEETS ·RECIPES	·MEAT & FISH ·CONDIMENTS	·OILS & SPICES ·HEAT & SERVE	·BAKED GOODS ·PANTRY

TastesOfChicago.com Tastes of Chicago by Lou Malnati's · 800-568-8646

Promising "nationwide delivery of all your Windy City favorites," this site starts, of course, with deep dish pizza from Lou Malnatto's Pizzarilla, but goes on to include Carson's ribs, Vienna's hot dogs, Eli's cheesecake, Portillo's beef and steak from Wildfire. If you've never been to Chicago, the names will mean nothing to you. If, however, you regularly yearn for the meaty tastes of the Second City, order in advance; the lack of overnight delivery means you're going to have to plan against your next craving.

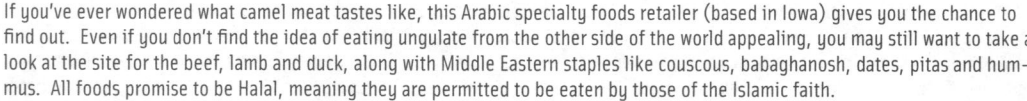

·MEAT & FISH	·HEAT & SERVE		

Tayeeb.com Tayeeb Foods · 866-328-42525

If you've ever wondered what camel meat tastes like, this Arabic specialty foods retailer (based in Iowa) gives you the chance to find out. Even if you don't find the idea of eating ungulate from the other side of the world appealing, you may still want to take a look at the site for the beef, lamb and duck, along with Middle Eastern staples like couscous, babaghanosh, dates, pitas and hummus. All foods promise to be Halal, meaning they are permitted to be eaten by those of the Islamic faith.

·SWEETS	·MEAT & FISH	·RECIPES	·PANTRY

TheFreshLobsterCompany.com The Fresh Lobster Company · 508-451-2467

There's more to this Gloucester, Massachusetts, company than lobster, but with its offer to overnight fresh and even live orders of the shellfish, everything else can be easy to overlook. Try not to, though, because elsewhere on the site you'll find an even greater variety of fresh seafood and pre-prepared gourmet dishes. More remarkable may be the sushi-grade tuna, eel, sea urchin, octopus and roe, and most remarkable might be the prices. Ordering fish through the mail never seemed so appetizing.

·MEAT & FISH	·DELICACIES	·HEAT & SERVE	

847-328-3711 · The Spice House

TheSpiceHouse.com

Shopping for spices online can prove a surprisingly bland experience, with alphabetical lists and subtle varietal distinctions that are only minimally explained. Although this Midwest chain has been operating fifteen years as a brick-and-mortar retailer, it's responsible for the most user-friendly spice site going. Hit the Our Spices link and you'll find the typical alphabetical browsing option; however, you'll also find the spices sorted by Cuisine Type, ranging from Barbecue and Cajun to Indian and Thai. A Product Type menu lists out individual types of spices, such as Paprika or Peppercorns, then actually tells you why one form of the spice is different from the rest. The results are delicious and educational.

·OILS & SPICES   ·RECIPES

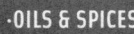

011-207-221-4448 · The Spice Shop

TheSpiceShop.co.uk

It may seem counterintuitive to shop for spices from England of all places, but this homegrown shop offers such an extensive array of whole and blended spices from points international that the serious spice hound should be more than willing to pay the modest overseas shipping rates. In particular, you may appreciate a healthy assortment of paprikas and curries, plus an entire section devoted to "leaves, bark, roots, powders, seeds and berries." Your meals will never taste the same.

·OILS & SPICES

888-472-1022 · Tienda.com

Tienda.com

Spain has certainly not contributed as much to the world's culinary landscape as its Mediterranean neighbor, France, but with many centuries' worth of influence from Celtic, Moroccan and Catalan cultures, the Iberian melting pot turns out some of the most intriguing dishes Europe has to offer. At the forefront, of course, is paella, which receives special attention from this Spanish food specialist, including starter kits covering the basic ingredients, tools and cooking procedures. But the site also features a grocery store filled with a wide variety of regional mainstays, which, coupled with a comprehensive collection of recipes, will have you turning out Spanish meals to cover every taste, from pork-stuffed empanadas to a cadre of tapas, the Spanish word for snacks.

·SWEETS   ·MEAT & FISH   ·OILS & SPICES   ·RECIPES
·CONDIMENTS   ·SNACKS

800-952-2842 · Tsar Nicoulai Caviar

TsarNicoulai.com

Enjoying caviar is the key to enjoying this gourmet specialist and, to the uninitiated, the beautiful little pyramids of roe pictured on the site may not seem appetizing. To those of us who know, however, they could not seem more delicious. Despite what the company's name might suggest, most of this caviar does not hail from Russia, rather from a sustainable sturgeon farm in California. You may find some imported Sevruga caviar, along with the high prices you might expect; then again, if you're hooked on the stuff, chances are you can afford it.

·MEAT & FISH   ·DELICACIES

UptownPrime.com

Uptown Prime · 877-987-8696

If you go looking for prime-grade beef in your local supermarket, you're only setting yourself up for disappointment. The best-quality meats can only be obtained from a great butcher, and even then restaurants usually snap them all up. This site gives you a shot at eating the finest cuts of steak available, whether Kobe beef, rib eye, New York strip, filet mignon or top sirloin. Everything offered here tastes amazing, so all you really need to do is decide whether you want to order the fresh, dry aged or frozen varieties.

 ·MEAT & FISH

VirginiaTraditions.com

S. Wallace Edwards and Sons · 800-222-4267

The culinary tradition of the South is kept alive by this purveyor of bacon, sausage, ham, smoked turkey, barbecue pork and ribs. Roughly eight decades after starting out in a rural Virginia town, this smokehouse retail chain and catalog surely knows what it's doing, preparing savory meats you'll want to cook or heat up for breakfast, lunch and dinner. Most of the categories let you know exactly what cuts of meat you're after, but we'd recommend you don't miss the Specialty Meats section, which offers brisket, pork chops and tur-duc-ken and other classic barbecue essesntials.

  ·MEAT & FISH | ·RECIPES | ·HEAT & SERVE

VosgesChocolate.com

Vosges Haut Chocolate · 888-301-9866

If you find yourself growing bored with traditional chocolate, maybe it's time to spice things up a bit—literally. This gourmet chocolatier offers chocolate infused with spices such as chili powder, wasabi and ginger. The confections and "haut-chocolat" are similarly creative, often incorporating ingredients like cheese in the mix. You simply do not find these sorts of flavors everwhere. Sure, you could experiment with a Hershey bar and your spice rack, but we're guessing the end results will be far less tantalizing.

 ·SWEETS

WallyWine.com

Wally's · 888-992-5597

The West Los Angeles liquor store behind this web site pays keen attention to the ins and outs of wine tasting, so you don't have to. Anytime you're looking for a top-rated bottle of recent years, or even an older vintage, one short visit should net you a terrific red or white, domestic or import. You may browse regional appellations by price or vintage, or, if you want to cut straight to something impressive, sort the selections by Parker or *Wine Spectator* scores, either of which will turn up those bottles favored by the experts. As for the spirits, beer and gourmet delicacies also available here, you'll have to make up your own mind.

   ·TOBACCO | ·DELICACIES | ·ALCOHOL

773-275-6100 · **Wikstroms' Scandinavian Food & Gifts**

WikstromsGourmet.com

Of all the notable European cuisines, traditional Scandinavian tastes probably get the least amount of international recognition, but in a way, this makes the Swedish, Norwegian, Danish and Finnish foods featured here all the more exotic to the American palate. For example, most of us would not even be able to describe lefse or limpa breads, let alone identify the spices typically used in the region's native dishes. Thus, this site winds up providing an interesting culinary education in addition to its many varied products. You'll find such rarely seen items in addition to the slightly more recognizable foodstuffs like Danish cheeses, gravlax salmon, pickled herring, lingonberries and a long list of condiments courtesy of the great white north.

·SWEETS ·DELICACIES	·MEAT & FISH ·CONDIMENTS	·BAKED GOODS ·SNACKS	·RECIPES ·PANTRY

888-980-9463 · **Wine Library**

WineLibrary.com

True to its name, this terrific specialty retailer offers a wealth of information to go with its incredible selection of wines. Shop by the best-selling, best-reviewed or most-coveted collector's wines and you may easily discover great bottles to fit your price range and tastes, complete with short but thorough reviews detailing every little nuance in flavor. More experienced oenophiles may want to take advantage of a search feature allowing you to track down a particular vintage from a lengthy list of international and domestic varietals. Either way, it's easier than the Dewey decimal system.

·ALCOHOL			

800-255-8278 · **William Greenberg, Jr., Desserts**

WmGreenbergDesserts.com

Best known for its famous black-and-white cookies, this Manhattan bakery has been adding pounds to New Yorkers since 1946, when William Greenberg returned from World War 2 with a pocketful of poker winnings to cover startup costs. The local mainstay can finally be shared coast to coast with this simple but tantalizingly effective site. Each page in the Baked Goods section shows pictures of delectable morsels, beginning with cookies and brownies and going on to offer babkas, pound cake, angel food cake, rugelach and some amazing-looking cupcakes. It's a safe bet.

·BAKED GOODS			

888-636-8162 · **Zingermans.com**

Zingermans.com

To find out why this Michigan deli sells more than 20,000 loaves of bread per week, take a look at its fresh, hearth-baked selection of ryes, sourdoughs, french breads, sweet breads and multigrains. Dip them in some of the finest vinegars and olive oils available on the planet, or top them with a slice from the site's equally impressive cheese selection, which combines international flavors with those of the Zingerman's own creamery. Finally, hit the Edible Add-ables category for meats, mustards and other condiments to make great bread even better.

·SWEETS ·CONDIMENTS	·MEAT & FISH ·PANTRY	·OILS & SPICES	·BAKED GOODS

NOTES:

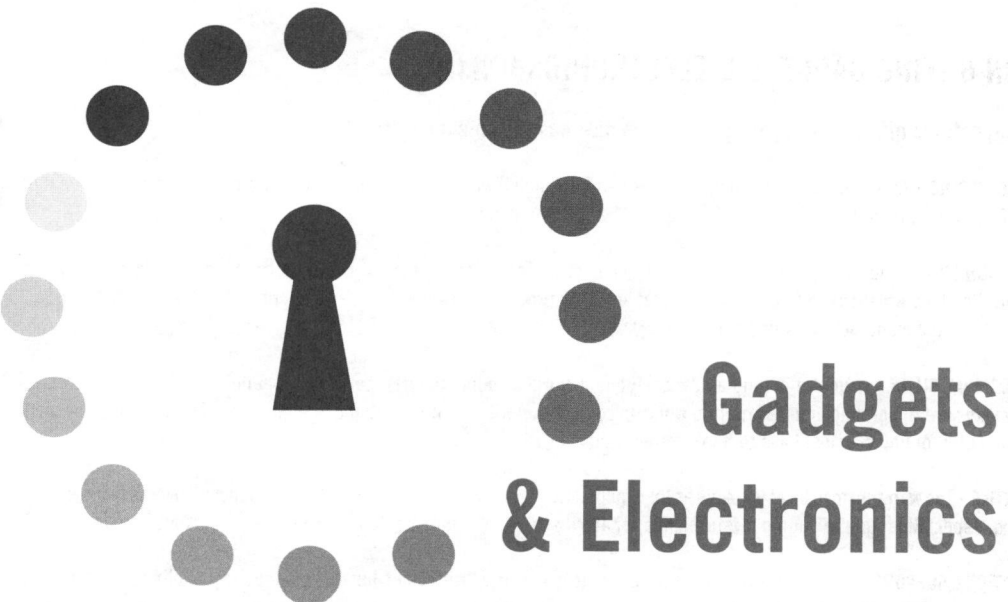

Gadgets & Electronics

In case anybody hasn't noticed, the third millennium is in full swing, making it official: we live in the future. The high-tech world surrounding us is all but unrecognizable to those of us who were alive only fifty years ago. Back then, being able to pause a television broadcast, chart your global position by satellite or speak on the phone to someone while driving was the stuff of science fiction. Today we take these innovations for granted.

If the pursuit of technology revs your engines, take a good look at this collection of next-generation retailers. The first thing you may want to do is use your computer to buy a better computer. By ordering online, you can custom-build a machine to your exact specifications, soup it up to smoothly perform your favorite tasks and even deck it out like a 21st-century hot rod. Set it up properly, and you can run your entire house through your computer, configuring everything from home security to your entertainment system to operate through a single remote control. You can fill your home with high-fidelity sound, watch movies on massive high-definition screens or get lost in videogames that move you. For those of us on the move, technology has become better, stronger, faster… and smaller, giving us PDAs, digital cameras, MP3 players and smart phones that are a little bit of everything. This world is getting pretty amazing, and there's no easier way to keep up than by shopping the sites in this section—some of them are so advanced they read like science fiction themselves. You can literally order tomorrow's technology today.

 **TIPS ON BUYING GADGETS & ELECTRONICS ONLINE**

These suggestions may prevent your electronics purchase from short-circuiting.

• **INSURE SHIPPING** • As always, when a big purchase is involved, you'll want to make sure that your product is insured while it is shipped. Electronics, in particular, consist of some very fragile merchandise.

• **COMPARISON SHOP** • The site where you find the perfect electronics equipment may be different from the best place to buy this equipment. Use **thepurplebook** to find other sites that sell your product, to compare prices and options. Also, it may be a good idea to check out the manufacturer's web site.

• **CHECK COMPATIBILITY** • If you're buying a new component for your home theater, computer, phone or any other electronics systems, make sure the product you're ordering works in conjunction with the products you already own. If not, you may be able to find an adaptor, or you may just have to find another product.

• **WARRANTIES** • The warranty may be as valuable as the equipment it protects. Check to see that your product is covered if something goes wrong, especially if you're buying it refurbished, or at a discount—and then don't lose the warranty documents!

• **INSTALLATION & SUPPORT** • Electronic devices have the power to make life a little easier, but assembling and installing them can send you over the edge. When in doubt, try to stick to products that offer good instructional and technical support, be patient and don't throw away the instruction manual. If all else fails, some sites offer referrals to local installers who can do the work for you.

• **BATTERIES** • It sounds silly, but check to see that the personal electronics devices you order come with batteries, especially if they're product-specific and/or rechargeable. On request, some sites will make sure the batteries are charged when they arrive.

• **AUTHORIZED RETAILERS** • Many online shops offer great prices on products by popular brand-name manufacturers, but be careful: if the site in question is not an authorized dealer of a specific brand, the product may not be covered by any warranty or subject to any technical support. A few bucks extra is usually worth it for the security of manufacturer support.

• **FINDING THE BEST PRICES** • Seasonal sales are aggressively advertised, but the best electronics discounts may usually be found in early January or June. Individual items may be found at great prices in the month leading up to the release of next-generation technology.

• **RECYCLE OLD EQUIPMENT** • Discarded computer and electronics equipment can be damaging to the environment, and should not be thrown away with regular trash. Look to ElectronicsRecycling.com and EIAE.com to find local recycling locations.

>> SITES THAT MAY COME IN HANDY

The following URLs may be useful when you shop for electronics.

CNet.com	Personal electronics info and product reviews
ConsumerReview.com	Consumer electronics info and reviews
Cristina.org	Donate used computers to underprivileged children
DCResource.com	Digital camera product info
eCoustics.com	Audio product reviews
eHow.com	Maintenance, repair and installation guides
HomeTheater.About.com	Home theater news, features and links
HomeTheaterInfo.com	Home theater tips and info
JiWire.com	Locate WiFi hotspots
MonsterCable.com/HookUp_Learning	Home theater installation
NetLingo.com	Glossary for internet terms
oFoto.com	Digital photo printing and sharing
Phones4Charity.org	Donate your old cell phone
PhotoWorks.com	Digital photo printing and sharing
Shutterfly.com	Digital photo printing and sharing
SnapFish.com	Digital photo printing and sharing
TechBargains.com	Locates good deals for electronics products
WhatIs.com	Glossary for computing terms
ZDNet.com	Computing info and product reviews

>> POPULAR ELECTRONICS RETAILERS & MANUFACTURERS

You may buy brand name electronics at the following sites.

Apple.com
BestBuy.com
Brookstone.com
CircuitCity.com
CompUSA.com
Dell.com
Gateway.com

HPShopping.com
IBM.com
PalmOne.com
RadioShack.com
SharperImage.com
SonyStyle.com

*For in-depth reviews of these sites and more, check out www.thepurplebook.com.

SECTION ICON LEGEND

Use the following guide to understand the rectangular icons that appear throughout this section.

COMPUTER PRODUCTS

Stores devoted to computers (desktops, laptops, network servers, etc.) can be found under this icon, whether they offer hardware, software, peripherals, components, networking products, accessories or, as is typically the case, all of the above.

GADGETS

Ranging from spy gadgets to pocketknives (which no spy should be without), this icon will point you toward nifty and ingenious executive toys and tools that help the modern man be better prepared than any Boy Scout.

HOME SECURITY & AUTOMATION

Your home has the potential to be smarter than you think—all it takes is a few electronic upgrades. Automation products will allow you to control your home's climate, lighting, entertainment, curtains and other internal systems with a remote control, while security devices will keep that remote safe.

HOME THEATER

Home theater equipment, including all audio and video components and accessories, is covered by this icon, whether you prefer to buy individual components or packaged sets, bare bones technology or ultrahigh fidelity.

PERSONAL ELECTRONICS

Any portable electronic devices, such as cell phones, personal music players, handheld recorders, video cameras and videogames fall under this icon.

LIST OF KEY WORDS

The following words represent the types of items typically found on the sites listed in this section. You will find them listed in the orange strip at the bottom of each entry, as appropriate.

ACCESSORIES	Computer, home theater and personal electronics devices require a wide range of accessories, including batteries, carrying cases, adapters, cables and many other hard-to-define products. Stores offering thorough selections of such products will be tagged with this key word.
AUDIO	All audio products or components, whether audio players, stereo speakers, headphones, amplifiers or recorders.
COMPONENTS	Parts to improve the performance of audio or computer systems, including hard drives, preamplifiers, audio receivers, networking devices, video cards, etc.
COMPUTERS	Full desktop or laptop computer systems.
CUSTOM	Sites that allow you to build a custom-model computer, home automation or home theater system from available components.
EXECUTIVE TOYS	Gadgets that are typically intended for technophiles, especially professionals, including massage devices and shower radios.
GAMING	Videogame software, accessories, controllers and consoles.
HANDHELDS	An expanding range of portable electronics devices, including MP3 players, PDAs and other technological innovations.
PERIPHERALS	Computer devices, including printers, scanners, keyboards, mice, track balls and other external hardware that expand or improve a computer's functionality.
PHONES	Cell phones and accessories, fax machines, answering machines, satellite phones and pagers, in addition to standard telephones.
PHOTOGRAPHY	All cameras and photography equipment, including film, digital, video and digital video.
REFURBISHED	Used and repaired computer and electronics merchandise.
SECURITY	Any installed home security systems and integrated automation systems, as well as remote controls.
SOFTWARE	Computer and PDA software, either available for download or on a disc.
VIDEO	All video recording or playback devices, whether televisions, DVD players, DVRs or cameras.

KEY WORD INDEX

Use the followings lists to locate online retailers that sell the gadgets and electronics you seek.

ACCESSORIES

5Inch.com
AbesOfMaine.com
AcousticalSolutions.com
Adorama.com
AllStarShop.com
AudioCubes.com
Batteries.com
BHPhotoVideo.com
Blank-CD-CDR.com
CablesToGo.com
CableWholesale.com
CDW.com
CellPhoneShop.net
ColorWarePC.com
ConsoleSource.com
Crutchfield.com
DJMart.com
eBatts.com
eTronics.com
Expansys-USA.com
GadgetFreeks.com
GadgetUniverse.com
Geeks.com
HannSpree-USA.com
Headphone.com
HelloDirect.com
HerringtonCatalog.com
iGadget.com
InkFarm.com
JR.com
LetsAutomate.com
LetsTalk.com
Lik-Sang.com
MacConnection.com
MobilePlanet.com
MonarchComputer.com
OregonKnifeShop.com
PCNation.com
PDAParts.com
ShopLaptop.net
SmartHome.com
SoundCity.com
TigerDirect.com
Tweeter.com
UltimateEars.com
WeLoveMacs.com

AUDIO

5Inch.com
AbesOfMaine.com
AcousticalSolutions.com
AudioCubes.com
BestBuyPCs.com
BHPhotoVideo.com
BigBangElectronics.com
Blank-CD-CDR.com
CablesToGo.com
ColorWarePC.com
Crutchfield.com
DigMind.com
DJMart.com
EtonCorp.com
eTronics.com
Expansys-USA.com
GadgetFreeks.com
GadgetUniverse.com
Headphone.com
iGadget.com
JR.com
LetsAutomate.com
MacConnection.com
MobilePlanet.com
Shop.NPR.org
SmartHome.com
SoundCity.com
SpyTechAgency.com
Tweeter.com
UltimateEars.com

COMPONENTS

AllStarShop.com
AudioCubes.com
BestBuyPCs.com
BHPhotoVideo.com
BigBangElectronics.com
Blank-CD-CDR.com
CableWholesale.com
CDW.com
Crutchfield.com
DJMart.com
eTronics.com
Geeks.com
JR.com
LetsAutomate.com
MemoryX.net
MobilePlanet.com
MonarchComputer.com
PCNation.com
PDAParts.com
SmartHome.com
SoundCity.com
ThinkGeek.com
TigerDirect.com
Tweeter.com
Weaknees.com
WeLoveMacs.com
Xoxide.com

COMPUTERS

AbesOfMaine.com
BestBuyPCs.com
CablesToGo.com
CDW.com
ClearanceClub.com
ColorWarePC.com
ConsoleSource.com
Geeks.com
GetConnected.com
JR.com
LetsAutomate.com
Lik-Sang.com
MacConnection.com
MobilePlanet.com
MonarchComputer.com
PCNation.com

COMPUTERS (cont.)

SmartHome.com
ThinkGeek.com
TigerDirect.com
VelocityMicro.com

CUSTOM

ColorWarePC.com
MonarchComputer.com
VelocityMicro.com
Xoxide.com

EXECUTIVE TOYS

CellPhoneShop.net
GadgetUniverse.com
HerringtonCatalog.com
iGadget.com
MyTypewriter.com
OregonKnifeShop.com
SpyTechAgency.com
Spyville.com

GAMING

ColorWarePC.com
ConsoleSource.com
GadgetUniverse.com
Lik-Sang.com
PocketGear.com

HANDHELDS

AbesOfMaine.com
BestBuyPCs.com
CDW.com
eTronics.com
Expansys-USA.com
GadgetFreeks.com
Handango.com
JR.com
LetsTalk.com
Lik-Sang.com
MemoryX.net
MobilePlanet.com
PCNation.com
PDAParts.com
PocketGear.com
TigerDirect.com

PERIPHERALS

AbesOfMaine.com
AllStarShop.com
Blank-CD-CDR.com
CDW.com
eTronics.com
Geeks.com
InkFarm.com
JR.com
MacConnection.com
MonarchComputer.com
PCNation.com
ThinkGeek.com
TigerDirect.com
Webopolis.com
WeLoveMacs.com
Xoxide.com

PHONES

1-NoveltyPhones.com
CellPhoneShop.net
Expansys-USA.com
GadgetFreeks.com
GetConnected.com
HelloDirect.com
LetsTalk.com
MobilePlanet.com
SpyTechAgency.com
Spyville.com

PHOTOGRAPHY

AbesOfMaine.com
Adorama.com
BestBuyPCs.com
BHPhotoVideo.com
eTronics.com
Expansys-USA.com
JR.com
Lomography.com
MobilePlanet.com

REFURBISHED

Adorama.com
ClearanceClub.com
Crutchfield.com
Geeks.com
MonarchComputer.com
MyTypewriter.com
TigerDirect.com

SECURITY

AAARemotes.com
AbesOfMaine.com
BestBuyPCs.com
BigBangElectronics.com
CablesToGo.com
iGadget.com
LetsAutomate.com
NorcoAlarms.com
SecurityAndMore.com
SmartHome.com
SpyTechAgency.com
Spyville.com

SOFTWARE

AllStarShop.com
AtomicPark.com
BHPhotoVideo.com
BuyCheapSoftware.com
CDW.com
DownloadStore.com
eTronics.com
Handango.com
Lik-Sang.com
MacConnection.com
MobilePlanet.com
PCNation.com
PocketGear.com
SpyTechAgency.com
WeLoveMacs.com

VIDEO

5Inch.com
AbesOfMaine.com
Adorama.com
BestBuyPCs.com
BHPhotoVideo.com
BigBangElectronics.com
Blank-CD-CDR.com
CablesToGo.com
Crutchfield.com
eTronics.com
GetConnected.com
HannSpree-USA.com
LetsAutomate.com
NorcoAlarms.com
SmartHome.com
SoundCity.com
SpyTechAgency.com
Spyville.com
Tweeter.com
Weaknees.com
Webopolis.com

1-NoveltyPhones.com

If you're like most modern Americans, you've not only acquired a mobile phone but have started to make all of your phone calls using cellular technology, which means your land line no longer serves much of a function. Well, then, it might as well win points for style. If you're going to plug a phone in at all, make it one of the stylish, kitschy or unrepentantly goofy phones found on this bizarre specialty site. Categories like Sports Phones, Animal Phones, Vehicle Phones, Antique Reproductions and Famous Character phones deliver exactly what they promise: because if you're going to hold a piece of molded plastic next to your face, it may as well match your interests and tastes.

·PHONES			

5Inch.com

Personal devices that play MP3s and video files may have pushed CDs and DVDs out of your mind for a while, but this blank media specialist is likely to push you right back. Rather than offer you blank discs with the name of some giant corporation printed across the top, this shop offers an assortment of CD-Rs in a variety of colors that are just as blank across the top. Better yet, you may opt for discs with cool silkscreen-printed designs, or even custom order media with your own illustrations printed across the top. If you've got a band or a business or have made your own straight-to-DVD film, you'll want to remember this site.

·ACCESSORIES	·AUDIO	·VIDEO	

AAARemotes.com

Deep in our hearts, we know that most remote controls are really unnecessary indulgences. After all, how much trouble is it to change the channel really? Getting out of a car to open a garage door, on the other hand, qualifies as grueling labor, which is why we feel obligated to bring your attention to this all-too-important site. Specifically, these guys sell remote-control garage and gate openers, and like us you will be surprised just how many different kinds there are. Whether you're opening the garage of a house, or the heavy, wrought-iron gate of an apartment building, this site's certain to have your model, even if it's hopelessly out-of-date, obsolete and unavailable in the rare retail store that carries such items.

·SECURITY			

AbesOfMaine.com

Going all the way to Maine just to get good prices on camera and video equipment hardly seems worth it. Going to this web site, on the other hand, is definitely worthwhile. It offers a wide assortment of digital and SLR cameras, with prices about as competitive as they get. What's that you say? You wish they offered computers, personal electronics and small appliance selections as well? You're in luck. We can only imagine this electronics superstore has been doing it right all along; we've just been too far away to notice.

·COMPUTERS ·PERIPHERALS	·ACCESSORIES ·AUDIO	·PHOTOGRAPHY ·VIDEO	·HANDHELDS ·SECURITY

800-782-5742 · Acoustical Solutions

AcousticalSolutions.com

Whether you live in a noisy environment or want to create one, controlling sound can be a big problem for the dedicated audio-phile. In a busy neighborhood, outside noise can seriously hinder your listening pleasure. In a quiet area, your high-fidelity recordings and room-rumbling bass can quickly turn neighbors against you. The solutions offered by this online specialist include foam panels and vinyl sheets specifically designed to dampen unwanted sound waves and enhance the desirable ones, enabling pro and amateur audio producers and aficionados to control their environments to every concerned party's benefit.

·ACCESSORIES	·AUDIO			

800-223-2500 · Adorama

Adorama.com

Shopping for cameras, video cameras and all related photo equipment can be a daunting and confusing task under the best condi-tions. Well, this site offers the best conditions, which means if you do go in knowing what sort of products you want, you will find them easily and precisely, narrowing down a massive selection by using the helpful product filters located on the right side of the page within each category. If you're not sure what you want, shopping may still be complicated, but you can at least learn the names of the myriad features you don't yet understand.

·ACCESSORIES	·PHOTOGRAPHY	·REFURBISHED	·VIDEO	

800-424-7188 · Allstar Microelectronics

AllStarShop.com

Ordering computer components in a time-sensitive situation can be a huge frustration, as most reasonably priced computer su-perstores operate slowly, and often won't even have the part you need in stock. This retailer offers same-day shipping and other customer service perks that make it a fantastic place to shop if you're in a jam. Better still, the prices are easily competitive, and often better than you might get visiting a store in person. Worth a look.

·SOFTWARE	·ACCESSORIES	·PERIPHERALS	·COMPONENTS

888-322-4250 · AtomicPark

AtomicPark.com

Finding user-friendly software is a feat in itself. Finding a user-friendly software retailer online is near-impossible. Finding this online software retailer was a blessing. Featuring a full complement of the major software brands (more than fifty of them), this site carries works for Windows, Mac, Linux and Palm operating systems, which it offers to deliver free with a "30-Day Happiness Guarantee." All this with a beautiful-to-view, easy-to-use interface that makes other software sites look utterly miserable. Not that they needed the help.

·SOFTWARE				

AudioCubes.com

If you're looking for the world's most advanced consumer electronics, you typically will have to search across the Pacific, to "the world's most innovative electronics producing country," also known as Japan. Over there, new products appear often a year or two before we ever see them in US stores; except this one. Boasting "Japan's best kept secrets," this unique shop secures a terrific selection of stylish, high-end audio gear, anything from wireless headphones and designer speaker systems, and a variety of personal MP3 players and accessories. Of course, if you look regularly, you may just find something you never anticipated, because nobody else on this side of the International Date Line even knows it exists yet.

·ACCESSORIES	·AUDIO	·COMPONENTS	

Batteries.com

Mobile technology may have changed the ways we travel, do business and even communicate, but it would be nothing without one key component that was invented more than one hundred years ago: the battery. This brilliant site keeps you up to date on just about all of your battery needs, and we're not just talking about your alkaline double-A's. General categories include Cordless Phones, Camcorders, Cellular Phones, Digital Cameras, Watches, PDA Products and Notebook Computers. Yes, these devices all tend to require manufacturer specific, rechargeable batteries, and that's just what you'll find. With several easy ways to shop, you can fill your most basic battery needs at the same time as you tackle some of the tougher ones.

·ACCESSORIES			

BestBuyPCs.com

Even if this site did carry only PCs, we'd list it here by virtue of its better-than-competitive prices and a selection that wants nothing to do with poor-quality merchandise. As it turns out, they don't even offer many desktop PCs, and only a few notebook brands. Nice of them, then, to carry a great deal of home theater, digital photography, video and home security equipment as well, including some valuable digital video editing suites and intriguingly hi-tech surveillance gear. A bit of personal electronic gadgetry rounds out the selection, but will be easily forgotten when you get a gander at the TVs....

·COMPUTERS ·VIDEO	·PHOTOGRAPHY ·COMPONENTS	·HANDHELDS ·SECURITY	·AUDIO

BHPhotoVideo.com

That this site offers video and camera equipment, you may already have guessed. Less obvious is the great amount of audio gear found within these pages. The New York City–based retailer excels in all three areas, offering professional-quality merchandise as well as consumer products. So, if you're looking to light up a studio, set up a darkroom or edit video sequences on your computer, no problem. Or, if you merely want to peruse an exhaustive selection of portable audio and video products, you can do that too. Any way you go you'll find a cleanly designed and organized site that's more than prepared to earn your repeat business.

·SOFTWARE ·VIDEO	·ACCESSORIES ·COMPONENTS	·PHOTOGRAPHY	·AUDIO

888-314-2620 · Big Bang Electronics

BigBangElectronics.com

We've seen dozens of consumer electronics dealers that try to cover every audio and video category, and even those that don't fail miserably and completely usually overlook a product here and there. This unique retailer, on the other hand, seems to excel in otherwise overlooked categories. While you may find an occasional deal on more common items like televisions or DVD players, the most satisfying and intriguing components here consist of universal remotes, boom boxes, video projectors, DVRs, headphones and what may be the best selection of rock-shaped outdoor speakers found anywhere. If your regular electronics dealer has let you down, this one might just be able to pick up the slack.

·AUDIO	·VIDEO	·COMPONENTS	·SECURITY

626-581-0702 · Blank-CD-CDR.com

Blank-CD-CDR.com

Pretty much every computer these days comes standard with a CD writer built in, if not a CD-RW or DVD-RW, meaning just about everybody is out there burning audio, video and other transferable data. As you may have guessed, this site specializes in blank media for such projects, in particular unbranded and bulk orders, so you can get dozens and even hundreds of blank discs at affordable prices, without the manufacturer's name stamped all over them. You'll find ink jet printable discs, colorful discs, dual-layer discs and more, as well as plenty of hardware that will write, rewrite and copy multiple discs at once. You'll also find the ink jets, printer ink, blank labels and cases that enable you to create professional-looking media from start to finish.

·ACCESSORIES ·COMPONENTS	·PERIPHERALS	·AUDIO	·VIDEO

888-999-2611 · BuyCheapSoftware

BuyCheapSoftware.com

These guys mean it like they say it, and even with tax and shipping you stand a good chance of saving some money on your software purchases. We're not even talking about fringe software brands that haven't managed to compete with the industry standards; this is the real stuff, as you can see by the menu of popular software manufacturers running down the left side of the page. There's the rub. They didn't bother to divide the products here into usable categories, meaning that you need to know which brands make the sorts of programs you need. Basically, there's no room for comparison. If you know what you want, absolutely shop here. Otherwise, keep it in the back of your head.

·SOFTWARE			

800-293-4970 · Cables To Go

CablesToGo.com

The more electronics you buy, and the more new technologies become available, the more you're going to need new ways to connect it all together. The sad truth is, even your local electronics superstore may not have all the necessary cables and adaptors to connect your various audio, video and computer components. It's a safe bet, though, that this incredibly comprehensive cable specialist will. Dozens of categories each lead to dozens of subcategories, making it easy to find exactly what you're looking for, assuming you know what that is. If not, a beautifully illustrated Connector Guide will help you figure out the naming of all the various plugs or sockets they keep inventing.

·COMPUTERS ·SECURITY	·ACCESSORIES	·AUDIO	·VIDEO

CableWholesale.com

CableWholesale.com · 888-212-8295

Cables, switchboxes, adaptors: these are the things that can make a computer system look like a tangled mess of confusion to the casual observer. Of course, these same items are absolutely necessary if you intend to expand your computing capacity, or get your home theater gear involved. Aside from an S-Video adaptor here and gender changer there, you can easily find stuff like extension cables or surge protectors, which is good considering the site demands a ten-dollar-minimum purchase of products that often cost less than a buck. In almost every case, though, it will be worthwhile to buy at least that much.

·ACCESSORIES   ·COMPONENTS

CDW.com

CDW Computer Centers · 800-840-4239

These guys have a lot to offer for your computing needs, with all kinds of networking equipment, software, peripheral devices and computer components, as well as an enormous selection of increasingly powerful desktops, laptops and handhelds. Visiting this site, you may be reasonably assured you've found the best, strongest, most up-to-date machine available, and at a decent price. The problem lies in finding it. Despite earnest efforts to narrow selections down to manageable numbers, you'll still have to wade through pages of different options. Different, wonderful options. Most times, it's worth it.

·COMPUTERS   ·SOFTWARE   ·ACCESSORIES   ·HANDHELDS
·PERIPHERALS   ·COMPONENTS

CellPhoneShop.net

Cell Phone Shop · 888-989-1584

This site explores an unforeseen side effect of cellular phone technology: accessories. Certainly, our home phones never got this much attention, but today's mobiles (many of which can be purchased here) can be outfitted to match your lifestyle, if not your outfit. Selecting by phone brand and model number, you'll find yourself perusing a choice of faceplates, hands-free kits, car chargers, holsters, wind-up chargers, radiation blockers and a wealth of other products ranging from essential to useful to excessively flashy (decorative antennas, for example). Your land line will be jealous.

·PHONES   ·ACCESSORIES   ·EXECUTIVE TOYS

ClearanceClub.com

Clearance Club · 877-855-0230

At the rate modern computers become obsolete, it's all but impossible to keep up with the state of the art. So, maybe you don't have to. If you don't feel the pressing need to own this year's top-of-the-line model, you'll want to visit this site. Here, all of the computers and peripherals are factory refurbished, overstock or closeout models, meaning you'll save a lot of money buying machines that the techno-hip are prematurely ready to pass up. All the machines of today will be past their prime tomorrow, anyway, so you might as well get a head start on being behind, and save money in the meantime.

·COMPUTERS   ·REFURBISHED

888-452-6567 · ColorWare

ColorWarePC.com

Most computer operating systems allow you to customize the colors of your backgrounds, menus and windows, but the results only emphasize the dullness of your beige, white or metallic notebook case or monitor. Not so with these machines. As impossible as it may seem, this site has actually found a way to improve upon the already design-friendly lines of Apple desktops and laptops by altering them to feature your choice from dozens of colors. In addition, you'll find several home videogame consoles and iPods, which include options for matching controllers and headphones, respectively. Of course, you'll pay a small premium for this custom service, but when you get a glimpse of the beautifully rendered product previews, you won't want to do without it.

·COMPUTERS ·AUDIO	·ACCESSORIES	·GAMING	·CUSTOM

888-779-1377 · ConsoleSource.com

ConsoleSource.com

Keeping track of the changing face of videogames can be tough on the uninitiated, but whether you're waiting for the next generation in the escalating platform wars or complementing the gear you already have and love, this site offers clean, easy browsing to hook you up with hardware, controllers, games and accessories for each of the major competitors. An esoteric menu of brand names may still confuse newcomers, so we'd recommend consulting a teenager before just diving in.

·COMPUTERS	·ACCESSORIES	·GAMING	

888-955-6000 · Crutchfield.com

Crutchfield.com

If you're one of those nitpicky online shoppers who values things like selection, detailed information, ease of navigation and great prices, with this site you may finally have found an electronics retailer worthy of your time. Somehow these guys have managed to bundle loads of information onto each page without making it impossible to decipher and, while not every portable and home-electronics product you might want exists in great supply, most of the big items give you plenty of options and enough detail to distinguish between them. Special sections for AV-equipped computers, Outlet items and Scratch & Dent discounts round out this stellar home theater specialist. If you find better, do let us know.

·ACCESSORIES ·COMPONENTS	·REFURBISHED	·AUDIO	·VIDEO

760-603-9100 · Digital Mind Corporation

DigMind.com

There are plenty of places online to find an MP3 player, but only one place to find "the world's largest capacity digital audio player." This powerful little machine is available with up to 100GB of storage (as of this writing), with enough battery life to last 22 hours when fully charged. It plays a wide variety of audio files—not just MP3—and can store any digital format in its massive, easily replaceable hard drive. Additionally, it boasts direct line recording capability, along with a built-in microphone, and an FM receiver, making this some smart MP3 player. And that's just one of the models available from this tiny but impressive proprietary line of personal electronics.

·AUDIO			

DJMart.com

DJs may be viewed as audiophiles who've gotten a little bit carried away with the capabilities of audio equipment. However, the rest of us can benefit from their dedicated hi-fi prowess with this site, which accommodates the techno lust of these ardent gear-heads. Aside from the obvious (turntables, headphones and powerful speakers), you will find a fantastic array of audio cables and adaptors, as well as quality microphones and recording devices. Most of the audio components listed go above and beyond what the normal home-theater enthusiast requires, but we like the idea that by checking here, we can make sure we're not missing anything.

·ACCESSORIES   ·AUDIO   ·COMPONENTS

DownloadStore.com

Is there such a thing as too much software? This site makes the case for it. While it offers a fantastic wealth of downloadable software, it takes a lot of patience to find the best available to suit your interests. While your purchases here are almost immediately gratified, every category—whether antivirus software, educational programs, voice recognition applications, games or clip-art selections—is well stocked but disorganized, offering hundreds of choices in no better order than alphabetical (if that), and even the Search feature doesn't help much. Consequently, shopping takes longer than delivery, which is almost never true anywhere else.

·SOFTWARE

eBatts.com

The world of portable electronics would be worthless without batteries, and increasingly phones, camcorders, laptop computers and other personal devices require unique, proprietary battery models that are difficult to replace. Rather, were difficult. Here you'll easily find the specific battery you need, or even a better, longer-lasting model that is compatible with your device. Just browse by manufacturer to narrow in on the apparatus you wish to free from the wall socket, or find a decent AC adapter in order to plug it back in.

·ACCESSORIES

EtonCorp.com

If you're looking to listen to the radio with simplicity, style and small equipment, take a quick look at the small selection of table-top radios available from this manufacturer/distributor site. These types of radios have been surging in popularity over the past couple of years, as they're versatile enough to plug in to any room of the house, and deliver sharp sound out of a tiny package. Particularly interesting are the models equipped to receive a satellite radio signal, which is perfect for a cabin or other remote getaway locations.

·AUDIO

800-323-7669 · etronics.com

eTronics.com

Here's the rare electronics superstore that stands out; not for having the hugest number of products, the widest breadth of merchandise or the lowest prices, though it does fairly well on all accounts. The most interesting thing about this Manhattan-based retailer is its offering of unique and memorable home audio, video, photography and personal electronics gear. Stuff like wireless speakers, novelty turntables and waterproof radios are only some of the fascinating products to be found on this deceptively basic site. Browsing is rarely so much fun.

·SOFTWARE ·PERIPHERALS	·ACCESSORIES ·AUDIO	·PHOTOGRAPHY ·VIDEO	·HANDHELDS ·COMPONENTS

309-820-7913 · eXpansys USA

Expansys-USA.com

The field of pocket-size personal electronics represents some of the most exciting technological advances of our time, whether you're trying to organize your life, keep up your on-the-go correspondence or simply listen to music. Of course, the truly tech-savvy devices combine all functions into a single, powerful design; kind of like this site, which is built to satisfy all handheld computing, entertainment and communications needs, along with all the desirable accessories. Palmtop computers, smartphones, Bluetooth devices and MP3 players are fairly standard here, with a surprising number of manufacturers and models represented. You'll have to log on for yourself to see what the latest catchy gizmo looks like.

·PHONES ·AUDIO	·ACCESSORIES	·PHOTOGRAPHY	·HANDHELDS

212-406-8255 · Gadgetfreeks

GadgetFreeks.com

It's tough to say exactly when it was that mobile phones became "smart," but we do know that it's happened, and that your wireless life may never be the same. A smartphone may take your calls, play your music, organize your calendar—just about everything but do your laundry. While it may be bigger than the average cell phone, it makes many of your other personal gadgets obsolete, so there will suddenly be a lot of room available in your pocket. This shop is great in that it serves up just about every conceivable phone and wireless accessory, ranging from book smart to brilliant, but as you'll have to browse through dozens of brand names to see them all, the site itself turns out to be not so bright.

·PHONES	·ACCESSORIES	·HANDHELDS	·AUDIO

800-429-1139 · Gadget Universe

GadgetUniverse.com

Your futuristic home doesn't necessarily stop at a super-powerful computer, top-shelf home theater system or even a centralized home automation system. If your idea of modern living includes ionized air, memory foam and personal climate control devices, this may just be the shop for you. A perfect spot to find gifts for yourself or your gadget-loving friends, the selection of this forward-thinking web shop is constantly changing, so you'll want to check back when yesterday's world of tomorrow becomes today.

·ACCESSORIES	·EXECUTIVE TOYS	·GAMING	·AUDIO

Geeks.com

ComputerGeeks.com · 760-726-7700

The word *geek* has undergone quite a transformation in the past two decades. Any negative connotations to the term are all but gone and, in fact, when you find yourself in dire need of technological assistance or advice, the geek is almost revered. We think you'll look kindly upon this user-friendly computer site, which is anchored by a fine selection of refurbished computers and bolstered by a wide assortment of necessary and indulgent accessories, components and peripheral devices. The prices are pretty phenomenal, even with regard to new items, which isn't likely to hurt the image of geeks anywhere.

·COMPUTERS ·COMPONENTS	·ACCESSORIES	·PERIPHERALS	·REFURBISHED

GetConnected.com

GetConnected · 800-775-2506

Considering all the different ways there are to get connected, it's pretty impressive to uncover a site that offers most of them. That's what you'll find here, with plenty of phone, internet and television plans to browse—you just need enter your zip code to see what's available locally. Mostly, though, the focus here is on cell phones, and whether you're interested in starting a new plan or upgrading the phone for the plan you're on, this site can hook you up in a matter of minutes. However, shipping is often an unknown here, as the products and services available are distributed through local providers. At the very least, it behooves you to take advantage of this shop's tremendous reference guides and other resources.

·COMPUTERS	·PHONES	·VIDEO	

Handango.com

Handango · 817-280-0129

As PDAs and smartphones have established themselves as more than just flash-in-the-pan executive toys, it's no surprise a site like this one would thrive. With an unwavering devotion to palmtop computing, regardless of operating system or design, you might have trouble finding any actual devices here, you will have no trouble finding software for whichever palmtop operating system you favor. Which is to say, you'll have no trouble spotting the huge selection of software. With thousands of titles available, finding the programs you want can be a daunting task, but if you rely heavily on the site's thorough organization, you may just come across something that makes your life on the go even easier than expected.

·SOFTWARE	·HANDHELDS		

HannSpree-USA.com

HANNSpree · 510-360-3080

Just when you think televisions are only as exciting as what's on the screen, a site like this comes along to wipe out all of your preconceptions. With highly stylized LCD TVs, this unique manufacturer offers televisions of fantastic appeal. To start, you'll find a curious array of ultramodern sets that seem to be out of a science fiction film, and a few nostalgic designs that deliver crystal-clear picture from a wood panel box. But the most memorable TVs here are the sports and children's models, which come shaped like baseballs, basketballs and a variety of stuffed animals. If you want to know what they've done to remote controls you'll have to see for yourself.

·ACCESSORIES	·VIDEO		

800-828-8184 · HeadRoom

Headphone.com

Here's the site your neighbors want you to know about. As gratifying as it may be to share your music with the entire block, it's at the very least polite to keep it to yourself. As it turns out, you may be doing yourself a favor, as in many ways a quality pair of headphones can outperform even high-end speakers in terms of clarity. You can read all about it in this site's excellent Buying Guide, which distinguishes between the types of headphones best suited for portable devices, home theaters or during exercise, as well as offering convincing arguments for splurging on the good stuff. These guys will make a quiet convert out of you.

·ACCESSORIES	·AUDIO			

800-435-5634 · HelloDirect.com

HelloDirect.com

Chances are, if you bought a telephone this year it was a cell phone. But as this site proves, there are still plenty of reasons to keep your land line turned on. Fax machines, conferencing devices and expandable multiple-line phones combine with cordless phones, wireless headsets and answering machines to make this traditional phone site technologically up to date. Keep this site handy, because chances are, if you need to update a phone next year, it'll probably be the one you've been neglecting at home.

·PHONES	·ACCESSORIES			

800-903-2878 · Herrington

HerringtonCatalog.com

This home page of this gift and gadget catalog gets it right when it says, "Our site isn't fancy, but with its ease of navigation and quickness, it's respectful of your time." While it's tough to typify the sort of products you'll find here any given season, with a variety of quality products handpicked by the progressively old-fashioned proprietors, like-minded individuals can be sure to track down a few nifty examples of technology, ingenuity or flat-out charm. We found some waterproof casings for your iPod, a pocketknife with a foldout flash memory stick and an electronic rangefinder for golfers who want to know exactly how far it is from tee to hole.

·ACCESSORIES	·EXECUTIVE TOYS			

877-775-7779 · iGadget.com

iGadget.com

If you think that the height of technological splendor has been achieved in the confines of your CPU, then you haven't been paying attention. From extraordinarily hi-tech to downright kitschy, these guys have got toys and utilities the likes of which once existed only in science fiction. Take, for example, wireless weather stations, briefcase alarms and binocular cameras. While not every-thing here specifically fits the "gadget" label, with plenty of products for personal grooming, day-to-day living and sheer fun, your shiny, sparkling future has arrived.

·ACCESSORIES	·EXECUTIVE TOYS	·AUDIO	·SECURITY	

InkFarm.com

These guys serve one purpose: replacing your printer's toner and ink cartridges. After all, you're bound to run out eventually, and they figure if they make it easy enough, you'll look to them when you do. They make it rather easy, offering a menu of product manufacturers and, subsequently, model numbers, so you can simply follow a path to the correct printer and make your purchase. It works the same way if you're looking for paper, whether of regular stock or something better. You may want to pause and wonder at the ridiculous costs of such things, but then, you'd do that anyway.

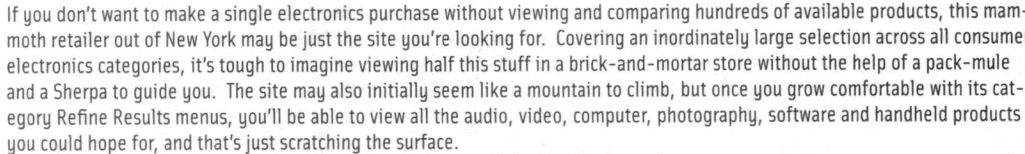

·ACCESSORIES	·PERIPHERALS		

JR.com

If you don't want to make a single electronics purchase without viewing and comparing hundreds of available products, this mammoth retailer out of New York may be just the site you're looking for. Covering an inordinately large selection across all consumer electronics categories, it's tough to imagine viewing half this stuff in a brick-and-mortar store without the help of a pack-mule and a Sherpa to guide you. The site may also initially seem like a mountain to climb, but once you grow comfortable with its category Refine Results menus, you'll be able to view all the audio, video, computer, photography, software and handheld products you could hope for, and that's just scratching the surface.

·COMPUTERS ·PERIPHERALS	·ACCESSORIES ·AUDIO	·PHOTOGRAPHY ·COMPONENTS	·HANDHELDS

LetsAutomate.com

If you revel in the ultimate and unyielding power that is push-button remote control, you will be primed to enjoy this site, which offers several home automation solutions. Basically, the concept takes advantage of your home's internal wiring structure so that you can centralize command of systems like lighting, security and climate control. Then, in conjunction with motion detectors, timers and even your computer, you can act like a true omnipotent master of your domain, even when away, ensuring that your home never rests on its laurels. Be careful, though, this company ships from the UK, and it can be quite expensive.

·COMPUTERS ·COMPONENTS	·ACCESSORIES ·SECURITY	·AUDIO	·VIDEO

LetsTalk.com

Cell phones have come a long way in the past few years, to the point that actual wireless communication between people almost seems like a secondary function. Of course, all the phones and rate plans you'll find here will put you in touch with the world at large, but even better it can help you find the best combination of features and accessories to suit your wants and needs. Shop By Feature and you may quickly peruse phones compatible with your service plan that offer downloadable ringtones, MP3 players, cameras, video cameras, games, IR ports, speakerphones, Bluetooth adapters and/or much more. Better yet, take a look at their smartphone selection to find the latest, greatest combination of features that fit into a handset.

·PHONES	·ACCESSORIES	·HANDHELDS	

877-545-7264 · Pacific Game Technology

Lik-Sang.com

Why would you buy something from an Asian-based gaming shop when there are so many closer to home? The real question is, why would a gamer shop locally when all the best stuff comes out of Asia? Thanks to free worldwide shipping, the decision's relatively easy. While shopping for consoles may not be the best idea (some platforms are only available in foreign versions), shopping for accessories is a must, particularly with regard to controllers. We're not just talking about the sort of thumb-waggling, two-handed controllers most commonly associated with home gaming, but also floor pads that you dance on, drums that you beat on and swords you can swing. Who needs buttons?

·COMPUTERS ·HANDHELDS	·SOFTWARE	·ACCESSORIES	·GAMING

718-522-4353 · Lomographic Society International

Lomography.com

Sure, your point-and-shoot camera may get the job done, but just how much fun can you have with it? If you're interested in taking on a more creative role in your amateur photography, follow the Shop link of this site. Here you'll find a small but captivating selection of cameras offering a variety of special features, including panoramic lenses, lensless "pinhole" designs, manual shutter controls, color tinted lenses, tinted flashes and 80mm exposures. These amazingly cool cameras make taking amazingly cool images a snap, and make digital cameras seem positively dull in comparison.

·PHOTOGRAPHY			

888-213-0259 · PC Connection

MacConnection.com

If you're looking for a good reason to shop here for Mac- and iPod-compatible peripherals, components, software and accessories, just remember three simple words: *third party products*. The Apple web site proves virtually unbeatable when you want to buy Apple products, but variety is limited. Here, you'll find a much greater selection of printers, monitors, networking equipment, input devices, memory upgrades and carrying cases that may not bear the Apple logo, but do work with all of your Mac products. Of course, there may be one better reason to browse these competing brands: price.

·COMPUTERS ·AUDIO	·SOFTWARE	·ACCESSORIES	·PERIPHERALS

866-636-6799 · Memory Ten

MemoryX.net

One unforeseen aspect of the digital age has been that we've become less reliant on our brains to remember things. Cell phones store our phone numbers, email programs keep our contacts straight and personal organizers remind us when and where our appointments take place. The opposite is true when it comes to our computers and handheld devices, as advanced software capabilities require more and more memory with which to operate. Rather than declare your low-memory machine obsolete, you might want to shop from this terrific memory specialist, which offers RAM upgrades and flash storage for just about every personal computing device under the sun. All you need to remember is the make and model of your computer.

·HANDHELDS	·COMPONENTS		

MobilePlanet.com

Mobile Planet · 800-675-2638

This site's specialization in mobile computing and communications has automatic appeal, as its wares represent technologies that advance every year, usually in time for the holiday gifting season. What with smartphones, Wi-Fi, Bluetooth and flash memory, there's always going to be a buzzword here to make the tech-savvy drool, but if you're just catching on to the wireless revolution, the Resource Center link should catch you up pretty quickly, so that, soon enough, you'll be drooling too.

·COMPUTERS ·PHOTOGRAPHY	·SOFTWARE ·HANDHELDS	·PHONES ·AUDIO	·ACCESSORIES ·COMPONENTS

MonarchComputer.com

Monarch Computer Systems · 800-611-0875

If you fancy the image of a mad scientist assembling pieces of machinery for arcane purposes, perhaps you will enjoy this site. Its most markedly intriguing feature is a custom desktop builder that "allows you to fully customize your new PC from start to finish." Such an undertaking is quite complicated, even if they do assemble and set up the machine for you. Fortunately, you don't need to start from scratch to enjoy the site's considerable selection of occasionally refurbished desktop components, peripherals and accessories, whether you seek to boost, repair or simply spruce up your machine or network. It's fairly simple shopping on a site that seems at times pieced together from unused parts...

·COMPUTERS ·REFURBISHED	·ACCESSORIES ·COMPONENTS	·CUSTOM	·PERIPHERALS

MyTypewriter.com

myTypewriter.com · 703-930-3484

A typewriter may seem as archaic as an 8-track cassette, but if you can think of a more charming machine on which to type, you'll have to let us know. This unique specialty shop offers a small but beautiful variety of vintage typewriters and, yes, they do work, each repaired and restored to original condition for your typing pleasure. You'll also find all the necessary ink ribbons for your portable or desktop, though if you still prefer your computer word processor and laser printer, these tend to work just as well as a decorative conversation piece.

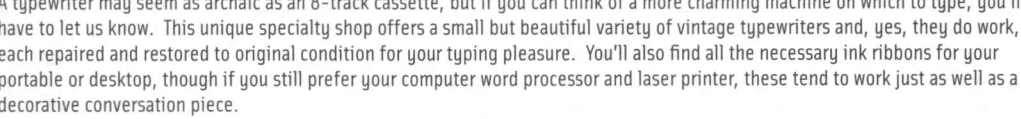

·EXECUTIVE TOYS	·REFURBISHED		

NorcoAlarms.com

Norco Security Products · 888-501-7870

Here's your chance to turn your home into the type of impenetrable fortress depicted in heist movies, complete with motion detectors, video surveillance systems and sensory light beams that will be undetectable to anybody without chalk dust. Buying the stuff here is much easier than setting it all up, and a good few of these items would probably qualify as "going overboard." But sometimes peace of mind may be procured along with some intriguing technology, and this site will fit the bill for those looking to protect their property and person.

·VIDEO	·SECURITY		

877-235-5723 · MDX Industries

OregonKnifeShop.com

You might call Swiss Army knives the original gadgets; yet they still prove inordinately useful, even with the advent of all sorts of advanced personal electronics technologies. If you think simple is better, maybe you'd prefer to keep your pocket filled with functional tools like these Swiss Army products and leatherman gadgets. Or maybe you like things a little complicated—that works too. Here you'll discover that the time-tested pocketknife has kept up with the times, and now you'll find stuff like flash memory cards folding out alongside the classic penknife, screwdriver, tweezers and scissors combo. Some things never become obsolete.

| ·ACCESSORIES | ·EXECUTIVE TOYS | | |  |

800-235-4050 · PCNation.com

PCNation.com

To the uninitiated, tech specs can be quite boring, if not downright frustrating and confusing. So, a word of caution: if you don't know the difference between gigahertz and gigabytes, this impressively stocked megastore is not for you. If, however, you know some of the general specifications you would like in a computer, MP3 player, printer, networking hub or digital camera, a quick and easy Advanced Search filtering system will show you a list of all products that meet your requirements, within your specified price range. Thus you can apply your grasp of the information technology spectrum to something useful for a change: shopping.

| ·COMPUTERS ·PERIPHERALS | ·SOFTWARE ·COMPONENTS | ·ACCESSORIES | ·HANDHELDS | |

408-852-9595 · AX Micro Solutions

PDAParts.com

Now that handheld PDAs have become commonplace, so have minor accidents and misplacements, such as a cracked screen, burnt-out battery or a broken button. No problem. This site offers a full range of replaceable PDA parts and accessories for just about every popular brand and model, including Casio, Samsung, Handspring and Palm, and they're even starting to include digital music players, like the iPod. If you think the mechanics of such repair jobs are beyond your scope, check out the site's repair guides and videos before you decide; in most cases, they're easier than you think.

| ·ACCESSORIES | ·HANDHELDS | ·COMPONENTS | | |

800-746-7646 · Motricity

PocketGear.com

How much can you fit into your pocket? Your keys? A wallet? Maybe a pack of gum? How about a translation guide, or a board game? Or an encyclopedia? With a pocket-size PDA you may fit a remarkable number of nifty tools, games and resources into a single handheld computer, and this software specialist offers hundreds of programs designed to make your digital life on the go both more fun and easier. Sadly, the ease doesn't start until you begin to download the software, as browsing this massive selection almost requires a reference guide in and of itself.

| ·SOFTWARE | ·GAMING | ·HANDHELDS | | |

SecurityAndMore.com

Ever wonder what it is that goes bump in the night? With some of the security and surveillance equipment available from this site you can detect and record the late night happenings on your premises without having to be around or awake for them. Alarm systems and safes will keep you and yours out of the grasp of those who would lurk in the shadows, giving you peace of mind, while the hi-tech camera equipment will show you that it's probably just raccoons doing the lurking and rooting through your garbage.

·SECURITY

Shop.NPR.org

If you're a fan of good radio, it makes sense that you shop from the nation's chief producer of good radio, which just so happens to offer some great radios. While proceeds from this site support National Public Radio programming, the prices are the same or better as you'd find in a typical retailer. In the meantime, you get a beautiful selection of portable and tabletop radios, including models by Tivoli and Boston Acoustics, which combine functional listening with superior class. You might even find a few similarly elegant satellite radios in the mix, because there's no better broadcast than a commercial-free one.

·AUDIO

ShopLaptop.net

When it comes to mobile computing, the only real limitation these days seems to be your power source. Whether you wish to operate your laptop on a longer-life battery, through your car's DC power source or simply need to replace a lost or broken AC adaptor, this specialty site most likely carries a product compatible with your specific brand and model computer. If, once you're powered up, you decide your machine doesn't have enough operating memory (RAM), chances are you'll find an upgrade for that here too. It's not always pretty, but this site will easily get the job done and send you on your way.

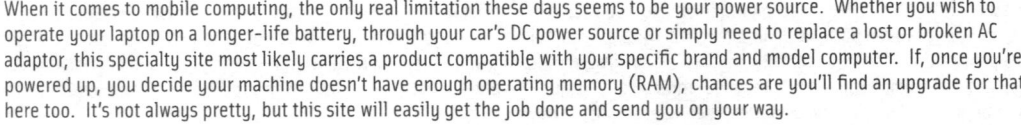

·ACCESSORIES

SmartHome.com

Not to insinuate that your home is dumb, but can it control its own internal climate in response to external weather conditions, tend its own garden, feed your pets, or turn the lights off when you leave the room? These are only a few of the automation options available from this site that upgrades your home for the new millennium. On the basic level you can update your home security, and for the advanced there's a chance to integrate nearly every electric system in your house into one remote control, with particular attention paid to your home theater. However, if your house starts talking to you, don't expect it to be interesting.

·COMPUTERS ·ACCESSORIES ·AUDIO ·VIDEO
·COMPONENTS ·SECURITY

800-542-7283 · Sound City

SoundCity.com

Consumer electronics is big business, and a culture of unscrupulous characters marketing defective and counterfeit merchandise is well documented internationally. When shopping online, it's all the more impossible to tell if you're getting the real deal, and there's really only one way to make sure you get the right equipment with a valid warranty: shop from an authorized dealer. This site fits the bill, with hundreds of high-end and popular brands covering a full range of home audio and video products, including quality home theater components and prepackaged systems. The site will match any price offered by other authorized dealers, but if you're willing to take a chance on a better deal, follow links to the store's Outlet site.

| ·ACCESSORIES | ·AUDIO | ·VIDEO | ·COMPONENTS | |

888-878-2779 · Spy Tech Agency

SpyTechAgency.com

As the age of Big Brother approaches, it may sometimes seem like someone is always watching, listening and following you in your daily routine. Well, probably not. However, if your paranoia proves to be grounded in reality, it's nice to know you can fight back against "them." This site offers remarkable technological toys, the likes of which used to exist only in spy movies. With the gear found here, you may encrypt your phone calls, digitally mask your voice and detect phone taps. But that's only the start. You'll also find surveillance equipment, locksmithing tools, tracking devices and hidden microphones. Shop here, and give "them" a taste of their own medicine.

| ·SOFTWARE ·VIDEO | ·PHONES ·SECURITY | ·EXECUTIVE TOYS | ·AUDIO | |

866-779-8455 · Spyville

Spyville.com

Somewhere between the home protection instincts and your sense of paranoid delusion you may appreciate this site, which offers an intriguing array of nifty spy gadgets as well as an entirely functional assortment of home security equipment. The motion-activated video recorders speak for themselves, whereas the phone recorders, bug detectors and hidden cameras may require a bit more explanation to loved ones. Most of this stuff actually seems kind of fun, in a Cold War sort of way.

| ·PHONES | ·EXECUTIVE TOYS | ·VIDEO | ·SECURITY | |

888-433-5788 · ThinkGeek, Inc.

ThinkGeek.com

Leave it to the makers of this site to slip a *Star Wars* reference into their About Us page. These guys unabashedly serve geeks, defined as the "people out there who were on the front line and in the trenches as the Internet was forged." Basically, the site offers a vast array of gadgets, alongside PC modifications, components and peripherals, including some pretty high-end, tech-forward stuff that we won't even try to keep up with here. Suffice to say, if you didn't assemble your computer personally, you may not be able to find your way around. For the geeks out there, browsing is no more difficult than bull's-eyeing womp rats with a T-16.

| ·COMPUTERS | ·PERIPHERALS | ·COMPONENTS | | |

TigerDirect.com

With sections of this computer superstore labeled Overstock, Recertified and Open Box, you immediately get the feeling you can find a good deal here. You can, but you needn't always stalk these discount sections to find it. Well-stocked categories and conveniently broken-down subcategories guide you to a fine selection of affordable computers, components, peripheral devices and accessories, along with plenty of handheld devices, cell phones and personal MP3 players. There's enough here to keep you busy for hours of productive browsing, but it's the ease on your pocketbook that will keep you coming back.

·COMPUTERS ·REFURBISHED	·ACCESSORIES ·COMPONENTS	·HANDHELDS	·PERIPHERALS

Tweeter.com

Quality home audio and video products are quite easy to buy from this authorized electronics dealer. Though the selection is small by web shop standards, the novice home theater enthusiast should be able to find satisfactory gear without having to fret much about technical specs or shoddy merchandise. Ironically, the site's comprehensive Research section gives you a chance to read up on such things, at which point you may desire a broader array of products with which to test your newfound expertise. More likely, though, you'll realize this shop offers everything you need to satisfy your entertainment needs.

·ACCESSORIES	·AUDIO	·VIDEO	·COMPONENTS

UltimateEars.com

Headphones come in many shapes and forms, but we're guessing you haven't seen any that look quite like this. Without a doubt the most expensive you'll ever see, the distinctive ear buds you'll find here are molded to fit the irregular shape of the human ear, thus creating a better fit and seal than the standard round bud designs. True audiophiles may even consult an audiologist for your personal ear canal impressions to be used to fashion a custom set. Either way, the site promises "the ultimate in high definition and precise sound reproduction." At these prices, we sure hope so.

·ACCESSORIES	·AUDIO		

VelocityMicro.com

According to this site, every silicon computer chip is not the same, and whereas the poorly performing ones might just be used in your current computer, the cream of the crop may be found in these machines. Well, we can't be sure how much better or long lasting these desktops and laptops truly are, but we can attest to the ease and versatility of the proprietary shop's customization feature, which allows you to build a fast, powerful machine for personal use, gaming or business, with plenty of slick add-ons to make it worth your while. However well these computers compare to industry standards, it's nice to know you won't have to work hard to buy one.

·COMPUTERS	·CUSTOM		

888-932-5633 · weaKnees

Weaknees.com

If you've seen any television ads lately, we're guessing you haven't got a DVR yet. The wildly proliferating digital video recording technology has people all over the country pausing and rewinding live television broadcasts, as well as fast-forwarding effortlessly through commercials. But, you probably already know this. What you may not know is that on this TiVo specialty site, you may upgrade your existing DVR's memory, or buy a new one with incredible deals and rebates that make it more affordable than a single month of cable.

·VIDEO	·COMPONENTS		

866-595-5289 · Webopolis

Webopolis.com

Harkening back to a day when TVs and radios "were furniture that added warmth, beauty and character to a room," this site offers a very limited, but undeniably appealing product range: wooden computer monitors, mice and keyboards. As unlikely as it sounds, you may find these fully functional and oddly gorgeous LCD displays and USB input devices in genuine, satin-finished sapele, beech or ash, and you may never look at molded plastic the same way again. You can't even find TVs made of real wood anymore; unless you shop here. The site carries those too.

·PERIPHERALS	·VIDEO		

866-636-6799 · We Love Macs

WeLoveMacs.com

It's always nice to see an online retailer maintain an emotional attachment to its products, and this Apple computers and electronics specialist expresses its devotion with doting detail. While you won't actually find any computers or iPods for sale here, you will find a comprehensive selection of compatible accessories, components and peripheral devices; even more products than are carried by the official Apple site. Browsing is not as easy as we usually expect from a specialty shop, which just goes to show: sometimes it takes more than love to make a relationship work.

·SOFTWARE	·ACCESSORIES	·PERIPHERALS	·COMPONENTS

610-353-1634 · Xoxide.com

Xoxide.com

Most of us think of computer modifications as switching to a new web browser or changing the photo on your desktop. But to those in the know, it involves much more interesting alterations to your physical machine. This site offers plenty to work with, including clear, acrylic cases; silent, fan-free cooling systems; sound-reactive internal light sources and UV sensitive cables for that neon, glow-in-the-dark vibe. The site also offers a good assortment of stylized, high-performance mice and keyboards to match your machine's makeover while offering superior functionality. It's tough for anyone to look cool while sitting in front of a computer; this may be as close as you ever get.

·CUSTOM	·PERIPHERALS	·COMPONENTS	

NOTES:

Health & Beauty

Judging from all the recent media coverage, health is becoming something of a national obsession, which puts it just below beauty on our list of priorities. In the following pages, we tried to find a balance between the two, opting for a variety of sites that demonstrate the breadth of human health issues and a long list of beauty sites representing just about every skin care, body care and cosmetics brand we've ever heard of.

Online pharmacies head up the list of general health sites we found, along with the virtual equivalents of corner drugstores and even traditional apothecaries. Other sites focus on individual parts of the body, offering the sorts of dental, orthopedic and ocular appliances recommended by doctors. Or, if you're fed up with modern medicine, there are plenty of alternatives, ranging from ancient to new age treatments. Beauty, of course, covers a holistic approach to health, because we always seem to feel good when we look our best. There is a plethora of products available to keep us feeling clean and smelling fresh, offering sensory experiences that range from basic to inventive, subtle to striking, and innocent to sensual. We're particularly excited this year to have seen a surge in the number of such products springing up to serve men, and not just with regard to shaving. True, most men will still have no reason to browse the many online cosmetics counters, but if the rest of the sites on the following pages are used right, the good looks of great health might just catch on, and nobody will need to wear makeup at all anymore.

 ## TIPS ON BUYING HEALTH & BEAUTY PRODUCTS ONLINE

These suggestions may help keep your health and beauty purchases from getting ugly.

• **CONSULT YOUR PHYSICIAN** • Information on the web is not always reliable, so you'll definitely want to keep the lines of communication open with a licensed physician before you embark on any course of treatment afforded online. In particular, supplements aren't regulated by the FDA, so consult a doctor about any potential side effects or harmful drug interactions before you ingest anything.

• **CHECK FOR BEAUTY PRODUCT SAMPLES** • Some bath, body care and skin care products can run high in price. Many of the online retailers offer to send you a sample, or travel-size portions of the product. Take them up on this and try it out before committing to a big jar of the stuff. Same goes for fragrances, which alter in reaction to individual skin chemistry.

• **SPOT TEST NEW SKIN PRODUCTS** • Try new skin products on a small patch of skin on your arm before applying them to your face and body, to make sure you suffer no adverse reactions.

• **MAKE SURE SKIN CARE PRODUCTS ARE RIGHT FOR YOU** • Everybody's skin works in different ways, and certain products may not be right for you. When in doubt, consult the customer service of the site offering the product, check the site to determine proper application techniques, and check the ingredients list to avoid allergic reactions. If you can't find answers online, seek counsel elsewhere, either through a dermatologist, aesthetician or other knowledgeable source.

• **BE WARY OF SITES OFFERING NARCOTICS** • Narcotic medications, such as Vicodin and Demerol, cannot be legally purchased online at this time. If you see a site offering such medications, chances are that something shady is afoot. Exercise caution.

 ## POPULAR BEAUTY BRANDS

The following sites offer proprietary cosmetics, bath-and-body and skin care products.

Avon.com	Lush.com
ChidoriaWorld.com	MDFormulations.com
CaswellMassey.com	NaturoPathica.com
CrabtreeAndEvelyn.com	Origins.com
ElizabethW.com	SabonNYC.com
FlorisOfLondon.com	Sensia.com
FrenchSoap.com	ShopAccaKappa.com
Kiehls.com	SimoneFrance.com
Lather.com	ThreeCustom.com
LippmanCollection.com	

*For in-depth reviews of these sites and more, check out **www.thepurplebook.com.**

>> SITES WITH A SINGLE FOCUS

The following sites excel at selling one or two specific products.

HeadHunterSurf.com	Sunscreen
HeartMonitors.co.uk	Heart monitors
KauaiSoap.com	Handmade soaps
OnlineMagnets.com	Magnet therapy
SupportPlus.com	Leg support garments

>> SITES THAT MAY COME IN HANDY

The following URLs may be useful when you shop for health and beauty products.

ACOG.com	Women's health resources
AllAboutVision.com	Vision info and resources
AMA-Assn.org	American Medical Associatiion provider directory
Cancer.gov	Informative cancer resource
Clairol.com	Virtual hair color model
ClinicalTrialResults.org	Results of clinical drug trials
eHealthInsurance.com	Health insurance info and quotes
FDA.gov	FDA consumer warnings and news
Healing.About.com	Alternative health info and resources
HealthGrades.com	Ratings of hospitals and doctors
HealthInsurance.org	Health insurance info and quotes
HolisticNetwork.org	Locate alternative health providers
InteliHealth.com	Medical info and definitions
Ivanhoe.com	Medical news
KidsHealth.org	Children's health info
MakeupAlley.com	Consumer cosmetics reviews
MayoClinic.org	Medical info and definitions
MedicineNet.com	Medical info and definitions
MedlinePlus.gov	Medical info and definitions
NABP.net	National Association of Boards of Pharmacies
NCCAM.NIH.gov	Alternative health info and resources
PharmacyChecker.com	Price comparison for online pharmacies
Pollen.com	Local pollen forecasts
SmartSkinCare.com	Reviews of skin care products
WebMD.com	Medical info and definitions

>> SECTION ICON LEGEND

Use the following guide to understand the rectangular icons that appear throughout this section.

ALL-NATURAL PRODUCTS
Many products available in Health & Beauty have been made without the inclusion of any chemical agents. This icon makes them easier to find.

MEN'S GROOMING
Most of the Beauty sites and some of the Health-oriented shops focus on products designed largely for women. To make it easier for men, this icon lets you know when male items, like cologne, shaving gear, toiletries, hair treatments and various skin care products, are available.

HEALTH
With the vast number of grooming and cosmetics sites out there, it can be easy to lose sight of the health-related shops. This icon should help them stand out a bit.

WOMEN'S BEAUTY
This icon will turn up a lot, and hopefully women will revel in the great variety of cosmetics, fragrances and skin care products available to them. Men, however, may wish to avoid these sites whenever possible.

 ## LIST OF KEY WORDS

The following words represent the types of items typically found on the sites listed in this section. You will find them listed in the orange strip at the bottom of each entry, as appropriate.

ALTERNATIVE	If you prefer ancient healing, all-natural and/or homeopathic treatments to modern medicine, check out the sites noted by this key word.
BATH & BODY	Soap is about as basic as it gets in this selection of products aimed at making you feel clean, soft and aromatic.
CHRONIC	Ranging from poor vision to aching joints, a bad back, allergies, asthma and high blood pressure, these are conditions that just won't go away, and you'll find treatments on these sites.
COSMETICS	Makeup, including nail polish, foundation, mascara, eyeliner, blush, lipstick and more.
DENTAL CARE	Your teeth will thank you for visiting these sites, especially if you've been going through our Epicurean section.
FRAGRANCES	You can't download a fragrance, but you can definitely buy perfumes, colognes, incense and other aromatic items online.
GROOMING	From shaving to clipping your toenails and plucking your eyebrows, this key word marks sites that help keep you clean-cut.
HAIR CARE	Shampoo and conditioner are just the beginning; there are also plenty of salon and styling products on these sites, and some baldness prevention/cures.
PHARMACY	These are sites that will grant you online access to prescription medications, sometimes at better prices than you'll find elsewhere.
SEXUAL CARE	There are plenty of birth control options on these sites, including condoms and pills, but there are also some more intriguing, adult-oriented items....
SKIN CARE	If you want to put your best face forward, there are plenty of sites offering high-quality skin care treatments, ranging from moisturizers and exfoliants to cleansers and toners.
SUPPLEMENTS	Vitamins, herbs and various other supplemental products are available to help improve your health and/or achieve personal, physical goals like losing weight, gaining muscle or quitting smoking.

KEY WORD INDEX

Use the followings lists to locate online retailers that sell the health and beauty products you seek.

ALTERNATIVE

BigelowChemists.com
CosmeticMall.com
eBubbles.com
Elixir.net
Fragrance.net
InterNatural.com
LEF.org
MakeMeHeal.com
NaturalUnity.com
RelaxDepot.com
SaffronRouge.com
SmallFlower.com
TheOrganicPharmacy.com
VitaCost.com

BATH & BODY

Aedes.com
BathSplendor.com
Bathtopia.com
BeautyExclusive.com
BeautyHabit.com
BeautyMark.ca
BeautyOfASite.com
BeBeautiful.com
BigelowChemists.com
BlissWorld.com
Body-Systems.net
CarolsDaughter.com
CosBar.com
CosmeticMall.com
DHCCare.com
DiamondBeauty.com
Drugstore.com
eBubbles.com
eGentlemen.com
Folica.com
FourSeasonsProducts.com
HQHair.com
LadyPrimrose.com
LafcoNY.com
MensEssentials.com
NaturalUnity.com
OleHenriksen.com
RelaxDepot.com
SaffronRouge.com

BATH & BODY (cont.)

SAMSoap.com
Sephora.com
SkinStore.com
SmallFlower.com
Sophee.com
SpaLook.com
SpiralHairCase.com
TheBodyDeli.com
TheOrganicPharmacy.com
VitaCost.com

CHRONIC

AllergyBuyersClub.com
Elixir.net
EyeSave.com
FootSmart.com
HealthCheckSystems.com
LEF.org
NationalAllergySupply.com
RelaxTheBack.com

COSMETICS

BeautyMark.ca
BeautyOfASite.com
BeBeautiful.com
BigelowChemists.com
BlissWorld.com
CosBar.com
CosmeticMall.com
DiamondBeauty.com
EyesLipsFace.com
FourSeasonsProducts.com
Gloss.com
HQHair.com
MakeUpHeaven.com
NaturalUnity.com
SaffronRouge.com
Sephora.com
SkinStore.com
SmallFlower.com
StrawberryNet.co.uk
VarnishNails.com

DENTAL CARE

BigelowChemists.com
ClassicShaving.com
DentalDepot.com
DermaDoctor.com
NaturalUnity.com
SaffronRouge.com
SkinStore.com
SmallFlower.com

FRAGRANCES

Aedes.com
BathSplendor.com
BeautyExclusive.com
BeautyHabit.com
BigelowChemists.com
Body-Systems.net
CarolsDaughter.com
CosBar.com
CosmeticMall.com
DHCCare.com
DiamondBeauty.com
eBubbles.com
FourSeasonsProducts.com
Fragonard.com
Fragrance.net
Gloss.com
HQHair.com
LadyPrimrose.com
LafcoNY.com
LusciousCargo.com
NaturalUnity.com
Penhaligons.com
RelaxDepot.com
Sephora.com
SpaLook.com
StrawberryNet.co.uk
TheOrganicPharmacy.com

GROOMING

AfroWorld.com
BeautyHabit.com
BeautyOfASite.com
BeBeautiful.com
BigelowChemists.com
BlissWorld.com
ClassicShaving.com
CosBar.com
CosmeticMall.com
DermaDoctor.com
DiamondBeauty.com
Drugstore.com
eBubbles.com
eGentlemen.com
Folica.com
HQHair.com
MensEssentials.com
NaturalUnity.com
Penhaligons.com
SaffronRouge.com
Sephora.com
ShavingCream.com
SkinStore.com
SmallFlower.com
SpaLook.com
SpiralHairCase.com
TheShaveBeverlyHills.com
VarnishNails.com

HAIR CARE

AfroWorld.com
BeautyExclusive.com
BeautyHabit.com
BeautyMark.ca
BeautyOfASite.com
BeBeautiful.com
BigelowChemists.com
BlissWorld.com
CarolsDaughter.com
ClassicShaving.com
CosBar.com
CosmeticMall.com
CurlMart.com
DermaDoctor.com
DHCCare.com
DiamondBeauty.com
Drugstore.com
eGentlemen.com
Folica.com
FourSeasonsProducts.com
Fragrance.net
HQHair.com
LadyPrimrose.com

HAIR CARE (cont.)

MakeMeHeal.com
MensEssentials.com
NaturalUnity.com
SaffronRouge.com
Sephora.com
SkinStore.com
SmallFlower.com
Sophee.com
SpiralHairCase.com
TheOrganicPharmacy.com
TheShaveBeverlyHills.com

PHARMACY

CanadaMeds.com
DermaDoctor.com
Drugstore.com

SEXUAL CARE

Condomania.com
DermaDoctor.com
Drugstore.com
Elixir.net
LEF.org
MakeMeHeal.com
WorldHealthProducts.com

SKIN CARE

Aedes.com
AfroWorld.com
BathSplendor.com
Bathtopia.com
BeautyExclusive.com
BeautyHabit.com
BeautyMark.ca
BeautyOfASite.com
BeBeautiful.com
BigelowChemists.com
BlissWorld.com
Body-Systems.net
Borba.net
CarolsDaughter.com
CosBar.com
CosmeticMall.com
DermaDoctor.com
DHCCare.com
DiamondBeauty.com
Drugstore.com
eBubbles.com

SKIN CARE (cont.)

eGentlemen.com
Folica.com
FourSeasonsProducts.com
Fragrance.net
Gloss.com
HQHair.com
LadyPrimrose.com
LEF.org
LipMedic.com
MakeMeHeal.com
MensEssentials.com
NaturalUnity.com
OleHenriksen.com
RelaxDepot.com
SaffronRouge.com
SAMSoap.com
Sephora.com
SkinStore.com
SkinTerra.com
SmallFlower.com
Sophee.com
SpaLook.com
SpiralHairCase.com
StrawberryNet.co.uk
TheBodyDeli.com
TheOrganicPharmacy.com
WorldHealthProducts.com

SUPPLEMENTS

Borba.net
Elixir.net
InterNatural.com
LEF.org
SaffronRouge.com
SmallFlower.com
TheOrganicPharmacy.com
VitaCost.com
VitaminShoppe.com
WorldHealthProducts.com

Aedes.com

Aedes De Venustus · 212-206-8674

The high-end fragrances, skin care and bath-and-body products available from this site will ensure that any woman leaves a lovely bouquet in her wake. Within each category, you may choose from a lengthy list of brands, each with a fine and distinctive scent. However, by following the Try Before You Buy link, you can order samples of any fragrance that intrigues you to make sure you love it before making a larger investment. The skin care and bath items will require a bit more faith.

·BATH & BODY	·FRAGRANCES	·SKIN CARE	

AfroWorld.com

Afro World · 800-228-9424

For women of African origins, hairstyling has become at once an art form and a science unto itself. Of all styles, probably the easiest to cultivate is the Afro, which, contrary to the site's name, is not accommodated here. Rather, categories like Weaving, Bonding & Fusion Supplies feature hair extensions in a wide assortment of colors, shapes and textures, while elsewhere on the site you can find products and information to aid in braids, twists, dreadlocks or any combination thereof, as well as some general shaving and skin care items. Finding what you want isn't too difficult, considering that the really hard part comes after delivery.

·GROOMING	·HAIR CARE	·SKIN CARE	

AllergyBuyersClub.com

AllergyBuyersClub.com · 888-236-7231

Sneezing is fun the first few times you do it; after that it becomes a lifetime nuisance. Puffy eyes, asthma and skin rashes are awful from the start, so if you experience any of these symptoms due to allergies, this specialized health retailer proves to be more necessity than luxury. The focus here is not in stopping your body's reaction to allergens, but in removing them from your home environment, particularly dust mites, molds and pollens that overload the air, get into your rugs and cling to your bedding. This site blesses you before you sneeze.

·CHRONIC			

BathSplendor.com

Bath Splendor · 800-576-0771

If the thought of animal testing on bath and body products gives you frown lines, check out this Chicago-based aggregator of humane, American-made soaps, lotions, shaving products and bath additives. You can shop by product type, skin type or brand name, but the most satisfying shopping experience may be found using the Fragrance menu. It's remarkable just how many scents you can add to your bath, and if you look closely you'll discover interesting additional benefits to each one, for instance that Gardenia "promotes spirituality" and Peppermint "Promotes energy and mental clarity." It's a heck of a way to relax.

·BATH & BODY	·FRAGRANCES	·SKIN CARE	

888-717-2284 · Bathtopia
Bathtopia.com

If you love to be pampered, even when it's you doing the pampering, this proves a great site to find a unique assortment of sumptuous bath and spa products designed with both comfort and style in mind. The beautiful packaging alone will win you over, and at the very least will make for a great gift. However, you wouldn't want to bestow a gift like this upon a good friend unless you'd first tested it out on yourself to ensure quality. It's only the right thing to do.

·BATH & BODY	·SKIN CARE			

888-874-6723 · Beauty Exclusive
BeautyExclusive.com

It's always been our understanding that beauty is nonexclusive; however, if you pick up a few of these products you might just get an edge up. Primarily through the use of natural ingredients, this assortment of spa-oriented skin, hair, footcare, bath additives and body products does not typically turn up in your local beauty shop, nor even on most comparable web retailers, which is a shame, given the beautiful packaging. Brands like Tocca Beauty, Roger & Gallet and Eskander are probably a bit more familiar in Europe; but even there, only the beauty products, not the concept, are proprietary.

·BATH & BODY	·FRAGRANCES	·HAIR CARE	·SKIN CARE	

800-377-8771 · BeautyHabit.com
BeautyHabit.com

Beauty is indeed an addicting pursuit, and the trouble is, it's an appetite that just gets tougher to satisfy as time passes. Offering "only the finest and most sought after personal care products from all over the world," this site might just help you stay on a steady diet of bath-and-body products, cosmetics, skin cleansers, tonics, shampoos and conditioners, sun protection and fragrances. Granted, this can be a pricey habit to get started on, but if you opt for the best products now, you may be able to avoid some really expensive treatments a few years down the line.

·BATH & BODY ·SKIN CARE	·FRAGRANCES	·GROOMING	·HAIR CARE	

877-823-2889 · Beautymark
BeautyMark.ca

Here's another fine site with a wide range of upper-end cosmetics and beauty products (we found a whole lot of these). However, this one's from Canada, which alone makes it exotic enough to mention. More importantly, it offers some quite desirable brands that are hard to come by online, let alone domestically. If names like Jing Jang, Monyette Paris, Paula Dorf, Principessa and Savasana don't mean anything to you, then you can take this site or leave it. If, however, you've been looking all over for these product lines, your search is over.

·COSMETICS	·BATH & BODY	·HAIR CARE	·SKIN CARE	

BeautyOfASite.com

If you like to shop for your beauty products based on magazine recommendations, perhaps you will enjoy this site, which offers an As Seen In the Press section, wherein you can view monthly selections from *InStyle*, *Allure*, *Lucky*, *Cosmopolitan*, *Glamour* and *Elle*. Or, you can view a list of celebrities and learn about products you could use to emulate their looks. Lastly, you could shop through the standard means, by category and brand, but what's the fun in that?

·COSMETICS ·SKIN CARE	·BATH & BODY	·GROOMING	·HAIR CARE

BeBeautiful.com

When this internet retailer offers "a vast selection of the most advanced, top-of-the-line professional beauty products," it's not playing around. The site claims most of the products here are the same brands used by spas and salons all over the country, and if you check out the Spa and Professional categories you'll see what that means. But the other sections are worth a look as well, whether you stop in Skincare, Haircare, Hand & Nail, Pedicure, Makeup or Tanning. The site can load slowly and be difficult to use at times, but wouldn't judging that just be superficial?

·COSMETICS ·SKIN CARE	·BATH & BODY	·GROOMING	·HAIR CARE

BigelowChemists.com

The very fact that this shop refers to itself as a chemist clues you in to its age, but get this: it also claims to be "the oldest apothecary in America." For more than 160 years, this New York City West Village store has been serving locals and knowing visitors with tried-and-true beauty, grooming and homeopathy products, both procured elsewhere and of its own devise. It's spent considerably less time online, and it shows, as navigation consists of easily misunderstood category names and lengthy brand lists. These brands, however, are known to be good ones, as many of them have been pleasing customers for decades.

·COSMETICS ·GROOMING	·BATH & BODY ·HAIR CARE	·ALTERNATIVE ·DENTAL CARE	·FRAGRANCES ·SKIN CARE

BlissWorld.com

If you're a fan of spas, but just can't seem to get away these days, leave it to the internet to bring the cleansing and relaxing features of a spa to you. Based on Bliss Spas, located on the East Coast, this site features products you might be pampered with during body or skin care treatments at one of their facilities. You will also find a selection of makeup and beauty tools designed to keep you looking hip and beautiful. The site isn't entirely easy to use, but when you compare it to the utter indulgence you could be experiencing in a day spa, really, what could possibly match up?

·COSMETICS ·SKIN CARE	·BATH & BODY	·GROOMING	·HAIR CARE

605-484-6742 · Body Systems Company

For spa products as fresh as your produce, check out this South Dakota company's line of exfoliants, moisturizers, cleansers, toners, bath additives and aromatherapy products. "Passionate about providing only natural products made fresh for each order," the company provides a lengthy list of favorite ingredients, including some extracted from roses, hemp seeds, eucalyptus, jojoba, bamboo, ginseng, pomegranate and sage. This appetizing variety of seeds, salts, waxes, clays and oils scrubs and soothes even the most sensitive skins without any reaction stronger than a lovely aroma.

·BATH & BODY	·FRAGRANCES	·SKIN CARE	

212-239-4531 · Borba

This skin care line springs from the philosophy, "the key to true beauty is found in the right melding of the inner and outer person." Hence the line's Cosmeceuticals and Nutraceuticals, external and internal skin treatments designed to clear, firm and replenish skin. Treated water and fortified gummi candies compliment more standard cleansers and creams to take a holistic approach to your dermologic care, with natural active ingredients such as lychee, acai, green tea, cherimoya and pomegranate to add flavor as well as skin tone.

·SUPPLEMENTS	·SKIN CARE		

877-542-3330 · CanadaMeds.com

Because the Canadian government regulates the cost of prescription drugs, we "can save up to 90%" of the cost for the same medication in US markets by shopping from Canadian pharmacies, such as this one. While finding your particular drug here is easy, the ordering process gets rather complicated, as you must fax a prescription and fill out questionnaires with your order, after which the site's staff will contact your doctor, meaning you may have to wait several weeks before receiving your medication. In most cases you'll want to order locally, but if you want to save some serious money on long-term prescriptions, this is the place to do it.

·PHARMACY			

718-857-0282 · Carol's Daughter

Described as a "labor of love," this homegrown line of beauty products started as one woman's experiments at making perfume in her kitchen. Well, the experiments apparently smelled too good to resist, and now, thanks to the advent of online business, it's expanded into a family-and-friend-operated venture, selling unique self-made bath treatments, multiple fragrances, massage oils, aromatherapy items and plenty of products for hair and skin. Not as notable as, say, Chanel, but why smell like everybody else anyway?

·BATH & BODY	·FRAGRANCES	·HAIR CARE	·SKIN CARE

ClassicShaving.com

ClassicShaving.com · 760-288-4178

The advent of disposable and electric razors have taken all the romance out of what used to be a very classy gesture. If you or someone you love still view shaving as a sign of sophistication, do not miss the fantastic selection of straight razors, strops, hones, shaving brushes and mugs available on this web site, which was "established in response to the current worldwide rediscovery of and increased interest in classic traditional wet shaving methods and products." The often beautiful items actually do a great job cutting a close shave, and plenty of instructional articles found within these pages should help you avoid any more serious cuts.

·GROOMING	·HAIR CARE	·DENTAL CARE	

Condomania.com

Condomania · 800-926-6366

We're not sure that anyone's ever exhibited a mania for condoms, but if buying the right condom can improve the quality of your sex life, this site sure is something to get excited about. Chief among reasons to shop here is selection, with nearly two dozen brands represented, featuring latex and nonlatex varieties, different colors, pleasure producing shapes, a wide range of sizes and even a few female condoms. But if you really want something special, download the Fit Kit and measure yourself to order from "the world's first Sized-to-Fit condom line." It's remarkable how fun safe can be.

·SEXUAL CARE			

CosBar.com

The Cos Bar · 800-722-8982

If you'd like to cut through all the excess beauty products in the world to look at a selective group of only the best, do what visitors to Aspen, Vail, Maui and Santa Fe have done for years: shop at The Cos Bar. The small chain of boutiques is known for its devotion to quality skin care that will stand up to the rigors of sun, wind and snow. Makeup, fragrances, bath and body products round out a selection that features top brands such as Chanel, Laura Mercier, Lancôme, Origins and Yves Saint Laurent at prices that are tough to beat.

·COSMETICS ·HAIR CARE	·BATH & BODY ·SKIN CARE	·FRAGRANCES	·GROOMING

CosmeticMall.com

CosmeticMall.com · 800-805-5493

We just knew we were going to love this all-over beauty supersite when we saw they carry New York City's infamous Frozen Hot Chocolate by Serendipity. What the cold, sweet beverage has to do with skin care, hair, body, fragrance or cosmetics products is besides the point; we just like the style. As it turns out, the shop carries a seemingly limitless number of products from hundreds of the most popular and lesser-known brand names of beauty, from low-end items to the very expensive. You should have no trouble finding your inner beauty with this one's help.

·COSMETICS ·GROOMING	·BATH & BODY ·HAIR CARE	·ALTERNATIVE ·SKIN CARE	·FRAGRANCES

512-371-7545 · NaturallyCurly.com

CurlMart.com

Do you ever feel as if your naturally curly hair warrants special attention? This site wholeheartedly agrees, offering a vast array of hair care products designed specifically with the full-bodied coif in mind. Of course, any straight heads that have caught on to the beauty of curls will find perm-friendly treatments among these shampoos, conditioners, gels, lotions, creams and oils. Shop wisely for your most reliable brand names and when you walk down the street you will undoubtedly receive all the attention you deserve.

·HAIR CARE

800-210-5897 · DentalDepot.com

DentalDepot.com

Recognizing "that most stores do not carry complete lines of dental products," the Massachusetts dentist behind this web retailer put together an inventory filled with all the products he'd been recommending to his patients over the years. Much more than just toothpaste and dental floss, you'll find categories devoted to Waterpiks, Interdental Brushes, Tongue Care, Electric Brushes, Stimulators, Xerostomia (Dry Mouth) and Halitosis. This could save you a lot of future time in the dentist's chair.

·DENTAL CARE

877-337-6237 · DERMAdoctor.com

DermaDoctor.com

Striving "to bring you the latest in proven skin care technology and provide information and products to help you achieve healthy skin," this specialty site has the backing of a qualified dermatologist to win your trust. As if that weren't enough, the site is filled with an unbelievable amount of reading about every conceivable skin and hair topic, but if you still can't find the answers you're looking for, you may type in specific questions and await a professional's response. Oh yeah, first and foremost this is a web store, with a wealth of reliable products you may browse by brand name, product type or condition, but by the time you get around to shopping you'll practically be an expert yourself.

·GROOMING ·SKIN CARE	·HAIR CARE ·PHARMACY	·SEXUAL CARE	·DENTAL CARE

800-342-2273 · DHC

DHCCare.com

Inspired by the many benefits of olive oil, this Japanese mail-order skin care company promotes "an ideal balance that can bring harmony to any skin type." Not surprising in itself, but what's a bit stunning is just how diverse a selection of products such thinking can lead to. Categories like Skincare, Hair Care, Body Care, Fragrance and Makeup are each filled with a tasty selection of products including ingredients such as ginseng, cucumber, rosemary and green tea. Of course, these are beauty products we're talking about, but if they should make you hungry, there is a tiny Fine Foods section that should tide you over until dinner.

·BATH & BODY	·FRAGRANCES	·HAIR CARE	·SKIN CARE

DiamondBeauty.com
Diamond Beauty · 800-669-6638

If you've ever looked at a celebrity and wondered, "How does she manage to look like that?" you might be able to find out on this site. With hundreds of brands available, you can search through them each and find out what famous faces fancy their products, or you can search through an extensive list of celebrities and click on those that have made you wonder. The site is a little hectic at first, but it's easy to figure out where everything is, whether you want to peruse the glossary of beauty terms or learn about the past hundred years of beauty history. Finally, you can take part in regular chat sessions, so you can talk about it all with experts and gossip with fellow beauty fans.

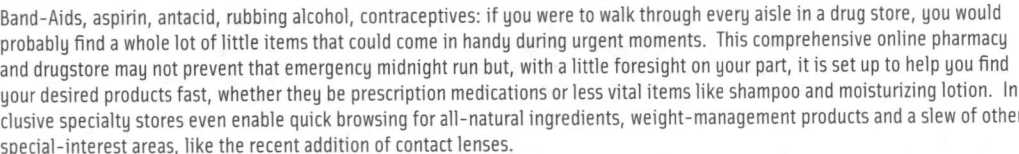

·COSMETICS ·HAIR CARE	·BATH & BODY ·SKIN CARE	·FRAGRANCES	·GROOMING

Drugstore.com
Drugstore.com · 800-378-4786

Band-Aids, aspirin, antacid, rubbing alcohol, contraceptives: if you were to walk through every aisle in a drug store, you would probably find a whole lot of little items that could come in handy during urgent moments. This comprehensive online pharmacy and drugstore may not prevent that emergency midnight run but, with a little foresight on your part, it is set up to help you find your desired products fast, whether they be prescription medications or less vital items like shampoo and moisturizing lotion. Inclusive specialty stores even enable quick browsing for all-natural ingredients, weight-management products and a slew of other special-interest areas, like the recent addition of contact lenses.

·BATH & BODY ·SKIN CARE	·GROOMING ·PHARMACY	·HAIR CARE	·SEXUAL CARE

eBubbles.com
eBubbles.com · 888-403-8701

If a bubble bath seems like the greatest form of luxury you can imagine, visit this bath, body and spa specialist for some ideas that meet and expand upon the notion. With nods to aromatherapy, massage and the intriguing "fizzies," relaxation takes many forms here, and with dozens of enticing product categories, if you're not careful you may run out of water. The best thing about this shop is that it offers the ultimate in indulgence for quite reasonable prices, so there's nothing to say you can't relax almost every minute of the day.

·BATH & BODY ·SKIN CARE	·ALTERNATIVE	·FRAGRANCES	·GROOMING

eGentlemen.com
eGentlemen · 323-269-7943

Gentlemen never discuss their romantic conquests, but even less so do they discuss their grooming regimens. Online shops always keep your secrets, so you may discreetly fill your medicine cabinet with hair-styling products, antiaging treatments, facial scrubs, body lotions, moisturizers and bronzers (even a few concealers—shhh). Easier to talk about is the very masculine selection of top-tier shaving products, including anything from brushes and shaving creams to preshave oils and aftershave ointments. After all, the well-kempt gentleman is more likely to have something not to talk about.

·BATH & BODY	·GROOMING	·HAIR CARE	·SKIN CARE

310-657-9300 · Elixir Tonics & Teas

Elixir.net

This site may be the modern-day version of traveling shysters selling tonic and elixir "miracle cures" out of the backs of horse-drawn wagons. Then again, this could be the dawn of a new era in American health care, one in which people are becoming increasingly disenchanted with insurance and pharmaceutical companies, and are ready to turn to some long-standing and natural remedies for minor ailments. The answer probably lies in your willingness to pursue this course of therapy, combined with your body's ability to sustain a healthy and natural balance. Either way, these guys are here, and their products are available, and you might just feel better knowing so.

·ALTERNATIVE	·SUPPLEMENTS	·SEXUAL CARE	·CHRONIC	

888-821-7283 · Eyesave

EyeSave.com

Once associated with nerdiness, in the modern era glasses are known to make people look smart, mostly because they're associated with reading. Well, whether or not the association is warranted, this site's specialty happens to be reading glasses, and its selection is certainly not lacking in smart-looking frames. Check out a variety of reading glasses categories like Half-Readers, for the otherwise well sighted; Folding Readers, for those on the go; Budget Readers, for the fiscally smart; and Sun Readers, which features great-looking shades, so you can read at the beach and still look cool in the process.

·CHRONIC				

800-231-4732 · e.l.f.

EyesLipsFace.com

For some reason, in all the business world, cosmetics companies in particular are prone to mixing a bit of metaphysical outlook into their business plans. So far as corporate philosophies go, this one's "beauty comes from within" isn't the most original. Fortunately, the line of accompanying products are designed to work on external beauty, with eye, lip, nail and face makeup. Perhaps more importantly, the lip liners, nail lacquers, mascaras, bronzing powders and associated tools are some of the best bargains in the world of cosmetics.

·COSMETICS				

888-919-4247 · Folica Beauty Supply Stores Online

Folica.com

Whether you're trying to straighten, curl, remove, regenerate, clean, condition, color, relax or shape your hair, this site can help in a big way. You'll find an amazing selection of hair gels, mousses, spritzes, sprays, pomades, shampoos, conditioners, dyes, tools and appliances. On the flip side are waxes, razors, depilatories, tweezers, bleaches and electrolysis tools. The same diligence is applied to bath-and-body and skin care items for both men and women, ensuring that customers of this web superstore have nary a hair out of place, nor any patch of skin untended.

·BATH & BODY	·GROOMING	·HAIR CARE	·SKIN CARE	

FootSmart.com

Foot Smart · 800-230-4077

Feet are only the beginning for this retailer specializing in "smarter, better products for lower body health." Orthopedic shoes, insoles and arch supports head up an incredibly thorough selection of physical remedies for foot pain, corns, bunions and foot odor, but the product categories continue upward, covering the ankles, calves, knees and on up to the back. While your head might not be explicitly covered, the bottom line is that every structural part of your body will feel better as a result of shopping here, saving you any number of headaches.

·CHRONIC			

FourSeasonsProducts.com

Four Seasons · 800-555-8082

When you get tired of seeing the same set of beauty products everywhere you look, pay a visit to this very worldly web shop. Although at first glance it seems like your standard, well-assembled bath, cosmetics, hair and skin care boutique, a deeper look reveals various product lines you never see anywhere else. These international brand names may not be especially trendy or over-hyped as competing selections, but by and large they have been doing the beauty thing longer than most, incorporating natural products when it wasn't cool to do so, and using a whole-body approach to help you achieve a glow not usually associated with one who shops on a computer.

·COSMETICS ·SKIN CARE	·BATH & BODY	·FRAGRANCES	·HAIR CARE

Fragonard.com

Fragonard · 011-33-92-42-34-34

Possessing the "secrets of the creation of perfume, mysteries of a magical knowledge, from antiquity to the present," this Parisian parfumeur has been turning out some of the world's finest fragrances for eighty years. Here, its online Boutique offers the new along with the tried and true, each portrayed with rich, detailed descriptions that seem to have been concocted with as much inspiration as the scents themselves. The result is perfume shopping that proves surprisingly enticing considering smells cannot currently be downloaded. When in doubt, just remember, it's French.

·FRAGRANCES			

Fragrance.net

Fragrance.net · 800-987-3738

With "over 5,000 brand name fragrances, skin care" and other items, free shipping, gift wrapping and free gifts with each purchase, there are plenty of reasons to buy perfume and cologne from this site, if you're going to buy online at all. Boasting "no imitations," this might just be the most thorough selection of original fragrances anywhere. What's more, they offer a wide array of mini sizes as well. This may be a good idea, as you can buy a selection of samples to try out before spending big money on the regular sizes. Finally, a decent way to avoid the guerrilla tactics of perfume counters.

·ALTERNATIVE	·FRAGRANCES	·HAIR CARE	·SKIN CARE

888-550-4567 · GLOSS

Gloss.com

Though it initially seems as feminine as can be, we were somewhat surprised to find a small but valuable stash of men's hygiene and fragrance products on this site (you may have to look under Gifts to find it). Ladies will have an easier time finding cosmetics, skin care and fragrances by the likes of Chanel, Estée Lauder, Clinique, M-A-C and Bobbi Brown, among others. Male or female, it's hard to go wrong here.

·COSMETICS	·FRAGRANCES	·SKIN CARE	

718-339-5570 · HealthCheck Systems

HealthCheckSystems.com

Keeping track of heart rate, blood pressure and body fat index is an integral part of a healthy routine for some people, and technology can help. This health monitor specialist offers digital tools to help with these and other tasks, including glucose monitors, insulin injectors, cholesterol gauges, thermometers, otoscopes, nebulizers and scales. Chances are, if you know what some of these things are, you or someone you love could use the device for daily use, and should be able to find one at a reasonable price here.

·CHRONIC				

011-44-20-7292-8770 · HQHair

HQHair.com

Hair gets the greatest attention from this UK salon turned online retailer, but it's by no means where the product selection ends. Categories include Beauty & Skincare, Shave & Groom, Accessories and Electrical, and though many different product types are encompassed by each, this is where the organization ends. Unless you're aiming for a specific brand name. While you'll find a host of the regular suspects, there are also a few lines represented here that are much harder to find on this side of the Atlantic, making this a great place to go for those special products you've thus far only heard about.

·COSMETICS ·HAIR CARE	·BATH & BODY ·SKIN CARE	·FRAGRANCES	·GROOMING

800-643-4221 · Internatural

InterNatural.com

This alternative health superstore has been in business for more than two decades, and thus is "NOT new to the industry trying to make some fast bucks as part of the 'Internet boom,'" and it shows. Rather, these guys are quite serious about the aromatherapy, biomagnetics, massage therapy, herbal supplements and other natural healing products they carry, to the point that the massive selection is underscored by a wealth of information. Unfortunately, there's neither a pill you can take nor an incense to burn that will make browsing easy, so you may want to meditate on the virtue of patience before you log on.

·ALTERNATIVE	·SUPPLEMENTS		

LadyPrimrose.com

The art of packaging perfumes has been around almost as long as the fragrances themselves, and you won't find anyone that does it better than this English company, which bears the full name Lady Primrose's Royal Bathing & Skin Luxuries. A luxe variety of moisturizers, bath salts, shower gels and of course fragrances boast the "highest quality contents, which include royal jelly, honey, lactic acid and crushed silk." Prices are remarkably fair, especially when you consider the beautiful crystal decanters, jars, urns and pumps that contain them. Whether you refill them with Lady Primrose products, or something from another line altogether, nothing will look better on your vanity table.

·BATH & BODY	·FRAGRANCES	·HAIR CARE	·SKIN CARE

LafcoNY.com

The New York boutique behind this site offers exclusive soap, bath and fragrance products from internationally renowned lines Trilogy, Maria Novella, Lorenzo Villoresi and Claus Porto. Finding these products elsewhere will prove quite the difficult task, and the truth of the matter is, actually finding the products on this convoluted and inconsistent site is darn near impossible. Rest assured, they're in there, somewhere, and if you're familiar with these aromatic beauty items you'll know why it's worth looking.

·BATH & BODY	·FRAGRANCES		

LEF.org

It turns out LEF stands for the Life Extension Foundation, which is a tough concept to argue with. While they have a plethora of great items geared toward this goal, it's very easy to get distracted by an abundance of health-related news and articles. Look for the Product Finder, to select from one of many topics, such as Skin Care, Weight Management, Anti-Aging and Growth Hormones. Okay, some sections may be worth avoiding, but others are can't-miss.

·ALTERNATIVE ·CHRONIC	·SUPPLEMENTS	·SEXUAL CARE	·SKIN CARE

LipMedic.com

With "over 500 lip balms in more than 100 fantastic flavors," this site without a doubt has your lips covered. Shopping by flavor turns up such tantalizing tastes as cantaloupe, cranberry, ginger mango, passion fruit, pear, pomegranate, pineapple and chai, and that's not even taking into consideration the many more interesting balms to be found in the Exotic & Foreign section. Browsing the fantastic assortment can be fun and very affordable, and it's made all the better with the help of customer reviews that let you know whether a particular tube, jar or tin is as delicious as it sounds. Pucker up.

·SKIN CARE			

770-886-6202 · Luscious

LusciousCargo.com

Who knows what nefarious means cosmetics counters have for selecting their fragrances? Are there kickbacks? Backroom deals? It can make you wonder. But there's no wondering with this site; its founder has a nose for scents, an obsession with aroma dating back to childhood, and pays close attention to every smell she comes across. The best make it to this site, which offers perfumes, body oils and sprays, or as the site slogan goes: "Swank Fragrances & Gifts." This one's worth shopping for all the right reasons.

·FRAGRANCES

866-363-4325 · Make Me Heal

MakeMeHeal.com

As of this writing there isn't a way to have cosmetic surgery performed online. As we've discovered with this site, however, you can find products to aid in the recovery from such procedures. Whether you've been the recipient of skin treatment, body augmentation, body reduction, hair replacement or any anatomical reconstruction, there are plenty of products here to promote quicker healing, minimize scarring, alleviate discomfort and provide physical support to vulnerable areas. Chances are, your doctor will tell you what you might need, and with easy browsing categories you should have no trouble finding it here.

·ALTERNATIVE | ·HAIR CARE | ·SEXUAL CARE | ·SKIN CARE

904-655-7744 · Makeup Heaven

MakeUpHeaven.com

If you're into makeup, particularly into trying new makeup, but generally rely on the recommendations of your girlfriends, this site may prove valuable to you. All the products offered here represent hip, well-received cosmetics brands. More importantly, all have been tried out by the self-described "makeup junkies" who run the site, so you know they come recommended by people who have an idea of what they're talking about. Now you can be the one making the recommendations.

·COSMETICS

877-449-6599 · MenEssentials Corporation

MensEssentials.com

Men aren't generally known for their devotion to hair, body or skin care products, and as a result options are limited in local markets. This site offers a tremendous selection of male-specific products to be delivered wherever you live. A Shop By Skin Type function helps you narrow down the wealth of options, and clear organization makes it otherwise easy to order the products you need, which is great, because sometimes it's easier not to buy this stuff in person.

·BATH & BODY | ·GROOMING | ·HAIR CARE | ·SKIN CARE

NationalAllergySupply.com

National Allergy Supply, Inc. · 800-522-1448

Allergies are the bane of many an existence, and any sufferer has undoubtedly been through the full cornucopia of prescription and over-the-counter remedies. While you'll find a rich assortment of such products on this site, most of the selection is based on the premise that "the reduction of airborne contaminants is the number one method of relieving allergy symptoms." Hence, this company focuses more on air filters, HEPA vacuums, humidity controls and a host of hypoallergenic products including personal care treatments, bedding and household cleaners. One thing's for sure: if you can fight allergens without having to take any more pills you'll breathe easier.

 ·CHRONIC

NaturalUnity.com

Natural Unity · 011-845-0602-8805

Citing the statistic that "sixty percent of what we put on our skin finds its way into the bloodstream" as "reason enough" to stick to natural and organic products, this UK site is as convincing as it is thorough. Cosmetics, dental care, toiletries, sun block, hair care, depilatories, massage oils, herbal tinctures, lip balms, essential oils and first-aid products pick up where comparable skin care specialists leave off. Of course, the bath-and-body selection is so complete even men may take advantage of the all-natural selection, which is rare as some of the hard-to-find brand names available here.

·COSMETICS ·GROOMING	·BATH & BODY ·HAIR CARE	·ALTERNATIVE ·DENTAL CARE	·FRAGRANCES ·SKIN CARE

OleHenriksen.com

Ole Henriksen Face/Body · 800-327-0331

Representing the "facialist to the stars," this simple, colorful and elegant site makes it easy to access some of the fine skin and body products relied upon by some of the most beautiful women in the world (Christy Turlington and Charlize Theron, for example), as well as some of the most photogenic men (Leonardo DiCaprio and Eminem). These products are heavenly for the hands, face, lips and eyes, and cleansing for the entire body. There may be no better way in LA.

·BATH & BODY	·SKIN CARE		

Penhaligons.com

Penhaligon's London · 877-736-4254

Founded in the late 19th century, this upscale British perfumer claims its products, "share a timeless elegance which represents a rich history whilst acknowledging a very contemporary taste for exclusive style." In other words, it's often hard to describe how things smell, but these perfumes and colognes come in beautiful bottles. Men and women are served equally well, with even a few unisex scents and home fragrances in candle, oil and potpourri forms, all from a lovely site with an easy-to-remember name.

·FRAGRANCES	·GROOMING		

888-207-3529 · Relax Depot

RelaxDepot.com

This could easily become your favorite site, especially if the stresses of everyday life leave you longing for respite. Massage products, sleep aids, bath additives, spa products, aromatherapy products and more fill this site with hundreds of ways to let the perils of the day to day melt into the background. While there's a lot here to consider and browsing in itself could prove a source of irritation, we're sure that, once you've ordered, just knowing help is on the way will give you some moments of relief.

·BATH & BODY	·ALTERNATIVE	·FRAGRANCES	·SKIN CARE

    (WISH)

800-222-5728 · Relax the Back

RelaxTheBack.com

Whether your daily routine consists of scouring the internet for the best in online retail, or something less strenuous, like heavy construction, it's quite likely that at the end of the day you could use a little recuperative therapy on the old back muscles. This site hears the creaking of your spine and has the answer...well, several answers, really. From braces and supports to massage products and ergonomic furniture, many of these products seem to have been specifically designed to elicit sighs of relief. You can't go wrong.

·CHRONIC			

866-322-3227 · Saffron Rouge

SaffronRouge.com

While you might typically associate the word *organic* with your grocer's produce section, this site proves that you can opt for sustainable beauty and health care, as well as fruits and vegetables. Products here delve into dental care, hair care, cosmetics, acne treatments and lip balms, all chemical free and never tested on animals. It's an incredibly slick site that arranges its products by category as well as brand name, but we mostly like it because it helps to make you feel good even as you look good.

·COSMETICS ·GROOMING	·BATH & BODY ·HAIR CARE	·ALTERNATIVE ·DENTAL CARE	·SUPPLEMENTS ·SKIN CARE

877-726-7627 · SAM Soap

SAMSoap.com

Anyone who is particularly picky about skin care products should enjoy this specialty site, which allows you to custom build your own soaps, scrubs and shower gels, right down to the name on the label. Using "only the finest quality herbs, nuts, clays and other ingredients from all over the world," the resulting all-natural products will suit your particular skin care needs and even your sense of smell. The custom ordering tools are pretty easy to use, but online consultations are available should you need one.

·BATH & BODY	·SKIN CARE		

Sephora.com

Sephora · 877-737-4672

With a different color of lipstick for every day of the year, the Sephora line of beauty products has grown into one of the world's most popular, largely due to the success of nonaggressive salesmanship in its stores. Forutnately, the site pushes a little harder, which ultimately will help you to navigate the thousands of products available, including those of the finest and best-known beautifying brands on the globe. One consumer-friendly Sephora trait does, however, remain: the price. In particular, if you're a fan of French cosmetics, you can find them here at drugstore prices. *Chouette!* This site sets the standard.

·COSMETICS ·HAIR CARE	·BATH & BODY ·SKIN CARE	·FRAGRANCES	·GROOMING

ShavingCream.com

ShavingCream.com · 877-326-8785

Thanks to the stodgy stocking practices of local drugstores, most men probably don't realize just how many diverse shaving products are available in the world. This site can single-handedly change all that with its superior selection of shaving creams, aftershave lotions and beautifully crafted razors. More than that, the site covers hair care, skin care, fragrances, sun care and body washes, making it a complete one-stop shop for the guy interested in something a little better than medicine-smelling foams and alcohol-infused aftershaves.

·GROOMING			

SkinStore.com

SkinStore.com · 888-586-7546

Founded by "a team of physicians who recognized that by using the internet they could bring dermatologist-created and recommended skin care products to a much larger audience," the fact this site boasts such expertly endorsed skin, hair and nail items could almost get lost in the massive size of the catalog. Fortunately, this is about the most user-friendly skin supersite we've seen, with products parsed by product type, skin condition, price range and active ingredients as well as brand name. Whether you seek makeup, better hygiene, stronger nails, fuller hair, treatment for mild conditions or simply radiant skin, make this shop your first stop.

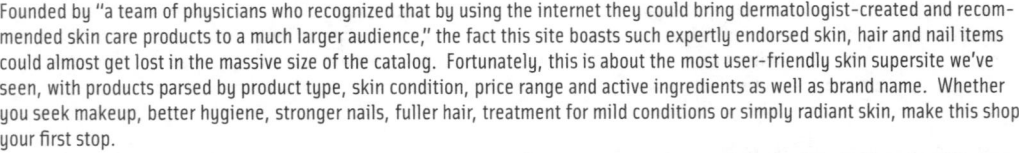

·COSMETICS ·DENTAL CARE	·BATH & BODY ·SKIN CARE	·GROOMING	·HAIR CARE

SkinTerra.com

Skinterra · 888-216-8174

This site will appeal to anybody who likes the idea of clean, pure and smooth skin—in other words, everybody. Simply fill out a brief survey about your own skin, and a customer service representative will contact you shortly to assist in your skin care purchases and regimen. If you'd rather get started right away, a shorter, less in-depth form will guide you to a range of products generally recommended for your skin type. The products themselves are high-end and very specific, ranging from acne treatments to antiaging treatments, with some masks, scrubs and moisturizers thrown in to aid in the quest for perfection.

·SKIN CARE			

800-252-0275 · **Merz Apothecary**

SmallFlower.com

While this Chicago apothecary has only been online for less than a decade, it's been in business for more than a century. Though the site is by no means technologically advanced, its selection has kept up with an ever-changing world of beauty and hygiene, without losing sight of the time-tested, all-natural toiletries, dental health, makeup, bath, skin and hair products that have helped the store flourish for so long. We're particularly glad to find them online as, frankly, we're not sure if their aging building can safely house the huge amount of health and personal care products we found here.

·COSMETICS ·GROOMING	·BATH & BODY ·HAIR CARE	·ALTERNATIVE ·DENTAL CARE	·SUPPLEMENTS ·SKIN CARE

877-867-6743 · **Sophee Corporation**

Sophee.com

As the metrosexual age commences, and the stigma of men's beauty products wanes, we're finding a lot more sites like this, which focus on male cleansers, creams, shampoos and lotions. If this stuff is new to you, don't be intimidated; a Tips & Trends section offers articles pertaining to different treatments and conditions, and if your needs aren't covered, an Expert Advice feature allows you to email specific questions to their in-house makeup artist. Relax—nobody's suggesting it's time for men to start wearing makeup… yet.

·BATH & BODY	·HAIR CARE	·SKIN CARE	

800-709-1865 · **Spalook**

SpaLook.com

There are literally thousands of beauty, bath and skin care products on the market, and nearly as many sites selling them. This one may not offer the most products, and it may not offer all the best products, but it fits nicely in between, offering great quality at reasonable prices. Best of all, this is the rare beauty site that will actually help you choose from the glut of available options by allowing you to browse by Skin Type or Skin Problem, so you can quickly narrow a huge selection down into manageable portions, saving you time and ensuring you get the best for your money.

·BATH & BODY	·FRAGRANCES	·GROOMING	·SKIN CARE

866-590-6963 · **Spiral Haircase**

SpiralHairCase.com

There are so many products covering so many brand names on this personal care site that we don't know where to begin. Clearly, there's a strong focus on hair care, and getting lost in this section is almost assured. However, you'll also find a huge nail care selection, as well as bath-and-body products, grooming tools and accessories and enough skin care to keep you glowing all year. Shopping by Brand makes the site tough to browse, though, so you might want to have a particularly beauty line in mind before you shop.

·BATH & BODY	·GROOMING	·HAIR CARE	·SKIN CARE

StrawberryNet.co.uk

This Hong Kong site claims to be "the world's largest provider of discounted skin care, makeup, cosmetics and fragrance," and we won't dispute anything but the grammar. With a selection so deep you could spend days browsing it, we recommend you do just that. After all, the site offers free shipping on every order, with a discount if you order just three products, and a further "loyalty bonus" discount every time you come back for more. Just pick up whatever you find in a single sitting, then return later for the rest.

·COSMETICS	·FRAGRANCES	·SKIN CARE	

TheBodyDeli.com

Perhaps the only line of bath and skin care that's almost good enough to eat, this stuff is not just made of all-natural products, but organic products at that. For proof, we refer you to the Ingredient Glossary. Though it includes a few off-putting names, like Ascorbyl Palmitate and Azulene, it explains how these substances are extracted from more comforting sources, such as citrus fruit, chamomile, plums, roses and cacti. Thanks to this spa-quality fare, you no longer have to put anything on your skin that you wouldn't put in your stomach.

·BATH & BODY	·SKIN CARE		

TheOrganicPharmacy.com

An organic pharmacy sounds too good to be true, and in actuality this British shop focuses more on skin care, hair care and homeopathy than conventional medicine. Nevertheless, a great source of organic bath-and-body products and herbal remedies can prove a valuable resource, and this one may be more valuable than most. In addition to a thorough list of products, various articles and ingredient descriptions let you know exactly why all-natural, nontoxic, preservative-free products that have never been tested on animals can be beneficial to your daily hygiene regimen.

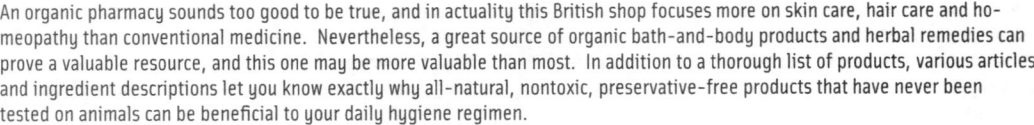

·BATH & BODY ·HAIR CARE	·ALTERNATIVE ·SKIN CARE	·SUPPLEMENTS	·FRAGRANCES

TheShaveBeverlyHills.com

Just when you think the art of shaving was lost from the barber's chair, comes along this Beverly Hills take on the "gentlemen's barbershop," which actually treats locals to classic wet shaves, complete with hot towels and badger brushes. Of course, the purpose of the Online Store here is to sell you such products as you need to get a close, elegant shave at home, which means a strong supply of top-end implements, creams and aftershaves. More important may be the site's Shaving Tips section, which finally puts the shave with-or-against-the-grain argument to rest.

·GROOMING	·HAIR CARE		

800-593-9822 · Varnish

VarnishNails.com

For a trendy Hollywood nail salon that gets regular press in magazines like *InStyle*, *Lucky*, *Women's Wear Daily* and *Allure*, the proprietary line of nail polish offered by this animated site are rather inexpensive. The page design might be a little too dynamic for most tastes, but if you can patiently scroll through the eighty different hues, a few of them at least are sure to suit you. Easier to browse, and possibly more useful, is the "wickedawesome" selection of nail grooming kits designed "for every gal who likes to get nailed."

·COSMETICS	·GROOMING			

800-793-2601 · VitaCost

VitaCost.com

Unless it requires a prescription, if it can be taken in pill form to improve your nutrition, aid in the effectiveness of your exercise, help you reach your sexual potential or make that diet easier to swallow, it can probably be found here. The massive supplements shop offers vitamins, herbs, over-the-counter remedies, homeopathic treatments, sports supplements and even standard toiletries and grooming tools. Of course, any of these should only be taken in addition to a wholesome, well-rounded diet, but this proves a terrific resource if you prefer to hedge your nutritional bets.

·BATH & BODY	·ALTERNATIVE	·SUPPLEMENTS		

800-223-1216 · Vitamin Shoppe

VitaminShoppe.com

Not just vitamins, ye olde shoppe (in cyberspace) offers a variety of nutritional supplements, ranging from herbs, minerals and bodybuilding powders to personal care items. You'll find products arranged by general and sometimes specific product types, and by brand. A Quick Reorder feature makes keeping up your regular supply much less complicated, though if you spend a few hours here you may start to wonder if your Zinc Picolinate levels are running low, or whether you could maybe use a little Creatine in your diet. If it's not in your food, it might be here.

·SUPPLEMENTS				

888-811-4286 · WorldHealthProducts.com

WorldHealthProducts.com

If you buy into the use of hormones, power bars, protein powders and other such stuff to improve your strength and tone, then this place will seem to you a muscle-bound playground. All of a bodybuilder's favorite supplements can be found here, whether you're looking to lose weight or add bulk. There are also sections devoted to Anti-Aging products, Sleep Aids and Sexual Enhancers. If you like biotechnology to keep you beautiful and fit, check here and eat creatine to your heart's content.

·SUPPLEMENTS	·SEXUAL CARE	·SKIN CARE		

NOTES:

Home & Garden

Like most species of birds, we humans have strong instincts to nest. However, while birds may fly hither and thither collecting leaves, twigs and pine needles, we've found a better way to build and furnish our homes: e-commerce. This section is easily the biggest in the book and, if we weren't incredibly discriminating, the book would be too large to fit on a bookshelf. We found several distinctive retailers for every style of furniture under the sun, from traditional rustic pieces to conceptual modern designs, and for every furniture shop there seemed to be a dozen sites offering accents, dinnerware, table linens, bedding, rugs, window treatments and lighting to complement your personal style. If you already have all the furniture you want, you can always upgrade the house itself with a fine assortment of decorative hardware, wallpapers, flooring and plumbing fixtures. It's truly remarkable just how much a motivated interior decorator can find online, whether you're changing your habitat to reflect a growing family, changing tastes or just to better organize all your stuff.

And that's just inside the house. It turns out your backyard is actually a personal oasis just waiting to happen. It can be as simple as the right patio furniture and a few colorful plants, or as extravagant as a koi pond and gazebo. Not to mention, if you're really ambitious, installing a pool, spa or sauna can be arranged within just a few minutes of browsing. The right web sites can turn you into a landscape artist, roofer or topiary gardener, and by the time you finish with every part of the house you may be ready to start again from scratch. The way that birds do.

TIPS ON BUYING HOME & GARDEN PRODUCTS ONLINE

These suggestions may help you maintain a very, very, very fine house.

• **SHIPPING CHARGES** • This section contains a lot of very heavy furniture, meaning that shipping time may be long and the costs high, accordingly. Some of the better deals can be found on sites that have local affiliations with stores that can drive a truck to your home. If you're already paying a lot, check in to White Glove Service, which includes delivery and any setup/assembly that may be required.

• **SHIPPING INSURANCE** • With large and delicate items in particular, make sure the site insures your purchases before they undergo the many potential ravages of shipment.

• **SEASONAL & REGIONAL PLANTS** • Some varieties of plants are only available in certain seasons, while others can thrive only in certain environments. Check to make sure any plants you may order are ready for shipment and can survive in your planting zone.

• **PRECISE MEASUREMENTS** • Window treatments and other customizable home fixtures typically require very precise measurements in order to fit. These fixtures can be very expensive, so you'll want to get it right the first time around. It may be necessary to call a store's customer service line before confirming your order.

• **COLOR COORDINATION** • As always, the colors represented on your screen may differ from the actual color of the object you're purchasing, due to discrepancies between the site's color settings and those of your computer monitor. Whenever possible, it may behoove you to request fabric swatches.

• **RETURN POLICIES** • At the risk of stating the obvious, we'd like to remind you to be aware of a site's return and exchange policies before purchasing anything, particularly big-ticket items.

• **TABLEWARE** • When purchasing china, dinnerware, flatware, glass and stemware sets, you may wish to add a few replacement pieces, as specific patterns and designs are commonly discontinued, no matter how great they are.

>> ## SITES THAT MAY COME IN HANDY

The following URLs may be useful when decorating or improving your home.

Appliance411.com	Household appliance information, instruction and repair
BudgetTruck.com	Moving truck rentals
CPSC.gov	Product recalls and household safety checklists
DesignerPreviews.com	Locate an interior decorator
DoItYourself.com	Home improvement resources
Earth911.org	Directory for local recycling and conservation resources
EERE.Energy.gov/consumerinfo	Energy conservation and alternatives
FreeTreesAndPlants.com	Surplus plant giveaways
Furniture.com/common/roomplanner	Virtual room planner
GetOrganizedNow.com	Tips and resources to help organize your home
GreenChoices.org	Resources for eco-friendly living
HGTV.com	Decorating, home improvement and gardening tips and ideas
HomeSaver.com	Fireplace safety resource and chimney-sweep locator
HouseholdProducts.NLM.NIH.gov	Health and safety information on building materials
MocoLoco.com	Online modern design magazine and resource
MovingScam.com	How to avoid moving frauds
MrHandyman.com	Locate a handyman
MyGardenGuide.com	Gardening instruction and tutorials
OnlineOrganizing.com	Locate an organizational expert
OrganizedHome.com	Tips and resources to help organize your home
Phals.com	Orchid care guide
Redo.org	Locate recycling and salvage centers
ServiceMagic.com	Locate contractors and receive online bids
UPack.com	Moving truck driving service
WallCoverings.org	Wallpapering guide

NATIONAL CHAINS & CATALOGS

The following sites offer online sales for familiar retailers.

Anthropologie.com	MarthaStewart.com
BallardDesigns.com	PBTeen.com
BBQGalore.com	Pier1.com
BedBathAndBeyond.com	PlowHearth.com
BombayCo.com	PotteryBarn.com
Burpee.com	RestorationHardware.com
CeramicaDirect.com	WHotelsTheStore.com
CountryCurtains.com	SincerelyYours.com
CrateBarrel.com	SmithAndHawkin.com
CuddleDown.com	SurLaTable.com
Gumps.com	TheCompanyStore.com
Horchow.com	WestElm.com
ImprovementsCatalog.com	Williams-Sonoma.com
JacksonAndPerkins.com	WinterthurGifts.com
LampsPlus.com	WSHome.com
LnT.com	zGallerie.com

OTHER SITES WE RECOMMEND

The following sites excel at selling one or two specific products.

Abizaks.com	Contemporary furniture
AllPicnicTables.com	Outdoor furniture
AmericanMeadows.com	Wildflower seeds
AnnieGlass.com	Tableware/dinnerware
ApplianceAccessories.com	Parts and accessories
ArenaRoses.com	Roses
BambooSourcery.com	Bamboo plants
BeHome.com	Traditional furniture
BlindsGalore.com	Window coverings
BluDot.com	Modern furniture
Boltz.com	Modern furniture
BoxesDelivered.com	Moving boxes and supplies
BrassBedShoppe.com	Beds
BroadwayPanhandler.com	Kitchenware
BrownSafe.com	Safes
CedarStore.com	Outdoor furniture
CooksGarden.com	Seed catalog
CopperPans.com	Copper cookware
CottageChicStore.com	Lighting
DaviStudio.com	Tableware/dinnerware
DayBeds.com	Daybeds and bedding
DecorateToday.com	Accents/design
DelMarFans.com	Ceiling fans and lighting
DesignerStencils.com	Interior decorating

DishesOldAndNew.com	Vintage tableware
DomenicaRosa.com	Table linens
Domestique.com	Aprons
eTopiary.com	Lawn and garden
FauxStore.com	Interior decorating
FinePaintsOfEurope.com	Interior and exterior house paint
FountainGallery.com	Fountains
FunkySofa.com	Contemporary seating
GivingTreeOnline.com	Bed, bath and table linens
GoodHomeStore.com	Natural household cleaning
GoodWoodProducts.com	Clean-burning wood and charcoal
HammerTown.com	Contemporary furniture
Hangers.com	Clothing hangers
HeatersNFans.com	Climate control
HomefrontDesigns.com	Mailboxes
HomeHarvest.com	Garden equipment and supply
HooverFence.com	Fencing supplies and materials
IndustrialHouse.com	Industrial furniture/housewares
iRoomDividers.com	Partitions and screens
ItalyDesign.com	Modern furniture
JiffySteamer.com	Clothing steamers
JoanneHudson.com	Tableware/dinnerware
LampShop.com	Lamp shades and kits
LuxPillow.com	Exotic skin and fur pillows
ModernSofa.com	Custom sofas
OutdoorFabrics.com	Patio fabric
PartyLights.com	Decorative string lights
PersonalizedDoormats.com	Door mats
PeterBoroBasket.com	Baskets
PortableHeaters.com	Heaters
RainforestfFora.com	Plants
RareSeeds.com	Vegetable and herb seeds
SafeSmith.com	Security
SafetyZone.com	Safety and security
SchoolHouseElectric.com	Lighting
SimonPearce.com	Glassware/accents
StencilEase.com	Stencils and supplies
SureFit.com	Slipcovers
TheIronShop.com	Spiral staircases
TheJungles.com	Media storage
UncommonGoods.com	Housewares/accents
VictorPest.com	Pest control
VintageCargo.net	Tableware and furnishings
WallpaperStore.com	Interior decorating
Wallter.com	Modern wall accents
WhiteFlowerFarm.com	Patio and garden
WineStuff.com	Glassware and accessories
WMBoundsLtd.com	Salt and pepper mills
WoodsideNursery.com	Daylilies
WoodSpoon.com	Wooden cooking utensils

*For in-depth reviews of these sites and more, check out **www.thepurplebook.com**.

SECTION ICON LEGEND

Use the following guide to understand the rectangular icons that appear throughout this section.

HARDWARE
This icon includes tools, power tools, screws, nuts, bolts, nails, hooks, fasteners, cleaning supplies, decorative hardware and plenty of other materials that hold your home together and keep it operating properly.

INTERIOR DECORATING
This icon indicates the sale of furniture, furnishings, decor, accents, lighting and miscellany that goes into assembling and decorating the interior of your home.

PATIO, YARD & GARDEN
Whether garden-related or more for the lawn, pool or patio, this icon illuminates the sites that offer florae, furniture and all kinds of accessories for the outdoors, including but not limited to: stoneware, fencing, fertilizer, spas, ponds, ornaments and outdoor grills.

PREPARATION & SERVICE
From fine china to simple barware, this icon indicates a selection of serving tools—such as plates, glasses and silverware—that may help you entertain guests and/or fill a bridal registry.

LIST OF KEY WORDS

The following words represent the types of items typically found on the sites listed in this section. You will find them listed in the orange strip at the bottom of each entry, as appropriate.

ACCENTS	Accents include baskets, rugs, clocks, mirrors, throw pillows, room dividers, vases and more.
APPLIANCES	Appliances and parts for the kitchen, laundry, climate control or household cleaning.
BED & BATH	Bedding, towels and other decorative features for the bedroom and bathroom.
CLEANING	Tools, solvents, detergents and other household cleaning accoutrements.
COOKING	Cutlery, cookware, kitchen gadgets, baking tools, cake decorations and more.
DECORATIVE	All manner of decorative hardware for the inside and outside of your home.
ECO-FRIENDLY	Stores offering environmentally responsible products.
FLORAE	Plant, tree, bush, herb, fruit, vegetable and flower seeds, bulbs, cuttings and seedlings.
FURNITURE	Furniture for every room of the house, ranging from rustic to modern and designer.
GLASS & BAR	Drinking glasses, including stemware, and any home bar necessities.
HARDWARE	Includes hand tools, power tools, garden tools, as well as home improvement materials such as wallpaper, flooring, plumbing, paints, roof hardware, wiring, shutters and trim.
LAWN & GARDEN	Tools and decor for landscaping, gardening, ornamentation and more.
LIGHTING	Indoor and outdoor lighting, including lamps, sconces and chandeliers.
MODERN	Contemporary and conceptual decorative styles dating back to the mid-20th century.
ORGANIZATION	Storage and organization gear for closets, files, media, wine, garbage, laundry and more.
PATIO & POOL	Outdoor accents, furniture and tools, including pools, spas, wind chimes, hammocks and umbrellas.
SECURITY	Includes alarm systems, household safety gear, safes, fencing, locks and emergency equipment.
TABLEWARE	Includes flatware, dinnerware, china, pottery, tabletop accessories, linens, service trays and carts.
TRADITIONAL	Keep an eye out for this key word to find rustic, vintage, European and other classic decorative styles.
WINDOWS	Window treatments, drapes, curtains, blinds and related hardware.

 KEY WORD INDEX

Use the followings lists to locate online retailers that sell the home and garden items you seek.

ACCENTS

2Modern.com
After5Catalog.com
AntiqueRoom.com
ARusticGarden.com
BelgianHuis.com
Bellacor.com
BoDanica.com
CabinAndLodge.com
CarolinaRustica.com
CB2.com
CharlestonGardens.com
Chiasso.com
Clocko.com
CoastalDecorShop.com
CountryDoor.com
CrystalClassics.com
CurranOnline.com
DeLaEspada.com
DesignPublic.com
DirectFromMexico.com
DWR.com
EnglishCreekGardens.com
FineGardenProducts.com
FrenchGardening.com
Frontera.com
Frontgate.com
FurnitureFind.com
GraciousStyle.com
HighbrowFurniture.com
HomeFiresUSA.com
iFloor.com
Importu.com
InterfaceFlor.com
InvitingHome.com
JamaliGarden.com
JonathanAdler.com
JustMorocco.com
LavenderFieldsOnline.com
LSFabrics.com
Marston-And-Langinger.com
MaxwellSilverNY.com
MichaelAram.com
MichaelianHomeRetail.com
ModernEssentials.com
ModernRugs.com
MossOnline.com

ACCENTS (cont.)

NaturalAreaRugs.com
Nova68.com
OrangeSkin.com
OutdoorDecor.com
Pendleton-USA.com
PierreDeux.com
PillowsAndThrows.com
PioneerLinens.com
RetroModern.com
RoomAndCompany.com
RoomServiceHome.com
RugsUSA.com
SilkTrading.com
SilverQueen.com
SisalCarpet.com
SmithAndNoble.com
SourcePerrier.com
Stencil-Library.com
StoreHouse.com
TabulaTua.com
TheMagazine.info
TheWellAppointedHouse.com
Umbra.com
UnicaHome.com
VelocityArtAndDesign.com
Vivavi.com
WaterGarden.com

APPLIANCES

AAAVacs.com
AltEnergyStore.com
AmericasBestBBQ.com
BBQGuys.com
BodumUSA.com
ChefsCatalog.com
ChefsResource.com
CompactAppliance.com
Cooking.com
CooksWorld.com
CulinaryParts.com
Fitzsu.com
Frontgate.com
GreenBuildingSupply.com
KnifeMerchant.com
LakelandLimited.com

APPLIANCES (cont.)

McMaster.com
RepairClinic.com
TeakWickerAndMore.com
WholeLatteLove.com
WokShop.com
WaterWarehouse.com

BED & BATH

2Modern.com
ABed.com
AntiqueDraperyRod.com
BelgianHuis.com
BetweenTheSheetsInc.com
Boxport.com
CarolinaRustica.com
CathKidston.com
CB2.com
Chiasso.com
CoastalDecorShop.com
CountryDoor.com
DesignPublic.com
Fitzsu.com
Frontgate.com
GraciousStyle.com
LavenderFieldsOnline.com
LinenPlace.com
MaxwellSilverNY.com
MichaelianHomeRetail.com
ModernEssentials.com
OrangeSkin.com
PeacockAlley.com
Pendleton-USA.com
PillowsAndThrows.com
PioneerLinens.com
RoomServiceHome.com
SchweitzerLinen.com
ShowerPresents.com
SourcePerrier.com
TheWellAppointedHouse.com
Umbra.com
UnicaHome.com
Vivavi.com
Wisteria.com
Wrapables.com

CLEANING

AAAVacs.com
CasaBella.com
CharleysGreenHouse.com
Fitzsu.com
FlorStor.com
GreenBuildingSupply.com
LakelandLimited.com
Organize-Everything.com
ToolsPlus.com
UnicaHome.com
WaterGarden.com
WaterWarehouse.com

COOKING

AmericasBestBBQ.com
BBQGuys.com
BoDanica.com
BodumUSA.com
CB2.com
ChefsCatalog.com
ChefsResource.com
CompactAppliance.com
Cooking.com
CooksWorld.com
CountryDoor.com
CulinaryParts.com
Fitzsu.com
Frontgate.com
Hanneby.com
KnifeMerchant.com
Korin.com
LakelandLimited.com
MossOnline.com
OrangeSkin.com
TabulaTua.com
WokShop.com

DECORATIVE

AntiqueDraperyRod.com
ArchitecturalDepot.com
ARusticGarden.com
BauerWare.com
Bellacor.com
BeniciaGarden.com
BuyHammocks.com
CabinAndLodge.com
CarolinaRustica.com
CharlestonGardens.com
CoastalDecorShop.com
DirectFromMexico.com
DirectionsHG.com
Faucet.com
FaucetDepot.com
FineGardenProducts.com
FireplaceScreens.com
FixturesDirect.com
HomeFiresUSA.com
HouseOfAntiqueHardware.com
iFloor.com
InvitingHome.com
JustMorocco.com
LAHardware.com
LeeValley.com
MichaelAram.com
MosaicTileMarket.com
NordicStyle.com
OutdoorDecor.com
SilkTrading.com
TheMagazine.info
Umbra.com
VanDykes.com
VelocityArtAndDesign.com
VintageWoodWorks.com
WalpoleWoodWorkers.com

ECO-FRIENDLY

AdirondackChairs.com
AltEnergyStore.com
CasaBella.com
CharleysGreenHouse.com
CleanAirGardening.com
GardenersEdge.com
GardensAlive.com
GreenBuildingSupply.com
LeeValley.com
SafetyCentral.com
SeedsOfChange.com
Vivavi.com

FLORAE

AlmostEdenPlants.com
BeniciaGarden.com
BrentAndBeckysBulbs.com
DirectGardening.com
DutchGardens.com
FrenchGardening.com
HighCountryGardens.com
JohnnySeeds.com
JohnScheepers.com
KitazawaSeed.com
Ponds2Go.com
RainTreeNursery.com
SeedsOfChange.com
SelectSeeds.com
SongSparrow.com
WindowBox.com

FURNITURE

2Modern.com
AdirondackChairs.com
After5Catalog.com
AntiqueRoom.com
ArtisanCountryPineFurniture.com
ARusticGarden.com
BuyHammocks.com
CabinAndLodge.com
CarolinaRustica.com
CB2.com
CharlestonGardens.com
Chiasso.com
Circa50.com
CoastalDecorShop.com
CountryCasual.com
CountryDoor.com
CurranOnline.com
DeLaEspada.com
DesignPublic.com
DirectFromMexico.com
DWR.com
FransWicker.com
Frontera.com
Frontgate.com
FurnitureFind.com
GardenSide.com
GreenBuildingSupply.com
Hammock-Company.com
HighbrowFurniture.com
HoldEverything.com
Importu.com
JustMorocco.com
MaineCottage.com
Marston-And-Langinger.com
MichaelAram.com

FURNITURE (cont.)

ModernEssentials.com
MossOnline.com
NordicStyle.com
Nova68.com
OrangeSkin.com
OutdoorDecor.com
PierreDeux.com
Plexi-Craft.com
PopsFurniture.com
RoomAndCompany.com
RoomServiceHome.com
SmithAndNoble.com
SourcePerrier.com
SpinKeeper.com
SpiritElements.com
StoreHouse.com
TeakWickerAndMore.com
TheMagazine.info
TheWellAppointedHouse.com
VelocityArtAndDesign.com
Vivavi.com
WalpoleWoodWorkers.com
WineEnthusiast.com
Wisteria.com
WoodClassics.com

GLASS & BAR

After5Catalog.com
BoDanica.com
CabinAndLodge.com
CathKidston.com
CB2.com
ChefsResource.com
Clio-Home.com
CoastalDecorShop.com
Cooking.com
CooksWorld.com
CrystalClassics.com
eTableTop.com
Fitzsu.com
Frontgate.com
Gearys.com
ManorHG.com
MossOnline.com
OrangeSkin.com
PoshChicago.com
RetroModern.com
SilverQueen.com
SourcePerrier.com
SpiritElements.com
TabulaTua.com
TCStore.com

GLASS & BAR

TheMagazine.info
TheWellAppointedHouse.com
UnicaHome.com
WineEnthusiast.com
Wrapables.com

HARDWARE

AltEnergyStore.com
AntiqueDraperyRod.com
ArchitecturalDepot.com
ARusticGarden.com
BauerWare.com
BeniciaGarden.com
BuyHammocks.com
CabinAndLodge.com
CharlestonGardens.com
CleanAirGardening.com
CoastalTool.com
CountryHomeProducts.com
CulinaryParts.com
DirectFromMexico.com
DirectionsHG.com
Faucet.com
FaucetDepot.com
FineGardenProducts.com
FixturesDirect.com
GrandBrass.com
GreenBuildingSupply.com
HomeFiresUSA.com
HouseOfAntiqueHardware.com
iFloor.com
InvitingHome.com
JohnnySeeds.com
LAHardware.com
LeeValley.com
McMaster.com
MichaelAram.com
OutdoorDecor.com
RepairClinic.com
SeedsOfChange.com
ServiceLighting.com
SilkTrading.com
SmithAndNoble.com
SpiritElements.com
Stencil-Library.com
ToolsPlus.com
TreeHelp.com
Umbra.com
VanDykes.com
VintageWoodWorks.com
WalpoleWoodWorkers.com

LAWN & GARDEN

ArizonaPottery.com
ARusticGarden.com
BeniciaGarden.com
CarolinaRustica.com
CharlestonGardens.com
CharleysGreenHouse.com
CleanAirGardening.com
CountryHomeProducts.com
DirectFromMexico.com
DirectGardening.com
DirectionsHG.com
EnglishCreekGardens.com
FiberglassPlanters.com
FineGardenProducts.com
FrenchGardening.com
GardenersEdge.com
GardensAlive.com
JamaliGarden.com
JohnnySeeds.com
LeeValley.com
Marston-And-Langinger.com
Nova68.com
OutdoorDecor.com
Ponds2Go.com
RoomServiceHome.com
SeedsOfChange.com
SpiritElements.com
TeakWickerAndMore.com
TreeHelp.com
VelocityArtAndDesign.com
WalpoleWoodWorkers.com
WaterGarden.com
WindowBox.com
WoodClassics.com

LIGHTING

2Modern.com
After5Catalog.com
Alluminare.com
AntiqueRoom.com
Bellacor.com
BuyHammocks.com
CabinAndLodge.com
CB2.com
CharlestonGardens.com
Chiasso.com
CircaLighting.com
CountryDoor.com
CrystalClassics.com
DirectFromMexico.com
DirectionsHG.com
DWR.com
FormPlusFunction.com

LIGHTING (cont.)

FurnitureFind.com
GrandBrass.com
HighbrowFurniture.com
Importu.com
InvitingHome.com
JonathanAdler.com
JustMorocco.com
LampStore.com
LightingUniverse.com
Lightology.com
Marston-And-Langinger.com
McMaster.com
Nova68.com
PierreDeux.com
PillowsAndThrows.com
RoomAndCompany.com
ServiceLighting.com
SilverQueen.com
SmithAndNoble.com
SourcePerrier.com
StoreHouse.com
TeakWickerAndMore.com
TheMagazine.info
TheWellAppointedHouse.com
UnicaHome.com
VanDykes.com
VelocityArtAndDesign.com
Vivavi.com
WalpoleWoodWorkers.com
WaterGarden.com
Wrapables.com

MODERN

2Modern.com
After5Catalog.com
Alluminare.com
BauerWare.com
Bellacor.com
BoDanica.com
BodumUSA.com
CasaBella.com
CathKidston.com
CB2.com
ChefsCatalog.com
Chiasso.com
Circa50.com
CircaLighting.com
Clio-Home.com
Clocko.com
CooksWorld.com
DeLaEspada.com
DesignPublic.com
DWR.com

MODERN (cont.)

eTableTop.com
FireplaceScreens.com
Fitzsu.com
FormPlusFunction.com
FurnitureFind.com
Hanneby.com
HighbrowFurniture.com
InterfaceFlor.com
JonathanAdler.com
LampStore.com
LightingUniverse.com
Lightology.com
LinenPlace.com
ManorHG.com
MaxwellSilverNY.com
MichaelAram.com
ModernEssentials.com
ModernRugs.com
MossOnline.com
Nova68.com
OrangeSkin.com
PeacockAlley.com
PillowsAndThrows.com
Plexi-Craft.com
RetroModern.com
RoomAndCompany.com
RugsUSA.com
SabiStyle.com
ShowerPresents.com
SilverSuperStore.com
SmithAndNoble.com
SpinKeeper.com
SpiritElements.com
Stencil-Library.com
StoreHouse.com
TabulaTua.com
TheMagazine.info
Umbra.com
UnicaHome.com
VelocityArtAndDesign.com
Vivavi.com
Wrapables.com

ORGANIZATION

CabinAndLodge.com
CarolinaRustica.com
Chiasso.com
ContainerStore.com
Cooking.com
CountryDoor.com
DesignPublic.com
DWR.com
Fitzsu.com

SECURITY

FransWicker.com
Frontgate.com
GladiatorGW.com
HoldEverything.com
McMaster.com
MichaelAram.com
Nova68.com
OrangeSkin.com
Organize-Everything.com
RetroModern.com
SpinKeeper.com
TheWellAppointedHouse.com
Umbra.com
UnicaHome.com
VelocityArtAndDesign.com
Vivavi.com
WineEnthusiast.com
Wrapables.com

PATIO & POOL

After5Catalog.com
AmericasBestBBQ.com
ARusticGarden.com
BBQGuys.com
BuyHammocks.com
CharlestonGardens.com
CoastalDecorShop.com
CountryCasual.com
CurranOnline.com
FineGardenProducts.com
FormPlusFunction.com
FransWicker.com
Frontgate.com
FurnitureFind.com
GardenSide.com
Marston-And-Langinger.com
OutdoorDecor.com
PoolWarehouse.com
SpiritElements.com
TeakWickerAndMore.com
TheMagazine.info
WalpoleWoodWorkers.com
WaterWarehouse.com
WoodClassics.com

SECURITY

McMaster.com
SafetyCentral.com
ToolsPlus.com
WalpoleWoodWorkers.com

TABLEWARE

AllTeaPots.com
BelgianHuis.com
BetweenTheSheetsInc.com
BoDanica.com
CarolinaRustica.com
CathKidston.com
CB2.com
ChefsResource.com
Chiasso.com
Clio-Home.com
Cooking.com
CooksWorld.com
CountryDoor.com
CrystalClassics.com
DirectFromMexico.com
eTableTop.com
EverythingChopsticks.com
Fitzsu.com
Gearys.com
GraciousStyle.com
Hanneby.com
iFloor.com
Importu.com
ItalianPottery.com
JonathanAdler.com
Korin.com
ManorHG.com
Marston-And-Langinger.com
MaxwellSilverNY.com
MossOnline.com
OrangeSkin.com
PierreDeux.com
PioneerLinens.com
PoshChicago.com
Replacements.com
RetroModern.com
RoomServiceHome.com
RudisPottery.com
SabiStyle.com
SchweitzerLinen.com
ShowerPresents.com
SilverQueen.com
SilverSuperStore.com
SourcePerrier.com
SpiritElements.com
TabulaTua.com
TCStore.com
TheMagazine.info
TheWellAppointedHouse.com
UnicaHome.com
VelocityArtAndDesign.com
Vivavi.com
Wisteria.com
WokShop.com
Wrapables.com

TRADITIONAL

AntiqueDraperyRod.com
AntiqueRoom.com
ArtisanCountryPineFurniture.com
ARusticGarden.com
BelgianHuis.com
Bellacor.com
CabinAndLodge.com
CarolinaRustica.com
CharlestonGardens.com
CircaLighting.com
Clocko.com
CountryCasual.com
CountryDoor.com
CrystalClassics.com
CurranOnline.com
DirectFromMexico.com
EnglishCreekGardens.com
FineGardenProducts.com
FireplaceScreens.com
FransWicker.com
FrenchGardening.com
Frontera.com
FurnitureFind.com
GardenSide.com
Gearys.com
GraciousStyle.com
HomeFiresUSA.com
HouseOfAntiqueHardware.com
Importu.com
InvitingHome.com
LampStore.com
LavenderFieldsOnline.com
LightingUniverse.com
LinenPlace.com
ManorHG.com
Marston-And-Langinger.com
NordicStyle.com
OutdoorDecor.com
PeacockAlley.com
Pendleton-USA.com
PierreDeux.com
PioneerLinens.com
PopsFurniture.com
Replacements.com
RoomServiceHome.com
RugsUSA.com
SchweitzerLinen.com
ShowerPresents.com
SilverQueen.com
SilverSuperStore.com
SmithAndNoble.com
SourcePerrier.com
SpinKeeper.com
SpiritElements.com
Stencil-Library.com

TRADITIONAL (cont.)

TabulaTua.com
TheWellAppointedHouse.com
VintageWoodWorks.com
WalpoleWoodWorkers.com
Wisteria.com

WINDOWS

AntiqueDraperyRod.com
ArchitecturalDepot.com
FabricsAndHome.com
JamaliGarden.com
LavenderFieldsOnline.com
LSFabrics.com
McMaster.com
Pendleton-USA.com
SilkTrading.com
SmithAndNoble.com
StoreHouse.com
Umbra.com
VanDykes.com

2Modern.com

Since there's no such thing as too modern, we dig this small but appealing furniture and accents site that weighs heavy on embellishments. You'll find plenty of popular ultracontemporary designers on hand, whether you're looking for a new bed, decorative geometric prints, conceptual lighting, superslick trash bins or a gaggle of throw pillows. There may not be anything formal about these sorts of furniture and accents, but it's at least the sort of casual you work hard to achieve.

·LIGHTING ·MODERN | ·ACCENTS | ·FURNITURE | ·BED & BATH

AAAVacs.com

Most of the products offered on this site suck, literally. Vacuums are the primary focus, whether the traditional upright or the cyclonic Dyson models, which promise never to stop sucking. A long menu runs down the left side of the page offering different brand names and product types, alphabetically. Among the well-known and not-so-familiar names, you may notice vacuum replacement parts, steam cleaners and air purifiers, but only if you pay close attention. While this menu is thorough, it's neither pleasing to the eye nor very helpful, so while this may be a great place to buy a vacuum, it's not that nice a place to look for one.

·APPLIANCES | ·CLEANING

ABed.com

As you may have guessed, this site sells beds. More specifically, it sells bed mattresses, but not just your typical mattresses. Primarily, this proves an effective online source of memory foam, that miraculous space age material that conforms to the shape of your body to provide even pressure and pure comfort. Full memory foam mattresses are typically very expensive, so if you'd simply like to add to your current mattress's comfort, you might want to look into the shop's selection of Memory Foam Toppers, which apply just enough of the technology to add a little something to your slumber, without taking too much away from your bank account.

·BED & BATH

AdirondackChairs.com

 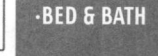 

The unmistakable slatted style of Adirondack furniture is impressively represented by this outdoor furniture specialist, which has no qualms claiming the mantle, "Largest Adirondack Chair Selection Online." A beautiful assortment of chairs, rockers, tables and swings offer just about every conceivable variation on the classic outdoor look developed by upstate New York resorts. The pieces are available in cedar, pine, cypress, spruce, oak, aspen and mahogany, and if you prefer plastic, it's nice to know that these plastic chairs were made from recycled materials.

·FURNITURE | ·ECO-FRIENDLY

866-523-8370 · After 5

After5Catalog.com

If you wish to establish your home as a swinging bar-away-from-bar, you'll absolutely need to shop from this specialty retailer of cocktail accoutrements, glassware, bar furniture and decor. Whether outdoor or indoor, lit by tiki torches or neon, the home bar you build with the help of this site will be perfect for that poolside barbecue, and particularly inviting for that after-hours night-cap. The shop even offers some recommended listening, but the greatest thing about assembling your own cocktail lounge is that the soundtrack is up to you.

·LIGHTING ·PATIO & POOL	·ACCENTS ·MODERN	·FURNITURE	·GLASS & BAR

866-797-4084 · A Bit of Britain

AllTeaPots.com

Tea service is an artistry that has been finally developed across many cultures, but ask anyone who does it best and you'll get the same two answers every time: England and Japan. It's no surprise then that the wares of both countries are beautifully represented by this teapot specialist out of Colorado, which offers a vast assortment of elegant fine china as well as decidedly more modern, even funky options. However, the astounding thing about this site might be its inclusion of less-likely nations, with plenty of pots hailing from places such as Africa, South America and Eastern Europe. It will take a lot of clicking too view them all, but it's definitely worth the effort.

·TABLEWARE			

866-526-7748 · Alluminare

Alluminare.com

Want a little control over your home lighting? This sites gives you that and more, with an excellently conceived web shop that allows you to begin with a simple lamp shape, then add color and trim to your own specification. Hanging light, wall sconce, table and floor lamp designs may be matched with shades of silk, bamboo, lemongrass, cane, linen or other fabrics printed with a designer pattern. Or, if you've already got a lamp you love, simply pick up a new shade, with or without fringe, at just the size you need. The only hitch? You can't view your final selection before you buy. Fortunately, a liberal return policy should entice you to risk it; check it out before you buy.

·LIGHTING	·MODERN		

337-462-8255 · Almost Eden Plants

AlmostEdenPlants.com

While nowhere as pretty as the products it sells, and truthfully a far cry from paradise, this site does do a decent job filling its awkward pages with a fantastic selection of cacti, succulents, vines, shrubs, trees and tropical plants. Despite being huge, the pictures of these plants and flowers don't usually offer a great depiction of the flora in question, and are only occasionally accompanied by verbal descriptions. Still, for satisfying your floral and vegetative landscaping needs, this shop proves all but necessary.

·FLORAE			

AltEnergyStore.com

The Alternative Energy Store · 877-878-4060

When energy costs get you down, don't forget about this excellent source of alternative energy sources. Whether you're trying to power a rural cabin, RV, boat or even your home, the solar, wind and hydropower gear here may seem a little complicated at first, but will ultimately give you a sustainable power supply completely independent of your local utility company, which may even be willing to buy any excess electricity from you. Easier, less expensive ways to take advantage of this truly progressive shop is to make use of its batteries, composting equipment and energy efficient products, which are all good for the planet as well as your pocketbook.

| ·APPLIANCES | ·HARDWARE | ·ECO-FRIENDLY | |

AmericasBestBBQ.com

America's Best Barbecue · 800-814-6815

It is our duty to inform you that your backyard barbecue is probably not among America's best. How do we know? Because among the startling selection of grills, roasters and smokers found on this site are some that could make a brush fire seem rinky-dink. Freestanding electric, propane and charcoal grills mix it up with both built-in and portable models, with extensive variety in every category. On top of this, you can find patio coolers, torches and beer dispensers to help keep the party outdoors well past cooking time.

| ·APPLIANCES | ·COOKING | ·PATIO & POOL | |

AntiqueDraperyRod.com

Antique Drapery Rod Co. · 214-653-1733

Though not technically antique, the drapery and window hardware that stocks this site looks good enough to be mistaken as old. The luxurious drapes and bed canopies come in suede, velvet, hemp and silk, while the finials, rods, rings and brackets may be procured in wood, iron, stone or bamboo. Considering the aesthetic value of these wares, we'd expect the site to show them off with enticing images and glowing descriptions. Instead, with many of these products your imagination will have to do the work; not too bad if your imagination is up to the task.

| ·HARDWARE ·TRADITIONAL | ·BED & BATH | ·DECORATIVE | ·WINDOWS |

AntiqueRoom.com

Antique Room · 718-875-7084

In the past hundred years or so, furniture design has undergone myriad changes, not only in style and materials, but in concept as well. Well, forget all that. This site's specialty is 19th-century antique furniture. Predating the age of mass production, this stuff is not just extremely expensive, but exquisitely high quality, with ornate, hand-carved trim boasting an artisanship long since lost to 20th-century "progress." The fine array of furniture and accents are categorized into aesthetic movements such as Classical, Renaissance, Gothic, Neo-Greco and Rococo, though all may be considered "La Crème de la Crème of the Victorian Era."

| ·LIGHTING | ·ACCENTS | ·FURNITURE | ·TRADITIONAL |

800-294-1098 · ArchitecturalDepot.com

ArchitecturalDepot.com

Your home improvement projects are only limited by two things: your imagination and your pocketbook. Normally, we'd include the options available to you as a limiting factor, but after looking at this site we're not really sure there are that many options left to explore. With house hardware including all manner of decorative trim for your ceilings and walls; siding, shutters and roof hardware for your exterior; and a huge assortment of door knockers and bells, we'll be surprised if your home doesn't go through quite the makeover now that you know about this shop.

·HARDWARE	·DECORATIVE	·WINDOWS	

800-420-1808 · Arizona Pottery

ArizonaPottery.com

When we think of Arizona plant life, pretty much all we can think of is cacti, so we were as surprised as anyone to discover that this is the best source of planters online. The extensive selection of sizes and styles makes it so, but just as important is the stellar organization. Categories like Red Clay, Brown Clay, Tan Clay, Black Clay, Brushed Clay and Glazed make finding the right style of pot incredibly easy, especially as they're all beautifully photographed and arranged together on visually oriented pages. We'd like to see another state do better.

·LAWN & GARDEN			

866-477-8407 · Artisan Country Pine Furniture

ArtisanCountryPineFurniture.com

Fans of pine furniture have a great find in this web shop, which offers a terrific assortment of pieces for the entire house. Browsing by room proves quite easy, as you view available items, styles and sizes. But the real fun begins once you've chosen the bed, dresser, table or desk you like best, and move on to select your preferred finish from two dozen options including Dark Roast, Chocolate Cherry, Light Walnut, Dark Laurel, Sierra Brown and Honey. This site always makes the perfect addition to any room easy to find.

·FURNITURE	·TRADITIONAL		

217-773-3766 · A Rustic Garden

ARusticGarden.com

Nothing says *rustic* like wrought iron, and this site says it with verve, offering a good deal of decorative patio furniture, garden ornaments, landscaping elements and home hardware, much of it antique. It's not all wrought, and you will find occasional materials other than iron, including stepping stones, shutters and baskets. But mostly you will find the heavy metal, bent or cast into beautiful and functional shapes, which means that shipping will be on the expensive side, even at standard postal rates. Such is the price we pay for traditional elegance online.

·HARDWARE ·DECORATIVE	·ACCENTS ·PATIO & POOL	·FURNITURE ·TRADITIONAL	·LAWN & GARDEN

BauerWare.com

This site will open your eyes to new ways to open your doors and cabinets. The highly original, funky and/or fashionable knobs and pulls featured here come in a variety of "whimsical" shapes and colors that will inspire you to upgrade any boring, purely functional hardware found in your home. These decorative pieces are almost a revelation, available in unheard-of designs. Glazed ceramic, glass and a variety of metals contribute to the dazzling assortment, and even the site's "Traditional" selection is sure to exceed all expectations.

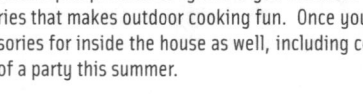	·HARDWARE	·DECORATIVE	·MODERN	

BBQGuys.com

Playing with fire is rarely so appealing as this specialty cookware site makes it seem. A truly exhaustive selection of grills make the shop impossible to ignore if you intend to barbecue like a pro, while it turns out to be the fine assortment of grilling accessories that makes outdoor cooking fun. Once you've built your patio kitchen, however, there are plenty of culinary tools and accessories for inside the house as well, including cookware of every conceivable variety and barware that will help you throw one heck of a party this summer.

	·APPLIANCES	·COOKING	·PATIO & POOL	

BelgianHuis.com

Squeezing every possible use out of the concept of linens, this Belgian importer delivers fine woven fabrics for your bed, bathroom, kitchen and dining table, for starters. Belgian crystal, lace and tapestries also populate the site, and if you're not familiar with the luxurious quality of products manufactured in the nation that gave birth to the stock market, odds are you're missing out. Certainly, browsing is risk free; except it's almost a sure thing that one of these exquisite tablecloths, sheet sets or bathrobes will inspire an investment.

	·ACCENTS	·BED & BATH	·TABLEWARE	·TRADITIONAL

Bellacor.com

With more than 500,000 products from 700 manufacturers, it can be tough to know where on this massive home furnishings site to begin. Might we recommend the Lighting section? Find your way through the thousands of floor lamps, table lamps, ceiling fans, sconces and chandeliers, and you'll be ready to tackle the mirrors, clocks and other decorative accents available elsewhere on the site. The key is understanding their very well-organized product filters, which take into account elements of Style, Finish (material) and Price Range, as well as which room in the house you'd like to accommodate. Or, you can tell one of the on-staff Personal Shoppers what you'd like, and let them find it. It's easy enough, either way.

	·LIGHTING ·TRADITIONAL	·ACCENTS	·DECORATIVE	·MODERN

707-747-9094 · Benicia Garden & Nursery

BeniciaGarden.com

It's not often you find a garden shop that offers plant, herb and vegetable seeds, and backs them up with a tasteful selection of decorative garden accents. After all, if you don't supplementally adorn your garden space, you'll simply be looking at soil while you wait for those seeds to sprout. You'll even find a fantastic selection of wind chimes, so your garden will sound beautiful, and some stylish gardening apparel, so you can look the part while preparing your flowerbed, rather than just like a grown-up playing in the dirt.

| ·HARDWARE | ·LAWN & GARDEN | ·FLORAE | ·DECORATIVE | |

949-640-9999 · Between The Sheets

BetweenTheSheetsInc.com

A case could be made that quantity and quality rarely overlap, but when you're talking about bed linens the two go together beautifully. This Southern California retailer brings an extraordinarily high sense of comfort and style to its fine array of bedding, with comparable quality found in its stellar bath towels, robes and tablecloths. Price must be no object if you're to risk shopping from this site, and with sheets boasting up to a 1020 thread count, you can expect to pay at least a dollar a thread for a sheet set or duvet.

| ·BED & BATH | ·TABLEWARE | | | |

800-654-4674 · Bo Danica

BoDanica.com

Featuring brands such as Simon Pearce, Annieglass and Rosenthal, this San Diego area housewares retailer offers a small but surprisingly diverse range of dinnerware, flatware, tabletop accessories, serving pieces, stemware, linens and home accents, "from modern urban to Mediterranean casual." But the true story here is the delicate balance between fine china sets that never get too stuffy, and modestly priced dinnerware imbued with an almost refined charm. Formal and casual selections never had so much in common.

| ·ACCENTS ·MODERN | ·COOKING | ·TABLEWARE | ·GLASS & BAR | |

800-232-6386 · Bodum

BodumUSA.com

Making and selling their own tabletop items, cooking tools and small appliances, these guys are proficient at both. Whether it's coffee machines, fondue pots or *plat ménages*, these products and this web site are equally slick, with clean lines and exquisitely functional design. Best may be their Coffee and Tea sections, featuring grinders, kettles and cups, but honestly all of the sections should satisfy, despite the fact that the selection is slim and that you may not think you like this sort of thing.

| ·APPLIANCES | ·COOKING | ·MODERN | | |

Boxport.com

Boxport · 415-772-1670

Striving "to deliver all the elements of a luxurious hotel stay to people at home," this uniquely structured bedding site brings five-star indulgence into your bedroom. Sheets, robes, towels and other hotel amenities are made available to retail customers, including the fine products used by the St. Regis, Kimpton and Loews hotels. Pick up some of these quality linens and, next time you stay at one of these fine accommodations, you'll be looking forward to returning to your own bed for a change.

·BED & BATH

BrentAndBeckysBulbs.com

Brent & Becky's Bulbs · 877-661-2852

Brent and Becky are a couple of perennial flower farmers from Coastal Virginia who proffer seasonal bulbs for some of your favorite blossoms, as well as some rare and unusual bulbs you may not be able to find anywhere else. You can browse by their seasonal catalogs, but that's really only useful if you know the scientific names of the flowers. The rest of us will prefer to search by Color, Height or, at the most, Nickname if we're to have any hope of finding the sort of flowers we want going in.

·FLORAE

BuyHammocks.com

Nicamaka Distributors · 866-377-1224

Outdoor living gets quite a bit more fun with the help of this patio leisure site. Hammocks are only one interesting part of this story, but you will find a great selection of home and camping hammocks, hammock chairs and stands. But you'll also find some more permanent outdoor furniture, as well as patio torches, outdoor heating, shade umbrellas, portable gazebos, pool toys and mosquito netting. Meanwhile, a slim indoor selection provides a surprising variety of fireplace accessories and bed canopies. We don't see the connection, but you won't hear any complaints from us.

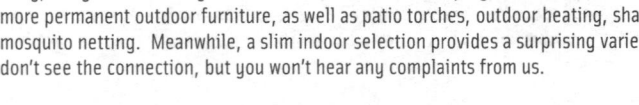

| ·LIGHTING ·PATIO & POOL | ·HARDWARE | ·FURNITURE | ·DECORATIVE |

CabinAndLodge.com

CabinAndLodge.com · 704-362-0734

Like the name would suggest, this site is devoted to lake cabins, mountain lodges or other nature dwellings, specifically, to the sort of furniture and home decor appropriate to such homes. This means a heavy rustic influence, with a lot of bear, moose, deer, duck and pine cone themes, along with a full complement of canoe-shaped bookcases and coffee tables.   The shop's remarkable breadth of products includes plenty of decorative drawer pulls, fireplace accessories, bedding and dinnerware, much of which might even look great in your city home.

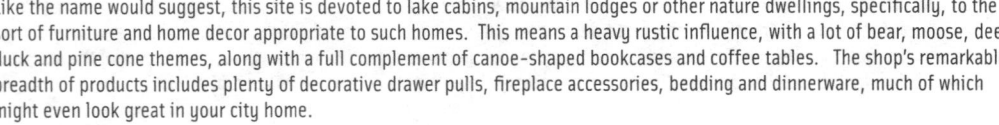

| ·LIGHTING ·ORGANIZATION | ·HARDWARE ·GLASS & BAR | ·ACCENTS ·DECORATIVE | ·FURNITURE ·TRADITIONAL |

800-205-7819 · Carolina Rustic

CarolinaRustica.com

North Carolina and furniture go together like wrought iron and wood. It all adds up to equal this shop, which features an outstanding assortment of home furnishings across the board. Beautiful decorative hardware, canopy beds, patio seating, attractive storage solutions, elegant lawn structures, magnificent fireplace accessories and a bevy of gorgeous home accents come together on a single site to provide the web with one of the best sources of rustic furniture and decor anywhere. Anyone who thinks traditional is boring hasn't seen this.

·ACCENTS ·TABLEWARE	·FURNITURE ·ORGANIZATION	·LAWN & GARDEN ·DECORATIVE	·BED & BATH ·TRADITIONAL

800-841-4140 · Casabella

CasaBella.com

Not that you're overly into the stuff, or anything, but...you wanna see some pretty cool mops and brooms? This place offers some of the more interesting home cleaning supplies you're likely to come across, whether it's a Duck Dustpan, Get Bent Cleaner or Magnet Broom. Actually, most of this stuff sounds weirder than it is, and though these are somewhat more than your run-of-the-mill designs, at the root of it they have some functional cleaning tools, and one spectacularly clean-looking site.

·CLEANING	·ECO-FRIENDLY	·MODERN	

  ★

212-343-0223 · Cath Kidston Limited

CathKidston.com

This Notting Hill London company started out selling secondhand furniture and vintage fabrics, but in time Ms. Kidston began designing her own products, and the results have undoubtedly been more inspired. She brings her bright, fun and feminine style to a variety of products, and we're particularly impressed with the towels, table linens and dinnerware she brings to this site, recently redesigned to serve US customers. This one's a must-shop for fans of cute, contemporary housewares.

·BED & BATH	·TABLEWARE	·GLASS & BAR	·MODERN

800-606-6252 · Crate and Barrel

CB2.com

We don't exactly know why Crate & Barrel felt the need to create a second shop to house this funky, modern collection of furniture and housewares, but if you dig the contemporary urban vibe, at least this offshoot specialty shop will make it easy for you to find what you're after. The selection covers a lot of ground, but not always with a lot of options. So, while you may find a decent number of shower curtains to chose from, if you're shopping for bedroom furniture, you may soon run out of options. A good place to shop if you're of particular tastes, but not if you're picky.

·LIGHTING ·BED & BATH	·ACCENTS ·TABLEWARE	·FURNITURE ·GLASS & BAR	·COOKING ·MODERN

CharlestonGardens.com

The founder of this lawn-and-patio shop refers to Charleston, South Carolina, as a place "where classic home and garden furnishings are an essential part of a gracious lifestyle." To get an idea of what she's referring to, take a look at the decidedly genteel patio furniture and lawn ornaments available from this classy, if somewhat clunky, site. You'll find wrought-iron, mahogany and teak tables and chairs, a wealth of beautiful fountains, elegant outdoor lighting options and planters that look great even without vegetation. No wonder most of the store's customers these days live outside the South.

·LIGHTING ·LAWN & GARDEN	·HARDWARE ·DECORATIVE	·ACCENTS ·PATIO & POOL	·FURNITURE ·TRADITIONAL

CharleysGreenHouse.com

You have to be a pretty determined gardener to erect a greenhouse on your property. If so, you'll want the options provided by this surprising online retailer. Select between a couple of primary structural styles, and whether the greenhouse should be attached to your home or freestanding, then explore the ample variety available in materials, colors and shapes. Just as important is the selection of tools, planters, accessories and climate-control devices that ultimately allow you to grow as you want to, to the envy of your flowerbed-tilling friends and neighbors.

·LAWN & GARDEN	·CLEANING	·ECO-FRIENDLY	

ChefsCatalog.com

If you occasionally find yourself describing pots and pans as beautiful, you are going to love this site, where function meets aesthetic appeal. A broad range of cooking tools and accessories accompanies a similarly great selection of kitchen gadgets and electrics, to help keep your kitchen up to par with your interior decoration. Thorough organization and a crystal-clear visual layout makes shopping here just as pleasurable as using these tools to cook up something great to eat. No promises that you'll enjoy the cleanup.

·APPLIANCES	·COOKING	·MODERN	

ChefsResource.com

You don't need to have a huge kitchen to shop on this site, but you'll want one. More nifty kitchen gadgets and accessories populate these pages than you probably know what to do with, stuff like bowl scrapers, cherry stoners and spaetzle makers. Follow the standard browsing to its finish, and you'll see plenty of fine cutlery and cookware as well, and a great assortment of countertop appliances that will hopefully make some of the other items obsolete. If you find cooking fun, this stuff will help make it more so. If you don't like to cook, this enormous quantity of chef's tools will practically do it for you.

·APPLIANCES	·COOKING	·TABLEWARE	·GLASS & BAR

800-654-3570 · Chiasso

Chiásso (the Italian word meaning "uproar") promises "inspired design for the home." It turns out that the inspiration covers most rooms of the house, with categories like Furniture, Home Accessories, Home Textiles and Kitchen & Bath leading to a variety of subcategories, via animated menus. A lot of this stuff looks expensive without actually being overpriced, making this a great place for the urban apartment dweller to find hip, modern housewares yet still have enough leftover cash to throw a party and show them off.

·LIGHTING ·TABLEWARE	·ACCENTS ·ORGANIZATION	·FURNITURE ·MODERN	·BED & BATH	

877-247-2250 · Circa50

It's tough to make sense of this convoluted site, what with their bizarre organization and inconsistent navigation. These products are generally too cool to skip, however, featuring ultrahip furniture designs by the likes of Herman Miller, Modernica and a host of others. If you're willing to embrace these expensive, confounding waters, there is sort of a game to be made out of locating the Ultra Lounge section. It's buried deep in there somewhere; can you find it?

·FURNITURE	·MODERN			

877-726-2323 · Circa Lighting

"Whether you are renovating, building or just searching for that one perfect piece," this Savannah, Georgia, lighting specialist has a fine array of floor lamps, table lamps and fixtures for in- and outside the home. Between the traditional, shaded lamps and more conceptual, modern creations, you should have no trouble finding plenty to work with, and some of it may be relatively inexpensive, though you must link to a detailed view for each of the hundreds of products before you'll know what alternative colors and materials are available, or just what is the price of perfection.

·LIGHTING	·MODERN	·TRADITIONAL		

214-370-0530 · Clean Air Gardening

If gasoline prices have got you down, why pay at the pump to keep your lawn manicured? This site offers plenty of Earth-friendly ways to tend your yard and garden. While a push-reel mower might seem like a lot of effort, an electric mower is simple to charge when you need it, giving one cause to wonder why gas mowers were invented in the first place. It doesn't stop at mowers, with plenty of tillers, trimmers and blowers contributing to your curb appeal without polluting the air. Ecological purists will also benefit from composting materials, rain barrels and pumps, and everyone will appreciate the yard-and-garden tools and ornaments that populate the rest of the site.

·HARDWARE	·LAWN & GARDEN	·ECO-FRIENDLY		

Clio-Home.com

Clio Home · 212-966-8991

You can always get by with your great-grandmother's fine china, or something just like it, but if you prefer to serve your special-occasion meals on something of a more modern taste, take a look at the unique options afforded by this SoHo, Manhattan, boutique. "A treasure trove of plates, glasses, bowls, serving pieces, flatware, vases, table linens, lamps and more" may be found on these pages, all featuring savvy design and a confluence of old and new tastes. Think of it as something you may pass along to your grandchildren.

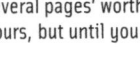

	·TABLEWARE ·	·GLASS & BAR	·MODERN	

Clocko.com

Clocko Clock Company · 888-899-7483

It's all clocks all the time on this unique specialty site, whether you're a fan of contemporary timekeeping or prefer nostalgic styles. An entire section of the site is devoted to grandfather clocks alone, while the regular Clock section proves anything but typical. You'll find clocks that double as tables, clocks with musical chimes and clocks that tell the weather. In fact, you'll find several pages' worth of cuckoo clocks, each more intricately ornate than the last. There's enough here to keep you occupied for hours, but until you buy one you won't notice the seconds ticking by.

	·ACCENTS	·MODERN	·TRADITIONAL	

CoastalDecorShop.com

Cyber Island Shops · 888-974-3557

Though maddeningly slow to load, this virtual seaside site usually makes it worth the wait, with great beach-themed home furniture and accents. If you're decorating a coastal house or condo you shouldn't miss it, and if you only wish you had such a home, the shop can at least make it feel like you live close to the water. We're particularly fond of the shower curtains, assorted decorative hardware and a spectacular selection of Adirondack chairs, which are available in several distinctive colors and styles; perfect for lounging with a cocktail and watching the sunset.

	·ACCENTS ·GLASS & BAR	·FURNITURE ·DECORATIVE	·BED & BATH ·PATIO & POOL	·TABLEWARE

CoastalTool.com

Coastal Tool · 877-551-8665

The most important thing to note in regard to this thoroughly well-stocked tool retailer is that their shipping policy is based on the price of the order, not the weight of it. This, if for no other reason, makes it a necessary stop when doing price comparisons with other shops, as the shipping costs on heavy power tools elsewhere can prove prohibitive, to say the least. As for actually shopping here, you should generally go away happy, unless you ultimately utilize these wares to destroy rooms in your home.

	·HARDWARE			

800-297-6076 · CompactAppliance.com

CompactAppliance.com

While these guys do offer a great variety of miniature appliances, perfect for dorm rooms, RVs and tiny apartments, there are also a few less compact machines; refrigerators, dishwashers and washer/dryers, for example. And despite the high costs associated with having any sizable appliance sent through the mail, these guys offer incentives that might inspire you. Basically, whether rotisserie ovens, induction cooktops, steam vacuums or beer coolers, they have plenty to choose from.

·APPLIANCES	·COOKING			

888-266-8246 · Container Store

ContainerStore.com

Whether you're trying to organize a CD collection, a closetful of clothes, kitchen utensils, dirty laundry, hardware or that personal stuff everybody else on the planet might refer to as "junk," you'll want to store it as efficiently and out of your way as possible. This site can help minimize the clutter, with a focus on storage and organization items to cover every product in every room of the house. While not all of these products may be considered aesthetically pleasing, you can bet they're a lot nicer to look at than a stack, pile or disheveled mess, so if you want to keep your place neat and clean you can either forsake all of your material possessions, or shop here.

·ORGANIZATION				

800-663-8810 · Cooking.com

Cooking.com

You get the feeling, as you look over all the various resources of this rather large site, that its proprietors would take it as an effrontery to find out there was a cooking tool they'd somehow left out of their catalog. After all, they feature an entire section devoted to Egg Tools, so they obviously approach their work with a thorough discipline. If there is anything missing, only the most experienced cook will notice. For the rest of us, the site proves nothing short of revelatory, complete with recipes, advice and general how-to articles. Feast your eyes on this one, and your stomach will follow.

·APPLIANCES ·GLASS & BAR	·COOKING	·TABLEWARE	·ORGANIZATION	

800-825-1833 · Cooks' World

CooksWorld.com

If you like your chef's tools and appliances like you like your home—stylish—you'll flip for this hip provider of cooking accoutrements. Whether bakeware, cutlery, kitchen utensils or juicers, this catalog of functional items pays close attention to the finer details of aesthetic appeal, opting for a modern reinterpretation of the boring old designs. You'll make waffles, dice onions, scoop ice cream and boil water the same way you always have, but look cooler in the process. This site has the power to turn your home food preparation into a spectator sport.

·APPLIANCES ·MODERN	·COOKING	·TABLEWARE	·GLASS & BAR	

CountryCasual.com

If you're a fan of teak, log on to this site immediately to feast your eyes upon some of the most beautiful outdoor furniture you're likely to find anywhere. If you're not a fan of teak, prepare to be won over. From a gorgeous array of outdoor dining sets to some surprisingly nice trash receptacles, it's all teak here and it's all incredibly well made. We particularly recommend the fantastic gliders, rockers and porch swings, each of which are appealing enough to inspire dreams of early retirement.

·FURNITURE   ·PATIO & POOL   ·TRADITIONAL

CountryDoor.com

Built by and for "down-to-earth, country-loving folks just like you," this specialty furniture and housewares retailer offers "unique products that reflect a love of traditions and celebrate the family." It may sound like a Republican campaign speech, but this site turns out to be the genuine article, offering old-fashioned decorative items as well as lovely furniture and beautiful serving pieces. Best of all, the shop's reasonable prices ensure you can return time and again to keep your family living and eating in a style befitting true values.

·LIGHTING ·BED & BATH	·ACCENTS ·TABLEWARE	·FURNITURE ·ORGANIZATION	·COOKING ·TRADITIONAL

CountryHomeProducts.com

If you look out upon the verdant acreage of your property and think, "Let me at it," you'll want to pay a visit to this site that specializes in the heavy machinery of the landscaping outdoorsman. With the relatively low-key array of lawn mowers and hedge trimmers distinctly butched up by an assortment of burly power tools like chain saws, wood chippers and stump grinders, there's no question this is a selection made for tough individuals who're ready to tame nature.

·HARDWARE   ·LAWN & GARDEN

CrystalClassics.com

When only the best serving pieces will do, turn to this impressively stocked crystal and fine china retailer based in Ohio. With brands such as Waterford, Kosta Boda, Orrefors, Swarovski and Wedgwood available, you may be certain that the stemware, barware, flatware and dinnerware you find here will be among the highest-class available. If you like that, perhaps one of the gorgeous crystal chandeliers will make its way into your home to complement one of the many brilliant candlesticks. Thanks to this site, the web literally sparkles.

·LIGHTING ·TRADITIONAL	·ACCENTS	·TABLEWARE	·GLASS & BAR

866-727-8435 · Culinary Parts Unlimited

CulinaryParts.com

Finding small kitchen appliances is a cinch with this well-stocked specialty site, whether you're planning to press waffles, slice meat, make your own ice cream, toast bread or brew espresso. However, the best part might be the option to buy replacement parts for all such appliances. Not that these new products are likely to fall apart anytime soon, but if your coffee pot happens to break or your deep fryer filter clogs, it's great to know you can quickly find the part you need for hundreds of models ranging across dozens of brands.

·APPLIANCES	·HARDWARE	·COOKING		

800-555-6653 · Curran

CurranOnline.com

This home catalog grew out of modest beginnings in 1996 when a considerate manufacturer's representative "put a little flier together" to show some of his friends the great furniture he had access to. Clearly, word spread quickly over the past ten years, and that small flier for twenty people has grown into a popular biannual catalog. The great dining, living room and patio furniture still ships from the manufacturer, though, meaning you can get a great price on this stuff even before the free freight shipping. Consider Jeff Curran a friend to us all.

·ACCENTS	·FURNITURE	·PATIO & POOL	·TRADITIONAL	

212-625-1039 · De La Espada

DeLaEspada.com

White oak and black walnut provide the inspiration and foundation for the sleekly designed furniture on this manufacturer's site. Like a great poet can inspire creativity and insight within the structural confines of a rhyming couplet, these guys manage to deliver warm and appealing designs despite an almost fanatical devotion to right angles—squarish, simple and elegant. Simply select All Our Products from the Products drop-down menu to view living room, dining room and bedroom furniture in its lovely entirety.

·ACCENTS	·FURNITURE	·MODERN		

800-506-6541 · Design Public

DesignPublic.com

Encouraging you to "take an active role in personalizing your space and be happy dwelling in it," this San Francisco-based home shop seeks to help you do both with a host of fresh, modern furniture and accents. Designer bedding, wallpaper and lamps head up a selection punctuated by hip barstools and slick coffee tables, and though the small shop has only recently gotten off the ground, the proprietors do try to impress you with great values, despite the fact that reasonable prices are impossible to come by with such stellar wares.

·ACCENTS ·MODERN	·FURNITURE	·BED & BATH	·ORGANIZATION	

DirectFromMexico.com

If you're going for a Southwestern decorating scheme in your home, no room will be complete without a good selection of Mexican furnishings, straight from the source, by way of Arizona. This fantastic shop offers gorgeous varieties of wood, tin and earthenware items, ranging from furniture and lighting to decorative hardware, pottery and service accessories. Familiarizing yourself with the site's organization may take a bit of focus, but don't give up until you've at least seen the exquisite selection of hand-painted Talavera ceramics; they're good enough to inspire a complete redesign of your home.

·LIGHTING ·LAWN & GARDEN	·HARDWARE ·TABLEWARE	·ACCENTS ·DECORATIVE	·FURNITURE ·TRADITIONAL

DirectGardening.com

If you're in the market for a breath of fresh air, this site offers a variety of young trees to plant on your property. Ranging from one to three feet high when they arrive, the firs, spruces, willows, poplars and even redwoods are simple to find within these pages, and at prices low enough to procure a forest. Only slightly less inexpensive are trees bearing fruits (apple, cherry and lemon) or nuts (walnut, hazelnut and pecan). You may also find shrubbery, edibles that grow closer to the earth, as well as plenty of groundcover, including the Walk-On-Me plant, which gives off the aroma of thyme when trod upon, should you prefer a breath of fresh, scented air.

·LAWN & GARDEN	·FLORAE		

DirectionsHG.com

Without a doubt, you've always been curious just which company is "the nation's #1 weathervane and cupola manufacturer." Well, wonder no more. Here you'll find a variety of vinyl cupola designs, which prove easier to attach to your home than you might imagine. Meanwhile, weathervanes come is a variety of elegant shapes, while some beautiful brass finials, drainage heads and rain chains provide unique aesthetic upgrades to your roof. But the delightful site boasts more than just roof accents; you'll also find decorative mailboxes, wind chimes, birdhouses, fire pits and custom gazebos. It's little wonder these guys are at the top of their field.

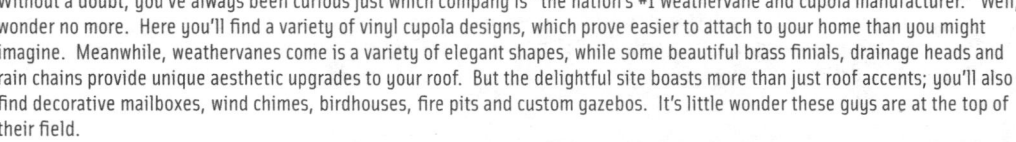

·LIGHTING	·HARDWARE	·LAWN & GARDEN	·DECORATIVE

DutchGardens.com

Given the name of this site, you'd expect to find a lot of tulips, and you can, unless they're out of season, in which case you'll have to settle for the lovely selection of begonias, dahlias, gladiolus, peonies, roses and lilies. Browsing is easy enough, but if you're supremely impatient, the Plant Finder search function enables you to search for florae based on height, color and light requirements, as well as by season, so you can go ahead and plan for those tulips, and have a replacement flower ready when those finish blooming.

·FLORAE			

800-944-2233 · Design Within Reach

DWR.com

Are you ready for a slick shopping experience? That's what there is to be found at DWR, aka Design Within Reach, a San Francisco-based seller of upscale European furniture. Apparently, Europeans have a better grasp and/or appreciation of fine designs, and these guys want to bring it to the rest of us. They do so with aplomb, offering what may be the best online selection of designer furniture we've seen—neither run-of-the-mill, nor overly conceptual. Each product is beautifully displayed, generously described, and never difficult to find.

·LIGHTING ·MODERN	·ACCENTS	·FURNITURE	·ORGANIZATION

800-610-8610 · English Creek Gardens

EnglishCreekGardens.com

Whether you have the luxury of a yard in which to pursue your botanical interests or wish to dress up the inside of your home with a thriving garden of sorts, this English-themed shop provides an excellent array of planters and topiary to work with. Most interesting among these wares are the terrariums, cloches, Wardian cases and apothecary jars, in which you may present, protect and/or preserve your plants and flowers in the most elegant fashion. Traditional gardeners and even the slightly less traditional sort will not be let down.

·ACCENTS	·LAWN & GARDEN	·TRADITIONAL	

212-251-0621 · eTableTop

eTableTop.com

Founded on the principle that "tableware doesn't need to be expensive or fancy, but it should be a reflection of your personal style," this internet retailer delivers a unique assortment of modern service-wares that run the gamut from inexpensive to moderately inexpensive. The flatware, glassware, dinnerware, serving trays and table linens are ultimately arranged by brand, so finding the best items to enhance your personal expression may take some time, but since we're talking about fashionable brands like Rosenthal, Versace and Jonathan Adler, you may wish to do so anyway.

·TABLEWARE	·GLASS & BAR	·MODERN	

541-221-9806 · *Everything Chopsticks.com*

EverythingChopsticks.com

You might not expect a site that focuses entirely on chopsticks to be this big; but between Chinese, Japanese and Thai varieties, there are dozens of the beautifully ornate utensils, ranging in cost from two to eleven dollars per pair. You definitely wouldn't expect that such a site would come from Eugene, Oregon, but that's the case with this retailer that also offers chopstick rests, bamboo coasters and several other Asian table accessories, available individually or as part of a gift set. But, as it turns out, at every turn this "Largest Selection of Chopsticks on the Internet" exeeds expectations.

·TABLEWARE			

FabricsAndHome.com

Brought to us by "New York City's largest suppliers of home decorative fabrics, designer wallpaper, custom window treatments" and more, this site offers an incredible abundance of fabrics by the yard, with relatively easy shopping. The shop also seems to offer custom-ordered bedding and window treatments, and while these are difficult enough to order by virtue of the fact you must enter your own measurements, we also couldn't find a place to select which of the fine fabrics for the company to use when making your order. Hopefully, this will change soon, but if not, we'd recommend sticking to the fabrics.

·WINDOWS

Faucet.com

Some massive web shops offer everything but the kitchen sink—this one offers the sink. A huge assortment of sinks, faucets and other fixtures for the kitchen or bath may be found here, along with plenty of cabinet and door hardware to help with most of your home improvement projects. However, just when you think you've got this site pegged, it turns up full selections of fireplace accessories, indoor fountains, mirrors, clocks and a huge inventory of lamps and lighting fixtures. No end of your home will look the same when you're done shopping here.

·HARDWARE ·DECORATIVE

FaucetDepot.com

Life would be lovely if we didn't need to have things like toilets and running water in our home, but life sure gets ugly fast when we don't. This site helps keep the pipes running in both directions, and even manages to cast a pretty light on it all. Decorative fixtures for the kitchen and bathroom add chrome, brass and steel finishes to your faucets and handles, while sinks, toilets and other basins provide a variety of other options, including faux woods. Boost your showerheads or beautify your bidet; you'll be glad you checked this one out.

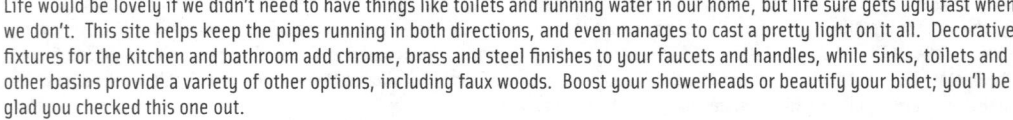

·HARDWARE ·DECORATIVE

FiberglassPlanters.com

A singular assortment of products dominate this unique specialty shop, and they're not as heavy as you might think. Although the bronze and cast-iron patinas seen on the many varieties of planter here may look as if they'd take an army to move, they're actually comprised mostly of fiberglass, and thus surprisingly light. Don't be mistaken in thinking these are of low quality, though—a sophisticated process bonds an outer layer of metal to the fiberglass, meaning these planters will look, feel and even age as if they were made entirely of bronze or iron, which might explain why you'll find some startlingly high prices here as well.

·LAWN & GARDEN

888-949-2999 · FineGardenProducts.com

FineGardenProducts.com

Expressing one of the sweetest sentiments on the whole world wide web, this site's tag line claims, "We want you to be happy." Well, it's a wonderful thing to say, and happiness comes to you in the form of garden decor or door knockers, get ready to be in a great mood. This variety of garden structures and other landscaping ornaments stands up to any you'll find online, and the assortment of decorative hardware promises to spruce up your house from the outside in. The aesthetic appeal of these items is off the chart, making this site good enough to cheer up just about any landscaping grouch.

·HARDWARE ·PATIO & POOL	·ACCENTS ·TRADITIONAL	·LAWN & GARDEN	·DECORATIVE

800-485-7217 · FireplaceScreens.com

FireplaceScreens.com

"Add a dash of style and warm ambience to your home," courtesy of the fine assortment of fireplace accessories offered by this specialty shop. With hundreds of items available, you may easily sort the beautiful selection of fireplace tools and screens by materials such as Wood, Brass, Iron, Steel and Copper, or shop by fireplace height or width. Perhaps the best browsing options, however, are style options including Antique, Traditional and the modern Designer's Touch. It's enough to make you excited for winter.

·DECORATIVE	·MODERN	·TRADITIONAL

323-655-1908 · Fitzsu

Fitzsu.com

Not many shops will make the effort to offer beautiful toilet brushes, but that's just the kind of store this is. Nontraditional design enthusiasts will get a huge kick out of just about everything seen here, from service-ware to cooking tools and accents to ashtrays, the shop makes for a fantastic out-of-the-ordinary bridal registry. In other words, whenever your friends come over, this stuff will put their typical housewares to shame.

·APPLIANCES ·ORGANIZATION	·COOKING ·CLEANING	·BED & BATH ·GLASS & BAR	·TABLEWARE ·MODERN

888-649-0882 · Improvement Direct

FixturesDirect.com

Is your bathroom as beautiful as it can be? How about your kitchen or bar? If your fixtures and faucets are in need of an upgrade, this site will be a great help. Heck, if you were to visit this site by chance, you'll probably wind up deciding to upgrade anyway. It helps to know what you're doing with regard to your home's plumbing dimensions, but if you don't, a customer service representative is available for a chat consultation during regular hours on most days. Factor in the wholesale prices, and there's hardly a reason left not to improve the beauty and quality of your showers, tubs and sinks.

·HARDWARE	·DECORATIVE		

FlorStor.com

Cleaning the floor is rarely as easy as it sounds, especially when you're trying to renew the perfection of your finer surface materials. This site offers solutions in the form of solutions designed to clean Hardwood, Laminate, Vinyl and Stone & Tile. In many cases, the solvents come recommended by top flooring manufacturers, and usually with each floor type you'll have multiple options. However, once you select the surface in question from the site menu, you must do the rest of your shopping by brand name, at which point it's tough to say for sure whether one cleans cleaner than the other.

·CLEANING

FormPlusFunction.com

"From understated modern design classics to exuberant low-voltage chandeliers," this site offers "Contemporary lighting for every room of your home," so much so that shopping could take all day. It's not very user-friendly for so regimented a site, but this may mostly be attributed to the wide selection, which includes a terrific assortment of track lighting and ceiling fans in addition to lamps, sconces, chandeliers and patio lighting that range from clean and cool to downright funky. It's definitely worth a good, long look.

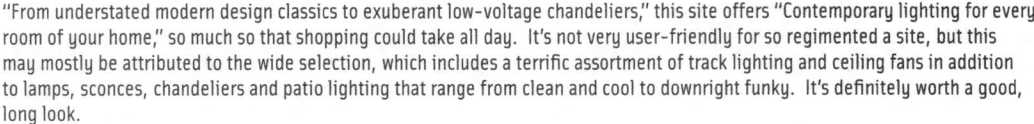

·LIGHTING   ·PATIO & POOL   ·MODERN

FransWicker.com

Fran has a brick-and-mortar store in New Jersey, but why go there when you can find all the wicker and rattan furniture you'll ever need on the store's no-frills web site? We're talkin' wicker chairs, tables, entertainment centers, hampers and even a wicker chaise longue. You can browse through it all pretty easily, and click on the thumbnail images to check out some of the largest and most detailed pictures of furniture we've seen online. In fact, if you notice on the large view that you're not pleased with the fabric of a seat cushion or ottoman, don't fret, just check out the Online Swatch Book to find the right alternative for special order. Looks like this site has some frills after all.

  ·FURNITURE   ·ORGANIZATION   ·PATIO & POOL   ·TRADITIONAL

FrenchGardening.com

A taste of French gardening may be found on this site, courtesy of its American founder, who endeavors to offer only French-made gardening products. The company, whose name means "The Green Studio," includes gardening apparel, planters, tools, accents and other garden-related gear. The best part, however, may be the access it provides to French vegetables and wildflowers. Considering that France has historically been responsible for cultivating some of the best gardens in the world, this one is imperative to the culturally sophisticated green thumb.

 ·ACCENTS   ·LAWN & GARDEN   ·FLORAE   ·TRADITIONAL

800-762-5374 · Frontera

Frontera.com

It's hard to say what passes for "traditional" these days, but whatever you imagine it to be, in terms of furniture, there's a good chance it's here. The only problem may be finding it. The navigation can be a little confusing, but with patience, it works, and actually offers you several different ways to find what you're after. The easiest would be to select the site's Indoor, Outdoor or Accessories options at the top of the home page. You then select a style (e.g., Rustic, Colonial, Contemporary, etc.) and then the room you're trying to furnish. The left side of the page features a bunch of different navigations that might work faster, but faster's not always better.

·ACCENTS	·FURNITURE	·TRADITIONAL	

888-263-9850 · Frontgate

Frontgate.com

Now this is living. Frontgate is a vendor of high-end "lifestyle accessories," basically the kinds of furnishings that everybody has, but better versions of them. This stuff is sleek, chic, and, of course, expensive. It's hard to beat this shop for entertaining, though, and so it's well worth the cost if you like to host a gathering here and there. You'll find plenty of service-ware, kitchen accessories, cleaning tools, furniture and accents here to turn any occasion into a fete, whether it's a pool party, dinner party, barbecue or just your friends coming over to watch the big game on TV.

·APPLIANCES ·BED & BATH	·ACCENTS ·ORGANIZATION	·FURNITURE ·GLASS & BAR	·COOKING ·PATIO & POOL

800-362-7632 · FurnitureFind

FurnitureFind.com

Aptly named, this site finds you an elaborate selection of furniture for just about every room in the house. Basic, functional stuff rules here, with no striking sense of style or adventure. If anything stands out, it would be the surprisingly thorough array of chandeliers, a good number of grandfather clocks and a wide, if not distinctive, selection of fireplaces. If your ISP can handle it, you can view all products in a single section. This will be particularly useful in behemoth categories such as Patio Furniture, Bedroom Furniture, and Dining Room Furniture.

·LIGHTING ·MODERN	·ACCENTS ·TRADITIONAL	·FURNITURE	·PATIO & POOL

888-556-5676 · Gardeners Edge

GardenersEdge.com

This all-around gardening site focuses primarily on the things you need most to tend your plants and flowers, covering just about everything except the actual plants and flowers. Plenty of shovels, shears, weeders and other tools may be found to help you get your hands dirty, as well as plenty of gardening gloves to keep them clean. The selection includes some helpful lawn care equipment, sprinkler parts, composting tools, pest control options, arbors, trellises and other garden accents. By anyone's estimate there's enough here to keep all your weekends busy for weeks to come.

·LAWN & GARDEN	·ECO-FRIENDLY		

GardensAlive.com

What does it take to make your garden grow? Obviously, there's water, sunlight and fertile soil, but what nature gives, nature can take away, in the form of insects, fungi and other botanical threats. The tendency is to add chemicals to the mix. But, come on, these plants flourished for millennia without the help of pollutant artificial supplements, so why should they stop now? Instead, check this site's "Environmentally Responsible Products That Work," for beneficial insects, nonchemical fungicides and other nature-friendly products to aid and protect your lawn and garden.

	·LAWN & GARDEN	·ECO-FRIENDLY		

GardenSide.com

In a word: *teak*. This outdoor furniture specialist sticks strictly to the weather-resistant wood, with benches, chairs, loungers, parasols, tables and planters to accentuate your deck, patio, lawn or garden. Browsing is about as simple as it gets, with a tremendous variety within each product category. While shipping seems a bit pricey, when you consider that it's rather sizable wood furniture going through the mail, the prices suddenly seem quite reasonable. Good stuff.

	·FURNITURE	·PATIO & POOL	·TRADITIONAL	

Gearys.com

For more than 75 years, this housewares retailer has been giving Beverly Hills a beautiful assortment of fine china, flatware, glassware, barware and other serving pieces. Here the upscale shop gives the rest of the world a chance to indulge in the posh tableware long appreciated by the entertainment industry elite. Although a bridal registry is available for online purchase, as of the time of this writing it appears that you can only actually register for gifts in the physical store; if and when this changes, this store will be even better.

	·TABLEWARE	·GLASS & BAR	·TRADITIONAL	

GladiatorGW.com

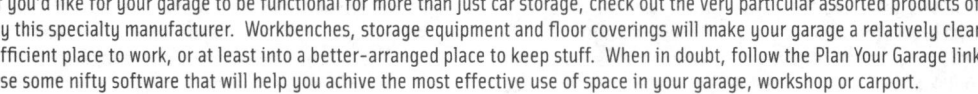

If you'd like for your garage to be functional for more than just car storage, check out the very particular assorted products offered by this specialty manufacturer. Workbenches, storage equipment and floor coverings will make your garage a relatively clean and efficient place to work, or at least into a better-arranged place to keep stuff. When in doubt, follow the Plan Your Garage link to use some nifty software that will help you achive the most effective use of space in your garage, workshop or carport.

	·ORGANIZATION		

888-828-7170 · Gracious Style

GraciousStyle.com

This purveyor of table linens, silverware, porcelain and crystal wares has the goal to "inspire discerning clients to create the perfect settings for celebrating a life of luxury, elegance and sophistication." As if that weren't enough of a mouthful, they intend to do this by capturing "the essence of fine living with its exquisite collection of tabletop accessories." Sounds to us like you've been issued a challenge. If you fancy yourself a "discerning client," check out their merchandise; odds are you won't be disappointed.

·ACCENTS	·BED & BATH	·TABLEWARE	·TRADITIONAL

212-226-2567 · Grand Brass Lamp Parts

GrandBrass.com

Industrious people may see this site as an opportunity to build a lamp from scratch; certainly, everything you need to do so resides in this catalog. We're talking armbacks, backplates, bobesches, bushings, check rings, crystals, reducers, risers, slip rings, sockets and more, each broken into the relevant subcategories. Now, if you don't know what any of these things are, you may not be ready to put together a custom lamp, but you might still manage to find a specific piece you want to replace on a lamp you already own, thanks to a couple of effective browsing techniques, and way, way more products than we ever thought necessary to light a room.

·LIGHTING	·HARDWARE		

800-405-0222 · Green Building Supply

GreenBuildingSupply.com

Construction of environmentally sound "green" buildings has only recently started to catch on, but thanks to this site it's not too late to improve your existing home's ecological compatibility. It can be as simple as using the nontoxic cleaning solvents, paints, sealers and stains, or as involved as installing low-water toilets, energy-conserving appliances and natural flooring. You'll find it all here, as well as some helpful air and water filtration systems, Earth-friendly insulation and lovely wood furniture. The site tends to offer too much information to make for easy shopping, but there shouldn't be any lasting damage for cluttering up the web.

·APPLIANCES ·ECO-FRIENDLY	·HARDWARE	·FURNITURE	·CLEANING

800-398-6004 · The Hammock Company

Hammock-Company.com

Putting a bed on your deck or in your backyard just doesn't make sense. Putting up a hammock, however, might just be the best idea you ever had. And this might just be the best spot to buy that hammock. The internet retailer based outside of Greenville, North Carolina, "the hammock capital of the world," offers a fantastic assortment of hammocks and porch swings of every look or design. With each rope, quilted or poolside hammock you'll be told how many people may fit comfortably, how much weight it can hold and which pillows or other accessories go best with it, so you may nap through those lazy afternoons in style.

·FURNITURE			

Hanneby.com

Hanneby · 713-213-4591

Believing that art can "be expressed in things and tools we use every day," this small and at times difficult retailer turns up a varied assortment of housewares for those in search of something a little special and different. Whereas most modern home specialists seem to feature a lot of the same concepts and designs, this one tends to deviate from all norms, which might make for an interesting bridal registry, if the shop offered such a service. However, apparently it's "Quality Function Design" mantra doesn't apply to web commerce.

	·COOKING	·TABLEWARE	·MODERN	

HighbrowFurniture.com

Highbrow, Inc. · 888-329-0219

If you're tired of sofas and chairs that look like every sofa and chair you've ever seen, check out this modern/designer catalog of furniture. Here, no shape is too abstract, no color overstated; every sitting piece is viewed as a work of art and as such has been crafted down to the minutiae. Seating, tables, rugs and a fascinating assortment of hanging lights and clocks will at times bewilder the eyes and boggle the imagination. On the other hand, you'll occasionally see what appears to be the most uncomfortable, mass-produced chair imaginable, but don't be fooled. If you find it here, it's definitely fabulous.

	·LIGHTING	·ACCENTS	·FURNITURE	·MODERN

HighCountryGardens.com

Santa Fe Greenhouses · 800-925-9387

Flowers are great, but if you're looking for a reasonable selection of interesting and beautiful groundcover, this may ultimately be the site you want to check out. Featuring a unique assortment of ornamental grasses, succulents, shrubs and perennials, this vegetation proves a great way to establish a Southwestern style to your landscaping schemes. Browsing can be cumbersome, so we recommend heading straight to the Online Store's Plant Finder search function, which enables you to narrow down specific plant types, colors, blooming seasons, soil types, climate conditions and other features relating to animals and fragrance. It's an easier alternative to floral gardens, but nicer-looking than lawn and dirt.

	·FLORAE			

HoldEverything.com

Hold Everything · 888-922-4117

If you spend a lot of time flipping through the pages of **thepurplebook**, your home will eventually be overflowing with so much great stuff that you'll have to consider knocking down some walls or moving to a bigger place. Not so fast! This shop is filled with ingenious solutions to the problems of organization and storage. Whether it's a handy set of shelves that can fit where you never imagined shelves before, or equipment that can optimize use of your closet space, the specialty shop can help keep your space neat and clean even after the biggest of shopping sprees.

	·FURNITURE	·ORGANIZATION		

800-749-4049 · Home Fires

HomeFiresUSA.com

When we're cold, we're likely to value heat over beauty, but isn't it nice when we can have it both ways? Thanks to this shop, we can. The site's focus is a slew of decorative fire baskets: polished metal fireplace accessories that combine 18th-century British charm with "gas coal burners" to provide a cleaner alternative to smoky wood fires, without forfeiting the romantic allure of open flames. It sounds complicated but looks fantastic, even if you explore the Electric Inserts option, which operate gas-free and even without a fireplace. These beat space heaters any day.

·HARDWARE	·ACCENTS	·DECORATIVE	·TRADITIONAL	

888-223-2545 · House of Antique Hardware

HouseOfAntiqueHardware.com

Doorknobs, cabinet pulls, heater vents, switch covers and electrical fixtures are the little embellishments that can add a bit of character to any home, assuming they're not the common, mass-manufactured variety. A full complement of decorative hardware pieces can be found on this site, enough to cover every entryway, bathroom accent and window in the house. You'll find both antique and replica items, and while the antiques certainly have more cachet, the replica pieces look just as beautiful, and take nothing at all away from the ultimate grandeur of a beautifully accented home.

·HARDWARE	·DECORATIVE	·TRADITIONAL		

800-454-3941 · iFloor.com

iFloor.com

If you're interested in drastically altering the feel of your home, one sure way to do so is to redo your floors. With help from this site, you can change your carpeted floors to hardwood, then to tile and back to carpet again. Okay, one change will be enough, but with the vast selection of carpets, area rugs, hardwoods, linoleum, ceramic, vinyl, bamboo, cork and even leather flooring options available here, you'll wish switching one floor for another was just that easy.

·HARDWARE	·ACCENTS	·TABLEWARE	·DECORATIVE	

866-467-6788 · importu

Importu.com

"Born from a love of travel, exotic cultures and a fascination with time-honored skills of craftsmanship," Importu got its start importing products from Morocco. Today, it culls home accents, furniture, lighting and service pieces from five continents, specializing in exactly the sort of exotic trinkets and artifacts of foreign cultures that Americans love to place tastefully around the house. These beautiful objects include some especially lovely lamps, serving trays and throw pillows, but you're likely to find nearly any sort of home furnishing, from just about every corner of the planet.

·LIGHTING ·TRADITIONAL	·ACCENTS	·FURNITURE	·TABLEWARE	

InterfaceFlor.com

InterfaceFlor · 866-281-3567

Mosaic meets rug on this curious site, which sells modular carpet, 380 square inches at a time. The roughly 20x20 inch self-adhesive squares come in a range of colors, and may be arranged and rearranged as you see fit. Cover a small area or go wall to wall; follow a checkerboard pattern or opt for a more complex crossword puzzle look; keep it simple or piece together a motley eight-color conceptual design. Presorted packages offer some pleasing color combinations at better costs, while ordering per tile allows you to flex your creative muscles ad infinitum.

·ACCENTS · ·MODERN

InvitingHome.com

Distinctive Interiors Group · 781-249 -0957

If you actually know what people are talking about when they refer to crown molding, friezes, corbels, appliqués, rosettes and wainscotting, you will really enjoy this site. With architectural adornments for your walls, mantels, stairs and ceiling, you may add a depth and class to your home that Oscar Wilde would have appreciated. Highlights include classical columns, wood carvings, wall niches, chandeliers and ceiling medallions, with fine assortments of fireplace accessories, mirrors, room dividers and decorative wall hangings to complete the look.

·LIGHTING ·TRADITIONAL · ·HARDWARE · ·ACCENTS · ·DECORATIVE

ItalianPottery.com

The Italian Pottery Outlet · 805-899-9170

When you find yourself in need of handcrafted pottery and dinnerware from across the Atlantic, take note of this site, whose buyers "scour the Italian countryside searching for the most interesting designs and patterns." From Tuscany to the Amalfi coast, most if not all regions of the country are represented, each with its own particular styles and colors. As it happens, you must browse by region, so sifting through the many beautiful plates and complimentary dishes can take awhile, but if you look upon it as a cultural education of sorts, you might find yourself having fun while you shop.

·TABLEWARE

JamaliGarden.com

Jamali Garden Supplies, Inc. · 212-979-0108

It's amazing how simple things, like stone groundcover or bamboo stakes, can beautifully embellish a home garden. These are just some of the fantastic garden accents that will draw your attention to this retailer based in New York City's flower district. You'll also find some remarkable vases and beautiful planters, along with some useful gardening supplies. Given the site's name, none of this is terribly surprising. However, the curtains, ribbons, baskets and table linens did catch us off guard. If this lovely shop's focus is expanding to include the indoors, all the better.

·ACCENTS · ·LAWN & GARDEN · ·WINDOWS

800-879-2258 · Johnny's Selected Seeds

JohnnySeeds.com

When you're ready to scour long lists of flowers and vegetables, go to this site, which offers just about all the seeds you could want to add beauty and/or nourishment to your garden. While the initial menus don't offer any visual assistance, within each plant name you'll find up to a dozen varieties to choose from, each beautifully photographed so you can be sure what the flower, fruit or veggie is supposed to look like when grown properly. Luckily, the site also offers a comprehensive assortment of tools and supplies; everything you'll need to keep your thumb as green as can be.

·HARDWARE   ·LAWN & GARDEN   ·FLORAE

860-567-0838 · John Scheepers

JohnScheepers.com

Nobody wants to go shopping for Reticulata bucharicas or Humilis alba coerulea oculatas when all you want are irises and tulips. That's one of the reasons we like this flower bulb site—it arranges all the various species of flowers into their respective, recognizable groups. Hence, you can browse a full variety of the above florae, as well as crocus, hyacinths, lilies and amaryllis, then view a splendid layout of vibrant images depicting the many varieties available, which have names that only botanists really know.

·FLORAE

877-287-1910 · Jonathan Adler

JonathanAdler.com

If you'd like to shop from a site with character for a change, take a look at this one and go straight to the About Jonathan Adler and Manifesto sections. Oh yeah, but don't leave without perusing the extraordinary assortments of the store's Pottery, Lighting, Lacquer and Textiles categories. Once you've gotten the idea of what this intriguing designer's all about, you'll probably want to venture into the Furniture, Handbags and Groovy Gifts sections as well, which hopefully will grow with time. Do all of the above and you should have a hard time leaving without buying something.

·LIGHTING   ·ACCENTS   ·TABLEWARE   ·MODERN

727-251-4803 · Justmorocco Imports Store

JustMorocco.com

"All handmade and imported from the souks and villages of Morocco," the wood-carved and wrought-iron furniture available from this site are enough reason to visit. But there's a lot more to be found here, beginning with some gorgeous hanging light fixtures, opulent couches and outstanding mosaic tables. But the most impressive stuff may be the decorative hardware. With tiles, ceiling arches and a truly wonderful assortment of doors, there are enough great goods here to help you fashion your own Moroccan palace, one piece at a time.

·LIGHTING   ·ACCENTS   ·FURNITURE   ·DECORATIVE

KitazawaSeed.com

Kitazawa Seed Company · 510-595-1188

They're not usually available in your local supermarket, and only rarely if ever to be found online. But if your recipe book calls for Asian vegetables, with the help of this site you may grow them in your garden. You may have to really scour that cookbook to find recipes requiring Edible Burdock, Japanese Mugwort, Komatsuna, Mibuna, Misome, Molokeyhia, Shiso, Poha Berry or Malabar Spinach, but seeing as you can find such rare and exotic veggie seeds here, you might just need to get a new cookbook.

·FLORAE

KnifeMerchant.com

The Knife Merchant · 800-714-8226

Buying a knife set is a fairly simple, straightforward matter: you simply choose whichever handles look nicer or are more comfortable, and voilà, you've got the basics covered. However, there are so many particular specialty blades called for by recipes or required by certain foods, and finding such knives can prove a hassle. Not so with this retailer, which offers knives by type and/or shape, meaning that you can first select a category such as Japanese Blades, Bread Knives or Paring/Garnishing, then view a plethora of knives with distinct shapes, metals and purposes. Then you can choose the handle you like best.

·APPLIANCES   ·COOKING

Korin.com

Korin Japanese Trading Corp. · 800-626-2172

When the finest Japanese restaurants in the country want cooking equipment, cutlery, service-ware and chef's apparel, this is the company most of them go to. This site allows all of us the same access to the best tools available for preparing Japanese cuisine, which of course uses some of the finest tools in the world. Whether you want a rice cooker, a nigiri sushi mold, beautiful lacquer dinnerware, a traditional tea set or just a very sharp knife, make this the first stop on your road to mastery of Asian cuisine.

·COOKING   ·TABLEWARE

LAHardware.com

Liz's Antique Hardware · 323-939-4403

Though the name of this decorative hardware boutique doesn't technically refer to Los Angeles, it does happen to reside in the smoggy Southern California city, and it turns out the home of Hollywood has had some of the world's best access to incredible hardware for years. Fortunately, this site does a good job presenting the antique, contemporary and reproduction door, cabinet and window pieces, so we may all re-outfit our homes with fantastic new (or old) knobs, pulls, switchplates, mailboxes and heating vent covers.

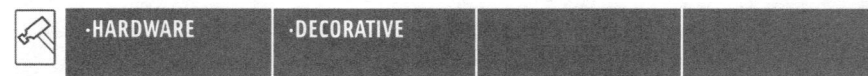

·HARDWARE   ·DECORATIVE

011-44-15394-88100 · Lakeland Limited

LakelandLimited.com

This "Creative Kitchenware Company" out of England may muddle you with its clever and cutesy category names, but in the end you'll find a wide assortment of handy and appealing cooking and cleaning equipment. Featuring bakeware, Tupperware, microwave cookware and a slew of tools for stirring, slicing, measuring and basting, we're forced to wonder how a country boasting a franchise such as this could be so renowned for having bad cuisine. As for the helpful cleaning supplies available here...well, they make more sense.

·APPLIANCES	·COOKING	·CLEANING	

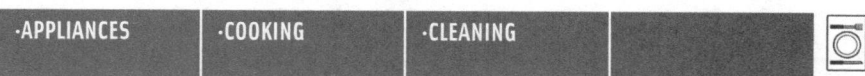

888-874-2676 · LampStore.com

LampStore.com

Been bumping your shins on furniture in the dimly lit corners of your home? Well, these guys would rather sell you a lamp than curse your darkness, and so have embraced the great advantage maintained by all specialty retailers: selection. There are only lamps for sale here, but in every traditional design you could imagine, as well as a few odd ones you couldn't. A simple, illustrative site design makes it easy to browse—you can shop by room (for example, kids' rooms, rec rooms or studies) or style (anything from Victorian to casual to contemporary). The lack of a search feature might keep you from immediately finding the lamp shade shaped like a stuffed shirt, but if your tastes are that specific, you're probably patient enough to find it on your own.

·LIGHTING	·MODERN	·TRADITIONAL	

866-898-5461 · Lavender Fields

LavenderFieldsOnline.com

"Located in the historic coastal hamlet of Port Jefferson, New York," this shop brings its quaint, small-town atmosphere to the web, with a lovely assortment of country chic blankets and home accents. You'll spot some furniture on the site as well, but as of this writing it was not available for online purchase. Whether or not this changes, there is plenty to keep you busy here, whether it's curtain panels, a multitude of household decorations or bedding by the likes of Rachel Ashwell, Bella Notte and Pine Cone Hill. Top off your order with some nontoxic cleaning agents and you'll be ready for an idyllic lifestyle even if you live in the city.

·ACCENTS	·BED & BATH	·WINDOWS	·TRADITIONAL

800-267-8735 · Lee Valley & Veritas

LeeValley.com

If you've ever walked into a football-field-size home improvement store and gotten lost among thousands of products stacked fifteen feet high, you know just how daunting it can be to find that single item you want. In most cases, you need a guide, and even then you may be dissatisfied with the results. Thanks to this enormous online hardware, woodworking and garden supply store from Canada, we can hunt for myriad hand tools and obscure hardware pieces with pretty favorable odds for success, and no one will have to send out a search-and-rescue party.

·HARDWARE	·LAWN & GARDEN	·ECO-FRIENDLY	·DECORATIVE

LightingUniverse.com

Allied Trade Group · 888-404-2744

Billing itself "The Professional's Lighting Source," this behemoth of a specialty store definitely seems to offer more than most, offering you a great opportunity to bypass your pro lighting guy and choose from a massive selection of sconces, lamps, bulbs, ceiling fans, track lighting and chandeliers yourself. While a few of these desirable designs aren't available online, the bulk of the catalog may be purchased as quickly as they may be found. While not strictly easy, the very thoroughly organized site shouldn't present any problems to navigate, even for the amateur.

	·LIGHTING	·MODERN	·TRADITIONAL	

Lightology.com

Lightology · 773-883-6111

If the lights in your home illuminate stylish, modern furnishings, you'll definitely want those lights to look as good as all they shine upon. This site won't let you down, offering a very cool and deep selection of contemporary lighting fixtures, lamps, ceiling fans and outdoor light sources. There is dedicated lighting for your closets, bathroom mirrors, artwork, lawn, desk and walls, and subcategories of the thoroughly organized catalog can usually be viewed on one page, which makes finding the right light here easier than finding a light switch in the dark.

	·LIGHTING	·MODERN		

LinenPlace.com

Linenplace.com · 973-696-3311

When we speak of luxury, it's easy to imagine things like diamonds, caviar and gentlemen's gentlemen, but once you've locked onto the idea of slipping between the smooth coddling warmth of silk sheets, everything else just seems like trivial comfort. This site leads you to plenty of quality bedding, boasting high thread counts and excellent materials. There are even some similarly indulgent towels, so that the coarsest fabric your skin ever needs make contact with will be the clothes you wear.

	·BED & BATH	·MODERN	·TRADITIONAL	

LSFabrics.com

Lewis & Sheron Textile Company · 877-256-8448

Get a new look for your old furniture with the help of this fabric specialist, which offers an incredible array of pattern and textures to suit your upholstering and drapery needs. Crewels, silks, damasks, toiles, suedes and linens are represented in Asian motifs, animal themes, stripes, plaids, checks, dots and florals, with myriad contemporary designs as well as traditional looks. Once you've selected any swatches you'd like to evaluate, meander on over to the trim section to peruse to assorted cording and fringe, which we found to be oddly captivating.

	·ACCENTS	·WINDOWS		

888-859-5522 · Maine Cottage

MaineCottage.com

With a summery palette and a sunny attitude to match, this small furniture business out of the Northeast has blossomed from a modest family enterprise into quite the purveyor of charm. It all starts with a tremendous selection of wicker furniture, which successfully combines quaint and contemporary styles. But a more solid selection of housewares includes great kid's beds, great sofas and plenty of fun accents that will be perfect in your vacation home, whether or not it's a separate entity from your regular home.

·FURNITURE

866-406-2667 · Manor Home & Gifts

ManorHG.com

The definition of what comprises fine china has loosened a little bit over the years to include a few more diverse designs. You'll rarely find better modern takes on special-occasion dinnerware than on this high-end service site. Excellent plates of contemporary and traditional patterns head up an outstanding assortment of flatware, stemware and ceramic table accessories. Just as styles range from classic to opulent, prices range from high to outright extravagant. This is definitely the bridal registry you want your rich relatives to see.

·TABLEWARE · ·GLASS & BAR · ·MODERN · ·TRADITIONAL

212-965-0434 · Marston & Langinger Limited

Marston-And-Langinger.com

Conservatories aren't just handy places to murder Colonel Mustard with a candlestick, but lovely, refreshing sunrooms where folks in less temperate climates may still enjoy the beauty, fresh air and natural light of a garden. Of course, the concept is championed by the perennially rained-in country of England, which is also responsible for the style maintained by the furnishings offered by this garden room specialty shop. Gorgeous rattan furniture, beautiful table linens, torch lamps and traditional plants head up the selection, and though an unusual ordering process can make shopping a hassle, the results are too calming to pass up.

·LIGHTING
·TABLEWARE · ·ACCENTS
·PATIO & POOL · ·FURNITURE
·TRADITIONAL · ·LAWN & GARDEN

212-799-1711 · Maxwell-Silver New York

MaxwellSilverNY.com

Chock-full of decorating advice like "square shapes in your decorating associates with earth and the feeling of being grounded," and "using the color green encourages growth and change," this excellent housewares shop out of New York brings selections from the city's "most interesting and exciting home decor boutiques" together on one site. Using these tips will be a delight if you're incorporating the service-ware and home accents brands found here, including Simon Pearce, Jonathan Adler, Dwell and Apartment 48—especially if you're adding items to your wedding registry.

·ACCENTS · ·BED & BATH · ·TABLEWARE · ·MODERN

McMaster.com

McMaster-Carr Supply Company · 562-692-5911

The truth of the matter is, this site probably does not deserve the Difficult user-friendliness rating we've given it, as its wares are highly organized, efficiently presented and very precisely detailed. However, such is the risk you run when you boast more than 420,000 products. To call this a hardware store is to misstate the point—it simply offers every imaginable gauge of tube, fastener, tool, switch, pump, sealant, hook, hinge, valve and filter you might need to rewire, refinish or rebuild your home. Successful shopping here requires a handiness most of us simply do not possess, but if you happen to have it, you'll blow through this inconceivably massive selection like a breeze.

·APPLIANCES ·SECURITY	·LIGHTING ·WINDOWS	·HARDWARE	·ORGANIZATION

MichaelAram.com

Michael Aram · 866-792-2726

Just because mankind has been fashioning tools out of metal since prehistoric times does not mean we haven't got any fresh ideas about how to do it. Just check out the incredibly innovative work of this metal craftsman. His line of service-wares is unlike anything you've probably seen before, and we're talking about the forks, knives and spoons. Aside from flatware, you'll find assorted table accessories, occasional accents, a limited selection of furniture and a number of intriguing decorative hardware pieces, including knobs, pulls and hooks that would make an interior decorator drool.

·HARDWARE ·DECORATIVE	·ACCENTS ·MODERN	·FURNITURE	·ORGANIZATION

MichaelianHomeRetail.com

Michaelian Home · 800-258-3977

A unique and interesting assortment of hooked rugs make this site a must-see for anyone searching for new floor coverings. Plenty of hand-woven shapes, sizes, colors and patterns fill these pages, and while no signature look or feel links the different selections, we think you'll agree that most are lovely to look at. If the rugs don't get you, a slim selection of blankets might, or even the surprisingly large assortment of throw pillows. Impressive needlepoint abounds on this unique specialty site, and you bet the prices reflect this.

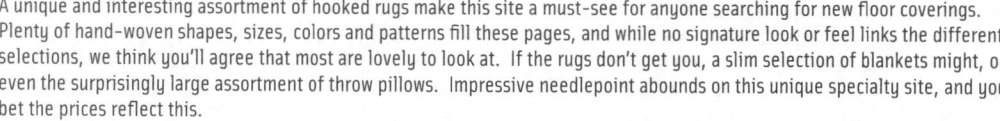

·ACCENTS	·BED & BATH		

ModernEssentials.com

Modern Essentials · 866-761-6151

It's tough to get excited about bedding, considering that the most thrilling options it tends to provide pertain to fitted elastic corners or high thread counts. But the linens, shams and duvet covers available from this eye-pleasing site will tempt even the masculine taste with easily matched colors and geometric patterns. This cool simplicity carries over into furniture and home accents as well, with particularly superb entertainment centers, mirrors that will look good even when your face isn't in them, and a great group of tables—yes, tables can be inspiring too. You'll have to check the site or take our word for it.

·ACCENTS	·FURNITURE	·BED & BATH	·MODERN

800-830-7847 · ModernRugs.com

ModernRugs.com

While you may have trouble stepping on artwork, this site invites you to get used to it, offering an interesting assortment of artistically rendered designer area rugs. Most are simply eye-catching abstract patterns, but still good looking enough that you may start asking visitors to remove their shoes before entering your home. You may not immediately notice any distinctions between the Modern Masters, World Rugs and Designer Rugs categories (although a great selection of Shag stands out), but once you get the hang of this visually oriented navigation, this site provides a pretty fun shopping experience.

| ·ACCENTS | ·MODERN | | | |

408-353-8428 · Mosaic Tile Market

MosaicTileMarket.com

If your kitchen or bathroom walls have gotten boring, here's a site that may offer everything you need to spruce things up a bit. With this extensive variety of mosaic tiles, it should be no trouble finding a color or texture that would go great in your space. Glass, porcelain and stainless-steel varieties may be purchased loose, to maximize your creativity, or in patterned sheets, which will be less labor intensive. Either way, the result should be colorful, exotic, and much more representative of your personality than any wallpaper or paint.

| ·DECORATIVE | | | | |

866-888-6677 · Moss

MossOnline.com

Perhaps the most rewarding high-concept store online is of course the virtual rendition of one of the most intriguing concept retail stores in the nation, the Moss store in SoHo, New York City. Appropriately enough, the store took over a gallery space; its mission is to show and sell an incredible selection of products that display industrial ingenuity. Its stock has grown with its reputation, and now the web site features a wealth of deliriously hip home accents, service-wares and furniture, some of which slightly skew classic looks, and others that simply dazzle.

| ·ACCENTS
·GLASS & BAR | ·FURNITURE
·MODERN | ·COOKING | ·TABLEWARE |  |

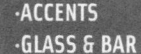

800-661-7847 · Natural Area Rugs

NaturalAreaRugs.com

Knowing it can be tough to pronounce some of the materials used in carpet fibers, we think you'll appreciate this natural alternative. Featuring easy-to-pronounce materials like wool, mountain grass, paper, sisal, jute and bamboo, you can be confident that these area rugs will feel as cool as they look, even if you don't exactly know what sisal and jute are. Available in many sizes, alongside a lovely assortment of shag rugs, these natural-fiber floor coverings may be some of the nicest things you ever step on.

| ·ACCENTS | | | |  |

NordicStyle.com

Nordic Style · 011-44-20-7581-1

This London-based shop was inspired by the "18th-Century neo-Classical look that was brought back to Sweden by King Gustaf III from the court of Queen Marie Antoinette," which of course will be glaringly obvious once you've seen the light grays, blues and whites that characterize this selection. Check Furniture Overview to find product categories, unless you'd rather check out the assortment of wallpapers, paints and upholstering fabrics, all of which adhere beautifully to the aforementioned Scandinavian color palette.

·FURNITURE	·DECORATIVE	·TRADITIONAL	

Nova68.com

NOVA68.COM · 917-518-4812

If you dig a bit of concept mixed in with the function and style of your home furniture, this modern home specialist can turn you on to some very slick pieces. You may have to browse for a while to find something you like enough to buy, but there's not enough merchandise to turn your visit into a major drag. If you do happen to tire of furniture and accents at any point, take a break and check out the very interesting selections of designer mobiles and toys, which will encourage your child's appreciation of modern design from an early age.

·LIGHTING ·ORGANIZATION	·ACCENTS ·MODERN	·FURNITURE	·LAWN & GARDEN

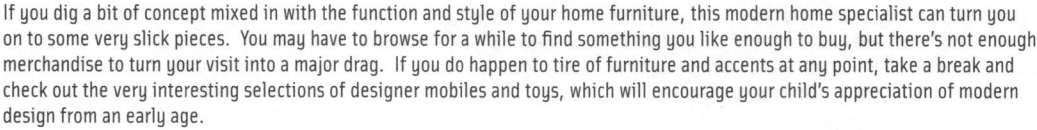

OrangeSkin.com

Orange Skin · 773-394-4500

Accessories for the home typically take rectangular shapes in a reliable palette of earthy or metallic colors. At least, that's how we see it in this country. Other countries apparently have a wildly different idea, as is represented by this site, which boasts "a cross-fertilization of contemporary Italian furniture and modern design objects" that cater "to the well-traveled and design savvy consumer." This translates to kitchen gadgets, tabletop accessories, sofas, CD racks and throw pillows in funky shapes and vibrant colors. Most of these things prove incredibly handy, almost in spite of their glossy looks, meaning that they should appeal even to us regular function-savvy Americans.

·ACCENTS ·TABLEWARE	·FURNITURE ·ORGANIZATION	·COOKING ·GLASS & BAR	·BED & BATH ·MODERN

Organize-Everything.com

Organize Everything · 800-600-9817

This site is an obsessive-compulsive's dream come true. As you may have gleaned from the name, here you will find the means to put a little organization into your household. As cleanly designed and well organized as you'd expect, the site offers Kitchen, Closet, Bath/Laundry and Garage categories, as well as the more general Storage Containers and Shelving sections. The selection generally values function over form, but don't be surprised to find that many of these products fit nicely into your decorative scheme, even if they happen to be trash bins or laundry hampers.

·ORGANIZATION	·CLEANING		

800-422-1525 · OutdoorDecor.com

OutdoorDecor.com

Though not unique in its devotion to outdoor decorative hardware and landscaping products, this site may be singularly good at it, with a wonderful selection of tasteful wood, metal and stone items, large and small. Whether your improvement project is as simple as a new door knocker or house number, or as grandiose as adding a cupola to your roof or an arbor to your garden, this site comes through in an easy way. Other highlights include fantastic outdoor faucets, beautiful stepping-stones and some comfortable-looking hammocks, so you can relax and enjoy your newly renovated grounds.

·HARDWARE ·DECORATIVE	·ACCENTS ·PATIO & POOL	·FURNITURE ·TRADITIONAL	·LAWN & GARDEN

800-652-3818 · Peacock Alley

PeacockAlley.com

When you're shopping here for bedding and linens, the key word is *quality*. After all, there's not a huge number of products to choose from, and though patterns range from modern to traditional, they're ultimately not very diverse. Of course, what they mostly have in common are good looks, and once you get these sheet sets and blankets home you'll forget what they look like, and focus instead on how luxuriously comfortable they can be. At these prices, they'd have to be.

·BED & BATH	·MODERN	·TRADITIONAL

800-649-1512 · Pendleton Woolen Mills

Pendleton-USA.com

If you're a fan of Native American-inspired products—curtains and blankets in particular—this site from Oregon has something for you. Simply look in the Blankets & Home section and browse until you see something you like (it won't take long). You can also buy fabric by the yard, so if you see a woven pattern you particularly like, you can turn it into a motif by reupholstering sofas, chairs, etc. It's beautiful proof that American culture isn't all about red, white and blue.

·ACCENTS	·BED & BATH	·WINDOWS	·TRADITIONAL

888-743-7732 · Pierre Deux

PierreDeux.com

Whether you describe it as "quaint," "charming" or "comfortable," French Country style almost always impresses, and will discourage houseguests from making a mess. From beautiful reproduction wood furniture to wrought-iron accents and exquisite serving pieces, you should easily sift through this simple variety to find items for your living room, dining room or kitchen. While the metal, wood and glass work will wow you, keep in mind that an array of colorful fabrics is also available, whether you opt for table linens, upholstered products, fabric by the yard, wallpaper or matching lampshades.

·LIGHTING ·TRADITIONAL	·ACCENTS	·FURNITURE	·TABLEWARE

PillowsAndThrows.com

Although the namesake selection of throw pillows on this website is rather remarkable, an unparalleled assortment of modern bedding is what should really bring you around. Full selections of top brands such as Dwell, Inhabit, Nygard, Lee Wilder and Koko Company inhabit the pages with gorgeous patterns and rich colors. Of course, the pillows tend to go well with the chic contemporary flavor of the bedding, as do the surprisingly cool assemblage of table lamps. Don't put the final touches on your hip bedroom without checking this out first.

	·LIGHTING	·ACCENTS	·BED & BATH	·MODERN

PioneerLinens.com

Here's a retailer with a better creation story than most. Founded as a hardware store in a frontier town, it initially sold a strange smattering of items like dynamite and chicken wire. As the town progressed, the store moved on into home furnishings, but with the Great Depression, downscaled its inventory to move affordable items like towels and linens. Now, nearly a century after its hard beginnings, the shop comes to us in internet form, softer than ever, featuring a plush assortment of towels, a wide variety of bedding and an extensive array of table linens; easily enough that any visit to this site should have a happy ending.

		·ACCENTS	·BED & BATH	·TABLEWARE	·TRADITIONAL

Plexi-Craft.com

We've seen plenty of wood furniture, upholstered furniture, metal furniture, wicker, glass and even some plastic, but this site might offer the first instance of Plexiglas furniture we've encountered. Tables, chairs, desks and barstools make up most of this very translucent, and very modern, collection, which also includes a few somewhat more conceptual storage items. We can't say for sure that Plexiglas furniture is the wave of the future, but we're pretty sure there hasn't been anything like it in our culture's past.

	·FURNITURE	·MODERN		

Ponds2Go.com

This site has everything you need to build, install and maintain a pond on your property, from hardware and plant life to decorations. Sound difficult? Well, you should also be able to find some helpful hints and interesting ideas to make the process relatively easy and somewhat fun, once you get the hang of browsing this site. Still not inspired? Well, just imagine relaxing in a chaise longue, drinking a beer and watching the sunset as you lie beside a body of water that you've named after yourself. Now imagine the jealous faces of your neighbors as they look over the fence, and then the fun of planning to build a higher fence. Oh yeah, building can be a blast.

	·LAWN & GARDEN	·FLORAE		

800-609-4917 · Pool Warehouse
PoolWarehouse.com

The most astounding thing about this site isn't that it can sell you a swimming pool online—we have, after all, seen a willingness of "e-tailers" to sell anything and everything over the internet. No, the real surprise here is just how many options you have in purchasing a pool, not to mention things such as diving boards, slides and spas. First of all, you have pool-building kits, perfect for the industrious do-it-yourself homeowner. Second, there are some easier-to-set-up aboveground pools. Finally, and this is great, you can have an entire fiberglass pool, available in dozens of different shapes and sizes, delivered to your home on a truck. Sure to make the neighbors jealous.

·PATIO & POOL

888-838-0707 · PopsFurniture.com
PopsFurniture.com

When it just becomes impossible to find acceptable tables, dressers, bookcases, hutches and seating stained to match the pieces you already own, pay a visit to this Los Angeles area unfinished-furniture specialist. The site offers a wide assortment of items for every room of the house as well as the patio, all representing classic, traditional and Southwest styles. Of course, the catch is, you'll have to finish this furniture yourself, but one plus is that "unfinished manufacturers must use a higher-grade lumber in furniture production," so you'll know your matching items will be virtually perfect.

·FURNITURE   ·TRADITIONAL

312-280-1602 · P.O.S.H.
PoshChicago.com

Looking for something a little different in tableware? This site might have it. "Found in such disparate places as old American china warehouses to the antique markets and auction houses of Europe," the one-of-a-kind or limited-edition dinnerware, flatware and glassware featured here ranges from a great bargain on restaurant china to something fun to chuckle over as you eat with your family. The inclusion of bizarre tabletop accessories and a healthy price range makes this a must-see site for the budget- and taste-conscious alike.

·TABLEWARE   ·GLASS & BAR

888-770-8358 · Raintree Nursery
RainTreeNursery.com

Toiling away on your garden proves a lot more fruitful if you're growing edible vegetation. With that in mind, this Washington state nursery specializes in fruit trees, selecting varieties "for flavor and ease of growing," so even the novice grower can cultivate something sweet. Berries, nuts, fruits and unusual edible plants fill several hastily assembled pages of the site, and if it weren't for the great low prices we might expect a better web design. However, without question, starting your amateur orchard is still easier than you might think.

·FLORAE

RepairClinic.com

If you've ever thought you might be handy with a little bit of home appliance repair, you can prove it with the help of this site. Whether the problem is your microwave, dryer, dishwasher, refrigerator or just about any other household machine that's on the fritz, it's probably just a matter of replacing one or two specific little pieces. It just so happens, this is the perfect place to find these replacement parts. All you really need to know is the make and model of your machine and have just enough of an understanding of it to know what's broken. Fortunately, you'll also find some diagnostic advice, repair directions and a handy repair guru to help you through the parts you don't quite get.

 | ·APPLIANCES | ·HARDWARE | | |

Replacements.com

In some cultures, appreciation for a good meal may be expressed by smashing the plates it was served on in a wine-fueled display of satiation. Too good a meal, and you may even see all your best china and flatware decimated by a feisty cadre of guests. Or, just invite some children over, and something's bound to be smashed. Point is, you can only protect your tableware so far; your sets will undoubtedly be missing some pieces before too long. The genius of this site is that you can buy individual pieces from "more than 180,000 patterns," keeping your fine china set intact in spite of the occasional dinnertime violence.

 | ·TABLEWARE | ·TRADITIONAL | | |

RetroModern.com

It can be presumed that the term *retro modern* here either refers to an attempt to emulate contemporary home styles of the past, or simply to take a look back at the styles themselves. In this case both are accurate, as vintage and new furniture, accents and service-ware harking back to the postwar era are on keen display on this site that wants to encourage a deeper understanding of and appreciation for 20th-century design. Simply select your favorite designer from their list, and enjoy his/her masterworks. Don't know who those people are? Well, you can shop by more conventional methods, browsing through categories, price range and looking at pictures, lots of pictures. The Vintage Design section alone will have you yearning for a higher credit card limit.

  | ·ACCENTS ·MODERN | ·TABLEWARE | ·ORGANIZATION | ·GLASS & BAR |

RoomAndCompany.com

This Northern California designer furniture chain offers a small, expensive and excessively cool assortment of enviable products. The selection of sofas and beds, in particular, merit a visit to this shop by anyone who's ever considered him- or herself modern, and the assorted vases, rugs, lamps, storage solutions and bric-a-brac will avail themselves well on the site, which has grown considerably easier to use over the years, finally lending credence to the notion that it makes "modern living simple."

| ·LIGHTING | ·ACCENTS | ·FURNITURE | ·MODERN |

800-588-1170 · Room Service Home

RoomServiceHome.com

Testament to what a couple of Texas mothers can accomplish when they put their heads, and their shared decorating tastes, together, this furnishings catalog was created to offer "products that provided comfort and style without much fuss." The shabby chic furniture, accents, service-ware and bedding selection is small in size but beautifully presented and seems incredibly cozy. If your style comes even remotely close to matching the fine assortment of designer country sophistication, you will be in heaven shopping here.

·ACCENTS ·TABLEWARE	·FURNITURE ·TRADITIONAL	·LAWN & GARDEN	·BED & BATH

800-631-2526 · Rudi's Pottery

RudisPottery.com

This site is easy to use, but only if you're shopping from the Bridal Registry section. If you're looking for a set of flatware, stemware or fine china, you might not have it so easy—unless you have a particular brand in mind. You can find Reed & Barton flatware, Waterford crystal and Wedgwood china, for example, as well as dozens of other brands. Unfortunately, you won't always be able to view the full range of a brand's set, nor will you even get to view a sample, in some cases, so you'll either want to stick to what pictures are available or simply use this site to complete a specific line of service-ware you've already started.

·TABLEWARE			

800-982-7210 · RugsUSA.com

RugsUSA.com

It's rare that we can emphatically say that shopping online for a home product is far easier than buying it in person, but if you can peruse a selection of rugs this big more easily in a brick-and-mortar store, more power to you. Here, there's no heavy lifting, no unrolling, no dust or sweat. All items are laid out visually, arranged by shape, weave or design, and available in multiple sizes. The only drawback we can see is that there are no carpet samples to match against your furniture and/or decor. But at the very least, you can easily research a list of brands and patterns you like, to make your offline shopping easier.

·ACCENTS	·MODERN	·TRADITIONAL	

310-659-9838 · Sabi Style

SabiStyle.com

Your standard ten-inch round plate and salad bowl works great if you're serving meat loaf and mashed potatoes. But if you're dishing up sushi or tempura, such dinnerware is incongruous. A bevy of gorgeous Japanese table-service pieces may be perused quite easily on this site. Chopsticks, coasters and sake sets beautifully complement the lacquered bowls and trays that enable you to present a variety of delicate entrees and condiments as elegantly as does any restaurant. After all, anything too good for our dishwashers is good enough for us.

·TABLEWARE	·MODERN		

SafetyCentral.com

Preparedness Industries · 707-472-0288

This is a site that's intriguing from top to bottom, beginning with its primary focus: home safety and preparedness. Emergency food storage, power generators and multiband radios would've gone over well during the Y2K craze, and antiterrorism protection equipment (gas masks and such) will probably stir some imaginations today. Not all of this stuff is so dire as stun guns and pepper spray, though, and the best of it consists of spy gadgets, outdoor/camping gear and some rather useful travel items. Whatever the case, you can feel prepared.

	·SECURITY	·ECO-FRIENDLY		

SchweitzerLinen.com

Schweitzer Linen · 800-554-6367

For those of us who demand that only the finest of fineries should come into contact with our persons, this Manhattan-based luxury retailer offers a dazzling array of bedding, table linens, towels and robes that should satisfy even the most discerning tastes. Finding these items proves as easy as one would expect from a high-end retailer, thanks to animated menus that roll down from the top of the page, allowing you to select specific types of items within each category. With plenty of alluring fabrics such as cashmere, sateen and silk, this is fine shopping at its finest.

		·BED & BATH	·TABLEWARE	·TRADITIONAL	

SeedsOfChange.com

Seeds Of Change · 888-762-7333

The greatest thing about this site is that all of its products are ecologically sound, promoting the preservation of genetic diversity in all manner of plants. Primarily seeds are for sale here. But these seeds are the result of natural, open-pollinated plants, grown without chemical or genetic manipulation. The result is a selection of healthy, natural seeds for plants, flowers and herbs that will produce more seeds once mature (most commercially sold seeds don't). There's a lot of environmentally-conscious gear here, as well, like watering timers and composting equipment. If you want your garden to be Earth-friendly, this is the first place you should look.

	·HARDWARE	·LAWN & GARDEN	·FLORAE	·ECO-FRIENDLY

SelectSeeds.com

Select Seeds · 800-253-5691

We're used to applying terms like *unique* and *heirloom* to jewelry, furniture and in some cases clothes, but we haven't often seen it refer to flowers before. However, this specialty nursery deals exclusively in antique plants, "open-pollinated seed varieties that originated fifty or more years ago." The beautiful selection is represented by seeds, bulbs and plants, depending on how patient and/or skilled a gardener you are, and when you see how lovely these heirloom lilies, dahlias, irises, geraniums and more can be, you'll want to get in on the tradition.

	·FLORAE			

800-838-0977 · Service Lighting

ServiceLighting.com

There's a popular, long-standing joke about the number of people it takes to complete a lightbulb installation, the implication being that it should only take one person of reasonable intelligence. With the help of this site, we lose the intelligence requirement. Well-defined categories tell you which sorts of bulbs you're browsing, coupled with pictures that explicitly show you. Take a look around, and you'll find everything you need to keep your space bright enough to see bad punch lines coming from way off.

·LIGHTING	·HARDWARE		

202-270-5020 · Jared Alon Designs

ShowerPresents.com

Sometimes it's tough to draw that line between traditional and modern. The best we can say about this site's very limited but delectable variety of housewares is that it gives traditional style a slight modern twist. In particular, you'll find Dash & Albert rugs, Pine Cone Hill bedding and Potluck Studios tableware, each of which offer bold splashes of color combined with country home sensibilities. You'd have a tough time finding any of this stuff anywhere else online, so if it's what you're after, log on immediately. If you're browsing for something nice, this site will take about two minutes to view, so be sure not to miss it.

·BED & BATH	·TABLEWARE	·MODERN	·TRADITIONAL

888-745-5302 · The Silk Trading Co.

SilkTrading.com

Can buying curtains online be easy and satisfying? Only if you shop here. With its Drapery-Out-of-a-Box and Drapery By Design sections, this site allows you to either choose from a lovely selection of ready-made styles or enter custom measurements, color and trim for the curtains of your dreams. If you have a more do-it-yourself mentality you may buy one of the shop's many fine fabrics, and if you wish to match your walls to your new curtains simply select from its many hues of paint. Lastly, if you'd rather just lounge back and imagine the window treatment of your desires, be sure to check the Pillows section.

·HARDWARE	·ACCENTS	·DECORATIVE	·WINDOWS

800-262-3134 · The Silver Queen

SilverQueen.com

In one of the great ironies of the internet, this site looks about as bad as they come, however it offers one of the most beautiful selections of fine china, sterling silver flatware and opulent crystal. We're forced to wonder why anyone would present such gloriously expensive service-ware in such a horrendously poor manner, but we can't argue too much, as the site works, whether you wish to register for a full set of top-tier goods, or simply need to add an extra setting or replacement to a collection of products you already own.

·LIGHTING ·TRADITIONAL	·ACCENTS	·TABLEWARE	·GLASS & BAR

SilverSuperStore.com

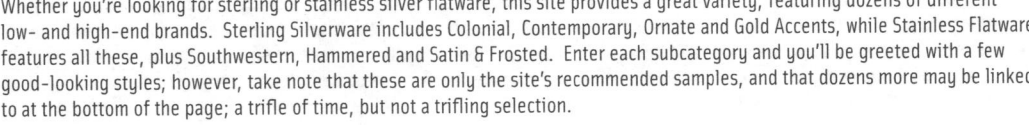

Whether you're looking for sterling or stainless silver flatware, this site provides a great variety, featuring dozens of different low- and high-end brands. Sterling Silverware includes Colonial, Contemporary, Ornate and Gold Accents, while Stainless Flatware features all these, plus Southwestern, Hammered and Satin & Frosted. Enter each subcategory and you'll be greeted with a few good-looking styles; however, take note that these are only the site's recommended samples, and that dozens more may be linked to at the bottom of the page; a trifle of time, but not a trifling selection.

	·TABLEWARE	·MODERN	·TRADITIONAL	

SisalCarpet.com

The choice between natural and synthetic sisal carpeting is only the first you'll make on this site; there'll be many more. You might decide to utilize the site's Pick a Room pull-down menu, which calls up a list of the site's recommended weaves and patterns as determined by foot traffic, comfort and quality. However, aside from a tiny bit of advice, it's just as easy to view the full range of carpets and rugs, available in multiple shapes and sizes, or custom ordered by the square foot. You can even choose to order a few free swatches, if you ultimately have trouble deciding from the smart-looking variety.

	·ACCENTS			

SmithAndNoble.com

All right, you've done everything to create the perfect interior design for your home—installed a new carpet, changed the light fixtures, redone the wallpaper and even replaced your switchplates. Everything lines up just right, and you have proven yourself a decorative genius...except for those pesky windows. Well, these guys will customize your window treatments, from blinds and shades to cornices and even shutters. From start to finish, they'll help you measure all the necessary dimensions, and even give you a glossary of terms so you can figure out exactly what the heck is going on. By the time you're through, you'll know a lot more about windows, and you can finally achieve absolute perfection from floor to ceiling. Now if you could only fix the view...

	·LIGHTING ·WINDOWS	·HARDWARE ·MODERN	·ACCENTS ·TRADITIONAL	·FURNITURE

SongSparrow.com

If you think you know what a peony looks like, you might want to think again. This site offers no fewer than 150 varieties of the flower, seasonally, and each is distinctive from the next, both in shape and coloring. Adding to the confusion are several dozen tree peonies, nearly one hundred daylilies and scores of other flowering and/or leafy plants like hostas and clematis. Getting a look at all of these varieties proves much less arduous than it sounds, as all are neatly and visually arranged for your viewing ease.

	·FLORAE			

888-543-2804 · Atwood International

Inviting yet sophisticated, the wares of this site cater to the beautifully livable home. Is it the sort of stuff you can keep around the house with small children around? Not at these prices, but where less messy adults are concerned you may manage to satisfy a high level of taste yet maintain an almost casual feel in your table service, bedding and furniture. It's tough to anticipate what you'll find within some of the site's product categories, but a well-executed, very visual layout makes browsing a cinch, allowing you to shop as comfortably as you live.

·LIGHTING ·TABLEWARE	·ACCENTS ·GLASS & BAR	·FURNITURE ·TRADITIONAL	·BED & BATH

845-351-5994 · SpinKeeper

Music, movie and literature enthusiasts know that, over time, a healthy entertainment collection can grow out of control and begin to consume your lovely household. This site steps in to curtail the ruin of your interior decor by offering a wide array of storage units and entertainment furniture that will neatly contain great amounts of CDs, LPs, DVDs, VHS tapes and/or books. The many browsable options include wood or metal storage racks to put your tastes on display, apothecary units to organize them in drawers and full-size cabinets to keep your collection behind closed doors and out of the way.

·FURNITURE	·ORGANIZATION	·MODERN	·TRADITIONAL

800-511-1440 · Spirit Elements

If your backyard is sitting empty, here's your chance to fill it in the best ways possible. Beginning with a fine selection of patio furniture, this hand-selected catalog has it all: gazebos, trellises, fences, planters, greenhouses, wood sheds, hammocks, ponds, spas, doghouses, kid playhouses and fountains. You'll also find some amazing new front doors, fireplace accessories, mailboxes, and custom pool tables. But most of the selection is definitely concerned with the outdoors, so much so that your yard may not be big enough.

·HARDWARE ·GLASS & BAR	·FURNITURE ·PATIO & POOL	·LAWN & GARDEN ·MODERN	·TABLEWARE ·TRADITIONAL

011-44-1661-844-844 · The Stencil Library

It may seem odd at first to reach across the Atlantic to find stencils designed to help paint patterns on your walls, but if you take a moment to check out the terrific variety of stencils available from this UK site, you'll see it's worthwhile. Sure, there are a few of the typical stencil designs you'd expect to find anywhere: leafy patterns, children's story characters, architectural shapes and such. But most of the selection could change your mind about stenciling altogether, with Chinese pictograms, animal prints, Art Deco designs and stencils made to emulate mosaic tiles, among others. There's even a Bad Attitude category, featuring camouflage, barbed wire and boot prints, in case colorful and pretty ain't your thing.

·HARDWARE	·ACCENTS	·MODERN	·TRADITIONAL

StoreHouse.com

Storehouse · 888-786-7346

T.S. Eliot might describe the wares of this all-encompassing contemporary furniture and accents shop as "neither diffident nor ostentatious." In other words, these products are perfectly suited to this time and place, without being boring or showy, with the possible exception of a surprisingly large assortment of somewhat gaudy rugs (worth seeing). Given just how comprehensive this selection is, it's fairly easy to browse items for the entire house, and a nifty House Planner software offers a fun way to position the site's various furnishings in an illustrated floor plan. It's almost poetic.

·LIGHTING ·MODERN	·ACCENTS	·FURNITURE	·WINDOWS

TabulaTua.com

Tabula Tua · 888-535-6590

The inspiration for this Chicago tabletop retailer occurred when the founder began shopping for quality dinnerware, only to find that "department stores have fine china (that never gets used) and low-end, mass-produced everyday ware." Like Goldilocks, she wanted something in between. Now, more than ten years later, she has built a fine selection of upscale service sets and accessories, beautiful stuff to dress your table, but nothing so fine as to be locked away for special occasions only. In other words, just right.

·ACCENTS ·MODERN	·COOKING ·TRADITIONAL	·TABLEWARE	·GLASS & BAR

TCStore.com

The Addison Collection · 800-994-3744

An overwhelming inventory and challenging organizational structure could easily prevent you from appreciating the deep assortment of products house by this purveyor of the "finest in collectibles, decorative home, and fine gifts." You'll find artisan glassware, decorative sculpture, occasional pottery and a scattered assortment of other household decor. In truth, you might want to avoid the difficult site, unless you happen to be impressed by names like Michael Aram, Murano Glass, Lalique, Lam Lee and Waterford.

·TABLEWARE	·GLASS & BAR		

TeakWickerAndMore.com

The Garden Cottage · 866-263-8325

The teak and wicker furniture available from this site might bring you in, but it's the more that may keep you coming back. Actually, there are many styles of patio furniture here, made from many materials, and though the web pages might seem rather busy at first, you'll soon realize that a bevy of helpful browsing techniques are set up to present you an extraordinarily well-organized selection. This stuff can only improve your backyard, as the New York City area retailer also delivers a wide variety of lawn ornaments, bird feeders, outdoor lighting, greenhouses and hammocks. Don't miss this one if you enjoy sitting outside.

·APPLIANCES ·PATIO & POOL	·LIGHTING	·FURNITURE	·LAWN & GARDEN

510-549-2282 · The Magazine

Presenting distinctive furniture designs that often feel straight out of a sci-fi flick, this Berkeley, California-based retailer offers nothing less than a glimpse into our near-distant future. Strictly speaking, nothing here could be described as all that affordable, but the great image attached to each of these fantastic products might be enough to convince you it's worth it. From striking entertainment centers to conceptual beds, and some seating options you'll have to see to disbelieve, even the shipping is pricey, but to buy items such as these from a primitive offline store would dash the ultramodern experience of shopping from the web site of tomorrow.

·LIGHTING ·GLASS & BAR	·ACCENTS ·DECORATIVE	·FURNITURE ·PATIO & POOL	·TABLEWARE ·MODERN

888-935-5277 · The Well Appointed House, LLC

As you may be able to tell by the name of this site, its many offerings tend to veer toward the upscale. As it happens, just about every room in the house is also well represented, whether you're looking for luxury bedding for the boudoir, or a decorative bench for your foyer. You'll also find plenty of lamps and lighting fixtures, a lovely assortment of tabletop accessories, formal mirrors, service trays and a surprising amount of tasteful trash bins, which, if you think about it, do play very important roles in keeping your house well appointed.

·LIGHTING ·TABLEWARE	·ACCENTS ·ORGANIZATION	·FURNITURE ·GLASS & BAR	·BED & BATH ·TRADITIONAL

800-222-6133 · Tools-Plus

The tool-loving internet shopper will have a field day with this comprehensively stocked "discount tool store." Categories such as Hand Tools, Cordless Tools, Air Powered and Automotive are bound to get a gearhead revving, while Power Tools, Metalwork Machines and Woodworking Machinery prove the site can cater to those with an entire workshop to fill. Pricing may vary, but a price-matching guarantee has the surprising effect of making comparison tool shopping an appealing proposition.

·HARDWARE	·CLEANING	·SECURITY	

877-356-7333 · TreeHelp.com

Sick trees can be a major headache, and while chopping them down may be the most absolute and expedient way of dealing with them, perhaps with the help of this site you can explore other options. A wealth of information about tree diseases can be found here, along with how-to articles, insect control tips and plenty of resources on particular tree species and their care. The site also offers plenty of tools and tree treatments, so even if you can't save one tree from a particular illness, maybe you can prevent other trees from catching it.

·HARDWARE	·LAWN & GARDEN		

Umbra.com

Umbra · 800-387-5122

When you enter a room, you're apt to notice any number of things right away: large furniture, wall hangings, lighting fixtures. But what about the minute details that fill out a room? Things like clocks, picture frames, knobs and trash cans tend to get second billing in any home, but this doesn't mean you need to take them for granted. At least, that's what the proprietors of this site would tell you. They offer a cool little selection of household accents on slick display, the kinds of finishing touches that can freshen up a modern decor by adding flashes of color and funk to otherwise dreary parts.

·HARDWARE ·DECORATIVE	·ACCENTS ·WINDOWS	·BED & BATH ·MODERN	·ORGANIZATION

UnicaHome.com

Unica Home · 888-898-6422

The upshot of filling your home with decorative accessories and functional furnishings is that you have to look at these items every day of your life. In the interest of making it all more interesting, here's a fine selection of intriguing ultramodern designs that should keep things fresh whether you're entertaining or just sitting around enjoying all your stuff. You can browse by general product ranges, from floor mats to barware and some especially hip lamps, or by the various designers and companies contributing items to this eclectic selection crafted to convince you that even something as dull as a wastebasket can look cool.

·LIGHTING ·ORGANIZATION	·ACCENTS ·CLEANING	·BED & BATH ·GLASS & BAR	·TABLEWARE ·MODERN

VanDykes.com

Van Dyke Supply Co. · 800-787-3355

"Specializing in unusual and hard-to-find products," this decorative hardware site covers a lot of ground, yet "continues to search out existing products of outstanding original hardware to have reproduced by highly skilled artisans from around the world." In other words, if you're in need of replacement door hardware, switchplates, vent covers, roof hardware, wood trim, window hardware or any number of decorative parts for the tiny decorative and functional embellishments to your home, there are good odds this site has got them, or will at least some day replicate them. While nothing in particular may be easy to find, everything in particular might just exist here, even if it's a piece of antique furniture.

·LIGHTING	·HARDWARE	·DECORATIVE	·WINDOWS

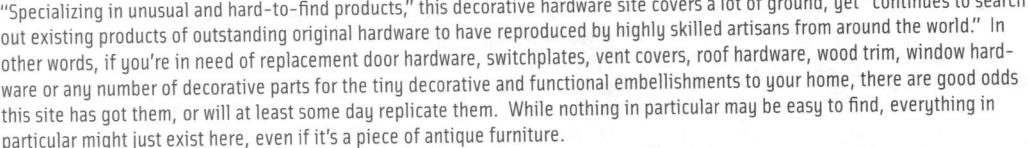

VelocityArtAndDesign.com

Velocity Art And Design · 866-781-9494

This fascinating contemporary furnishings showroom out of Seattle offers "a mix of the best of both timeless mid-century modern and what's modern today," with intriguing conceptual designs across a broad range of home products. From top to bottom, the site is entirely original, and though it's possible some of these items might turn up elsewhere, you certainly won't find anything like this in one place, online or off. Highlights include a funky assortment of clocks, some peculiar dinnerware, ultrahip furniture, the most unusual room dividers on record and the Groove Tube, a plastic device that, when placed over your television, turns whatever's onscreen into animated artwork, which may even be more mesmerizing than cable.

·LIGHTING ·TABLEWARE	·ACCENTS ·ORGANIZATION	·FURNITURE ·DECORATIVE	·LAWN & GARDEN ·MODERN

903-356-2158 · Vintage Wood Works

VintageWoodWorks.com

If you know what corbels are, or spandrels, brackets, bead boards, gable decorations, headers or running trims, find them in fine design and supply here. If you don't know, these are items used to give a house that old-time woodsy, fancy feeling. It's hard to describe, so you'll just have to check out the site to see. If it makes it any easier, though, there are also some incredible screen doors here, along with well-crafted shingles, porch posts, balusters, signs and rails aplenty. Your home will never look so good.

·HARDWARE	·DECORATIVE	·TRADITIONAL	

866-848-2840 · Vivavi

Vivavi.com

With "contemporary, sustainable furniture and home furnishings for the environment-minded modern lifestyle," this Brooklyn shop takes a love of designer furniture into the new millennium, ensuring that it suits the burgeoning demand for eco-friendly products. As of this writing, the broad assortment of household items was still pretty limited, but as great as it all looks, you're bound to fall in love with something. Maybe the three-dimensional wallpaper, the cat cocoon, a nontoxic cleaning solution or one of the many inspired, highly conceptual benches. You won't know until you pay a visit.

·LIGHTING ·TABLEWARE	·ACCENTS ·ORGANIZATION	·FURNITURE ·ECO-FRIENDLY	·BED & BATH ·MODERN

800-343-6948 · Walpole Woodworkers

WalpoleWoodWorkers.com

When it comes time to turn your home improvement ambitions and decorative tastes to the outside of your house, be sure not to miss this extraordinary woodwork and hardware site. While shipping sits on the expensive end of the spectrum, the product selection is usually exquisite enough to warrant the expense. Particularly worth noting is the great variety of fencing, from picket and post to metal palisades and gates. These go hand in hand with the many gazebos, arbors, trellises and birdbaths to be found, which typically match the patio furniture, as well as the cupolas, signposts, mailboxes and weather vanes. This is beautiful stuff, as easy to locate here as it is to look at.

·LIGHTING ·SECURITY	·HARDWARE ·DECORATIVE	·FURNITURE ·PATIO & POOL	·LAWN & GARDEN ·TRADITIONAL

423-870-2838 · The Water Garden

WaterGarden.com

If you've ever looked across the broad landscape of your yard and thought that a small body of water was just what it needed, you're in luck, because this site will set you up. Follow the Our Online Catalog link and you'll be able to browse for Pond Kits, if you're just getting started; you'll also find any number of liners, plants, stones and other decoration, from footbridges to lighting. There are plenty of pond maintenance items, too, including filters, pumps and treatments, both chemical and ultraviolet, against algae and bacteria. There's a variety of tabletop fountains as well, in case you want a small body of water indoors.

·LIGHTING	·ACCENTS	·LAWN & GARDEN	·CLEANING

WaterWarehouse.com

If you've got a pool, you know maintenance and upkeep can be a costly, laborious process. Leave it to this site to make things a little easier, whether you need to order an automated pool cleaner, replace your chemicals, upgrade to a solar heater or add a diving board. If you don't yet have a pool, don't worry about how much work it might be—you can simply order an aboveground pool here, and pick up plenty of pool toys along the way. Considering the shop offer free shipping on some pretty hefty products, we don't begrudge them a small handling fee on all orders; so long as they do all the heavy lifting.

	·CLEANING	·PATIO & POOL		

WholeLatteLove.com

Unless you possess a tremendous aversion to puns, this is a must-see site for any coffee lover. With an incomparable collection of articles, buying guides and reviews, this would be a worthwhile stop without a store. As it happens, the shop also features an unbeatable selection of coffee makers, espresso machines, coffee grinders and accessories. You'll quickly notice a long list of brands, but if you look further you'll find options to shop for French presses, thermal carafes, vacuum pots and milk frothers. With these guys' help, you'll make enough great java to leave you dazed and confused.

	·APPLIANCES			

WindowBox.com

Here's a site for those of us who lack one of the more important components of a home garden: land to grow it on. High-rise dwellers can find flowery relief in this site that caters to fans of potted plants and window gardens, starting with its selection of handcrafted window boxes, hanging baskets and planters. There're also many small garden tools, as well as the requisite herb, plant and flower seeds. If you're new to the indoor planting game, the site's Floracle feature will make recommendations based on your gardening diligence and local environment. If you still don't feel ready for the real thing, practice on a virtual plant in the Plant Game, "the slowest game on the web."

	·LAWN & GARDEN	·FLORAE		

WineEnthusiast.com

The proprietors of this site probably determined that Wine Connoisseur would be too difficult a name to spell, but connoisseurs are just who this shop aims to please. Whether you would like to add a wine cellar or bar to your home, or upgrade the one you already have, you can fairly easily browse an array of storage and cooling solutions here. You can also find some beautifully constructed bar furniture, as well as brilliant stemware sets and bar accessories. Stocking your home with fine wines and liqueurs will require the assistance of our Epicurean section.

	·FURNITURE	·ORGANIZATION	·GLASS & BAR	

800-767-5490 · Wisteria

Wisteria.com

With a penchant for home furnishings with "thoughtful, intriguing combinations of color, texture, whimsy, and history," the husband-and-wife team behind this steadily growing catalog engage in worldwide searches for such items. Aside from providing a splendid life for themselves, they've accomplished a pretty interesting collection of household items to behold. It's tough to describe a consistent style at play here, but suffice to say the Antiques section sets the tone, and even the more contemporary pieces will probably work better in a traditional home than a modern one.

·ACCENTS ·TRADITIONAL	·FURNITURE	·BED & BATH	·TABLEWARE

888-780-7171 · The Wok Shop

WokShop.com

Straight out of San Francisco's famous Chinatown, this family-owned-and-operated business "covers nearly every aspect of Asian cooking, including woks, clay pots, cleavers, bamboo steamers, wooden and bamboo cooking utensils, Oriental chinaware, Oriental vegetable seeds, and other hard to find items." It's simple, friendly and filled with exotic cookware that will improve your culinary skills tenfold. All you'll have to do now is flip to our Epicurean section to find some authentic Asian ingredients.

·APPLIANCES	·COOKING	·TABLEWARE	

800-385-0030 · Wood Classics & Teakscapes

WoodClassics.com

"Classics" in this site's name refers to the sort of classic embodied by porch swings, picket fences and rocking chairs. In fact, this teak garden furniture specialist provides all of these and more, and usually with a surprising variety, considering the consistency in style throughout the catalog. It's incredibly easy to sift through the many tables, chairs, benches, cushioned seating, planters, deck chairs and trellises available, and you'll even see some patio umbrellas on the way, to keep it all in the shade.

·FURNITURE	·LAWN & GARDEN	·PATIO & POOL	

877-411-9600 · Wrapables.com

Wrapables.com

You might consider this one of the better home-oriented gift shops out there, and you'll rarely find a better housewarming gift anywhere else. However, because it's so good, and some of these items so indispensable, we think you'd rather shop here for yourself. A bright array of fresh, colorful and fun home accents heads up the selection, including some ingenious clocks and truly impressive candlesticks. But every page you browse will reveal something fantastic, whether it's some especially hip paper lanterns, distinctive organizational accessories, casually cool dinnerware or the best selection of shower curtains you'll likely see this year. It's great to see out of the ordinary done so well.

·LIGHTING ·ORGANIZATION	·ACCENTS ·GLASS & BAR	·BED & BATH ·MODERN	·TABLEWARE

NOTES:

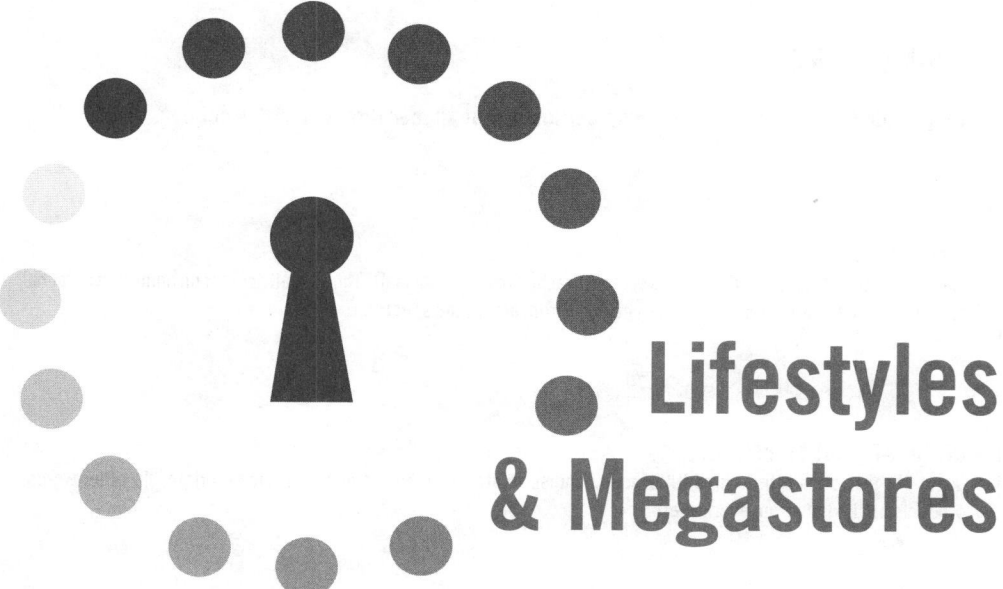

Lifestyles & Megastores

In a perfect world, every online shop would fit succinctly into one of the other nineteen **thepurplebook** categories. However, since they don't, we came up with this section, which includes those reputable web retailers that do a fine job covering three or more of the shopping areas we've addressed in this guide. Some of them are just incredibly ambitious, trying to sell every type of product they can get their hands on. Others were simply brought up that way, as they represent the online manifestations of popular catalogs, shopping networks, outlet warehouses and long-established department stores. A third group caters to particular lifestyles, stocking a variety of items that will appeal to surfers, cowboys or people fond of a particular nation or region. Across the spectrum you'll find stores offering incredible discounts, and others boasting unspeakable luxuries. In fact, the only thing most of these e-tailers really have in common is that you can pick up a long shopping list of items in a single online session, often saving time and consolidating shipping costs in the process. For this edition, we've left out a few of the old familiar sites you may already know about to make room for a great bunch of lesser-known megastores that should have no trouble capturing your attention and stoking your imagination... at least, when you're too busy to browse the boutiques and specialty shops featured in the rest of the book.

 ## SECTION ICON LEGEND

Use the following guide to understand the rectangular icons that appear throughout this section.

 ### MEGASTORES

Many of these are stores you're used to seeing attached to your local mall. They usually center on home and personal fashion products, but many deal in merchandise from across the spectrum.

 ### INTERNATIONAL MERCHANTS

Some of these sites offer a breadth of merchandise related only by national or regional origin. In other words: products of all kinds from everywhere.

 ### LIFESTYLE SHOPS

Whether you're a cowboy or simply a fashionista, we found a range of stores that cater to many walks of life, selling enough variety of products as to defy categorization.

 ### DISCOUNT & OVERSTOCK

We reckon this will be a popular icon by name alone. Surely, it will lead you to some of the best prices on the web, but usually on outdated or unpopular merchandise. Still, cheap is cheap.

 ## DEPARTMENT STORES & CATALOGS

These sites represent popular catalogs, shopping channels and department stores.

Bloomingdales.com	Kohls.com	SaksFifthAvenue.com
Dillards.com	LandsEnd.com	SamsClub.com
EddieBauer.com	LLBean.com	Sears.com
Gap.com	Macys.com	SeenOnTV.com
HSN.com	NiemanMarcus.com	SolutionsCatalog.com
HammacherSchlemmer.com	Nordstrom.com	Talbots.com
IAmUncleSam.com	Orvis.com	VermontCountryStore.com
JCPenny.com	QVC.com	Woolrich.com

*For in-depth reviews of these sites and more, check out **www.thepurplebook.com**.

LIST OF KEY WORDS

The following words represent the types of items typically found on the sites listed in this section. You will find them listed in the orange strip at the bottom of each entry, as appropriate.

ACCESSORIES	Offering everything from hats to shoes, alongside some jewelry, watches, eyewear and handbags/wallets to stow it all away.
APPAREL	Clothing for men and women.
ART & COLLECTIBLE	The original masterworks of the century, posters for your dorm room or collections of kitsch, including decorations and/or decorative investments.
CRAFTS & HOBBIES	Domestic crafts projects, musical instruments, art supplies, models and science hobbies.
ELECTRONICS	Computer hardware and software and/or electronics for your home or pocket, plus innovative gizmos.
ENTERTAINMENT	Music, movies and/or books, or possibly puzzles and games, as well as tickets to live performances.
EPICUREAN	Grocery items, gourmet foods, vintage wines and fine cigars, among other ingestible delights.
GIFTS	Anything from personalized letterheads, invitations and greeting cards to flowers, baskets and confections, with a few innovative ideas thrown in for those tough-to-shop-for special occasions.
HEALTH & BEAUTY	The pills, dressings and ointments it takes to keep your body healthy, as well as all the cosmetics, cleansers and fragrances you favor to keep you looking and feeling beautiful.
HOME & GARDEN	From home improvement to making your garden grow, including furniture, household tools or a bounty of landscaping gear.
MATERNITY	A thorough selection of fashionable clothing to help display the radiance of impending motherhood during nine months of changes.
MINORS	From infants through teens, and from clothes and toys to furniture and educational products.
PETS	May include supplies for birds, critters, fish and reptiles, but mostly for cats and dogs.
SENIORS	Offers products that may be useful to the aging.
SPORT & OUTDOOR	Home gyms, athletic equipment or outdoor gear, though sport-specific stores are often better.
TRAVEL	Booking a vacation may not be what they have in mind (there are exceptions), but luggage is pretty sure to be found.

KEY WORD INDEX

Use the followings lists to locate online retailers that sell the type of products you seek.

ACCESSORIES

Anthropologie.com
AzaleaSF.com
Barbwire.com
Barneys.com
BDJeffries.com
BergdorfGoodman.com
BlueFly.com
Costco.com
DuluthTrading.com
EcoChoices.com
Fortunoff.com
GreenFeet.com
GreenHome.com
KMart.com
LaylaGrayce.com
ModHaus.com
Overstock.com
PearlRiver.com
Ross-Simons.com
SageJewelry.com
SailorJerry.com
ShanghaiTang.com
Sheplers.com
ShopComposition.com
ShopKitson.com
SmartBargains.com
SoftSurroundings.com
Spiegel.com
StacksAndStacks.com
StandardStyle.com
StitchChicago.com
Swell.com
Target.com
UrbanOutfitters.com
UrbanStyle.com
Vivre.com
Yoox.com

APPAREL

Anthropologie.com
AzaleaSF.com
Barbwire.com
Barneys.com
BergdorfGoodman.com
BlueFly.com
DuluthTrading.com
EcoChoices.com
GreenFeet.com
GreenHome.com
KMart.com
LaylaGrayce.com
ModHaus.com
Overstock.com
PearlRiver.com
SageJewelry.com
SailorJerry.com
ShanghaiTang.com
Sheplers.com
ShopKitson.com
SmartBargains.com
SoftSurroundings.com
Spiegel.com
StandardStyle.com
StarsAndInfiniteDarkness.com
StitchChicago.com
Swell.com
Target.com
UrbanOutfitters.com
UrbanStyle.com
Vickerey.com
VivaTerra.com
Vivre.com
Yoox.com

ART & COLLECTIBLE

BDJeffries.com
Berings.com
EcoChoices.com
GuyBuys.com
ModHaus.com
Namaste.com
PearlRiver.com
Ross-Simons.com
ShanghaiTang.com
ShopComposition.com
UrbanStyle.com

CRAFTS & HOBBIES

DuluthTrading.com
GuyBuys.com
LaylaGrayce.com
RedhillGeneralStore.com

ELECTRONICS

Amazon.com
Comfort1st.com
Costco.com
eCost.com
GuyBuys.com
KMart.com
ModHaus.com
NewYorkFirst.com
Overstock.com
SmartBargains.com
Spiegel.com
Target.com
TheLeftHand.com
Wal-Mart.com

ENTERTAINMENT

Amazon.com
Costco.com
eCost.com
GuyBuys.com
HighVibe.com
KMart.com
Namaste.com
Overstock.com
ShopComposition.com
Wal-Mart.com
Yoox.com

EPICUREAN

Berings.com
HighVibe.com
KokoGM.com
Namaste.com
NapaStyle.com
NewYorkFirst.com
PearlRiver.com
SoftSurroundings.com
TwoKH.com
VivaTerra.com
Wal-Mart.com

GIFTS

Amazon.com
Barneys.com
BDJeffries.com
BergdorfGoodman.com
Berings.com
BlueFly.com
DuluthTrading.com
EcoChoices.com
Fortunoff.com
GreenFeet.com
GuyBuys.com
LaylaGrayce.com
ModHaus.com
Namaste.com
NapaStyle.com
NewYorkFirst.com

GIFTS (cont).

PearlRiver.com
Ross-Simons.com
SageJewelry.com
SailorJerry.com
ShanghaiTang.com
ShopComposition.com
SoftSurroundings.com
Spiegel.com
StarsAndInfiniteDarkness.com
StitchChicago.com
TheLeftHand.com
TwoKH.com
UrbanOutfitters.com
Vickerey.com
VivaTerra.com
Vivre.com

HEALTH & BEAUTY

Amazon.com
AzaleaSF.com
Barneys.com
BergdorfGoodman.com
Berings.com
Costco.com
EcoChoices.com
eCost.com
Gaiam.com
GreenFeet.com
GreenHome.com
HighVibe.com
HomelandPreparedness.com
KMart.com
KokoGM.com
Namaste.com
NewYorkFirst.com
PearlRiver.com
SageJewelry.com
ShopKitson.com
SoftSurroundings.com
Spiegel.com
StitchChicago.com
Target.com
TwoKH.com
Vickerey.com
VivaTerra.com

HOME & GARDEN

Amazon.com
Anthropologie.com
Barneys.com
BDJeffries.com
BergdorfGoodman.com
Berings.com
BlueFly.com
Comfort1st.com
Costco.com
DuluthTrading.com
EcoChoices.com
eCost.com
Fortunoff.com
Gaiam.com
GreenFeet.com
GreenHome.com
GuyBuys.com
HighVibe.com
HomelandPreparedness.com
KMart.com
KokoGM.com
LaylaGrayce.com
ModHaus.com
NapaStyle.com
NewYorkFirst.com
Overstock.com
PearlRiver.com
RedhillGeneralStore.com
Ross-Simons.com
SailorJerry.com
ShopComposition.com
SmartBargains.com
SoftSurroundings.com
Spiegel.com
StacksAndStacks.com
StitchChicago.com
Swell.com
Target.com
TheLeftHand.com
TwoKH.com
UrbanOutfitters.com
UrbanStyle.com
VivaTerra.com
Vivre.com
Wal-Mart.com

MATERNITY

Amazon.com
LaylaGrayce.com
StandardStyle.com
UrbanStyle.com

MINORS

Amazon.com
Barbwire.com
Barneys.com
DuluthTrading.com
EcoChoices.com
Fortunoff.com
GreenFeet.com
GreenHome.com
KMart.com
LaylaGrayce.com
RedhillGeneralStore.com
SailorJerry.com
Sheplers.com
ShopKitson.com
SmartBargains.com
Spiegel.com
StacksAndStacks.com
StandardStyle.com
StarsAndInfiniteDarkness.com
StitchChicago.com
Target.com
TwoKH.com
UrbanOutfitters.com
UrbanStyle.com
Vivre.com
Wal-Mart.com

PETS

Comfort1st.com
Costco.com
Gaiam.com
GreenHome.com
KokoGM.com
NewYorkFirst.com
RedhillGeneralStore.com
ShopComposition.com
StacksAndStacks.com
StarsAndInfiniteDarkness.com
Target.com
TwoKH.com
UrbanStyle.com
Wal-Mart.com

SPORT & OUTDOOR

Amazon.com
BDJeffries.com
Comfort1st.com
Costco.com
DuluthTrading.com
Gaiam.com
GuyBuys.com
HighVibe.com
KMart.com
Overstock.com
RedhillGeneralStore.com
StacksAndStacks.com
Swell.com
Target.com
TheLeftHand.com
UrbanStyle.com
Vickerey.com
Wal-Mart.com

TRAVEL

Comfort1st.com
Costco.com
DuluthTrading.com
EcoChoices.com
Gaiam.com
GuyBuys.com
Overstock.com
SmartBargains.com
StacksAndStacks.com
StitchChicago.com
Vivre.com
Wal-Mart.com
Yoox.com

TRAVEL

BDJeffries.com
CattleKate.com
Fortunoff.com
PearlRiver.com
Ross-Simons.com

Amazon.com

The first name in internet retail has come a long way from its origins as strictly a bookseller. Its expansion started, logically, with music and videos, but has gone on to include electronics, home-and-garden stuff, baby gear, toys and even cars (these last through partnerships with industry leaders). As it happens, these guys literally own the patent on "1-Click" shopping, and personal pages offer suggestions based on previous purchases. Of course, if you start taking recommendations from a computer, you'll likely end up with multiple copies of Tron.

·MINORS ·ELECTRONICS	·MATERNITY ·ENTERTAINMENT	·GIFTS ·HEALTH & BEAUTY	·SPORT & OUTDOOR ·HOME & GARDEN

Anthropologie.com

Drawing influence from different cultures around the globe, the designers of the exclusive Anthropologie line of products are always careful to accommodate the ever-changing fashions of contemporary urban America. The result is a youthful and stylish selection of apparel, accessories and home furnishings, each with bright colors and a tasteful flair, most of which is distinctly funkier than the franchise's primary competition. If this burgeoning promenade mainstay hasn't yet popped up in your town, log on now and see what great things you've been missing.

·ACCESSORIES	·APPAREL	·HOME & GARDEN

AzaleaSF.com

"A keen appreciation for timeless style" is not required to shop from this San Francisco boutique, but it will sure aid in your enjoyment of the several superhip designer collections found on its savvy site. Men and women both will benefit from the denim and other urban fashions filling these pages, which include such rarely seen labels as English Laundry and Milly alongside luminaries such as APC and True Religion. Men will also find some great belts, while the women's Accessories section features some truly stylish jewelry. As for who will benefit from the finely stocked assortment of skin care products found in the Beauty Bar, that's up to you.

·ACCESSORIES	·APPAREL	·HEALTH & BEAUTY

Barbwire.com

Showing us how "the west is wild again," this Arizona retailer turns traditional cowboy style on its ear. True caballeros might not know what to make of this stuff, but anybody with a hint of style and a Western romantic streak will gladly pay the price it takes to assemble the hottest of urban cowboy and cowgirl wardrobes. Principle items to watch out for include hats, boots and belts, of course, but all of the assorted accessories and attire here put extravagant colors and patterns into America's most celebrated mystique.

·ACCESSORIES	·APPAREL	·MINORS

888-222-7639 · Barneys New York

Barneys.com

Perhaps the best department store in the world, with only four locations outside of New York, most of us have been missing out on Barneys' magnificent selection of merchandise—until now. The fabulous designer apparel, top-end cosmetics and attention-getting accessories have been making their way to this high-tech site bit by bit, and we're hoping more will become available as time goes by. If not, the bright side is that we get to save money in the meantime; this is definitely not a discount department store.

·ACCESSORIES ·HEALTH & BEAUTY	·APPAREL ·HOME & GARDEN	·MINORS	·GIFTS

800-954-3004 · B.D. Jeffries

BDJeffries.com

This shop seems to have fashioned a lifestyle out of its beginnings as a crocodile and alligator accessories brand, and we won't complain. While you'll still find plenty of elegant belts and wallets, now you may also procure some great barware, wedding party gifts, home decor and the occasional antique. The site's not big enough to take up an afternoon, but promises to serve a variety of needs for the alligator-friendly, as well as just those who appreciate quality and style.

·ACCESSORIES ·SPORT & OUTDOOR	·GIFTS	·HOME & GARDEN	·ART & COLLECTIBLE

888-774-2424 · Bergdorf Goodman

BergdorfGoodman.com

There's more than one famous department store on Manhattan's Fifth Avenue, and this often overlooked upscale retailer brings a fantastic selection of designer women's wares to this uncomplicated site. In fact, a glance at the Designer Index is really all you need to know whether you want to shop here; names like Diane von Furstenberg, Elie Tahari, Jean Paul Gaultier, Emilio Pucci, Donna Karan, Vera Wang, Roberto Cavalli, Narciso Rodriguez and Oscar de la Renta don't even comprise half the list. Only those seeking the best cosmetics, perfumes, handbags, apparel, shoes and accessories will want to bother.

·ACCESSORIES ·HOME & GARDEN	·APPAREL	·GIFTS	·HEALTH & BEAUTY

713-665-0500 · Bering's

Berings.com

If we've learned anything in the past few years, it's that when Texas does anything, Texas does it big. That's what you'll discover with regard to this upscale Houston retailer, which delivers a great selection of fine gifts and products for the home, pantry and bathroom. There's nothing typical about the household goods, which include great fireplace accessories, mirrors, door knockers, small appliances, fine china, wind chimes and of course barbecues. Even by Texan standards, this one's a big winner.

·EPICUREAN ·HOME & GARDEN	·GIFTS	·ART & COLLECTIBLE	·HEALTH & BEAUTY

BlueFly.com

Bluefly.com · 877-258-3359

Whatever Blue Fly means is not important. What's important is that this site is an online outlet store, and that means that whatever you see here will be cheaper than it should be. Why? Who cares? Whether you're shopping for designer shirts, table linens, sandals, handbags or jewelry, you can find it here. And not just knockoff, fake-label items either—whether it's Gucci, Marc Jacobs, Vera Wang or Christian Dior, you can find it. Especially with the site's excellent organization, which lets you browse by designer or category, then narrow down the results on the basis of price, popularity and new arrivals.

		·ACCESSORIES	·APPAREL	·GIFTS	·HOME & GARDEN

Comfort1st.com

Z&M Enterprises · 443-539-1440

What starts out as a comfort specialist sort of balloons into an everything-under-the-sun megastore with this surprisingly big site. While the general lack of focus makes this a difficult store to shop, you still will find plenty of comfortable products, whether bed mattresses or hypoallergenic bedding. Beyond that you'll find plenty of appliances and cleaning tools to keep your home feeling comfortable, some medical aids to keep individual body parts comforted and even some things for your pets. How the sporting goods fit in we may never know.

		·TRAVEL ·PETS	·SPORT & OUTDOOR	·ELECTRONICS	·HOME & GARDEN

Costco.com

Costco · 800-774-2678

If you're already a member of Costco, you'll pretty much know what to expect from this online store. Those of you not so well acquainted should know a couple of things before you start shopping. See, in order to take advantage of their wholesale prices, you'll need to purchase a membership, usually for an annual fee. Otherwise, when you buy from the site, you'll be assessed an additional surcharge. As a result, while there is a limited range of large and/or electronic items, membership really makes sense if you want to shop here repeatedly for grocery and day-to-day items.

		·ACCESSORIES ·ENTERTAINMENT	·TRAVEL ·HEALTH & BEAUTY	·SPORT & OUTDOOR ·HOME & GARDEN	·ELECTRONICS ·PETS

DuluthTrading.com

Duluth Trading Company · 877-382-2345

If you're a rugged man, or know one, this site may make sense as a place to shop for traditionally masculine apparel, accessories and just general tough-as-nails merchandise. Stuff like workman's gloves, suspenders and workshop aprons fit alongside tool belts, winter coats and speed sensor baseballs to cover men's hobbies and recreation, as well as just hefty daily routines. There are even smaller versions of some products for the man's man in training.

	·ACCESSORIES ·TRAVEL	·APPAREL ·SPORT & OUTDOOR	·MINORS ·HOME & GARDEN	·GIFTS ·CRAFTS & HOBBIES

626-969-3707 · EcoChoices Natural Living Store

EcoChoices.com

The clear and important emphasis of this site is that living an ecologically sustainable lifestyle is a choice we can make as consumers; at least, now that we know about this lifestyle shop we can make the choice to purchase environmentally sound products. Most of the products here, such as the clothing and furniture, have been made from organic materials. Others are comprised of recycled materials, some made of hemp or, as in the case of the bath-and-body products, all-natural herbs and vegetables. Whether you're shopping for towels, coasters, toys or a new mattress, this shop can keep your shopping and your home green.

·ACCESSORIES ·TRAVEL	·APPAREL ·ART & COLLECTIBLE	·MINORS ·HEALTH & BEAUTY	·GIFTS ·HOME & GARDEN	

877-888-2678 · eCost.com

eCost.com

For a dot-com that's built its brand name around the notion of "cost," it's hard to get a bead on these guys' prices, as they change them often, sometimes more than once a day. The result is an all-around electronics superstore that probably offers its best incentives at times when the market is better conditioned to buyers than sellers. As such, it may prove worthwhile to check any purchases from other stores against the prices here. Since they offer a pretty elastic selection of computer gear, home electronics equipment, home and grooming appliances, you can get a pretty good idea of what's available and what it's worth, assuming you can see past the hectic exterior.

·ELECTRONICS	·ENTERTAINMENT	·HEALTH & BEAUTY	·HOME & GARDEN	

800-367-8866 · Fortunoff

Fortunoff.com

From modest beginnings as a neighborhood housewares store in Brooklyn, Fortunoff shops have expanded over nearly eight decades to finally bring their great selection and prices online. The site is well set up to help you find what you're looking for, whether by department or manufacturer, though it can really take a while before you actually click through to a product. If you have some idea of what you're looking for, you might want to stick to the advanced search so you can filter out any of the hundreds of items that might otherwise distract you. On the other hand, if you're getting married, you might just want to take your time, as a Fortunoff Gift & Bridal Registry is now available online, and you definitely don't want to miss out on anything.

·ACCESSORIES	·MINORS	·GIFTS	·HOME & GARDEN	

877-989-6321 · Gaiam.com

Gaiam.com

This increasingly popular online department store was created "to provide choices that allow people to live a more natural and healthy life with respect to the environment," and thanks to its growing selection of information, health products, fitness equipment and housewares, adhering to an eco-friendly lifestyle has never been easier. Proving that sustainable living is not just a fad, the excellently designed shop offers items as aesthetically pleasing as they are functional, which almost takes the fun out of curbing your reliance on chemicals and plastics for the sake of the planet.

·TRAVEL ·PETS	·SPORT & OUTDOOR	·HEALTH & BEAUTY	·HOME & GARDEN	

GreenFeet.com

greenfeet.com · 888-562-8873

Green is our other favorite color here at **thepurplebook**, in part due to this shop, which delivers a surprisingly comprehensive selection of "high-quality, truly natural products that you can trust." We're getting used to seeing the eco-lifestyle represented online, but every time we visit this site we're still surprised at just how deep its variety of environmentally friendly products is. With entire sections devoted to nontoxic cleaning supplies, all-natural personal-care products and items made entirely of hemp, and no less than six addressing different household needs, you'll be back here often.

·ACCESSORIES ·HEALTH & BEAUTY	·APPAREL ·HOME & GARDEN	·MINORS	·GIFTS

GreenHome.com

Green Home · 877-282-6400

As "your source for environmentally superior goods, services, and information," this excellent, multifaceted lifestyle shop shows us just how easy it can be to go green. It of course covers organic clothing, long-lasting lightbulbs, all-natural bath products, nontoxic cleaners and alternative energy sources, but as you browse these pages you soon realize that the combination of technology and green industry growth has brought the concept of sustainable living to a wider range of products than was previously imaginable. We'd recommend this site as your go-to home store and personal accessories source, and chances are, if you look here first, you'll find just about any functional product you need, and it will be green.

·ACCESSORIES ·HOME & GARDEN	·APPAREL ·PETS	·MINORS	·HEALTH & BEAUTY

GuyBuys.com

Guy Buys · 631-375-2803

Boasting "over 20,000 'guy approved' items," the size of this site isn't what matters. What is important is that the distinctly male focus allowed the site designers to build the browsing around categories that make sense to the uniquely unsubtle male mind. Hence you'll find a predictable array of products scattered across Sports, Electronics, Tailgating, Game Room, Videogames and more, including autographed memorabilia and loads of time-killing software and gaming accessories. Women should probably stick to the gift certificates.

·GIFTS ·ELECTRONICS	·TRAVEL ·ENTERTAINMENT	·ART & COLLECTIBLE ·HOME & GARDEN	·SPORT & OUTDOOR ·CRAFTS & HOBBIES

HighVibe.com

High Vibe Health and Healing · 212-777-6645

One of the toughest lifestyle changes any of us are bound to make in our lives revolve around diet and nutrition. Sure, we know processed foods, heavy oils, fructose, pesticides and preservatives wreak havoc on our bodies, but can we really flush them out of our system and start from scratch with a new, completely healthy approach? Maybe not, but with the help of this site you can come pretty damn close. The raw-foods and natural-products specialist covers a wide range of health and dietary concerns, with a breadth of products ranging from produce to skin care items, self-help books and exercise guides. Rare is the web site that can make you feel so good after visiting.

·EPICUREAN ·HOME & GARDEN	·SPORT & OUTDOOR	·ENTERTAINMENT	·HEALTH & BEAUTY

800-350-1489 · **Homeland Preparedness**

HomelandPreparedness.com

Gear up your home for any emergency with this safety and security specialist, and while you're at it go ahead and outfit your office, car and school. So complete is the shop's supply of disaster preparedness kits that they offer several that take your pet into consideration. Aside from the general first-aid-type supplies, you'll find food rations, water purifiers, sanitation supplies, emergency shelters and even a few gas masks. It ultimately offers an easy way for you to feel prepared in case of catastrophe, leaving you at ease to enjoy the mundane splendor of everyday life.

·HEALTH & BEAUTY	·HOME & GARDEN		

866-562-7848 · **Kmart**

KMart.com

Attention Kmart shoppers: you can now find many of the items you exect to see in your local store without having to leave your home, or even change out of your bathrobe. Children's clothes, household essentials and personal-care products top the list of items we found, but there's more for sale here than you could ever fit into a shopping cart. Blue light specials, of course, are always just a few clicks away.

·ACCESSORIES ·ELECTRONICS	·APPAREL ·ENTERTAINMENT	·MINORS ·HEALTH & BEAUTY	·SPORT & OUTDOOR ·HOME & GARDEN

800-210-0202 · **Kokopelli's Green Market**

KokoGM.com

These guys offer environment-friendly products to "detoxify your body" and "detoxify your world." Both seem to be good ideas, and what with the all-natural soaps, household cleaners, water filters and baby-care products found here, they seem to be fairly well executed. Further exploration uncovers other fantastic items such as biodegradable trash bags, sun-simulating Chromalux light bulbs and powerful air filters that will still keep your home's atmosphere chemical free if you happen to use a product you didn't buy here.

·EPICUREAN	·HEALTH & BEAUTY	·HOME & GARDEN	·PETS

801-474-1990 · **Layla Grace**

LaylaGrayce.com

This shop sort of adheres to the lifestyle mothers and their children share, which isn't to say guys are left out of the shopping experience—just the masculine products are left out. It makes sense to the founders, a couple of busy moms who stock the departments of this store as an act of self-expression, and so usually opt for soft, colorful, feminine fare, and supercute kid's stuff. Clothes may take up a good deal of your time on this slow-to-load site, but leave room in your schedule for the furniture and housewares, because they're good enough for even a man to love.

·ACCESSORIES ·GIFTS	·APPAREL ·HOME & GARDEN	·MINORS ·CRAFTS & HOBBIES	·MATERNITY

ModHaus.com

ModHaus.com · 617-822-9183

Do you feel cool? Do you want to? This site specializes in "the Mod," meaning vintage designer items from the 1950s-1970s that were ultrahip in their own time, and have lost little or no luster with age, even in the 21st-century. With sections devoted to jewelry, fashion, art, furniture and the aptly named Other Far Out Stuff, you can now easily decorate your life to look like a Fellini film (well, maybe not that far out). Current designs struggle to be as way cool as this stuff, so why bother with the new when the old mod outhips us all, man?

| | ·ACCESSORIES ·ELECTRONICS | ·APPAREL ·HOME & GARDEN | ·GIFTS | ·ART & COLLECTIBLE |

Namaste.com

Namaste.com · 866-438-4642

Desis will delight in this site, whose name loosely translated means "I bow to the divine in you." What's a Desi? Well, if you have to ask, the name probably doesn't apply to you, but that doesn't mean you can't enjoy this store devoted to Indian products of all kinds. Really, though, its best use lies in a bevy of community resources, which connects South Asians with local communities and organizations, offers special deals on things like international calling cards and makes it easy to order gifts for friends and family members in India without incurring high shipping costs. Great use of the web.

| ·EPICUREAN ·HEALTH & BEAUTY | ·GIFTS | ·ART & COLLECTIBLE | ·ENTERTAINMENT |

NapaStyle.com

Napastyle · 866-776-1600

The posh, laid-back style of the California wine country finds terrific representation with this lovely home and gourmet site. Among the many home accents and furniture pieces you'll find one of the web's best collection of wine racks, stemware, bar stools and decanters. But it's not all about the oenophile here; great wine is best served with great cooking, so the site includes a healthy assortment of gourmet condiments and spices, including a surprisingly diverse array of salts. Add the selection of nifty kitchen gadgets and beautiful serving-ware, and it's easy to see why domestic winemakers like to eat and drink in the comfort of home.

| ·EPICUREAN | ·GIFTS | ·HOME & GARDEN | |

NewYorkFirst.com

The New York First Company · 607-277-0152

It's the city so nice they named it twice, so no surprise that this New York-centric shop should offer a litany of fine products for your home, office and palate. In the Gotham Grocery section you'll find such local delicacies as H&H Bagels; the Mezzanine offers classic barware; the Curiosity Shop features an intriguing selection of Urban Toys; and City Stuff, of course, is filled with great souvenirs. Ultimately, you'll find a wide range of great gifts for yourself and friends, including one big healthy bite of the Big Apple.

| ·EPICUREAN ·HOME & GARDEN | ·GIFTS ·PETS | ·ELECTRONICS | ·HEALTH & BEAUTY |

800-989-0135 · Overstock.com

Overstock.com

The promise of extremely low prices makes the word *overstock* very attractive to the bargain shopper, but it's great design and thorough organization that make this the best discount superstore online. Of course, the low prices are there for all the excess inventory and factory-refurbished items, meaning you can find terrific deals on everything from clothes and accessories to home furnishings and consumer electronics. If you like the idea of saving a little money, you should bookmark this one as a comparison shopping site where you'll almost always have an inexpensive alternative.

·ACCESSORIES ·ELECTRONICS	·APPAREL ·ENTERTAINMENT	·TRAVEL ·HOME & GARDEN	·SPORT & OUTDOOR	

800-878-2446 · Pearl River

PearlRiver.com

This "first Chinese American department store" has been offering quality merchandise since before the US allowed trade with modern China, so you can imagine how good the store is now that the doors of international commerce are open. It's an excellent place to find home furnishings in particular, such as lamps, screens, blinds and straw mats. But there's plenty of everything to be found here, including clothes, herbal medicines, teas, stationery, wedding decorations and some incredibly beautiful slippers. This is the sort of extraordinary quality it takes thousands of years to fine tune.

·ACCESSORIES ·HOME & GARDEN	·APPAREL ·ART & COLLECTIBLE	·EPICUREAN ·HEALTH & BEAUTY	·GIFTS	

800-251-8824 · Red Hill General Store

RedHillGeneralStore.com

About as general as it gets, this multifaceted shop offers a wide range of essential items for your family and household. True to the general stores of old, the site offers quaint items like washboards, oil lanterns and large wooden water barrels as well as traditional farm equipment. You'll also find heating appliances, cleaning supplies, gardening equipment, kitchen tools and pet gear. Look hard enough and you'll even find a bevy of camping equipment to outfit your home away from home, or as you embark for a new life on the frontier.

·MINORS ·CRAFTS & HOBBIES	·SPORT & OUTDOOR	·HOME & GARDEN	·PETS	

800-835-1343 · Ross-Simons

Ross-Simons.com

Though maintaining a strong focus in silver, crystal and porcelain collectibles, the Ross-Simons catalog has expanded considerably to include a fine array of jewelry, housewares and keepsake gifts, making for a great bridal registry. However, the site hasn't improved much on user-friendliness, and with such a deep selection only minimally organized, you may have to spend a few hours filling that registry. If on first look you like what you see but haven't the patience to browse all day, they'll be all too happy to mail you a paper catalog every month to help with quick ordering from the site.

·ACCESSORIES	·GIFTS	·HOME & GARDEN	·ART & COLLECTIBLE	

SageJewelry.com
Sage Jewelry · 866-755-7243

"Kamikaze jeweler, clothing designer, perfumer, boutique owner, artist, and entrepreneur Sage Machado" is behind this bohemian Los Angeles boutique, which offers a unique assortment of her own products, almost enough jewelry, shoes, perfume, bath products and apparel to constitute a women's department store. If the slow-moving site starts to frustrate you, just remember that the self-started business has already attracted a great amount of attention, both from magazines and by celebrities, so if you don't persevere the limited quantities could easily sell out.

·ACCESSORIES	·APPAREL	·GIFTS	·HEALTH & BEAUTY

SailorJerry.com
Sailor Jerry · 215-923-6980

If you dislike the permanence of tattoos but adore the styles, this unique all-around retailer might just appeal to your quasi-roguish sensibilities. Inspired by the long-storied culture of tattoo art (particularly the sort brandished by sailors), the clothes, accessories and household items available here feature classic illustrations such as anchors, eagles and roses. Of course, there's no saying that somebody already sporting a lot of ink won't enjoy the styles found here; in fact, they may be right up your alley.

·ACCESSORIES ·HOME & GARDEN	·APPAREL	·MINORS	·GIFTS

ShanghaiTang.com
Shanghai Tang · 888-252-8264

"Interweaving traditional Chinese culture with the dynamism of the 21st-Century," this shop originated in Hong Kong and has spread worldwide with its outstanding selection of Chinese goods. The well-stocked department store caters to a full facet of apparel and fashionable accessories, championing functionality and putting a modern twist on traditional Asian styles. We can't say for sure whether American trends have impacted the designs of this stuff, but we can speculate that the emergence of web retailers like this will bring the Chinese influence home.

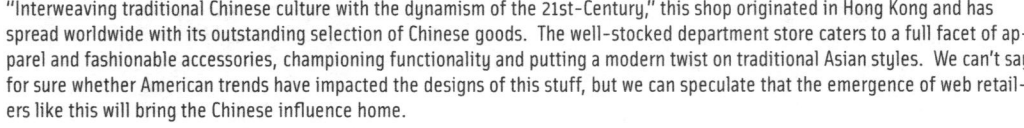

·ACCESSORIES	·APPAREL	·GIFTS	·ART & COLLECTIBLE

Sheplers.com
Sheplers · 800-833-7007

"Meeting the Western wear needs of America for over 55 years," this traditional Western lifestyle shop specializes in all the things that make a cowboy a cowboy; namely hats, belts and boots. Of course, there's more to wrangling and doing rodeo than the accoutrements, but getting the look down pat is about the best we can hope for from a web shop, and this one does it just fine. Men's, women's and children's garb is easy to find and brightly displayed, and even if you don't consider yourself a great Westerner, you're bound to love the rugged selection of blue jeans available for every member of the family.

·ACCESSORIES	·APPAREL	·MINORS	

303-894-0025 · Composition

ShopComposition.com

If this "neighborhood boutique" sprang up on your block, it would certainly give a new look to the community. The Denver shop brings a focus on design, and "has curated a diverse selection of modern goods from jewelry to laptop bags, housewares to footwear." Super funky across the board, the products are great to look at, even if they are a pain to shop for—see, even the web design works hard to be unique, which makes browsing a long, arduous process. As bad as it can be, once you've gotten a glance at some of these items, it's hard not to look at the rest.

| ·ACCESSORIES ·HOME & GARDEN | ·GIFTS ·PETS | ·ART & COLLECTIBLE | ·ENTERTAINMENT | |

877-754-8766 · Kitson

ShopKitson.com

If you're itching to shop at the trendy Los Angeles Kitson boutique, but wish to stay out of range of the paparazzi's zoom lenses, now you can. This rapidly improving site may not offer a casual encounter with any of the shop's famous in-store clientele, but it can grant you access to the same accessories, apparel and beauty products favored by some of the city's favorite tabloid headliners. Come and get it while it's still hot.

| ·ACCESSORIES | ·APPAREL | ·MINORS | ·HEALTH & BEAUTY | |

866-692-2742 · SmartBargains.com

SmartBargains.com

If you appreciate things like easy browsing and great prices in your online shopping session, this site's pretty much got it all. With a wide range of categories covering each room within your home, including the closets, this bargain department store should meet your simple electronics, furnishings and clothing needs, as well as the occasional decorative or accessorizing indulgence. While the catalog is wide and deep, it's excellently organized, meaning you'll find what you need quickly, and stumble across things you want almost by accident. Smart indeed.

| ·ACCESSORIES ·ELECTRONICS | ·APPAREL ·HOME & GARDEN | ·MINORS | ·TRAVEL | |

800-240-7076 · Soft Surroundings

SoftSurroundings.com

The world is tough enough without abrasive bed linens, uncomfortable shoes and dried-out hair. At least, that seems to be the premise behind this site, which specializes in the sort of soothing products especially favored by women after a long day of drudgery. Thus, they offer pleasantly comfortable after-work clothes, soothing bath products and moisturizers to put the harder days behind you. And, for when you need to go that extra step, they also offer comfort food in the form of chocolate truffles and bundt cakes.

| ·ACCESSORIES ·HEALTH & BEAUTY | ·APPAREL ·HOME & GARDEN | ·EPICUREAN | ·GIFTS | |

Spiegel.com

Having survived well more than a century as a successful Chicago department store and catalog, this online entity promises to maintain a long-existing standard of customer satisfaction. Offering such perks as delayed billing and upgraded substitutions for out-of-stock items, chances are that you'll find this a reliable retailer, whether you're browsing one robust section or another. Highlights include the Fashion & Accessories and For the Home sections, but generally there are no surprises and few, if any, letdowns.

·ACCESSORIES ·ELECTRONICS	·APPAREL ·HEALTH & BEAUTY	·MINORS ·HOME & GARDEN	·GIFTS

StacksAndStacks.com

This site is full of crates, carts, boxes, cabinets, shelves, racks and every other conceivable home storage utility. True to form, the site's excellently organized in conjunction with its products, with a healthy list of animated menus (our favorite kind) making it quite easy to view and delve into subcategories. Of course, this helps you realize that they have a lot more than just home storage options here, as many of these surprisingly innovative products are dedicated to eliminating disorder from your sporting activities, pet care and child rearing—which always verge on chaos.

·ACCESSORIES ·HOME & GARDEN	·MINORS ·PETS	·TRAVEL	·SPORT & OUTDOOR

StandardStyle.com

This "fashion forward boutique for the chic" may be headquartered in Kansas, but it definitely boasts "a West Coast vibe." Inspired by California fashions, the selection here is massive and thorough enough to outdo most California retailers, with a huge assortment of top labels for men, women, pregnant women, babies and children. The only apparent drawback is that you'll need to be well versed in each of the hundreds of brands represented, or find yourself wading through dozens of pages of clothes. This might be a problem if the garments in question weren't so hip

·ACCESSORIES	·APPAREL	·MINORS	·MATERNITY

StarsAndInfiniteDarkness.com

Aside from the requisite dot-com extension, this hip apparel site has a poetic name, and true to this spirit, it's definitely "not your typical store." For the most part this stems from the fact that the bulk of the items for men, women, babies and children are handmade by the designers at the time they're ordered. This means each graphic tee, bikini, skirt or hoodie is both unique and of high quality, but also that it will take a long time for you to finally receive it. It'll be worth the wait, though, because even the doggy apparel here is something special to behold.

·APPAREL	·MINORS	·GIFTS	·PETS

773-782-1570 · Stitch

StitchChicago.com

A Chicago boutique with a definite flair for the modern, the web site we found here isn't terribly fun to use, and in fact seems dreadfully serious about all its assorted products. This may be appropriate, however, as each bedding set, furniture piece, laptop case, tabletop accessory, handbag, children's toy, pen and wallet is designed to be extraordinarily clean, simple and otherwise contemporary. Of course, to the truly modern soul, all of these borderline sterile objects will seem just quite close to perfect.

·ACCESSORIES ·TRAVEL	·APPAREL ·HEALTH & BEAUTY	·MINORS ·HOME & GARDEN	·GIFTS

866-255-7873 · Swell

Swell.com

The passion for the world's greatest watersport, surfing, is powerful enough that it's spawned its own set of styles and customs, many of which may be addressed by this online surf shop. Although its fine selection of gear doesn't include surfboards, plenty of leashes, racks, wetsuits, and board bags should keep the coastal shopper satisfied, while an assortment of surfing DVDs prove as entertaining as they are educational. The site's real value, however, may be found in its many pages of guys' and gals' accessories and apparel, which cover the sorts of board shorts, bikinis, sneakers, sweatshirts and hats favored by dudes and hodads alike.

·ACCESSORIES	·APPAREL	·SPORT & OUTDOOR	·HOME & GARDEN

800-591-3869 · Target

Target.com

Even without its online presence, this department store chain has been gaining in popularity almost to the point of cult status, thanks to its enormous selection of affordable items for everyday life. Incredibly, with this web site it manages to carry even more than any individual retail store could, including a large assortment of furniture, mattresses, rugs and other household accoutrements. However, the real reason for the shop's recent success is probably the colorful, almost quirky designs behind many of its contemporary offerings—see the Red Hot featured products to see what we mean.

·ACCESSORIES ·ELECTRONICS	·APPAREL ·HEALTH & BEAUTY	·MINORS ·HOME & GARDEN	·SPORT & OUTDOOR ·PETS

239-985-9553 · The Left Hand

TheLeftHand.com

While it's widely assumed that righthanded and lefthanded people differ in their abilities to define patterns and interpret spatial relations, the proprietors of this site realize that the only established differences tend to involve the trouble lefthanders have using righthanded tools. Here, we get to browse a range of office supplies, culinary tools, computer accessories and baseball mitts created with the southpaw in mind. Lefthanders may only truly have an advantage when it comes to baseball, but with the help of this shop, they should be able to overcome any disadvantages.

·GIFTS	·SPORT & OUTDOOR	·ELECTRONICS	·HOME & GARDEN

TwoKH.com

II KH · 866-458-1017

Bringing "a new level of sophistication to the booming market of eco-friendly products," this environmentally conscious lifestyle shop capitalizes on the fact that sustainable living is not only more popular than ever, but has become socially appealing in the process; in other words, hip. Housewares, beauty products, pet shampoos, gourmet gifts and organic baby gear head up this small but growing collection of products that are even cooler than they look, if only by virtue of their attitude toward the earth and its resources.

	·MINORS ·HOME & GARDEN	·EPICUREAN ·PETS	·GIFTS	·HEALTH & BEAUTY

UrbanOutfitters.com

Urban Outfitters · 800-959-8794

Urban Outfitters has made a name for itself in the past few years, with franchise stores secured as mainstays in busy shopping districts wherever young people may yearn for butterfly chairs, disco balls or sassy graphic tees. Just go to the Apartment section and you'll easily find your way through any of their varied and vibrant housewares, all suitable to modern lifestyles. The Apparel and Accessories sections are self-explanatory, but better stocked than you probably think; it's worth a look.

	·ACCESSORIES ·HOME & GARDEN	·APPAREL	·MINORS	·GIFTS

UrbanStyle.com

Urban Style · 773-252-4800

The wide base of categories featured here draw directly from the catalogs of an ever-growing conglomeration of stylish boutiques that reside in the hip neighborhoods of Chicago. With names such as The Urban Gardener, Bourdage Pearls, Barker & Meowsky and Cradles of Distinction, it's not usually hard to figure out what sort of items reside within each store, but to avoid any confusion you may access the entire selection through some well-devised product categories, which provide easier travel between stores than the El ever will.

	·ACCESSORIES ·ART & COLLECTIBLE	·APPAREL ·SPORT & OUTDOOR	·MINORS ·HOME & GARDEN	·MATERNITY ·PETS

Vickerey.com

Vickerey · 800-963-1050

Initially, we couldn't figure out a connection between the various items for sale on this site, but then a trip to the About Us page set us straight: "This is the art of living the good life." The proprietors' view of the good life seems grounded in fantastic yoga apparel for men and women, a litany of high-end bath-and-spa products and some kick-ass stationery. The handpicked selection features some particularly nice journals and date books, but in truth every page of the store turns up something great, however good you like your life to be.

	·APPAREL	·GIFTS	·SPORT & OUTDOOR	·HEALTH & BEAUTY

800-233-6011 · VivaTerra

VivaTerra.com

Driven by a "dedication to living in harmony with nature," this eco-friendly lifestyle shop manages to offer environmentally sound home products, gifts and beauty products without seeming to sacrifice anything in terms of quality or appeal. By the looks of it, this could be any small department store, except you may shop here without a twinge of liberal guilt that you're contributing to the slow degradation of the world around us, which means it's just a little bit better than any department stores we're used to.

·APPAREL ·HOME & GARDEN	·EPICUREAN	·GIFTS	·HEALTH & BEAUTY	

    (WISH)

800-411-6515 · Vivre

Vivre.com

Short for L'Arte de Vivre, which any Frenchman will tell you means "The Art of Living," this luxury retailer isn't the sort of shop you come to when you need something in particular, but the sort of place you visit when you feel like spending money on something lovely and indulgent. Whether you're shopping for yourself or a loved one, you'll probably come across something you want for yourself, as this selection of apparel, accessories, home items and gifts proves seductive and pretty fun to browse. Ready your credit card and dive in; you'll be glad you did.

·ACCESSORIES ·TRAVEL	·APPAREL ·HOME & GARDEN	·MINORS	·GIFTS	

800-966-6546 · Wal-Mart

Wal-Mart.com

You know the store. After all, it's the largest retailer in the nation, offering extensive shopping opportunities from coast to coast, and you can't stay away. There's just something about being able to find all of life's accoutrements under one roof that is eminently appealing. And here it is, all on one web site, throughly organized for easy perusal and (occasionally) slow loading. A visit to one of their huge stores will certainly give you more exercise, at least until they build one in your backyard.

·MINORS ·ELECTRONICS	·EPICUREAN ·ENTERTAINMENT	·TRAVEL ·HOME & GARDEN	·SPORT & OUTDOOR ·PETS		

      (WISH)

866-900-9266 · YOOX

Yoox.com

"Europe's No. 1 online fashion destination" started out as a great place to find designer accessories of all sorts for both men and women, and over the years it has become an incredible place to get all that and more. Terrific improvements made to its navigation makes browsing a cinch, which may prove devastating to your bank balance, as you'll find page after page of ultradesirable products. Featuring an incomparable selection of designers, some of whom you know and others whom you'll quickly grow to love, if you haven't been to YOOX before you'll definitely want to check it out, and if you haven't seen it lately, your return visit promises to be the first of many.

·ACCESSORIES	·APPAREL	·TRAVEL	·ENTERTAINMENT	

NOTES:

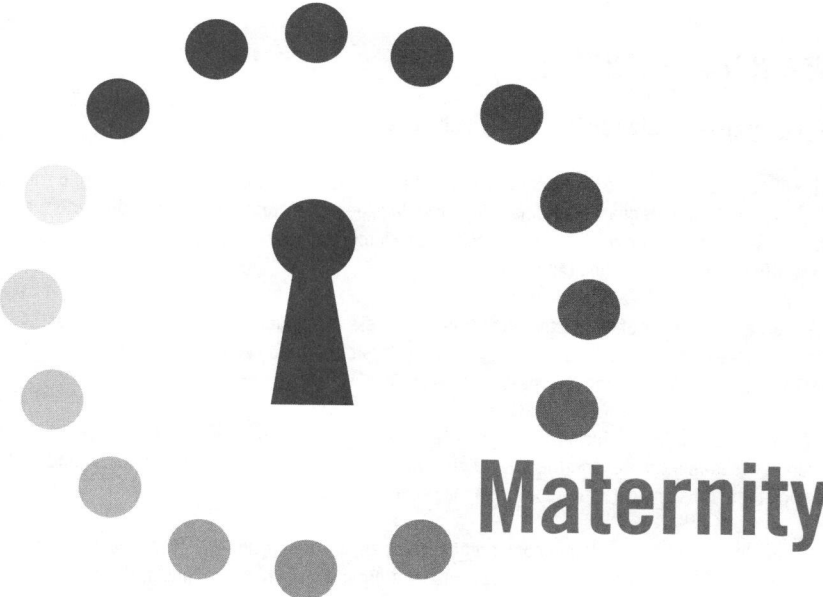

Maternity

There's no better excuse to buy a whole new wardrobe than becoming pregnant. Fortunately, with the great strides the maternity apparel industry has taken over the past decade, picking out clothes to fit a growing belly proves just as fun as shopping for regular sizes, if not more so. In this section we've been careful to include mommy-to-be clothing for the gamut of styles and occasions, mixing in designer evening wear sites with knockaround casual retailers, and including selections of lingerie, swimwear and athletic apparel. However, none of it beats the fantastic array of up-to-date fashions available for the hip, young impending mother. This stuff used to be tough to find in even the most sprawling metropolises; now it's conveniently located on a web site near you, featuring such glam wares as designer jeans, chic career apparel and plenty of sexy dresses that embrace the appeal of convex curves. If you find yourself feeling self-conscious about your pregnancy, merely slipping into one of these outfits can help you feel more comfortable, as can the occasional skin care treatments and maternity pillow. We've tried hard to cover everything, even pointing you to some great nursing apparel for your postpartum fashion requirements, but if you'd like to delve deeper into the world of maternity boutiques, keep an eye out for **thepurplebook: baby edition**, available in bookstores nationwide. This could be the best nine months your closet ever sees.

TIPS ON BUYING MATERNITY ITEMS ONLINE

These suggestions may help your pregnancy stay stylish through all seasons.

• **SIZING UP APPAREL** •The sizes for maternity clothing are set in parallel to a women's original size; in other words, a size 8 will find size 8 maternity selections. However, during pregnancy a woman can possibly expect to increase in size in addition to the room allowed for an expanding belly. As a pregnant woman's body is consistently changing, her exact size is nearly impossible to determine. When in doubt, it's a safe bet to buy a size you can grow into.

• **STOCK UP ON WARDROBE BASICS** •Part of the benefit of online shopping is easier access to updated styles in maternity wear. If you plan multiple pregnancies, though, take advantage of selections that feature classic styles and wardrobe staples, stuff that you'll feel comfortable adding back into your rotation on the next pass.

• **CHECK OUT THE MINORS SECTION** •In this section, we've included sites that feature items meant for a new or expecting mother. To this end, there is a bit of overlap between this chapter and the Infants portion of our Minors section, which focuses more on stuff for the child. Nevertheless, look there for some parenting tools that may come in handy.

• **FEEL BEAUTIFUL** • Comfort will be high on the list of priorities for any pregnant woman, and this includes a positive self-image. Despite the fact that most of humankind immediately sees the exquisite beauty inherent in a mother-to-be, physical changes can be daunting, and it may sometimes be difficult for a mother to see this beauty in herself. Ranging from sexy lingerie to glamorous evening gowns, there is plenty of clothing, as well as some beauty products in this section that will make a pregnant woman's appeal impossible to ignore. Take advantage of this. Pamper yourself—or better yet, have someone else pamper you.

SITES THAT MAY COME IN HANDY

The following URLs may be useful as you approach parenthood.

4Women.gov	Pregnancy health and nutrition information
ABOG.org	Locate a board-certified OBGYN
BabyNamer.com	Baby name resource
ClubMom.com	Parenting resource
Dona.org	Locate a doula
Dy-Dee.com	Cloth diaper resource
EatRight.org	Dietary advice
ePregnancy.com	Pregnancy info, resources and checklists
iParenting.com	Mothering resources, news and ideas
Lamaze.org	Locate a Lamaze class
MidwifeInfo.com	Locate a midwife
NursingBaby.com	Nursing info and tips
OtisPregnancy.org	Effects of common medications on pregnancy
PregnancyAndBaby.com	Pregnancy and motherhood resource
TheGreenGuide.com	Information on all-natural and eco-friendly products

BIRTH ANNOUNCEMENTS & BABY SHOWERS

The following sites offer online sales for familiar retailers.

2Chix.com
BabyShowerCakes.com
BestBabyShower.com
ButtercupKids.com

KAndTAnnouncements.com
NaptimeCards.com
StorkAvenue.com
TulipPress.com

*For in-depth reviews of these sites and more, check out **www.thepurplebook.com**.

SECTION ICON LEGEND

Use the following guide to understand the rectangular icons that appear throughout this section.

APPAREL

Ranging from stylish frocks to utilitarian wardrobe basics, the clothing featured in this section promises to keep a woman well dressed through all nine months of pregnancy, in any season.

EQUIPMENT

This icon refers to the equipment essential to a new mother for the purposes of nursing, hygiene and general small-baby care.

HEALTH

During pregnancy, myriad particular health issues may arise. These sites offer items to promote optimum health in expecting mothers, from skin care products to prenatal vitamins.

PREPARATION

It could be reading up on all the latest medical theories regarding childbirth, or choosing birth announcements. This icon gets you ready for your family's new addition, from functional to frivolous, with birth calendars, books, baby shower favors and more.

SPECIALTY SIZES

Refers to tall and/or plus-size maternity apparel.

 **LIST OF KEY WORDS**

The following words represent the types of items typically found on the sites listed in this section. You will find them listed in the orange strip at the bottom of each entry, as appropriate.

ACCESSORIES	Accessories for the new and impending mother, including strollers, diaper bags, pillows, carriers and baby shower favors (also see the Minors section).
ANNOUNCEMENTS	Birth announcements and baby shower invitations.
CASUAL WEAR	Casual maternity attire.
CHIC LABELS	Hip and designer label maternity attire and/or accessories.
EVENING WEAR	Formal maternity gowns, including some wedding dresses.
FITNESS	Athletic apparel and accessories for the expecting mother.
LINGERIE	Basic underwear, nursing bras and the occasional sexy lingerie for pregnant women.
NEWBORN CARE	Baby monitors, changing stations and other necessities for the care of a newborn (also see the Minors section).
NURSING	Nursing aids, tools, apparel and equipment, including nursing bras, breast pumps, sterilizers, bottles, bottle warmers, etc.
SKIN CARE	Includes stretch-mark treatments and other skin-related issues for the impending mother.
SWIMWEAR	Swimwear for the expecting mother.

KEY WORD INDEX

Use the followings lists to locate online retailers that sell the maternity items you seek.

ACCESSORIES

BabyStyle.com
BellaBluMaternity.com
BellyDanceMaternity.com
BreastFeedingExpress.com
DiaperBags.com
DueMaternity.com
GapMaternity.com
MomsNightOut.com
PumpStation.com
UnbuttonedMaternity.com

CAREER DRESS

Avenue-Des-Bebes.com
BabyStyle.com
BloomingMarvellous.co.uk
CadeauMaternity.com
Figure8Maternity.com
GapMaternity.com
JapaneseWeekend.com
MaternityAndNursing.com
MaternityMall.com
MotherWear.com
OldNavy.com

CASUAL WEAR

BabiesnBellies.com
BabyStyle.com
BecomingMommy.com
BellaBluMaternity.com
BellaMaterna.com
BellyDanceMaternity.com
BloomingMarvellous.co.uk
CadeauMaternity.com
DueMaternity.com
EuphoriaMaternity.com
Figure8Maternity.com
GapMaternity.com
Hello-Mommy.com
IsabellaOliver.com
ItsAMiracleMaternity.com
LizLange.com
MaternityAndNursing.com

CASUAL WEAR (cont.)

MaternityMall.com
MotherWear.com
NicoleMaternity.com
OldNavy.com
PumpStation.com
UnbuttonedMaternity.com
ZoeeMaternity.com

CHIC LABELS

AppleMaternity.com
Avenue-Des-Bebes.com
BloomingMarvellous.co.uk
CadeauMaternity.com
Carla-C.com
DiaperBags.com
DueMaternity.com
ElinOtto.com
EuphoriaMaternity.com
Figure8Maternity.com
Hello-Mommy.com
IsabellaOliver.com
ItsAMiracleMaternity.com
JapaneseWeekend.com
LizLange.com
MaternityMall.com
NaissanceMaternity.com
UnbuttonedMaternity.com

EVENING WEAR

Avenue-Des-Bebes.com
BellaBluMaternity.com
Carla-C.com
EuphoriaMaternity.com
Figure8Maternity.com
ItsAMiracleMaternity.com
JapaneseWeekend.com
MaternityMall.com
MomsNightOut.com
NicoleMaternity.com

FITNESS

BabyStyle.com
BecomingMommy.com
DueMaternity.com
EuphoriaMaternity.com
Figure8Maternity.com
FitMaternity.com
GapMaternity.com
JapaneseWeekend.com
LizLange.com
MaternityMall.com
OldNavy.com

LINGERIE

Avenue-Des-Bebes.com
BabyStyle.com
BecomingMommy.com
BellaMaterna.com
BellyDanceMaternity.com
BloomingMarvellous.co.uk
BravadoDesigns.com
DueMaternity.com
EuphoriaMaternity.com
Figure8Maternity.com
FitMaternity.com
GapMaternity.com
IsabellaOliver.com
JapaneseWeekend.com
MaternityAndNursing.com
MaternityMall.com
MotherWear.com
OldNavy.com
UnbuttonedMaternity.com

NEWBORN CARE

BabyStyle.com
BecomingMommy.com
BloomingMarvellous.co.uk
ErbaViva.com
Hello-Mommy.com
PumpStation.com
SelfExpressions.com

NURSING

BabyStyle.com
BecomingMommy.com
BellaBluMaternity.com
BellaMaterna.com
BloomingMarvellous.co.uk
BravadoDesigns.com
BreastFeedingExpress.com
DueMaternity.com
EuphoriaMaternity.com
Figure8Maternity.com
FitMaternity.com
GlamourMom.com
JapaneseWeekend.com
MaternityAndNursing.com
MaternityMall.com
MotherWear.com
PumpStation.com
SelfExpressions.com
UnbuttonedMaternity.com

SKIN CARE

BabyStyle.com
BelliCosmetics.com
DueMaternity.com
ErbaViva.com
EuphoriaMaternity.com
FitMaternity.com
MamaMio.com
UnbuttonedMaternity.com

SWIMWEAR

Avenue-Des-Bebes.com
BellaBluMaternity.com
BellyDanceMaternity.com
BloomingMarvellous.co.uk
DueMaternity.com
EuphoriaMaternity.com
FitMaternity.com
GapMaternity.com
IsabellaOliver.com
MaternityMall.com
NicoleMaternity.com
OldNavy.com

NOTES:

AppleMaternity.com

Finding hip new maternity styles can be pretty easy if you check out this site, which stays up to date with some of the more popular chic labels. The problem is, it may prove too easy, and with limited quantities available, some of the hotter items will sell out quickly once the rest of the pregnant world gets a look at them. Your best bet is to log on soon and often—it should only take you a few minutes a week to keep track of the best new looks—because in no time at all your maternity clothing will go out of style as nursing apparel becomes all the rage.

·CHIC LABELS				

Avenue-Des-Bebes.com

The French have somehow always managed to accomplish such a casual elegance in fashion that it should be no surprise they do it again here, this time for expecting mothers. Words like *sophisticated*, *sexy*, *stylish*, *funky* and *cute* may not always translate well across cultures, but there's no denying the clothes offered by this unforgettable clothing line will look good in just about any cultural environment. If you went shopping in Paris for your maternity wardrobe, this is what you'd buy. Just think how much money you'll save coming here instead.

·EVENING WEAR ·CHIC LABELS	·LINGERIE	·CAREER DRESS	·SWIMWEAR

BabiesnBellies.com

Simple, *cute* and *fun*; it's easy to find clothes that meet this description when you're a freewheeling young woman, but once you're dressing for two there sometimes seems to be a chasm between upscale designer maternity wear and floral-print muumuus. This site offers a happy medium vis-à-vis sassy and tasteful clothes for the impending mommy on a budget. Your greatest use of the site will involve top, lots of tops, and there are enough here to keep your eyes glued to the computer monitor for the bulk of an hour, comparing, contrasting and quite often succumbing to the web shop's suggestion that you "Buy Now!"

·CASUAL WEAR			

BabyStyle.com

From the day of conception until your child grows out of his or her car seat, this site proves a handy one-stop-shopping haven in the virtual universe. Despite inconsistencies in the megasite's shopping techniques, each browsing option suits the enormous category that it serves, and it should only take a slight bit of focus to switch from maternity clothing to personal care, and later on to nursing equipment, diaper bags, strollers, carriers and infant apparel. It's a great and enormous selection, and a good thing you'll have nine months to finish your shopping.

·CASUAL WEAR ·SKIN CARE	·LINGERIE ·FITNESS	·CAREER DRESS ·NEWBORN CARE	·ACCESSORIES ·NURSING

877-364-4923 · Becoming Mommy

BecomingMommy.com

This Pittsburgh boutique features "hip maternity and cool nursing clothes" for the fashionable young mother, beginning with a distinctly feminine assortment of dresses and including everything from sleepwear and swimwear to a bevy of funky tees. A designer index turns up favorites like Olian, Belly Basics and Tummi, as well as tougher-to-find labels such as Ripe, Rebel and Divine Duo, but the most helpful browsing technique may be to Shop by Size feature, which makes it easy to find petite and plus-size garments across all categories.

·CASUAL WEAR ·NURSING	·LINGERIE	·FITNESS	·NEWBORN CARE

888-678-0034 · BellaBlu Maternity

BellaBluMaternity.com

With a deep selection of fun, contemporary maternity clothes, including one of the biggest swimwear selections we've seen, this online boutique comes to the web as a labor of love, and it shows. With incredibly rich clearance selections to grab your attention, the truth is just about every page of items here is worth viewing, if only to get an idea of what's going on in the world of maternity apparel. Casual outfits or formal dresses, activewear or something light and sexy, this incredibly well-rounded shop may be the best thing to flatter your well-rounded belly.

·EVENING WEAR ·NURSING	·CASUAL WEAR	·SWIMWEAR	·ACCESSORIES

888-700-8438 · Bella Materna

BellaMaterna.com

Pregnant women get sexier every year; rather, our society seems to see it that way, and each year we find a growing selection of sensuous maternity apparel for the young woman who wishes to maintain her sultry style for the duration of her term. Here we find it in the form of camis, tanks and halter tops, with a few dresses and thong underwear to hammer the point home. There isn't a lot here, but it all looks great, so you may be inspired to keep shopping here postpartum for an equally hip assortment of nursing bras and tops.

·CASUAL WEAR	·LINGERIE	·NURSING	

425-313-5878 · Belli Cosmetics

BelliCosmetics.com

Nurturing your skin during pregnancy isn't just an soothing and indulgent way to pass the time, but a vital daily routine you'll be grateful for the rest of your life. There are few better ways to care for your growing surface area than those offered by this line of washes and creams meant to ward against stretchmarks, reduce swelling, prevent chloasma and keep your skin moist and radiant. After all, if your child is going to prematurely age you, it should do so the old-fashioned way: as a two-year-old.

·SKIN CARE			

BellyDanceMaternity.com

Belly Dance Maternity · 888-802-1133

Since we first started looking for maternity apparel online, things have changed considerably. For example, finding a good selection of contemporary clothing for the expecting mother used to be tough. However, if this site had existed five years ago there never would have been a problem. Fully stocked with a wide range of updated looks and colors, this site delivers on its promise to be an "answer for women who do not want to sacrifice their style while expecting," and offers a great starting point for an afternoon of fruitful online maternity shopping.

	·CASUAL WEAR	·LINGERIE	·SWIMWEAR	·ACCESSORIES

BloomingMarvellous.co.uk

Blooming Marvellous · 011-44-870-751-8966

This UK site has got the right idea about motherhood, so it may even be worth the high cost of transatlantic shipping to get a hold of some of these "marvellous" items. Vastly improved browsing makes the site an enjoyable exploration of all things baby related, including baby equipment and some adorable outfits. Of course, the fun begins with the lovely maternity apparel available. Covering a full range of clothes from evening and career wear to casual weekend garb and swimsuits, we're forced to imagine droves of well-dressed British moms-to-be parading the streets with beauty and grace. Now, thanks to this site, American moms don't need to be left behind.

	·CASUAL WEAR	·LINGERIE	·CAREER DRESS	·SWIMWEAR
	·NEWBORN CARE	·NURSING	·CHIC LABELS	

BravadoDesigns.com

Bravado Designs · 800-590-7802

This homegrown business grew out of the need for a nursing bra that was at once "comfortable, stylish and affordable," but that "didn't look like something your grandmother wore." The enterprising women behind the site realized they'd achieved their goals when they fashioned a comfortable, supportive nursing bra in a leopard print cotton/spandex blend. Since these auspicious beginnings they've dabbled in different colors and have added matching panties and nursing sleepwear for the discerning mom.

	·LINGERIE	·NURSING		

BreastFeedingExpress.com

Breastfeeding Express · 800-886-4474

When it comes to something as intimately functional as breast pumps, you'd think there'd be a huge variety available at every turn for the nursing mother. Unless you visit this site, there is not. Here you may browse varied models offered by several different brands, reading up on the advantages and disadvantages, and generally determining what you might feel comfortable with. Once that's done, check out the assorted breastfeeding accessories, baby carriers, diaper bags and strollers, which will assist in making your transition to motherhood a little easier and more comfortable.

	·ACCESSORIES	·NURSING		

866-622-3322 · Cadeau Maternity　　　　　　　　　**CadeauMaternity.com**

"Fashioned for the woman who refuses to part with her sense of style during the nine months of pregnancy," this upscale maternity label offers only a small seasonal selection, but one worth a look as you'll find classically simple styles assembled with unbeaten quality and future trends created as if on these pages. Fashion forward or not, we're betting your favorite part of the site will be the Sale section, where you'll commonly find slightly older garments for as low as half price, which can amount to the cost of an entire wardrobe elsewhere.

·CASUAL WEAR	·CAREER DRESS	·CHIC LABELS	

011-31-20-620-6020 · Carla C. Designer Maternity　　　　**Carla-C.com**

Though not very big, this top-of-the-line designer maternity label is too good to be ignored. A sleek line of chic apparel, this will be the perfect place to shop if you love to look sexy, particularly if you like to do so dressed all in black. There is the occasional splash of color here and there, and even some gorgeous wedding gowns. All of it's easy to find and nice to look at, although we noticed they occasionally sell out of some of the best items, so if you like something buy it now.

·EVENING WEAR	·CHIC LABELS		

270-303-6554 · diaperbags.com　　　　　　　　　**DiaperBags.com**

When shopping for a diaper bag, it's always a good idea to remember that you're going to be schlepping this thing around with you for at least a couple of years, so you might want to pick one—or several—to match your personal style. This site is great for doing just that, with a wide assortment of diaper bag designs and styles, including a dozen or so Daddy Bags, which will help new fathers grow accustomed to the new sensation of carrying an accessory on their shoulders.

·ACCESSORIES	·CHIC LABELS		

866-746-7383 · Due Maternity　　　　　　　　　**DueMaternity.com**

With a growing franchise of maternity boutiques, this purveyor of hand-selected fashions continues to spread the message that impending motherhood is "all about showing off and letting the whole world know you're pregnant." And they mean it, too. A terrific assortment of cute, sexy and fun casual, active and formal wear awaits, whatever your size, along with maternity lingerie, sleepwear, nursing attire and diaper bags. If you're looking for the most efficiently stylish maternity shopping experience, check it out; one visit can save you a trip to several other sites.

·CASUAL WEAR ·SKIN CARE	·LINGERIE ·FITNESS	·SWIMWEAR ·NURSING	·ACCESSORIES ·CHIC LABELS

ElinOtto.com

How much can be accomplished with a single idea and some simple, stretchy fabric? Judging by this site you can create a full line of maternity-friendly apparel. We say "maternity-friendly" because the site points out that the "Italian viscose stretch fabric… can be worn pre-pregnancy, during and after." Each top, bottom and dress (there aren't many) can be found in a small variety of easily mixed and matched colors, and promises to make you look every bit as sexy as you feel.

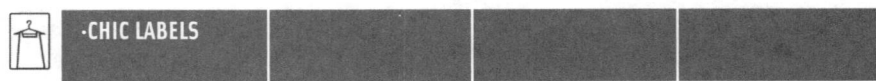

·CHIC LABELS

ErbaViva.com

If you're into naturals, and want your child to be as well, start by checking out this site, whose name means "living herbs." Basically, it offers soothing and sweet-smelling salves that are "100% pure, certified organic," so you can indulge yourself with skin- and body-care products without having to worry about your baby's exposure to any harmful toxins; at least until he or she is born. Even then, some of these bath essences, body rubs and aromatic oils are designated baby-friendly, so all you have to do is move out of the city, grow your own uncontaminated food and draw water from a well or mountain spring, and your kid can grow up the way nature, and homeopathy, intended.

·SKIN CARE | ·NEWBORN CARE

EuphoriaMaternity.com

For a great selection of top-quality maternity apparel labels, check out this outstanding retailer that offers clothes for a wide range of styles and occasions. Simple shopping categories guide you to visual lists of pants, tops, dresses and jeans, usually from such popular and respected brands as Juliet Dream, Olian Maternity, ChiaraKruza, Childish, Momzee, Ripe and Belly Basics. You'll also find a lovely selection of evening gowns, some great undergarments, fitness apparel, swimwear, sleepwear and—what the heck—diaper bags.

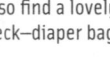

| ·EVENING WEAR | ·CASUAL WEAR | ·LINGERIE | ·SWIMWEAR |
| ·SKIN CARE | ·FITNESS | ·NURSING | ·CHIC LABELS |

Figure8Maternity.com

Figure8 · 888-816-6513

When a single shop can outfit a stylish pregnant woman for the office, gym, dinner and the bedroom, that's a great shop. This one even does it with a limited selection, meaning that virtually everywhere you look in these pages you'll run across something fabulous, whether it's flared jeans, velour yoga pants, a satin wrap dress or herringbone jacket. Of course, it all adds up to easy, fun shopping, especially when you spot the site's "infinite fit symbol," which indicates that a particular garment should still fit postpregnancy, so you can still stay stylish once you're a full-time mommy.

| ·EVENING WEAR | ·CASUAL WEAR | ·LINGERIE | ·CAREER DRESS |
| ·FITNESS | ·NURSING | ·CHIC LABELS | |

888-961-9100 · Fit Maternity & Beyond

FitMaternity.com

While pregnancy may not be the time to worry about keeping your girlish figure, there's no reason you can't pursue a healthy level of exercise while you're expecting. That being said, there's no reason you shouldn't be properly attired while you do stay fit, especially with this specialty site devoted to athletic wear for the new and expecting mother. Between nursing sports bras, fitness shorts and support girdles, you'll find everything necessary to make your physical exertions comfortable enough to actually become a routine.

·LINGERIE ·NURSING	·SWIMWEAR	·SKIN CARE	·FITNESS

800-427-7895 · The Gap

GapMaternity.com

We don't doubt that you already know what to expect from this ubiquitous mall retailer. However, we do like to point out that The Gap includes lovely casual and career wear for the pregnant woman among its cookie cutter selection. Affordable, classic and easy, there are no surprises here, with the possible exception of some swimwear and maternity undergarments. Best of all, since you probably know your Gap sizes, you can reliably get your shopping done here without having to go anywhere near a food court.

·CASUAL WEAR ·ACCESSORIES	·LINGERIE ·FITNESS	·CAREER DRESS	·SWIMWEAR

888-579-4666 · Glamourmom

GlamourMom.com

You may see every item available from this site within a minute of logging on, with time left over to check your email. So why bother looking? Because these innovative Nursing Bra Tanks (tops with built-in bras) offer support and easy access to the nursing mother, at the same time allowing her to reclaim her postpartum personal style as she waits for her body to adjust to myriad changes. While the tank is offered in a couple of models and even in dress form, the real variety may be found in the color menu; with a growing list of hues you may decide to order a few.

·NURSING			

303-323-1920 · Hello Mommy

Hello-Mommy.com

Complete with a beautiful page design and an appealing selection, this lovely small business out of Boulder, Colorado, has accomplished a seamless transition into a terrific online boutique. The site will win you over with a hip assortment of activewear for the impending mother, then keep your business with nursing apparel, adorable baby clothes, nursery furniture, strollers, prams and toddler beds. Shops like this make the web a better place.

·CASUAL WEAR	·NEWBORN CARE	·CHIC LABELS	

IsabellaOliver.com
Isabella-Oliver · 866-614-9387

Designers have been dressing the feminine form pretty much forever, and sometimes it can start to feel retread and stale. Maternity wear, on the other hand, is relatively new, so it still feels fresh and filled with new visions of what works. This relatively new line of upscale maternity apparel clearly works, as does the web site, which is just as simple, chic and sexy as the clothes. You may easily browse through a fantastic selection of tops, dresses, swimwear and intimates without losing interest for a second, which is just how a clothes shopping experience should be.

| | ·CASUAL WEAR | ·LINGERIE | ·SWIMWEAR | ·CHIC LABELS |

ItsAMiracleMaternity.com
It's A Miracle Contemporary Maternity · 888-409-8654

Catering both to a woman's need for a reliable and affordable basic wardrobe, and to her desire for stylish and hip outfits, this popular maternity label aims to "create fashionably modern and original designs that leave room for the imagination." Though not huge, the selection of Comfy Tees, Skirts, Dresses, Blouses, Pants, Blouses and Evening attire manages to cover a lot of ground, with classic looks and slightly more daring items that boast an almost bohemian touch. The easiest part? Mixing and matching these lovely, interchangeable garments throughout your term.

| | ·EVENING WEAR | ·CASUAL WEAR | ·CHIC LABELS |

JapaneseWeekend.com
Japanese Weekend · 800-808-0555

The full current seasonal collection of the incredibly popular Japanese Weekend maternity line may be found without hassle by making a trip to this simple site, which shows off the clothes to great effect. Career gals, casual chicks, fitness nuts and social butterflies all swear by the consistently great-looking label, and if you're not familiar with it yet, you will be. Once you take a look, you'll start to notice it everywhere you look, as boutiques nationwide try to stock as much of the brand's wares as possible. Be sure to come back here though: after all, where better to get something great than from the source?

| | ·EVENING WEAR ·NURSING | ·LINGERIE ·CHIC LABELS | ·CAREER DRESS | ·FITNESS |

LizLange.com
Liz Lange Maternity · 888-616-5777

As a former editor of *Vogue* magazine, Liz Lange certainly has plenty of experience when it comes to high fashion, so it should come as no surprise to anyone that hers is pretty much the first name in maternity apparel. The Collection drop-down menu will guide you to the full range of tops, dresses, skirts, pants and jackets, which includes career-appropriate attire and elegant apparel for the ever-important night out. With the help of this lavish line, you may find pregnancy to be the sexiest and most sophisticated time in your life.

| | ·CASUAL WEAR | ·FITNESS | ·CHIC LABELS | |

888-962-6264 · Mama Mio

MamaMio.com

Your body undergoes tremendous changes over a full term of pregnancy, and bladder aside, probably no single part of your body takes it harder than your skin. That's where this line of maternity skin products comes in. The science goes something like this: "the continual and plentiful use of Essential Fatty Acid-rich oils… nourish the lipid layer of your skin, helping maintain the suppleness and elasticity." You'll find formulas dedicated to breasts, bellies, full body moisture and a massage oil designed to soothe your legs, which will also be needing additional relief as the months go by.

·SKIN CARE				

888-806-2727 · Special Addition

MaternityAndNursing.com

Family owned and operated for more than a decade, this Austin, Texas, shop has accumulated a fine assortment of casual and active wear for the regular or plus-size mother-to-be, as well as stylish nursing attire to keep her both functional and pretty when she shows off her new baby to the world. Aside from all the fashionable considerations, the site also offers plenty in the practical sense, including support garments and breastfeeding equipment, so its customers may be assured of looking smart and feeling informed.

·CASUAL WEAR	·LINGERIE	·CAREER DRESS	·NURSING

800-466-6223 · MaternityMall.com

MaternityMall.com

This maternity megasite has swallowed some of our favorite maternity stores into one huge shop. As each of these lines appeal to different budgets or occasions, browsing requires getting to know the personalities of each store: iMaternity and Motherhood incorporate wardrobe basics with contemporary trends at low prices, both including plus sizes; Mimi sells higher-quality fashions and A Pea in the Pod offers the sort of high-end designer looks that celebrities such as Madonna and Catherine Zeta Jones favored during their pregnancies. Better yet, if you get tired of shopping, you'll find more articles and info than you can read in nine months.

·EVENING WEAR ·SWIMWEAR	·CASUAL WEAR ·FITNESS	·LINGERIE ·NURSING	·CAREER DRESS ·CHIC LABELS

212-744-6667 · Mom's Night Out

MomsNightOut.com

With separate categories for elegant dresses and evening gowns, this site makes shopping for that special-occasion attire just as fun for expecting moms as it is for everybody else. There is not a lot to see here but it's all excellently presented and certain to satisfy, whether you're going to a formal affair or just on a special date. Even the Bridal section will knock your socks off, with a small variety of gowns that are breathtaking and sophisticated—who knew the perfect wedding dress was designed for a pregnant woman?

·EVENING WEAR	·ACCESSORIES		

MotherWear.com

Motherwear · 800-950-2500

Breast-feeding is one of the most beautiful, natural interactions between humans, and there's absolutely no reason it should impinge upon a mother's style. With that in mind, this site offers a lovely selection of nursing bras, tops and dresses to allow the young mother some dressing options when she introduces her newborn to the world at large. There are no extraordinary or gaudy fashions here, just simple, classic designs that will fit seamlessly into most wardrobes, even if you just stick to the swimsuits and sleepwear.

·CASUAL WEAR	·LINGERIE	·CAREER DRESS	·NURSING

NaissanceMaternity.com

Naissance on Melrose · 800-505-0517

Where do hipster mommies-to-be in Los Angeles shop? Most likely this Melrose Avenue boutique that offers pregnant women "the kind of great clothes that make them feel pretty and sexy." Distinctly feminine, with the occasional rocker flair, these sassy dresses, tops, tees, skirts and trousers demand attention and will draw admiring gazes from all directions as you walk down the street, which is ironic, because walking down the street is a rare experience for the residents of Los Angeles.

·CHIC LABELS			

NicoleMaternity.com

Nicole Michelle · 888-424-8228

"Dedicated to making you look good so you feel good while you're pregnant," this regular and plus-size apparel brand offers current looks and sleek designs, and nearly every women's garment in this catalog justifies the site's use of words like *stylish*, *sexy* and *chic*. Included are some superslinky evening wear, sultry swimwear and out-of-this-world wedding gowns. Even the Clearance section has some great options, both formal and casual. It's all easy to see—just follow the link that says Shop and don't look back.

·EVENING WEAR	·CASUAL WEAR	·SWIMWEAR	

OldNavy.com

Old Navy · 800-653-6289

Sure, you may never see a pregnant woman in any of the ultracampy commercials, but that doesn't mean you won't find a lengthy list of maternity apparel on the Old Navy site. It's actually kind of shocking that they'd devote so much attention to impending mothers, as you may find comfortable career wear, swimwear and fitness apparel in addition to the to-be-expected casual and specialty-size attire. Simply follow the Maternity link to see what we mean; the rest of the site is just as self-explanatory.

·CASUAL WEAR ·FITNESS	·LINGERIE	·CAREER DRESS	·SWIMWEAR

877-842-7867 · The Pump Station

PumpStation.com

With the mission "to support and empower new mothers with quality information, outstanding products, and compassionate service," this web site representing the nation's first Lactation Center promotes healthy breastfeeding with an abundance of helpful information and expert guidance. Of course, more important for our purposes, they offer a terrific selection of nursing products—everything from breast pumps to nursing apparel—to assist the new mother in a very practical way, as well as some of the better baby carriers on the market, to support the child.

·CASUAL WEAR	·ACCESSORIES	·NEWBORN CARE	·NURSING

800-542-8368 · Self Expressions Nursing Supplies, Inc.

SelfExpressions.com

What's surprising about this site isn't that it offers nursing equipment alongside personalized baby gifts, but that it does such a good job with both. It's easy to miss the gift baskets and monogrammed blankets amid all the breast pumps, nursing bras and nipple treatments, but if you keep your eyes open you should come away happy whether you're shopping for the functional or memorable.

·NEWBORN CARE	·NURSING		

800-691-6269 · UnButtoned Maternity

UnbuttonedMaternity.com

Maternity fashions have just been getting better year after year. Don't believe us? Then we offer this site as proof. A hot selection of tops includes rocker tees as well as form-fitting blouses to go with distressed jeans or chic skirts. Comfortable sleepwear, sexy intimates and a few knockout dresses complete the maternity apparel collection, but you may also like some of the web boutique's skin care products, and you'll definitely want to pick up some of the beautiful nursing bras and incredibly hip diaper bags on your way out.

·CASUAL WEAR ·NURSING	·LINGERIE ·CHIC LABELS	·ACCESSORIES	·SKIN CARE

213-614-0733 · Zoee Maternity

ZoeeMaternity.com

The designer of this line for expecting mothers was looking to create clothes that she would wear "even if she wasn't pregnant." The result is a catalog of very stylish maternity apparel in seasonal designs suitable to the active, style-conscious woman. Don't think of it as clothing meant to conceal the physics of impending motherhood, though; if anything, it's the opposite. The site sums up its own attitude best: "Accentuate your belly. Proudly reveal your newfound figure. Celebrate your pregnancy in style."

·CASUAL WEAR			

NOTES:

Men's Apparel

For those keeping score, it's true: the Women's Apparel section of this book is bigger than the Men's. While women clearly still have an advantage when it comes to wardrobe selection, the good news is that menswear is rapidly catching up. Plenty of online retailers cater to a wide range of men's styles, covering the savvy professional, the old-school tailored-suit type, the clean-cut family man and the kickaround casual guy's guy. Most of all, though, we're impressed by the far-reaching selection of contemporary fashions afforded urban hipsters and trendsetters. The internet is positively ripe with men's designer garb and a burgeoning assortment of fresh labels that will make a guy look like he walked out of a fashion magazine.

Of course, this is all a manner of taste, and some men would rather resort to sweatpants than spend a hundred bucks on a pair of jeans. The point of this section is just to make these options apparent, and shopping for them easy. Because in a matter of minutes the internet can make everything available to the man in need of new attire, always in a variety of colors and in a size that fits. With such ease and convenience, we suspect that even those men who loathe the mall will secretly start to enjoy shopping.

TIPS ON BUYING MEN'S APPAREL ONLINE

These suggestions may help keep your clothes shopping experience from going south.

• **ORDERING REGULAR SIZES** • Most of us know our sizes for familiar brands, but many clothing lines have differing views on what constitutes a large, medium, small, etc. When in doubt, look for the manufacturer's site to find a size/measurements chart, or call the customer service number.

• **ORDERING SUITS & DRESS SHIRTS** • Purchasing a suit online can oftentimes save you a bit of money, but as standard sizes for such apparel can be unforgiving, most will require additional tailoring, so you'll still have to take them into a local shop for a fitting (some sites offer custom-tailoring at the time you order–see the icon legend).

• **ORDERING CUSTOM APPAREL** • Custom-tailoring is a great option once you've ascertained your personal measurements (this can most easily be done by a professional tailor, or see Sites That May Come in Handy below). However, once a retailer has put the time and effort into altering apparel, it's not likely to offer refunds if you're unsatisfied with the items in question. Before committing to an order, be sure to note the site's return policies with regard to tailored clothing.

• **COLOR COORDINATION** • As always, the colors represented on the screen may differ from the actual color of the object you're purchasing, due to discrepancies between the site's color settings and those of your computer monitor. Whenever possible, it may behoove you to request fabric swatches.

• **SPECIALTY SIZES** • The internet is a great place to buy men's big-and-tall sizes, for obvious reasons: price and availability. But it's better than you may realize, as many popular stores and brand names that don't offer specialty sizes in brick-and-mortar stores do offer these sizes through the web. The same goes for shoes (see the Shoes & Accessories section).

• **e-NEWSLETTERS** • Adding yourself to the mailing list of a web shop allows them to send you special offers and notfications of new stock. If you do it often, however, it can really fill up your email inbox; we'd suggest dedicating a separate email account.

 ## SITES THAT MAY COME IN HANDY

The following URLs may be useful when you shop for men's apparel.

AskMen.com/fashion/index.html	Men's fashion articles
BakerPrecision.com/measure.htm	Taking measurements for suits
FiberGypsy.com	Clothing size charts
SarnoTux.com/glossary.asp	Formal attire glossary of terms
SoYouWanna.com/site/syws/menssuit/menssuit.html	Guide to buying a suit
SuitYourself.com/mens_clothing_sizes.asp	Men's size chart
TieANeckTie.com	How to tie a tie
TopButton.com	Information on buying designer samples
WardrobeSupplies.com	Clothing care supplies
Xposed.com/styleg	Men's fashion articles

GRAPHIC T-SHIRT SITES

The following sites specialize in graphic and designer t-shirts.

Workmen.com
80sTees.com
AfrodisiakClothing.com
BarkingIrons.com
BlueCollarDistro.com
DestroyClothing.com
Gama-Go.com
GravyFactory.com
HeavyTees.com
Honest-Ts.com
ImageExchange.com
ImaginaryFoundation.com
ImperfectArticles.com

JohnnyCupcakes.com
JustAnotherRichKid.com
KiserNY.com
KrudMart.com
MiltonCarter.com
MinoriTees.com
MomiMomi.com
MudflapBoys.com
Option-G.com
Sudaca.com
TheCast.com
TheLittleIdiot.com
YouDon'tKnowShirt.com

NATIONAL CHAINS & CATALOGS

The following sites offer online sales for familiar retailers.

BananaRepublic.com
BrooksBrothers.com
DrJays.com
EddieBauer.com
Gap.com
Guess.com
KennethCole.com

JCrew.com
LandsEnd.com
LLBean.com
LuckyBrandJeans.com
MensWearhouse.com
PacSun.com
WilsonsLeather.com

*For in-depth reviews of these sites and more, check out **www.thepurplebook.com**.

SECTION ICON LEGEND

Use the following guide to understand the rectangular icons that appear throughout this section.

CUSTOM TAILORING

Any time clothes can be cut to your measurements through an online order, this icon appears. It's particularly handy for suits and dress shirts, but you'll find some custom casual attire as well.

DRESS ATTIRE

Not all as boring as it sounds, this icon highlights a variety of suits and components of a workplace wardrobe or formal event, ranging from the fashionable to the functional.

SPECIALTY SIZES

Bigger, taller and shorter men will be able to find better fits at stores tagged by this icon.

WARDROBE STAPLES

Whether it's boxers, briefs, boxer-briefs, socks, t-shirts, jeans or pajamas, this is the stuff nearly every guy wears, regardless of personal style or interests.

STYLISH THREADS

This icon merely serves to point out sites that will be of use to the fashionably inclined man, and covers a variety of styles.

LIST OF KEY WORDS

The following words represent the types of items typically found on the sites listed in this section. You will find them listed in the orange strip at the bottom of each entry, as appropriate.

ATHLETIC	Fitness apparel, including shorts, sweats, tracksuits, bicycle shorts, tanks and athletic supporters.
CASUAL	Casual wear for men, including t-shirts, cargo pants, sweaters, jeans, shorts, polo shirts, Hawaiian shirts, bowling shirts, rugby shirts, sports jerseys and more.
DENIM	Refers to any item of clothing made of denim, usually jeans or jackets.
DESIGNER	All manner of apparel made by top designers, whether dressy or of a casual style.
FORMAL	Generally refers to tuxedos and accompanying accessories (the occasional cufflinks, pocket squares, cummerbunds and bow ties).
LEATHER	Applies to all leather-crafted apparel, usually jackets, but occasionally pants.
OUTERWEAR	All jackets, coats and heavy sweatshirts/sweaters, including raincoats, windbreakers, bomber jackets, denim jackets, leather jackets, parkas and hoodies.
PROFESSIONAL	All appropriately professional attire, including suits, sports coats, and dress shirts.
SLEEPWEAR	Refers to lounge wear, including pajamas and robes.
SOCKS & UNDIES	Various underthings, ranging from boxers to briefs, boxer-briefs, thongs and socks.
SWIMSUITS	Swim trunks and other swimwear for men.
TIES	Silk ties, designer ties, conversational ties, bow ties, bolo ties, clip-ons and regular styles.
URBAN STYLE	Sellers of hip, contemporary men's styles, usually a step above casual, both in fashion and price.
VINTAGE	Stores that offer used and vintage attire for men.

 **KEY WORD INDEX**

Use the followings lists to locate online retailers that sell the type of apparel you seek.

ATHLETIC

AE.com
BigTallDirect.com
CasualMale.com
Daddyos.com
FLCrooks.com
FredPerry.com
GoClothing.com
HighAndMighty.co.uk
HisRoom.com
KillerDana.com
KingSizeDirect.com
NeighborHoodies.com
Section219.com
ShortSizesInc.com
SolisStyle.com
VintagePimp.com

CASUAL

2KTShirts.com
80sTees.com
AE.com
AmericanApparel.net
ArmaniExchange.com
BBClothing.com
BenShermanUSA.com
BigTallDirect.com
Buckle.com
CarrollAndCo.com
CasualMale.com
ClarksRegister.com
CoolestShop.com
Daddyos.com
EmmettShirts.com
Fabric8.com
FLCrooks.com
GBySolis.com
GoClothing.com
HighAndMighty.co.uk
HouseOfStyle.com
JohnSmedley.com
JosBank.com
JRansomLA.com
KarmaLoop.com
KillerDana.com
KingSizeDirect.com

CASUAL (cont.)

KrudMart.com
MonsterVintage.com
MyCubanStore.com
NeighborHoodies.com
PaulFredrick.com
PaulStuart.com
PenguinClothing.com
RevolveClothing.com
Section219.com
ShortSizesInc.com
SolisStyle.com
SplurgeInc.com
SuitYourself.com
T-Shirts.com
TheGiantPeach.com
Triple5Soul.com
Tyrwhitt.com
VineyardVines.com
VintagePimp.com
VintageTrends.com
WinterSilks.com

DENIM

AE.com
BBClothing.com
BigTallDirect.com
Buckle.com
CarrollAndCo.com
CasualMale.com
FLCrooks.com
GBySolis.com
GoClothing.com
HouseOfStyle.com
JRansomLA.com
KarmaLoop.com
KingSizeDirect.com
Kultic.com
MonsterVintage.com
Oki-Ni.com
RevolveClothing.com
ShortSizesInc.com
SolisStyle.com
SplurgeInc.com
VintagePimp.com
VintageTrends.com

DESIGNER

2KTShirts.com
AgnesB.com
ArmaniExchange.com
BBClothing.com
EmmettShirts.com
FLCrooks.com
GoClothing.com
HighAndMighty.co.uk
Kultic.com
LeeAllison.com
MarkShale.com
Menswear-Discounts.com
MisterShop.com
Oki-Ni.com
RevolveClothing.com
Ties.com
TopDrawers.com
TuxedosOnline.com
WildTies.com

FORMAL

BeauTiesLtd.com
JosBank.com
JPressOnline.com
Menswear-Discounts.com
MisterShop.com
MonsterVintage.com
MyShirtMaker.com
PaulFredrick.com
RustyZipper.com
SuitYourself.com
TuxedosOnline.com
Tyrwhitt.com

LEATHER

BenShermanUSA.com
CasualMale.com
Danier.com
FLCrooks.com
JosBank.com
KingSizeDirect.com
MarkShale.com
MonsterVintage.com
PaulStuart.com
VintagePimp.com
VintageTrends.com

OUTERWEAR

AE.com
ArmaniExchange.com
BenShermanUSA.com
BigTallDirect.com
Brora.co.uk
CarrollAndCo.com
CasualMale.com
CoolestShop.com
Danier.com
Fabric8.com
FLCrooks.com
FredPerry.com
GBySolis.com
HouseOfStyle.com
JohnSmedley.com
JosBank.com
JRansomLA.com
KarmaLoop.com
KillerDana.com
KingSizeDirect.com
MarkShale.com
Menswear-Discounts.com
MonsterVintage.com
PaulStuart.com
PenguinClothing.com
ShortSizesInc.com
SolisStyle.com
SplurgeInc.com
SuitYourself.com
Triple5Soul.com
VintagePimp.com
VintageTrends.com

PROFESSIONAL

BigTallDirect.com
CasualMale.com
ClarksRegister.com
EmmettShirts.com
HighAndMighty.co.uk
JosBank.com
JPressOnline.com
KingSizeDirect.com
LeeAllison.com
MarkShale.com
Menswear-Discounts.com
MisterShop.com
MonsterVintage.com
MyShirtMaker.com
PaulFredrick.com
PaulStuart.com
PenguinClothing.com
RustyZipper.com
ShortSizesInc.com
SuitYourself.com
Tyrwhitt.com
WildTies.com
WinterSilks.com

SLEEPWEAR

BathrobesOnline.com
BigTallDirect.com
CarrollAndCo.com
CasualMale.com
HighAndMighty.co.uk
RustyZipper.com
WinterSilks.com

SOCKS & UNDIES

AE.com
BigTallDirect.com
Brora.co.uk
Buckle.com
CasualMale.com
FreshPair.com
GBySolis.com
HighAndMighty.co.uk
HisRoom.com
JosBank.com
JPressOnline.com
JRansomLA.com
KingSizeDirect.com
ShortSizesInc.com
SockCompany.com
SolisStyle.com
SuitYourself.com
TopDrawers.com
WinterSilks.com

SWIMSUITS

BenShermanUSA.com
BigTallDirect.com
GBySolis.com
KillerDana.com
MonsterVintage.com
PenguinClothing.com
SauvageWear.com
VineyardVines.com

TIES

BeauTiesLtd.com
JosBank.com
JPressOnline.com
LeeAllison.com
MisterShop.com
PaulFredrick.com
PaulStuart.com
SuitYourself.com
Ties.com
TuxedosOnline.com
Tyrwhitt.com
VineyardVines.com
WildTies.com

URBAN STYLE

BBClothing.com
CoolestShop.com
Fabric8.com
GBySolis.com
GoClothing.com
HouseOfStyle.com
JRansomLA.com
KarmaLoop.com
KrudMart.com
MyCubanStore.com
NeighborHoodies.com
Oki-Ni.com
PenguinClothing.com
RevolveClothing.com
SolisStyle.com
TheGiantPeach.com
Triple5Soul.com

VINTAGE

Daddyos.com
MonsterVintage.com
RustyZipper.com
VintagePimp.com
VintageTrends.com
ZootSuitStore.com

2KTShirts.com

2K by Gingham · 877-258-7447

Graphic t-shirt fans will find plenty to look at with this fashion-friendly specialty shop, which houses a great variety of print designs arranged by artist. While a few names stand out, such as Yoko Ono, Jean-Michel Basquiat and Bjork, the best offerings here may be attributed to names you've probably never heard. This doesn't necessarily make browsing a quick or easy experience, but if you're willing to take the time to wade through each page of shirts, it sure can be fun.

| ·CASUAL | ·DESIGNER | | |

80sTees.com

80sTees.com · 866-807-8337

Promising "great t-shirts for the kid in us all," this radical site offers a treasure trove of nostalgic graphic tees dating back to the 1980s and beyond. Popular rock bands, cartoons, comic book characters, TV shows, videogames, junk food and movies are thoroughly covered in t-shirt form, as are pop culture phenomena such as MTV, Evil Knievel, Ronald Reagan and Patrick Nagel. The ever-expanding site even includes a few updated cult references such as Napoleon Dynamite and the Big Lebowski, and a "Retro Sucks" shirt, in case the idea of such a site doesn't appeal to you.

| ·CASUAL | | | |

AE.com

American Eagle Outfitters · 888-232-4535

Casual dressers on the hunt for a quick-and-easy shopping experience may revel in this site, which offers simple, affordable and durable clothes for the sporty, preppy set. Extra-small, large and tall sizes are available for most all of the brand's offerings, including track jackets, shorts, jeans, polos and more. This laid-back attire will allow you to get through the day without calling too much attention to yourself, unless your friends find out about this site, in which case there's a real danger you could wind up wearing the same shirt.

| ·CASUAL ·SOCKS & UNDIES | ·OUTERWEAR | ·ATHLETIC | ·DENIM |

AgnesB.com

agnès b. · 212-431-4339

It takes a mighty well-informed man to understand why he'd want to drop a bundle of cash on the extremely savvy attire found on this French designer site. He could realize that the clean, simply fashioned garments are "modern and pure, elegant but not conventional," or he could genuinely relish the exquisitely cut clothes as simply being better made than the average mall fare. Or, he could just take a leap of faith that it's nearly impossible to look anything but hot in French designer apparel. That's reason enough for us.

| ·DESIGNER | | | |

213-488-0226 · American Apparel

AmericanApparel.net

Getting back to basics doesn't get better than with this "Sweatshop Free" casual outfitter. A thorough selection of classic designs begins with the short-sleeved tee and includes different varieties of tanks, ringers, long sleeves, ribbed tees, hoodies, raglans and more. Color schemes vary from earth tones and pastels to the fairly universal blacks and whites, and yet the clothes manage to cull a sense of style out of the simplicity. Sexy, cool and compliant to both your budget and your principles, this site could supply your wardrobe staples for years to come.

800-717-2929 · Armani Exchange

ArmaniExchange.com

Giorgio Armani long ago set a standard for men's dress fashions, his name having become almost synonymous with a fine suit. Can he do the same for upscale hipster styles? The answer may be found on this site, which boasts an offering of the A|X label, a slick but downplayed assortment of high-quality casual apparel including jeans, jackets and tees, as well as some club-friendly shirts and trousers. Ironically, these fine-hewn garments may prove more impressive if the Armani label is kept under wraps.

·CASUAL   ·OUTERWEAR   ·DESIGNER   ·DENIM

866-966-2787 · BathrobesOnline.com

BathrobesOnline.com

There haven't been too many design innovations to bathrobes over the years, so, all things being equal, you may just want to head straight to the clearance section of this site, where you might luck onto a perfectly reasonable robe in your size at a great price. However, since the point of this site is that you can easily find a robe in the color you want, in a cut that suits your style and comfort, it might behoove you to delve a little deeper, where you'll find more luxurious fabrics and a greater variety of colors.

·SLEEPWEAR

011-44-1625-859185 · Brown Bag Clothing

BBClothing.com

This UK site offers "designer menswear... at discounted prices," though between the transatlantic shipping costs and conversion to pounds sterling, any discounts may actually be hard to come by. The upscale apparel, on the other hand, can be found in abundance, including top labels like Versace, Burberry, Prada, Boss, Dolce & Gabbana and Armani. A knowledge of such brand names will be helpful when browsing, as the site's organization pretty much consists of an assortment of logos. Of course, if you're willing to pay this much for shirts and trousers, you've probably already got a designer in mind.

·CASUAL   ·DESIGNER   ·URBAN STYLE   ·DENIM

BeauTiesLtd.com

Designed "for unique gentlemen who understand the difference between standing out and sticking out," this site endeavors to make wearing bow ties seem cool. Whether it succeeds is entirely subjective, but it does offer some pretty cool silk ties, so if you favor the once classic look you may don it with aplomb. For the rest of us, there also happens to be a great selection of standard ties, as well as ascots, cravats and even some out-of-the-ordinary, made-to-order cummerbunds. This one's for the rare man indeed.

 ·FORMAL | ·TIES | |

BenShermanUSA.com

It's rare that you'll find quality dress and casual wear on the same site, let alone by the same brand. Somehow, Ben Sherman manages to succeed on both ends, offering tailored dress shirts for the upscale professional, polo shirts for the casual weekender and thin graphic t-shirts for the ultra casual. Prices range accordingly, but however you prefer to dress (we like to think that a single man can be comfortable with all three looks), you can count on the label's classic appeal to suit you in any social climate.

  ·CASUAL ·LEATHER | ·OUTERWEAR | ·SWIMSUITS | ·DENIM

BigTallDirect.com

Jeans, dress shirts, slacks, swim trunks and underwear are pretty easy to find just about everywhere—unless you're looking for big-and-tall sizes, which are only easy to find here. Simply select a product type and size and you may go straight to a solid assortment of dress and casual attire that will fit without costing an arm, leg or even an inch from your waistline. You may also browse by brand name, the long list of which includes Levi's, Nautica and Polo. All of life should be this easy.

   ·PROFESSIONAL ·SWIMSUITS | ·CASUAL ·DENIM | ·OUTERWEAR ·SLEEPWEAR | ·ATHLETIC ·SOCKS & UNDIES

Brora.co.uk

If you like sweaters, you'll find a sweater you'll like here—which wouldn't be all that remarkable if the site had hundreds of garments for you to choose from, but these guys only offer a dozen or so different designs, in only a handful of colors. However, these items are constructed from two-ply Scottish cashmere, and cover just enough of your basic design elements (V-neck, round neck and hooded) to win you over at least once or twice. Better yet, even when you incorporate transatlantic shipping costs, this is about as inexpensive as quality cashmere gets.

 ·OUTERWEAR | ·SOCKS & UNDIES | |

800-522-8090 · Buckle

Buckle.com

What you will find here is denim, some t-shirts, shorts, boxers, khakis and cargo pants. Basically, the kind of clothes you can kick around in, the stuff you'd like to be wearing all the time, if anyone cared to ask. Since this site focuses on jeans, they make it really simple for you to find pairs in your size, by a particular fit (wide leg, baggy, bootleg, etc.), or brand. This is key, as none of us really wants to spend all day shopping for clothes we intend to destroy slowly with a lifestyle of bruising activity and/or couch sitting.

·CASUAL	·OUTERWEAR	·DENIM	·SOCKS & UNDIES

 WISH

800-238-9400 · Carroll and Company

CarrollAndCo.com

Complete with Italian trousers and cashmere sweaters, this men's sportswear shop out of Beverly Hills doesn't offer a lot of merchandise, but does tend to stick to the high end of casual attire. If you find sweatpants here they are probably velour, and if you see a robe it will be called a "dressing gown." This classy contributor is not difficult to use, though the pictures usually depict folded apparel, and without the beaming written descriptions it would be difficult to tell what you're getting into. That being said, these are classic, gentlemanly staples, so we should all know what to expect.

·CASUAL	·OUTERWEAR	·DENIM	·SLEEPWEAR

800-767-0319 · Casual Male Big & Tall

CasualMale.com

Men who've been shopping big-and-tall sizes for a few years have come to take it for granted that finding a large selection of truly fashionable apparel will require a huge budget, and even then will pale in comparison to regular off-the-rack attire. This site does a great job attempting to put those days behind us, with great clothes, low prices and even an enjoyable shopping experience. The catalog is not enormous, but the jackets, jeans, pajamas, underwear and suit offerings may be pinpointed by size, so you won't have to waste time looking at anything unavailable in yours. Men of height and girth may always find their options limited, but at least here they'll be limited to a decent variety.

·PROFESSIONAL ·DENIM	·CASUAL ·LEATHER	·OUTERWEAR ·SLEEPWEAR	·ATHLETIC ·SOCKS & UNDIES

 WISH

877-243-9060 · Clark's Register

ClarksRegister.com

There are the sort of casual clothes you wear to walk the dog or work on the car, and then there's the casual apparel you wear on a date to the movies or to a friend's barbecue. This site offers the latter. Featuring versatile, high-quality garb in simple yet sophisticated styles, this catalog clothier succeeds where others fail, delivering fresh styles that may be comfortably worn by men over thirty on a variety of occasions. This stuff is priced in such a way that you won't want to spill any BBQ sauce on it, but it's worth it, as you cannot find these clothes anywhere else.

·PROFESSIONAL	·CASUAL	·DENIM	

CoolestShop.com

These guys have a bold name, and consequently we were ready to tear them down, fault by uncool fault. Um, as it turns out, we're not able to. They kind of won us over with a persistently hip selection of wall art, home decor, accessories, shoes and, of course, apparel. Catering to men and women, the site's selection has fallen off a bit recently, and it seems there are not too many cool things here in any specific category, but then, just how many cool things are there in the world? Either way, it's still cooler than most.

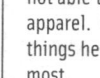

	·CASUAL	·OUTERWEAR	·URBAN STYLE	

Daddyos.com

If you don't think bowlers are cool, you clearly have not seen the shirts they wear. Take a gander, hepcat, because this site will knock your socks off. Traditional bowling-shirt styles may be found alongside somewhat more fun designs, including some campy numbers and retro favorites that follow a flames motif. So break out the pomade and start your engines; with one of these shirts on your back you can be swingin' with style in perpetuity, even if you're not a roller.

	·CASUAL	·VINTAGE	·ATHLETIC	

Danier.com

Leather, leather, leather. There's not a whole lot of it here, but it's all you will find, and it's all you will care about once you've perused the selection. Consisting of trench coats, blazers, jackets, bombers and even some pants (for the brave), this selection is not likely to go out of style anytime soon, and if it does you have only to wait a season before it comes back. Animal enthusiasts may wish to avoid this site, but if you've eaten a steak lately, these garments give you a chance to use more parts of the cow.

	·OUTERWEAR	·LEATHER		

EmmettShirts.com

It could be easily argued that all dress shirts are essentially the same, so you could shop here or there and, label aside, it wouldn't really make any difference. Well, this site easily shoots down that argument, offering a full complement of surprisingly diverse business and "smart casual" cotton weaves. Vibrant colors convey many textures in solids, checks, stripes and a few innovative (usually well-conceived) patterns. The kicker is that London designer Robert Emmett only produces twenty-five shirts in each fabric, ensuring an evolving selection of limited-edition garments.

	·PROFESSIONAL	·CASUAL	·DESIGNER	

888-554-4321 · Fabric8

Fabric8.com

This San Francisco-based "boutique of independent design" offers what a lot of retailers don't: a place for guys to find understated club wear. A few of these outgoing designs may be a bit wild, but for the most part the clothes err on the side of casual, offering shirts, pants and jackets just interesting enough to attract attention but not so noticeable that you feel like a fraud. A clean site matches the clothes' simple designs, while a bevy of goofy and decidedly not-super models give the shop itself some character as well.

·CASUAL	·OUTERWEAR	·URBAN STYLE	

800-320-6902 · Crooks Clothing Co.

FLCrooks.com

This site may not have the most trustworthy name in the clothing business, but it does have one of the better assortments of hip casual apparel. However, while you may shop brand by brand from a list of popular designer labels, you don't get a chance to browse by category. Hence, it's not immediately obvious that the shop's a good source of jeans, leather jackets, casual trousers, hoodies and memorable shirts. Don't come here expecting to find any steals, but if you like Tommy Hilfiger, Tommy Bahama or Ecko Unltd., check it out.

·CASUAL ·DENIM	·OUTERWEAR ·LEATHER	·DESIGNER	·ATHLETIC

011-44-20-7632-2800 · Fred Perry

FredPerry.com

This high-style athletic apparel brand from the UK will ensure you look good when you go to the gym, with ultrahip track jackets and jerseys that will do their part in keeping you warm, cool and/or dry. Heck, these slim-fitting tops might even keep you looking good after you've run up a good sweat. Browsing is a workout all its own though, as you must click to enter the home page, then to enter the shop, and then follow the Shop Home link to get a look at the actual garments, which are arranged by perplexing terms such as Sports Authentic and Modern Authentic. But, it's like they say: no pain, no gain.

·OUTERWEAR	·ATHLETIC		

866-373-7472 · Freshpair.com

FreshPair.com

Even if you're still wearing the same clothes you've owned since 1980, your socks and underwear have hopefully been replaced and replaced again, at least a couple of times. This niche retailer just makes it easier to keep the drawers in your drawers fresh, and your socks comfortably new. With more than a dozen brands and a wide variety to choose from, the sites slow-loading pages could make shopping a hassle, but if you prefer to don the same brand of socks and underwear you have for years, the free shipping makes this one a site for your favorites file.

·SOCKS & UNDIES			

GBySolis.com

None of us expected to find one of the hippest apparel retailers online to be based in Indiana, but that's exactly the case with this stylish, affordable and easy-to-use web shop. The well-organized site distributes sought-after labels like Le Tigre, Von Dutch, Ben Sherman, The Original Penguin and Modern Amusement across well-organized categories so that jeans, jackets, shirts, socks, swim trunks, underwear and hoodies may each be viewed on a single page. Even New Yorkers could benefit from shopping here.

·CASUAL ·DENIM	·OUTERWEAR ·SOCKS & UNDIES	·URBAN STYLE	·SWIMSUITS

GoClothing.com

When you enter the Mens category of this flavorful designer threads retailer, you'll notice a long list of hip labels running down the left side of the page. If you're a fan of Michael Kors, Theory or Sharagano in particular, this will help. If you're like the 90 percent of men who don't know what these names mean, keep scrolling down to the Category menu. Not only will this cut through the labels, but it will give you the entire selection of shirts or pants on one screen, allowing you to buy excessively cool clothing in less time than it takes to shave.

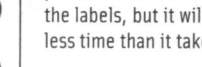

·CASUAL ·DENIM	·DESIGNER	·URBAN STYLE	·ATHLETIC

HighAndMighty.co.uk

Domestic men's shops that specialize in big-and-tall sizes could learn a little something from this UK retailer: a sense of style. It begins with the terminology, as big sizes become king sizes, but more importantly, it extends to the selection, which includes some of the more popular fashion designers available to the medium and large range. Pierre Cardin, Yves Saint Laurent and Ben Sherman are only some of the big names featured on this winning and well-stocked site that gives both large casual and professional men the royal treatment.

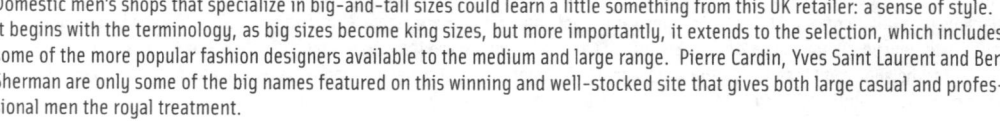

·PROFESSIONAL ·SLEEPWEAR	·CASUAL ·SOCKS & UNDIES	·DESIGNER	·ATHLETIC

HisRoom.com

Most men may not be ready for the amount of underwear choice offered by this well-stocked specialty retailer. Boxers, Briefs and Boxer Briefs may account for the main shopping categories, but within each you'll find underwear organized into a long list of available brands, and into dozens of applicable features such as Contour Pouch, Low-Rise, Hi-Cut, Fly-Front, Silk, Spandex, Lycra, Padded, Stretch, Support and Thongs. We're not even sure if many women would know what to make of so many undergarment options, but it's still nice to know the options are out there.

·ATHLETIC	·SOCKS & UNDIES		

877-463-8460 · Let's Go Clothing & Footwear

HouseOfStyle.com

Though Southern California may best be associated with surfer fashions, this San Diego retailer proves it can hang with the most cosmopolitan of looks. A variety of upscale clothing labels provide shirts, pants and jackets of a style suitable to any summer clime, however far you happen to be from the Pacific Ocean. Better yet, this hip selection is big enough to offer plenty of variety, but small enough to be viewed on just a couple of pages, giving us plenty of time to surf—or web surf—elsewhere.

·CASUAL	·OUTERWEAR	·URBAN STYLE	·DENIM

011-44-16-2953-4571 · John Smedley

JohnSmedley.com

Oh, it must have been back in late 18th century Derbyshire when two businessmen, Smedley and Nightingale, inspired by the successes of Sir Richard Arkwright, determined to make sweaters in a garment factory located in the village of Lea. But isn't this how nearly all success stories begin? As charmingly British as they are, these also happen to be great sweaters, whether you prefer cotton or wool, with just enough colors and styles to make it interesting; after all, if a company's survived centuries on sweaters alone, you know they have to be worth it.

·CASUAL	·OUTERWEAR		

800-999-7472 · Jos A. Bank

JosBank.com

For a century, Jos. A. Bank has offered low prices on quality men's apparel, which they attribute to their practice of purchasing fabrics straight from the factories; but there's no need to concern yourself with all that. All you need to know is what you're looking for, whether it's a sport coat, trousers, business dress (corporate or casual) or a tux. Making it easier is their Suit Builder, which boasts "six simple steps to the perfect suit," and a similarly fashioned Shirt Builder, which does it in five. You can also beef up your weekend wardrobe, and even your golf attire, though it will do nothing for your game.

·FORMAL ·LEATHER	·PROFESSIONAL ·TIES	·CASUAL ·SOCKS & UNDIES	·OUTERWEAR

212-687-7642 · J. Press

JPressOnline.com

You can tell the sort of apparel a man can expect to find from this site just by the names given to its menu categories. For example, instead of Socks, you should follow Hose; and rather than ties you should look for Neckwear. Gloves, underwear and hankies are easy enough to find within Accessories, while Belts & Braces is fairly self-explanatory, assuming you know *braces* means *suspenders*. Essentially, the classy, professional dresser will find plenty of finely crafted shirts and other haberdashery here, and if you don't know what that means, you probably don't want to.

·FORMAL	·PROFESSIONAL	·TIES	·SOCKS & UNDIES

JRansomLA.com

J. Ransom · 323-936-1675

In a moment of frank admission uncharacteristic of many retailers, this hip Los Angeles boutique caters to customers who "desire unique brands and styles and are willing to pay higher prices for it." It turns out what you're paying for is designer jeans, cooler-than-average shirts and occasionally jackets featuring labels that superfashionable women will recognize and envy. Browsing by these brand names will only be easy if you also know a little something about them, but we anticipate the hardest part will be the cost-benefit analysis when deciding to purchase any of these very expensive garments.

·CASUAL ·SOCKS & UNDIES	·OUTERWEAR	·URBAN STYLE	·DENIM

KarmaLoop.com

Karmaloop · 877-465-2762

Labeling it a "boutique to outfit cutting edge culture" it would seem the proprietors of this stylish web shop started the site mostly to "get free clothes." With clothes like this, it's tough to blame them. The hard part of using this site is trying to find something that's not hip or fashion-forward, as you'll easily find plenty of sought-after labels to go along with more obscure up-and-comers. With great jeans, pants, shirts and especially jackets, you can be assured this one will keep up with the current trends; the owner's wardrobe depends on it.

·CASUAL	·OUTERWEAR	·URBAN STYLE	·DENIM

KillerDana.com

Killer Dana · 800-228-7873

Based in the Orange County city of Dana Point, this "old-fashioned, sand on the carpet, California beach surf shop" contributes a mighty selection of beach-friendly attire through its site, with board shorts, wet suits and sandals you might expect. But this one's about more than just what you might want to wear in the sand; a deep selection of casual clothes offers plenty for any guy looking for an alternative to preppy or hipster styles, including long pants, woven shirts and sweaters. *Laid back* doesn't begin to describe it.

·CASUAL	·OUTERWEAR	·ATHLETIC	·SWIMSUITS

KingSizeDirect.com

King Size · 800-677-0249

For the man who can't find anything in the puny measurements of "regular" stores, this site features your standard, everyday kinds of clothes in bigger, longer sizes. Here you'll find what you need to dress up, dress down, go to work or work out, with a tremendous variety across the board, including some "rugged gear" and NFL branded apparel. The site's easy to browse, and well-stocked enough that you may create your own personal sense of style out of a wide (and/or tall) range of pants, shirts, sweaters and jackets.

·PROFESSIONAL ·DENIM	·CASUAL ·LEATHER	·OUTERWEAR ·SOCKS & UNDIES	·ATHLETIC

716-417-1569 · The Krudmart

KrudMart.com

This shop's name isn't likely to win over any highbrow shoppers, nor is it intended to. Rather, the target audience here is the beat-loving brandisher of t-shirts. Carrying brands such as Soul Rebel, Local Celebrity, Brown Sound and Ubiquity, the graphics printed on these tees owe allegiance to no particular product or logo, opting instead for savvy images and/or provocative witticisms. Sizes and colors are limited; fortunately, all designs may be viewed on just a few pages, so you can just check back every now and then to see if there's anything new worth wearing.

| ·CASUAL | ·URBAN STYLE | | |  |

305-776-6047 · Kultic

Kultic.com

To most men, spending an extra hundred bucks on a pair of jeans doesn't seem worth it— they all look the same, right? The thing is, most women somehow know how to tell the difference. If you think it's worth it to be noticed, you may appreciate this designer jeans site that offers prices we might term "reasonable" were they not already so inflated by brand awareness. If names like Chip & Pepper, Paper Denim, True Religion and 7 For All Mankind mean anything to you or the woman you want to impress, take a glance at this fine selection before you buy elsewhere.

| ·DESIGNER | ·DENIM | | |  |

888-434-8437 · Lee Allison

LeeAllison.com

Ties are rarely that interesting to look at, let alone talk about. However, the "whimsical but sophisticated" designs available from this top-tier tie maker may just start some interesting conversations. You'll initially speak of the quirky and colorful patterns to be browsed among these pages, but eventually you'll have to discuss the fact that they're woven rather than printed, meaning each silk creation is akin to a piece of artwork, "like a tapestry." Some simpler, solid colored ties may also be found, as well as a fine assortment of dress shirts, but these prove decidedly less interesting to explain.

| ·PROFESSIONAL | ·DESIGNER | ·TIES | | |

888-333-6964 · Mark Shale

MarkShale.com

The proprietors of this shop encourage consumers to opt for quality over quantity when it comes to your wardrobe. The theory seems to be that, although you may buy several items of clothing for every one or two purchased here, you won't enjoy them as much, and it's better to wear great clothes often than a different set of mediocre clothes every day. It may not make much sense on paper, but when you get a look at the clothes featured on this slickly designed site you might just be won over. Fine upscale and designer threads look as comfortable as they do cool, and with new ones coming each season, you may start to wonder just how many days in a row you can get away with wearing the same pair of pants.

| ·PROFESSIONAL | ·OUTERWEAR | ·DESIGNER | ·LEATHER | |

Menswear-Discounts.com

Discount Designer Menswear · 866-761-1500

The word *menswear* sounds generic and dull, which doesn't in any way apply to the fine designer duds offered by this site. *Discounts*, on the other hand, gets the adrenaline pumping, and a bargain is exactly what you can expect to find here. From short to big sizes, and plenty between, browsing these rudimentarily built pages will turn up a bevy of great, reasonably priced dress suits and formal wear, featuring brand names such as Ralph Lauren, Oleg Cassini and Nino Cardi suits and tuxedoes. Tons of cachet, not so much cost.

·FORMAL	·PROFESSIONAL	·OUTERWEAR	·DESIGNER

MisterShop.com

Norridge Mister Shop · 800-715-7975

If finding a designer suit at a reasonable price is important to you, this site will become important to you. With categories featuring Ralph Lauren, Calvin Klein and Ben Sherman, the simple but effective navigation can guide you quickly to a limited number of prestigious ensembles. We wouldn't recommend this shop if you value huge assortments of suits in every conceivable style and color. However, don't miss it if you expect a good deal on fine threads; low prices and shipping fees are exactly what makes this one worthwhile.

·FORMAL	·PROFESSIONAL	·DESIGNER	·TIES

MonsterVintage.com

MonsterVintage.com · 503-236-7542

Don't go thinking that classic tastes can't be accommodated by online shopping. If this site's any indication, you can still piece together a slick, nifty and/or keen wardrobe without leaving your home. Covering vintage styles across the board, including Motorcycle and Westernwear, we're particularly impressed with the Oregon shop's Suits, Hawaiian Shirts, Outerwear, Denim and Big & Tall sections. Browsing may take some time, but as each item is pictured with exquisite detail and described with exact measurements, we're pretty sure you'll like what you'll find.

·FORMAL ·VINTAGE	·PROFESSIONAL ·SWIMSUITS	·CASUAL ·DENIM	·OUTERWEAR ·LEATHER

MyCubanStore.com

Mi Tienda Cubana · 800-657-0292

Think what you will about Cuban politics, music and even cigars; there's little denying that the classic Cuban style is tough to beat. It's all about linen, and here you'll find a slight but fantastic selection of linen shirts and pants, as well as several ultracool fedoras and panama hats. Clothes like this look great on any man, and if you live outside of Florida you might even stand out in a crowd. The authenticity of these garments are without question, but don't worry, this site's based in the USA.

·CASUAL	·URBAN STYLE		

888-744-7897 · The Custom Shop

MyShirtMaker.com

We give this one a "difficult" rating because you can never get a clear picture of exactly what you're ordering. You must also have a clear knowledge of your own measurements before you can complete the custom shirt feature, as well as an understanding of choices like cuff style, collar style, pocket styles, sleeve placket buttons (or not), front styles, button colors and where you prefer your monogramming, if any. However, the result is a dress shirt, made to order in a choice of several fabrics; for the price, this is about the closest you'll get to the perfect shirt.

·FORMAL	·PROFESSIONAL		

718-722-7277 · Neighborhoodies

NeighborHoodies.com

Give it up for this site, which gives locals a chance to represent, in the form of personalized hoodies. These hooded sweatshirts are available in a variety of colors and styles, but the key thing to remember is that you get to emblazon them with the name of your favorite city or neighborhood, or any personal message you want to wear with pride. This service is extended to a smattering of t-shirts, at times with soccer numbers on the back. The site is slow-moving but easy, though it already seems to be growing from its homegrown Brooklyn roots.

·CASUAL	·URBAN STYLE	·ATHLETIC	

011-44-20-7494-1716 · Oki-Ni

Oki-Ni.com

Every once in a while, we find a site that we don't necessarily want to tell everybody about, because when you're dealing with an exclusive and limited selection, shopping becomes a competitive sport. For example, this UK design group, which "works in collaboration with a range of globally renowned brands" to create an exclusive assortment of amazing clothes and shoes, will quickly and easily sell out of any product it carries. So, if we tell you about it, we're just going to miss out on any brilliant future designs. Oh well...this is what we do.

·DESIGNER	·URBAN STYLE	·DENIM	

800-247-8162 · Paul Fredrick MenStyle

PaulFredrick.com

The Paul Fredrick line of clothes is known to be a quality set of dress attire, but don't make the mistake of thinking they're stuffy. Somehow, these guys have managed to blur the boundaries between professional and casual, with dignified but breezy designs that will have you looking and feeling more comfortable than anybody else in the office. Of course, the great benefit of this is that you can then easily make the transition into regular life, still looking sharp but with an air of indifference. It's nice to know style can transcend the restrictions imposed by the traditional suit and tie.

·FORMAL	·PROFESSIONAL	·CASUAL	·TIES

PaulStuart.com

Paul Stuart · 866-278-8278

This domestic men's clothier offers some incredibly dapper suits of the sort you don't normally see this side of the Atlantic, which makes sense when you get a look at the prices. The quality shows, though, whether you opt for a full suit or stick to the dress shirts, trousers, sweaters and sport jackets, and it would be impossible not to seem incredibly classy in this fine garb. A fine choice for the American who wants to look like a million bucks rather than a million pounds.

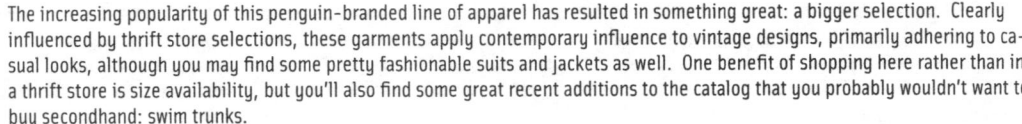

·PROFESSIONAL ·TIES | ·CASUAL | ·OUTERWEAR | ·LEATHER

PenguinClothing.com

An Original Penguin · 732-933-1100

The increasing popularity of this penguin-branded line of apparel has resulted in something great: a bigger selection. Clearly influenced by thrift store selections, these garments apply contemporary influence to vintage designs, primarily adhering to casual looks, although you may find some pretty fashionable suits and jackets as well. One benefit of shopping here rather than in a thrift store is size availability, but you'll also find some great recent additions to the catalog that you probably wouldn't want to buy secondhand: swim trunks.

·PROFESSIONAL ·SWIMSUITS | ·CASUAL | ·OUTERWEAR | ·URBAN STYLE

RevolveClothing.com

Revolve Clothing · 888-442-5830

We can think of dozens of reasons to shop from this generously stocked purveyor of urban styles, the foremost being: free shipping, free returns and a price match guarantee. But most of the reasons have to do with selection, and the Men section of the shop features a long list of designers known to be popular with the fairer sex. If you're out of the fashion loop you may be in for a long day, as the organization doesn't stoop to help the novice shopper. Stick with it, though, and you'll find a great assortment of cool clothes that won't fail to impress.

·CASUAL | ·DESIGNER | ·URBAN STYLE | ·DENIM

RustyZipper.com

Rusty Zipper Vintage Clothing · 503-233-2259

There aren't many stores where you can find leisure suits, disco shirts, Hawaiian shirts and 80s-style windbreakers all in one place. This is just such a store. Featuring one of the best vintage apparel selections available anywhere, the site takes it a step further, offering a quick-and-easy search function that allows you to pick through thousands of items by decade, clothing article, size and price range without even a second thought. Individual items are displayed well, both in text and pictures, with special note given to the garment's condition: in most cases, very cool.

·FORMAL | ·PROFESSIONAL | ·VINTAGE | ·SLEEPWEAR

858-514-8229 · Sauvage

SauvageWear.com

While you spend the bulk of your time on this site browsing the women's section, you might begin to suspect the guy's swimsuits will be a little skimpy to actually wear. Indeed, if you do feel like showing off all the time you spent in the gym this year, you'll find some tight-fitting suits that also happen to be quite stylish, featuring a variety of cool patterns and cuts, both colorful and classic. Fortunately for the rest of us, many of these trunks also manage to cover enough flesh that we'll feel comfortable wearing them even if we don't resemble the muscular, chiseled models seen here—women shopping here don't get that option.

·SWIMSUITS				

877-653-5646 · Classic Sports Logos

Section219.com

Some people wear sports shirts to show their allegiance to their favorite local teams; others wear obscure graphic t-shirts to demonstrate their reverence for the unknown or underappreciated. This site offers an interesting combination of the two, boasting an unparalleled selection of logos representing defunct minor league teams from a variety of sports. Just browse casually and you'll immediately wonder: at what point was it that sport logo designs ceased to be great? These classic designs demonstrate regional loyalty as well as artistic merit, and prove that even sport shirts can be stylish.

·CASUAL	·ATHLETIC			

440-605-1000 · Short Sizes Inc.

ShortSizesInc.com

Standing in stark contrast to big-and-tall shops, this store's worthy mission is to furnish the man under five-eight with clothes that fit without need of hem or belt. A full range of clothes adequately suits smaller frames, thin or stout, but there are definitely limits on color and style variety, as well as occasional size disparities. Bottom line, there's nothing perfect about this site, but there are enough simple, essential professional and casual elements that it's not to be overlooked.

·PROFESSIONAL ·DENIM	·CASUAL ·SOCKS & UNDIES	·OUTERWEAR	·ATHLETIC	

888-472-5678 · The Sock Company

SockCompany.com

What can be said about socks that hasn't been said before? What can be said about socks in the first place? Well, they protect your feet from both the cold and excessive odors, and sometimes they match other articles of clothing. This site is even less interesting than this, and not even that easy to use or understand. However, they have socks and underwear in abundance, and for very low prices, plus flat-rate shipping (free if you do a year's worth of shopping at once). Socks are never very exciting, so when in doubt, go for variety.

·SOCKS & UNDIES				

SolisStyle.com

Solis Company · 310-909-8558

Succeeding in its mission to offer "high-quality and stylish products at better than reasonable prices," this web company features a widely varied list of sought after brands including 2(x)ist, FCUK, Calvin Klein, Ben Sherman, Fubu, Von Dutch, Hilfiger, Sean John and dozens more. Sadly, poring through them all is not an enviable proposition, as even though each category is well organized, slow-loading pages will test your patience when it eventually dawns on you that "reasonable prices" is a relative term when it comes to clothing this cool.

| ·CASUAL ·DENIM | ·OUTERWEAR ·SOCKS & UNDIES | ·URBAN STYLE | ·ATHLETIC |

SplurgeInc.com

Splurge Inc. · 866-619-5913

While most of the men who will appreciate this fashionable apparel retailer are too young to afford it, those with a little bit of a clothing budget and a yen for trends might just be willing to fork it over it here, hence the "splurge." Getting around the site is easy as can be, and the computer-savvy individual should be able to browse the entire selection within ten minutes, which works fine because, in this day and age, any young man who can afford this stuff is almost certain to be working in computers.

| ·CASUAL | ·OUTERWEAR | ·DENIM | |

SuitYourself.com

SuitYourself.com · 203-255-8889

Refined gentlemen and fashionable professionals alike will appreciate this men's clothier that offers a wonderful selection of smart-fitting suits, sport coats, overcoats and tuxedos. These aren't your bargain-basement, generic-cut jacket-and-trouser combinations, and the distinction shows. Single and double-breasted designs are available by fine labels like Baroni, Belvest and Ermenegildo Zegna, among others, alongside some similarly fine but decidedly more casual polo shirts and a surprising variety of boxer shorts, which boast an even more universal appeal.

| ·FORMAL ·TIES | ·PROFESSIONAL ·SOCKS & UNDIES | ·CASUAL | ·OUTERWEAR |

T-Shirts.com

T-Shirts.com · 800-588-1857

When it comes to t-shirts, fashion has less to do with fabric and color than it does with what gets printed on the shirt. Perhaps that's why we're such fans of this custom tee shop, which allows even the most casual of computer users to rather simply upload graphics to build a personally expressive t-shirt that nobody else will be wearing, anywhere. The Design Your Own link will get you started, but if you get stuck for ideas your can always peruse the huge variety of clever and popular printed tees also available here: not as personal, but almost as fun.

| ·CASUAL | | | |

510-465-9070 · The Giant Peach

TheGiantPeach.com

Independent hip hop artists and labels find an outlet for their merchandise here, whether it's 12-inch vinyl singles or logo apparel. Browsing proves quite difficult by category, and even if you do opt to shop by artist, label or clothing line, the site moves with all the hustle of a slow jam, with pages taking enough time to load that you might think the link is broken. Still, there's no denying the quality music, graphic tees and hoodies of the not-so bling bling hip hop underground, including the likes of Mos Def, Jurassic 5, Blackalicious and Aesop Rock, along with labels such as Rawkus and Ninja Tune, just to name a few.

·CASUAL	·URBAN STYLE			

888-686-8437 · Ties.com

Ties.com

The name of this site may seem a little obvious and bland, but we can promise it's the only remotely boring thing about this site. After all, boredom stems from the feeling something is wasting our time, and given the excellent organization of this specialty shop, it's virtually impossible to spend any more time here than you want to. Any method you might use to pick out a tie is accounted for, beginning with a long list of colors, and including designer, pattern and price range. You may even browse by thematic categories including Golf, Holidays, Science and Animals. Your suit may never be dull again.

·DESIGNER	·TIES			

604-684-4861 · TopDrawers.com

TopDrawers.com

Though teeming in pictures of men with hairless chests and washboard abs, this site actually has underwear for just about everyone, whether you're a boxers or brief type of guy, or even of a thong ilk. With plenty of designer and popular name brands, the occasional shape-enhancing pair of briefs and a plethora of colors, a few clicks should guide you to the drawers that you look good, or at least feel comfortable, wearing. If nothing else, this site will make you ponder the invigorating life of the underwear model.

·DESIGNER	·SOCKS & UNDIES			

718-218-9066 · Triple 5 Soul

Triple5Soul.com

The fifteen-year history of this Brooklyn-grown brand/retailer may be plotted by the list of hip hop luminaries who have passed through its doors, from Fab 5 Freddy to Mos Def. Street cred aside, the smooth layout and stylish apparel exhibited by this site is enough to warrant a glance from anyone looking to enhance his wardrobe without any second-guesswork. Hoodies, sweaters and jackets offer the best sampling of styles available here, while backpacks and record bags highlight the accessories section. This site gets it right.

·CASUAL	·OUTERWEAR	·URBAN STYLE		

TuxedosOnline.com

It's not hard to guess this site's specialty, nor is it hard to shop here. Once you know your rudimentary measurements, browsing the various Classic, Contemporary, Colored, Designer, White and Cutaway tuxedos is a simple matter, and each may be ordered with a variety of options including cummerbunds, vests and/or suspenders. A $100 Tuxedos category may prove particularly alluring to those on a tight budget, but you may also find an incredible deal in the Used Tuxedos section. Do it right the first time and you should never need to shop here again.

·FORMAL	·DESIGNER	·TIES	

Tyrwhitt.com

As a British shirt maker, you might expect this revered Jermyn Street label to be overly starchy. Not so. While the differences between its Formal, Weekend and Friday Shirts are minimal, this dressy apparel might surprise you with its engaging patterns and color combinations, and we're not just talking about the ties. Drawing a fine distinction between dressing well and doing so with charm, this pleasing site should even have crass Americans looking dapper again.

·FORMAL	·PROFESSIONAL	·CASUAL	·TIES

VineyardVines.com

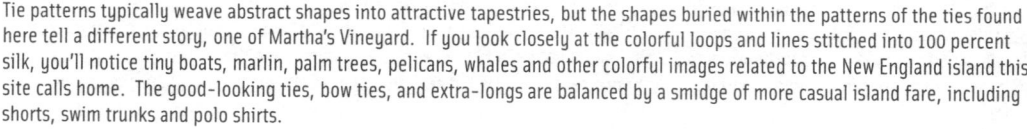

Tie patterns typically weave abstract shapes into attractive tapestries, but the shapes buried within the patterns of the ties found here tell a different story, one of Martha's Vineyard. If you look closely at the colorful loops and lines stitched into 100 percent silk, you'll notice tiny boats, marlin, palm trees, pelicans, whales and other colorful images related to the New England island this site calls home. The good-looking ties, bow ties, and extra-longs are balanced by a smidge of more casual island fare, including shorts, swim trunks and polo shirts.

·CASUAL	·SWIMSUITS	·TIES	

VintagePimp.com

If you're looking for clothes to match your checkered Vans, visit this site and ready yourself for a flashback to the 1980s, where breakdancing apparel and Member's Only jackets rule. The more classic pimps among you may prefer some of the 60s and 70s vintage attire found here, including entire sections devoted to ruffled shirts and leather pants. The site doesn't make it easy to browse the entire selection, but we'd encourage you to stick with it, as you never know what's going to turn up behind any given link and, given the abundance of funky threads populating the site, you really do want to find out.

·CASUAL ·ATHLETIC	·OUTERWEAR ·DENIM	·URBAN STYLE ·LEATHER	·VINTAGE

323-562-0065 · Vintage Trends

VintageTrends.com

Finally, we have a site willing to explain the semantic and price discrepancies between thrift store and vintage clothing. While both sets of apparel are used, vintage garments are "hand picked... for their quality, desirability and historical significance." In other words, only the rarest and most fashionable secondhand clothes are elevated to vintage status, which is why you'll like the shirts, jeans, trousers, jackets and robes featured here. The clothes here are so extensively organized that browsing the dozens of subcategories may turn you off even if the prices don't, but if you can patiently appreciate this outstanding array of old clothes, you'll almost certainly leave happy.

| ·CASUAL ·LEATHER | ·OUTERWEAR | ·VINTAGE | ·DENIM | |

877-945-3843 · Wild Ties

WildTies.com

A sure sign that times they are a-changin', this site claims to be "the oldest Internet tie store in the world." Most such statements would be used to signify some sort of Old World elegance, or time-tested grandeur, but then, this is the Internet. The site's product line tends to be "novelty and conversational neckwear." No, you won't find any ascots here, but you may find a salmon tie (the fish, not the color), or one covered with *South Park* characters. Easy and funny, this site's tamer selections include solid colors and polka dots; but really, a suit only offers one expressive item of clothing, so sometimes you just gotta go wild.

| ·PROFESSIONAL | ·DESIGNER | :TIES | |  |

888-782-2224 · WinterSilks

WinterSilks.com

If there's anybody on this planet who doesn't like silk, he alone will fail to appreciate this specialty retailer. The rest of us may delight over the many ways the smooth, luxurious fabric is represented here. At the heart of the site's selection are longjohns of various weights and blends, but as this is actually a shop for all seasons you will find plenty of underwear for every climate, along with shirts, sweaters, pajamas and bedding. The best reason to buy it in silk? Others will enjoy touching it as much as you enjoy wearing it.

| ·PROFESSIONAL | ·CASUAL | ·SLEEPWEAR | ·SOCKS & UNDIES | |

800-408-8933 · ZootSuitStore.com

ZootSuitStore.com

We're not sure if it was zoot suits that went out of style, or the rest of us that did, but this site brings back the panache of the boldly-colored suits famous for their baggy pants and long jackets. You needn't go so far as to order a suit, as you'll find some retro-style shirts among the overall selection, but if you do want the full shebang, you'll need all the pertinent accoutrements offered here as well, and by this we mean hats with turned-down brims and long watch chains (more commonly used these days with wallets). More importantly, you'll need some swagger.

| ·URBAN STYLE | ·VINTAGE | | |

NOTES:

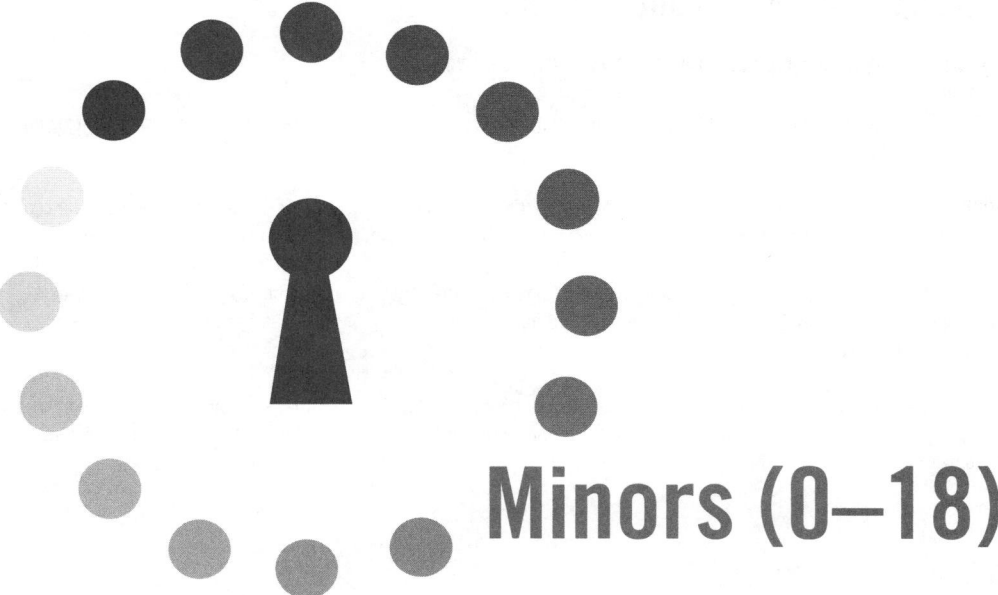

Minors (0–18)

Being a kid is all about discovery, and the internet provides the ultimate portal to explore. Not only is it a fantastic learning tool for kids, but once they have locked on to an interest, it is an exceptional place to supply them with the goods to enhance and equip the experience. On the pages within this section, we have selected sites that will inspire children's curiosity, excite their senses, encourage them to express their personal style and make it easy for you to keep track of their interests. Babies are the easiest to please, so we've provided sites that sell basics and necessities to satisfy your parenting preferences, whether you seek stimulating developmental toys or a layette made of organic materials. Once a child begins school there are other things to think about. Uniforms, dress attire, knockaround casuals and sneakers are all well represented here, as are sporting goods sites just for kids, and furniture and decor retailers that provide stylish selections with youthful sensibilities. We have paid special attention to shops promoting a kid's creativity and intellectual growth by offering educational toys, science kits and art supplies. Adolescents may want to look to the rest of **thepurplebook** to satisfy a lot of their burgeoning interests, but we've found a good number of teen and tween sites that can help them hold on to that youthful imagination for just a little while longer.

Ultimately, we know parents will spend a lot more time browsing the sites of this section than kids will, and new parents may want to check out **thepurplebook: baby** for even more great shopping opportunities. However, today's children are more likely than ever before to have their own opinions on what to buy, and even their own styles. If you can get them to go online shopping with you, it can be a process of shared discovery. After all, if they have a hand in picking it out now, they're more likely to appreciate it later.

TIPS ON BUYING MINORS' PRODUCTS ONLINE

These suggestions may help keep your children from turning on you.

• **EUROPEAN SIZES** • Bear in mind that much of the more charming children's clothing comes from Europe and uses a different sizing structure. See IslandChild.net/sizing.cfm for reference.

• **AGE APPROPRIATE TOYS** • Take note: toys and games are often constructed for particular age ranges. Some toys are too advanced and even can be dangerous for younger children. Others are meant for younger kids and will simply embarrass a teenager.

• **TAKE A DEEPER LOOK** • There is truly a bounty of unique products listed in this category. It may be easy to find typical, cookie-cutter clothes, toys and educational products, but just a little digging on your part could be greatly beneficial to your child's lifestyle and creative development.

• **GET YOUR CHILDREN INVOLVED** • Your children may be too impatient for you to take them clothes shopping, but if you shop on-line you can simply point them to the computer screen, and let them look at items you're considering, to see what they like best. They're sure to like the clothes better if they helped pick them out.

NATIONAL CHAINS & CATALOGS

The following sites offer online sales for familiar retailers.

AmericanGirl.com
AeroPostale.com
BackToBasicsToys.com
BombayKids.com
ChildrensPlace.com
CompanyKids.com
Fisher-PriceStore.com

GrowingUpGarnetHill.com
Gymboree.com
HannahAndersson.com
HasbroToyShop.com
KBToys.com
MagicCabinDolls.com
OldNavy.com

OneStepAhead.com
OshKoshBGosh.com
PBTeen.com
PotteryBarnKids.com
RightStart.com
Scholastic.com
WetSeal.com

SITES WITH A SINGLE FOCUS
The following sites excel at selling one or two specific products.

BloomingBows.com	Hair accessories
eSwak.com	Camp care packages
FlynnOhara.com	School uniforms
FrenchToast.com	School uniforms
GuideCraft.com	Wood toys
HighChairs.com	High chairs
JRayShoes.com	Classic children's shoes
JudiBoisson.com	Quilts and bedding
Milswear.com	School uniforms
OdysseyToys.com	Historical action figures
PapoDAnjo.com	Sunday best clothing
SafeSand.com	Sandbox sand

>> SITES THAT MAY COME IN HANDY

The following URLs may help out parents and their children.

ACACamps.com	Summer camp directories
BrainPop.com	Online homework assistance
CFSLoans.com	School loans
CollegeLoanCorp.com	College loans resource
CollegeSavings.org	College savings plans
CollegeSummit.org	College fund resource for low-income families
CyberPatrol.com	Online content filter
Encarta.MSN.com	Online encyclopedia
Encyclopedia.com	Online encyclopedia
FaceTheIssue.com	Resources on coping with teen issues
FunPlaydates.com	Activities and other fun resources
GoCityKids.com	Children's city guide
IslandChild.net/sizing.cfm	European size conversions
KiddoNet.com	Online homework assistance
KidNeeds.com	Resources for parents of children with special needs
KidsCamps.com	Summer camp directories
KidsHealth.org	Children's health information
KidStockMontana.com/sizing.htm	Clothes and shoes size guides
MTNA.org	Locate a music teacher
Ology.AMNH.org	Online science homework assistance
ParentingToolBox.com	Parenting advice
Petersons.com	Info on colleges and test prep courses
PublicLibraries.com	Public libraries directory
Safety-Identification-Products.com	Identification kits and tools
ToyPortfolio.com	Educational toy guide
UrbanBaby.com	Baby-friendly city guides
USSportsCamps.com	Sports camp guide
YoungInvestor.com	Educational tool about investing money

*For in-depth reviews of these sites and more, check out **www.thepurplebook.com**.

SECTION ICON LEGEND

Use the following guide to understand the rectangular icons that appear throughout this section.

CHILDREN
Most of the stores in this section include toys, furniture, clothes and more for children between the ages of three and twelve.

BABIES
Easy enough to remember, this icon indicates that a store offers merchandise designed for little ones under the age of three.

PERSONALIZED
This icon indicates that a site's prepared to personalize items, with names, images, initials or otherwise.

TEENS
This is a rare enough icon, as most interests for those aged thirteen through eighteen are included in other sections throughout the book, but there are still a few worth highlighting here.

LIST OF KEY WORDS

The following words represent the types of items typically found on the sites listed in this section. You will find them listed in the orange strip at the bottom of each entry, as appropriate.

ACCESSORIES	Children love to accessorize, and they are sure to like at least one of the following: shoes, hats, jewelry, watches, hair clips, bags and backpacks.
BABY NECESSITIES	Focuses on the very particular needs of babies (and their parents), and necessary products such as blankets, bottles, diapers, food, strollers, carriers, baby monitors and more.
BOOKS & MEDIA	Picture books, juvenile fiction and educational videos, software and texts. See the Entertainment section for more selection, including frivolous videos and software.
CLOTHES	Apparel for teens, kids and babies.
EDUCATIONAL	A selection of educational items, whether books, media, toys or recreational equipment.
FURNITURE	Decorative accents and furniture for the nursery, kids' rooms and teens can be found here, as well as in our Home & Garden section.
HEALTH & SAFETY	Health and personal safety items for children and babies turn up on a few of the sites in this section, and may also be located in the Health & Beauty and Home & Garden sections, respectively.
NURSERY	Furniture, decor and other pertinent items found in a baby's nursery.
RECREATION	Recreational items including swing sets, tetherballs, sprinkler toys, playground equipment and other items designed to keep children jumping, running and climbing. You can also find some of these things in the Sports & Outdoors section.
SUNDAY BEST	Dressier baby and children's clothes and accessories, including religious and ceremonial dress.
TOYS & GAMES	The types of toys and games available are too numerous to mention, but you can use this in conjunction with the Educational key word to locate some of the best selections.

 **KEY WORD INDEX**

Use the followings lists to locate online retailers that sell the baby & children's products you seek.

ACCESSORIES

2LittleMonkeys.com
AChildsCloset.com
AllAboardToys.com
Alloy.com
BabyAlexandra.com
BabyAnt.com
BabyBecause.com
BabyCenter.com
BabyCZ.com
BabyGeared.com
Bebenique.com
BeckerSurf.com
Cloz.com
CraftsburyKids.com
CustomGlamGirl.com
Delias.com
DPAM.com
ElegantBabyGifts.com
ElegantChild.com
FloraAndHenri.com
GoJane.com
HearthSong.com
HotTopic.com
InFashionKids.com
JanieAndJack.com
JenKlairKids.com
Journeys.com
KidsFirstInternet.org
LaLaLing.com
LifeSizeKids.com
LillianVernon.com
LilliputSoHo.com
LimitedToo.com
LunchBoxes.com
MadisonAndFriends.com
MignsonAndCo.com
MurikWebStore.com
NaturinoLosGatos.com
Oliebollen.com
OnaToko.com
PinkTaffyDesigns.com
PokkaDots.com
PolkaDotWhale.com
PoutyChild.com
RagsLand.com
RainBee.com
Robeez.com

ACCESSORIES (cont.)

RosenberryRooms.com
SandPailKids.com
Sanrio.com
Showroom64.com
Sparkability.com
TheTrendyBaby.com
TotShop.com
TuttiBella.com
UnderTheNile.com
WickedCoolStuff.com

BABY NECESSITIES

ABaby.com
BabyAnt.com
BabyBecause.com
BabyBunz.com
BabyCenter.com
BabyGeared.com
BabyRide.com
BabyUniverse.com
CraftsburyKids.com
DiaperWare.com
InFashionKids.com
KidsFirstInternet.org
NetKidsWear.com
Oliebollen.com
PiccoliniOnline.com
RainBee.com
SafeBeginnings.com
Sparkability.com
TotShop.com

BOOKS & MEDIA

AllAboardToys.com
AsiaForKids.com
BabyBunz.com
BabyCenter.com
BabyUniverse.com
BooksOfWonder.net
ChinaBerry.com
DiscountSchoolSupply.com
eLearningToys.com
FamilySafeMedia.com
HearthSong.com

BOOKS & MEDIA (cont.)

HotTopic.com
Just-For-Kids.com
MindWareOnline.com
MuseumTour.com
MusicForLittlePeople.com
Oliebollen.com
SensationalBeginnings.com
Toys2Wish4.com

CLOTHES

2LittleMonkeys.com
AChildsCloset.com
AllAboardToys.com
Alloy.com
Anichini.net
BabyAlexandra.com
BabyAnt.com
BabyBecause.com
BabyCenter.com
BabyCZ.com
BabyGeared.com
BabyUniverse.com
Bebenique.com
BeckerSurf.com
BibisBabywear.com
BunkLine.com
BuyCostumes.com
Cloz.com
CottonFactory.com
CraftsburyKids.com
CustomGlamGirl.com
Delias.com
DPAM.com
ElegantChild.com
FloraAndHenri.com
GoJane.com
Grammies-Attic.com
HotTopic.com
InFashionKids.com
JanieAndJack.com
JenKlairKids.com
Journeys.com
LaLaLing.com
LifeSizeKids.com
LillianVernon.com

CLOTHES (cont.)

LilliputSoHo.com
LimitedToo.com
MadisonAndFriends.com
Malinas.com
MarieChantal.com
MignonAndCo.com
ModernSeed.com
MurikWebStore.com
MyLittleDucks.com
Natalys.fr
NaturinoLosGatos.com
NetKidsWear.com
NonchalantMom.com
Oliebollen.com
OnaToko.com
OneOfAKindKid.com
OrientExpressed.com
PiccoliniOnline.com
PinkTaffyDesigns.com
PokkaDots.com
PolkaDotWhale.com
PoutyChild.com
Prom-Dresses.com
RachelRiley.com
RagsLand.com
RainBee.com
RawSugarOnline.com
SandPailKids.com
Showroom64.com
TheTrendyBaby.com
TotShop.com
TuttiBella.com
UnderTheNile.com
WickedCoolStuff.com

EDUCATIONAL

AsiaForKids.com
ChinaBerry.com
CreativeKidStuff.com
CreativityForKids.com
DiscountSchoolSupply.com
DiscoverThis.com
DragonflyToys.com
EducationalInsights.com
eLearningToys.com

EDUCATIONAL (cont.)

FAO.com
GeniusBabies.com
HearthSong.com
InsectLore.com
LakeshoreLearning.com
LillianVernon.com
MasterMindToys.com
MindWareOnline.com
MuseumTour.com
MusicForLittlePeople.com
NeuroToys.com
PhysLink.com
RagsLand.com
RainBee.com
SensationalBeginnings.com
SpeedyDog.net
StoreForKnowledge.com
Toys2Wish4.com

FURNITURE

2LittleMonkeys.com
ABaby.com
AllAboardToys.com
BabyAlexandra.com
BabyAnt.com
BabyBecause.com
BabyGeared.com
BabyRide.com
BabyUniverse.com
BibisBabywear.com
BooksOfWonder.net
CraftsburyKids.com
DiscountSchoolSupply.com
ePlayFurniture.com
JenKlairKids.com
KidsDecor.net
KidsFirstInternet.org
LandOfNod.com
LillianVernon.com
MiniTots.com
ModernNursery.com
ModernSeed.com
MyLittleChild.com
NetKidsWear.com
Oliebollen.com
OneOfAKindKid.com
PBTeen.com
PiccoliniOnline.com
PinkTaffyDesigns.com
PlatesPlus4Kids.com
PoshTots.com
QualityInflatables.com
RainBee.com
RosenberryRooms.com

FURNITURE

Sanrio.com
SensationalBeginnings.com
Sparkability.com
TheTrendyBaby.com
TuttiBella.com
ZacAndZoe.com

HEALTH & SAFETY

BabyAnt.com
BabyBecause.com
BabyBunz.com
BabyCenter.com
BabyGeared.com
BabyUniverse.com
FamilySafeMedia.com
KidsFirstInternet.org
NetKidsWear.com
PokkaDots.com
SafeBeginnings.com
SensationalBeginnings.com

NURSERY

2LittleMonkeys.com
ABaby.com
BabyAlexandra.com
BabyAnt.com
BabyBecause.com
BabyCenter.com
BabyGeared.com
BabyUniverse.com
BibisBabywear.com
CraftsburyKids.com
DiscountSchoolSupply.com
ElegantBabyGifts.com
GeniusBabies.com
InFashionKids.com
JenKlairKids.com
KidsFirstInternet.org
LandOfNod.com
MiniTots.com
ModernNursery.com
ModernSeed.com
NetKidsWear.com
Oliebollen.com
OneOfAKindKid.com
PiccoliniOnline.com
PinkTaffyDesigns.com
RainBee.com
RosenberryRooms.com
Sparkability.com
TheTrendyBaby.com
TuttiBella.com
ZacAndZoe.com

RECREATION

BabyRide.com
BunkLine.com
Cloz.com
CreativeKidStuff.com
DiscountSchoolSupply.com
eLearningToys.com
GopherSport.com
HearthSong.com
LakeshoreLearning.com
LillianVernon.com
Maximum-Velocity.com
Mobileation.com
MuseumTour.com
MusicForLittlePeople.com
QualityInflatables.com
RagsLand.com
SensationalBeginnings.com
WildPlanet.com
ZebraHall.com

SUNDAY BEST

Anichini.net
BibisBabywear.com
Grammies-Attic.com
InFashionKids.com
JenKlairKids.com
LittleGirlDresses.com
MadisonAndFriends.com
MignonAndCo.com
OneOfAKindKid.com
OrientExpressed.com
PolkaDotWhale.com
Prom-Dresses.com
RachelRiley.com
RagsLand.com
TheTrendyBaby.com
TuttiBella.com

TOYS & GAMES

ActiveToys.com
AllAboardToys.com
AsiaForKids.com
BabyAnt.com
BabyBecause.com
BabyGeared.com
BabyRide.com
BuildABear.com
CraftsburyKids.com
CreativeKidStuff.com
CreativityForKids.com
DiscoverThis.com
DragonflyToys.com
EducationalInsights.com

TOYS & GAMES (cont.)

eLearningToys.com
ElegantChild.com
ePlayFurniture.com
FAO.com
FreeBears.com
GeniusBabies.com
GrowingTreeToys.com
HearthSong.com
InsectLore.com
LakeshoreLearning.com
LifeSizeKids.com
LillianVernon.com
ManhattanDollhouse.com
MasterMindToys.com
Maukilo.com
Maximum-Velocity.com
MignonAndCo.com
MindWareOnline.com
MiniTots.com
Mobileation.com
ModernNursery.com
ModernSeed.com
MuseumTour.com
MusicForLittlePeople.com
MyLittleChild.com
NetKidsWear.com
NeuroToys.com
NonchalantMom.com
Oliebollen.com
PetraToysUSA.com
PhysLink.com
PiccoliniOnline.com
PinkTaffyDesigns.com
PokkaDots.com
PoshTots.com
PuppetUniverse.com
RagsLand.com
RainBee.com
RedWagons.com
RoboToys.com
Rockimals.com
SandPailKids.com
Sanrio.com
SensationalBeginnings.com
Sparkability.com
SpeedyDog.net
StoreForKnowledge.com
TheTrendyBaby.com
TotShop.com
Toys2Wish4.com
UnderTheNile.com
WickedCoolStuff.com
WildPlanet.com
ZacAndZoe.com

2LittleMonkeys.com

2 Little Monkeys · 480-361-2656

This is a site that clearly understands furniture and bedding for young children and infants. Hand-painted furniture and round cribs are typical finds, and truth is, most of the stuff here has a lot of imagination, whether it's a rug shaped like a race car, or a loft bed shaped like a castle, with a ladder up one side and a slide down the other. If you don't like castles, you can get one shaped like a fire station.

·CLOTHES	·FURNITURE	·ACCESSORIES	·NURSERY

ABaby.com

aBaby.com · 877-552-2229

A lot of internet-only retailers try to appeal to customers by throwing a lot of products at them, and usually, for one reason or another, it doesn't work. However, on this site it works rather well, as you can essentially find vast selections of all the bigger baby items that come to mind: strollers, carriages, high chairs, cribs, cradles, bassinets, changing tables and bedding. The great selection applies to some older children's products as well, particularly with fun stuff like racecar-shaped beds, banana-shaped beanbag chairs, sports-themed rocking chairs and rocking horses shaped like snails, dragons and unicorns.

·TOYS & GAMES	·FURNITURE	·NURSERY	·BABY NECESSITIES

AChildsCloset.com

A Child's Closet · 888-300-5960

Poor web design meets some of the cutest kids' clothes you've ever seen on this jumble of a site. While browsing allows you to shop for Girls, Boys or Shoes, missing is the option to pinpoint specific selections such as baby clothes, although if you look close you'll spot swimsuits, underwear and tights. For the most part, though, you'll have to shop by brand, which is ultimately the saving grace of the site, as there are many fine and designer children's labels representing the United States and Europe, all of them worth the hassle of shopping here.

·CLOTHES	·ACCESSORIES		

ActiveToys.com

Bruder Toys · 877-858-8697

Toy technology may have changed by leaps and bounds in the past century, but at least one thing holds true: little boys love their toy trucks. The eighty-year-old German toy manufacturer hasn't forgotten, retaining the high standards that earned its line the "spiel gut" commendation, which is just another way European toy experts have of calling this the "finest selection of toy trucks on the internet." Divided into age-appropriate ranges and including construction vehicles, garbage trucks, tractors and—everybody's favorite—fire trucks. What kid wouldn't be happy?

·TOYS & GAMES			

800-416-7155 · AllAboardToys.com

AllAboardToys.com

Here it is, a store devoted to Thomas the Tank Engine. "Thomas the what?" you may ask. Well, to those in the know, this popular character is featured in product categories such as Video & Music, Train Tracks, Puzzles & Games, Clothing and on and on. The most promising items, however, will most likely be found in the Books section, as these will best answer any questions as to the origins and purpose of this steam engine with a grin. Can such a character really warrant its own web site? We think it can, we think it can, but you'll also find merchandise for Madeline, Bob the Builder, Dora the Explorer and more.

·TOYS & GAMES ·ACCESSORIES	·CLOTHES	·FURNITURE	·BOOKS & MEDIA

(WISH)

888-502-5569 · Alloy

Alloy.com

Teenage girls have a lot to talk about, but that doesn't mean anybody needs to hear it. Fortunately, there are sites like this, which offer endless adolescent-friendly content to go along with a cute, funky and sassy selection of clothes and accessories. The good news for budget-conscious parents is your daughter won't spend all her time here shopping. The bad news is that there's enough content to keep her coming back and plenty of cool clothes to entice a mini-shopping spree at any moment. Fortunately, reasonable prices still make this a safer bet than the mall.

·CLOTHES	·ACCESSORIES		

(WISH)

011-39-055-284-977 · Anichini

Anichini.net

This oldest children's clothing store in Florence, Italy, offers a fine selection of traditional European styles for boys, girls, and babies who prefer the more refined and venerable look of a young aristocrat on the make. Available in a variety of high-quality fabrics and colors, these ceremonial baby gowns and fine-tailored dress clothes should probably not be left on a child unsupervised; given the high cost and lengthy delivery process, these aren't clothes you want to sacrifice to your kids' attraction to dirt.

·CLOTHES	·SUNDAY BEST		

800-888-9681 · Asia For Kids

AsiaForKids.com

"Your key to cultural connections," this site may be just what you need to help teach your kids that there's more to this planet's history than the eternal struggle between cowboys and Indians. It actually proves to be an excellent place to find materials relating to a variety of unique cultures from all over the planet. Country-by-country browsing will turn you on to aspects such as food, music, languages and arts. Ultimately, the site may prove particularly useful to the adoptive parents of international children, as a means both to keep in touch with a mutually unfamiliar culture and to ensure none of us lose sight of where we've come from.

·TOYS & GAMES	·BOOKS & MEDIA	·EDUCATIONAL	

BabyAlexandra.com

The Baby Alexandra Company · 561-626-4466

The web extension of a Palm Beach, Florida, baby boutique, this site is "designed around a beautiful and fun lifestyle," offering cute baby clothes, accessories and furniture to the parent looking to make those first few years as adorable as can be. Unique gifts and decorative items top an inventory that includes every nursery furnishing imaginable, each easy to find even if you do come across the occasional blurry photo. Slow-to-load pages give you a chance to ruminate about the special items contained in this ultimately terrific shop.

  ·CLOTHES ·FURNITURE ·ACCESSORIES ·NURSERY

BabyAnt.com

BabyAnt.com · 866-609-0410

This multifaceted retailer offers baby gear just the way you want it: as cute as can be. With selections covering clothes, toys, furniture, safety, health and travel, you may easily browse through a great assortment of products every baby needs and every parent wants. We won't speculate as to which section of the store is the strongest, but we can tell you the Gifts section seems entirely unecessary, as the bulk of the products offered here make a terrific gift for a newborn or toddler.

 ·TOYS & GAMES ·ACCESSORIES ·CLOTHES ·NURSERY ·FURNITURE ·BABY NECESSITIES ·HEALTH & SAFETY

BabyBecause.com

BabyBecause · 866-734-2634

You child's environmental awareness may not kick in until sometime during grammar school, but your adherence to environmentally friendly products can start from birth. The key component to this site's success is its organic cloth diapers. Sure, they may not offer the convenience of the disposable variety, but when has saving the planet ever been easy? Also available are natural health and hygiene products, some great baby gear and an abundance of adorable, organic cotton baby clothes; some of which may jump start your child's fashion sense.

 ·TOYS & GAMES ·ACCESSORIES ·CLOTHES ·NURSERY ·FURNITURE ·BABY NECESSITIES ·HEALTH & SAFETY

BabyBunz.com

Baby Bunz & Co. · 800-676-4559

Whether out of concern for health or the environment, cloth diapers are becoming more popular these days than they've been since disposables crinkled their ways into our lives. This family run business out of the Pacific Northwest makes it easier for all of us to embrace a more natural and less polluting way to control the pre-potty years. Striving to offer only products that are "environmentally sensible, practical, and pleasing to the senses," the specialty shop carries a wide range of cloth diapers and diaper covers, including plenty of all-natural, organic options, and several toilet-training aids that will help make your laundry safe again.

 ·BOOKS & MEDIA ·HEALTH & SAFETY ·BABY NECESSITIES

866-241-2229 · BabyCenter

BabyCenter.com

With a full arsenal of baby-raising equipment to peddle, BabyCenter.com sets out to win your repeat business with technological assistance, community and informative content. To start with, if you enter your baby's due date or birth date, the entire site will be customized to feature products and information pertinent to his or her stage of development at any time you log on. If a $5 flat shipping rate doesn't encourage you to stock up on supplies, their extensive list of relevant articles and expert advice may, or the community chats and message boards might do it. They also offer extras like a baby-naming software, child-care and doctor finders, a vaccine guide and everything else they can come up with to keep you satisfied and coming back time and again.

·TOYS & GAMES ·ACCESSORIES	·CLOTHES ·NURSERY	·BOOKS & MEDIA ·BABY NECESSITIES	·HEALTH & SAFETY

877-822-2929 · Baby CZ

BabyCZ.com

Comprised of the "softest cashmere, cotton, and silk," this lovely line of baby accessories and apparel is just about perfect. Ivories, pinks and baby blues dominate the selection of clothes, hats and booties that adhere to traditional designs, yet often manage to add distinctly modern and cultural elements to create contemporary baby fashions that prove as comfortable as they are adorable. Shop by size, material, color or prematched ensemble to get started, then bookmark the site, because you'll probably be back for more right up until your child grows out of 4T.

·CLOTHES	·ACCESSORIES	

888-868-8139 · babygeared

BabyGeared.com

Offering "essentials for the urbane parent from world-renowned designers and manufacturers," this intriguing shop offers a modern slant on baby accoutrements. From conceptual toys to designer crib sets, you'll find a startling interpretation of baby gear, with stuff like Dyson vacuums, Dwell bedding and modern decorative prints thrown in for kicks. It really is mostly about the baby here, though, as nontraditional as it seems sometimes, and if your home already features a "form-follows-function" sensibility you're going to need this shop to make your nursery fit in.

·TOYS & GAMES ·ACCESSORIES	·CLOTHES ·NURSERY	·FURNITURE ·BABY NECESSITIES	·HEALTH & SAFETY

800-721 7444 · BabyRide.com

BabyRide.com

This homegrown enterprise aims to provide online shoppers "with a wide selection of products and brands—even in special needs models—at the lowest available prices." Clearly, we like that. The site proves an excellent source of baby travel necessities such as baby carriers, strollers, carriages and car seats, with long lists of terrific products and deals. You'll also find high chairs and novelty furniture to keep things cute inside the home. Last but not least is a tremendous selection of some superfun outdoor gear, including playhouses and ride-on toys that will delight your youngsters for hours at a time.

·TOYS & GAMES	·FURNITURE	·RECREATION	·BABY NECESSITIES

BabyUniverse.com

Baby Universe · 877-615-2229

You may just want to head straight for the Search feature on this one, because this selection of baby wares is as large as the name would indicate. To give you an idea, we found five different types of jogging strollers that were made specifically to hold twins. So, it goes that we can only imagine how much variety can be found in sections and subsections devoted to clothing, diapering, feeding, healthcare, bedding, bathing supplies and nursing aids. Fortunately, we only have to imagine; browsing through it all—well, that's up to you.

·CLOTHES ·NURSERY	·FURNITURE ·BABY NECESSITIES	·BOOKS & MEDIA	·HEALTH & SAFETY

Bebenique.com

Bebenique · 866-843-2323

Traditional and contemporary baby styles meet at this terrific online clothes and gifts boutique where the common threads are quality and good looks. Supercute and comfortable layette garments give way to utterly adorable toddler outfits that usually stick to modern trends, but with classic flourishes. The clothes make great gifts by their own rights, but if you're looking for something more memorable you'll find a wide assortment of beautiful trinkets here, including personalized paintings, ceramics and some truly unforgettable patchwork quilts.

·CLOTHES	·ACCESSORIES		

BeckerSurf.com

Becker Surf · 888-673-0225

Even if you don't live on a coastline, you might have kids who've adopted the surfer lifestyle. As such, you may want to check out this virtual beach shop, which offers a great deal of beachy attire and accessories for kids and teens, including swimsuits, hoodies, baggy shorts, sandals and shades. Though it moves a bit awkwardly, the site generally makes it easy to find what you need, and the selection is pretty good, if you're into the bonfire scene. Dude.

·CLOTHES	·ACCESSORIES		

BibisBabywear.com

Bibi's Babywear · 866-544-2229

With a lot of products to sort through, this cute baby destination out of New Jersey offers much more than what an infant might wear, featuring a huge inventory of nursery furniture, accents and bedding. A long, detailed menu down the left side of the page guides you to some deep assortments of very particular items as well as slim selections of some general items, and you'll pretty much have to resign yourself to a good hour's worth of browsing in order to see how it all pans out. We can tell you that wall decor, cribs, bassinets and Moses baskets are absolutely worth a first look.

·CLOTHES	·SUNDAY BEST	·FURNITURE	·NURSERY

800-207-6968 · Books of Wonder

BooksOfWonder.net

It's tough to say your child will value $300 first-edition signed copies of their favorite picture books, but if you'd like to get your kid started on an early book collecting habit, this New York City bookshop might be the place to do it. More likely, you just want exposure to the finest in children's literature, whether it's contemporary or an ageless favorite. Again, this site can help you out, with a fantastic selection of award winners and recommended picks covering a variety of styles and subject matter. Of course, if you are determined to buy something indulgent that everybody can appreciate, the store also offers an exquisite selection of original illustrations from some of the greatest picture books of our era.

| ·FURNITURE | ·BOOKS & MEDIA | | | |

888-560-2327 · Build-A-Bear Workshop

BuildABear.com

This site is somewhat of a misnomer. It's not that you can't customize, or "build" a teddy bear, complete with one of several cute outfits (including NBA uniforms, a fishing outfit and a bikini)—you can, and easily at that. But, among the many bear options, are pandas and koalas, which are technically not bears. Okay, okay, so we're nitpicking. But what do you say to the fact that among these "teddy bear" options are also included a monkey, bunny, cow, elephant, pony, tiger and turtle? If you're anything like us, you'll say, "Cool!" These dolls are almost as much fun to shop for as they are to own.

| ·TOYS & GAMES | | | |

800-435-6888 · Bunkline Camp Outfitters

BunkLine.com

This summer camp outfitter has got it all for those kids who are ready to step out into cabin life, while you relearn what it means to have a minute to yourself and a home that stays clean. Of course, you'll use your free time to worry about them, but you'll worry less knowing that they have warm sleeping bags, rugged clothes and protective outdoor equipment. Best of all, you won't have to suffer that recurring nightmare, where your kid shows up at camp and discovers that he or she doesn't have any extra underwear.

| ·CLOTHES | ·RECREATION | | | |

800-459-2969 · BuyCostumes.com

BuyCostumes.com

Though not strictly for kids, this costume specialist is at its best when it's dressing up babies as famous characters from cartoons and fairy tales. Clearly, most of its business comes around Halloween, though you might just get a good deal if you plan ahead this year. Either way, you'll find an amazingly comprehensive selection of costumes inspired by history, literature and popular culture. Of course, whether or not you decide to buy anything, it's worth visiting just to see the hilarious and adorable photographs.

| ·CLOTHES | | | | |

ChinaBerry.com
Chinaberry · 888-481-6744

The staff of this children's book shop has actually read all of the books you'll find on its web site, as well as many others they didn't deem worth stocking. As a result "you won't find a single ho-hum or overly hyped, media-driven product" among the selection. Instead, you'll find a great assortment of age appropriate reading choices, with particular sections devoted to Reluctant Readers and Expanding Minds. The best part is, they've also provided insightful reviews of each book to help you better determine which of the massive selection you—and your child of course—would actually enjoy reading.

·BOOKS & MEDIA	·EDUCATIONAL		

Cloz.com
Cloz · 800-876-2267

You don't want to send your kids off to camp shorthanded, so while you're planning their summer away from home, you might as well log on to this site to pick out those sundry items that they'll need while they're exploring and experiencing the rustic life. Anything from durable clothes and sleeping bags to travel bedding and toiletries will leave them well equipped for months (in case they decide to extend their stay). Handily enough, when they do return, you can use this same site to buy school uniforms.

·CLOTHES	·RECREATION	·ACCESSORIES	

CottonFactory.com
The Cotton Factory · 800-441-3046

If you thought the days of Mr. T. "I Pity The Fool" t-shirts were long over, think again. This site doesn't just reinvigorate graphic tee proclamations like "Bowling Is For Lovers" and "Meat Is Murder," but offers a variety of images and slogans that only teens could get away with. Designs range from the cool (Atari) to the notoriously geeky (tuxedo tee), with plenty of mixed messages in between, such as "Keep on Tolkien" and "Even Dinosaurs Take Baths." Hey, if we understood them they wouldn't be teenagers.

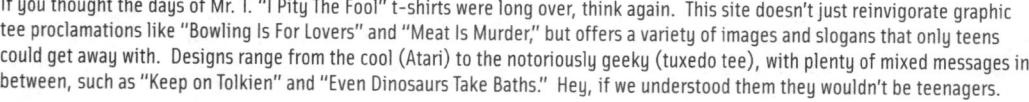

·CLOTHES			

CraftsburyKids.com
Craftsbury Kids · 800-549-3414

Beseeching us to "Celebrate the unique magic of childhood," this site offers a lovely alternative to "mass-produced toys" and "cookie-cutter chain stores." Though short on selection, the quality is high, as all of its products are handmade by a talented group of artisans. You'll find baby booties, little hats and a variety of other accessories, as well as a few cute garments, toys and nursery decorations. A gift purchased here is sure to have quite an impact.

·TOYS & GAMES ·NURSERY	·CLOTHES ·BABY NECESSITIES	·FURNITURE	·ACCESSORIES

800-353-0710 · Creative Kidstuff

CreativeKidStuff.com

Whether your children's imaginations are sparked by science, arts and crafts, fairy tales, sports, role-playing, music or games, this site offers some wonderfully inventive and fun games that should busy their minds as well as their hands. Shopping by Interest/Categories turns up themes like Knights & Castles, Science and Tech, Music, Puzzles and Travel, whereas a Shop by Age section may provide a more appropriate way to shop for kids with varied interests.

| ·TOYS & GAMES | ·EDUCATIONAL | ·RECREATION | | |

800-311-8684 · Faber-Castell

CreativityForKids.com

A rainy day doesn't have to portend drudgery; with the help of this kids arts-and-crafts brand it can become an opportunity for tons of fun. Featuring child-friendly modeling clay, paints, colored pencils, crayons, markers and a wide variety of other hands-on materials, this line of crafts kits may be found in most toy stores, but never with such a comprehensive selection. The site can be a pain to navigate, but compared to the hassle of kids trapped indoors with nothing to do, it's a cakewalk.

| ·TOYS & GAMES | ·EDUCATIONAL | | | |

800-796-8731 · Estephenie

CustomGlamGirl.com

Teen girls with a message for the world can make their statement in t-shirt, handbag, belt, sweatpants, undies and hoodie form with the help of this personalized accessories and apparel site. Browsing's easy as can be, with distinct categories leading you to pages filled with colorful and funny designs, each of which may be printed with the text of your choosing (be careful to check your spelling). Better yet, once your girl is sufficiently glammed out, you can turn your attention to the adorable Glam Baby section.

| ·CLOTHES | ·ACCESSORIES | | |  |

888-533-5427 · dELia*s

Delias.com

Well known for its trendy teen and tween styles, the truth is this mall mainstay is even a favorite of young adults, who will no doubt use the web site as an opportunity to buy some cute outfits on the sly. In addition to the colorful, fresh and fun clothes, you'll find a great assortment of shoes, sandals and boots, which fashion-friendly moms may see fit to borrow from time to time. Ultimately, the biggest reason to shop here is that the catalog has mastered the art of demonstrating an innocent appeal, offering a catalog that bridges the gap between parental sensibility and pop culture imagery; finally something you and your daughter can agree on.

| ·CLOTHES | ·ACCESSORIES | | | |

DiaperWare.com

How big can a homegrown cloth diaper business get? Surprisingly big. Boasting "mountains of diapers ready to ship," this small-time retailer has a wide enough assortment to put you off disposable diapers forever. Flannel, hemp and organic cotton selections include contoured and fitted diapers, plus a startling number of colors and patterns, lending credence to the site's assertion that diapers can be "cute." Mostly, the technology of the cloth diaper has caught up to modern needs and demands for convenience, featuring absorbent materials and stay-dry liners, making this perhaps the best place online to find nappies.

·BABY NECESSITIES

DiscountSchoolSupply.com

Though its name certainly won't inspire a lot of excitement in children, plenty of the products featured on this site will do the trick. It's not easy to get a bead on the shop's intentions, as any actual school supplies seem to be listed here as an afterthought. However, most of these toys, educational materials and furniture will help establish a healthy environment for kids to return to from school, and a lot of the sporting equipment, arts-and-crafts kits and role-playing toys might even distract them from heading straight for the television.

·TOYS & GAMES ·RECREATION	·FURNITURE ·NURSERY	·BOOKS & MEDIA	·EDUCATIONAL

DiscoverThis.com

Giving your children science kits to play with won't make them nerds... well, most of the time, anyway. But it can light a fire under their interest in learning and creativity, in most cases without the use of actual fire. With educational toys spread across categories such as Chemistry Sets, Ants & Bugs, Astronomy, Microscopes, Mechanics and the ever popular Dinosaurs, you just know these things are going to be so much fun that you'll take over as soon as the box is open. If you can restrain yourself just a little bit, though, your kids really do stand to learn a lot and have fun in the process.

·TOYS & GAMES	·EDUCATIONAL		

DPAM.com

What with the garish colors, difficult navigation and pricey transatlantic shipping, shopping from this European children and babies site may not be ideal. However, once you manage to click through to the actual clothing, you'll see why it's easily worth it. Terrific clothing selections offer styles we just don't see too often domestically, and they're unbelievably adorable. The Overstock section makes a good place to start, whereas the Shoe Store may warrant a quick glance on your way out.

·CLOTHES	·ACCESSORIES		

800-308-2208 · Dragonfly  **DragonflyToys.com**

Physically challenged and developmentally disabled children tend to have two things in common: they love to expand their horizons, and they love to have fun. From sensory exploration games to those aiding hand/eye coordination or just plain education, this site features toys and technology that promote healthy response and a broader grasp of the physical realm in youngsters with special needs. These games and devices, along with some truly useful daily living aids, can be easily found by creating an individual child profile that will guide you toward only relevant products.

·TOYS & GAMES	·EDUCATIONAL			

800-995-4436 · Educational Insights **EducationalInsights.com**

Your kid's school should provide the basic elements of academic learning, but it's widely accepted that a parent's involvement at home can make all the difference in a child's education. Whether a specific subject is causing distress or your overachiever wants to pursue some extracurricular interests, this all-educational shop offers games, toys and kits designed to promote a more in-depth understanding of basic and more advanced elements of reading, math, science and social studies. With these tools in hand, you can make sure your child grows up to be smarter than you.

·TOYS & GAMES	·EDUCATIONAL			

800-283-8155 · eLearningToys.com **eLearningToys.com**

For the eager minds of young children and toddlers comes this toy shop with an educational focus. Baby toys get matched up with picture books, art kits and science sets to cover the intellectual and physical development of children from birth through the age of seven, with some adorable options to contrast against the really cool stuff. The shop clearly favors wooden toys whenever possible, and the book section alone is worth the visit, especially for those kids who don't yet have a grasp of the alphabet, but can be attracted to pretty colors and pictures.

·TOYS & GAMES	·BOOKS & MEDIA	·EDUCATIONAL	·RECREATION	

800-827-0392 · Elegant Baby Gifts **ElegantBabyGifts.com**

True to its word, the gifts offered by this online boutique are quite elegant, a fact that will be more appreciated by parents than tots, we are sure. The personalized items, such as baby blankets, bibs, silver spoons or shawls can't be beat, and some of the bath accessories will be fun for everyone (albeit a classy sort of fun). The site is well sorted, allowing you to pinpoint a price range or shop by gender, but really browsing the entire selection in these pastel pages won't take very long, and nearly every page will turn up something great.

·ACCESSORIES	·NURSERY			

ElegantChild.com
The Elegant Child of Beverly Hills · 888-673-3273

Where do the stars turn for personalized baby attire and luxurious gift baskets? This Beverly Hills boutique, for one. With a clientele you'd expect to see at movie premiere or awards gala more than a baby gift shop, one might presume these adorable clothes, baby blankets, keepsakes and gift boxes cost more than the average new family could afford, but this isn't necessarily the case. While you'll spot some ultra-indulgent items that cost the moon, there are plenty of beautiful, reasonably priced options that make this a great destination for the entire planet.

·TOYS & GAMES	·CLOTHES	·ACCESSORIES	

ePlayFurniture.com
ePlayFurniture.com · 813-972-9090

This internet retailer's devotion to children's furniture makes it a great stop on your way to fixing up your kid's bedroom or playroom. Simple and beautiful desks, tables and chairs are complemented by more interesting items such as toy pianos, easels, play kitchens, cutesy vanities and the most adorable potty trainers you're likely to find. While the site ultimately comes a tad short of its goal "to provide the largest selection of playroom furniture for children anywhere," it might have succeeded in offering one of the web's best.

·TOYS & GAMES	·FURNITURE		

FamilySafeMedia.com
Family Safe Media · 800-828-4514

"Preserving family values in a media driven society," this specialty site offers a host of highly technological products designed to protect your kids' eyes and ears from harmful content, whether on television or the internet. You'll find DVD players designed to filter offensive material, devices that automatically mute profanity from any television broadcast and computer software that blocks obscene web sites based on your own set of definitions. Further controls may be found in the form of TV, videogame and internet time managers and even a gizmo that allows you to keep the internet under lock and key. They'll be more likely to hear bad words at school.

·BOOKS & MEDIA	·HEALTH & SAFETY		

FAO.com
FAO Schwarz · 800-876-7867

For more than 130 years, F.A.O. Schwarz has been one of the greatest toy stores in the whole wide world. It also happens to be one of the best on the world wide web. A Luxury Gifts section should be kept out of view of your children, as some of these toys may cost more than your home. However, in reality most of the toys across ages and price ranges are indulgent enough as it is, including giant plush toys, ride-on Porsches and life-size dinosaur models. Toys were not like this when we were growing up.

·TOYS & GAMES	·EDUCATIONAL		

888-749-9698 · flora and henri

FloraAndHenri.com

This children's clothing label decries the overuse of brand advertising in apparel, so you'll never see any ostentatious use of the flora and henri name sullying this charming attire. "Inspired by the charm and enduring qualities of vintage garments," these clothes are nice, but not too nice, as "the fine detailing and craftsmanship never make them too precious for climbing, digging, swimming, and running." The site works pretty well, too, with relatively click-free browsing that looks dull but really isn't, as it does a good job of showing off these clothes that we'd personally hate to see get dirty.

·CLOTHES   ·ACCESSORIES

866-340-2327 · FreeBears.com

FreeBears.com

With "over 900 teddy bears and stuffed animals," visiting this specialty toy shop in a no-brainer when you're looking for that perfect plush gift for a baby or child. Categories like Jungle Animals, Barnyard Animals, Sea World, Jumbo Animals, Birds, Bunnies and Monkeys will guide you through a terrific selection, and an Animal By Species menu will even take you straight to such creatures as Armadillos, Pandas and Skunks. Though none of the toys are free, many of them are certainly reasonably priced, and if your order tallies to fifty dollars or more the family-owned business will donate a teddy bear to a children's charity.

·TOYS & GAMES

704-573-4500 · GeniusBabies.com

GeniusBabies.com

This store seems to operate under the theory that a stimulating environment will improve a child's creative impulses and brain-power in general. Sounds plausible. And what could it hurt to surround your child with mobiles, colorful play-mats, soothing music and thought-provoking toys? Well, this is what you get when a bunch of devoted mommies band together to create a business concerned with the betterment of child-rearing—a pretty darn good business. Here's hoping the child-rearing part works as well.

·TOYS & GAMES   ·EDUCATIONAL   ·NURSERY

800-846-5263 · GoJane.com

GoJane.com

Adding "at least 50 new styles every week to keep you at the forefront of fashion," this internet retailer targets the ever-changing tastes of teenage girls with a cuter and sometimes daring selection of bold, sassy attire. From jeans and halter tops to gaucho pants and prom dresses, the site caters particularly well to a fickle shopper who might come back three times a week in search of something entirely different and be satisfied at every turn. Best of all, incredibly affordable prices make such repeat visits entirely possible, without doing too much damage to your pocketbook.

·CLOTHES   ·ACCESSORIES

GopherSport.com

Gopher Sport · 800-533-0446

As if the trauma of physical education in the schools wasn't enough, this site allows you to re-create the experience at home, offering all manner of children's recreational and athletic gear. For starters, you can find many sizes of those ubiquitous red, air-filled balls (known to many as the terror-inflicting "dodge ball"). Then, there are climbing walls, gymnastic stations, bowling carpets (to simulate indoor lanes), tetherball sets and even those big parachutes that teach youngsters the value of…something or other. Once you've filled your home and yard with this equipment, select from scoreboards and bleachers and invite other parents over to get worked into a frenzy over whose kid is best at what.

  ·RECREATION

Grammies-Attic.com

Grammie's Attic · 877-760-5259

Special occasions call for special attire, and for your infant or toddler you may not find lovelier garments than those offered by this odd-looking but surprisingly functional site. New, vintage and retro-inspired christening gowns, sailor suits, layette and pinafores may keep you cooing for the duration of your shopping session, as the detailed photos highlight the dainty and adorable charms of these clothes that see "babies dressed like babies instead of mini-adults."

 ·CLOTHES   ·SUNDAY BEST

GrowingTreeToys.com

Growing Tree Toys · 800-993-8697

Imagine a toy store bereft of the loud, obnoxious cartoon merchandise so aggressively foisted upon children by television shows and commercials. Now log on to this site and see the dream become reality. This toy shop offers plenty in the way of fun and enticement, without pandering to the interests of the giant toy makers and entertainment industry. The result is a terrific, well-rounded selection of dolls, puzzles, puppets, trucks, musical instruments, imaginative play items and educational sets that may not be on your children's wish lists, but only because they weren't advertised.

   ·TOYS & GAMES

HearthSong.com

Hearth Song · 800-533-4397

Having grown from a small homemade catalog into a mail order company servicing nearly twenty million customers, the primary philosophy of this retailer remains intact: that "children need time for creative, imaginative play." More importantly, it offers hundreds of products to back this up, including arts-and-crafts kits, musical instruction sets, developmental toys, games, puzzles and more. Rather than force genius upon your children, these products merely allow them to engage the world at their own natural paces, resulting in happy kids and fun for the whole family.

  ·TOYS & GAMES   ·BOOKS & MEDIA   ·EDUCATIONAL   ·RECREATION
·ACCESSORIES

800-892-8674 · Hot Topic

HotTopic.com

This mall shop turned online store should be able to satisfy the needs of any kind of alternative-music-loving teen, with its identity-establishing apparel and supplemental accessories. Punk, gothic, metal—there's a lot of black garb here, but the selection is constantly changing to keep up with new trends as they pass (gift certificates may be the only gift purchases that make sense). Whatever the scene, it all starts with the basic element of genre subculture: the band t-shirt, of which there are many to be found here.

| ·CLOTHES | ·BOOKS & MEDIA | ·ACCESSORIES | | |

908-371-1733 · In Fashion Kids

InFashionKids.com

This New Jersey–based retailer offers what could only be considered dapper dress clothes for boys, darling dresses for girls and adorable attire for tots. Category headings tell the rest of the tale, with fantastic Pajamas, plenty of Shoes and the ever-popular Boys' Tuxedos. The best, though, might be their Halloween Costumes section, which offers some classics, along with costumes such as Superman and Barbie that actually look like the character in question, as opposed to the dreadfully familiar plastic smock with the picture of the character on it. A must-see.

| ·CLOTHES
·BABY NECESSITIES | ·SUNDAY BEST | ·ACCESSORIES | ·NURSERY | |

800-548-3284 · Insect Lore

InsectLore.com

We have to warn you—if you easily get the creeps, you don't want your kids to find out about this one. After all, it's bad enough that animal-loving children can simply bring frogs and insects in from the yard and let them loose in the kitchen, but with this site they can actually order live insects through the mail. Without this site, you could go an entire lifetime without seeing a praying mantis, millipede or hissing cockroach in your home; here it's considered to be in the interest of science, part of a catalog including ant farms and giant tarantula puppets. If your kids do desperately want insects to learn from, maybe they'll be content with the ladybugs, silkworms and butterflies.

| ·TOYS & GAMES | ·EDUCATIONAL | | | |

877-449-8800 · Janie and Jack

JanieAndJack.com

Preppy styles take on tiny proportions with this offshoot of the Gymboree brand, with adorable toddler-size sundresses and baby boy deck pants heading up a selection of casually smart garments for your wee one. Though not very large, the selection manages to cover all the basics, ranging from clothes a kid can cake with mud to special-occasion attire a kid will probably want to cake with mud. Whether on their best behavior or up to your knees in mischief, there's little doubting how cute kids will look in these outfits.

| ·CLOTHES | ·ACCESSORIES | | |  |

JenKlairKids.com

Jen Klair Kids · 866-465-1263

The proprietress of this homegrown business has searched, "over the world for the most luxurious, handcrafted products for you and your child." The result is an exclusive collection of fine clothes, bedding, accessories and furniture for little ones that will satisfy parents with discerning taste. To wit, you may find a selection of personalized silver spoons, along with some beautiful Moses baskets and outstanding cribs. There are more than a thousand products here, so be sure not to overlook the Next Page links within categories, or you'll miss out on all the lovely items this site has to offer.

·CLOTHES ·NURSERY	·SUNDAY BEST	·FURNITURE	·ACCESSORIES

Journeys.com

Journeys · 888-324-6356

Hip kids need hip shoes or they become just kinda-cool kids. That's how it works. Well, from skate shoes to boots and even Heelys (the shoes with wheels embedded in the heels), this shop's got the stylin' footwear youngsters and teens tend to clamor for. Brands like Adidas, Vans, Dr. Martens, Converse, Puma and Timberland in particular stand out, but many more are well represented in this store that's known to reside in a mall or two. Better to shop from them online, because food courts just aren't cool.

·CLOTHES	·ACCESSORIES		

Just-For-Kids.com

Just For Kids Books · 847-803-8783

Although shopping from this kids-only book store requires more patience than taking a tired child for a day of shopping, visiting this dedicated web shop turns out to be a good idea on certain occasions. For example, if you're looking for a specific book, you'll probably find it here for a great price. Or if you would only like to browse Newbery, Caldecott and Coretta Scott King award winning titles, find your desired selection from the menu on the home page and you'll do so in no time. However, at this point you'll be faced with long text lists of titles with little product description at all, let alone pictures. It can be tough, but not worth throwing a tantrum.

·BOOKS & MEDIA			

KidsDecor.net

Kid's Decor · 866-837-5437

The vast amount of child and baby furniture and decor housed by this massive site can easily overwhelm, which is why we'd like to point out the handy menu running down on the righthand side of the page: the Top Decor Themes menu. This allows you to shop by adorable subjects such as airplanes, ballerinas, boats, cowboys, sea life, flowers, nursery rhymes and sports. You'll still find comprehensive selections, but they'll make more sense toward matching your own decorating intentions.

·FURNITURE			

866-543-7352 · Kids First Internet

KidsFirstInternet.org

"Passionate about providing a unique mix of an engaging parenting community with a great value shopping experience," this web retailer proves to be about as exciting as it sounds, however, it definitely provides a terrific selection and competitive prices. A focused buyer will uncover good deals on infant and children's bedding, along with enough furniture, safety products and baby equipment to warrant a deep look. Browsing can be inconsistent and convoluted at times, but it's nothing that will slow down the experienced internet shopper.

·FURNITURE ·BABY NECESSITIES	·HEALTH & SAFETY	·ACCESSORIES	·NURSERY

800-428-4414 · Lakeshore Learning

LakeshoreLearning.com

If you want to get an early start and/or take an active interest in your child's learning and skills development, this site offers a wealth of tools and toys that will help you do just that. From reading and language skills to physical coordination and introductions to musical performance, this stuff has the potential to give your child all sorts of educational advantages; but even more, it gives you a great excuse to spend some productive quality time together.

·TOYS & GAMES	·EDUCATIONAL	·RECREATION	

323-664-4400 · La La Ling

LaLaLing.com

"Providing Los Angeles with a unique, fresh and different hub of fashion, arts, and culture for cool kids… and their happening parents" this upscale baby boutique covers a lot of ground that's neglected by other shops. A truly remarkable selection of Hot Fashions includes infant and toddler apparel adhering to a variety of contemporary and retro looks, including hipster button-down shirts for boys and hand-embroidered girls' garments. These are some serious clothes that are way too good for daycare in any place but Hollywood.

·CLOTHES	·ACCESSORIES		

800-933-9904 · Land of Nod

LandOfNod.com

Most likely, there's only one room in the house that kids can call their own: their bedroom. So why not decorate it to their tastes and interests? Beginning with some fantastic beds, cribs and bedding, kids' rooms get the treatment here, with pint-size furniture and pleasant colors at every turn. Separated into Girls, Boys and Babies, if you use the animated menus provided at the top of the page, browsing should run fairly smoothly, though at any given time you'll probably still trip over something left on your son's or daughter's floor.

·FURNITURE	·NURSERY		

LifeSizeKids.com

Life Size · 323-651-3698

Recognizing that hip parents would like to have hip children, this offshoot of the chic Los Angeles department store Fred Segal "has an incredibly fashionable and stylish clientele, who also happen to be underage." Featuring a long list of highly sought after designers, this shop is meant for babies and toddlers who dress better than most adults, whether it's in the coolest graphic tees, the hottest jeans, the freshest kicks, a motorcycle jacket or the most laid-back onesies an infant would want wear to a movie premiere. We'd have to say this nearly perfect shop is actually bigger than life.

·TOYS & GAMES	·CLOTHES	·ACCESSORIES	

LillianVernon.com

Lillian Vernon · 800-545-5426

Lillian Vernon created a mail-order empire back in 1951 with a simple ad selling personalized leather belts and handbags. In fifty years, her line of merchandise has made its way to the internet and expanded to include a vast array of gifts and decorations for the home, and a surprisingly fun selection of products for kids. You may question the catalog's evolution from offering monogrammed belts to featuring children's water toys, but inflatable waterslides, water balloon machines, and "stay afloat swimsuits" are just some of the things available here that you just don't see anywhere else. The site also features educational toys, clothes, and a bunch of other stuff your kids will love, as long as you don't mention where you got it.

·TOYS & GAMES ·RECREATION	·CLOTHES ·ACCESSORIES	·FURNITURE	·EDUCATIONAL

LilliputSoHo.com

Lilliput SoHo Kids · 212-965-9201

Few neighborhoods are as trendy as New York City's SoHo district, and it may just be the only place in the country that could pull off this sort of children's boutique. Boy-size Italian suits and sequined dresses for girls are just a few of the upscale items you're likely to encounter here. You'll otherwise find designer jeans, trendy shirts, luxurious sweaters and other such fashion staples of well-to-do Manhattanites. There's no telling whether your town is ready for children this well-dressed, but here's an easy way to find out.

·CLOTHES	·ACCESSORIES		

LimitedToo.com

Limited Too · 866-458-3866

Shopping for adolescent girls may be the most impossible venture known to adultkind. Fortunately, this mall shop seems to be fairly serviceable to the so-called tween set, offering clothes and accessories almost rebellious enough to make a parent shudder, but not so crazy that there'll be any phone calls from the school. Actually, this stuff is cute, colorful and fun, just like the seven-to-fourteen-year-old girls it markets to, so what we have here just may be a great solution to that ageless gifting problem.

·CLOTHES	·ACCESSORIES		

866-239-1253 · Little Girl Dresses

LittleGirlDresses.com

Do little children enjoy dressing up for fancy occasions? Usually not. But that doesn't keep us from making them do it. Probably because they look so darn cute, we subject them to wearing white satin dresses and three-piece suits, then take them to churches, weddings and other dressy events and show them off with style. This site offers a lovely variety of such apparel, and not just for little girls. Communion dresses and suits are backed up by christening gowns, bris gowns and even ring-bearer tuxedos. It's all easy to browse; in fact, the only hard part will be keeping them clean.

·SUNDAY BEST				

323-908-3916 · Lunchboxes.com

LunchBoxes.com

Brown paper bags are out. Nothing carries your meals as well as a lunch box and thermos, and no lunch box is complete without cartoon or movie characters adorning its lid. Here you'll find boxes covering everything from the Simpsons to Harry Potter, along with such unlikely fare as *King Kong*, *Casablanca* and da Vinci's *Last Supper*. Fortunately for those who don't appreciate garish merchandising, there are plenty of plain, classic designs that will keep your kids' food from getting smushed on the bus.

·ACCESSORIES				

888-332-8610 · Madison and Friends of Chicago

MadisonAndFriends.com

This Chicago boutique initially offered designer fashions for babies and toddlers, but like the children it catered to, the shop quickly outgrew its own selection. Now it offers hip apparel and shoes for babies on through preteens, featuring top labels most of us won't be able to find locally, or even elsewhere online. For example, we've seen a lot of James Perse, Sean John, Diesel and Lacoste apparel on adult clothing sites, but not in children's sizes. Here, such items simply blend in with the designer jeans, cool shoes and other upscale kiddie attire that makes this site a must-see for the fashion set.

·CLOTHES	·SUNDAY BEST	·ACCESSORIES		

310-395-5965 · malina

Malinas.com

It's tough to make baby clothes that don't look extremely cute on an infant or toddler, so telling you how adorable this baby attire is probably won't make this site stand out in your mind. What will is the fact that a lot of the outfits offered by this site are fashioned of cashmere and silk. Do we have your attention? Truly, the cotton clothes here are great in their own right, but if you can appreciate classic baby styles rendered in luxe fabrics, this shop should be your next stop.

·CLOTHES				

ManhattanDollhouse.com

If you feel threatened by dollhouses that look better than your own home, you might shy away from this miniature niche retailer. A whole neighborhood's worth of houses is available, including townhouses, rustic farmhouses, country cottages, log cabins, Tudor-style homes and full-blown mansions. Some are offered prebuilt while others require detailed assembly, and while the site itself isn't soundly designed, you should be able to tell the difference.

·TOYS & GAMES

MarieChantal.com

Ever wonder what sort of baby and toddler clothes are good enough for royalty? This endlessly appealing clothing line, founded by and named for the wife of a Greek prince, might just be your answer. These high-quality play clothes and special occasion outfits have been worn by the children of European aristocrats and international celebrities, and thanks to this elegant-looking site everybody's baby can dress like a prince or princess.

·CLOTHES

MasterMindToys.com

Here's a Canadian toy store chain offering a wide assortment of products "that awaken creativity, encourage curiosity, enhance motor skills, develop imagination, challenge thinking and offer a child hours of fun." Categories names such as Science Toys, Theatre & Puppets, Dinosaurs, Dress Up, Arts & Crafts and Puzzles pretty much paint the picture, while the enigmatic Cool Toys section is simply too good to pass up. If more toy stores in the US stocked such creative and educational selections, we'd probably have a nation of supergeniuses.

·TOYS & GAMES   ·EDUCATIONAL

Maukilo.com

Anyone hip to the idea of having their kids play with wooden toys rather than plastic will be doubly impressed by this lovely little site, which sells a great selection of European wooden toys. With building blocks, wood dolls and developmental baby toys, you child will be well on the way to a wholesome upbringing. Of course, it's not all solid here, and you will find the occasional soft toy mixed in. Certainly though, you won't find this stuff being manufactured by a lot of American companies.

·TOYS & GAMES

623-587-9261 · Maximum Velocity

Maximum-Velocity.com

The need for speed starts at an early age, and industrious youngsters may take a great interest in pinewood derby cars. Not just for Boy Scouts anymore, these small wooden cars racing each other down an inclined track becomes less a test of male aggression and more about craftsmanship, engineering and, though it won't help you win, style. You'll find basic plans and materials, plus no shortage of inspiration for piecing together your own design. Working on a derby racer could be just the ticket for some parent-child bonding.

| ·TOYS & GAMES | ·RECREATION | | | |

888-662-6326 · Mignon and Compagnie

MignonAndCo.com

If you want to shower your little princess with the adorable clothes and toys she deserves, take a good look at this fanciful web retailer that wholeheartedly embraces the girly girl. Age-based browsing makes it simple to shop for your darling daughter from birth up through preteen, whether you're dressing her up, playing dress-up or giving her all the toys and tools to add the royal touch to her imaginative play. It's a wonderful source of gifts, and a particularly good source of christening gowns, Sunday attire, swimsuits and the type of precious outfits that will make Daddy proud.

| ·TOYS & GAMES | ·CLOTHES | ·SUNDAY BEST | ·ACCESSORIES | |

800-274-6123 · MindWareOnline.com

MindWareOnline.com

Offering "Brainy toys for kids of all ages," this proves a great site to find brainteasers and building toys designed to get children thinking creatively and analytically. Ironically, the site requires little or no thought on your part, as the navigation guides you effortlessly through categories such as Early Learning, Reading and Coloring Books, even prompting gift ideas along the way. It all falls under the notion that one day your kids will be significantly smarter than you.

| ·TOYS & GAMES | ·BOOKS & MEDIA | ·EDUCATIONAL | | |

866-307-8687 · Mini Tots

MiniTots.com

Despite overpriced shipping and relatively slow-loading pages, this site is not to be missed if you're in the market for baby and children's furniture. With thorough selections of sturdy beds, chests, desks and armoires, you'll find pretty much all you'll need to furnish and decorate your schoolchild's room. However, the best part of the site falls under the Nursery heading. With hand-painted cribs, an awesome assortment of cradles and endless pages filled with all kinds of nursery necessities, you'll not be disappointed.

| ·TOYS & GAMES | ·FURNITURE | ·NURSERY | | |

Mobileation.com

Mobileation · 888-886-6245

Some kids are easy to please; others require a little extra effort. None will be disappointed by the extravagant toys featured by this specialized web retailer. The focus here is anything a child can ride upon, and while most of them are fairly simple and traditional, such as big wheels, tricycles, red wagons and rocking horses, others easily raise the bar. Pedal-operated cars are the least of it; among the many options found within these pages are kid-size construction vehicles, rideable electric trains (and track), motorized airplanes (they don't actually fly) and battery cars to match just about anything Mom or Dad may have in the driveway.

·TOYS & GAMES	·RECREATION		

ModernNursery.com

Modern Nursery · 877-663-2224

Offering to help your child "begin life in style," this unique specialty shop certainly doesn't miss a beat, with an infinitely appealing assortment of conceptual, designer and modern baby furniture, bedding and decor. Unique designs abound whether you're looking at cribs, high chairs, mobiles or wall stickers, and though there may not be a lot available within each category, we're betting you'll still be bowled over by what you see, whether or not the rest of your home is already outfitted with the sleek, clean designs of the modern age.

·TOYS & GAMES	·FURNITURE	·NURSERY

ModernSeed.com

Modernseed · 510-547-4445

While it's impossible to predict what will pass as modern when your kids come of age, this shop offers plenty of children's furniture and decor that suits the current definition just fine. The selection covers most furniture a child could want, and extends to include some nifty conceptual toys and wall art. Babies can get in on the act with some terrific crib sets and an assortment of mobiles that you might even want to hang up over your bed.

·TOYS & GAMES	·CLOTHES	·FURNITURE	·NURSERY

MurikWebStore.com

Murik Children's Store · 415-395-9200

Though based in San Francisco, this kid's boutique has a direct line to Northern Europe, which for some reason excels in children's fashions. The result includes an unusually stylish selection of clothes for children of all ages, plus hats, underwear, shoes and, not surprisingly, a decent selection of cold weather attire. The site itself has a few quirks that prevent us from calling it user-friendly, but if you shop for clothes by size, you should find everything you like almost immediately.

·CLOTHES	·ACCESSORIES		

888-444-5500 · Informal Education Products

MuseumTour.com

This site simply offers "educational toys and museum gifts that stimulate curiosity, provide aesthetic pleasure and enhance the joy of learning," and like the word *museum* itself, this makes it sound much duller than it actually is. In essence, these products are the sorts of "hands on" toys, games and science kits that intrigue children of all ages at the best science and educational museums in the country. This is a great place to find wondrous family activities across a broad spectrum of subjects, including art, history and physical fitness, as well as a few things that are just plain fun.

| ·TOYS & GAMES | ·BOOKS & MEDIA | ·EDUCATIONAL | ·RECREATION | |

800-409-2457 · Music For Little People

MusicForLittlePeople.com

They say Mozart composed his first piece of music at the age of five. While we don't propose you put such pressures on your budding virtuoso, if you would like to support your youngster's early interest in music, this proves a great site to visit. With a lovely selection of kid-size instruments including guitars, keyboards, drums and harps, you'll find plenty of options (earplugs sold separately). If your child's musical interest is not so ambitious, a deep catalog of kid-friendly recordings may also be found, along with the occasional imaginative toys, which are quieter if less educational.

| ·TOYS & GAMES | ·BOOKS & MEDIA | ·EDUCATIONAL | ·RECREATION | |

310-383-8343 · My Little Child

MyLittleChild.com

When it comes to toys your toddler or small child can sit on or pull, this site's got all the other ones beat. There are plenty of pedal-powered cars and airplanes, a bunch of little red wagons, some tricycles, bicycle caddies and some adorable rocking chairs. However, the best selection has to be in the Rocking Toys category, where you'll find rocking circus animals, cars, airplanes, trains, jeeps and even motorcycles. Yes, you'll find a few rocking horses mixed in, but isn't a rocking zebra even better?

| ·TOYS & GAMES | ·FURNITURE | | |  |

561-386-2243 · My LittleDucks

MyLittleDucks.com

Just like in the female-dominated grown-up apparel market, clothing retailers usually pay more attention to little girl's fashions than they do boys'. Not so with this all-guy site. It focuses entirely on clothes and accessories for males, whether they be infants, toddlers, little boys or daddies looking for a masculine diaper bag. This alone might make the site stand out, but rest assured, it's the cute, affordable selection that you'll remember the most.

| ·CLOTHES | | | | |

Natalys.fr

Natalys · 011-33-147-24-6262

If you speak French, the infant and toddler attire found on this French retail chain will seem extra special; otherwise, look to the bottom of the home page to link to the English version of the site. You almost don't need to, though, as the appeal of these precious European garments speaks for itself. The finely tailored outfits range from provincial style to hipper, more sophisticated fashions, dressing little boys and girls so adorably that photo ops will become a daily routine. Translating exchange rates and transatlantic shipping costs could prove a bit complicated, but to find clothes like this it's worth it.

·CLOTHES			

NaturinoLosGatos.com

Naturino Los Gatos · 877-236-6830

Like a baby taking its first tenuous steps, this colorful and playful site doesn't always seem quite balanced, but once you get a look at its fantastic selection of European children's shoe brands such as Naturino, Moschino and Oilily, you'll see it's nicely up and running. Wading through the entire site may net you some cool clothes and the odd child's accessory, but we'd suggest sticking to shoes, socks, tights and hair accessories for starters.

·CLOTHES	·ACCESSORIES	

NetKidsWear.com

Childrenswear Centre · 732-203-9677

By the name, you might think this site caters to older children; however, the real focus here is babies. In particular, it proves an excellent site to visit when putting together your baby's room, as the top-notch selection of cribs, baby bedding, gliders, rockers, mobiles, bassinets, cradles and other imperative nursery items is virtually unmatched, online or off. New parents will also benefit from a bevy of baby health and safety supplies; ensuring you'll come back in a couple of years to peruse the terrific children's beds and ride-on toys.

·TOYS & GAMES ·NURSERY	·CLOTHES ·BABY NECESSITIES	·FURNITURE	·HEALTH & SAFETY

NeuroToys.com

NeuroToys · 303-772-6271

If you know a child who gets excited at the mention of robots or dinosaurs, imagine how excited that kid might get at the notion of building robot dinosaurs. This is a perfect site when shopping for such scientific and curious children, as it focuses on building, mechanical and electronics kits like Erector and Robotix sets that help develop a better understanding of circuit boards and engineering. Of course, this stuff may be way over our heads, but that's why they don't market it to adults.

·TOYS & GAMES	·EDUCATIONAL		

401-783-6632 · NonchalantMom

NonchalantMom.com

This hip baby retailer is relatively new to the game, but its great beginnings hold the promise much more to come. Already it offers a cool assortment of interesting designers such as Lucky Wang, Marimekko, Erica Tanov and Splendid, which promise "no frills or chills, just clothing for children that match your nonchalant lifestyle." It's still small and thus fairly simple to browse, and with quality apparel at such reasonable prices, now is the time to peruse one of the web's brightest recent additions.

| ·TOYS & GAMES | ·CLOTHES | | | |

877-543-2665 · Oliebollen

Oliebollen.com

When they were handing out domain names, it seems this seller of "cool things for kids" was last in line. But with excellent design, wacky presentation and amusing illustrations, this site named for a Dutch fried pastry (literally translated, "oil flour balls") won't soon be forgotten. Its proprietor, "a former stay-at-home mom with a stubborn addiction to childish living," is intent on avoiding second-rate mass-market items, offering only handpicked toys, books, clothes and accessories of the highest quality. Such classic titles as *Good Night, Gorilla* or *The Stinky Cheese Man* are for sale in the Books section; you'll find fresh, modern furnishings in Home Goods; or just get caught up in our favorite section: Hip Toys.

| ·TOYS & GAMES ·ACCESSORIES | ·CLOTHES ·NURSERY | ·FURNITURE ·BABY NECESSITIES | ·BOOKS & MEDIA | |

011-852-9220-9330 · OnaToko Company

OnaToko.com

Have you seen what girls are wearing on the streets of Seoul and Tokyo this year? Maybe it's time to pay attention. This Asian Pacific specialty shop is devoted to the fashion-forward thinking of Eastern pop culture, which definitely has its own distinct take on modern couture. Not that it's a world so far removed from our own—they follow many of the same celebrities and magazines as we do—but more interesting than the overlap is the opportunity to see what sort of fresh looks a different worldview can respond with. This one never gets boring.

| ·CLOTHES | ·ACCESSORIES | | |  |

800-344-8894 · One of a Kind Kid

OneOfAKindKid.com

If other children keep showing up in the same clothes as your one-of-a-kind child, it may be time to switch to this impressively comprehensive online boutique. Aside from having unique selections, they have incredibly deep varieties of apparel for children and babies of all sizes, so it would take a remarkable coincidence to see the same garments on a neighbor's kid. However, there's some fantastic furniture here as well, including an outstanding variety of rocking chairs, beds and the most interesting cribs we've seen (one of them is round!). We tend to think of boutiques as being small, but this one can keep you shopping for days on end.

| ·CLOTHES | ·SUNDAY BEST | ·FURNITURE | ·NURSERY | |

OrientExpressed.com

Orient Expressed Imports · 888-856-3948

The schoolteachers behind this wonderful Louisiana retail shop first started selling clothes to help finance a vacation to the Far East back in the late seventies, and the business has since blossomed into one of the best deals in children's and toddlers' clothing. When you consider just how many hours of labor go into each of the hand smocked and embroidered garments found here, the price tag will stun you. Even if you don't think about it, the costs of these beautiful fun-time and special-occasion clothes seem reasonable enough that you'll buy a lot of them.

·CLOTHES	·SUNDAY BEST		

PBTeen.com

Pottery Barn Teen · 866-472-4001

The Pottery Barn catalog isn't for everyone, but with the addition of this youth-oriented shop, it's for a few more people at least. What makes this merchandise teen furniture and decor as opposed to adult furniture and decor is entirely subjective. Suffice to say this stuff is a lot more colorful, and often less expensive than "adult" furniture (but there's no saying your friends will notice if you do a little shopping for your "grown-up" apartment). This evolving selection seems to be for more people than it may have intended.

·FURNITURE			

PetraToysUSA.com

Petra Toys · 908-862-3277

Those on the hunt for a different sort of toy store will find it with this site, which boasts "over 300 nostalgia toys mostly imported from Europe." This includes a broad assortment of wooden toys and jigsaw puzzles, but for the most part what should draw you here is a love of puppets. In imaginative hands, this selection of hand puppets, finger puppets, cone puppets and marionettes will delight young children and, complemented with various puppet theaters and props, will provide older children with hours of creative amusement that sock puppets just can't compete with.

·TOYS & GAMES			

PhysLink.com

PhysLink.com · 888-300-4561

While the term *physical science* may invoke memories of geodes and the excessive yawning associated with geodes, this site might just change your perception about how interesting and entertaining natural phenomena can be. More important, the eStore of this site can inspire your kids to embrace the many splendors of science. We found plenty of fun, educational sets with intriguing names like: Make Your Own Bubble Gum, the Sumo Robot Kit, the Human Powered Light Bulb and several Levitating Globes (hint: they involve magnets). Now don't you wish you'd stayed awake in high school?

·TOYS & GAMES	·EDUCATIONAL		

877-294-7079 · Piccolini Online

PiccoliniOnline.com

If you're looking for proof that modern design doesn't have to be cold and impersonal, look no further than this baby-gear retailer that offers hip, urban styles that prove just as fun as your tot. The Pennsylvania boutique offers a fantastic web presence, fully showing its "commitment to creating a warm environment for children and their parents coupled with great design, style and dependability." High-concept mobiles, sleek nursery furniture, surprisingly fashionable baby slings, hilarious onesies, organic clothes and the funkiest selection of plush toys anywhere give you plenty of reasons to visit, and more than enough incentive to come back again and again.

·BABY NECESSITIES ·CLOTHES ·FURNITURE ·NURSERY ·TOYS & GAMES

WISH

831-425-4441 · Pink Taffy Designs

PinkTaffyDesigns.com

This family-owned e-boutique "was created with an inspiration to design magical nurseries and bedrooms." The resulting hand-picked selection is sure to delight any indulgent parent with a surprisingly wide range of lavish baby gear, including some adorable bibs, hooded towels, Moses baskets, crib bedding and nursery decor. If extravagances like satin/chenille and silk brocade baby blankets don't get you, the extraordinarily pretty, hand-painted cribs might. Just make sure there's room on your credit card first.

·TOYS & GAMES ·CLOTHES ·FURNITURE ·ACCESSORIES
·NURSERY

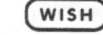

WISH

718-428-1018 · PlatesPlus for Kids

PlatesPlus4Kids.com

You wouldn't serve a children's dinner party with your fine china, but that doesn't mean a special set of plates isn't appropriate. This site specializes in novelty dinner sets, featuring plenty of popular cartoon personalities like Dora the Explorer, Bob the Builder, Jimmy Neutron, Kim Possible, Scooby Doo, SpongeBob, Winnie the Pooh and Mickey Mouse. Of course, these are merely a fraction of the colorful characters available, either in plate form or in the assortment of backpacks and lunch boxes also offered by this peculiar and very vibrant specialty shop.

·FURNITURE

WISH

530-274-7179 · Pokkadots

PokkaDots.com

If you feel like looking at cute pictures of babies, check out this site. While you're here, you might also glance at all of the darling baby things, mostly clothes and toys, with a few skin care products to round out the selection. Cuteness definitely reigns here, however, and it's tough to tell whether this stuff will make your baby more adorable or the other way around. Suffice it to say, when you put the two together, the result will be plenty of photo opportunities.

·TOYS & GAMES ·CLOTHES ·HEALTH & SAFETY ·ACCESSORIES

PolkaDotWhale.com

For baby gift shopping that neither takes a long time nor scrimps on variety, check this homegrown purveyor of "classic and contemporary, unique, handcrafted and heart-felt baby gifts that put the joy back into the task of carefully selecting and giving." Even something so simple as a baby blanket can provide terrific shopping on a site filled with a huge pastel variety, and if you would like to go a step further a great variety of picture frames, booties, layette and bath products may also be found. Or just select one of the fantastic gift sets and be certain to please any new parent with a moment's notice.

	·CLOTHES	·SUNDAY BEST	·ACCESSORIES	

PoshTots.com

Boasting "the most extraordinary children's furnishings in the world," this site backs up its claims and then some. Quite simply, you will not believe the tremendous imagination and quality of this furniture, which includes items that appear straight out of a storybook, such as a carrot-shaped dresser, the biggest selection of tuffets you'll ever see and a Fantasy Coach bed that seems apt to turn back into a pumpkin any minute. If you don't find the fanciful furniture eye-popping, the prices will certainly do the trick; but then, stuff this good is only affordable in fairy tales.

	·TOYS & GAMES	·FURNITURE		

PoutyChild.com

A pouting child is rarely fun, but this San Diego boutique has something a little different in mind. With a wide assortment of terrific designer accessories and apparel for kids and tots, any pouting here would be the sort a model uses to look hip on the catwalk. Fortunately, your youngsters will look great regardless of mood, as these remarkable clothes have been culled from some of the best and most popular children design brands. Swimwear, shoes and hats complement an extensive selection of clothing for newborns on up through tweeners, and your kids will never look more fashionable.

	·CLOTHES	·ACCESSORIES		

Prom-Dresses.com

History, tradition, peer counseling and common sense all tell us that finding the right dress for the prom is going to be a nightmare, or at least a very expensive headache. Hopefully, this site can stave off some of the difficulty, offering a decent assortment of simple, contemporary designs. If a girl doesn't find a great prom dress on this site, at the very least you can get an idea of what sort of look she's after, and roughly what it should cost. Or, you might just luck out, and this site will do the trick. Either way, consider it practice for finding the right wedding dress.

	·CLOTHES	·SUNDAY BEST		

866-478-7738 · Puppet Universe

PuppetUniverse.com

It's a puppets' world, and we just live in it. At least, it seems that way when you log on to this terrific specialty retailer offering more puppets than you could shake a stick at… or over. Hand puppets, finger puppets and marionettes all get special treatment, divvied up into different subcategories like Cartoon Characters, Farm Animals, Mythical Creatures and Zoo Animals. Shopping, then, becomes almost as entertaining as playing with these puppets, though not quite as much fun as watching your children respond to them.

 ·TOYS & GAMES

800-728-6009 · Quality Trading

QualityInflatables.com

Summertime fun involves a lot of backyard watersports, and whether you have a pool, want a pool or will settle for some lawn sprayer games, check out this site for a wide assortment of beat-the-heat options. Inflatable swimming pools and pool toys make up the bulk of the selection, some of them proving to be as fun for adults as they are for children. But a bright variety of sprinkler toys and slip'n'slides offer low-budget options that will keep your kids splashing and squealing happily until the next school session starts.

·FURNITURE ·RECREATION

212-534-7477 · Rachel Riley

RachelRiley.com

Anglophiles take note: the proper English child may be well outfitted by this British line of dapper apparel, even if that child happens to be American. Follow the US Store link of this site to enter the prim world of velvet cardigans, tweed pea coats, classic pajamas, herringbone blazers, quilted pinafores, baby bonnets and short trousers. You may browse the assorted high-quality, smocked and embroidered knits by infant, child and teen sizes, then sort by color to match the various browns, reds and blues. Good show!

·CLOTHES ·SUNDAY BEST

800-589-5085 · Rags Land

RagsLand.com

Offering "styles to suit any occasion embellished with custom smocking, appliqué, and embroidery," this Louisiana clothing label specializes in the sorts of preppy and traditional apparel you might more commonly associate with Great Britain or the Northeast US. However, aside from the occasional "additional shipping charge" attached to smocked garments and patterned sweaters, you'll find better prices among these baby and children's clothes. You'll also find a fantastic selection of play clothes, as well as arts-and-crafts kits, imaginative play toys, plush toys and adorable layette items.

·TOYS & GAMES ·RECREATION ·CLOTHES ·ACCESSORIES ·SUNDAY BEST ·EDUCATIONAL

RainBee.com

RainBee.com · 877-724-6233

Featuring brand names such as Munki Munki and HM Woggle Bug, there's a distinct possibility that shopping from this all-children's retailer can get confusing. While the navigation for the site has generally improved, it still can't quite keep up with the wide range of products available, which is a shame, because it turns out the above oddly named brands and the others offered here make some pretty fine and fun clothes, accessories, toys, educational materials, furniture and decor, along with some indispensable parenting tools, also known as pacifiers.

·TOYS & GAMES ·ACCESSORIES	·CLOTHES ·NURSERY	·FURNITURE ·BABY NECESSITIES	·EDUCATIONAL

RawSugarOnline.com

Raw Sugar · 866-867-8427

A lot of clothes will make your little ones look cute, whereas this site gives you the option to dress your infant or young child to look hip as well. Founded to provide an alternative to the mass-produced child's fashions manufactured by national chain retailers, this store instead seeks out upcoming local designers and their wares. Consequently, the quality of selection varies, but if you View All within each category you may quickly browse through dresses, t-shirts, sweaters and pants to outfit your urban youngster in style.

·CLOTHES			

RedWagons.com

Red Wagons · 708-366-7700

The little red wagon is a mainstay of American childhoods, and if you wish to pass the tradition on to your child, the particular devotion of this shop to the full line of Radio Flyer models will allow you to choose between traditional and cargo wagon designs, as well as from a slew of modern innovations involving plastic, canopies, all-terrain wheels and bed pads. Whichever you decide on, the fun will be in watching how your son or daughter puts his or her own imaginative twist on playing with a classic toy.

·TOYS & GAMES			

Robeez.com

Robeez Footwear · 800-929-2649

If you're looking at a site that sells no product other than baby shoes, it better be one terrific site. This one is. An immense and truly inspired variety of soft-soled leather shoes and slippers for infants and toddlers will have parents reaching for their credit cards faster than a kid can get into trouble. With colorful, often cartoonish designs and exceptional quality, these baby booties are something special, so much so that we won't be able to do them justice just writing about them; you'll have to take a look for yourself.

·ACCESSORIES			

818-769-5563 · RoboToys

RoboToys.com

Robots have come a long way since the first steam-powered man was built in 1865, but nowhere have they been made so accessible to children of all ages than this robo-dedicated retailer. Featured are robot models, robot toys, robot science kits, robot pets and, perhaps most importantly, robot appliances designed to take household work out of your hands. Sadly, as of this writing, the latter group consists mostly of vacuums. But that's okay—you have children to do the housework, and plenty of robot toys available here to offer as a reward.

·TOYS & GAMES

813-972-9090 · Casam

Rockimals.com

A classic children's toy gets the royal treatment with this rocking horse specialty site. You'll find beautiful, built-to-order, hand-carved horses, along with less-expensive personalized options, molded carousel models, wooden horses and plush varieties. Of course, another benefit of such a site is that you don't have to stick to horses at all. A thorough assortment of rocking toys includes dogs, elephants, pigs, bears, boats, trucks and cars. Price options exist in as much variety as the designs, textures and colors here, and whichever toy you settle on it's guaranteed to rock.

·TOYS & GAMES

866-967-6667 · Rosenberry Rooms

RosenberryRooms.com

Do not miss this site if you are planning a nursery, upgrading your nursery to a kid's bedroom or have any interest whatsoever in sprucing up you children's environment. With the absolute best selection of nursery and children's decor, this shop's focus on the "world of imagination, fantasy and make-believe" makes it a must-see destination for any parents who wish to make their little ones' bedroom or playroom a magical place. You'll find competitive assortments of furniture and bedding, but the real treat will be all the wall hangings, growth charts, decorative hardware, bathroom accents, clocks, lighting and rugs. You can't lose.

·FURNITURE ·ACCESSORIES ·NURSERY

800-598-8911 · Safe Beginnings

SafeBeginnings.com

Your baby will spend the vast majority of its infancy in the home, so you'll want to make it as safe a place as possible. You can get rid of all your furniture and possessions, pad the walls, put down safety mats and clean everything with a soft, wet towel, or you can be sensible about it and shop from this site. Specializing in home safety products, with a few travel safety products tossed in for good measure, the shop offers safety gates, corner cushions, electrical outlet covers, cabinet locks and more to keep harm out of a crawling and toddling child's way.

·HEALTH & SAFETY ·BABY NECESSITIES

SandPailKids.com

Summertime brings all kinds of fun for parents and children, a good portion of which will require bathing suits. This swimsuit-dedicated site offers plenty to work with for all ages of child, from infant to preteen. Sun protection swimsuits, floating swimsuits and swim diapers add to an already comprehensive assortment of cute and colorful trunks, one-pieces, bikinis and sarongs. Shopping proves quite easy despite the fact this may be the largest collection of suits you see in or out of season.

·TOYS & GAMES	·CLOTHES	·ACCESSORIES	

Sanrio.com

If you're not already well acquainted with Hello Kitty, this is your chance to move along before you get caught up in something big. Everyone else, brace yourselves, because you're about to enter the source. The shockingly popular Japanese icon may even turn up on more merchandise here than you would have thought. Sure, there are the expected Kitty-laden backpacks, pencil cases, address books, wallets, stickers and key rings aplenty. But you'll also find Hello Kitty mobile phones, alarm clocks, aluminum foil and hundreds of other, curious pastel pink items. There's no going back now.

·TOYS & GAMES	·FURNITURE	·ACCESSORIES	

SensationalBeginnings.com

Brandishing "toys and tools that celebrate the wonders of childhood," this catalog features "products for infants and toddlers that stimulate their senses while promoting interaction between parent and child." It's really not as dull as it sounds, though it may seem so if you use the navigational tabs at the top of the page (probably the first to catch your eye). Instead, if you stick to Shop by Age or Shop by Category, you'll find a vibrant, fun selection of stuff endorsed by a nurse (even if she is the site's founder). Better yet, shop here in the months preceding Halloween and find the best children's costume selection going.

·TOYS & GAMES ·RECREATION	·FURNITURE ·HEALTH & SAFETY	·BOOKS & MEDIA	·EDUCATIONAL

Showroom64.com

"The hottest and hippest baby clothes" are to be had from this chic London baby boutique that's probably best known for its "chunky gift boxes" and celebrity clientele. However, with cheeky tees, onesies, and bibs; personalized knit caps and a small but delicious assortment of cashmere items, gift ideas certainly abound for shoppers of any price range, even if you prefer to assemble and wrap them yourself. Shopping should be a snap, regardless—all you need to do is keep an eye out for the View All link.

·CLOTHES	·ACCESSORIES		

800-852-3769 · **Shiny Things**

Sparkability.com

Fed up with finding "cheap, plastic, throw-away products" when shopping for their kids, the founders of this shop set about assembling a catalog where parents could find a "cohesive collection" of "inspiring designs." They did an excellent job. While there's not enough here to please everyone, the site does offer some amazing hand-selected items for infants and young children, ranging from a bevy of great mobiles to some brilliant furniture and what may be the best assortment of ride-on toys you'll ever see. Shop here for some special children's gifts.

·TOYS & GAMES ·BABY NECESSITIES	·FURNITURE	·ACCESSORIES	·NURSERY	

805-557-0779 · **Speedydog Corporation**

SpeedyDog.net

Many of us grew up with ant farms, or with bugs we captured and put into a jar, and sure, it was illuminating, even educational. Only when you get a look at the products available on this "best science toys and gizmos" site will you realize how much more fun you could have been having. Here, an ant farm comes standard, but you may also opt for an Xtreme Ant Farm, an Ant Village or a Giant Ant Farm. It gets better. You'll find a Bug Town to replace that jar, or a small replica beach (complete with surfboard) where you may raise a tadpole to a frog. The concept is applied to aquariums so that your pet fish may appear to be swimming in space or around a volcano. It almost makes a pet dog seem boring.

·TOYS & GAMES	·EDUCATIONAL			

800-392-8739 · **S4K**

StoreForKnowledge.com

Beginning with life-size models of dinosaur skeletons, this educational kid's shop repeatedly demonstrates a capacity to dazzle even the most skeptical of learners. You'll find kits devoted to magnets, wildlife, spy gadgets, remote-control toys and robots, as well as some brainteasers and more traditional science sets. Whatever the age, you can impress your child with the phenomena of the natural world, as well as the unmitigated splendor of man-made technology.

·TOYS & GAMES	·EDUCATIONAL			

201-612-8019 · **The Trendy Bébé**

TheTrendyBaby.com

If you prize a great selection above all else, you will love this massive homegrown baby site. Featuring "unique, trendy, hard-to-find baby products" across a number of categories, the dozens and dozens of pages here offer no shortage of items for you to look at, whether you're searching for clothes, blankets, nursery furniture or decor. Then, just when you think you've finally seen all your choices, you'll realize that a great number of these items can be personalized, making this one of the best one-stop gift shops for tots online.

·TOYS & GAMES ·ACCESSORIES	·CLOTHES ·NURSERY	·SUNDAY BEST	·FURNITURE	

TotShop.com

Compiling an assortment of kid and baby clothes and accessories by some of the brightest designers and boutiques from New York City and beyond, this site's savvy selection wins a lot of points for originality and style. You have to understand this, because trying to browse items using the convoluted navigation might frustrate you enough to give up and go somewhere else. If you can stick it out, you will surely be rewarded with a fantastic variety, and in time may even find the perfect gift or garment for the apple of your eye.

	·TOYS & GAMES	·CLOTHES	·ACCESSORIES	·BABY NECESSITIES

Toys2Wish4.com

Most kids wish for a lot of toys, and to such wishes this behemoth toy shop has all the answers. With no fewer than eight subcategories within each of its more than a dozen categories, browsing here can be overwhelming, so it's best to have some idea of the sort of toys you would like to buy going in, whether educational, creative or just plain fun. Otherwise, you can shop by age range, or stick strictly to a category called Award Winners, which is sure to feature toys that somebody liked a lot.

	·TOYS & GAMES	·BOOKS & MEDIA	·EDUCATIONAL	

TuttiBella.com

With a fairly thorough assortment of elaborate, high-quality clothing and accessories for infants and toddlers, this site, which offers "Everything beautiful for baby," definitely excels when it comes to aesthetic appeal. The clothing in particular makes this one of the best baby shops online, a long list of available brands features many you won't readily find elsewhere, including Cakewalk, Charlie Rocket, Zutano and Oink! Look deeper, and you'll find some nursery bedding and decor that meet the same sophisticated standards as the wonderful clothes.

	·CLOTHES ·NURSERY	·SUNDAY BEST	·FURNITURE	·ACCESSORIES

UnderTheNile.com

Bringing a bit of altruism into the manufacture of baby apparel, this green company offers 100 percent cotton clothing and accessories that promise to be all-natural and organic, as well as supportive of free trade practices. Does this mean these wares lack in quality? Definitely not. If you're looking for such basics as cloth diapers, layette, baby blankets, hats and bibs this site will prove a welcome sight on your internet horizon. It even offers a few similarly responsible plush toys that you can trust in your child's mouth.

	·TOYS & GAMES	·CLOTHES	·ACCESSORIES	

877-894-2533 · WickedCoolStuff.com

WickedCoolStuff.com

Teenage boys are notoriously tough to shop for, and while this site may not be a panacea, it offers an approach too radical not to work: it offers products nobody but an adolescent male could possibly love. Bobble-head dolls, obnoxious t-shirts, useless car accessories and novelty items up the wazoo. Nothing will make sense to a parent, no matter how cool (or uncool) you think you are, so your best bet might be to go with a "wicked cool gift certificate…" just don't make the mistake of saying that out loud.

·TOYS & GAMES	·CLOTHES	·ACCESSORIES	

866-463-3563 · Wild Planet Toy Store

WildPlanet.com

Aiming to create "products that spark the imagination," this innovative toymaker has easily hit the mark. Its several distinct lines of toys may be found here, including Waterball & Outdoor Antics Pool Toys, Off The Map Adventure Gear, Battle Crawlers (fighting insect robots) and our favorite, the Spy Gear brand of espionage toy gadgets. You'll also find a little something called SpongeBob SquarePants. Most of this stuff will be appealing to imaginative and rambunctious boys, but it's tough to envision any kid who wouldn't have a blast with any of these toys.

·TOYS & GAMES	·RECREATION		

917-438-9149 · Zac and Zoé

ZacAndZoe.com

Specializing in "timeless, unique pieces that still retain the air of childhood," this small web boutique is "wild over creative pieces," and it shows. Cute, funky and fun nursery furniture, decor and bedding heads up a colorful assortment of baby stuff, while some beds, toys and kiddie work tables play more to the toddler crowd. Great product details will inspire you to shop, while excellent customer service will encourage you to come back time and again for functional items that will keep your children's spirits up.

·TOYS & GAMES	·FURNITURE	·NURSERY	

800-834-9165 · Zebra Hall

ZebraHall.com

This "extraordinary toy shop" truly offers a unique range of toys for your child or toddler, bouncing between classic designs and ingenuity as effortlessly as you may browse these pages. Everything here seems to offer a little bit of style and a lot of fun, covering categories like the Menagerie, Wardrobe and Parlor, which translates to Stuffed Toys, Wearable & Role Play and Games & Puzzles, respectively. A great spot to find a delightful and memorable gift for a clever child, even those aged "10 To Adult."

·TOYS & GAMES	·RECREATION		

NOTES:

Pets

Our affinity for animals can be so fickle. Take rats, for example: some of us keep them as pets, some of us set traps to keep them dead and out of our cereal boxes, yet others of us use them to feed the giant snakes we keep as pets. Increasingly, the distinction drawn between beastly creatures and pets has more to do with how we feel about them than how they feel about us. Yes, we love to turn animals into our own little unconditional friends. Studies even show that people who have pets live longer, happier lives. While cats and dogs remain the most popular pets, birds, reptiles, rodents, fish, horses and even spiders have become veritably commonplace. And you can buy food, health and hygiene products for any of them online, which means you'll never have to shlep that heavy bag of dogfood from your car again.

Of course, if you feel the urge to spoil your pets rotten, there's no better resource than the web. Gourmet treats, superfun toys, palatial doghouses, animal furniture and even fashionable attire make up just a few of the material items we've found to help shower our pets with love. And if yours isn't acting so well behaved, you can find stuff like muzzles, leashes and training supplies that will help you shower it with tough love. Perhaps most important is the tremendous array of health products to be found, which range from prescription medications to all-natural supplements and grooming supplies.

But if we had to pick a favorite category, it would be all the fun items that you can use to form those enduring bonds with the nonverbal members of your family (and parrots, lots of stuff for parrots). Really, if you take a look at everything, you'll eventually come to the same conclusion we have: Noah could have used this section to stock the Ark.

 ## TIPS ON BUYING PET PRODUCTS ONLINE

These suggestions may keep your pet product purchases from coming back to bite you.

• **IS IT EDIBLE?** •Anything you buy for your pets will almost assuredly end up in their mouths at some point; that's why they're called animals. Be careful, then, about buying something that could be harmful if ingested, whether pointy, indigestible or flat-out poisonous.

• **CONSULT A VET** •Sure, there's a bunch of health-related merchandise for your pet, and some fun treats, but as you would for yourself, be sure to consult a licensed medical professional to avoid feeding your animals anything potentially hazardous.

• **ADOPT A PET** •Now that you've got all this access to great stuff, wouldn't it be nice to add another member to your household? Check the Pet Adoption link below, or contact your local Humane Society or animal rescue to save a lovely creature from a lonely, imprisoned peril.

• **IDENTIFY YOUR PET** • Losing a pet is a tough deal for everybody. The easiest way to keep your pet from getting lost forever is keeping it in a collar, which can be bolstered by registering your animal with local agencies. If your pet doesn't like wearing a collar, technology can help, with harmless microchips that can be implanted under the animal's skin, to identity you as your pet's owner.

• **BUY IN BULK** • Purchasing pet items like food and hygiene products in bulk can be cheaper and save you shipping in the long run.

 ## SITES WITH A SINGLE FOCUS
The following sites excel at selling one or two specific products.

ArtPaw.com	Pet portraits
BuyGoDogGo.com	Dog ball-throwing machine
CleanRun.com	Dog agility-training equipment
FancyPaws.com	Pet doors
FenixResearch.com	Pet feeding bowls
GroomersChoice.com	Grooming supplies
PawsAboard.com	Pet boat gear
PetCareInsurance.com	Pet insurance
PetInsurance.com	Pet insurance
SmallDogMall.com	Small dog apparel
TheHonestKitchen.com	Dehydrated pet food
ThreeDog.com	Dog bakery

>> SITES THAT MAY COME IN HANDY

The following URLs may be useful when you shop for certain pet products.

AHVMA.org	Resources for pet holistic medicine
AnimalPlaza.com	Locate dog breeders
AVCADoctors.com	Locate a pet chiropractor
CityDog.net	Guide to dog parks and dog-friendly establishments
DogFocused.com	Locate a dog park
DogFriendly.com	Locate pet-friendly lodging
DogGoneFun.com	Guide to pet-friendly travel
FamilySafety.com	Pet and child safety resource
GreatPets.com	Pet info, resources and communities
IVAS.org	Locate a pet acupuncturist
MyPetStop.com	Pet info, resources and communities
PetFinder.org	Pet adoption
PetPlace.com	Pet health info and vet locator
PetsOnTheGo.com	Pet travel resource
PuppyTravel.com	Pet travel resource
TravelDog.com	Pet travel resource
UrbanPuppy.com	Animal training resource

SECTION ICON LEGEND

Use the following guide to understand the rectangular icons that appear throughout this section.

ALL-NATURAL
If you maintain an all-natural lifestyle, you'll probably want the same for your pet, and there are a lot of options available online. Locate them when you find this icon.

EXOTIC PETS
These sites may or may not include stuff for dogs and cats, but they'll definitely carry supplies for one or more of the following: reptiles, amphibians, insects, critters, fish, birds and then some.

HEALTH
Highlighting products that promote your animal's continued health, this icon covers everything from pet pharmaceuticals to pet health insurance.

PET LUXURIES
You may find plenty of pet products that your animal could do without but are too much fun to pass up. Use this icon to find things like gourmet treats, doggy clothes, squeaky toys and other pet indulgences.

PET NECESSITIES
This icon allows you to locate items you need for pet control, grooming, feeding and housing your pet, whether it's an aquarium, leash, birdseed or more.

LIST OF KEY WORDS

The following words represent the types of items typically found on the sites listed in this section. You will find them listed in the orange strip at the bottom of each entry, as appropriate.

BIRDS	Cages, feed, perches, mirrors and other necessities and accessories for the pet bird.
CATS	Cat stuff includes food, collars, litter boxes, scratching posts, feeding dishes, catnip, cat beds, toys and more.
CRITTERS	Habitat, food and other equipment for small mammals, like gerbils, hamsters, rabbits, mice, guinea pigs and ferrets.
DOGS	Most of these sites cater to dogs, offering collars, leashes, grooming tools, medicine, training gear, pet apparel, doghouses, dog doors, beds, feeding dishes, treats, toys and much more.
EQUIPMENT	Equipment for a variety of pets, including leashes, food dishes, safety barriers, litter boxes, exercise wheels and more.
FISH	All fish-related merchandise, including food, aquarium, filters, etc.
FOOD	Refers to food available for any and all animals.
GROOMING	Grooming items, including brushes, claw clippers, shampoos, etc.
HABITAT	Aquariums, cat beds, doghouses, bird cages, Habitrail tubes and then some.
HORSES	Grooming, tack and stable accessories.
MEDICINE	Refers to over-the-counter and prescription medications for a variety of pets, as indicated.
PET APPAREL	Animal apparel is most commonly available for dogs, though occasionally garments for other animals turn up.
REPTILES	The rarest of pets, reptiles, are only catered to by a few sites, each noted by this key word.
TOYS & TREATS	Most toys and treats are intended for dogs or cats, but occasionally you'll be able to find them for other pets too.
TRAINING & SAFETY	Mainly devices used to train and contain your animals, including leashes, electric fences, household barriers, doggy doors and more.
TRAVEL	Travel items for pets, including small dog carriers, travel crates and the occasional car restraints or outdoors gear.

KEY WORD INDEX

Use the followings lists to locate online retailers that sell the pet products you seek.

GROOMING

BowsaWowsa.com
CallingAllDogs.com
FerretStore.com
GeorgeSF.com
GWLittle.com
HealthyPooch.com
Horse.com
JakesDogHouse.com
LesPoochs.com
McMurrayHatchery.com
NaturalPetMarket.com
PetCareRx.com
PetFoodDirect.com
PetSafe-Warehouse.com
PetVetSupply.com
QuintessentialPet.com
SitStay.com
TheBirdBrain.com
ThePamperedPup.com
TrixieAndPeanut.com
ValleyVet.com
VetAmerica.com

HABITAT

AudubonWorkshop.com
BarkerAndMeowsky.com
BowsaWowsa.com
CallingAllDogs.com
CoolPetStuff.com
DrsFosterSmith.com
ExoticFish.com
FuturePets.com
GeorgeSF.com
GWLittle.com
McMurrayHatchery.com
PetSafe-Warehouse.com
PetsR4U.com
PetStreetMall.com
PostmodernPets.com
QuintessentialPet.com
RexInTheCity.com
SafePets.com
SitStay.com
ThatPetPlace.com
TheBirdBrain.com
ThePamperedPup.com
TrixieAndPeanut.com
ValleyVet.com

HORSES

FuturePets.com
Horse.com
JeffersPet.com
MyPetPrescriptions.com
NaturesPet.com
PetClick.com
PetVetSupply.com
RevivalAnimal.com
UPCO.com
ValleyVet.com
VetAmerica.com

MEDICINE

1800PetMeds.com
DrsFosterSmith.com
FerretStore.com
FuturePets.com
HealthyPooch.com
Horse.com
McMurrayHatchery.com
MyPetPrescriptions.com
NaturalPetMarket.com
NaturesPet.com
PetCareRx.com
PetRx.com
PetVetSupply.com
RevivalAnimal.com
ThatPetPlace.com
TheBirdBrain.com
ValleyVet.com
VetAmerica.com

PET APPAREL

BarkerAndMeowsky.com
BowsaWowsa.com
CallingAllDogs.com
Diva-Dog.com
DogBar.com
GeorgeSF.com
GWLittle.com
JakesDogHouse.com
MrsBones.com
QuintessentialPet.com
RexInTheCity.com
SitStay.com
ThePamperedPup.com
TrixieAndPeanut.com

REPTILES

CoolPetStuff.com
DrsFosterSmith.com
FuturePets.com
JeffersPet.com
PetFoodDirect.com
PetsR4U.com
PetStreetMall.com
ThatPetPlace.com
UPCO.com

TOYS & TREATS

AdvancedPetProducts.com
BarkerAndMeowsky.com
BowsaWowsa.com
CallingAllDogs.com
CatToys.com
CleanRun.com
DogBar.com
GeorgeSF.com
GWLittle.com
JakesDogHouse.com
Lafeber.com
LesPoochs.com
NaturalPetMarket.com
NaturesPet.com
PetSafe-Warehouse.com
PetVetSupply.com
SitStay.com
ThePamperedPup.com
TrixieAndPeanut.com
ValleyVet.com

TRAINING & SAFETY

CleanRun.com
FerretStore.com
GWLittle.com
Horse.com
MightyPets.com
PetCareRx.com
PetClick.com
PetProvide.com
PetSafe-Warehouse.com
PetStreetMall.com
PetTags.com
PetVetSupply.com
RevivalAnimal.com
SafePets.com
SitStay.com
UPCO.com
ValleyVet.com
VetAmerica.com
YourActivePet.com

TRAVEL

BowsaWowsa.com
CallingAllDogs.com
CleanRun.com
DogBar.com
FerretStore.com
GeorgeSF.com
GWLittle.com
PetSafe-Warehouse.com
PostmodernPets.com
QuintessentialPet.com
TheBirdBrain.com
ThePamperedPup.com
TravelinPets.com
TrixieAndPeanut.com
UPCO.com
YourActivePet.com

1800PetMeds.com

1-800-PetMeds · 800-738-6337

"America's Largest Pet Pharmacy" turns out a pretty good web site here. With a bevy of nonprescription medicines and some vaccines that should preclude use of prescription drugs, caring for your hypochondriac pet just got a little easier and a whole lot cheaper. The Online Catalog pull-down menu makes it easy to shop for specific needs such as Anxiety Relief, First Aid and Odor Control. But there are a lot of prescription-only products here as well, and you should definitely visit the vet before treating any ailment that's hindering your animal's quality of life.

	·DOGS	·CATS	·MEDICINE	

AdvancedPetProducts.com

Advanced Pet Products · 800-982-1906

If you browsed our Gadgets & Electronics section and felt that your pet was left out, check out this site. It offers only a couple of products (the tech gadget market is still catching up to the animal kingdom), but what you will find is at least worth checking out. Take, for example, a remote-control cat toy that lets you play with your feline without getting off the sofa (your cat wishes it could do the same). But the most intriguing gizmo here has to be the Bow-Lingual dog translator, which alleges to analyze the emotional nuances of your pet's barks to interpret their meaning. Hard to tell if it's accurate, but you know what they say: "Woof woof, growl, arf."

	·DOGS	·CATS	·TOYS & TREATS	

AudubonWorkshop.com

Audubon Workshop · 812-537-3583

Birds seem to be everywhere, all the time, flying all over the world and back and, occasionally, right through your backyard. What this essentially means is that you don't need a cage to enjoy their beauty and music, just a backyard feeder and the right ingredients to attract the ones you like. What better group could there be to help you attract birds to your home than the Audubon Society? The group's web site acts as a shop and information source for dedicated and casual birdwatchers alike; just spend a few sessions here and you'll be able to view wild birds as the pets you never had.

	·BIRDS	·EQUIPMENT	·HABITAT	

BarkerAndMeowsky.com

Barker & Meowsky · 773-868-0200

The name, and even the home page, seems to imply that this site caters to cats as well as dogs. But the small online pet boutique out of Chicago didn't feature any kitty products we could find. The one exception might be the Collars & Leashes section, which is the best part of the shop overall, with a broad variety of colors and materials and, yes, a few collars for small dogs that would probably fit a feline. Other notable offerings include better-than-average food and water dishes, assuredly tasty treats (some have apparently been tasted by the shop's human staff) and some novelty chew toys that are funny enough to turn your pooch into a pet comedian.

·DOGS ·PET APPAREL	·EQUIPMENT	·HABITAT	·TOYS & TREATS

818-997-8916 · Bowsa Wowsa

BowsaWowsa.com

Here's a Los Angeles-based boutique that was founded by a pair of canine-friendly aesthetes, which means that all of the hand-picked selection has been creatively conceived and/or is pleasing to the eye, whether it's a chew toy, dog bed or grooming tool. Of course, there's a precious element to it as well, with doggy-size sleeping bags and tee shirts that say things like "I'm a lover, not a biter." In all the world, there's at least one spot where the world of dog lovers and the world of art lovers overlap, and this is it.

·DOGS ·TOYS & TREATS	·EQUIPMENT ·GROOMING	·HABITAT ·PET APPAREL	·TRAVEL	

800-965-8596 · Calling All Dogs, Inc.

CallingAllDogs.com

If pampering your dog is a priority, take a look at the extraordinarily indulgent range of products available from this well-stocked site. Canopied beds may be found, as well as sweaters, cedar doghouses, jewelry, chenille robes, elevated dog bowls and spa products. While the page design is inconsistent, it's not too difficult to use, and you might even be able to browse for functional items, like the wonderful selection of travel equipment. Not to worry, not all of this stuff is strictly utilitarian. Some of it is designer travel equipment.

·DOGS ·TOYS & TREATS	·EQUIPMENT ·GROOMING	·HABITAT ·PET APPAREL	·TRAVEL	

877-364-8697 · CatToys.com

CatToys.com

There are several clear advantages to buying your cat toys from this niche retailer, the most obvious of which is selection. But a great shopping experience requires more than just tossing a bunch of products on a web page, and this site's great success stems from its incredibly well conceived browsing options. The first involves shopping by specific breed, ranging from Abyssinian to York Chocolate, while others guide you through several types of Toys (such as mouse or feather) and Treats. Our favorite is the Personality menu, which features toys catering to various kitty character traits such as Extremely Active, Couch Potato and Insists on Playing at Night. It might be nice if adult toys were arranged in such a way.

·CATS	·TOYS & TREATS			

800-311-6503 · Clean Run

CleanRun.com

Want your dog to be the type seen lunging headlong through the air to catch a Frisbee in its mouth, but it's more inclined to lie in the grass and chew on flowers? This site's products are aimed specifically at increasing your pooch's agility, with both training programs and equipment designed to push the limits of its speed and flexibility. Playing with this stuff will probably be the most fun your pet will have all day, and you may even find yourself getting some exercise in the process. What's more, the Store here is a great source of variable-length leads, as well as different sizes/types of balls and Frisbees, to really get those tired dogs leaping.

·DOGS ·TRAINING & SAFETY	·EQUIPMENT	·TRAVEL	·TOYS & TREATS	

CoolPetStuff.com

According to this site, "cool is a clever new design or idea to make the time you spend with your pet even more fun," and we think the family-owned and -operated web shop is onto something. Plenty of memorable products for dogs, cats, fish, birds and critters sit alongside a whole lot of the essential ones that make caring for these pets possible. However, at times the limitations of a homegrown business avail themselves, so you'll wind up shopping elsewhere for the boring stuff and just come here for the fun.

·DOGS ·CRITTERS	·CATS ·FISH	·BIRDS ·EQUIPMENT	·REPTILES ·HABITAT

Diva-Dog.com

This site proudly proclaims its dedication "to creating stylish leather dog collars and accessories for your favorite obsession, your best friend, the reason you get up at 6:30 in the rain." With collar categories like Cowhide, Ribbon, Colorful and Lizard, you can be sure the products are top-notch, and large images do their best to show the quality is in the details. If you do shop here, the more recent addition of mink collars and doggy coats beg the question: is your doggy really the diva in this scenario, or are you?

·DOGS	·PET APPAREL		

DogBar.com

Beyond its cartoonish façade, this Florida pet shop describes itself as a "24-hour luxury online pet department store featuring the finest and most unusual dog and cat products the world has to offer." Indeed, some of its wares are quite charming, including some amusing doggy graphic tees and a better-than-average selection of beds and feeding dishes. However, we like it for dog food, treats and toys, which are incredibly easy to find and found in great variety. Interpret this site as you will; it's definitely worth a look.

·DOGS ·TRAVEL	·CATS ·TOYS & TREATS	·EQUIPMENT ·PET APPAREL	·FOOD

DoggieFood.com

Although the concept is simple enough for even your doggy to understand, the pages themselves can be a little confusing. But if any such thing as quality dog food exists, it is probably stocked by this massive dog gourmet pet food specialist. A variety of kibble, mixes, treats and supplements are scattered haphazardly across the home page, where they occasionally lead to deep selections and sometimes don't. If you have something specific in mind or time to browse, you'll discover any number of healthy alternatives or additions to your dog's diet, just don't look for it in the shop's index.

·DOGS	·FOOD		

800-381-7179 · Doctors Foster & Smith

DrsFosterSmith.com

If you find the expert advice of veterinarians reassuring when shopping for your pet, this site may be the web's best destination for animal health supplies. Judging by this selection, you can treat many mild illnesses and ailments yourself, including some simple vaccinations. Aside from medicine, the Drs. Foster and Smith have selected products to cover everything from pet furniture to treats and toys, meaning all of your pet's basic needs may be accompanied with a pro recommendation; valuable enough even if these pros do happen to own the store.

·DOGS ·CRITTERS	·CATS ·FISH	·BIRDS ·MEDICINE	·REPTILES ·HABITAT	

888-442-3474 · Jeff's Exotic Fish

ExoticFish.com

We've looked long and hard for a really good pet fish site, and when we found this one we looked at it long and hard. However, despite the less-than-ideal navigation, we found everything we could possibly hope for in online fish sales and more. Specifically, these guys actually offer to ship some of the world's beautiful, exotic species of fish, coral and other sea life to your doorstep. Sure, it's a scary, and quite expensive prospect, and impossible to guarantee something shipped alive will still be that way when you open the box, but some of these pictures may be enticing enough that you'll want to try. Just make sure you order and set up the proper habitat for your animals before they arrive.

·FISH	·EQUIPMENT	·HABITAT		

888-833-7738 · FerretStore.com

FerretStore.com

Just when you think, "Hey, it's about time ferrets got their own store, devoted exclusively to the fuzzy little rodents," the first thing you notice on the home page is, "We're not just for ferrets!" Yes, it's true; while ferrets definitely get the special treatment on this site, all of your typical pets are also represented: dogs, cats, birds, other critters, reptiles, hermit crabs… you name it. Each category is very thoroughly organized, which may lead you to believe the selection is wider than it actually is. But if you don't like to be bogged down by excessively luxurious options your pet won't even appreciate, this turns out to be a good one-stop shop for just about any animal's essentials.

·DOGS ·MEDICINE	·CATS ·TRAVEL	·BIRDS ·GROOMING	·CRITTERS ·TRAINING & SAFETY	

888-738-3976 · FuturePets.com

FuturePets.com

Shopping for your dog or cat from this endlessly detailed pet superstore can be an all-day affair—while the site features thousands of useful items, a lefthand menu stretches way down each section alphabetically by brand name and/or very specific product type. However, if you're shopping for fish, birds, reptiles, horses, ferrets or other critters, you'll find the overwhelming selection to be something special as these animals are typically underrepresented in online stores. Fish sections are even divided between standard aquarium species and those allowed to swim free in ponds; we can only wish every section was so handily dedicated.

·CATS ·HORSES	·BIRDS ·FISH	·REPTILES ·MEDICINE	·CRITTERS ·HABITAT	

GeorgeSF.com

George · 877-322-3232

We don't normally associate words like *gingham*, *corduroy*, *organic* or *leather* with pet shops, but this is no ordinary pet shop. The fine range of functional products found on this cleanly designed site prove that dogs and cats can live stylishly as well, and some of the food dishes, pet beds and grooming equipment may even match your home's decorative sensibilities. Also to be found are healthy treats, sophisticated ID tags, some funky dog sweaters and toys that you'll never find obnoxious. With the help of this San Francisco retailer, you can love your pet without being overly cute about it.

·DOGS ·TRAVEL	·CATS ·TOYS & TREATS	·EQUIPMENT ·GROOMING	·HABITAT ·PET APPAREL

GWLittle.com

G.W. LITTLE · 866-495-4885

If you're looking for the type of small-dog boutique that features product categories such as Ultrasuede and Celebrity Dog, you just found it. The terrific upscale doggy lifestyles catalog delivers on its promise to provide the "finest pet couture" with products such as canopy dog beds, shea butter conditioner, crystal tiara hairclips, faux mink doggy purses and cashmere collars. The great thing is, though, it also offers some good quality functional items, like canine car seats and weight management plans, so you can shop here for their own good but come away with something indulgent as well. Talk about class!

·DOGS ·TOYS & TREATS	·EQUIPMENT ·GROOMING	·HABITAT ·PET APPAREL	·TRAVEL ·TRAINING & SAFETY

HealthyPooch.com

Mountain Skies · 800-738-7883

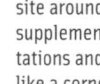

It's tough enough these days to know what's healthy for humans, let alone animals, so we're grateful to have this dog-and-cat site around to make keeping your pet feeling fine relatively easy. Follow the Go Shopping link to access a simple menu of food, supplements, shampoos, salves, medicines and other treatments intended to tackle pesky problems such as bad breath, skin irritations and fleas. More serious issues should be confronted with the help of a vet, but for day-to-day ailments, this site operates like a corner drugstore for your pet.

·DOGS ·GROOMING	·CATS	·FOOD	·MEDICINE

Horse.com

Country Supply · 800-637-6721

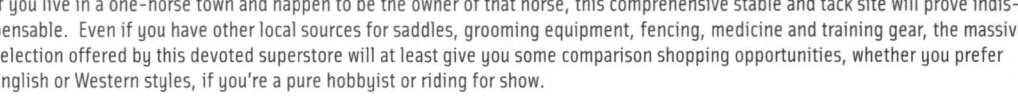

If you live in a one-horse town and happen to be the owner of that horse, this comprehensive stable and tack site will prove indispensable. Even if you have other local sources for saddles, grooming equipment, fencing, medicine and training gear, the massive selection offered by this devoted superstore will at least give you some comparison shopping opportunities, whether you prefer English or Western styles, if you're a pure hobbyist or riding for show.

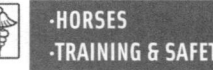

·HORSES ·TRAINING & SAFETY	·EQUIPMENT	·MEDICINE	·GROOMING

800-734-5253 · Jake's Dog House

JakesDogHouse.com

Jake's got himself a fairly convincing tag line, "Cool Stuff for Cool Dogs," but "Masculine Stuff" might be more accurate. This small, simple shop is full of fun toys and treats like Bow Wow Bistro Cigars that'll give your dog some fun while providing you some macho photo ops. Then, there are dog-friendly footballs and hockey pucks that give Fido a few butch alternatives to tennis. The kicker, though, is that Jake has outfitted this house with a lot of professional league team logo gear for your pooch. These collars, leashes and tags may be the best way to teach your dog about what's important in life: sports.

| ·DOGS | ·TOYS & TREATS | ·GROOMING | ·PET APPAREL | |

800-533-3377 · JeffersPet.com

JeffersPet.com

There is a lot of merchandise available from the Jeffers Pet Catalog; easily enough to overload your senses. You'll need to know specifically what you want to buy when you get here, to avoid being bogged down with choices; each of the subcategory lists reads suspiciously like an index, going so far as to draw distinctions between things like General Cages and Midwest Cages. Even if you're looking for unusual pet items such as cat colognes, canine costumes for Halloween, or hoof picks for your horse (should you need any), the same rule applies: the only easy thing to find is selection. Look here when every other site has failed you.

| ·DOGS
·CRITTERS | ·CATS
·HORSES | ·BIRDS
·FISH | ·REPTILES
·EQUIPMENT | |

800-842-6445 · Lafeber Company

Lafeber.com

Named for the birdbrain—er, veterinary avian specialist that created it, this is a line of nutrient-heavy feeding pellets, cakes, seed and vitamins for tropical birds like parrots and cockatoos. You end up reading more about the Dr. Lafeber than the foodstuffs at first, but you can just skip down the page to the Bird Food & Toys link. Chances are, feed your bird with this and he'll never shut up; if you want it quiet, by all means, just give Polly a cracker.

| ·BIRDS | ·FOOD | ·TOYS & TREATS | | |

800-745-4512 · Les Poochs

LesPoochs.com

Right about now, you're wondering just what sort of dog items one might want to purchase from France. Well, the same kinds of things humans like to buy: fragrances and shampoos. Actually, lots of different grooming supplies are here, with the added feature of a Breed Glossary to let you know which products are appropriate to your dog's skin and hair particularities. Many of the treatments and rinses you'll find here are naturally derived, some hypoallergenic, and you'll even find some organic treats that'll help entice your pooches into their new, sweeter-smelling bath.

| ·DOGS | ·TOYS & TREATS | ·GROOMING | | |

McMurrayHatchery.com

We're guessing you don't have a favorite, reliable poultry-as-pets site to shop from. All that's about to change. This Iowa-based specialist offers everything you could possibly need to raise chickens, turkeys, ducks, geese and game birds, and that includes the birds themselves or fertilized eggs (you decide which comes first). Some of these animals must be purchased in numbers exceeding ten, so you'll probably want at least a little bit of space available, whether you're populating a pond with a family of ducks or simply wish to lower your future grocery bills.

·BIRDS ·HABITAT	·EQUIPMENT ·GROOMING	·FOOD	·MEDICINE

MightyPets.com

Most of the pet training and containment sites we've seen offer great products. However, they usually don't offer more than one or two options within each category. That's what makes this site stand out, as it will usually offer electronic fences, bark collars and other training materials by a variety of brand names, allowing you to compare and contrast, and ultimately choose the one that best suits your needs. On the flipside, that makes this site harder to browse and, as the products aren't terribly different, your decision making will only occasionally add value to the shopping process. It's best to check here only if you enjoy being thorough.

·DOGS	·TRAINING & SAFETY		

MrsBones.com

While this upscale pooch boutique may just offer the best selection of doggy strollers online, the real reason to visit is the site's specialty: luxury custom collars. These finely patterned collars offer such indulgences as satin linings, brass hardware and personalized embroidery, but the real reason you'll like them is they offer beautiful and fashionable alternatives to the boring old leather or polyester models you'll find in most pet stores. As you might expect, the shop features a few other opulent items, including velvet leashes, crystal charms, rubber-soled lily boots and whatever else "the best dressed dogs are wearing."

·DOGS	·PET APPAREL		

Muttropolis.com

As its name would suggest, this site is all about having fun with your pets, and in truth it makes a better dog or cat gift source than anything else. Great page design makes it quite easy to sift through the several categories of products represented, including grooming products, treats, feeding bowls, beds and pet apparel, and almost all of it just as cute as the puppy or kitty you adore. But ultimately, your best finds will probably be in one of the Toys sections, which offer easy, affordable gifts certain to please animals and owners alike.

·DOGS	·CATS		

877-666-2501 · MyPetPrescriptions.com

MyPetPrescriptions.com

This site really contains two separate stores. The first will be found in the Prescription Items link, which leads you to a no-nonsense list of medicines that won't make any sense to you unless you're under the guidance of a veterinarian, or reading the name off your pet's prescription. The second is the Non-Prescription Items, in which over-the-counter products may be viewed by categories like Allergy Relief, Skin Care and Flea & Tick. While this is user-friendly to a point, product descriptions require deeper browsing, so choosing between an abundance of nonprescription treatments could take you longer than a stay in a vet's waiting room.

·DOGS	·CATS	·HORSES	·MEDICINE	

630-534-6682 · Natural Pet Market

NaturalPetMarket.com

If you're used to shopping for environmentally friendly and all-natural products for yourself, you'll be thrilled to discover this site, which offers a comprehensive selection of green foods, treats, grooming supplies and health products for dogs and cats. If you're not in the habit of buying eco-conscious products, perhaps your pet can lead the way, as this shop proves especially valuable for animals that are particularly sensitive to chemicals, which kind of makes you wonder why anyone would expose their pets, or themselves, to such things to begin with.

·DOGS ·TOYS & TREATS	·CATS ·GROOMING	·FOOD	·MEDICINE	

201-796-0627 · NaturesPet.com

NaturesPet.com

The home page proclaims, "Modern physics, various eastern philosophies and ecology all have shown that we live in a unified field," and it's immediately clear that this site serves pet owners who adhere to natural and holistic healing products. According to the owners of one brand featured here, "animals are herbalist by nature but domestication prohibits them from instinctively seeking the botanical diversity their bodies require." All right, this one does deviate from the beaten path a bit, but you can't shake a stick at natural products and treatments for a variety of animals. Unless, of course, shaking a stick is one of the recommended treatments.

·DOGS ·FOOD	·CATS ·MEDICINE	·BIRDS ·TOYS & TREATS	·HORSES	

800-844-1427 · PetCareRx.com

PetCareRx.com

Shopping for your pet's health and medical needs is not usually an easy thing to do, and if your animal is suffering we don't suggest waiting for its medicine to be delivered by a web site. That being said, if you are planning ahead, or want to replenish a dwindling supply of prescription medication, over-the-counter medications, vaccines, vitamins or grooming supplies, this handy site makes it incredibly easy, whether you're shopping for a cat, dog, bird, fish or critter. Take a look at it today and bookmark it for future reference: your pet's well-being deserves it.

·DOGS ·FISH	·CATS ·MEDICINE	·BIRDS ·GROOMING	·CRITTERS ·TRAINING & SAFETY	

PetClick.com

While one of the primary concerns of pet ownership has always been what comes out of the animal, here's a site that turns the focus to what goes in. Specializing in all-natural foods for your dog, cat, bird, fish, rodent or horse, this veterinarian-endorsed shop offers that rare assurance that you are absolutely doing right for your pet, in particular if you're raising a dog or cat from youth through adulthood, with the added benefit that production of this food is probably not hard on the planet either. The only thing we can't vouch for is taste.

| ·DOGS | ·CATS | ·BIRDS | ·CRITTERS |
| ·HORSES | ·FISH | ·FOOD | ·TRAINING & SAFETY |

PetFoodDirect.com

Do not be fooled—behind this web shop's goofy exterior lies the cold, calculating heart of a fully functional product database, and not just for food, as the name would imply. While the layout can leave you scanning endlessly for different menu options, and searches will yield dozens upon dozens of results, those with moderately fast connections should breeze through these pages with just a few well-placed clicks. Basically, if an animal fits in your house, you can find products to please it here…and prices to please you.

| ·DOGS | ·CATS | ·BIRDS | ·REPTILES |
| ·CRITTERS | ·FISH | ·FOOD | ·GROOMING |

PetProvide.com

If dogs didn't jump up, run around and bark every once in a while they wouldn't be any fun. That being said, an undisciplined animal is trouble for everybody and, as pop psychology would have it, dogs, like children, are happier if they have boundaries. This site specializes in training and obedience devices, ranging from bark control collars to invisible radio fences. Though there're limited options, you will be able to choose among items that utilize mild shocks (for larger and/or more exuberant pooches), or clicker training for dogs whose only goal in life is to find ways to please you.

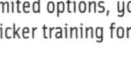

| ·DOGS | ·TRAINING & SAFETY | | |

PetRx.com

As its name would imply, this one turns out to be an invaluable animal pharmacy. As such, the fact that the site offers some very basic browsing techniques can be confusing, as in some cases over-the-counter medications are mixed in with the prescription selections. Whether you have the veterinary scrip or not, we recommend scrolling to the bottom of the lefthand menu and following the Prescription or Over-The-Counter links, respectively. This will make it easier for you to find the right ointment or pill for your dog or cat. Peanut butter to trick them into swallowing the pills will have to be purchased elsewhere.

| ·DOGS | ·CATS | ·MEDICINE | |

407-349-2525 · PetSafe

PetSafe-Warehouse.com

This may not be the site to suit your every pet-owning need, but when it comes to training, safety, containment and bark control, this is probably the most comprehensive end-user-friendly online shop available. Whether you need an electronic fence or automatic feeders, there are plenty of reasonably priced devices here to keep the dog or cat from getting hungry or into trouble when you're not around. It's just a bit of behavior modification with a technological assist, but for the safety of your pet and the delicate valuables in your home, it could be worthwhile.

·DOGS ·TRAVEL	·CATS ·TOYS & TREATS	·EQUIPMENT ·GROOMING	·HABITAT ·TRAINING & SAFETY

864-335-9697 · Pets R 4 U

PetsR4U.com

We like to shop at superstores when we need to buy a lot of items at once at reasonable prices; we shop boutiques when we want products with a bit more style or imagination. Here we find the best of both worlds represented with a massive pet store that offers better-than-average selection for a broad variety of pets without breaking the bank. A no-frills site gives you just exactly the tools you need to shop effectively and little else, resulting in a streamlined retail experience that can't fail an animal lover, especially when it comes to making your pet's habitat as stylish as your own.

·DOGS ·CRITTERS	·CATS ·FISH	·BIRDS ·EQUIPMENT	·REPTILES ·HABITAT

800-957-5753 · Pet Street Mall

PetStreetMall.com

It's probably a good thing a shop like this exists only online, because if you were forced to walk down the aisles of a brick-and-mortar store, you might wind up buying a lot more than you really need for your pet. On the site, however, you may simply choose your pet from a long list of varied creatures, then scroll down a menu until you find the specific type of product you seek. Thus you are able to ignore the wide range of interesting, fun, helpful and all-of-a-sudden essential items located throughout these pages.

·DOGS ·CRITTERS	·CATS ·FISH	·BIRDS ·HABITAT	·REPTILES ·TRAINING & SAFETY

800-227-4260 · PetTags.com

PetTags.com

When you're shopping for pet ID tags, you want two things: fun shapes and easy personalization. This tag specialist offers both. Simply browse among Traditional, Cartoon and Tie-Dye categories to find round-, heart-, bone- and fire-hydrant-shaped tags, then enter up to six lines of text to print on each. You'll likewise find personalized collars and leashes, plus a heavily red-white-and-blue Patriotic Collection section. The most fun, however, would be the Looney Tunes Collection, featuring popular characters like Bugs Bunny, the Tasmanian Devil and even Marvin the Martian.

·DOGS	·CATS	·TRAINING & SAFETY	

PetVetSupply.com

PetVet, Inc. · 800-283-2353

While many of the items found here overlap with the inventory of conventional pet stores, some surprising specialties are really what caught our attention. First of all, the inclusion of livestock is rare enough, but this site even features a full category devoted to llamas! Wild Birds also earned a focus, and it might be fun to compare this section to the one marked Poultry. Ultimately, while health and grooming supplies take precedence here, you should be able to find plenty of staple supplies for a fine variety of exotic pets.

·BIRDS ·TOYS & TREATS	·CRITTERS ·GROOMING	·HORSES ·TRAINING & SAFETY	·MEDICINE

PostmodernPets.com

Postmodern Pets · 650-331-3500

We've been pointing out modern and high-concept furniture stores for years and, now, thanks to this site, we can guide you to a great variety of pet gear to match. Highlights of the edgy designer pet store include architecturally interesting scratching posts, a wall-mounted fish bowl, space-age bird feeders and dog beds that would fit seamlessly into any hipster lounge. As usual, more attention is paid to canines and felines than to smaller pets, but that's definitely the only thing typical about this terrific web shop.

·DOGS ·HABITAT	·CATS ·TRAVEL	·BIRDS	·FISH

QuintessentialPet.com

The Quintessential Pet · 609-499-8885

If you don't feel you've spent enough money on your favorite little pooch, don't fret, this site's here to offer small dogs an opulence even Paris Hilton could appreciate. Whether it's providing a Poolside Cabana or terrycloth spa robe, "The Quintessential Pet" specializes in the trappings of material wealth, which is just like human wealth but seven times greater from a canine perspective. Crystal-embedded leather collars and bergamot perfume will be easy enough to find, but you may be thrown off by a link offering Your Majesty's Chifferobe, which is fancy language for upscale doggy apparel.

·DOGS ·GROOMING	·EQUIPMENT ·PET APPAREL	·HABITAT	·TRAVEL

RevivalAnimal.com

Revival Animal Health · 800-786-4751

We feature a lot of frivolous pet shops in this book, but with this site we find the responsible side of pet ownership well represented. All animals suffer from the occasional health issue, whether they're large or small, scaly, furry or feathery. Here you may find a fairly comprehensive selection of medicines, grooming supplies and training aids to ensure the safety and hygiene of your pet and everyone with whom it comes into contact. Serious problems may not be addressed by the shop, but most of your pet's day-to-day needs should easily be met.

·DOGS ·HORSES	·CATS ·FISH	·BIRDS ·MEDICINE	·CRITTERS ·TRAINING & SAFETY

646-216-9533 · Rex In The City

At first, we, too, groaned when we saw the name of this site. As it turns out, though, it's absolutely appropriate, as this small dog specialist offers enough designer pooch apparel to outfit your pet for a full season. While a small assortment of luxe dog beds is one of the best we've seen, the bulk of this boutique's selection may be browsed in the Couture Clothing category, where you'll see gingham dresses, cashmere sweaters, leather coats with fur trim and hip leather jackets. At this point we should reiterate that these are doggy clothes we're talking about. Look in our Women's Apparel section to populate your own closet.

·DOGS	·HABITAT	PET APPAREL		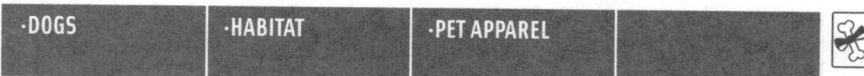

888-734-7650 · SafePets.com

While this site is called SafePets.com, what most of these products actually do is protect you, your stuff and your patience from the wily nature of your dog, cat or possibly pig. A range of options, for example, is there for you to contain your animal (with both actual or invisible fences). Likewise, you'll find different means of training your pet, including some oh-so-valuable bark control systems. They also offer controlled-entry pet doors, and a few devices designed to keep animals out of certain rooms or away from your valuables. Generally, this is all very useful, and mostly quite humane, but really some of these items may work best as a last resort.

·DOGS ·TRAINING & SAFETY	·CATS	·EQUIPMENT	·HABITAT	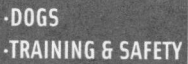

800-748-7829 · SitStay.com

A web-only one-stop shop for your pooch, this site touts itself as "where smart dogs do their business." Indeed, a comprehensive but moderately sized selection of equipment means you can find everything you need to get started with dog ownership without being overwhelmed. There's an excellent assortment of essentials like feeding, training, grooming supplies, as well as a few items veering more into the fun side of things, including cool chew toys and doggy sunglasses. A healthy Books & Videos Department even prepares you for the road ahead, meaning it's also a place where smart dog owners can do business.

·DOGS ·TOYS & TREATS	·EQUIPMENT ·GROOMING	·FOOD ·PET APPAREL	·HABITAT ·TRAINING & SAFETY	

800-733-3829 · That Pet Place

This particular pet place offers an exhaustive selection of necessities and indulgences for pretty much every animal that can legally be domesticated. In fact, the dog and cat sections are so big as to be exhausting as well, and the average pet owner may require a few weeks of training on other pet sites before tackling something so large. The lover of uncommon pets, on the other hand, will probably not find a better shop for fish, reptiles, birds and all manner of furry critters; and if you're brave enough to house all these animals under one roof, you will flat-out love it.

·BIRDS ·EQUIPMENT	·REPTILES ·FOOD	·CRITTERS ·MEDICINE	·FISH ·HABITAT	

TheBirdBrain.com

The Bird Brain · 888-923-2140

Here's one for the birds that talk, sing and swing; like parrots, canaries, macaws, lovebirds and cockatoos. Offering toys, perches, cages, food, health supplies, bowls and cleaners, this store is quite comprehensive in its selection. Better still, it proves an invaluable resource, even going so far as to separate items based on the type of bird you own, paying particular attention to its variable needs and interests. Excellent across the board, this is likely going to be the best place to buy bird-care items online for a long time to come.

	·BIRDS ·HABITAT	·EQUIPMENT ·TRAVEL	·FOOD ·GROOMING	·MEDICINE

ThePamperedPup.com

The Pampered Pooch · 561-833-9948

On this site you'll find just about everything you'd expect from a "Pawsitively Palm Beach" dog boutique, right down to the color pink. Essentially, if you're a stylish woman whose most treasured adornment has four paws, a tail and barks when it doesn't get its way, here you'll find everything necessary to pamper your pooch and fashionably accessorize the both of you. Highlights include an adorable selection of collars, some ultraluxurious dog beds, puppy spa products and a comprehensive assortment of small-dog fashions. Last but not least are what may be the most essential products of all: chic canine carriers tony enough to double as handbags even when you leave Precious at home.

	·DOGS ·GROOMING	·HABITAT ·PET APPAREL	·TRAVEL	·TOYS & TREATS

TravelinPets.com

Travelin' Pets · 866-738-7932

It only takes a moment to imagine the havoc that might ensue if animals were allowed to roam free on an airplane. As fun and carnivallike an atmosphere as this might be, it's probably for the best that pets are relegated to cages back in cargo. Such carriers are the specialty of this site, which also features pet car seats and restraints; vest carriers and backpacks (similar to those that people use to carry babies); and various pet travel items, like collapsible water dishes. It's a great place to go before you go anywhere with your dog or cat.

	·DOGS	·CATS	·TRAVEL	

TrixieAndPeanut.com

Trixie & Peanut · 212-979-1603

Two more dogs immortalized by the internet, Trixie and Peanut's owner put her experience in graphic arts toward this mail-order catalog turned web shop, placing an emphasis on clean design. The results include slick and pretty web pages with even better merchandise, including stylish collars, adorable beds, and plenty of apparel, jewelry, treats and toys. Exclusive products are supplemented by some of the industry's best to create one of our favorite dog-and-cat shops on the web.

	·DOGS ·TRAVEL	·CATS ·TOYS & TREATS	·FOOD ·GROOMING	·HABITAT ·PET APPAREL

800-254-8726 · UPCO

Before you pass this one over as "just another pet superstore," take into account the fact that we don't recommend it for dogs and cats. That's right, while they do offer a large, even unwieldy canine and feline selection, what we like about this store is its great selection of caged-animal products. Small animals, birds and reptiles get better treatment here than from most similar retailers, and even horses find a valuable online stable. It's a nice stop for those who take pet ownership off the beaten path, even if it does only lead to a Habitrail tube.

·BIRDS ·EQUIPMENT	·REPTILES ·FOOD	·CRITTERS ·TRAVEL	·HORSES ·TRAINING & SAFETY

800-419-9524 · ValleyVet.com

Sure, when most of us think of pets we imagine dogs, cats and small animals that won't end up on a grill. But to some, the cows and pigs that nuzzle the ground outside with their snouts are pets, of sorts, and for just such folk there is this site. Say you need an electric dehorner, udder treatment or sheep vaccine—it's important to know that the world of internet commerce hasn't forgotten you. There's also a huge section devoted to equine care and riding tack, as well as a thorough catalog devoted to "regular" pets. This one's humongous enough to serve you well whether you keep pets or livestock.

·HORSES ·HABITAT	·EQUIPMENT ·TOYS & TREATS	·FOOD ·GROOMING	·MEDICINE ·TRAINING & SAFETY

866-838-6337 · Vet America

If you don't think your pet is getting enough out of its regular diet, perhaps you'll want to include some nutritional supplements in its next meal. This is one of the several alternative health options provided by this veterinary supply retailer, alongside some more urgent traditional medical treatments including vaccines, flea-and-tick shampoos and other antiparasite solutions. As usual, dogs get the best treatment online, but the site also caters to cats, horses and even cattle, should your interest in animals rate a bit higher than simply playing fetch.

·DOGS ·GROOMING	·CATS ·TRAINING & SAFETY	·HORSES	·MEDICINE

877-288-2008 · YourActivePet.com

Does your dog like to run? Probably. Does it like to play in water? Some do. Well, maybe your dog would be into mountain hiking or whitewater rafting as much as you are? This site seems to think so, boasting "Adventure Gear for Your Dog." Stuff like hands-free leashes, canine boots and doggy life jackets enable you to take your faithful companion with you on your jaunts out-of-doors (because, really, where would a dog rather be?). They even offer equipment for something called skijoring, which gets your pets in on the act of cross-country skiing. Glad you didn't get a house cat?

·DOGS	·EQUIPMENT	·TRAVEL	·TRAINING & SAFETY

NOTES:

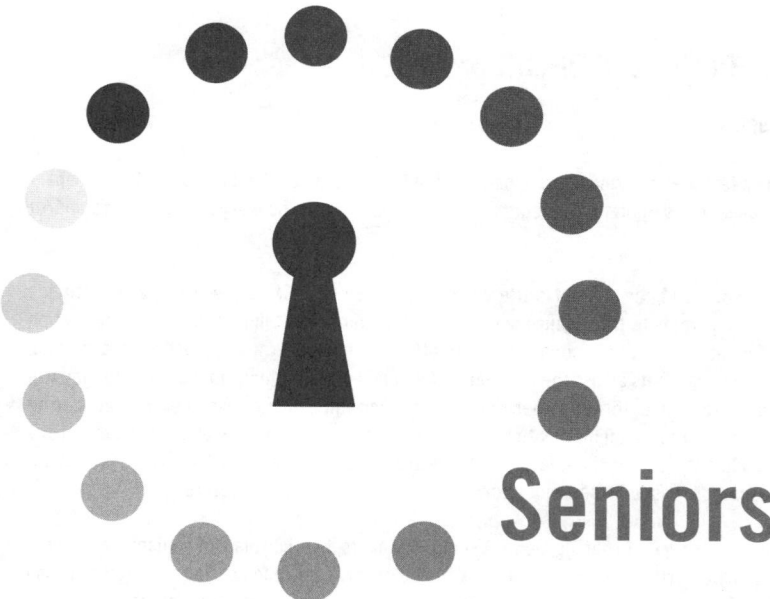

Seniors

The title of this section begs the question: what is a senior? It seems as though the age-based definition we might have used ten years ago no longer applies. The youthful demeanors, active lifestyles and over-whelming vitality of so many who've reached retirement age has changed the way we view our elders, and also the way they see themselves. In addition to living more physically fit, today's seniors are much more technologically savvy than in generations past, taking an increased interest in contemporary culture and marveling at the wonders of modern science. In fact, whereas computers used to be considered toys for youngsters, recent studies indicate that seniors made up the fastest-growing demographic of web shoppers last year. So why is this section so small?

The truth is, the entire book is for seniors as much as it is for anybody, and we hope most of their shopping habits will reflect this. However, we did find a small group of sites particularly devoted to the special needs of seniors, whether by establishing an online community based on shared interests, or offering items intended to help reclaim independence in the face of arthritis or other debilitating ailments associated with longevity. By and large, this hodgepodge of health, home, gadget and lifestyle sites tends to focus on useful products that can help people maintain their vigor well into the next century, where they may serve as an example to us all.

TIPS ON BUYING SENIORS' PRODUCTS ONLINE

These suggestions may prevent frustration.

• **GRANDPARENTING** • This section offers a few sites catering to grandparents, but by and large the best resources for grandparents will tune up in the Minors, Entertainment and Sports & Outdoors sections, many of which boast special children's and/or educational sections.

• **BEWARE OF INTERNET FRAUD** • As with the real world, the internet is littered with unscrupulous individuals who will take advantage of anybody just for a buck. However, avoiding problems takes only a few simple precautions. Most important is to use discretion when it comes to releasing personal information. All of the sites listed here offer secure credit card transactions that encode the information so that it's protected when it transmits across the internet. When you buy something from a web site, you will receive an email confirmation of your purchase, and notification when the item has been shipped. However, never respond to an email asking for your credit card number or other personal information. Emails are not secure, and more often than not, emails requesting credit card information are fraudulent. To be on the safe side, it helps to use the same credit card for every transaction, so you can keep track of internet purchases more easily. Also, print a copy of your order page for your records.

• **SENIOR DISCOUNTS** • Online transactions don't always explicitly mention senior discounts, but they may be available, especially with regard to travel bookings. It can often be worth a phone call to a site's customer service division to find out. You may also wish to check out some of the helpful sites listed on the opposite page to find more information on senior discounts.

>> SITES THAT MAY COME IN HANDY

The following URLs may be useful to seniors.

AARP.org	American Association for Retired People
About.com	General reference information and online resources
BenefitsCheckUp.com	Guide to governement programs for seniors
CareManager.org	Locate geriatric care managers
ElderCare.gov	Caregiver information and resources
HealthFinder.gov	Health and medicine web site directory
HelpGuide.org	Articles and information regarding healthy aging
LowVision.org	Resource for coping with vision impairment
Medicare.gov	Medicare official site
NAELA.com	Locate elder law attorneys
NetLingo.com	Glossary of internet terms
SeniorDiscounts.com	Search for local senior discounts
SeniorSite.com	Senior resources and community
SilverCross.com	Consumer info on wheelchairs, scooters and lifts
SpringStreet.com/seniors	Locate assisted-living and retirement communities
WebMD.com	Health and medical information
WhatIs.com	Glossary of computer terms
Zelgo.com	Online seniors community

SECTION ICON LEGEND

Use the following guide to understand the rectangular icons that appear throughout this section.

GIFT IDEAS
Our Stationery & Gifts section has much more to offer, but beside this icon you'll find sites offering plenty in the way of gifts designed specifically with the older individual in mind.

HEALTH & SAFETY
This icon makes it easier to locate items to protect seniors in or out of their homes, whether from outside elements or ill health. These products range from pill dispensers to money belts.

INDEPENDENT LIVING
Probably representative of the greatest value of this section, sites listed beside this icon offer helpful tools and appliances that make it easier for seniors to live alone while combating common ailments such as arthritis, hearing loss and deteriorating vision.

LIST OF KEY WORDS

The following words represent the types of items typically found on the sites listed in this section. You will find them listed in the orange strip at the bottom of each entry, as appropriate.

APPAREL	Seniors may of course benefit as well as anyone from the Men's and Women's Apparel sections in this book; the key word, however, denotes sites offering easy-to-put-on and easy-to-take-off clothes designed for independent seniors or those with caregivers.
HARD OF HEARING	Any site that offers products to help those suffering from hearing loss will turn up with this key word.
HEALTH CARE	Health-care items for seniors, including: pill dispensers, first-aid kits, medic alert bracelets, home health monitors, tools for caregivers and miscellaneous other health products.
HOBBIES	Tools and other accoutrements designed for popular senior hobbies, including cards, gardening, needlepoint and more.
HOUSEHOLD	Independent living tools, such as easy-grip devices, cleaning tools and cooking gadgets designed to make household chores and activities easier to perform.
MOBILITY	Wheelchairs, walkers, scooters, canes and relevant accessories.
NOSTALGIA	A wide range of products that refer to cultural events, people and occasions that remind seniors of their youth.
PERSONAL CARE	Items that make daily personal care and grooming routines easier to perform for those of limited mobility, modality or strength. Includes safety rails, easy-grip devices and dressing aids.
SECURITY	Home safety and security devices, as well as those that protect personal belongings away from home.

KEY WORD INDEX

Use the followings lists to locate online retailers that sell the senior products you seek.

APPAREL

BuckAndBuck.com
GoldenWearClothing.com

HARD OF HEARING

ActiveForever.com
DrLeonards.com
Dynamic-Living.com
EnablingDevices.com
EZLivingAids.com
MaxiAids.com
ProductsForSeniors.com

HEALTH CARE

A1-Medical-Supplies.net
DrLeonards.com
EnablingDevices.com
GoldViolin.com
IndependentLiving.com
RehabMart.com
SeniorShoppingNetwork.com
SeniorShops.com

HEALTH CARE

ActiveForever.com
Care4U.com
DrLeonards.com
Dynamic-Living.com
GiftIdeasForSeniors.com
GoldViolin.com
IndependentLiving.com
LifeSolutionsPlus.com
MaxiAids.com
ProductsForSeniors.com
SeniorShops.com
SeniorStore.com
SpinLife.com
WellHaven.com

HOUSEHOLD

A1-Medical-Supplies.net
ActiveForever.com
AidsForArthritis.com
Care4U.com
DrLeonards.com
Dynamic-Living.com
EnablingDevices.com
GoldViolin.com
IndependentLiving.com
LifeSolutionsPlus.com
MaxiAids.com
ProductsForSeniors.com
RehabMart.com
SeniorShoppingNetwork.com
SeniorShops.com
WellHaven.com

MOBILITY

1800Wheelchair.com
A1-Electric-Wheelchairs.com
A1-Medical-Supplies.net
ActiveForever.com
Care4U.com
DrLeonards.com
Dynamic-Living.com
EnablingDevices.com
IndependentLiving.com
MaxiAids.com
RehabMart.com
SeniorShoppingNetwork.com
SeniorShops.com
SpinLife.com

NOSTALGIA

GiftIdeasForSeniors.com
SeniorStore.com
WellHaven.com

PERSONAL CARE

1800Wheelchair.com
A1-Medical-Supplies.net
ActiveForever.com
AidsForArthritis.com
Care4U.com
DrLeonards.com
Dynamic-Living.com
EnablingDevices.com
EZLivingAids.com
GoldViolin.com
IndependentLiving.com
LifeSolutionsPlus.com
MaxiAids.com
ProductsForSeniors.com
RehabMart.com
SeniorShoppingNetwork.com
SeniorShops.com

SECURITY

ActiveForever.com
Care4U.com
Dynamic-Living.com
EnablingDevices.com
EZLivingAids.com
MaxiAids.com
ProductsForSeniors.com
SeniorShoppingNetwork.com
SeniorShops.com

VISION IMPAIRED

ActiveForever.com
Care4U.com
DrLeonards.com
Dynamic-Living.com
EnablingDevices.com
EZLivingAids.com
GoldViolin.com
IndependentLiving.com
MaxiAids.com
ProductsForSeniors.com
RehabMart.com
SeniorShoppingNetwork.com
SeniorShops.com
SeniorStore.com

NOTES:

_____

_____

_____

_____

_____

_____

_____

_____

_____

_____

_____

_____

_____

_____

_____

_____

_____

_____

1800Wheelchair.com

You probably won't encounter a more useful site when it comes to aiding a senior's mobility than this massive "one-stop, full service medical supply company." You'll find dozens of manual and powered wheelchairs here, but that's not even the half of it. There are scooters, canes, walkers, sports chairs and accessories for every mode of transport, as well as every conceivable associated product, like ramps, lifts, assistive furniture, safety rails and bathroom safety devices. Just when you think there could be nothing more, you'll notice personal-care tools and communications devices, all on an easy-to-use, all-around great shop.

	·MOBILITY	·PERSONAL CARE		

A1-Electric-Wheelchairs.com

A fine supply of wheelchairs, electric and otherwise, may be found on this comprehensive site. Wheelchair accessories include canopies, trays and storage attachments, while add-ons and seating options should help you get it just right. The site's value also extends to in-home mobility, with a collection of stair lifts, bath lifts, wheelchair lifts and adjustable beds, which can be expensive and complicated to install, but have the potential to make life much easier for seniors and caregivers alike.

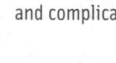	·MOBILITY			

A1-Medical-Supplies.net

This site used to cause as many pains as it would ease, but in its current form it's made itself almost indispensable to the health-conscious senior. The lefthand menu covers a host of ailments and concerns ranging from Aids to Daily Living and Blood Pressure to Wound Care and Urology. Going through the myriad products can be difficult for the vision impaired, but the site's otherwise well organized and laid out in a user-friendly manner. This is one site that can offer comfort where you'd least expect it.

	·MOBILITY	·PERSONAL CARE	·HOUSEHOLD	·HEALTH CARE

ActiveForever.com

As well stocked as this "life without limitations" web shop is, a senior could probably replace just about every object in his or her home with something less cumbersome and easier to use. With a focus on safety, comfort and independence, the hundreds of pages on this site offer personal-care tools, household cleaning equipment, kitchen gadgets, dressing aids, products promoting comfort and a great variety of items for hobbyists. A mobility section even offers an excellent assortment of walkers, scooters, wheelchairs and canes; so many that by time you get through them all they could be out of fashion.

	·MOBILITY ·SECURITY	·PERSONAL CARE ·HOUSEHOLD	·VISION IMPAIRED ·HARD OF HEARING	·HOBBIES

800-654-0707 · Aids for Arthritis

AidsForArthritis.com

Offering products "selected by medical professionals to promote joint preservation and energy conservation and reduce pain," this site should be a boon to anyone caught in the grip of arthritis. Categories here differentiate between products for Footcare, Dressing & Grooming, Communication and more, but in reality each section probably contains at least an item or two you'll find useful, and since this shop only selects the best, you know the products you buy will be reliable as well. You may want to bookmark this one.

·PERSONAL CARE	·HOUSEHOLD			

800-458-0600 · Buck & Buck Designs

BuckAndBuck.com

This comprehensive retailer "will acquaint you with clothing designs which promote independence for the self-dresser, as well as special closure items which make assisted dressing easier." It's a simple clothing catalog, except all the apparel is built to fit in such ways that those suffering arthritis or other restrictive ailments may put them on and take them off without much difficulty. Shopping is easy, as categories are split into garment selections as specific as sweaters, knit pants sets and velour sweatsuits. Shop here, and your only dressing limitations will be in terms of style.

·APPAREL				

877-538-6568 · Care4U

Care4U.com

The mission statement from these guys claims, "We will scour the world to find and offer useful, mostly unknown, products that sometimes cost very little but can be of great value to those who use them." Indeed, with a host of assistive functions ranging from playing cards and writing letters to opening jars and clipping nails, these products live up to the hype, offering solutions to common problems that may arise from time to time due to arthritis, impaired hearing/vision and decreased mobility, and offering comfort aids for sore joints that develop from an active lifestyle.

·MOBILITY ·SECURITY	·PERSONAL CARE ·HOUSEHOLD	·VISION IMPAIRED	·HOBBIES	

800-455-1918 · Dr. Leonard's

DrLeonards.com

"America's leading discount healthcare catalog" may not expressly serve seniors, but no other group may take better advantage of its multifaceted offerings. Categories like Mobility and Personal Care would be self-explanatory on any other site, but here they are filled with surprises, as is every category on the site, from General Merchandise to Exercise. In fact, we'd suggest taking a look at just about every product here, and picking out the ones that most astound you. With everything from gel cushions and denture cleaning kits to living will kits and rubber stair treads, chances are good you won't find stuff like this anywhere else.

·MOBILITY ·HOUSEHOLD	·PERSONAL CARE ·HEALTH CARE	·VISION IMPAIRED ·HARD OF HEARING	·HOBBIES	

Dynamic-Living.com

Dynamic Living · 888-940-0605

With "hundreds of kitchen products, bathroom helpers and unique daily living aids that promote a convenient, comfortable and safe home environment," this terrific site makes a wide range of helpful independent-living tools for the hard of hearing, vision impaired, arthritic or anyone weakened by surgery or other health issues related to age. In many ways, these helpful and often technological products are part of the home of the future, making daily routines easier and more convenient for people in every walk of life.

| ·MOBILITY | ·PERSONAL CARE | ·VISION IMPAIRED | ·HOBBIES |
| ·SECURITY | ·HOUSEHOLD | ·HARD OF HEARING | |

EnablingDevices.com

Enabling Devices · 800-832-8697

Between its Children's and Adult catalogs, this ingenious purveyor of assistive devices offers plenty of tools designed to promote physical rehabilitation and development. However, we're primarily intrigued by the selection of savvy electronic equipment designed to help its users achieve an otherwise complicated independence. For example, a voice-activated remote control removes the need to look for and press a lot of buttons, while large-key computer keyboards makes it a simpler matter to shop from **thepurplebook** sites. You won't find this stuff anywhere else—it's hard enough to find it on this poorly organized site.

| ·MOBILITY | ·PERSONAL CARE | ·VISION IMPAIRED | ·SECURITY |
| ·HOUSEHOLD | ·HEALTH CARE | ·HARD OF HEARING | |

EZLivingAids.com

Harris Communications · 800-825-6758

When your hearing and vision start to go, the simplest daily tasks around the home can become very complicated. This terrific product selection includes digital clocks with extra-large numbers and vibrating alarms, big-button phones and talking bathroom scales to help combat erosion of the senses without sacrificing independence. Most important may be smoke detectors and doorbells equipped with strobe lighting so that emergency situations will never go unnoticed. The world you don't see or hear can be scary, but not so much with the help of this dedicated retailer.

| ·PERSONAL CARE | ·VISION IMPAIRED | ·SECURITY | ·HARD OF HEARING |

GiftIdeasForSeniors.com

Gift Ideas For Seniors · 303-926-9301

While half of the gifts featured on this site seem to be corny poems on the topic of enduring love, or sappy odes to grandparents, there are a few legitimately sentimental gifts to be found here. A rolling selection of 50th anniversary–themed gifts is available, for example, which offers nostalgic items pertinent to the year of betrothal. Our favorite item is a framed newspaper, customized to a person's birth date and featuring the major headlines of the day; here's hoping the world celebrated on the day your recipient entered it.

| ·HOBBIES | ·NOSTALGIA | | |

204-953-4500 · Golden Wear Clothing

GoldenWearClothing.com

The difficulty of dressing and undressing those bound to wheelchairs or otherwise limited in mobility can be made easier with the garments available from this site. Intended for "for nursing home and home health care residents," these clothes open at the back so they may be easily slipped on and fastened with minimal help. The selection caters mostly to ladies, though a few male casual and sleepwear options may be found among the colorful, and for the most part very inexpensive, garb.

| ·APPAREL | | | |  |

877-648-8400 · Gold Violin

GoldViolin.com

There may not be a better shop online to find functional and elegant gifts for seniors than this small catalog created for those "who live rich long lives and inspire us with their experience and insights." Among the many functional independent-living aids you'll find stylish walking sticks, attractive reading glasses and many other thoughtful and appealing products that will be as gladly received as they are useful. Whether you or someone you love is challenged by impaired vision, decreased mobility or arthritis, something here will help, although our favorite section is aptly named All About Comfort.

| ·PERSONAL CARE
·HEALTH CARE | ·VISION IMPAIRED | ·HOBBIES | ·HOUSEHOLD | |

800-537-2118 · Independent Living Aids

IndependentLiving.com

This site boasts a catalog of "can-do" products, and to give you a clear idea of what this means, there are sections devoted to Cooking, Personal Care and Writing. There's plenty more, though, from computer accessories to household aids, with some fun stuff thrown in for, well, fun. Browsing by Department opens up several product links as well as some helpful explanatory text, and everything's organized well enough that you shouldn't have any trouble despite the fact that this site is chock-full of hundreds of useful products.

| ·MOBILITY
·HOUSEHOLD | ·PERSONAL CARE
·HEALTH CARE | ·VISION IMPAIRED | ·HOBBIES | |

877-785-8326 · LifeSolutionsPlus

LifeSolutionsPlus.com

This very earnest small business grew out of a need for "simple products that could make everyday tasks easier to accomplish." After "extensive research and product testing," the people behind this web shop have found a fantastic assortment of independent-living aids including jar openers, button hooks, pill organizers, long-handled brushes, magnifiers and easy-grip pens. A handy site for any senior to know, if you pay a visit anytime a daily task becomes frustrating, chances are you'll find the perfect solution within these pages.

| ·PERSONAL CARE | ·HOBBIES | ·HOUSEHOLD | | 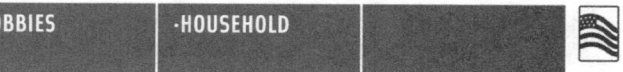 |

MaxiAids.com

The best way to operate this "Products for Independent Living" site is to use the menu that runs across the top of the page, which includes categories such as Low Vision, Hard of Hearing, Mobility, Medical/Health, Household and Technology. Within each section, a submenu running down the left side of the page will guide you to a valuable selection of particular products that run the gamut from arthritis aids to senior-friendly hobby items, computer input devices, walkers, appliances and even furniture. It all adds up to an independent life that's easier to live.

·MOBILITY ·SECURITY	·PERSONAL CARE ·HOUSEHOLD	·VISION IMPAIRED ·HARD OF HEARING	·HOBBIES

ProductsForSeniors.com

At first glance, it seems that this web site doesn't offer very many products for seniors after all. Though the catalog is not incredibly deep, it is easy to miss the bulk of the merchandise because only a few items will appear on each page. Look close, however, and you'll see that a small "Next" arrow appears at the top of most pages; this link will turn up more products like large-print playing cards, toilet lifter seats and automobile window tint. Most of this stuff is purely functional, even if the web site doesn't always seem to be.

·PERSONAL CARE ·HOUSEHOLD	·VISION IMPAIRED ·HARD OF HEARING	·HOBBIES	·SECURITY

RehabMart.com

"Owned and operated by therapists," the excellent customer service offerings of this assistive equipment specialist is tough to beat, as you may use the Contact Us link to send them a detailed email describing the circumstances and special needs of your loved one or yourself, and shortly receive a response outlining the best products to help rehabilitate and maintain independence following surgery or illness. This may come in handy, as the massive assortment of mobility, low-vision, safety, fitness, health, home and personal-care aids can be daunting to browse, and it's all, most assuredly, worth finding.

·MOBILITY ·HEALTH CARE	·PERSONAL CARE	·VISION IMPAIRED	·HOUSEHOLD

SeniorShoppingNetwork.com

A better-than-average selection of independent-living aids await you on this site, including some that offer a touch more style than most. Categories such as Health Management Products, Magnifying Products and Mobility don't hold a lot of surprises, but Magnetic And Aroma Therapy turns up some interesting alternatives to standard arthritis treatments. Ultimately, it's function that counts with these types of products, and the site guides you to plenty of items that will with time become indispensable.

·MOBILITY ·HOUSEHOLD	·PERSONAL CARE ·HEALTH CARE	·VISION IMPAIRED	·SECURITY

800-894-9549 · Senior Shops

SeniorShops.com

Boasting "over 900 gifts and products for the elderly," the Senior Shops catalog lists anything from air purifiers and orthopedic supports to bed rails and heating pads. Categories, including Feel Better, Hear Better, See Better, Move Better, Work Better and Play Better (obviously the most exciting of the bunch), break down into more helpful subcategories like Dressing & Grooming Aids, Exercise Equipment, Talking Products and Medication Accessories. There are so many subcategories, in fact, that it will take a few minutes just to read them all. Beyond that, though, browsing this fantastic selection is a no-brainer.

·MOBILITY ·SECURITY	·PERSONAL CARE ·HOUSEHOLD	·VISION IMPAIRED ·HEALTH CARE	·HOBBIES

303-926-9301 · SeniorStore.com

SeniorStore.com

This is a lot like any of the other sites in this section that sell innovative items and ergonomic designs to help seniors maintain independence and security into longevity—with one exception: it tends to be more fun. Shopping by Person (Grandma or Grandpa, for example), Occasion (Retirement, Anniversary) or Product Type (Games, Books, etc.) makes it simple to narrow down your focus to things that seniors may both use and enjoy, whether receiving them as gifts or buying them for themselves.

·VISION IMPAIRED	·HOBBIES	·NOSTALGIA	

800-850-0335 · SpinLife.com

SpinLife.com

If you're getting around on a set of wheels, you may find a lot of stuff on this site to soup up your ride and put a nice spin on wheelchair use (sorry—horrible pun unfortunately intended). Whether manual chairs, sport chairs, powered chairs or scooters, all are offered with a variety of options and designs, along with accessories ranging from cushions to "urologicals." Best of all, live customer support is always available, so any question may be promptly answered, almost before it's asked.

·MOBILITY	·HOBBIES		

888-564-1500 · Wellhaven

WellHaven.com

Offering "gifts that seniors will truly appreciate," this specialty gift shop makes it easy for anyone to find that special something for that person of ageless taste and humor. With sections devoted to special birthdays and anniversaries, as well as a bevy of age-appropriate gag gifts, getting through the charming assortment proves easy and quick. And, although we've grown accustomed to the sort of independent-living aids available here, these happen to be designed particularly with style and taste in mind, as well as function; something that even beats out nostalgia when it comes to giving and receiving.

·HOBBIES	·HOUSEHOLD	·NOSTALGIA	

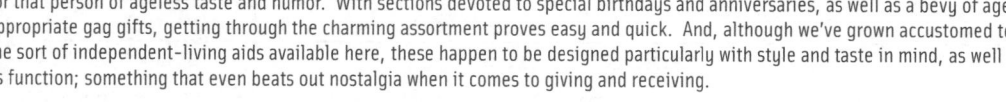

NOTES:

_____

_____

_____

_____

_____

_____

_____

_____

_____

_____

_____

_____

_____

_____

_____

_____

_____

_____

Shoes & Accessories

Of all the ways we express ourselves, the clothes we wear might be what those around us notice the most—at least they would be if it weren't for our accessories. Sometimes it seems that if you wore a burlap sack with a great pair of shoes, nobody would mention the sack and everyone would compliment the shoes. With this in mind we have done our best to find as many unique accessories as can be purchased online. This section is filled with terrific selections of hats, gloves, handbags, belts, glasses, watches, wraps, scarves, wallets and jewelry. Varieties range from the inexpensive to the absolutely indulgent, including styles you'd find in fashion magazines and vintage items you might expect to read about in Victorian novels.

The shoe stores were particularly thrilling to research, as there are enough sneakers, sandals, slippers, boots and dress shoes out there to keep an enthusiastic shopper busy for days, including some designs so elaborate and original you may want to construct whole outfits around them. With so many great designer sites and online boutiques to sort through, we had to make a lot of tough decisions to ensure we only included the best, most popular and most affordable options. We leave the daunting task of choosing from the immense assortment to you. It may not always be easy, but showing it off later will definitely be rewarding.

TIPS ON BUYING ACCESSORIES ONLINE

These suggestions may help keep your accessory buying experience from turning sour.

• **SHOES** •Buying shoes online can be a little scary, given the variety in shapes and sizes demonstrated even by a single manufacturer. The most important thing to take note of before buying footwear online is the store's return policy. In most cases, it shouldn't be a problem of fit; but when in doubt, don't hesitate to call the customer service number and ask some direct questions. However, just to be sure, try on your new shoes indoors, on clean floors, as soiled shoes will be tough to exchange or return.

• **DESIGNER LABELS** •Many of our sites offer designer label products, and in most cases the prices reflect the high stature of such items. Before purchasing, check to make sure the site is prepared to back up any claims of authenticity, preferably with a guarantee, to make sure you get what you pay for. If a product proves to be counterfeit or otherwise questionable, contact the seller immediately.

• **WATCHES & FINE JEWELRY** •Before making a large investment, it's wise to educate yourself about the quality and reputation of certain jewelry and watches (not to mention knowing a person's ring size before you shop!). This may require a lot of tedious research, but knowing the market and grading systems can prove worthwhile, amounting to thousands of dollars in savings. Additionally, you may wish to inquire into payment options, which often work similarly to car loans. As always, you'll want to research any store's return policy/guarantees before purchase.

• **EYEWEAR** • You can't try them on, so get to know the return policies of an eyewear shop before you commit to a set of frames, or you could be stuck with some goofy and expensive glasses. Also, take note that prescription lenses are available in many cases but are not necessarily refundable, even if the frames are.

POPULAR SHOES & ACCESSORIES BRANDS

The following sites offer online sales for familiar brand names.

Adidas.com
BirkenstockExpress.com
ColeHaan.com
Coach.com
Fossil.com
Gucci.com
Hermes.com
JohnstonMurphy.com

KateSpade.com
LeSportSac.com
NineWest.com
Oakley.com
Puma.com
SteveMadden.com
Swatch.com
Tiffany.com

*For in-depth reviews of these sites and more, check out **www.thepurplebook.com**.

>> SITES THAT MAY COME IN HANDY

The following URLs may be useful when you shop for certain accessories.

AllAboutVision.com	Guide to vision correction and preservation
CoutureJeweler.com	Research trends in jewelry design
DavidMorgan.com/hatsizing.html	Hat size measurements
DiamondReview.com	Diamond buying guide
Gem.net	Gemstone facts and symbolic meanings
GIA.org	Gemological Institute of America
Kovels.com	Guide to estate and vintage jewelry
OnlineConverters.com	Adult shoe sizes and conversion
Overstock.com/ringsize.html	Determine ring size
Style.com	Fashion news and trends
SullivanGlove.com/html/glove_size_.html	Determine glove size
TheHatSite.com	Hat resource
WatchReport.com	Watch resource
Zappos.com/measure.zhtml	Shoe size conversion chart

>> SITES WITH A SINGLE FOCUS
The following sites excel at selling one or two specific products.

AmyJoGladstone.com	Slippers
ATierney.com	Preppy accessories
BeverlyFeldmanShoes.com	Designer shoes
Charm-Express.com	Bracelets and charms
ClogWild.com	Wood clogs
Cufflinks.com	Cufflinks
DavidZ.com	Casual shoes
Emitations.com	Replica jewelry
FootCandy.com	Toe rings
FrenchSoleShoes.com	Ballet flats
GaraDanielle.com	Designer jewelry
Harputs.com	Vintage sneakers
HeatherBMoore.com	Designer jewelry
LaurenScherr.com	Evening bags
PlanetJill.com	Photo jewelry
Portolano.com	Cold-weather accessories
ThaiGem.com	Loose gemstones
TiffiniDooris.com	Designer jewelry
WalkerBags.com	Mesh totes and cosmetic cases
WatchesPlanet.com	Name-brand watches

SECTION ICON LEGEND

Use the following guide to understand the rectangular icons that appear throughout this section.

FOOTWEAR
Making it easier to find the most universally worn accessories, this icon represents any or all of the following: athletic shoes, casual shoes, dress shoes, bridal shoes, heels, pumps, slides, sneakers, slippers, sandals and boots, as well as shoe care and accessories.

JEWELRY & WATCHES
Look for this icon if you want to find fine, vintage, estate, costume or fashion jewelry, or if you're on the lookout for watches.

MEN'S ACCESSORIES
Used to elucidate which of the entries cater in part or exclusively to male consumers, sites marked with this icon may include ties, cufflinks, hats, pocket squares, wallets, watches, belts, umbrellas, backpacks, travel cases, organizers, briefcases, eyewear, key chains, jewelry and gloves among their wares.

WOMEN'S ACCESSORIES
By and large, most of the sites in this section offer something for the ladies, but we use this icon to point them out anyway. This icon denotes at least one of the following products for women: bags, wallets, belts, hats, hair accessories, eyewear, scarves, wraps, gloves, etc.

LIST OF KEY WORDS

The following words represent the types of items typically found on the sites listed in this section. You will find them listed in the orange strip at the bottom of each entry, as appropriate.

BAGS & WALLETS	Wallets for men and women, plus a variety of handbags, totes, clutches, evening bags, cosmetics cases, designer handbags, backpacks and briefcases.
BELTS	Belts for men or women.
BOOTS	Most of the boots are leather, but there are some faux leather options.
DESIGNER	Any decent selection of designer accessories.
DRESS SHOES	Dress shoes, including traditional men's styles and women's formal heels.
EYEWEAR	Most eyewear in this section consists of sunglasses, but there are also some standard eyeglass frames and color contacts.
FASHION JEWELRY	Fashion jewelry is typically made with less expensive materials, and includes contemporary designs, as well as costume jewelry and knockoffs.
FINE JEWELRY	This jewelry is made from precious metals and stones, and includes vintage and estate jewelry, as well as items such as engagement rings.
GLOVES	Gloves for men and women fit here, whether for fashion or to keep hands warm.
HAIR ACCESSORIES	Hair clips, bands, barrettes, pins, forks, tiaras and other jeweled hair accessories.
HATS	Hats for men and women, including cowboy hats, baseball caps, straw hats as well as conversational and traditional styles for both sexes.
KIDS	Any children's shoes or accessories.
LEATHER	We found an abundance of leather items across all accessories categories.
SANDALS	Sandals for both men and women, both in specialty shops and large shoe stores.
SCARVES & WRAPS	Scarves and wraps, including shawls, pashminas, boas, stoles and more.
SHOES	Footwear, including loafers, sneakers, moccasins, slippers, pumps, mules, slides and athletic shoes.
SMALL GOODS	Key rings, date books, phone cases and other functional items.
WATCHES	Fine and fashion watches, watchbands and winders for men and women.

 **KEY WORD INDEX**

Use the followings lists to locate online retailers that sell the type of accessories you seek.

BAGS & WALLETS

1154Lill.com
Ashford.com
CrisNotti.com
DellaModa.com
DeviKroell.com
EspadrillesEtc.com
FashionFlairs.com
FlipFlopTrunkShow.com
Forzieri.com
Ghurka.com
GinaShoes.com
Isharya.com
JacquelineJarrot.com
JemzNJewels.com
JenniferKaufman.com
JosephineOnline.com
KoloBags.com
LedererDeParis.com
LunaBoston.com
MadImports.net
MooRoo.com
MoynaBags.com
Mulberry-England.co.uk
NaughtySecretaryClub.com
PeterBeaton.com
PinkMascara.com
PlazaToo.com
Raffaello-Network.com
ScotlandShop.net
She-Works.com
ShoppingAllure.com
StephanieJohnson.com
StyleDrops.com
Timbuk2.com
TwelveNYC.com
YakPak.com
Zappos.com

BELTS

BootBarn.com
FashionFlairs.com
Forzieri.com
JacquelineJarrot.com
JemzNJewels.com
LargeFeet.com
LunaBoston.com
LynGaylord.com
MoynaBags.com
NicNorman.com
PeterBeaton.com
PlazaToo.com
Raffaello-Network.com
SouthwesternJewelry.net
Vegetarian-Shoes.co.uk

BOOTS

AshleyDearborn.com
BootBarn.com
DeviKroell.com
Faith.co.uk
FootCandyShoes.com
GinaShoes.com
JildorShoes.com
JosephineOnline.com
LargeFeet.com
OfficeHoldings.co.uk
OnlineShoes.com
PlazaToo.com
Sassanova.com
ShiekhShoes.com
ShoeBuy.com
ShoeTrader.com
StyleDrops.com
Vegetarian-Shoes.co.uk
WalkingCo.com
WideShoes.com
Zappos.com

DESIGNER

AllysonSmith.com
APairOfShades.com
Ashford.com
AshleyDearborn.com
BrellaBar.com
DellaModa.com
DeviKroell.com
EllenChristine.com
EyeGlasses.com
FootCandyShoes.com
Forzieri.com
Fragments.com
GinaShoes.com
GivingTreeGallery.com
GuenveurFurst.com
HeiressVault.com
JacquelineJarrot.com
JannaConner.com
JemzNJewels.com
JenniferKaufman.com
JildorShoes.com
JodySingleton.com
JosephineOnline.com
MinuJewels.com
MoondanceJewelry.com
MooRoo.com
PinkMascara.com
PlazaToo.com
Raffaello-Network.com
RobertaChiarella.com
RoyalOrder.com
Sassanova.com
ShoeMine.com
ShoppingAllure.com
StyleDrops.com
TinaTang.com
TresJolie.us
Ylang-Ylang.com
ZubieNYC.com

DRESS SHOES

DellaModa.com
JosephineOnline.com
LargeFeet.com
OddBallShoe.com
OfficeHoldings.co.uk
OnlineShoes.com
Raffaello-Network.com
ShoeBuy.com
StyleDrops.com
ToBoot.com
Vegetarian-Shoes.co.uk
WideShoes.com
Zappos.com

EYEWEAR

APairOfShades.com
Ashford.com
EyeGlasses.com
FramesDirect.com
Raffaello-Network.com
ShoppingAllure.com
StyleDrops.com

FASHION JEWELRY

AllysonSmith.com
BoucherJewelry.com
DilseyCoal.com
FashionFlairs.com
Forzieri.com
Fragments.com
GivingTreeGallery.com
GuenveurFurst.com
HeiressVault.com
Ice.com
Isharya.com
JacquelineJarrot.com
JannaConner.com
JemzNJewels.com
JenniferKaufman.com
JodySingleton.com
LunaBoston.com
MinuJewels.com
MoondanceJewelry.com
MooRoo.com
MorningGloryJewelry.com
NaughtySecretaryClub.com
PinkMascara.com
PlazaToo.com
PreciousAccents.com
RobertaChiarella.com
RoyalOrder.com
ShoppingAllure.com
SouthwesternJewelry.net
TalismanUnlimited.com
Tateossian.com
TinaTang.com
TresJolie.us
TrueFaux.com
Versani.com
Ylang-Ylang.com
ZubieNYC.com

FINE JEWELRY

Adin.be
AntiqueAndEstate.com
AntiqueJewelryExch.com
Ashford.com
Boodles.co.uk
DeNatale.com
GoldAvenue.com
GoldSpeed.com
Ice.com
Longmire.co.uk
LynGaylord.com
Mondera.com
MoondanceJewelry.com
SolomonBrothers.com
Ylang-Ylang.com

GLOVES

Forzieri.com
HartfordYork.com
Vegetarian-Shoes.co.uk

HAIR ACCESSORIES

FranceLuxe.com
GoldAvenue.com
HairBoutique.com
JacquelineJarrot.com
JenniferKaufman.com
MoynaBags.com
NaughtySecretaryClub.com
RobertaChiarella.com

HATS

BootBarn.com
EllenChristine.com
Goorin.com
HartfordYork.com
HatsInTheBelfry.com
JemzNJewels.com
JHHatCo.com
LockHatters.co.uk
PeterBeaton.com
ScotlandShop.net
VillageHatShop.com

KIDS

APairOfShades.com
BootBarn.com
EspadrillesEtc.com
EyeGlasses.com
FlipFlopCo.com
FlipFlopTrunkShow.com
FramesDirect.com
OnlineShoes.com
ShiekhShoes.com
ShoeBuy.com
Vans.com
WalkingCo.com
YakPak.com
Zappos.com

LEATHER

BootBarn.com
Faith.co.uk
Ghurka.com
HartfordYork.com
LargeFeet.com
LedererDeParis.com
Mulberry-England.co.uk
OfficeHoldings.co.uk
OnlineShoes.com
PlazaToo.com
She-Works.com
StubbsAndWootton.com
StyleDrops.com
ToBoot.com
WideShoes.com

SANDALS

AshleyDearborn.com
Canfora.com
ClassicSportsShoes.com
EspadrillesEtc.com
Faith.co.uk
FlipFlopCo.com
FlipFlopTrunkShow.com
FootCandyShoes.com
JacquelineJarrot.com
JildorShoes.com
JosephineOnline.com
LargeFeet.com
OddBallShoe.com
OfficeHoldings.co.uk
OnlineShoes.com
PlazaToo.com
Sassanova.com
ShoeBuy.com
ShoeTrader.com
ShoppingAllure.com
StubbsAndWootton.com
Vegetarian-Shoes.co.uk
WalkingCo.com
WideShoes.com
Zappos.com

SCARVES/WRAPS

Forzieri.com
HartfordYork.com
Isharya.com
JacquelineJarrot.com
JemzNJewels.com
MoynaBags.com
ScotlandShop.net

SHOES

AshleyDearborn.com
ClassicSportsShoes.com
ClogWorld.com
DellaModa.com
DeviKroell.com
EspadrillesEtc.com
Faith.co.uk
FlipFlopTrunkShow.com
FootCandyShoes.com
FrenchSole.com
Ghurka.com
GinaShoes.com
JemzNJewels.com
JildorShoes.com
JosephineOnline.com
LargeFeet.com
OddBallShoe.com
OnlineShoes.com
PlazaToo.com
Raffaello-Network.com
Sassanova.com
ShiekhShoes.com
ShoeBuy.com
ShoeMine.com
ShoeTrader.com
SportieLA.com
StubbsAndWootton.com
StyleDrops.com
ToBoot.com
Vans.com
Vegetarian-Shoes.co.uk
WalkingCo.com
WideShoes.com
Zappos.com

SMALL GOODS

Ashford.com
BrellaBar.com
CrisNotti.com
DeNatale.com
Ghurka.com
KoloBags.com
LunaBoston.com
Mulberry-England.co.uk
She-Works.com
Timbuk2.com
UmbrellaStand.com

WATCHES

Adin.be
AntiqueJewelryExch.com
APairOfShades.com
Ashford.com
Boodles.co.uk
FashionFlairs.com
FinerTimes.com
Forzieri.com
GoldAvenue.com
GoldSpeed.com
Ice.com
JacquelineJarrot.com
JewelryService.com
Joseph-Watches.com
LunaBoston.com
NaughtySecretaryClub.com
PreciousAccents.com
Raffaello-Network.com
USAWatchCo.com
WorldOfWatches.com
WristWatch.com

NOTES:

1154Lill.com

Having trouble matching a handbag to your favorite outfit? Not anymore. This small business turned outstanding web site began in the late 90s when founder Jennifer Velarde started handcrafting bags out of her condo at 1154 W. Lill St. The hip and functional handbags were an almost immediate success, but it wasn't until Velarde started offering "design-your-own" accessories that the business really took off. The concept translates even better online, where you may choose from more than a dozen handbag designs and nearly a hundred different incredible fabrics. This is easily the most fun handbag shopping experience you'll ever have.

 ·BAGS & WALLETS

Adin.be

Among Western European nations, Belgium is easy to overlook when it comes to high fashion. However, this fantastic estate jewelry retailer reminds us not only that the lowland country exists, but that it's worth noticing. In particular, special jewelry pieces such as lockets, religious pendants and engagement rings exist here in abundance and will blow your mind. As it happens, any specific type of piece you're looking for should be easy to find, as the site's browsing filters let you wade through a potentially complicated assortment of fine vintage jewelry without much hassle.

 ·FINE JEWELRY   ·WATCHES

AllysonSmith.com

Like a Southerner transplanted to New York City, the semiprecious jewelry available from this designer's site stands out with a burst of color against cold urban gray. Which makes sense, seeing as the Louisiana-born designer in question has taken the Big Apple by storm with her bright, dazzling and especially stylish bracelets, earrings and necklaces. We wish there were more to see (there are fewer than 200 pieces here), but this is just one inspired woman with an eye for fashionable jewelry, so we suggest taking a look at the full collection, buying everything you like and counting yourself lucky.

 ·DESIGNER   ·FASHION JEWELRY

AntiqueAndEstate.com

Billing itself as "Your source for one of a kind jewelry," this site runs a real risk of setting your expectations too high. Except, this unique antique and estate jewelry selection is fine, beautiful and constantly changing, and we dare you to be disappointed. Probably the best place to shop for an engagement ring for that girl with vintage tastes (you'll need to have it resized locally), and wedding bands beyond the pale. However, one boast the site can't make is excellent browsing, and while these rings and some elegant watches turn up without hassle, finding the delightful handful of bracelets, necklaces, brooches and earrings may test your patience. But it's worthwhile.

 ·FINE JEWELRY

800-809-4190 · Antique Jewelry Exchange

AntiqueJewelryExch.com

Jewelry is a very popular family heirloom, which generally means that the best jewelry gets handed down through the generations and never again sees the light of a marketplace. Appropriate, then, that this family-owned-and-operated business is one that specifically seeks out antique and estate jewels, to create one of the richer and finer jewelry selections online. Specializing in platinum and watches, they certainly have lovely items to display in either category, and though many items are sold out, those remaining still display a character and charm seldom seen in contemporary catalogs.

·FINE JEWELRY	·WATCHES		

888-742-3370 · A Pair of Shades

APairOfShades.com

Between the extensive lists of designer sunglasses and designer frames (you know, for the regular kind of glasses), you might just miss out on the secondary offerings of this simple but effective site, watches and contact lenses, each of which are quite well represented. Of course, sunglasses really are the best reason to show up, by a long shot, and with popular brands such as Gucci, Oakley and Vuarnet to be had, it's not tough to see why. But these are just three of roughly one hundred designer labels you'll find, which means you can spend a fun-filled hour hunting for that perfect pair of shades, and probably find three or four that fit the bill.

·EYEWEAR	·WATCHES	·DESIGNER	·KIDS

866-274-3673 · Ashford

Ashford.com

Claiming to sell more than 15,000 products covering "over 400 luxury brands," you wouldn't automatically think this is shop for bargain hunters. However, the site also claims you can "save up to 60 percent on brand names." Ultimately, this means if you're willing to spend a little you can save a lot on brands like Prada, Gucci, Fendi and Burberry, with such desirable products as designer sunglasses, handbags, fine watches and jewelry. With the added bonus of a custom engagement ring feature, two month's salary never bought so much.

·FINE JEWELRY ·DESIGNER	·EYEWEAR ·SMALL GOODS	·BAGS & WALLETS	·WATCHES

212-625-8595 · Ashley Dearborn

AshleyDearborn.com

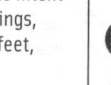

If commonplace shoes are bringing down your fabulous ensemble, you might need to upgrade your footwear with one of the extravagant pairs of heels, boots or sandals from this outstanding and fresh designer. A self-avowed shoe fanatic, Dearborn is intent on bringing "color, femininity, attitude and individuality back to the shoe market," and judging by inaugural seasonal offerings, she goes above and beyond her goals. You won't find a lot here, and it will be expensive, but for artwork you wear on your feet, it's absolutely worth a look.

·SHOES	·DESIGNER	·BOOTS	·SANDALS

Boodles.co.uk

It seems the fine jewels and watches offered by this two-centuries-old British manufacturer are good enough to warrant a browsing rate of one product per page. In truth, this actually may be the best way to present these breathtaking items, as the engagement rings, cufflinks, watches and other jewelry mainstays cost a fortune. So, when they are beautifully presented with large, colorful photographs that highlight every detail, the attention is absolutely warranted; after all, you'd hate to have any doubts with so many zeroes involved.

·FINE JEWELRY	·WATCHES		

BootBarn.com

There's no getting around this boot specialist, which offers a huge assortment of classic and modern takes on the time-tested footwear. Clearly, a big fraction of these are cowboy boots, but you'll see many styles including those meant for motorcycles, work, hiking, combat or just scintillating fashion. A variety of browsing filters makes it easy to wade through any boots you don't want; start by selecting your preferred style, followed by your size. Finally, choose the color you desire and you will have whittled thousands of pairs down to only a dozen or two. Not bad for a shop that compares itself to a barn.

·BELTS ·BOOTS	·HATS	·KIDS	·LEATHER

BoucherJewelry.com

Inexpensive, fashionable jewelry can be hard to come by for the cool customer. But discriminating accessorizers on a modest budget should find plenty of good bracelets, earrings and necklaces on this quirky site whose name is apparently French for "butcher" (we don't know why, we're just sayin'). Categories are split into color themes, including those redolent of the Beach and Honey. Or, check out the Pearls & Bridal section for a whole other level of elegant. You'll probably make return visits.

·FASHION JEWELRY			

BrellaBar.com

If, when the threat of rain looms, you're of the mind that just any umbrella will do, you probably won't want to shop here. On the other hand, those of us with discerning tastes will gladly pay a premium for the incredibly elegant and—dare we say—cool umbrellas found on this upscale specialty site. Some of these cost up to fifty times the amount you might expect to pay to keep your head and shoulders dry, but when you take a good look at the fashionable canopies and exquisitely designed crooks of what may be the world's best umbrella selection, you may decide it's worth it to see your prevent your personal style from being all wet.

·DESIGNER	·SMALL GOODS		

011-39-081-837-0487 · CanforaCapri.com

Canfora.com

The sassy and stylish handmade sandals offered by this one-of-a-kind retailer nearly qualify as jewelry for your feet. Based on the Mediterranean island of Capri, these sandals consist of flat, Italian leather soles and are inlaid with costume jewelry. But it's the incredible-looking designs that make them work, and they are so beautiful you won't even blanch when you see the high in-Euro price tags. You might flinch a little bit when you see the shipping charges, but as you will not find these anywhere else, it's worth it to have this precious footwear.

 ★

·SANDALS

888-266-5295 · ClassicSportsShoes.com

ClassicSportsShoes.com

With "over 10,000 pair of retro & fashion sneakers," this North Carolina–based web shop is to sneaker fetishists what the Louvre is to fans of Renaissance artwork. Except here you may actually purchase these artifacts of cultural history as created by Vans, Adidas, New Balance, Asics, Converse, Puma, Kangaroos and Keds. The classic sneaker styles will appeal to collectors and anyone else looking to add nostalgic appeal to his or her accessories wardrobe. Izod shirts and Member's Only jackets sold separately.

 ★

·SHOES   ·SANDALS

888-256-4748 · Clogworld.com

ClogWorld.com

The word *clog* typically brings to mind wooden shoes made in some Scandinavian country, but if you're looking for proof that clogs have gone global, this is it. Brands such as Birkenstock, Dr. Marten, Ecco, Dansko and Ugg may be better known for other styles of footwear, but you'll find them here in clog form, along with dozens of other brands. There are rubber and cork soles in addition to the traditional wood, complemented with leather, suede and faux leather tops and straps. You'd have trouble finding a greater clog variety in Amsterdam.

·SHOES

818-506-0862 · Cris Notti

CrisNotti.com

Hopefully, you've experienced the pleasure of carrying a handbag cool enough to turn your girlfriends green with envy; if you would like to attribute the same endorphin rush to your cosmetics case, this is the place to shop. Rising above pure functionality, these cases, totes and even sleeping masks take advantage of hip, colorful patterns to give you a stylish edge in front of the ladies' room mirror. All your friends will ask where you got them, but you might want to keep the answer to yourself, as these items do tend to sell out fast.

·BAGS & WALLETS   ·SMALL GOODS

DellaModa.com

DellaModaInc.com · 310-622-4490

If the word *outlet* sends chills up your spine, wait until you get a look at this one. Procuring designer and luxury overstock items from a variety of domestic and European sources, the shop specializes in handbags, wallets and shoes from luxe brands such as Prada, Fendi, Marc Jacobs and Christian Dior. While you may find some great deals here, the meaning of the word *discount* is relative, and since we're talking about some pretty posh items here, it stands to reason that the site's Shop By Price menu bottoms out at the $100 to $200 range.

| ·BAGS & WALLETS | ·SHOES | ·DESIGNER | ·DRESS SHOES |

DeNatale.com

De Natale Jewelers · 800-828-2930

For fine jewelry with no dearth of color, check out this high-end bauble site that offers gorgeous and elegant necklaces, bracelets, rings and earrings inlaid with vibrant precious stones. It also proves an excellent source of extravagant wedding bands, not to mention some engagement rings that deviate from the norm in an unparalleled manner. Alas, the site's only detriment may also be one of its strengths—namely, a relatively diminutive selection in most categories. What this ultimately means is that it shouldn't take you long to figure out whether or not you love this stuff as much as we do.

| ·FINE JEWELRY | ·SMALL GOODS | |

DeviKroell.com

Devi Kroell · 212-228-3201

Many sites have given us pause to wonder just how high-end can luxury shoes and handbags get. With this site we may have found the answer. With barely a dozen different products available at any given time, and a penchant for selling out, the incredibly upscale line could attribute its astronomical prices to the impeccable elegance of its wares. We're sure that plays a big part, but our best guess is that these items are as sought after as they are expensive due to the exotic materials involved: alligator, Astrakhan wool and python skin.

| ·BAGS & WALLETS | ·SHOES | ·DESIGNER | ·BOOTS |

DilseyCoal.com

Dilsey Coal · 704-334-8991

"Stocked with standout jewelry from emerging designers," this Charlotte, North Carolina, boutique features a small but mesmerizing assortment of baubles for fans of contemporary styles and sophisticated tastes. As up to date as any garment, handbag or shoes you're likely to pick up this season, these gemstone, gold and silver trinkets are often heralded by fashion magazines and coveted by celebrities, and are sure to make your daily outfit a special-occasion ensemble.

| ·FASHION JEWELRY | | |

212-242-2457 · Ellen Christine

EllenChristine.com

Do you ever get the feeling you're not spending enough on hats? Here are some handmade designs that should take care of that, and greatly increase the glamour of your head in the process. Inspired by the sort of styles fancied in a time when headwear was actually fashionable, these sculpted straws, cloches and traditional men's hats force us to wonder why they ever fell out of favor. High prices might have something to do with it, but as is often the case with products meant for lavish adornment, you get what you pay for.

·HATS	·DESIGNER		

011-34-965-690-158 · La Alpargateria de Aigües

EspadrillesEtc.com

This Spanish footwear boutique describes espadrilles as "effortlessly stylish, informally chic and the essence of Mediterranean allure," and they may be underselling the beachy shoes. Fantastic, and somehow affordable despite the transatlantic shipping, this is casual footwear that will turn heads. Despite a fairly simple design incorporating jute soles and canvas tops, you'll find a distinct variety of women's espadrilles, and a smaller but no less charming assortment of men's and children's designs. All you'll need now is a sunny place to wear them.

·BAGS & WALLETS	·SHOES	·KIDS	·SANDALS

888-896-3885 · Eyeglasses.com

EyeGlasses.com

Probably no accessory gets as much wear as your prescription eyewear, and absolutely none more affects the way you look. So how come it's so tough to find the perfect pair? If you'd like to see how easy it could be to find the right pair of glasses or sunglasses, take a look at this terrific frames and prescription lenses site. Initial browsing may not seem very useful or special, but that's why they offer the Feature Search. It's easily overlooked but incredibly powerful, enabling you to cut through the shop's huge variety with a compound search for frame styles, shapes, materials, colors, prices and more. Still uncertain? Upload a photo of yourself and through the miracle of technology get a glimpse of the frames on your face before you buy.

·EYEWEAR	·DESIGNER	·KIDS	

011-44-800-289-297 · Faith

Faith.co.uk

Designed for "the girl who is fun, sexy and mad about shoes," this British label delivers a comprehensive selection of fashionable footwear for those willing to suffer the calculations of a currency converter and endure the long wait for transatlantic delivery. It's easily worth the hassle, though, as this collection of boots, sandals, pumps and flats is versatile enough to cover any of your wardrobe's extremes, with a flair not typically found in UK brands, or US ones for that matter.

·SHOES	·LEATHER	·BOOTS	·SANDALS

FashionFlairs.com

Names like Aaneta, Ankh, Melie Bianco, Charm and Luck, Mae and J, Christiana, Besso and Loop NYC Design may not yet be on your fashion radar, but these emerging brands are making an impact in the world of style, sometimes featured in magazines and usually available from this constantly evolving web shop. Belts, watches, jewelry and most of all handbags may be found on a site that looks easier to use than it is, but if you take the time to figure out what sort of looks these labels represent, it will only get easier to stay on top of the newest accessory trends.

| ·BAGS & WALLETS | ·BELTS | ·WATCHES | ·FASHION JEWELRY |

FinerTimes.com

The amusing double meaning of this site's name aside, if you value a vintage watch design, you will find a great selection to work with here. With over 500 samples of charmingly outmoded wristwatches and classic pocket watches listed over fifty pages, by the time you go through the entire selection whatever watch you're wearing might be considered vintage. However, a Price Range filter can keep your browsing within an acceptable budget, while a Power Search allows you to do so while sticking to certain case metals, watch styles and movement types, if you happen to expect a watch that's both fetching and practical.

| ·WATCHES | | | |

FlipFlopCo.com

If it's been a while since a web shop has surprised you, maybe this one will do it. Devoted to footwear's most underrated design, the flip flop, the specialty site may not offer every thong design on the planet, but it has certainly managed to assemble much more than we're used to seeing in one place. Split among Men's, Women's and Children's categories, it should take you no time at all to browse through foam, wood, tatami and rubber soles with a variety of different strap materials and colors. Finally, we can match our flip flops to our bathing suits and hit the beach in style.

| ·KIDS | ·SANDALS | | |

FlipFlopTrunkShow.com

"Celebrating the unparalleled allure of women's thongs, slides and mules," this internet boutique is "all sandals all the time!" Well, they also offer a few beachy handbags, amusing graphic tee shirts and some other cute accessories. But flip-flops definitely rule the day, along with any other open-toed shoe that can be worn poolside, at a resort or, as the site insists, anywhere at any time. You'll have fun wearing them, and appropriately enough you'll have fun shopping for them here.

| ·BAGS & WALLETS | ·SHOES | ·KIDS | ·SANDALS |

707-963-2040 · Footcandy Shoes

FootCandyShoes.com

Since most of us believe you can't have too many shoes, here's a women's designer shoe site that may quickly become your favorite. While a look in the Manolo Blahnik section turns up a disappointing "In Store Only" message, shopping online for the likes of Isaac Mizrahi, Miss Sixty, Guiseppe Zinotti, Narciso Rodriguez, Moschino and many more is not just doable but highly fun, and with prices that seem almost fair, considering the upper echelon of fashion involved. If you're not immediately satisfied, check out the 50% Off sections; we think that ought to do it.

·SHOES	·DESIGNER	·BOOTS	·SANDALS

(WISH)

800-476-1718 · Forzieri

Forzieri.com

Italy. The long-standing global epicenter of fashion is celebrated in this Florence–based store that offers the finest in hand-crafted Italian designer accessories. Sure, the site can run kinda slow, but what's the rush if it's Italian? Take your time browsing the ties, ascots and scarves, or cufflinks, tie clips and belts. Or look at handbags and briefcases; what difference does it make? Man or woman, you're sure to find something in your price range or color preference, in your favorite materials, always made by Italy's finest, its designers.

·BAGS & WALLETS ·WATCHES	·GLOVES ·DESIGNER	·BELTS ·FASHION JEWELRY	·SCARVES/WRAPS

866-966-4688 · Fragments

Fragments.com

We've encountered many lines of hip fashion jewelry on many individual web sites—literally too many to mention. We like this site because it takes fresh necklace, bracelet and earring designs from these collections and includes them on one site: what a novel idea! These are designers and brands such as Chan Luu, Jane Diaz, Clear Metals, Greenbeads and Mallary Marks. You'll probably recognize some of these items from your favorite fashion magazines; only this site gives you the opportunity to wear it before you see it.

·DESIGNER	·FASHION JEWELRY		

800-248-9427 · Frames Direct

FramesDirect.com

With "Over 65,000 models for you to choose from," these guys make a pretty good case to support their claim of being the "world's leading online eyeglass store." Having a couple of brands in mind is pretty much the only way you'll find any sunglasses, though, without having to actually browse through those tens of thousands of options. You can also look for frames particular to such activities as golf, skiing and tennis, as well as peruse some contact lens brands and prescription-ready frames for those less-than-sunny days.

·EYEWEAR	·KIDS		

• Shoes & Accessories •

FranceLuxe.com

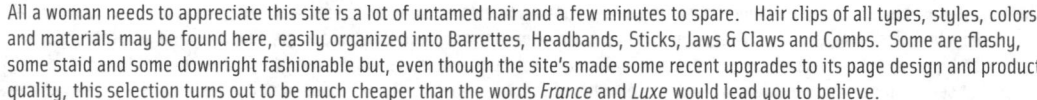 The Finest Accessories · 888-884-3653

All a woman needs to appreciate this site is a lot of untamed hair and a few minutes to spare. Hair clips of all types, styles, colors and materials may be found here, easily organized into Barrettes, Headbands, Sticks, Jaws & Claws and Combs. Some are flashy, some staid and some downright fashionable but, even though the site's made some recent upgrades to its page design and product quality, this selection turns out to be much cheaper than the words *France* and *Luxe* would lead you to believe.

 ·HAIR ACCESSORIES

FrenchSole.com

 French Sole · 011-44-118 988 88 0

You don't need to be a dancer to appreciate ballet-style footwear, and one look at this site will make you a believer even if you don't know a pirouette from croise devant. The European shoe specialist features a beautiful selection of ballet flats that apply a multitude of fabrics and patterns to a single, classic style, the result being extremely elegant shoes that don't require a heel to make a lasting impression. There's no saying they'll make you more graceful or postured, but they will add to your fashionable ensemble while keeping your feet comfortable for a change.

  ·SHOES

Ghurka.com

Ghurka · 800-587-1584

If fine craftsmanship and quality leather mean anything to you, you'll want to spend plenty of time browsing this manufacturer's site before you buy your next briefcase, handbag, cosmetics case, backpack, travel bag, wallet or pair of moccasins. The Connecticut workshop offers "heirloom quality products," which means they look great now but will only get better with age as the vegetable-tanned leathers grow soft and "mellow into an unmistakable luster." Knowing this should at least take some of the bite out of these items' exorbitant price tags.

   ·BAGS & WALLETS | ·SHOES | ·LEATHER | ·SMALL GOODS

GinaShoes.com

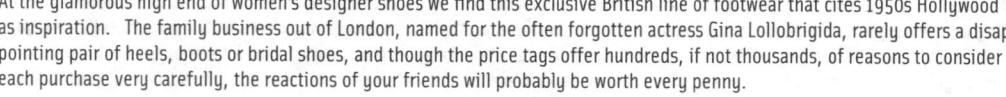 Gina · 011-44-20-7235-2932

At the glamorous high end of women's designer shoes we find this exclusive British line of footwear that cites 1950s Hollywood as inspiration. The family business out of London, named for the often forgotten actress Gina Lollobrigida, rarely offers a disappointing pair of heels, boots or bridal shoes, and though the price tags offer hundreds, if not thousands, of reasons to consider each purchase very carefully, the reactions of your friends will probably be worth every penny.

  ·BAGS & WALLETS | ·SHOES | ·DESIGNER | ·BOOTS

888-246-3551 · Giving Tree Gallery

GivingTreeGallery.com

Celebrating the artistry of designer jewelry, this labor of love has evolved from a small business run out of a Cape Cod gallery space into quite an amazing and slick web presence. The long list of featured designers will immediately impress those in the know, and even if you come in blind there are plenty of descriptive bios explaining exactly why each artist's work is appreciated, both by the proprietors and the world at large. Hence the New Discoveries and Exclusives sections are always worth visiting but, ultimately you should shop by Jewelry Type and just relish the beautiful bounty picture by picture, page by page.

·DESIGNER	·FASHION JEWELRY		

011-41-22-718-3314 · Produits Artistiques de Métaux Précieux

GoldAvenue.com

Most fashionable jewelry is composed of relatively inexpensive materials, which makes sense as trends tend to change with the seasons. Well, this Switzerland-based jeweler seems to let weather worry about seasons, preferring to combine fine gold and gemstones into elaborate, contemporary designs that are prone to bold statements. The jewelry provides fairly simple browsing, while other categories will uncover some fascinating pendants, charms and watches that will keep track of time regardless of the style du jour.

·FINE JEWELRY	·HAIR ACCESSORIES	·WATCHES	

800-465-3340 · Goldspeed.com

GoldSpeed.com

At first glance, this site isn't all that different from several others that just throw truckloads of jewelry at you and expect you to find something you want to buy. However, this site turns out to be better for one little reason: taste. These myriad lovely pieces seem to have a higher standard than other, comparable selections, and we're not just talking about higher prices. If you're going to spend a day browsing through many, many pages of fine jewelry, cufflinks and watches, you'd do well to do it here. Besides, the browsing is better.

·FINE JEWELRY	·WATCHES		

800-862-0100 · Goorin Brothers

Goorin.com

This site forces you through a bit of a rigmarole before letting you view and purchase its outstanding array of hats, then apparently won't allow returns, so you'll get no second guesses. This means you'll have to delve deep into all the superhip headwear, which ranges from urban hipster to ironic chic styles. We'd suggest following the Order link from the outset, then viewing all the seasonal and archived selection. New windows will open up and you'll be clicking links all over the place, almost never certain when you've reached the end, but since just about every hat will look good on somebody's head, browsing may be worth an hour of your time.

·HATS			

GuenveurFurst.com

Guenveur Furst · 214-328-6611

There's nothing new or unique about hanging semiprecious stones from earrings and necklaces, but the dynamic design duo behind this line of fashionable accoutrements has managed to add an original twist to a popular contemporary motif, one that makes a look at this site entirely worthwhile. The gist of it is that you get more stones, evenly dispersed, which has the effect of spreading vibrant color across the whole of the necklace chain, or the entire dangle of the earring, as it were. You must see it to truly understand, but that's what we're trying to get at: take a look!

·DESIGNER	·FASHION JEWELRY		

HairBoutique.com

HairBoutique.com · 866-469-4247

This helpful hair site offers news and tips about growing thick, lustrous hair, but if you enter the site's Marketplace, you can find a variety of hair accoutrements to help you tame it. The hair bands, ties, scrunchies, barrettes and pins are spread across several pages in the Accessories section, and upon first glance there may only appear to be a few dozen items. However, these are merely the "Most Popular" choices; you'll notice a right-side menu that offers Bobby Pins, Bridal Accessories, Bungee Bands, Bun Wraps, Sidecombs and much, much more, ranging from the purely functional to the sublime.

·HAIR ACCESSORIES			

HartfordYork.com

Hartford York Headwear · 800-936-5646

Here's a men's haberdasher with classic appeal, although according to the owner of this small business, "these days people wear more and different kinds of hats than in the past." We're not so sure about that, but his theory is well tested by a fantastic selection of popular headwear reflecting the past two centuries, including porkpie hats, newsboy caps, fedoras, fur caps, tweed hats, beret, felts, hunter's caps and plenty more time-honored designs. You'll also find scarves, gloves and a few more decidedly anachronistic items like walking sticks.

·GLOVES	·HATS	·SCARVES/WRAPS	·LEATHER

HatsInTheBelfry.com

Hats In The Belfry · 888-999-4287

Among the first things we noticed while checking out this site was a conical wizard's cap, a purple Mad Hatter's hat and one of those star-spangled top hats that curry favor on the July 4th holiday. A little crazy? More than a little. However, alongside the Sherlock Holmes caps, Kaiser helmets and French Foreign Legion hats, there are plenty of legitimate, sober headwear choices, from cowboy hats and cloches to ivy caps and berets, presuming berets can be considered legitimate headwear. The site runs a little slow, but otherwise is pretty well on top of things, whether your headwear interests are earnest or in jest.

·HATS			

800-561-4278 · The Heiress Vault

Featured on this vintage jewelry site are some of the best-known designers of 1940s and 1950s costume jewelry. Names like Trifari, Margaret Rowe and Miriam Haskell may only be remembered by a select few, but it's not just collectors who revel in these high-end fashion artifacts, as trendsetting celebrities and other style mavens are occasionally known to don this classic mid-century jewelry. To many of us, it's a bit surprising to see such high prices on pieces that lack any precious materials, but if the enduring quality of this work is not lost on you, everything on this site may excite you.

·DESIGNER	·FASHION JEWELRY	

800-539-3580 · Ice

With a name like Ice, you'd expect this site to be very cool, clean and crisp. It's all those things; a very slick site with excellent browsing and search options covering a fine selection, and terrific looks at some equally slickly designed rings, necklaces, bracelets, watches, etc. Despite the good-looking wares, though, the prices on this site are far from overblown and, should you find cause to disagree, they're willing to set you up with a monthly payment plan. Think of this as the rare jewelry store that exceeds expectations.

·FINE JEWELRY	·WATCHES	·FASHION JEWELRY

415-462-6294 · Isharya

"Founded by two moms who passionately believe that family and fashion should never be at odds," this small line of clothing, jewelry and accessories endeavors to create simple, stylish and affordable products for active mothers. As it happens, the results are a bit more dangerous than that, with killer scarves, to-die-for handbags, drop-dead-gorgeous tunics and terminally beautiful jewelry. It all may be too much for carpool, but if you refuse to accept motherhood as a death knell to your groovy youth, this will keep you looking as hot as ever.

·BAGS & WALLETS	·SCARVES/WRAPS	·FASHION JEWELRY

866-522-7768 · Jacqueline Jarrot

This small string of upscale accessories shops out of Los Angeles has enjoyed phenomenal success over the years and is regularly featured in popular fashion magazines, attracting fashionistas, socialites and young starlets alike to browse "the hottest merchandise from over 1000 designers." Now that this web site smoothly delivers the same wide assortment of handbags, hair clips, wallets, jewelry, watches, scarves, shawls, shoes and belts, you can pretty much buy an item as soon as you see it in your favorite celebrity fashion feature.

·BAGS & WALLETS ·WATCHES	·BELTS ·DESIGNER	·SCARVES/WRAPS ·FASHION JEWELRY	·HAIR ACCESSORIES ·SANDALS

JannaConner.com

Janna Conner Designs · 323-255-0374

The Los Angeles–based jewelry designer behind this site offers jewelry for women "who are influenced by trends yet are not ruled exclusively by them." In other words, many of these contemporary, colorful and feminine pieces set their own trends. You'll find dozens of pages on this site filled with necklaces, bracelets and earrings, and it will be worth every click to see the entire selection. Little wonder her jewelry has been picked up by the world's most popular upscale department stores... but this is still the best place to find it online.

·DESIGNER	·FASHION JEWELRY	

JemzNJewels.com

Jemznjewels · 800-488-8265

Fairly limited in terms of jewelry, this is actually a great site for couture accessories of many kinds: bags, shoes, scarves, hats and belts. A bevy of recognizable designer brands will immediately command your attention, whether Chanel, Prada or Louis Vuitton, and most of the items will keep you current and looking good. Better yet is the selection of vintage accessories, mostly handbags, which recall some of the fine designs of the past yet still stand the scrutiny of today's looks; they may even lend you an air of accomplished indifference to passing trends. As quantities are quite slim, you might want to keep this one to yourself.

·BAGS & WALLETS ·SHOES	·BELTS ·DESIGNER	·HATS ·FASHION JEWELRY	·SCARVES/WRAPS

JenniferKaufman.com

Jennifer Kaufman · 310-854-1058

Likening itself to a "no calorie candy shop," this site easily backs its claim with a colorful and delicious-looking assortment of designer jewelry. Though limited in variety, the brilliantly vivid baubles deliver massive amounts of design appeal, with simple ingredients like rope and glass beads mixing it up with precious metals and gemstones. Consequently, you'll find moderate prices mixed in with a few higher-end items. Regardless, it's a terrific place to shop when you want to treat yourself to a new trinket for that next night out; you'll just have to decide how big a treat you deserve when you get here.

·BAGS & WALLETS	·HAIR ACCESSORIES	·DESIGNER	·FASHION JEWELRY

JewelryService.com

Jewelry Service Centers · 877-768-6400

This web page actually hosts a conglomeration of sites that are fairly self-explanatory: AllWatchbands.com, WatchBattery.com, AllReligiousJewelry.com and AllCharms.com. The watch batteries and religious jewelry are fairly predictable, but the wide selection of charms more than meets expectations while the selection of watchbands far exceeds them. The latter may be ordered to size and color specifications, browsed either to match your particular watch brand or by a number of materials as boring as metal or plastic and as exotic as lizard, alligator, ostrich or shark. Overall, this web retailer's not nearly as boring as it sounds.

·WATCHES			

307-733-7687 · Jackson Hole Hat Co.

JHHatCo.com

Getting a cowboy hat from Wyoming is like getting a face-lift in Beverly Hills; it just feels authentic. But there's another great reason to buy a hat from this Jackson Hole retailer in particular: customization. You'll find an array of felt cowboy hat designs, ranging in styles from Derby, Fedora and Top Hat to all the various sheriff and outlaw looks you've seen in any movie; and all are available made-to-fit. You can also select from dozens of colors and hatbands, and can adjust the brim size to suit your own bent, pardner.

·HATS

877-569-4880 · Jildor Shoes

JildorShoes.com

If half the fun of having great shoes is shopping for them, then this designer shoe site offers twice the fun. Offering an enormous selection, the Long Island retailer has been working more than fifty years to develop a selection featuring some great assortments of the most popular labels in ladies' footwear. Emilio Pucci, Jack Rogers, Kate Spade, Michael Kors, Stuart Weitzman, Uggs and Vera Wang are but a sampling of the many pumps, flats, sandals, mules and boots on hand at this decidedly foot-oriented super-store.

 ★

·SHOES ·DESIGNER ·BOOTS ·SANDALS

212-683-2363 · Jody Singleton

JodySingleton.com

With a client list that reads like the *Billboard* top twenty, this unique designer creates "one of a kind pieces of jewelry with an urban edge." Incorporating such materials as leather, feathers, minerals and Fender guitar picks, you won't find anything resembling this selection in a typical jewelry store. It's little wonder these hand-crafted necklaces, earrings and cuffs have attracted the attention of the music world—wear one and you'll probably feel a bit like a rock star yourself.

·DESIGNER ·FASHION JEWELRY

011-34- 971-602-627 · Gisbert A. Joseph

Joseph-Watches.com

Representing a British workshop that has been refurbishing vintage wrist and pocket watches for twenty years, this web site doesn't always make it easy to view its thousands of available timepieces. You may filter your search to stick to one of the hundreds of brands represented, limit your hunt by whichever decade the watch was made or pinpoint specific face shapes or case materials. However you choose to look, chances are you will miss out on at least some fraction of the amazing selection, and will be equally flummoxed the next time you visit. Still, we can't help but think it's worth it.

·WATCHES

JosephineOnline.com

Josephine · 312-274-0359

This Chicago shoe salon takes its inspiration from "old Hollywood glamour," the result being a collection of high-end women's footwear that all but transcends fashion. Featuring designers such as Oscar de la Renta, Valentino, Christian Laboutin and Stella McCartney, the pumps, flats, sandals, boots and evening shoes cannot fail to thrill a shoe-loving gal, which makes this an excellent spot to pick up a gift certificate for a friend or loved one. The occasional designer handbag doesn't hurt either.

·BAGS & WALLETS ·SANDALS	·SHOES ·DRESS SHOES	·DESIGNER	·BOOTS

KoloBags.com

Kolobags · 866-405-5656

The advantage of owning a laptop is its portability, but who wants to lug a boring, ugly laptop case everywhere you go? Not the people who shop from this functional but fashionable accessory specialist. Laptop-ready briefcases, messenger bags, backpacks and totes allow you to keep your machine at the ready without sacrificing your sense of style. Dig deep and you'll find an assortment cool enough to match your wardrobe, but choose carefully—the cost of savvy mobile computing is high enough you probably won't want to buy two.

·BAGS & WALLETS	·SMALL GOODS		

LargeFeet.com

Friedman's Shoes · 800-886-3668

Boasting a clientele seemingly ripped from the pages of *Sports Illustrated*, this Atlanta specialty shoe store has been serving the extra-large feet of some very well known extra-large men for three-quarters of a century. But while the endorsement of big fellas like Shaquille O'Neal and Charles Barkley is exciting, more so is the selection of large-size shoes, which includes dozens of popular regular-size brands such as Puma, Adidas, Birkenstock, Cole Haan, Kenneth Cole, Nike and Timberland. Of course, the women's selection is a bit smaller, but still sufficiently big and wide.

·BELTS ·SANDALS	·SHOES ·DRESS SHOES	·LEATHER	·BOOTS

LedererDeParis.com

Lederer de Paris · 888-537-6921

Boasting the "finest European handcrafted goods since 1898," this NYC outfit enters its second century with an incredible and accomplished selection of briefcases, alongside some prim and, for lack of a better word, appropriate handbags. You'll probably find their ties atrocious (no offense if you're a fan), but they also have a few classy pieces of luggage that'll complement your professional polish. At any rate, do be sure to glance at the ties, at least, especially the one with a frog print. It could make a good gag gift.

·BAGS & WALLETS	·LEATHER		

011-44-20-7930-8874 · James Lock & Co.

LockHatters.co.uk

When the oldest family-owned-and-operated business in the world makes a place for itself on the web, you know internet shopping has arrived. Established in 1676, this British hat maker can still sell you some of the headwear styles in vogue when the original shop opened, including a variety of top hats, smoking caps and tweed pageboy caps. A historical selection continues with porkpies, panama hats, trilbys, homburgs and of course fedoras. Men's haberdashery cannot possibly be more classic than this.

| ·HATS | | | |  |

011-44-20-7930-8720 · Longmire

Longmire.co.uk

How much are you wiling to spend on cufflinks? Wait—don't answer that until you've taken a good, long look at this English specialty jeweler's site. Among this astronomically expensive selection you'll find timeless silver looks, high-concept modern designs, startlingly appealing novelty pieces and even a few great-looking monogrammed models. Of course those featuring gemstones are the priciest on the site, but when you're looking at arguably the finest men's jewelry you expect a staggering cost; you just hope it's not going to be in pounds sterling.

| ·FINE JEWELRY | | | |  |

866-910-3900 · Luna Boston

LunaBoston.com

This shop is intriguing in that it opened online and as a Boston-area boutique simultaneously, hedging its bets and embracing a business plan we like to consider the future of small entrepreneurial enterprise. More importantly, it's also got the goods, specifically when it comes to handbags, belts, fashion jewelry and functional accessories. A brilliant shopping experience allows you to browse from a long list of popular and/or hard-to-find designers, but you may also easily shop by product Type, Price and Use, as well as by personal Style, including Bohemian, Classic, Retro and Trendy. Whatever your look, you'll like the way these guys operate.

| ·BAGS & WALLETS ·SMALL GOODS | ·BELTS | ·WATCHES | ·FASHION JEWELRY |  |

203-853-3264 · Lyn Gaylord Accessories

LynGaylord.com

If you've found yourself lamenting the fact that your belt buckles or cufflinks simply aren't cute enough, this might be the site for you. The ornate metalwork depicts such things as horses, dogs, hearts, teddy bears, butterflies and turtles. Categories like Romantic and Whimsical tell the story, while a Mens section offers a slightly more subdued array of silver items. These are the sorts of things you usually only find in Beverly Hills and online.

| ·FINE JEWELRY | ·BELTS | | | |

MadImports.net

Since you probably won't be making it to Madagascar this year, we'd like to tell you about this web retailer, which offers to bring handbags from the island nation to you. These bags "blend the traditional weaving talents and contemporary techniques... enables families to gain economic independence and generates funding for community development projects." More importantly, the straw totes, clutches and travel bags look really cool, with clean, contemporary designs and beach-friendly colors.

 ·BAGS & WALLETS

MinuJewels.com

If the elegant, handcrafted semiprecious jewelry featured by this site reminds you of any ancient Mediterranean cultures, it's no mistake. The mother-daughter designers behind the site often travel to the region for raw materials and inspiration, the results "reflective of the ancient Egyptian, Arabic [and] Bedouin" influence. What the international effort really boils down to is jewelry offering beautiful stones and excellent craftsmanship presented by the type of small-business storefront only afforded by the world wide web.

 ·DESIGNER   ·FASHION JEWELRY

Mondera.com

Whatever your taste or price range, the odds are good this site will suit your jewelry needs. This should prove particularly handy for betrothed couples looking for the right set of wedding bands, or for grooms-to-be to build a custom engagement ring. Outside of marital items, you may browse by jewelry type or material, which works out fairly well whether you're looking for men's or women's items. Additionally, each category gives you the option of sticking to a particular price range, a fact that men may want to keep from their fiancées.

    ·FINE JEWELRY

MoondanceJewelry.com

If there are any treasure maps to Los Angeles, they probably all guide you to this Santa Monica designer jewelry retailer. Boasting both a lengthy list of designers and celebrity clientele, the only problem seems to be that you almost require a map to get through all the wonderful pieces made available on the site. If you happen to have a few favorites among these top jewelry crafters you'll have it easy, otherwise you'll have to set aside some serious browsing time to sort through this trove of riches.

  ·FINE JEWELRY   ·DESIGNER   ·FASHION JEWELRY

866-666-7661 · Moo Roo

MooRoo.com

You may be familiar with the sort of conceptual art that hangs on museum walls, but how about the kind that hangs off your elbow? The handbags and clutches here draw inspiration from unlikely sources, including flamingos, sushi rollers and rainbow-colored foxes. By the sound of it, you might expect these items to be tacky or kitschy—but, in truth, they're more likely to be seen on the arms of celebrities than pop culture fetishists. As for the wide assortment of conceptual brooches, we'll leave them for you to judge.

·BAGS & WALLETS	·DESIGNER	·FASHION JEWELRY	

505-296-2300 · Morning Glory Antiques

MorningGloryJewelry.com

Proving that even antique and vintage fashion jewelry can be as refreshingly cool as the newest modern designer baubles, this modest-looking site actually turns up a fantastic selection of products ranging from bracelets and brooches to cameos and hair clips. Most of these items are probably older than you are, and often their retro looks reflect an era gone by. However, even if you prefer something more sleek and sophisticated there will be more great finds here, and with great, reliable customer service, the keen fashionista can hardly afford to miss it.

·FASHION JEWELRY			

212-967-0760 · Moyna

MoynaBags.com

"Individually hand beaded and embroidered by skilled artisans in India," this incredible assortment of handbags is of such fine quality you might have to upgrade your wardrobe to match. Simply put, there is nothing ordinary among these purses, evening bags, bridal handbags and totes, whether they're adorned by glass beads, silver sequins, feathers, semiprecious stones or embroidered suede. For that matter, there's nothing ordinary about the small variety of belts, hair clips, scarves and shawls, either. Don't miss this one.

·BAGS & WALLETS	·BELTS	·SCARVES/WRAPS	·HAIR ACCESSORIES

011-44-17-4934-0500 · Mulberry

Mulberry-England.co.uk

Leather bags, briefcases and wallets are pretty much classy by definition, but when these items are made in Great Britain and designed with great finesse, their elegance increases exponentially. Purchasing these wares generally indicates that you're willing to go out of your way to show some sophistication, especially as shipping them across the Atlantic is a pricey proposition. Will owning such upscale products make you more organized or better equipped to handle important situations? No. But they sure will make you seem so.

·BAGS & WALLETS	·LEATHER	·SMALL GOODS	

NaughtySecretaryClub.com

Not just a web shop with a hilarious name, the power of this site may be summed up with the notion of "revamped vintage." In other words, any of the kitschy jewelry, purses or watches of the past century may be refurbished or returned to vogue by the quirky and vigilant eyes of the site's ironically hip proprietors. We spotted fruit basket barrettes, butterfly brooches and an elephant watch but, sadly, these items sell out quick so you'll have to check back often to find your next ultracute accessory.

		·BAGS & WALLETS	·HAIR ACCESSORIES	·WATCHES	·FASHION JEWELRY

NicNorman.com

Is your belt buckle doing enough? Maybe it fastens your belt, and maybe it holds up your trousers, but if it's one of the funky, fashionable belts available from this Los Angeles retailer it also displays a lovely piece of pop art in the process. As good as this site looks, browsing can be an arduous task, and if you don't feel like looking through all the artistically rendered images available, you may simply opt to add your own to the mix by following the Custom Belts link and uploading a digital image to include with your preferred belt-and-buckle combination.

·BELTS			

OddBallShoe.com

Do guys with big feet have any fashion sense? They do if they shop here. Founded by a couple of oversize siblings in Portland, Oregon, this exquisitely designed site serves sizes 12–20 with aplomb, featuring popular brands like Converse, Dr. Martens, Adidas, New Balance, Vans and plenty more, granting big feet fashionable options where there once were none. Don't think they can help? They'll even custom-order shoes for larger sizes, and have been known to boast having once sold a pair of size 56s.

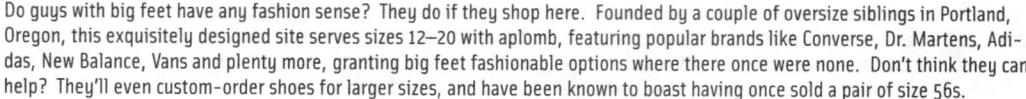

		·SHOES	·SANDALS	·DRESS SHOES	

OfficeHoldings.co.uk

Some people take their shoes very seriously, and will search for the perfect pair even if it means going across the Atlantic to do so. Here's a little something for them. It's not so much that one can't find these brands in American shoe stores; the models available just don't usually have the same cachet as those featured on this UK site. This exquisite footwear is hip to an international groove, and will look good anywhere. Too bad about the excruciatingly slow and yet extraordinarily expensive shipping...but it's still cheaper than a trip across the pond.

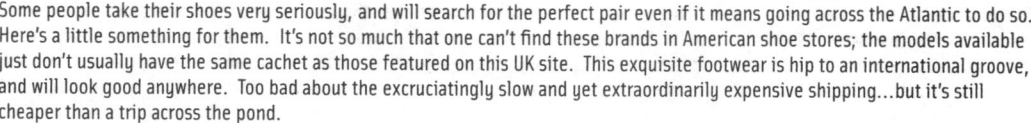

			·LEATHER	·BOOTS	·SANDALS	·DRESS SHOES

800-786-3141 · OnlineShoes.com

OnlineShoes.com

If a shoe store this big existed in the real world, you would wear out your soles walking around the store, and be forced to buy some new footwear just to have something to walk home in. Okay, this may be a slight exaggeration; but the fact is, this online behemoth does offer a great selection in each of more than three dozen brands, from Adidas to Uggs, including sandals, boots, dress shoes, casual shoes, athletic shoes and slippers. Your best bet is to use the Advanced Search to focus on something in your size, width, shoe type and/or price range. After that, it's simply a matter of style.

·SHOES ·SANDALS	·KIDS ·DRESS SHOES	·LEATHER	·BOOTS

888-723-2866 · Peter Beaton Hat Studio

PeterBeaton.com

If you're in the market for a lovely straw hat, check out these head toppers designed in Nantucket. Inspired by the sunny New England isle and its genteel culture, these ribboned sunhats will take you back to the country days of old, and to help maintain the illusion the site also offers striped sailor shirts, ribbon belts and straw tote bags, along with the requisite wicker hat boxes. However, this isn't to say these wares don't suit a modern setting, as these dozens of hats exhibit styles as charming as they are timeless.

·BAGS & WALLETS	·BELTS	·HATS

866-740-7465 · Pink Mascara

PinkMascara.com

Featuring a specialized but dazzling assortment of "in the know" fashions, this colorful retailer hosts a bevy of hip handbags by designers on the verge. Reputations may very well be established by the bags seen here, and judging by the publicity materials of this site, you'll appreciate this chance to get one of them before they're all snatched up by celebrities. Also available are a collection of dangling earrings and lovely necklaces, also said to be the next thing. You may not care about the buzz, but you still might dig the styles.

·BAGS & WALLETS	·DESIGNER	·FASHION JEWELRY

800-972-4179 · Plaza Too

PlazaToo.com

For seven decades this family-owned retailer has been serving the female fashion community with its smattering of boutiques scattered around the New York City metropolitan area. Here you'll find the same handpicked assortment of designer shoes, boots, belts, sandals and handbags without having to set foot anywhere near the Big Apple. Dozens of highly sought after designer labels are on hand, including Jack Rogers, Anne Klein, Marc Jacobs, Stuart Weitzman and Vera Wang. Check here to get a clear idea of the cost of high fashion.

·BAGS & WALLETS ·FASHION JEWELRY	·BELTS ·LEATHER	·SHOES ·BOOTS	·DESIGNER ·SANDALS

PreciousAccents.com

Precious Accents · 866-707-6001

Fans of gold and silver jewelry and the people who love them ought to remember this site, which makes shopping for the precious metal necklaces, bracelets and pins a simple and rewarding task. Chief among reasons to visit this shop, though, is the wide, terrifically organized assortment of pendants and charms. In particular, look under the Rembrandt Charms link, and you'll find lockets, photo charms, religious symbols, zodiac signs, good-luck charms and plenty of shapes representative of personal hobbies and interests. The most precious part may come at the end of the shopping process, when you get to choose between silver, gold-plated and multiple gold versions of each product, with prices commensurate.

·WATCHES	·FASHION JEWELRY		

Raffaello-Network.com

Raffaello · 888-855-7056

If you're under the impression that Italian fashion is tops in the world, you won't find a better accessories shop online. As unusual as it sounds, men apparently get preferential treatment here, but if you scroll down the page you'll see that women's accoutrements are also represented in abundance. Looking at this stuff can be a bear, as within each category you can only view one specific designer at a time, and vice versa. The thing is, you just don't find better designers. Including names like Gucci, Versace, Prada, D & G, Dior, Ferre, Ferragamo, Fendi and Armani, this selection of belts, wallets, shoes, ties, watches, sunglasses, jewelry, briefcases and handbags just doesn't come along every day.

·EYEWEAR	·BAGS & WALLETS	·BELTS	·SHOES
·WATCHES	·DESIGNER	·DRESS SHOES	

RobertaChiarella.com

Roberta Chiarella · 877-725-3935

Incorporating Austrian crystals into earrings, necklaces, bracelets and hair accessories, Roberta Chiarella's designs have had fantastic exposure in magazines, movies and television shows, and have been seen on too many celebrities to mention. The good news for us is that this site gives us the opportunity to browse through her entire colorful catalog, in particular the splashy dangling earrings that highlight the collection. You'll find dozens of pieces, but you'll have to look for them, as browsing proves to be a page-by-page ordeal; if it's any consolation, it's much easier than flipping through magazine pages.

·HAIR ACCESSORIES	·DESIGNER	·FASHION JEWELRY

RoyalOrder.com

Royal Order · 310-855-0850

This West Hollywood designer jewelry outfit exists at the point where heavy metal meets heavy metals, "the undeniable union of rock'n'roll and fashion." In this case, the metals are thickly cast sterling silver and 18K gold, whereas the rocks are diamonds, pearls and semiprecious stones. Probably the only place you'll find a $2700 wallet chain, this stuff can get quite expensive, which owes more to the generous portions of precious materials than the skull shapes embedded in many of the pieces. Your best bets are to stick to the rings, bracelets, earrings, cufflinks and pendants. And maybe an elaborate silver rosary if you're the religious rocker type.

·DESIGNER	·FASHION JEWELRY		

202-471-4400 · Sassanova

Sassanova.com

"Frustrated by the omnipresence of chains and sick of journeying to suburban department stores for designer shoes," self-professed "shoe junkies" Sassy Jacobs and Sarah Cannova put together a startlingly good collection of boots, flats, sandals, mules, wedges and heels when they opened this Washington, D.C., footwear boutique. In only a few years the store has managed to compile a succinct assortment of desirable shoes by an impressive list of hard-to-find designers, and we suggest you take advantage of this great site to make it hard for them to keep shoes in stock.

·SHOES	·DESIGNER	·BOOTS	·SANDALS

 ★

011-44-1890 860770 · ScotlandShop.net

ScotlandShop.net

Each of your tartan dreams may be fulfilled on this all-things-Scottish specialist, which caters to men, women and children in need of kilts and the like. While women will seem to benefit the most from the varied selection of apparel, the accessories available should please the whole family. Scarves and knit caps in particular give you all the plaid your wardrobe can handle, with plenty of socks to match (and, no, not all of them argyle). Sadly, you'll have to pick up your set of bagpipes elsewhere.

·BAGS & WALLETS	·HATS	·SCARVES/WRAPS	

800-201-3669 · She-Works

She-Works.com

"Run by working women, for working women," this surprisingly diverse accessories site offers a new sense of fashion where there once was none. Beginning with female-friendly briefcases and notebook computer carriers, the prim, colorful and highly functional selection caters to the style-savvy sophisticate who has ocassional funky tendencies. Such a range of products would not be complete without mobile phone cases, daily organizers, carry-on luggage, wallets and cosmetics cases, and these may be found with satisfaction and ease. It works.

·BAGS & WALLETS	·LEATHER	·SMALL GOODS	

510-732-8900 · Shiekh Shoes

ShiekhShoes.com

It's a good sign when an online shoe store offers so many options that you get tired of looking before you've seen them all. Such is the case with this growing retailer, which covers everything from casual to dressy shoes and does so with modest prices across the board. Boots, sandals and athletic shoes are also included, representing such popular brands as Adidas, Converse, Lacoste, Fila, Puma, Ecko and Timberland. When you come back for a second visit to view the rest, keep your eyes open for special sales and other deals that make the shop even more affordable.

·SHOES	·KIDS	·BOOTS	

ShoeBuy.com

ShoeBuy.com · 888-200-8414

With hundreds of name brands and thousands of products, what more could you want from this, "The World's Largest Site for Shoes?" How about free shipping and returns? Yes, the massive shoe shop makes great strides to provide strong customer service—but how are the shoes? Well, if your feet are large, small, narrow, wide or average, you'll find a great selection. If you're a man, woman or child, you'll find a great selection. And, if you're looking for dress, casual or athletic shoes, slippers, sandals or boots, you'll find a great selection. Come to think of it, you might want to use the Advanced Search feature to shop here.

·SHOES ·DRESS SHOES	·KIDS	·BOOTS	·SANDALS

ShoeMine.com

Shoe Mine · 866-975-7463

This spirited retailer from Park Slope, Brooklyn, makes up for its meager selection by making it fun, funky and slightly unusual. With a small number of brands you won't find elsewhere, and a small number of shoes for each brand you do, the shop is mainly useful to fringe-thinking fashionistas who are not among the one in 119 Americans currently living in New York City's most populous borough. If you want the all-encompassing shoe shopping experience, this won't be it. But if you want to see something a little different, this one will only take up a couple of minutes of your day, and no subway ride.

·SHOES	·DESIGNER		

ShoeTrader.com

ShoeTrader.com · 866-210-2664

Upon further inspection, the deep selection of ladies' footwear available from this Tuscon, Arizona–based web shop proves even wider than it looks. Literally, most pairs of boots, sandals, slippers, slides, pumps and athletic shoes are available in wider-than-average sizes, ensuring your foot the comfort it deserves. As if this wasn't reason enough to appreciate the site, it offers excellent prices, free shipping and even free returns, encouraging us to take a chance on any pair we like and making sure we find something that fits.

·SHOES	·BOOTS	·SANDALS	

ShoppingAllure.com

ShoppingAllure.com · 877-475-7018

A seemingly never-ending selection of terrific designer handbags and clutches is all the reason you'll need to shop from this family-owned web shop, but while you're here you might find some great belts, jewelry or flip flops as well. Featuring the sort of wares you'll spot in popular fashion magazines like *In Style* or *Us Weekly*, the proprietors strive to add new products daily, even offering pre-orders on items they anticipate will sell out fast, so handbag fiends will want to devote a couple of minutes each week to this regularly updated site.

·EYEWEAR ·SANDALS	·BAGS & WALLETS	·DESIGNER	·FASHION JEWELRY

800-781-8883 · Solomon Brothers Fine Jewelry

SolomonBrothers.com

If you'd like to "avoid the middleman" in your diamond jewelry purchases, this Atlanta-based jeweler offers "diamonds directly from the mines in South Africa," which should cut down on markup costs. A mildly complex search function guides you to decent browsing through the jewelry selection, which may be used to find some gorgeous wedding bands and engagement rings. Or, if you prefer a finely polished loose diamond, another search makes it simple to find an array of round, oval, emerald, marquise, radiant or Asscher cuts, among others, though beyond that you'll really want to know something about carat, color and clarity before making any purchase... at which point a middleman might come in handy.

·FINE JEWELRY

347-256-0127 · Southwestern Jewelry

SouthwesternJewelry.net

Browse through any number of jewelers and gift shops in the Southwest United States and you'll find yourself lost in a sea of turquoise. The same opportunity presents itself with this website, which offers a healthy amount of silver and turquoise rings, bracelets, necklaces, earrings and belt buckles. Beautifully rendered (and occasionally featuring other colors), the shop's lovely assortment of Native-American items includes modern designs in addition to its traditional pieces. However, whether it's high concept or vintage, authenticity is guaranteed.

·BELTS ·FASHION JEWELRY

323-651-1553 · Sportie LA

SportieLA.com

The Sportie LA retail store, located in Hollywood's famous Melrose shopping district, is cramped and disorganized, but always filled with enthusiastic shoppers. Why? Because it's got the best selection of sneakers in the city. It turns out the same fantastic selection is available on their web site, with one major difference: browsing here is an easy and comfortable experience. Pages of desirable brands like Puma, Adidas, Vans, New Balance and Asics are represented, generally in some of the hippest models available. You won't want to miss this.

·SHOES

888-637-2668 · Stephanie Johnson

StephanieJohnson.com

Life on the go gets a bit more colorful and a lot more fashionable thanks to this line of travel bags and cosmetics cases that may be recognized by their knotted ribbon zipper pulls. Founded by a former corporate executive, the initial aim of these bags was to "elevate the status of the cosmetic bag from something unseen to something that must be seen," a goal that's been clearly accomplished and then some. Shop by Style to pick your favorite items, or Select By Fabric to find your cute or funky pattern of preference; either way you'll have an easy time perusing the entire selection.

·BAGS & WALLETS

StubbsAndWootton.com

"A multitude of rich fabrics, embroideries, needlepoints and leathers" go into the crafting of this exquisite shoe line, and without a doubt the quality shows. Mules, slides, heels and espadrilles populate the Ladies portion of the site with amazing design after amazing design, some casually kitschy and others just breathtakingly cool. But it might be the slippers, available for men and women, that you'll most remember. Intricate patterns and quality fabrics combine to create loungewear for the foot so beautiful you'll be dying for a chance to show it off outside the home.

·SHOES	·LEATHER	·SANDALS	

StyleDrops.com

What do you get when you put sunglasses, shoes, wallets and handbags by some of Italy's finest designers all in one place? This web shop, for one. With a succinct assortment of wares for men and women, the site sometimes seems to have been slapped together out of spare parts and photographs, but here and there one of these fine items leaps out to grab your attention, especially if you stick to the Sunglasses section, which boasts deep selections of labels like Gucci, Prada, YSL and Chanel, to name only a few.

·EYEWEAR ·LEATHER	·BAGS & WALLETS ·BOOTS	·SHOES ·DRESS SHOES	·DESIGNER

TalismanUnlimited.com

The founders of this oft-celebrated jewelry design firm credit their success to "the synergy of expertise, tenacity, extraordinary resources, and good fortune," but we'd have blame their achievements on a much simpler combination: gold and semiprecious stones. A vast selection of elegant jewelry takes such favored gems as pearls, citrine, topaz, amethyst, tourmaline and peridot and matches them with 14 and 18 karat gold to create modern but timeless pieces that will easily accomplish jewelry's highest goal: attracting attention.

·FASHION JEWELRY			

Tateossian.com

British jewelry designer Robert Tateossian offers a small but intriguing selection of women's necklaces and earrings that hold their own against any comparable wares you may find. However, it's the men's supply that truly stands out, specifically the extensive and gorgeous array of cufflinks that go above and beyond the call of duty. Ranging from classy to avant garde, the precious metal, stone, fiberglass and leather cufflinks offer an expression of style men usually have to turn to ties for. Particularly impressive are the sophisticated Watch Cufflinks, whereas the sentimental may appreciate the Picture Frame model.

·FASHION JEWELRY			

415-252-4300 · Timbuk2 Designs

Timbuk2.com

The messenger bag has been gaining in popularity the past couple of decades, and if you take a look at this bag manufacturer's site it's almost certain you'll want one too. After all, the Build Your Own feature is so fun and easy to use you'll have to take it for a test drive, selecting your bag's size, coordinating its color scheme and adding on accessories. Then you'll get a good look at your finished product, imagine you can do better, repeat the process and ultimately decide you have designed the perfect messenger bag, and who could pass that up?

| ·BAGS & WALLETS | ·SMALL GOODS | | | |

212-645-6890 · Tina Tang

TinaTang.com

Hollywood couldn't tell a better story. Tina Tang turned her back on a Wall Street career (with Goldman Sachs, no less) to follow her dream of becoming a jewelry designer. Now this daring spirit has been captured in her collection of chokers, necklaces, bracelets and earrings. She uses handpicked crystal, glass, pearls and semiprecious stones to find a sort of cosmic harmony in her designs, and whether she expresses this with bold colors or elegant silverwork, her "bliss" shines through, for all (including you) to see.

| ·DESIGNER | ·FASHION JEWELRY | | |  |

877-464-3293 · Adam Derrick

ToBoot.com

Don't be misled by the name—this site doesn't actually offer any boots; at least, only a few high-top shoes may be found here. Instead, there's a selection of well-crafted leather footwear for the masculine professional, including dress shoes (suitable even for black-tie occasions) and a few casual designs. In truth, the "casual" offerings here don't typically fall under our usual interpretation of the word, as they're pretty dressy by most accounts. But we suppose if you're going to get that promotion, even your weekend shoes need to look imposing.

| ·SHOES | ·LEATHER | ·DRESS SHOES | | |

323-655-1110 · Trés Jolie Jewelry and Accessories

TresJolie.us

Up-to-the-minute jewelry designs find their way into this Los Angeles shop, which has fashioned a business out of dealing hot new items to the ultrachic. It's possible you won't like the first bracelets, rings, earrings and necklaces you see in the Merchandise pages, but keep looking. The styles do change the deeper you go, and nearly every modern taste may be accounted for, whether you prefer a peridot chain or a bracelet composed of wood charms. Buy it here, before you spot it in a magazine.

| ·DESIGNER | ·FASHION JEWELRY | | | |

TrueFaux.com

It's tough for a jewelry shop to be unique these days, even on the web. This one's devotion to vintage costume jewelry makes it so. Like a peculiar museum filled with the artifacts of a distant culture, each of these pages seems to offer a new, intriguing collection of pieces for perusal, ranging from sort of kitschy to extravagant and extraordinary. The hard part is knowing these earrings, necklaces, rings, bracelets, pendants and pins are in limited supply or even one of a kind. If you don't buy what you like immediately you may not have a second chance.

★

 ·FASHION JEWELRY

TwelveNYC.com

Boasting an array of products that "reflects the marriage of the practical and affordable with the joy of color and pleasing lines," the creator of this small collection of handbags doesn't use flashy designs or fancy fabrics to express her sense of style. Rather, she relies on functional simplicity and a made-to-order palette that allows you to put together the perfect everyday totes, messenger bags, laptop cases and more. As luck would have it, the site goes a step further to make it simple for you to order a canvas or nylon bag that will match your wardrobe with a bag classic enough even to outlast its own durability.

 ·BAGS & WALLETS

UmbrellaStand.com

If any people know about good umbrellas, they live in the Pacific Northwest. That's one good reason to shop from this Oregon-coast specialty retailer. The better reason is the fun that can be had with umbrella shopping. You wouldn't think there could be much variety; crooks, shafts and canopies don't tend to deviate in anything but material and color. However, here you'll easily get a glimpse of the differing degrees of quality and fabrics, with kooky patterns, many different hues of solid and some sophisticated designs that you'll need to see for yourself.

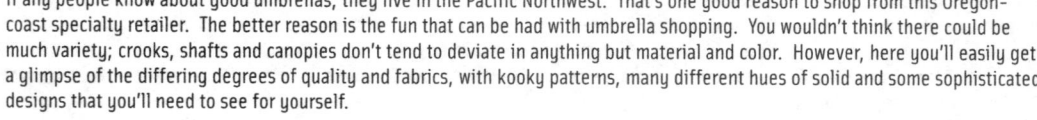

 ·SMALL GOODS

USAWatchCo.com

It's easy to get lost in the long list of watch brands available from this site, which, ironically, features mostly European timepieces. However, it might be worth losing yourself for awhile, for even though several of the brands shown were not actually available for purchase on our last visit, the great-looking watches we did see more than made up for any missing items. Sadly, there's no better way to browse than by brand name, and the more products offered by a manufacturer the harder it is to get through them all.

  ·WATCHES

800-826-7800 · Vans

Now heading into its fifth decade, Vans still offers many of the original styles that made the shoe line famous, and why not? They're still radical. In fact, this site allows you to custom order the classic Vans slip-on, whether you go for the retro checkerboard pattern or opt to mix and match a variety of colors. Of course, this was originally a skate shoe brand, and it's still not entirely for posers. Elsewhere on the site you'll find new and standard skate shoe designs, plus plenty of other fashionable models of sneakers for men, women, children and even your cooler-than-average babies.

| ·SHOES | ·KIDS | | | |

011-44-12-7369-1913 · Vegetarian Shoes

Take a quick glance at this site and you'll see a better-than-average selection of fashionable leather shoes, boots and sandals. Of course, appearances can be deceiving. Look deeper and you'll discover this specialty footwear shop's secret is that not a single piece of animal skin can be found here. But don't tell anyone; these faux suede and leather wares look as good if not better than the real thing, and usually wind up being cheaper. A small collection of belts and jackets complete the leather illusion, but have no doubt: the Birkenstocks featured here may be worn proudly by hippies anywhere.

| ·GLOVES ·SANDALS | ·BELTS ·DRESS SHOES | ·SHOES | ·BOOTS | |

877-837-7264 · Versani

As pristinely clean and shiny as the predominantly silver wares of this site may be, the page design casts a sort of murky texture that makes you want to overlook the strong selection within. Very little information is offered about each item, and the pictures are often blurred, so in some regards it's a test of faith to make a purchase. If you see something you (think) you like, don't be shy about harassing a customer service representative, as the site seems willing to offer exchanges, but may be reticent about refunds.

| ·FASHION JEWELRY | | | | |

888-847-4287 · The Village Hat Shop

Not to give this California hat shop chain a big head, but it's got one of the largest selections of headwear we've seen, or at least the widest. Where else can you find Viking helmets, pith helmets, fezzes and tricorner patriot hats all in one place? Novelty hats aside, the assortment really is meant to impress, with cowboy, panama, straw, top, rain and golf hats in addition to berets, fedoras, trilbys, walkers, beanies, bucket caps, visors, ball caps and pageboys, and that's just for men. Women, of course, can get away with wearing all these and more, with the possible exception of the Viking helmets.

| ·HATS | | | | |

WalkingCo.com

It's just hard to get things done when your feet hurt, which is why we recommend this comfort-driven shoe store to all those with sore soles. Sandals, moccasins and hiking shoes comprise the bulk of the catalog, catering just as well to men, women and children. Dozens of brands are featured, including those known to be most comfy, such as Tevo, Timberland, Uggs, Echo, Dansko, Cole Haan, New Balance and Birkenstock. Your feet stand to reap the benefits.

·SHOES	·KIDS	·BOOTS	·SANDALS

WideShoes.com

If narrow-minded shoe stores have got you down, take a good look at this men's footwear retailer with a specialty of generous proportions. Whether you shop for Athletic, Casual, Dress Shoes, Sandals, Slippers or Boots, when you do so here you get the option of selecting Width as well as Size. While sizes only rarely go above 14, shoes as small as a size 5 may be found in widths ranging from EEE to EEEEEE. Talk about an expansive selection....

·SHOES ·DRESS SHOES	·LEATHER	·BOOTS	·SANDALS

WorldOfWatches.com

This specialty web retailer is quick to point out that it's not an authorized dealer of the vast number of watches you'll find throughout it pages. However, the very same fact explains why the e-shop can offer "up to 60%" savings on brands ranging from Casio and Seiko to Bulgari and Cartier. It proves a great source of casual watches as well as finer timepieces, watch winders and straps. We recommend it as a comparison-shopping site or, if you utilize the Advanced Search feature, a good place to find exactly the sort of watch you've been looking for without breaking the bank.

·WATCHES			

WristWatch.com

The modern watch can be highly conceptual or highly functional, and if it's really good a combination of the two. This expansive selection of contemporary timepieces give you a chance to own a technologically advanced watch with classic looks or a very simple watch with a futuristic feel. You may shop by Brand or by Type, which in most cases sorts watches into appropriate gift occasions. But we prefer the Watches by Function menu, where categories like Kinetic, Atomic, Altimeter and Digital Compass make the concept of the second hand seem antiquated.

·WATCHES			

800-292-5725 · Yak Pak Concept Store

YakPak.com

Specializing in backpacks, messenger bags and DJ bags, this Brooklyn-based manufacturer embraces the mobile urban lifestyle, offering young and colorful alternatives to briefcases and purses. You may notice a lot of cobranding going on, with labels such as Wrangler, Penguin, Dickies and MTV in the mix, but it all amounts to the same thing: stylish and durable bags that have a way of proving themselves indispensable whether you plan to traverse the city by train, bus, bike or on foot.

·BAGS & WALLETS	·KIDS			

972-980-0819 · Ylang-Ylang

Ylang-Ylang.com

When "price is no object," you ought to head over to this upscale designer jewelry store based in Dallas, where fine gemstones and precious metals meet their matches in creativity and style. While you may find an affordable pair of earrings or modestly priced necklace, your best bet here is indulgence, and in that you can almost do no better. You may shop by designer, or through better-known categories, and either way you'll wind up clicking through a lot of pages of beautiful merchandise. Just don't ask us how to pronounce this shop's name.

·FINE JEWELRY	·DESIGNER	·FASHION JEWELRY		

888-492-7767 · Zappos.com

Zappos.com

Do you like a humongous shoe selection? Do you want there to be so many shoes in the style you seek that just when you think you've seen them all you realize you're only halfway through? That is just the sort of experience this self-proclaimed "Web's most Popular Shoe Store" can deliver. Each individual shoe subcategory is like a giant shoe store all by itself, with hundreds of brands interspersed among these pages, covering boots, sandals, slippers, dress shoes, loafers, sneakers, wide shoes, large shoes, evening shoes, kids' shoes, flats and pumps. And since there's no limit to virtual space, they've managed to add a comparably humongous selection of handbags, briefcases, backpacks, socks, wallets and belts.

·BAGS & WALLETS ·SANDALS	·SHOES ·DRESS SHOES	·KIDS	·BOOTS	

212-579-9824 · Zubie NYC

ZubieNYC.com

You enter the colorful world of semiprecious jewels when you log on to this relatively simple to use designer-baubles site, and no matter which hue you prefer you should be satisfied. Shop for earrings, necklaces and bracelets and you'll find selections sorted by color and price range. There aren't enough brooches to warrant such categorization, but some of these one-of-a-kind pieces prove memorable indeed. However you choose to browse, it will be hard to find something you dislike among the lovely assortment of chunky trinkets.

·DESIGNER	·FASHION JEWELRY		

NOTES:

Sports & Outdoors

Computers have changed the ways many of us live, and the chief impact may be seen during the workweek, which many of us spend crouched over a keyboard, staring at a monitor. Is it any wonder then that our spare time is increasingly spent pursuing our favorite athletic activities? It's tough to justify spending too much time on the sofa when there are so many great games to be played, mountains to climb, fish to be caught and waves to be ridden.

As always, the internet is here to help, and we tracked down a huge assortment of online retailers dedicated to outfitting the ardent adventurer, gym rat, team player, winter sportsman, outdoorsman or person of leisure. Whether you're in it for personal fitness or the sheer thrill of competition, you'll be able to easily locate sporting goods to help you get to the next level. If you love to explore your physical side in nature, dozens of shops specialize in tents, sleeping bags, hiking boots, kayaks and other outdoor accoutrements that will help you subsist through extreme conditions. Every activity we could imagine is represented, and we even discovered a few new sports that surprised us. From fan gear to safety equipment, for the novice or expert, this section is uniquely oriented to get your heart pumping and put that workweek behind you.

 ## TIPS ON BUYING SPORTS & OUTDOORS EQUIPMENT ONLINE

These suggestions may prevent your Sports & Outdoors items from leaving you out in the cold.

• **SIZE, WEIGHT & SHIPPING** •Weights are incredibly heavy by design, and fitness machines can be mighty bulky by necessity. Either are going to run up shipping costs like you wouldn't believe. Different retailers have learned to deal with this in different ways. Whenever possible, opt for merchants that can get this gear to you cheap, whether they distribute it locally or incorporate shipping costs into their competitive price structure.

• **COLD WEATHER RATINGS** •Stuff like sleeping bags and snowsuits are designed to keep you warm in cold conditions; however, some are suitable for colder weather than others. Keep an eye on such products' temperature ratings to make sure you don't end up in a 20 degree bag on a minus-20 degree mountain.

• **USE EQUIPMENT WITH CARE** •We've provided listings in this book for some stores that offer powerful, potentially dangerous equipment. Whether hunting, climbing, skiing, diving, boxing, hiking, skating or otherwise, please take care not to reap harm upon yourself or others. In other words: if you don't know or are unsure about how a piece of equipment is properly and safely used, find somebody who does know before attempting anything foolish. You may also want to buy all the necessary safety equipment, e.g., helmets, padding, etc. Thank you.

• **WARRANTIES & REPAIRS** • As with all big-ticket items, be sure there is a warranty on expensive orders, especially stuff like personal fitness machines that might easily be damaged in some way. It's not like any of us need another excuse not to exercise....

• **SIZE DOES MATTER** • Make sure that the equipment you purchase is appropriately sized for the body that will use it, whether in terms of grip, weight or fit, or it could be difficult to avoid injury.

 ## NATIONAL BRAND, CHAIN & LEAGUE SITES

The following sites offer online sales for familiar retailers and brands.

Adidas.com	NHL.com
FilaStore.com	Nike.com
FootLocker.com	Puma.com
MLB.com	Reebok.com
NASCAR.com	ShopPGA.com
NBA.com	TheAthletesFoot.com
NFL.com	

*For in-depth reviews of these sites and more, check out **www.thepurplebook.com**.

>> SITES THAT MAY COME IN HANDY

The following URLs may be useful when you play and explore.

AdventureCycling.org	National bicycle route network
FishingWorks.com	Fishing licenses, guides and information
FitnessOnline.com	Personal fitness and nutrition info
GoCampingAmerica.com	Locate campgrounds in the US
HealthClubs.com	Locate a health club or gym
NationalBikeRegistry.com	Bicycle registry and theft prevention resource
OneDayHikes.com	Locate hiking destinations
OnTheSnow.com	Ski reports and gear reviews
PlayGolfAmerica.com	Golfer's resource
RulesCentral.com	Sports rules
Sports.Yahoo.com	Sports news, schedules, scores and standings
SurflLine.com	Surf reports and destinations
VideoFitness.com	Reviews of fitness videos
WetSand.com	Surf reports

SECTION ICON LEGEND

Use the following guide to understand the rectangular icons that appear throughout this section.

APPAREL
Some of the apparel we wear for sports and outdoor activities is skintight, some quite bulky and heavy. From waterproof waders, leg warmers and helmets to running shoes, wet suits and ski masks, stores marked by this icon can keep you covered from head to toe.

OUTDOOR ACTIVITIES
There are plenty of activities worth doing outside, but we're referring to those that pit humans against nature and the elements. Hence, this icon will lead you to camping equipment, hiking gear, fishing tackle and essential tools for climbing, kayaking, diving, skiing and plenty of other natural excursions that offer an element of danger.

SAFETY GEAR
Outdoor and athletic activities can be incredibly healthy, but they can also be damaging. This icon will guide you to stores offering safety gear, whether its a helmet, padding, goggles, guards, harnesses or face masks.

SPORTING GOODS
Strength, flexibility, cardiovascular health and physical appearance are just some of the reasons we exercise, whether done alone, as part of a class or in the heat of competition. Most of these activities require some amount of sporting equipment, and you can find it on sites marked by this icon.

LIST OF KEY WORDS

The following words represent the types of items typically found on the sites listed in this section. You will find them listed in the orange strip at the bottom of each entry, as appropriate.

ADVENTURE	Adventure sports, including hiking, rock climbing and other harrowing adventures we can only imagine.
APPAREL	Apparel for a number of different sports and outdoor activities.
CAMPING	Tents, sleeping bags, camp stoves and other equipment to carry you through the long haul.
COURT SPORTS	Basketball, volleyball, racquetball and tennis, among others.
FAN GEAR	Apparel and accessories related to your favorite team or athlete.
FIELD SPORTS	Football, baseball, soccer, lacrosse and rugby are the best-known field sports, along with track and field.
FOOTWEAR	Athletic footwear can be found, as well as hiking and climbing boots (also see Shoes & Accessories).
GYM & STUDIO	The wide variety of sports and disciplines generally takes place in a gym or studio, often as part of a class, including dance, yoga, aerobics, Pilates, martial arts, wrestling and boxing.
INSTRUCTION	Instructional media, such as yoga videos, as well as training equipment, such as pitching machines.
KIDS	Sports and outdoors sites that cater to children as well as adults (see also our Minors section).
LEISURE SPORTS	Strictly speaking, these sports are competitive, but they tend to be taken at a leisurely pace, on sunny days, with a lot of conversation. This includes golf, bocce, lawn bowling, croquet, and horseback riding.
OUTDOORSMEN	These sites are for fishermen, hunters and other outdoors sportsmen (and women).
PROTECTIVE	Refers to safety apparel and equipment to protect us from the world, each other and ourselves.
PERSONAL FITNESS	Individual fitness equipment and apparel, whether in the form of exercise machines or jump ropes.
RECREATION	These activities may err more on the side of fun than athleticism, but there's an element of competition and/or education; includes bowling, Ping-Pong, paintball, kite-flying and children's activities.
ROAD SPORTS	Road sports include cycling, skateboarding, roller-skating, inline skating and other asphalt activities.
WATER SPORTS	Whether swimming competitively, boating, kayaking, waterskiing, windsurfing, body boarding, wakeboarding or surfing, this key word has your water sports covered.
WINTER SPORTS	Including warm clothes, the sites referred to here also offer skis, snowboards, ski-boards, jet skis, ice skates and other winter activity equipment.

KEY WORD INDEX

Use the followings lists to locate online retailers that sell the type of sports & outdoors equipment you seek.

ADVENTURE

66NorthUS.com
ActionGear.com
BackpackersPantry.com
BDEL.com
EMS.com
GreatOutdoorsDepot.com
MGear.com
MountainBoardShop.com
PalosSports.com
PrincetonSki.com
RealKiteboarding.com
SierraTradingPost.com
TrailFoods.com
Tramdock.com
TravelCountry.com
Wickers.com

APPAREL

66NorthUS.com
A2ZSportsDirect.com
AllAboutDance.com
BigToeSports.com
BikeSnob.com
BowlersParadise.com
Bowling.com
CapezioRVC.com
DoverSaddlery.com
GolfSmith.com
HockeyGiant.com
JHHE.com
JWhiteCricket.com
K-BeeLeos.com
KarateDepot.com
MartialArtsSupplies.com
PrincetonSki.com
RugbyImports.com
Ruggers.com
SaddleSource.com
SkateBuys.com
Soccer.com
SportsKids.com
SuperGo.com
TennisCompany.com
VSAthletics.com
WrestlingOne.com

CAMPING

66NorthUS.com
ActionGear.com
BackpackersPantry.com
BassPro.com
Cabelas.com
EMS.com
FlyFishingOutfitters.com
GreatOutdoorsDepot.com
RockyMountainTrail.com
SierraTradingPost.com
SportsBasement.com
TrailFoods.com
TravelCountry.com

COURT SPORTS

A2ZSportsDirect.com
GolfSmith.com
NikeTown.com
PacificSports.com
PalosSports.com
PrincetonSki.com
SportEyes.com
SportsKids.com
TennisCompany.com
TennisWarehouse.com
VolleyHut.com
WrestlingOne.com

FAN GEAR

A2ZSportsDirect.com
BeAPro.com
BigToeSports.com
HockeyGiant.com
JWhiteCricket.com
Lacrosse.com
LacrosseUnltd.com
PalosSports.com
RugbyImports.com
Ruggers.com
Soccer.com
SportEyes.com
SportsKids.com
VSAthletics.com
Wickers.com
WrestlingOne.com

FIELD SPORTS

A2ZSportsDirect.com
BeAPro.com
BigToeSports.com
HockeyGiant.com
JWhiteCricket.com
Lacrosse.com
LacrosseUnltd.com
PalosSports.com
RugbyImports.com
Ruggers.com
Soccer.com
SportEyes.com
SportsKids.com
VSAthletics.com
Wickers.com
WrestlingOne.com

FOOTWEAR

ActiveMailOrder.com
AllAboutDance.com
Austads.com
BDEL.com
BigToeSports.com
Blades.com
BoardersParadise.com
BowlersParadise.com
Bowling.com
Cabelas.com
CapezioRVC.com
DogFunk.com
EMS.com
GreatOutdoorsDepot.com
HockeyGiant.com
Lacrosse.com
LacrosseUnltd.com
MGear.com
MonsterSkate.com
Nashbar.com
NikeTown.com
PacificSports.com
PrincetonSki.com
RingSide.com
RoadRunnerSports.com
RugbyImports.com
Ruggers.com
SaddleSource.com
SierraTradingPost.com
SkateBuys.com
Soccer.com
SportsBasement.com
TennisCompany.com
TennisWarehouse.com
TGW.com
The-House.com
TitleBoxing.com
Tramdock.com
TravelCountry.com
VolleyHut.com
VSAthletics.com
WrestlingOne.com

GYM & STUDIO

A2ZSportsDirect.com
AllAboutDance.com
BalazsBoxing.com
BarefootYoga.com
BodyTrends.com
CapezioRVC.com
HuggerMugger.com
K-BeeLeos.com
KarateDepot.com
MartialArtsSupplies.com
MatsMatsMats.com
NewYorkYoga.com
NikeTown.com
PalosSports.com
PilatesEquipmentDirect.com
RingSide.com
SkateBuys.com
SportEyes.com
SportsBasement.com
TitleBoxing.com
Wickers.com
WrestlingOne.com

INSTRUCTION

4Swimwear.com
ActionGear.com
Austads.com
BalazsBoxing.com
BarefootYoga.com
BeAPro.com
BigFitness.com
BigToeSports.com
BikeParts.com
BoatUS-Store.com
BodyTrends.com
Bowling.com
DoverSaddlery.com
eAngler.com
eBodyBoarding.com
FlyFishingOutfitters.com
Go2Marine.com
KarateDepot.com
LaneFour.com
MGear.com
MonsterSkate.com
NewYorkYoga.com
PilatesEquipmentDirect.com
RealKiteboarding.com
RingSide.com
RoadRunnerSports.com
RugbyImports.com
Ruggers.com
SailNet.com

INSTRUCTION (cont.)

Sissel-Online.com
Soccer.com
SportsKids.com
TennisWarehouse.com
TGW.com
TitleBoxing.com
VolleyHut.com
VSAthletics.com
Windsurfing-Direct.com
66NorthUS.com

KIDS

A2ZSportsDirect.com
ActiveMailOrder.com
AllAboutDance.com
Austads.com
BassPro.com
BigToeSports.com
BowlersParadise.com
Bowling.com
CSSkiEquipment.com
DiversDirect.com
DogFunk.com
eBodyBoarding.com
EMS.com
GreatOutdoorsDepot.com
HockeyGiant.com
IntoTheWind.com
K-BeeLeos.com
LaneFour.com
Lids.com
MGear.com
MonsterSkate.com
NikeTown.com
Overtons.com
PalosSports.com
PrincetonSki.com
RoadRunnerSports.com
SierraTradingPost.com
SkateBuys.com
Soccer.com
SportsBasement.com
SportsKids.com
TennisWarehouse.com
Tramdock.com
Wickers.com
Windsurfing-Direct.com
WrestlingOne.com

LEISURE SPORTS

Austads.com
BoatersWorld.com
CSSkiEquipment.com
DoverSaddlery.com
GigaGolf.com
GolfSmith.com
JaquesAmerica.com
JHHE.com
SaddleSource.com
SportEyes.com
TGW.com

OUTDOORSMEN

66NorthUS.com
ActionGear.com
BassPro.com
BoatersWorld.com
BoatUS-Store.com
Cabelas.com
CSSkiEquipment.com
eAngler.com
FlyFishingOutfitters.com
GreatOutdoorsDepot.com
RockyMountainTrail.com
SierraTradingPost.com
TheFlyShop.com

PERSONAL FITNESS

BigFitness.com
BodyTrends.com
EMS.com
K-BeeLeos.com
KarateDepot.com
MatsMatsMats.com
NewYorkYoga.com
NikeTown.com
PalosSports.com
RingSide.com
Sissel-Online.com
SportEyes.com
SportsBasement.com
SportsKids.com
TitleBoxing.com
Wickers.com
WorkoutWarehouse.com
WrestlingOne.com

PROTECTIVE

66NorthUS.com
A2ZSportsDirect.com
ActionGear.com
ActiveMailOrder.com
BalazsBoxing.com
BDEL.com
BeAPro.com
BigToeSports.com
BikeParts.com
Blades.com
BoardersParadise.com
BoatersWorld.com
BoatUS-Store.com
Cabelas.com
DiversDirect.com
DogFunk.com
DoverSaddlery.com
eAngler.com
eBodyBoarding.com
EMS.com
FlyFishingOutfitters.com
Go2Marine.com
GreatOutdoorsDepot.com
HeavyGlare.com
HockeyGiant.com
JHHE.com
JWhiteCricket.com
KarateDepot.com
Lacrosse.com
LacrosseUnltd.com
MartialArtsSupplies.com
MGear.com
MonsterSkate.com
MountainBoardShop.com
Nashbar.com
NewYorkYoga.com
PacificSports.com
PaintballExpress.com
PalosSports.com
PrincetonSki.com
RealKiteboarding.com
RingSide.com
RockyMountainTrail.com
RugbyImports.com
Ruggers.com
SaddleSource.com
SailNet.com
SierraTradingPost.com
SkateBuys.com
Soccer.com
SuperGo.com
Team1Newport.com
TennisCompany.com
The-House.com

PROTECTIVE (cont.)

TitleBoxing.com
Tramdock.com
TravelCountry.com
VolleyHut.com
Wickers.com
Windsurfing-Direct.com
WrestlingOne.com

RECREATION

BowlersParadise.com
Bowling.com
CSSkiEquipment.com
DoverSaddlery.com
Go2Marine.com
IntoTheWind.com
Overtons.com
PaintballExpress.com
PalosSports.com
SkateBuys.com
SportsKids.com

ROAD SPORTS

ActiveMailOrder.com
BikeParts.com
BikesDirect.com
BikeSnob.com
Blades.com
CSSkiEquipment.com
EMS.com
HockeyGiant.com
MonsterSkate.com
Nashbar.com
Nirve.com
RacksForAll.com
SierraTradingPost.com
SkateBuys.com
SportEyes.com
SportsBasement.com
SuperGo.com
The-House.com

WATER SPORTS

4Swimwear.com
BassPro.com
Blades.com
BoardersParadise.com
BoatersWorld.com
BoatUS-Store.com
Cabelas.com
CSSkiEquipment.com
DiversDirect.com
eAngler.com
eBodyBoarding.com
EMS.com
FlyFishingOutfitters.com
Go2Marine.com
GreatOutdoorsDepot.com
LaneFour.com
Overtons.com
PacificSports.com
PrincetonSki.com
RacksForAll.com
RealKiteboarding.com
SailNet.com
SierraTradingPost.com
SportEyes.com
SportsBasement.com
Team1Newport.com
The-House.com
TheFlyShop.com
TravelCountry.com
Windsurfing-Direct.com

WINTER SPORTS

66NorthUS.com
A2ZSportsDirect.com
BDEL.com
Blades.com
CSSkiEquipment.com
DogFunk.com
GreatOutdoorsDepot.com
HockeyGiant.com
MGear.com
PrincetonSki.com
RacksForAll.com
RockyMountainTrail.com
SkateBuys.com
SportEyes.com
SportsBasement.com
Team1Newport.com
The-House.com

NOTES:

4Swimwear.com

4 Seasons Swimwear · 800-352-8868

If you shop for a swimsuit more for how it will impact your water speed than for how it will affect your tan lines, this competitive swimming specialist might just carry the suit you're looking for. Ironically, while the women's suits here tend to reveal less skin than those found in most clothing stores, the men's suits tend to be tighter and skimpier. Of course, the truth is that you have to be pretty fit to look good in a suit like this; fortunately, if you're just getting started with your swimming career, the swim caps and goggles should give you some degree of anonymity.

·WATER SPORTS	·INSTRUCTION		

66NorthUS.com

66° North · 203-431-1766

You don't need to visit Iceland to know it gets pretty cold there—it does sit, after all, right on the Arctic Circle (located at latitude sixty-six degrees north, in case you were wondering). It stands to reason, then, that the residents of the remote island would make some of the best winter-weather apparel in the world. That's exactly what gives the "Technical Outdoor Clothing" featured on this site so much credibility. Developed in Iceland, the stylish and warm jackets, coats, pants and undergarments promise to protect men, women and children from the harshest of elements, whether it's freezing where you're going or cold where you live.

·PROTECTIVE ·CAMPING	·WINTER SPORTS ·OUTDOORSMEN	·ADVENTURE	·KIDS

A2ZSportsDirect.com

A2Z Sports & Apparel · 866-618-0702

An emphasis on customized team uniforms completely validates this otherwise dubious sporting goods site, which offers a wider selection of products than it actually keeps in stock, and a spotty assortment of the items it does. While a smattering of sports actually are well represented in terms of game equipment and protective gear, the uniforms really do prove your best bet here, covering football, basketball, baseball, soccer, volleyball, lacrosse, track and cheerleading. This one could be especially valuable for the kids.

·PROTECTIVE ·KIDS	·WINTER SPORTS ·COURT SPORTS	·APPAREL ·GYM & STUDIO	·FIELD SPORTS

ActionGear.com

Brigade Quartermasters · 800-228-7344

Some survivalists like to be prepared for any difficult situation that might develop; a more aggressive type likes to search for difficult situations to overcome. Both should enjoy shopping from this distinctive outdoor outfitter. Part safety specialist and part military surplus store, the slow-loading site is equipped to outfit hunters, hikers, campers, climbers and a variety of adventurers and outdoorsmen with MREs, first-aid kits, rappelling lines, bivouacs, camouflage, pocket tools and night vision goggles. Whether you seek out danger or are patient enough to let it come to you, you'll be glad you shopped here.

·PROTECTIVE ·INSTRUCTION	·ADVENTURE	·CAMPING	·OUTDOORSMEN

800-588-3911 · Active Mail Order

ActiveMailOrder.com

Here's a skate shop about as well designed as its wares, which is saying a lot in the context of this extremely style-conscious and self-expressive sport. Whether you buy a board preassembled or by component, you'll find a solid selection of brands and designs; plenty, at least, to rival the variety in any local store. The good selection doesn't stop at skating hardware either, but carries over into the clothes, accessories and even shoes sections. A good thing, since stylin' kicks are as important as anything else.

·PROTECTIVE ·KIDS	·FAN GEAR	·FOOTWEAR	·ROAD SPORTS

800-775-0578 · All About Dance

AllAboutDance.com

When this site claims to be All About Dance, it's not kidding; ballroom, ballet, tap and jazz styles are equally well covered here, as are associated disciplines such as gymnastics and cheerleading. The shoes, workout wear, undergarments and costume apparel cover a full complement of popular brands to outfit men, women and children for competition as well as practice, and some instructional media should help you take every step in the right direction, or at least provide the appropriate soundtrack.

·APPAREL	·FOOTWEAR	·KIDS	·GYM & STUDIO

800-759-4653 · Austad's Golf

Austads.com

The more your golf hobby becomes an obsession, the better this site looks, with a great variety of gear across the board that can keep you browsing and researching products for hours at a stretch. More casual shoppers may find themselves overwhelmed by the sheer number of performance-oriented clubs, shoes and even balls available, but if you happen to be shopping for the golf enthusiast in your life, you may enjoy sifting through the plethora of apparel, accessories and other gift items without ever having set foot on the links.

·FOOTWEAR	·KIDS	·LEISURE SPORTS	·INSTRUCTION

800-641-0500 · Backpacker's Pantry

BackpackersPantry.com

Unless you're planning to hunt or forage for food on your next camping trip, you'll want to pack in a few meals to keep your nourishment up. Even fishermen might want to supplement the catch with a tasty side dish, dessert or—should the fish not be biting—an alternative entrée. Fortunately, this site offers an elaborate menu of vitamin-fortified, dehydrated meals that pack light and in some cases even taste good. A variety of brands are represented, and as you browse the menus of each you'll come across freeze-dried, gourmet and even some kosher options, as well as equipment to prepare them properly over the campfire.

·ADVENTURE	·CAMPING		

BalazsBoxing.com

Balazs Boxing · 888-466-6765

This shop offers a very simple and neatly arranged selection of boxing and martial arts necessities, which is a good thing as you'll still be able to shop after taking a few blows to the head. Simply follow the Gear link to find protective, training and exercise equipment meant to fine tune your body for some of the most physically demanding sports you'll ever encounter. As sturdy as this stuff will make you, we would recommend making a head guard your first purchase.

·PROTECTIVE	·INSTRUCTION	·GYM & STUDIO	

BallCap.com

Cooperstown Ball Cap Co. · 800-264-8294

With a singular devotion to baseball caps, this is an easy site to overlook, but we're here to tell you: don't miss it. To begin with, this isn't your typical major league sports merchandise. While you will find some pro baseball logos, they're all vintage, harking back to the days the Dodgers played in Brooklyn and the Washington Senators wore painter's caps. Even more intriguing are caps representing the Negro League, the Women's League and plenty of semipros, including fictional teams like the Bad News Bears and the Mudville squad of "Casey at the Bat" fame. Better yet, these caps offer custom sizing, including the option of leather hat bands and full or short hat volume, leaving no doubt that the ballcap aficionado will find his or her idea of perfection.

·FAN GEAR			

BarefootYoga.com

Barefoot Yoga · 877-227-3366

Certainly, yoga doesn't require any special dress code or decorative equipment, but reality being what it is, if you show up to a session feeling self-consciously shabby it's tough to focus on your breathing. If you prefer a fashionable presentation with your meditation, this is one site you don't want to miss. With patterned mats and rugs, stylish practice apparel and even a few funky mat bags, the small but hip retailer covers every relevant yoga accessory, so you'll never enter a class without looking a merely a stretch away from being in balance with the universe.

·INSTRUCTION	·GYM & STUDIO		

BassPro.com

Bass Pro Shops · 800-227-7776

Aspiring to be the "leading merchant of outdoor recreational products," this site acts pretty much as a one-stop shop for that breed of people who take pleasure in tracking down, capturing and/or killing animals for sport (and hopefully for eats as well). Whether you prefer to pit your wits against the likes of fish, waterfowl, deer or wascally wabbits, this shop can hook you up with lures, calls, decoys, camouflage and other sundry sporting equipment. Be careful, though—the great irony here is that the more you buy, the less sporting it gets.

·WATER SPORTS	·KIDS	·CAMPING	·OUTDOORSMEN

800-775-7625 · Black Diamond Equipment Online

BDEL.com

For that special brand of outdoor athlete who likes to go up mountains in the summer and down them in the winter, we found this employee-owned shop with a devotion to climbing and skiing. Based in Utah, the proprietors of this shop regularly give this gear a rigorous workout, offering sort of a de facto approval of the entire inventory (and knowledgeable customer service). This is important, as you'll want to know your gear is reliable when you're skiing the backcountry, digging your crampon into ice and dangling over a ledge at 200 feet. This one's for the rugged and the brave.

·PROTECTIVE	·WINTER SPORTS	·ADVENTURE	·FOOTWEAR

888-423-2776 · beapro.com

BeAPro.com

With literally thousands of products to offer, this site offers baseball players a better selection of bats and mitts than they'll ever find in a single brick-and-mortar store. On the one hand (right or left), this is a great thing, as any individual athlete may find precisely the style he or she seeks. On the other hand, it can prove a bit overwhelming to wade through many pages of a single product. It's best to browse mitts by glove size and/or position, while bats are divided into categories like T-Ball, Softball, Fungo and Wood. Distinguishing between the dozens of pitching machines may be a little tougher to do.

·PROTECTIVE	·FIELD SPORTS	·INSTRUCTION	

800-731-0098 · BigFitness.com

BigFitness.com

This site sells pretty much any type of equipment you might expect to find in your local gym, and most of it ships for free. However, some of the heavier items do not (begging the question, "Who buys weights online?" The answer: "Dumbbells," of course). If you don't want to pay exorbitant shipping fees on stuff you're not yet strong enough to lift, there are plenty of more home-oriented fitness products, like videos, jump ropes or chin-up bars that fit in doorways.

·PERSONAL FITNESS	·INSTRUCTION		

800-444-0365 · Big Toe Soccer

BigToeSports.com

Known around the world as football and "the beautiful game," we in the US still call it soccer, and we're getting better all the time. This site's keen devotion to the planet's most popular sport will help soccer players at every level get a hold of good gear, from head to—of course—toe. There's training equipment to make you better, shin guards to make you safer and even replica jerseys to make you look good to other fans. However, the real kicker may be the full catalog of game equipment, team jerseys, whistles and even referee uniforms, so you can start a league and maybe give your hometown an alternative to that other football.

·PROTECTIVE ·FOOTWEAR	·FAN GEAR ·KIDS	·APPAREL ·INSTRUCTION	·FIELD SPORTS

BikeParts.com

Peak Cycles · 303-216-1616

This online arm of a Colorado bike shop "carries over 11,000 bike parts from leading manufacturers," and though a good number of them may be out of stock at any particular time, browsing here still makes for a great shopping experience. Even if you can't wait, the in-stock items prove easy to find, as product categories may be filtered to focus on parts for cruisers, downhill-mountain, road, BMX or mountain bikes. Adding to its user-friendliness are articles about biking, trail recommendations and repair tips. If you're serious about your bicycle, this site may be exactly what you need.

·PROTECTIVE	·ROAD SPORTS	·INSTRUCTION	

BikesDirect.com

BikesDirect.com · 281-587-6808

Unlike a lot of the biking sites featured in this collection, these guys don't require you to know all the different specific parts and brands you might want incorporated into your bicycle (what's a derailleur?). Here, you can simply browse between sections for Road Bikes, Mountain Bikes (MTB), Comfort Bikes, Cruisers and Hybrid Bikes. These fairly cool bikes won't win any races or break any speed records, but they should be somewhat comfortable, and judging by the pics offered here, look pretty good as well. Easy as can be.

·ROAD SPORTS			

BikeSnob.com

BikeSnob · 281-851-3815

Cycling apparel is usually designed to be aerodynamic, quick to dry and highly visible to motor vehicle drivers. The featured products of this specialty shop take visibility to the next level. A surprisingly vast selection of cycling jerseys will not merely attract a driver's notice, but will often inspire a second glance. Images of birds, fish and various mythological creatures are just a few of the designs printed in bright colors on the fronts and backs of these shirts; you'll also find flames, beer logos, assorted patriotic graphics and at least a couple different rock bands. We couldn't exactly call this stuff stylish, but the term *self-expressive* might apply.

·APPAREL	·ROAD SPORTS		

Blades.com

Blades Board & Skate · 888-552-5233

Here's a site that goes all out to represent its favorite sports of snowboarding, skateboarding and rollerblading, offering complete selections in each respective section, including quality equipment, footwear and apparel. Less obvious is that the site also covers ice hockey, quad roller skating, wakeboarding, sledding and other snow or water sports. Not only that, but you'll find plenty of shopping guides and other useful resources for your preferred sport, so you know these guys know what they're talking about. Lastly, whether you prefer to carve, shred or grind, you'll want to take a look at the great prices in the Outlet section.

·PROTECTIVE ·ROAD SPORTS	·WATER SPORTS	·WINTER SPORTS	·FOOTWEAR

877-835-3780 · Boarders Paradise

BoardersParadise.com

If you get your thrills being towed behind a speedboat, this is the site for you. With wakeboards, water skis and almost every conceivable safety product or accessory to go with them, the specialty retailer has established a great web presence for towsport beginners and enthusiasts. They've even included a Toys section for the adventurous or recreational rider, highlighted by hydrofoils, knee boards and comfortable inner tubes. All you'll need to provide yourself is the water, the boat, and maybe a life jacket.

·PROTECTIVE	·WATER SPORTS	·FOOTWEAR	

877-690-0004 · BoatersWorld.com

BoatersWorld.com

This isn't a shop for most of us, as its entire selection is pretty much geared toward boat owners. But should you be lucky enough to fit this demographic, the site should serve you well. Whether you take the boat out for water sports, fishing or just to break out of national waters so you can freely cultivate your interests in nude suntanning and/or cockfighting, this site not only provides the equipment to get you out there, but also any necessary for repairs, safety and navigation, to ensure you make it back.

·PROTECTIVE	·WATER SPORTS	·OUTDOORSMEN	·LEISURE SPORTS

800-937-2628 · Boat U.S. Online Store

BoatUS-Store.com

This superstore is a boater's dream, including options for boat insurance and towing service (kind of like AAA for the water), as well as a huge selection of important (and some luxuriously less important) gear. From Anchoring & Docking products to Paint & Maintenance and Watersports, the multitudinous categories will get you just about anything you need to set sail or start your engines (sadly, the only boats actually sold here are Dinghies and Inflatables). Perhaps the most fun stuff can be found in the onboard Electronics section, which features such scintillating devices as surround-sound speaker systems, autopilots and night-vision goggles.

·PROTECTIVE	·WATER SPORTS	·OUTDOORSMEN	·INSTRUCTION

800-549-1667 · BodyTrends.com

BodyTrends.com

You may not automatically think of exercise techniques as trendy, but if you think back to the proliferation of phenomena like isometrics, step aerobics, inversion therapy, tai-bo, spinning, and now Pilates, it becomes pretty clear that keeping up with the fitness regime du jour requires both vigilance and additional equipment. This site should help you with both, offering information and instructional materials on the use of stuff like fitness balls and elliptical trainers, as well as most of the aforementioned trends that still hold water. After all, even yoga was once considered a fad.

·PERSONAL FITNESS	·INSTRUCTION	·GYM & STUDIO	

BowlersParadise.com

We're not entirely certain what comprises a bowler's paradise, but we're guessing there's a snack bar there. This site won't serve up any food, but it sure can deliver on bowling balls, bags, shoes and ancillary accessories. Having them drill holes in your new ball is an option, but one you may want to consider only if you're very familiar with your hand size and personal preferences. Novices will still find plenty to like, though, including a Ball Guide for Beginners to get you started on the right foot. You'll want to take lessons to make sure you finish on the right foot.

·RECREATION	·APPAREL	·FOOTWEAR	·KIDS

Bowling.com

You can argue all day long whether bowling is a sport, a hobby or a lifestyle, but there's no arguing the deep selection of bowling gear available from this lane-friendly specialty site. It begins, of course, with balls, whether for children, the competitive athlete or the budget conscious, some with a bit of character and some just ready to roll. Then of course there are back and wrist supports, ball towels and other ancillary necessities. Last but not least, fashion comes to play, with the shirts and shoes. You might find better styles elsewhere, but you'll be hard-pressed to pick up better values.

·RECREATION	·APPAREL	·FOOTWEAR	·KIDS
·INSTRUCTION			

Cabelas.com

Chock-full of articles and stories about hunters and their predilection for using very large guns with powerful ammo, this site actually seems to be a gamesman's best bet in cruising the web for hunting supplies. Loads of equipment and information is neatly organized—a bit better than it should be, actually—so that little patience need be wasted on shopping, and may be better spent out in nature. Big game, small animals, fish or waterfowl; this is one site that'll almost let you forget there's a dirty side to the sport.

·PROTECTIVE	·WATER SPORTS	·FOOTWEAR	·CAMPING
·OUTDOORSMEN			

CapezioRVC.com

This all-dance, all-the-time site caters to your every step, whether it be ballroom dancing, breakdancing or ballet. Under Footwear, you'll find tap shoes, jazz shoes, pointe shoes and more, while Bodywear includes skirts, leotards, tights, tutus and slinky dresses. Even male dancers can find what they need in terms of dance belts, footed tights and thong leotards (these last will take up to two weeks to make, so be sure to order them ahead of time). Bear in mind you'll be practicing in front of a mirror.

·APPAREL	·FOOTWEAR	·GYM & STUDIO	

888-208-4770 · Cool Sports Equipment

CSSkiEquipment.com

While the name of this site implies a devotion to skiing, it turns out the real focus of the shoddy-looking retailer is to be found in the "CS," or "Cool Sports." In particular, you'll find innertubes for sledding or for towing behind boats, as well as scooters, snorkeling gear, small watercraft, kites, bocce sets, stilts, pogo sticks, croquet sets and summer sleds, which are like regular sleds except with wheels, so you can ride down hills at breakneck speeds no matter what the season. You won't find another one like this.

·WATER SPORTS ·KIDS	·WINTER SPORTS ·OUTDOORSMEN	·RECREATION ·LEISURE SPORTS	·ROAD SPORTS

888-241-8807 · Distant Replays Retro Sports

DistantReplays.com

If you liked sports better the way they were before today's batch of superstars were even born, or if you thought it was a terrible idea for the Houston Astros to give up their colorful home jerseys, this is the fan site for you. Featuring the retro authentic and replica styles you just don't see anymore, here you can actually track down jerseys for superstars like Pistol Pete Maravich, Dr. J and Joe Namath. This thrillingly nostalgic selection even includes defunct leagues such as basketball's ABA and baseball's Women's and Negro Leagues. The historic selection changes often, so it's worth repeat visits.

·FAN GEAR				

800-348-3872 · Divers Direct

DiversDirect.com

Life below sea level begins with this retailer of scuba gear, snorkels and other underwater equipment. While not terrifically laid out, it's actually pretty easy to browse through the fins, masks and wetsuits presented here. More difficult would be earning your diver's certification, which is required in order to buy some of the more complicated pieces, like tanks and regulators. If you know what you're doing, though, you can shop here without so much as getting your feet wet; simply fax your C-Card and ID, and hold your breath while awaiting delivery.

·PROTECTIVE	·WATER SPORTS	·KIDS		

877-364-3865 · DogFunk

DogFunk.com

We've seen a lot of snow sports shops and a lot of board sport shops, but this site sticks strictly to snowboarding, and this alone almost makes it the best place online to find snowboards and related accessories. What actually does make it the best is a tremendous selection of boards, easy navigation, customer product reviews and a clearly expressed love of the sport. You'll also find a very impressive selection of winter clothes for the whole family, meaning a few ski and sledding enthusiasts may still benefit from this snowboarder haven.

·PROTECTIVE	·WINTER SPORTS	·FOOTWEAR	·KIDS

DoverSaddlery.com

Dover Saddlery · 800-989-1500

Unless you're Lady Godiva, any equestrian activity involves at least some small amount of outfitting for both horse and rider. This specialty retailer offers all the requisite safety equipment, apparel and tack for recreational riding, show riding and even fox hunting. You'll also find plenty of grooming and stable supplies, horse medicine and some instructional training media. If you don't own or wish to own a horse, the site probably won't hold any interest, unless you've figured out a way to incorporate riding apparel into your everyday wardrobe.

(WISH)

·PROTECTIVE ·INSTRUCTION	·RECREATION	·APPAREL	·LEISURE SPORTS

eAngler.com

eAngler · 877-979-3474

Bait and boat fishermen in particular will enjoy this full-service shop, which offers terrific prices on rods, reels and tackle. You'll also find a good variety of boating gear, whether you're heading out to the deep sea in a large vessel or just plan to troll around a lake for awhile in your canoe, kayak or inflatable. Hardcore enthusiasts may find some of the selection lacking, but the seasonal outdoorsman will find just about everything he needs to do battle with a fish except a license and a six-pack of beer.

·PROTECTIVE	·WATER SPORTS	·OUTDOORSMEN	·INSTRUCTION

eBodyBoarding.com

ebodyboarding.com · 877-326-2734

For those who like to do it on their stomachs, this bodyboarding specialty shop will prove a great find. Their expected selection of boards, wetsuits, fins and skegs are bolstered by the likes of portable showers, car roof racks and repair kits. They even offer a Buyers Guide section that can match your height and weight with different board options, as well as other tips to help novices on their way (what's a skeg?). Between this, the webzine, and the ultrahelpful Interact section, this should be all a bodyboarder needs.

·PROTECTIVE	·WATER SPORTS	·KIDS	·INSTRUCTION

EMS.com

Eastern Mountain Sports · 888-463-6367

If it can be done in the mountains, odds are good this site has the equipment to do it, whether you're going up or down, in winter or summer. The ski and snowboard selections may not compete with those of dedicated winter sports retailers, but the shop's assortment of winter wear, snowshoes and sleds make it worth the trip. Still, the real advantage of this site may be found when you visit the Camping, Hiking, Kayaking and Climbing sections, which all offer valuable equipment, safety gear and apparel that could save your life, or at least make you a little more comfortable at high altitudes.

·PROTECTIVE ·FOOTWEAR	·WATER SPORTS ·ROAD SPORTS	·PERSONAL FITNESS ·KIDS	·ADVENTURE ·CAMPING

866-672-1959 · Leland Fly Fishing Outfitters

FlyFishingOutfitters.com

Fly fishing fanatics won't want to miss this high-end specialty shop. With top-tier rods, reels, waders and even outfits, this will be your first stop on the search for quality gear, especially if you're just a novice who can afford to do things right the first time. If you like to match wits with the fish with careful fly selection, though, don't expect too much. While fly kits offer a great variety of tackle that will appeal to particular fish, the wily fisherman won't be able to choose individual flies, nor find many materials to let you tie your own.

·PROTECTIVE ·INSTRUCTION	·WATER SPORTS	·CAMPING	·OUTDOORSMEN

800-724-3085 · GigaGolf

GigaGolf.com

If you're getting serious about your golf game, you probably want to stop playing with your off-the-rack clubs, but think buying a custom set will cost you great amounts of time and money. This site aims to change your mind, making it incredibly easy to buy quality, custom-assembled clubs at prices lower than most top brands sell for secondhand. Simply select your club head, grip, shaft, flex and length from a long list of options and piece together a full set made to suit you precisely. Order one club at first for a test drive; if you like it, you'll almost certainly be back.

·LEISURE SPORTS			

877-780-5670 · Go2Marine.com

Go2Marine.com

The customers of this site all have one thing in common: they're a seafarin' lot. Landlubbers need not look to these pages for anything but a lifejacket in case they tread too close to the water's edge. Mariners, on the other hand, should take a good, long look at the great bounty of boating gear to be had. Ropes and Rigging Hardware are only two of the many categories offering high-tech electronics gear, mechanical equipment and the occasional item that hasn't been improved upon in centuries. Enthusiasts of any level should enjoy the site, but if you know how your boat works down to the minute details, you won't want to shop anywhere else.

·PROTECTIVE	·WATER SPORTS	·RECREATION	·INSTRUCTION

800-813-6897 · Golfsmith International

GolfSmith.com

This growing sporting goods specialty chain recently added tennis to its repertoire and, just like it did for golf, it's put together a top-notch selection of gear for amateurs up to experts. Whether you're in the market for a club or a racquet, you'll find the right gear for your grip, plus all the necessary accessories to optimize your performance. The shop still caters more heavily to golfers, with pre-owned and custom fit clubs, but you could make the argument that the tennis apparel section has drastically improved the overall fashion of the site.

·APPAREL	·LEISURE SPORTS	·COURT SPORTS	

GreatOutdoorsDepot.com

Great Outdoors Depot · 888-546-2267

Sure, there are about a million fun activities you could partake in close to home, but if you're anything like us, one look at this site will make you want to head up to the mountains. With extensive varieties of camping equipment, rock and ice climbing tools, inflatable watercraft, hiking gear and cold weather wear, the call of the wild never seemed so easy to appease. While first-aid kits, mosquito repellants and freeze-dried foods are there to remind us that it's not all a walk in the park, if a retail site can inspire us to leave our comfort zones, you know it's got to be good.

·PROTECTIVE ·FOOTWEAR	·WATER SPORTS ·KIDS	·WINTER SPORTS ·CAMPING	·ADVENTURE ·OUTDOORSMEN

HeavyGlare.com

Heavy Glare · 888-548-0558

The reason to visit this site is crystal clear: prescription eyewear for sports. Because vision should not be an impediment to athletic pursuits, this web shop offers a much more comprehensive assortment of sporting sunglasses and goggles than any brick-and-mortar retailer could. An incredibly deep selection of brands covers sports ranging from running and cycling to swimming and snowboarding, and it's a safe bet you can find the prescription lenses you need for your pursuits without any unnecessary effort.

·PROTECTIVE			

HockeyGiant.com

HockeyGiant · 800-633-5999

You couldn't really ask for a bigger selection of hockey gear than the one offered by this "giant" retailer, which includes ice and roller hockey equipment among its many wares. The products are succinctly divided by type, and then split into Senior, Junior and occasionally Intermediate sizes, which means that, aside from a few clicks, you'll find sticks, jerseys, pucks, gloves, masks, cages, pads and an incredible variety of skates fairly easily. We rated then as having expensive shipping due to a small handling fee added to every order, but if you order enough merchandise the actual shipping will be free, so you may want to stock up, eh.

·PROTECTIVE ·FIELD SPORTS	·FAN GEAR ·FOOTWEAR	·WINTER SPORTS ·ROAD SPORTS	·APPAREL ·KIDS

HuggerMugger.com

Hugger-Mugger Yoga Products · 800-473-4888

It's no stretch for us to recommend this slickly designed yoga shop, which offers a tidy selection of equipment and attire for novice, expert and fashion-conscious practitioners alike. You'll find a variety of mats and rugs, carrying bags and assorted props including blocks, support pillows and resistance bands. If you're unfamiliar with such exercise-oriented accessories, you might still enjoy those catering to the lifestyle, such as herbal eye bags, Neti nasal wash pots and Tingsha bells. Then again, maybe the clothes will be enough.

·GYM & STUDIO			

800-541-0314 · Into The Wind

IntoTheWind.com

This might be the best place online to buy a kite. That is, if you're impressed with such things as a terrific selection of box kites, stunt kites, flying animal shapes and traditional designs (i.e., diamond shapes). Or would it thrill you to notice that there's a healthy sampling of kites that'll fly when there's almost no wind at all? Or maybe you don't like actively battling the wind for position and would rather sit by, sipping a lemonade, watching a windsock or spinner from your porch or patio? From boomerangs to lawn ornaments to the special kite designs that'll soar so high you'll need binoculars to see them, this site humbly serves your kite-flying needs and then some.

·RECREATION	·KIDS			

877-374-8881 · Jaques America

JaquesAmerica.com

If you're like most people, you commonly lament just how difficult it is to find a decent regulation croquet set. Well, kind sirs and madams, let your grieving stop here. This North American distributor for Jaques of London offers all the finest in the gentle sports: badminton, leisure boule, home skittles and, yes, garden skittles (also commonly referred to as lawn bowling). Yes, you get what you pay for, which turns out to be ludicrous amounts of money. But if the alternative is letting your finely manicured green lawn go to waste, what other choice is there for a gamer of class?

·LEISURE SPORTS				

888-342-7656 · Jackson Hole Horse Emporium

JHHE.com

Proving once and for all that shopping for your polo pony can be as fun as shopping for yourself, this site devoted to everybody's favorite equestrian team sport offers a small but very particular assortment of goods for both horse and rider. This is important, because polo is a very particular sport. Sure, you'll find saddles, helmets, bridles, mallets and spurs, but then there are the fashionable considerations, such as polo shirts and white trousers. Ultimately, this shop is all about the horse, though, whether you're in need of grooming gear or blankets, leg wraps and liniments to keep your four-legged fellow athlete in good shape.

·PROTECTIVE	·APPAREL	·LEISURE SPORTS		

516-867-1608 · JWhiteCricket.com

JWhiteCricket.com

Seen by many of us as baseball's mutant cousin, Great Britain's popular cricket actually predates our own ball-and-stick sport, and could very easily have become the favorite national pastime in this country if the gentrified outfits been easier to find. With this site, the clothes and bats are within reach of everyone, meaning we could potentially experience a cricket resurgence in this country and soon be able to field a national team able to compete with the likes of India, Pakistan, Australia and other former colonies that in recent years have literally beaten the Brits at their own game. At least check it out to see how much you like the sweater vests.

·PROTECTIVE	·APPAREL	·FIELD SPORTS		

K-BeeLeos.com

k_bee Leotards · 888-523-3536

If you know the difference between a leotard and unitard, chances are you will greatly appreciate this site, which offers a tremendous selection of both. Divided into subcategories like Solid Colors, Prints, Rhinestone, Camisole & Halter and the sure to impress Hologram & Glitter, young girls and grown women alike will find plenty of choices for training as well as performance, in a variety of colors and fabrics, at very reasonable prices. All on a site that's easier to navigate than a balance beam.

 | ·PERSONAL FITNESS | ·APPAREL | ·KIDS | ·GYM & STUDIO |

KarateDepot.com

KarateDepot.com · 877-216-2669

Promoting strength, speed, agility and hand-eye coordination, individual sports like boxing and the martial arts are really less about violence than they are about ultimate fitness, discipline and self-reliability. This would explain the excellent selection of exercise equipment found on this site, including jump ropes, medicine balls and even yoga gear. Of course, controlled violence does play a big part in these activities, so the site offers plenty of protective pads to go along with gloves, foot pads, bags and uniforms, whether you're into boxing, Tai Chi, Muay Thai, Tae Kwon Do, Judo, Kendo, Kung Fu or Ninjitsu.

   | ·PROTECTIVE ·GYM & STUDIO | ·PERSONAL FITNESS | ·APPAREL | ·INSTRUCTION |

Lacrosse.com

Great Atlantic Lacrosse Company · 800-955-3876

This site, of course, is devoted to lacrosse, the sport that America forgot about. Well, nearly forgot about. Here you can buy a stick complete or assemble one from your favorite shafts, heads and stringing combinations. Then there are the helmets and pads that remind us just how brutally violent this sport can be, alongside other apparel that may be necessary to improve your game. And if you can't improve your game, you'll at least toughen it up.

   | ·PROTECTIVE | ·FIELD SPORTS | ·FOOTWEAR |

LacrosseUnltd.com

Lacrosse Unlimited · 877-932-5229

Perhaps the most versatile of the many lacrosse specialty retailers online (there are at least two of them), this one excels by offering custom stringing and coloring of your stick's head, giving you even greater visibility to your numerous fans. More important, though, is the solid selection of cleats, gloves, helmets and assorted padding that, regardless of color, should help you compete at a high level without getting injured at a high level.

| ·PROTECTIVE | ·FAN GEAR | ·FIELD SPORTS | ·FOOTWEAR |

800-284-3115 · Lane Four

LaneFour.com

Generally speaking, swimming requires little more than your body and a pool of water; competitive swimming, however, can get a bit more complicated. If you're looking for an aquatic advantage, the products offered by this site may suit you just right. Aside from a generous supply of top-brand swimwear at discounted prices, you'll find goggles, caps, fins and plenty of training equipment designed to improve your breathing, stroke and kick. And when you want to get less serious about your underwater endeavors, check out the snorkeling equipment.

·WATER SPORTS	·KIDS	·INSTRUCTION	

888-564-4287 · Hat World

Lids.com

These guys have your sports-loving head covered. Whether you prefer the NHL, NFL, NBA, Major League Baseball, the NCAA or NASCAR, there's a great chance you'll find a variety of hats here representing your favorite teams and/or stars. Or, you can attempt to combine all your sporting loves into one love with the Lids Create Your Own section, where you may add your own graphics and text to a variety of hat shapes and colors, to let everybody know you're a fan of your own home team.

·FAN GEAR	·KIDS		

877-223-4528 · MartialArtsSupplies.com

MartialArtsSupplies.com

From padded weapons to sparring gear, this martial arts specialist offers plenty of equipment that allows you and your friends to beat on each other and yet be left intact for the next round of practiced violence. They also have a fantastic selection of outfits, from kendo armor to ninja uniforms, which you can order and simply wear to feel cool. Or, if you possess a sense of honor, check out the Free Links page to find more information and instruction on how this gear is meant to be used.

·PROTECTIVE	·APPAREL	·GYM & STUDIO	

877-777-6287 · MatsMatsMats.com

MatsMatsMats.com

Do you get the feeling these guys sell mats? Well, you're right. Whether the mat in question is meant for wrestling, yoga, Pilates, gymnastics or just plain exercising, you'll find a good selection that ranges in thickness, softness and size to suit your needs. There are occasional additional products like gym balls and gymnastics props, but mostly the site really does cover mats, mats and more mats, as the name would suggest. Because sometimes the floor is just too hard.

·PERSONAL FITNESS	·GYM & STUDIO		

MGear.com

Your journey up from sea level to the sky will probably involve a lot of the equipment sold in this Mountain Gear store. Hiking and climbing tools and apparel can get you up to the top safely and comfortably, while skiing and telemarking (also known as free-heel skiing) gear pretty much serves to get you back to the bottom, fast. Meanwhile, when you are at the top, you may just want to cook, camp, drink water or wear warm clothes; fortunately, this store can outfit you for such extreme activities as well.

·PROTECTIVE ·KIDS	·WINTER SPORTS ·INSTRUCTION	·ADVENTURE	·FOOTWEAR

MinorLeagues.com

Despite the name, this retailer actually has mostly Major League Baseball fan gear for sale (plus some NBA, NFL and college brand merchandise). Still, for the fan whose town rallies around a development league, it's one of the few places anywhere (let alone online) to find caps representing teams like the Durham Bulls, Michigan Battle Cats, Toledo Mudhens, Lakewood Blue Claws, Quad City River Bandits and others. The site's not perfect, but then, neither are the players. Except that they're truly in it for love of the game.

·FAN GEAR			

MonsterSkate.com

This cleanly designed site appears to have been assembled with the same amount of skill and precision necessary to land a nollie frontside 180 kickflip; possibly more. This one is all about skateboarding, lest you forget that it's one of the most daring sports on the planet. They offer everything you need here, with a robust selection of the brands that sponsor your favorite pros, and some that just offer cool deck designs. Highlights may be the shoes, apparel and videos, but the opportunity to custom-build boards will never get tired.

·PROTECTIVE ·INSTRUCTION	·FOOTWEAR	·ROAD SPORTS	·KIDS

MountainBoardShop.com

We're guessing most of our readers will never have any reason to shop from this narrow specialty retailer that covers a sport so obscure, we had to create a new index word to represent it. We shouldn't be surprised: board sport enthusiasts have already mastered riding snow, water, wind and asphalt; it seems natural that they'd find a way to take a board offroading as well. Sort of like skateboards outfitted with burly wheels, if your mountain adventure just doesn't seem harrowing enough, try riding one of these for some seriously rough downhill action. Or, use this site in conjunction with one of the kiteboarding sites we found and let the wind carry you up the mountain.

·PROTECTIVE	·ADVENTURE		

800-627-4227 · Bike Nashbar

Nashbar.com

This is one of the better bike shops online, except that it doesn't seem to offer any bikes for sale. Of course, if you really wanted to, you could shop through this selection and assemble your own bike piece by piece, starting with the frame and continuing through to a variety of brakes, chains, derailleurs, fenders, forks, hubs, handlebars, pedals, saddles and wheels. An excellent source of parts and accessories (for safety and/or fun), we'd recommend getting the bike elsewhere and just relying on these guys for upgrades, replacements and repairs.

·PROTECTIVE	·FOOTWEAR	·ROAD SPORTS	

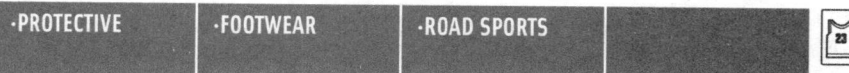

212-717-9642 · New York Yoga

NewYorkYoga.com

Can inner peace be achieved while looking at a computer screen? This question may be answered with this site, which offers yoga instruction online through streaming video. Classes are available for beginners on through intermediate and advanced levels (even prenatal), as well as by particular schools like Anusara, Ashtanga and Hatha, as well as Pilates and Vinyasa. All you need is a mat (which they conveniently offer for sale), as clothing is optional (assuming you're streaming this into your home). You may need to set your screen saver to activate at wider intervals, or you'll be forced to toggle your mouse in the middle of a stretching exercise; and that's no way to practice a meditation.

·PROTECTIVE	·PERSONAL FITNESS	·INSTRUCTION	·GYM & STUDIO	

800-806-6453 · Nike

NikeTown.com

If you're one of the few and shrinking number of people on this planet who isn't already well acquainted with the Nike swoosh, then we're almost sorry to be introducing you to it here. Chances are, though, that you've owned at least one pair of Nike sneakers in your life, or at least coveted the Air Jordans of another. Here you'll find virtually every Nike product available, including the infamous Nike iD sneakers, which now may be custom built to your color and style specifications. Although, with over 150 pairs of shoes to choose from in the Men's section alone, it's a good bet your perfect athletic shoe already exists somewhere on the site.

·FAN GEAR ·COURT SPORTS	·PERSONAL FITNESS ·GYM & STUDIO	·FOOTWEAR	·KIDS	

888-296-4783 · Nirve

Nirve.com

This is not a bicycle shop for squares. For starters, here you will find a good proprietary selection of BMX bikes, the best for taking moguls and jumps on dirt tracks. For the extreme rider of smooth surfaces, they offer a series of Freestyle (FS) bikes (all of these bikes bear the Nirve brand name), which can be made to do any number of miraculous, high-flying tricks/combinations. Rounding out the selection on a much chiller, primarily stylish tip is their line of Cruisers that, if you think about it, put most cars to shame. This is a fantastically slick, well-executed site for a great line of merchandise.

·ROAD SPORTS				

Overtons.com

With nearly 80 percent of this planet covered in water, mankind has devised myriad tools and toys to make floating, diving and swimming in the stuff more fun. And this online retailer carries a great deal of them. Claiming to be "The World's Largest Water Sports Dealer," a quick glance at the home page menu turns up Boating, Paddle Sports, Wakeboards and Skis, and this barely tells half the story. Look deeper in the chaotically organized pages to find snorkeling and scuba supplies, kayaks, pedal boats, pool toys, floating trampolines and plenty else to turn any river, lake or ocean into your own personal playground.

·WATER SPORTS	·RECREATION	·KIDS	

PacificSports.com

Given the name, it would seem appropriate if this site catered to activities such as surfing or tanning, but, in truth, the focus is on indoor racquet sports. It works, though, whether you prefer (or know the differences between) racquetball, squash, handball or paddleball. Aside from a hefty selection of racquets, you'll find plenty of shoes, gloves, protective eyewear and other necessary accessories. And, in case you feel that tennis, badminton, volleyball and wallyball have been unfairly left out, just follow the More Sports link.

·PROTECTIVE	·WATER SPORTS	·FOOTWEAR	·COURT SPORTS

PaintballExpress.com

Part cathartic exercise, part strategic workout, paintball gives new meaning to the "art of war," allowing us to nurture our violent sides without any more potential for harm than a spoiled wardrobe. This specialty shop offers a full complement of gear for the recreational warrior, whether you're a new recruit or wizened veteran. The guns, accessories, protective equipment and of course paintballs may only be viewed by brand, which is the only drawback to this otherwise exemplary shop that promises it "won't be undersold."

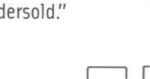

·PROTECTIVE	·RECREATION		

PalosSports.com

On the flipside of sports and fitness that requires discipline, focus and a serious mindset, we find this site, which isn't a lot to look at, but which proves a terrific source of fun for the active child or adult. Covering such diverse sports as archery, gymnastics, climbing and volleyball, the beauty of this site isn't in its adherence to the best high-tech equipment available to help optimize your performance. Rather, this selection's about giving something new a try, participating in a sport that might otherwise seem out of reach and just plain having a good time. Which explains why you'll also find playground equipment, game tables and lots of floor safety mats.

·PROTECTIVE ·FIELD SPORTS	·PERSONAL FITNESS ·KIDS	·RECREATION ·COURT SPORTS	·ADVENTURE ·GYM & STUDIO

800-718-1710 · Pilates Superstore

PilatesEquipmentDirect.com

To the uninitiated, the pronunciation of the word *Pilates* (Pill-ought-ease) seems as unintuitive and mysterious as the practice itself. Named after the man who devised it, Pilates comprises a system of exercises designed to build strength in muscles most of us have never knowingly used, which in turn promotes better health and balance. On this site you'll find some instructional materials to get you started, plus plenty of equipment, including full machines that will potentially boost your overall fitness for decades to come.

·INSTRUCTION	·GYM & STUDIO		

888-255-7547 · Princeton Ski Shops

PrincetonSki.com

Probably the only ski shop known to have outfitted both Olympic athletes and roller-skating chimpanzees, this Manhattan shop has been doing business for more than 75 years. It's tough to say at which point it expanded its selection to include rollerskates, nor ice skates, skateboards, kayaking and ultimately snowboarding, but they certainly approach each activity with enough enthusiasm to carry a modest but quality selection. We definitely don't know what inspired the proprietors to delve into tennis equipment and apparel, but if they accelerate the expansion process, maybe one day this'll qualify as a superstore.

·PROTECTIVE ·APPAREL	·WATER SPORTS ·FOOTWEAR	·WINTER SPORTS ·KIDS	·ADVENTURE ·COURT SPORTS

888-486-1264 · Racks For All

RacksForAll.com

When your outdoor sports and activities get big enough that they no longer fit into your trunk, you'll be glad to know about this shop, which specializes in roof racks for cars, trucks, RVs, vans and SUVs. Simply select your activity from a list including water sports, winter sports, cycling and boating, or browse by vehicle type, and you'll see a small but valuable selection of roof, trunk and hitch-mount racks made to transport your gear to the distant mountains, winds and waters you wish to conquer.

·WATER SPORTS	·WINTER SPORTS	·ROAD SPORTS	

866-732-5548 · Real Kiteboarding

RealKiteboarding.com

It's easy to assume that most of our readers have not tried this sport. After all, the recently developed activity requires a lot of courage, skill and expensive gear, and even then you would have to go somewhere with a lot of wind and water to practice. If, however, you're in possession of all the necessary components, this niche retailer's Gear section offers a good assortment of equipment to get the beginner started. On the off chance we do have a couple of advanced kiteboarders reading, we should mention the site has a few good kite and board upgrades as well, and a burgeoning snow kite section that can take the sport to new, mountainous heights.

·PROTECTIVE	·WATER SPORTS	·ADVENTURE	·INSTRUCTION

RingSide.com

Ringside.com · 877-426-9464

This site is all about boxing. Whatever your weight class, however unpolished your skills, you can find plenty of training materials here to step up your fight, along with medical gear to repair busted lips, close cuts and reduce swelling. Categories such as Gloves, Headgear, Hand Wraps, Jump Ropes, Mouth Guards, Punching/Speed Bags, Coaches & Cornermen Supplies and Boxing Rings should give you plenty enough reason to check this one out, assuming you like to scuffle a bit. Be careful, though: buy a lot and Don King may take an interest.

·PROTECTIVE ·GYM & STUDIO	·PERSONAL FITNESS	·FOOTWEAR	·INSTRUCTION

RoadRunnerSports.com

Road Runner Sports · 800-636-3560

They claim to be the "World's Largest Running Store," and we're gonna take their word for it. We can vouch for their tremendous selection of fitness footwear, whether you're running on the street, in the sand or through the forest. Many major brands are represented for men, women and children, and the prices definitely do not suck. Better yet, animated menus and great search functionality make finding your ideal runner or cross trainer easier than tying a shoelace. A bevy of fitness apparel choices can complete your exercise outfitting, while a forum and runner-friendly articles may answer questions about performance and safety, but probably not about style.

·FOOTWEAR	·KIDS	·INSTRUCTION	

RockyMountainTrail.com

RockyMountainTrail.com · 866-797-7625

Ultimately, there are three things you absolutely need when going on a long mountain hike: a warm jacket, a backpack and everything that goes in the backpack. This site can help with the first two, offering a long list of packs designs for general or very specific purposes, such as hunting, skiing or hydration. To some degree, the jackets all tend to serve the same purpose, but there are enough here that you may make style a consideration as you keep the cold out. Then again, if you are concerned with looking fashionable, perhaps you could use a longer hike.

·PROTECTIVE	·WINTER SPORTS	·CAMPING	·OUTDOORSMEN

RugbyImports.com

Rugby Imports · 800-431-4514

Since we are talking about rugby, the word *imports* here seems redundant. Nevertheless, you should be easily able to track down a selection of balls, training equipment, apparel and some protective gear, which will minimize bruises and breaks even as you reap the scorn of hardcore ruggers domestically or abroad. While the site is definitely meant for enthusiasts, anyone who likes the style of rugby shirts should check it out.

·PROTECTIVE ·FOOTWEAR	·FAN GEAR ·INSTRUCTION	·APPAREL	·FIELD SPORTS

877-784-4377 · Ruggers.com

Ruggers.com

"Ruggers" is sort of a cutesy name for the not-so-cutesy sport of rugby, to which this site owes an unwavering devotion. As such, you'll find plenty of appropriately durable shirts here, as well as fan gear for teams most of us probably haven't even heard of. Using occasionally brutal product descriptions to rate things like boots, tackle bags and scrum machines (whatever those are), it's difficult to say whether this site paints a scarier-than-necessary picture of this tough-guy sport, or whether it's entirely under-stated the matter.

·PROTECTIVE ·FOOTWEAR	·FAN GEAR ·INSTRUCTION	·APPAREL	·FIELD SPORTS

800-336-3882 · Rick's Heritage Saddlery

SaddleSource.com

With a deep selection of horse riding gear and apparel, from bridles and stirrups to snaffles and other rare things only riders have heard of, this site's steadily progressed since we first visited and can now be called one of the best equestrian shops online. Of course, we say this primarily for its unrivaled selection of saddles, including a thorough used selection that will save you some money on what may be the most expensive sporting endeavor represented in these pages. To wit, you'll have to buy your horse elsewhere.

·PROTECTIVE	·APPAREL	·FOOTWEAR	·LEISURE SPORTS

800-234-3220 · SailNet

SailNet.com

This comprehensive boating site goes deep, very deep. Some from its extensive list of categories actually have up to three levels of subcategorization, and there's plenty to choose from all the way. Thus, this selection ranges from Anchors and Sextants to the more obscure Pintles & Gudgeons, Flanged Spade Connectors and Stanchions & Rail Fittings. Fortunately for those of us who are confused by such language, the site also offers buying guides, articles and resources, so that none are left adrift in a sea of confusion. More like a sea of comfort, actually, as sections like Galley or Cabin & Cockpit play more to a home decorator than a hearty seaman.

·PROTECTIVE	·WATER SPORTS	·INSTRUCTION	

800-713-4534 · Sierra Trading Post

SierraTradingPost.com

For those of us who can't imagine outdoor gear and apparel going out of style, this retailer consolidates name-brand closeouts and overstocks and makes them available here at discounted prices. A Search By Percent Of Savings option tells the story, with discounts of up to 70 percent on items ranging from athletic apparel to camping equipment. Other browsing options will serve you better, though, as there's really a lot to behold here, including inline skates, wetsuits, climbing gear and cycling apparel, all new, and all a bargain.

·PROTECTIVE ·ROAD SPORTS	·WATER SPORTS ·KIDS	·ADVENTURE ·CAMPING	·FOOTWEAR ·OUTDOORSMEN

Sissel-Online.com

The fact this site represents a single brand of personal fitness equipment means you can rule out comparison shopping. However, this does make it remarkably easy to find your desired product from a full range of quality products like small dumbbells, balance boards, medicine balls and stretching gear. Better yet, the site offers a full complement of exercises to go with these products, articles promoting a better understanding of your well-rounded fitness and instructional DVDs covering yoga, Pilates and aerobics. The only thing missing is your motivation to get fit.

·PERSONAL FITNESS	·INSTRUCTION		

SkateBuys.com

If you're looking for a site that simultaneously meets the needs of a large, burly hockey player and a diminutive figure skater, you've found it. With products representing every conceivable skating possibilty, this specialty shop offers a superior selection of ice, roller and inline skates, whether built for hockey, speed, grace or for purely recreational purposes. You'll also find plenty of protective gear to suit every skating athlete, as well as leotards and dancing outfits, which are probably meant more for the figure skating set than the hockey players.

·PROTECTIVE	·WINTER SPORTS	·RECREATION	·APPAREL
·FOOTWEAR	·ROAD SPORTS	·KIDS	·GYM & STUDIO

Soccer.com

Soccer may be more popular in other countries, but that isn't to say we can't buy soccer equipment, apparel and merchandise with the best of them. This site certainly gets us started, with an amazingly comprehensive selection of soccer boots, balls, protective equipment and jerseys. It goes beyond just playing the sport though, and verges on living it, with a surprising amount of practice equipment, warm-up outfits, rule books, instructive videos, medical accessories and loads of fan gear. With a little bit of luck, and a lot of shopping from this terrific specialty retailer, perhaps the next generation of men, women and children will fully and finally embrace that beautiful game the rest of the world thinks of as football.

·PROTECTIVE	·FAN GEAR	·APPAREL	·FIELD SPORTS
·FOOTWEAR	·KIDS	·INSTRUCTION	

SportEyes.com

This retailer of "sports specific eyewear" will appeal to you on many fronts. Primarily, the fact that they offer prescription lenses for the myopic athlete should be enough, but then they'll try to sell you on the notion that you may "look cool while you play." Whether or not this is true, it's hard to complain about a range of products made specifically for ball sports, cycling, fishing, diving, snow sports, swimming and more. Ironically, the layout of their categories makes it hard to see where the actual products come in. Squinting should help.

·WATER SPORTS	·WINTER SPORTS	·PERSONAL FITNESS	·FIELD SPORTS
·ROAD SPORTS	·LEISURE SPORTS	·COURT SPORTS	·GYM & STUDIO

800-869-6670 · Sports Basement

SportsBasement.com

If the high prices of technologically savvy athletic apparel gets you down, turn to this site which regularly offers a full catalog of personal fitness, swimming, cycling, hiking and winter gear at discounted prices. The San Francisco Bay Area shop buys "overstock and excess inventory," meaning you might occasionally find some of these items on sale elsewhere for less, but you'll have to go looking for specific items, and once all is said and done it's just easier to log on here to browse for great deals in the first place.

·WATER SPORTS ·ROAD SPORTS	·WINTER SPORTS ·KIDS	·PERSONAL FITNESS ·CAMPING	·FOOTWEAR ·GYM & STUDIO

888-543-2173 · SportsKids.com

SportsKids.com

This site may be way behind in terms of web design, but if you can get past its clumsy coding and low-quality looks, you'll find a tremendous resource for the athletic youngster. With kid-size sporting goods and training equipment, there's plenty here to get your children well on their way to competitive play in just about every sport you can imagine. In fact, a Camps & Leagues finder helps you discover local leagues where your kids can pit their newfound skills and equipment against those of other peoples' kids. To this end there's one other thing the site excels at: remembering to keep it fun.

·FAN GEAR ·FIELD SPORTS	·PERSONAL FITNESS ·KIDS	·RECREATION ·INSTRUCTION	·APPAREL ·COURT SPORTS

800-326-2453 · Supergo Bike Shops

SuperGo.com

Due to limitations imposed by most manufacturers, it's sometimes hard to find bicycles you can actually buy online, so most of the cycling shops we've viewed focus on components, safety gear and apparel. This site actually does it all, offering a healthy selection of road and mountain bikes, as well as all the appropriate equipment and accessories. However, the biggest surprise of this specialty retailer is that, despite an abundance of products, it's very well organized and even easy to use. Hard to imagine better.

·PROTECTIVE	·APPAREL	·ROAD SPORTS	

800-847-4327 · Team One Newport

Team1Newport.com

This "foul weather gear" specialist located in Rhode Island can keep you warm and dry when you're embracing the natural beauty of harsh elements, but it can also keep you cool when you're exerting yourself in a controlled climate. Thermal layers, boat shoes and waterproof jackets for men, women and children prove indispensable when navigating rough waters or winter storms, while some of the more temperate sporting gear available here will fit well everywhere from the gym to your sofa.

·PROTECTIVE	·WATER SPORTS	·WINTER SPORTS	

TeamStore.com

Sports fans find another avenue toward advertising their loyalty thanks to this site, which keeps it simple while representin' pro sports merchandise. Whether you're a fan of the MLB, NFL, NBA, NHL or NASCAR you have only to choose your team of choice and browse away. Some amateurs get involved as well, whether collegiate or Olympian, and even a few minor league teams and a little something called the AFL (Arena Football league). Hats, shirts, pins and replica jerseys are only the beginning. Show your love.

·FAN GEAR

TennisCompany.com

This may not be the best tennis shop on the web, but it might lead you to the best deals. While it offers Used Racquets, we'd actually steer you away from that, as this shop actually makes it more worth your while to buy a new racquet. Its selection can be beat, but its prices won't, and since we're talking about Wilson, Prince, Head, Dunlop and Yonex brands, most customers should be satisfied. Of course, tennis shoes and accessories are also available, and there's little chance you'll get bogged down in anything so time-consuming as decision-making.

·PROTECTIVE   ·APPAREL   ·FOOTWEAR   ·COURT SPORTS

TennisWarehouse.com

When you're playing tennis, it's can be frustrating trying to compete with somebody who's better equipped than you are. This site's competitors must suffer the same feeling. The all-tennis retailer offers superior selections of racquets, shoes and apparel, exquisitely laid out with a low price guarantee, so if you actually manage to find all this stuff elsewhere, you can be certain to save money here. Other perks include a Learning Center to help with things like string options and racquet selection, and a Demo Program that allows you to try out certain racquet styles before you buy. Your tennis game only gets better from here.

·FOOTWEAR   ·KIDS   ·INSTRUCTION   ·COURT SPORTS

TGW.com

With a selection that seemingly never ends, you'll be glad this all-golf retailer has thoroughly organized its inventory to show you only what you need. When it comes to clubs, this means you may filter the available selection by club type, length, material, brand and price range, plus some more explicit details that will mean something only to an expert. Even still, you may find yourself debating several great options. The apparel is similarly arranged, but we can't vouch for the quality of any resulting selection; after all, we are talking about golf attire.

·FOOTWEAR   ·LEISURE SPORTS   ·INSTRUCTION

800-992-7245 · The House Boardshop

The-House.com

Board riders come in many forms, and this site serves just about all of them, beginning with snowboarders and continuing on to windsurfers, skaters and wakeboarders. The best part is, while quality design and proven name brands are a priority, this Minnesota specialty retailer never fails to take style into consideration with its boards or apparel, as evidenced by the dedicated Shoe and Sunglasses shops. In fact, with separate, dedicated shops for each activity, it seems the site should be easier to navigate than it is, but all the heavy clicking will be duly rewarded with huge, impressive selections across the board—or, boards.

·PROTECTIVE ·ROAD SPORTS	·WATER SPORTS	·WINTER SPORTS	·FOOTWEAR

800-669-3474 · The Fly Shop

TheFlyShop.com

Fly-fishing is a slowly acquired skill requiring patience, devotion and cunning wit, and shopping from this fly-fishing specialist will require many these same traits. Conquer the online catalog's layout, however, and you'll gain steady access to a variety of fly designs, tying materials, rods, reels, waders, nets and pontoons, mostly at terrific prices. Patient fly-fishermen take note: when you cast a fly on the river, there are no guarantees; log on to this site, and you're certain to find something you want.

·WATER SPORTS	·OUTDOORSMEN		

800-999-1213 · Title Boxing

TitleBoxing.com

A complete workout requires a complete web shop, and that's what boxing enthusiasts will find with this specialty fitness site that proudly proclaims, "If we don't have it, you don't need it!" They may be right. Beginning with exercise equipment to promote strength, conditioning and weight management, this store has everything you'll need to turn yourself into a lean, mean fighting machine, including punching bags, gloves, protective gear, handbags and instructional materials. The only thing you won't find here is a sparring partner.

·PROTECTIVE ·GYM & STUDIO	·PERSONAL FITNESS	·FOOTWEAR	·INSTRUCTION

877-363-7842 · Enertia Trail Foods

TrailFoods.com

When you're out in the wilderness around suppertime, you'll appreciate the offerings of this site. Far beyond granola, this trail foods specialist offers full and satisfying meals that will fit easily into your pack, yet still provide the sustenance you need to get back safely to civilization. A quick glance at the menu reveals entrees like bulgar, chowder, chili, soup, scallops, stroganoff and mush. Okay, so this doesn't sound very appetizing in comparison to every meal you've eaten in your life, but if you've been hiking through trees and shrubs for eight hours, these quick and hearty offerings will hit the spot.

·ADVENTURE	·CAMPING		

Tramdock.com

This might just turn out to be the best ski shop online. Granted, it may not boast the most outrageous attitude, nor stock snowboards, snow skates, mountain boards or sleds. But if you want to find good skis for someone of every size, shape and skill level, you won't likely do better. The avid winter athletes behind this site boast some of the best skis on the market, including fat skis, touring skis, high-performance designs, telemark skis and a few that are simply hard to find elsewhere. Add some quality boots, apparel and safety equipment and you don't even need to be a skier to recognize just how good this site really is.

| ·PROTECTIVE ·KIDS | ·WINTER SPORTS | ·ADVENTURE | ·FOOTWEAR |

TravelCountry.com

Adventurous campers will find a treasure trove of valuable outdoors equipment here, whether the objective is to keep warm in bitterly cold weather or to scramble deep into the wilderness. And we mean deep, as the site can set you up to add climbing and kayaking into your itinerary, packing loads of lightweight equipment in order to get to spots even the most determined hikers find hard to reach. As useful as this stuff is, it really takes someone exceedingly durable and tough to appreciate all of it at once; for the rest of us, this shop proves terrific one activity at a time.

| ·PROTECTIVE ·FOOTWEAR | ·WATER SPORTS ·CAMPING | ·WINTER SPORTS | ·ADVENTURE |

VolleyHut.com

You might say good service is the hallmark of this specialty retailer, which takes a devotion to volleyball to new heights. Whether you prefer to play indoors or out in the sand and sun, you'll find plenty of balls, nets, safety equipment, training equipment, instructional media and apparel to choose from. The single exception may be those extremely skimpy uniforms typically worn by professional women beach volleyball players, but, somehow, we don't think your game will suffer without them.

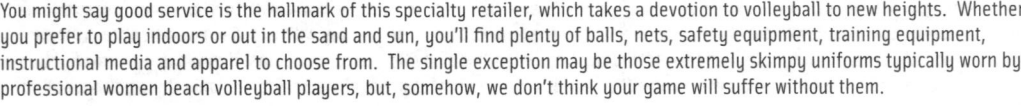

| ·PROTECTIVE | ·FOOTWEAR | ·INSTRUCTION | ·COURT SPORTS |

VSAthletics.com

Dedicated to athletes who run, jump and throw things, this track and field specialist covers every sport in the decathlon, with runner's spikes, relay batons, high-jump bars, discuses, hammers, shots, javelins, hurdles and vaulting poles among its wares. Like the aerodynamic singlets sprinters usually wear, the site is more functional than beautiful, its basic design allowing for quick browsing through quality gear. We wouldn't change a thing, though, as these guys manage to keep their prices low, proving that they fully understand the spirit of competition.

| ·APPAREL | ·FIELD SPORTS | ·FOOTWEAR | ·INSTRUCTION |

800-648-7024 · Wickers

Wickers.com

At first glance, the socks, undergarments and t-shirts available from this dedicated brand site seem like nothing more than just that: underwear. However, this underwear has been specially formulated to improve your thermoregulation, which means it can keep your body dry, warm and/or cool, depending on your activity and environment. Which makes it perfect for any of your indoor or outdoor physical activities, whether you need something lightweight for summer or heavyweight for winter and high altitudes. After all, what's the point of even wearing underwear if it's not going to contribute to your comfort and well-being?

·PROTECTIVE ·FIELD SPORTS	·WINTER SPORTS ·KIDS	·PERSONAL FITNESS ·GYM & STUDIO	·ADVENTURE

800-617-9463 · Windsurfing Direct

Windsurfing-Direct.com

Harnessing the power of water and the wind sounds like the stuff of mythological heroes, but truth is all it really takes is a modicum of athleticism and this windsurfing specialty site. You'll find boards, sails, masts and fins, or you may simply opt for an assortment of complete setups, including several entry-level packages (which include instructional DVDs). It's not an inexpensive sport, but nobody ever said mastery of the elements was going to come cheap.

·PROTECTIVE	·WATER SPORTS	·KIDS	·INSTRUCTION

800-999-3756 · WorkoutWarehouse.com

WorkoutWarehouse.com

Keeping fit was easy in the old days, when people had to hike forty miles to work in the fields lugging heavy equipment. Nowadays, with urbanization and the advent of the computer desk job, staying in shape is a task we must pursue during our leisure time. Fortunately, there's a great selection of home exercise machines available from this well-laid-out fitness specialist. Whether your intent is to bulk up or tone down, the site offers bikes, treadmills, skiers, steppers, weight machines and elliptical trainers to work into your daily regimen, and of course a few combo machines for that well-balanced look you could only otherwise achieve by going outside and participating in a variety of healthy activities.

·PERSONAL FITNESS			

800-759-8326 · WrestlingOne

WrestlingOne.com

The oft-maligned sport of wrestling finally gets its due with this full-service specialty site, and the most important thing you should know is that the bombastic personalities of professional wrestling have nothing to do with it. This shop's all about the Greco-Roman style favored by high school, collegiate and Olympian athletes, complete with singlets, protective headgear and special shoes. The biggest surprise may be the inclusion of Other Sports in this catalog, which include deep selections for those who love dance, cheerleading, field hockey, volleyball, tennis, soccer, softball and lacrosse, none of which suffer the public relations hit of steel-cage battle royales, but all of which should benefit from the retail exposure.

·PROTECTIVE ·FOOTWEAR	·PERSONAL FITNESS ·KIDS	·APPAREL ·COURT SPORTS	·FIELD SPORTS ·GYM & STUDIO

NOTES:

Stationery & Gifts

The act of giving is lovely in and of itself, and whether it's flowers, candy or a card, you really can't go wrong—especially if you get it from one of the exceptional traditional gift sites we've included in these pages, which offer ever-classier floral arrangements and ever-tastier gourmet confections. But if you really want to tap into the power of this section, you'll use it to track down something unique, personal and ideal for that special recipient in your life. The assortment of retailers here offer items ranging from lavish to outlandish, from thoughtful to romantic, from limited-edition to custom-made, and there's no question that browsing from web shop to web shop requires much less time and effort than driving around town only to be disappointed at every stop. Never mind how much easier it is to have an online retailer wrap and ship that perfect gift for you.

For those who prefer to package and deliver a present in person, we've made a special effort to include more shops that carry amazing gift bags, wrapping paper and ribbons. The paper selection only gets better with a fine array of stationery sites, where you'll find extensive varieties of invitations, note cards, journals, stationery sets and personalized letterheads. We're hoping these will inspire us all to keep in better touch with the people we care about, because receiving a handwritten letter is a great gift for any occasion.

TIPS ON BUYING STATIONERY & GIFTS ONLINE

These suggestions may help keep your gifts from coming back to haunt you.

• **THOUGHTFUL GIFTING** •There are quite a lot of gifting standards, and this book can help you find a gift quickly and easily. Use key words like Romantic and Creative to find selections of interesting and appropriate alternatives to old standbys like flowers and gift baskets.

• **GETTING IT THERE ON TIME** •Bear in mind that oftentimes even overnight delivery might not get a gift to its recipient on time (due to late-day orders and processing delays). If you want to make sure the gift you send arrives on time, you should probably order it at least a few days in advance (earlybirds can often arrange for a gift to arrive on a specific day). Delivery times vary by site, but for true last-minute orders, look for the gift certificate icon, since most of these sites offer email gift certificates that can be delivered electronically within a matter of minutes. Sure, recipients will know that it was a last-minute effort, but they won't mind so much if you send them shopping at a great online merchant.

• **GIFT RECEIPTS** •Obviously, it's a bit gauche to send a gift with the receipt included in the box, but most of these sites offer to include a gift receipt with the item even if they don't offer gift wrapping. A gift receipt doesn't include the price of an item but enables the recipient to arrange easy returns and exchanges should there be any problems related to size, color, defective parts or anything otherwise unsatisfactory.

• **STATIONERY PROOFS** • Personalized stationery is a popular feature offered by several of the sites listed here, and using the web-integrated software solutions of these sites usually works well to get you the look you want on your invitations, announcements or letterheads. However, there's always a considerable chance for error when computers are in the mix, so take these sites up on their offers to send you a proof copy of your stationery before the order is completed. It will take a bit longer to get everything, but you won't be stuck paying for a stack of misprints.

SITES THAT MAY COME IN HANDY

The following URLs may be useful when you shop for certain recipients.

Chocophile.com	Chocolate lover resource
ElegantAnniversary.com	Anniversary gift guidelines
GiftCertificates.com	Gift certificates of hundreds of on- and offline retailers
HappyBirthday.com	Online birthday reminder service
iFlorist.com/en/act/meaning	Symbolic meanings of flowers
Plaxo.com	Online address book
Shimojima.co.jp/english/wrapping/wrap00.htm	Gift wrapping instructions
SunMoments.com	Flower gift conventions
Surprise.com	Browse for gift ideas
Switchboard.com	Locate a mailing address
ThingsIWant.com	Wish list registry
USPS.com	United States Postal Service site
VerseIt.com	Verse and speech etiquette and ideas

▶▶ NATIONAL CATALOGS & BRANDS

The following sites offer online sales for familiar brands and gift catalogs.

1800Flowers.com	MrsFields.com
Discovery.com	OfficeDepot.com
DiscountOfficeSupplies.com	ProFlowers.com
FlaxArt.com	SFMusicBox.com
FranklinCovey.com	Staples.com
FTD.com	

▶▶ GIFT CONFECTIONS

The following sites offer sweet treats packaged as gifts.

BerryGourmet.com	Chocolate-dipped berries
CrazyBouquet.com	Candy bouquets
Fralingers.com	Boardwalk candy favorites
Ghiradelli.com	Chocolate
Godiva.com	Chocolate
GoodKarmal.com	Caramels
LadyFortunes.com	Cookie gifts
MrsFields.com	Cookies
SayItWithCheesecake.com	Cheesecakes
Sees.com	Chocolate
TinyTrapeze.com	Candies
WoodhouseChocolates.com	Chocolate

▶▶ SITES WITH A SINGLE FOCUS

The following sites excel at selling one or two specific products.

AKAGourmet.com	Unusual gift baskets
BarnesAndWagner.com	Glass gifts
BaileysBoxes.com	Gift boxes
CocoonOnline.com	Hostess gifts
DanielsonDesigns.com	Picture frames
EssenceDeProvence.com	Lavender gifts
FireLight.com	Glass candles
FlowersOfTheWorld.com	Unusual floral arrangements
GreatBigStuff.com	Supersize novelty gifts
GreatClubs.com	Gift-of-the-month clubs
HollywoodMegastore.com	Movie related gifts
McPhee.com	Novelty and gag gifts
RitaFordMusicBoxes	Music boxes
theSpaceStore.com	Space-related gifts

*For in-depth reviews of these sites and more, check out **www.thepurplebook.com**.

SECTION ICON LEGEND

Use the following guide to understand the rectangular icons that appear throughout this section.

STANDBYS

There are certain gifts that are appropriate for specific occasions, even expected. These include flowers, boxes of candy and gift baskets, as well as the occasional decorative housewarming gift. This icon will point out sites that offer the finest of anticipated gifts, which can help, particularly if you're in a rush.

PERSONALIZATION

Want to make sure your gift is not returned? Slap the person's name on it. This icon will point you to plenty of monogramming/engraving options, but in most cases it applies to various stationeries.

STATIONERY & OFFICE

This icon deals primarily in paper goods, with a few handy paper-related office supplies thrown in for good measure. Whether you're looking for personalized letterhead, packaging materials or a diary, this should point out some useful sites.

UNUSUAL GIFTS

If you want to surprise somebody with a unique and unexpected gift, this icon can help you find just the thing, even if you don't know what that thing is just yet.

>> LIST OF KEY WORDS

The following words represent the types of items typically found on the sites listed in this section. You will find them listed in the orange strip at the bottom of each entry, as appropriate.

ALBUMS/DIARIES	Photo albums, diaries and journals can be found on many sites throughout this section.
CANDLES/SCENTS	Includes both scented and unscented candles, plus other aromatic gifts.
CARDS	Primarily note cards, thank-you cards and invitations, as well as some greeting and personalized cards.
CONFECTIONS	You'll find plenty of sweets in our Epicurean section, but you'll find them here in pretty packages.
CREATIVE GIFTS	These gifts are meant for the creative people in your life, and include arts-and-crafts kits, as well as some more unusual fare.
EXECUTIVE GIFTS	Pens are the most common of these gifts, which generally denote the sort of gift you'd bestow upon a man's man.
FLOWERS	The age-old standby is easy to shop for, with some intriguing and exotic options, whether for same-day, overnight and/or international delivery.
GIFT BASKETS	We found gift baskets for men, women, children, babies and a variety of across-the-board interests (including food).
HOUSEWARMING	These gifts should prove appropriate for any gracious host or hostess.
OFFICE SUPPLIES	Refill your stapler, stock up on paper clips and pick up pretty much any other office necessity you might require from these shops.
ROMANTIC GIFTS	The most romantic gifts are personal, but sites marked by this key word should help if you're stuck.
STATIONERY	Personalized letterheads, handmade paper and other elegant paper goods make up the bulk of these products.
TCHOTCHKES	There's no easy way to describe this variety of trinkets, but you'll find them in stores labeled "Gift Shop."
UNIQUE GIFTS	These aren't gifts you generally plan to give, or receive, which is what makes them so great.

KEY WORD INDEX

Use the followings lists to locate online retailers that sell the stationery & gifts you seek.

ALBUMS/DIARIES

AimeeJ.com
DaisyArts.com
ExposuresOnline.com
FredFlare.com
FrenchGeneral.com
Galison.com
Gift-World-Collection.com
HillarysGifts.com
JenniBick.com
KatesPaperie.com
Levenger.com
LincolnStationers.com
LuxePaperie.com
PamelaBarsky.com
Paper-Source.com
PaperHaus.com
QuincyShop.com
RockScissorPaper.com
SeeJaneWork.com
SendAFrame.com
ShopHeidi.com
Smythson.com
SoleBerry.com
WingardHome.com

CANDLES/SCENTS

BlueChopsticks.com
CSPost.com
Illuminations.com
JapaneseGifts.com
PajamaGram.com
RedEnvelope.com
RobbSteck.com
RomanzaGifts.com
SproutHome.com
WingardHome.com

CARDS

AmericanStationery.com
CardSupply.com
CatfishGreetings.com
ChelseaPaper.com
EdiblesInc.com
ExposuresOnline.com
FabulousStationery.com
FineStationery.com
FireFly.bz
FredFlare.com
Galison.com
Gallery19.us
GreatArrow.com
ImpressInPrint.com
InvitationBox.com
Iomoi.com
KatesPaperie.com
LaughingElephant.com
LincolnStationers.com
LuxePaperie.com
MountainCow.com
MyGatsby.com
Paper-Source.com
PaperPresentation.com
PhotoWow.com
PlumParty.com
PulpFactory.com
RockScissorPaper.com
ShopHeidi.com
Smythson.com
SoleBerry.com
SugarPaper.com
TheStationeryStudio.com
Zazzle.com

CONFECTIONS

BeyondGourmet.com
BlackHoundNewYork.com
BlueChopsticks.com
Brownies.com
ChristopherNormanChocolates.com
DelightfulDeliveries.com
EdiblesInc.com
FlourPotDesign.com
GlobalExchangeStore.org
JosephSchmidtConfections.com
LulaBelleToffee.com
MarieBelle.com
NonniesTraditional.com
OrganicBouquet.com
Richart-Chocolates.com
RubyEtViolette.com
StarTreatment.com
zChocolat.com

CREATIVE GIFTS

BonsaiBoy.com
DaisyArts.com
ExposuresOnline.com
FredFlare.com
FrenchGeneral.com
Galison.com
JapaneseGifts.com
Levenger.com
MountainCow.com
NostalgicImpressions.com
Paper-Source.com
QuincyShop.com
WishingFish.com

EXECUTIVE GIFTS

BreakfastTray.com
DavidLinley.com
Gift-World-Collection.com
HillarysGifts.com
Joon.com
Levenger.com
LincolnStationers.com
MichaelCFina.com
NostalgicImpressions.com
OneShare.com
QuincyShop.com
RebeccaMoss.com
RedEnvelope.com
SeeJaneWork.com
StarTreatment.com
ThingsRemembered.com
TShipley.com
ZipperGifts.com

FLOWERS

1888Orchids.com
BBrooks.com
BlueChopsticks.com
BonsaiBoy.com
CalyxAndCorolla.com
CSPost.com
DelightfulDeliveries.com
Flower.com
HawaiianTropicals.com
LavaHut.com
NonniesTraditional.com
OrganicBouquet.com
SurroundingsFlowers.com
TeleFlora.com

GIFT BASKETS

BarrelsOfFun.com
BeyondGourmet.com
BlueChopsticks.com
Brownies.com
ChelseaMarketBaskets.com
DelightfulDeliveries.com

GIFT BASKETS (cont.)

Flower.com
FraicheGifts.com
GlobalExchangeStore.org
HillarysGifts.com
PajamaGram.com
RedEnvelope.com
StarTreatment.com
SurroundingsFlowers.com
TherapyInABox.com
TheWelcomedGuest.com
VansGifts.com

HOUSEWARMING

BeyondGourmet.com
BlackHoundNewYork.com
BonsaiBoy.com
CSPost.com
DavidLinley.com
DelightfulDeliveries.com
ElseWares.com
GiannaRose.com
GlobalExchangeStore.org
Illuminations.com
JapaneseGifts.com
MichaelCFina.com
ObjectsOfEnvy.com
Pylones-USA.com
RedEnvelope.com
RobbSteck.com
SproutHome.com
WingardHome.com
ZipperGifts.com

OFFICE SUPPLIES

BreakfastTray.com
DolphinBlue.com
HillarysGifts.com
JamPaper.com
Joon.com
KatesPaperie.com
Levenger.com
LincolnStationers.com
PaperHaus.com
PaperPresentation.com
RebeccaMoss.com
SeeJaneWork.com
TShipley.com
ZipperGifts.com

ROMANTIC GIFTS

BlackHoundNewYork.com
BreakfastTray.com
ChristopherNormanChocolates.com
CSPost.com
GiftSongs.com
GlobalExchangeStore.org
HawaiianTropicals.com
Illuminations.com
JapaneseGifts.com
LavaHut.com
LunarEmbassy.com
MichaelCFina.com
MusicBoxAttic.com
NostalgicImpressions.com
RedAmbrosia.com
RedEnvelope.com
RomanzaGifts.com
ShopLoveMe.com
StarRegistry.com
SurroundingsFlowers.com
ThingsRemembered.com
zChocolat.com

STATIONERY

AmericanStationery.com
CardSupply.com
ChelseaPaper.com
DolphinBlue.com
FineStationery.com
FireFly.bz
ForYourParty.com
FredFlare.com
HillarysGifts.com
Ink-Well.net
Iomoi.com
JamPaper.com
JapaneseGifts.com
KatesPaperie.com
Levenger.com
LincolnStationers.com
LuxePaperie.com
MountainCow.com
NostalgicImpressions.com
Paper-Source.com
PaperMojo.com
PaperPresentation.com
PaperStyle.com
QuincyShop.com
RockScissorPaper.com
SeeJaneWork.com
Smythson.com

STATIONERY (cont.)

SoleBerry.com
SugarPaper.com
TheStationeryStudio.com

TCHOTCHKES

BlueChopsticks.com
BroadwayNewYork.com
CSPost.com
DavidLinley.com
ElseWares.com
ExposuresOnline.com
ForYourParty.com
FredFlare.com
GagWorks.com
Gift-World-Collection.com
GlobalExchangeStore.org
HillarysGifts.com
Ink-Well.net
JapaneseGifts.com
LavaHut.com
MichaelCFina.com
ObjectsOfEnvy.com
PhotoWow.com
PlumParty.com
Pylones-USA.com
QuincyShop.com
RedEnvelope.com
ShopLoveMe.com
SpoonSisters.com
SproutHome.com
ThingsRemembered.com
WishingFish.com
ZipperGifts.com

UNIQUE GIFTS

BreakfastTray.com
BroadwayNewYork.com
ChristopherNormanChocolates.com
CSPost.com
EdiblesInc.com
ElseWares.com
ExposuresOnline.com
FredFlare.com
GagWorks.com
Gift-World-Collection.com
GiftSongs.com
GlobalExchangeStore.org
Ink-Well.net
JapaneseGifts.com
KaleidoVisions.com

UNIQUE GIFTS (cont.)

LavaHut.com
LunarEmbassy.com
NonniesTraditional.com
NostalgicImpressions.com
OneShare.com
PajamaGram.com
ParapluieDesigns.com
PhotoWow.com
Pylones-USA.com
QuincyShop.com
RedEnvelope.com
RobbSteck.com
ShopLoveMe.com
SpoonSisters.com
StarRegistry.com
TheMonogramShops.com
ThingsRemembered.com
WishingFish.com
Zazzle.com
ZipperGifts.com

WRAP/MAIL

AmericanStationery.com
APEC-USA.com
CardSupply.com
FredFlare.com
Gallery19.us
JamPaper.com
KatesPaperie.com
LuxePaperie.com
MasterStrokeCanada.com
MrGiftWrap.com
NostalgicImpressions.com
PaperMart.com
PaperPresentation.com
ParapluieDesigns.com
Photo.Stamps.com
PlumParty.com
PulpFactory.com
RibbonShop.com
ShopHeidi.com
SignatureByCrayon.com
SoleBerry.com
TheStationeryStudio.com
Trimorphos.com
Zazzle.com

1880Orchids.com

1880Orchids.com · 760-602-0837

Beautiful and mysterious, orchids capture the imagination like no other flower, and can even outdo the rose as an out of the ordinary romantic gesture. This orchid specialist out of "flower capital of the world" San Diego, California, offers you a way to do it right. Shipping directly from the grower, a wide variety of individual blooms are available for extremely competitive prices, usually with your choice of basket or pot. You'll also find a selection of beautiful planters, bonsai trees and the best assortment of leis online.

 ·FLOWERS

AimeeJ.com

aimeej, inc. · 913-897-0449

The inventory of this family-owned album and scrapbook specialist offers that special something that can never be faked: the human touch. The handmade assortment proves perfect for storing memories from the home front, while keepsake boxes preserve the three-dimensional artifacts of a life well spent. As you may already have surmised, this sort of thing would also be perfect for weddings and baby births—well, the designing mind behind this selection has created special items for just such occasions.

 ·ALBUMS/DIARIES

AmericanStationery.com

American Stationery Company · 800-822-2577

Thanks to rampant commercialism and kitschy pop culture, the words *American* and *elegant* aren't always thought of in the same context. This personalized stationery site is happy to disagree, offering fine and sophisticated letterheads, cards and paper at good, old-fashioned, affordable American prices. Whether you prefer embossed letterheads or decorative hand-drawn borders, the site offers a lovely selection that maintains the same great taste the shop has shown for more than eighty-five years. In other words, good taste that predates television.

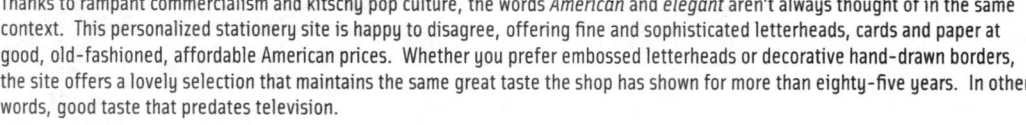
  ·STATIONERY · ·WRAP & MAIL · ·CARDS

APEC-USA.com

American Printing and Envelope Company · 800-221-9403

Who knew there was a company out there specializing entirely in envelopes and similarly constructed mailing products? Well, get ready to meet the American Printing and Envelope Company, "New York's hottest envelope manufacturer." Their selection of mailers, boxes, vellums and glassine envelopes would seem to be enough, and yet they supplement it with mailers specifically suited to compact discs, photos, films and negatives. If only they'd make an envelope suitable for sending cookies, we'd be all set.

 ·WRAP & MAIL

800-536-7386 · Barrels of Fun

BarrelsOfFun.com

Well, it appears these guys have come up with an innovative response to a burgeoning truth we are all, deep down inside, coming to terms with: baskets are not all that functional. Rather, they propose that you offer gift barrels instead. Yes, barrels. Not the wood-slatted sort with iron rings that lunatics like to ride over Niagara Falls, but a significantly smaller kind that comes with a sealing lid and all manner of goodies inside. Find them here for every occasion, and you won't waste one ounce of wicker in the process.

·GIFT BASKETS

888-346-3356 · B. Brooks

BBrooks.com

Behind the philosophy that "fine florists are artists and their medium is flowers," this San Francisco florist proves itself a cut above the rest by offering a small array of dazzling, meticulously arranged bouquets that will go out of their way to delight. Even the classic gift of a dozen long-stem roses is done finer here, with flowers chosen as much for their fragrance as their beauty, and coupled with the option to add lilies and exotic foliage to create a richer and, if possible, even more romantic gesture. Good luck trying to find better.

·FLOWERS

877-999-4940 · BeyondGourmet.com

BeyondGourmet.com

It's tough to imagine an occasion when a gift basket filled with delicious foods wouldn't be appreciated, which is why we dig this gourmet gift specialist. Wines, meats, cheeses, dried fruit and a variety of other fine treats abound in these infinitely appealing baskets, and whether the gifting event in question is somber, celebratory, conciliatory or obligatory, these cannot help but go over well. Shop by occasion, recipient or price, and the perfect gourmet gift will all but fall into your lap.

·CONFECTIONS   ·GIFT BASKETS   ·HOUSEWARMING

800-344-4417 · Black Hound New York

BlackHoundNewYork.com

The refined sweet tooth demands a quality confection, and this groundbreaking chocolatier is more than prepared to satisfy just about every nuance of flavor you could hope for. To help paint the picture, it may help to know that their signature gifts include a variety of chocolate truffle sauces, and a look at the ingredients list for any of their cookies will give you the munchies. We could go on to describe more, but the ensuing drool might short out our keyboards. Let's just say that these incredible gourmet sweets are prepared to charm any taste bud.

·CONFECTIONS   ·ROMANTIC GIFTS   ·HOUSEWARMING

BlueChopsticks.com

BlueChopsticks.com · 888-222-4185

Put just about every traditional gift known to Western civilization on a single web site and it might look like this. With easy gift choices for every conceivable occasion, you'll find a wide assortment of gift baskets, creative floral and confection arrangements, engravable items and plenty of other "chic gift products suited for the modern individual and lifestyle." It can actually be a bit overwhelming at first, but once you get your bearing this proves an easy site to return to when you need to select an appropriate gift, fast, and without too much effort.

·FLOWERS ·CANDLES/SCENTS	·CONFECTIONS	·GIFT BASKETS	·TCHOTCHKES

BonsaiBoy.com

Bonsai Boy · 800-790-2763

Giving flowers works for a variety of occasions, but ultimately they just look pretty for a while and then die. If you'd like to give something a bit more lasting from the plant world, consider the fantastic bonsai trees offered by this New York state nursery. Not only will the tree last for a long time with just a little bit of care, but if you include a bonsai tool kit with your gift, the creative person in your life will find trimming, pruning and training the miniature tree to be a wonderful, meditative outlet for years to come.

·FLOWERS	·CREATIVE GIFTS	·HOUSEWARMING

BreakfastTray.com

The Bed Tray Shoppe · 800-414-6886

We were as surprised as anybody to discover that the perfect executive gift and a terrific romantic gift may be found on the same site; in fact, in the same product! We're pretty sure this site offers the largest selection of bed trays you'll find anywhere, and the variety available is pretty impressive at that. These work great for serving the always romantic breakfast-in-bed gesture, but may just as easily double as a bedroom work desk for that lamp-burning executive who likes to work late in comfort. Regardless of your intentions, this exclusively online retailer is not to be missed.

·OFFICE SUPPLIES	·ROMANTIC GIFTS	·UNIQUE GIFTS	·EXECUTIVE GIFTS

BroadwayNewYork.com

BroadwayNewYork.com · 800-223-1320

Know a fan of the live theater? Or do they prefer "theatre"? Here, either perception of the art form is celebrated, from musicals to comedies, actors to authors. Posters, mugs, shirts and magnets bear logo graphics pertaining to celebrated works, while programs, cast albums and other souvenirs remember particular casts and productions. These gifts will absolutely thrill those friends of yours who're always singing show tunes, reciting lines and referring to obscure performers. Of course, look here and you could always buy them tickets to a show....

·TCHOTCHKES	·UNIQUE GIFTS		

800-324-7982 · Fairytale Brownies

Brownies.com

Brownies are probably not the first thing you think of when you brainstorm gift ideas, but once you get a load of the beautiful packaging offered by this homegrown brownie specialist, you may just make the chocolaty treat one of your favorite standbys. With Chocolate Chip, Amaretto, Coconut, Peanut Butter, Toffee Crunch and many more tantalizing flavors available, our top choice would be the Fairytale Dozen gift sampler, and although trying all of the the dense, rich cakes will be all too tempting to your weight-conscious loved ones, we have a feeling they'll forgive you.

·CONFECTIONS   ·GIFT BASKETS

800-877-0998 · Calyx & Corolla

CalyxAndCorolla.com

First and foremost, when you give the gift of a floral bouquet, it should look impressive. These do, and not in a gaudy way either. While the florists here match these classy arrangements with what seem to be the perfect pedestals and vases (according to the pictures), you are granted several options with each bunch, including whether or not to have a vessel at all (which will often be dependent on price). The second most important thing to consider when procuring a bouquet is the scent...but you'll have to take their word on that one.

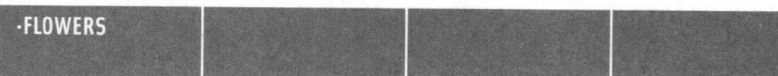

·FLOWERS

888-444-2273 · cardSupply

CardSupply.com

With a list of event-specific categories as long as our attention spans, it's a safe bet your invitation needs can be met with this "Internet's Largest Selection." The same could be said about the announcements, stationery and personalized holiday greeting cards found here. In each section there are several options to choose from, and yet somehow there doesn't seem to be a whole lot of variety. Erring on the side of simplicity, this shop prevents you from getting bogged down in excessive selection, and yet it all somehow seems potentially perfect.

·STATIONERY   ·WRAP & MAIL   ·CARDS

212-625-1800 · Cat Fish Greetings

CatfishGreetings.com

This independent stationer out of Manhattan's Nolita neighborhood offers note and greeting cards infinitely more distinctive than anything you'll find in a drugstore or chain gift shop. Hand made on fine paper, there are cards here designed to cover just about any occasion, with adorable illustrations, elegant sentiments and even an occasional bout of raunchy humor. As affordable as the greeting cards are, the boxed sets of blanks and thank-you cards offer unparalleled value for something that didn't come out of a machine.

·CARDS

ChelseaMarketBaskets.com

Chelsea Market Baskets · 888-727-7887

If you're going to successfully give somebody a gift basket, it must be tasteful. Few will taste better than the full selection of this Manhattan neighborhood specialist. Featuring classic New York treats, gourmet foodstuffs, fresh fruit, health foods and delectable snacks, the tremendous variety of epicurean gift baskets here are designed to make someone's mouth water, whatever his or her food preference may be. Shop by Recipient, food Category, Occasion or Price and you'll be sending the perfect basket in no time.

·GIFT BASKETS

ChelseaPaper.com

The Chelsea Paper Company · 888-407-2726

A lot of custom invitation and announcement retailers get the job done, but here's one that does so with aplomb. A great selection of raw materials starts with several dozen occasion-specific categories filled with a litany of brand-name stationeries, featuring such particular events as adoption anniversaries, bar mitzvahs, wine tastings and commitment ceremonies. The great range of options (tending toward "elegant" far more often than "fun") comes complete with online "proof sheets" that allow you to view how the cards will look once you've contributed your own lines of text.

   ·STATIONERY ·CARDS

ChristopherNormanChocolates.com

Christopher Norman Chocolates · 212-402-1243

★

This site doesn't just offer delicious confections, but also a great example of what happens when an artist turns to chocolate as a medium. Between hand-painted confections and ingenious gift boxing, this collection of pristinely designed sweets actually live up to its artistic pretensions. With candies shaped like dominoes, pyramids, walnuts and snowmen, these brilliant concoctions make for gifts more memorable than candy has a right to be.

  ·CONFECTIONS ·ROMANTIC GIFTS ·UNIQUE GIFTS

CSPost.com

CS Post & Co. · 888-419-2399

Though it calls itself a General Store, this Kansas retailer actually offers a "fresh variety of innovative finds for a sophisticated lifestyle." In other words, the sort of interesting and eclectic selection we're used to finding in gift shops. With plenty of quaint foods, household goods, specialty books, bath-and-body products and personal accessories, the shop delivers no shortage of unusual gift ideas for the not so unusual friend or loved one. And like any good General Store, it proves an excellent source of housewarming gifts in particular.

   ·FLOWERS ·TCHOTCHKES ·ROMANTIC GIFTS ·CANDLES/SCENTS
·HOUSEWARMING ·UNIQUE GIFTS

310-396-8463 · Daisy Arts

DaisyArts.com

Boasting a "unique quality and aesthetic that comes from hundreds of years of tradition," this intriguing album and journal producer offers leather, hand-bound books as made by Italian craftsmen. Impeccable gifts and stylish accessories to the creative, organized or nostalgic, the selection of photo albums, picture frames, sketchbooks and journals here exceed all others in terms of quality, if not quantity, and it's hard to imagine any writings or collections of photographs looking better anywhere else.

| ·CREATIVE GIFTS | ·ALBUMS/DIARIES | | | |

011-44-20-7730-7300 · David Linley

DavidLinley.com

Over the past twenty years, this British manufacturer "has become known for its imaginative use of wood," creating everything from furniture to desk sets. It's the household goods and executive gifts we focus on here, with extraordinarily elegant wood candlesticks, picture frames, dinnerware, decorative accents and cigar accessories. Be warned, though: such excessive quality does not come cheap, and many of these gifts cost more than most people pay for two months of rent, and that's in pounds sterling. This one's for extravagant shoppers only.

| ·TCHOTCHKES | ·HOUSEWARMING | ·EXECUTIVE GIFTS |  |

800-708-0024 · Delightful Deliveries

DelightfulDeliveries.com

When you put some of the best gourmet meal, cake, cookie and confection brands together into one online gift specialist, it's little wonder the result is the "America's #1 Gift Basket Website!" With selections from Mrs. Beasley, Mrs. Fields, Ghiardelli, Shari's Berries, A La Zing and more, these gift baskets make any occasion a delicious one, the packages overflowing with stuff like cookies, nuts, dried fruit, smoked salmon, filet mignon, cakes and chocolate, lots of chocolate. If it all doesn't seem enough, maybe you'll like the site's similarly tasty gift-of-the-month clubs.

| ·FLOWERS | ·CONFECTIONS | ·GIFT BASKETS | ·HOUSEWARMING | |

800-932-7715 · Dolphin Blue

DolphinBlue.com

If you are ecologically aware, you will definitely appreciate this site, which exclusively sells "Environmentally Responsible Office Supplies." Comprised largely of recycled and tree-free bulk printer paper, envelopes, post-its, organizers, folders and recycled toner cartridges, with this stuff you'll be able to get the job done, and at the same time know you're helping avoid excessive deforestation or landfill dumping. Their product selection continually grows, and in time you may be able to run a completely eco-friendly operation.

| ·STATIONERY | ·OFFICE SUPPLIES | | | |

EdiblesInc.com

Edibles · 800-858-4381

Tired of wasting paper on the greeting card industry? Here's an ingenious way to send the obligatory greeting with a literally sweet twist: these cards are actually cookies. They include everything you'd expect from a traditional card, including a funny little picture and a personalized greeting. The only real difference is that your recipient gets a tasty treat after reading it. The unique stationery/confections also make for incredible invitations and announcements; though of course you run the risk that your guests will eat the cookie and forget the party details.

·CONFECTIONS	·CARDS	·UNIQUE GIFTS	

ElseWares.com

Elsewares · 866-578-0730

This "catalog of unique products from independent designers and entrepreneurs" is capable of providing a most unusual gift to that funky friend or curious loved one, but in the end the best recipient of one of these diverse items might be yourself. Things like self-portrait mirrors are one of the myriad housewarming gifts you'll likely encounter here, while special custom-drawn comics could be the most extravagant greeting card you'll ever give. There's really no better way to describe this collection than to say it's eclectic, and we fear that doesn't even do it justice.

·TCHOTCHKES	·HOUSEWARMING	·UNIQUE GIFTS	

ExposuresOnline.com

Exposures · 800-572-5750

Everybody loves pictures, right? They preserve all those important moments for the ages so we don't have to rely upon our rapidly degenerating, um, you know. Well, this site brings you picture frames, albums, picture storage, displays and even mirrors so you can remember what you look like right now. We're not even getting into the "fun" options, like having a picture of your pet's face planted on a painting of a 17th-century nobleman. Sound crazy? What if we told you this image could then be printed on a pillow? This one you'll have to see for yourself.

·TCHOTCHKES ·UNIQUE GIFTS	·CREATIVE GIFTS	·CARDS	·ALBUMS/DIARIES

FabulousStationery.com

FabulousStationery.com · 800-521-5443

If you take note and thank-you cards seriously, you'll want to shop from this ad agency that has made its in-house stationery designs available to a public market. And there are plenty to choose from, all with bright colors and distinctive modern designs. As if the tremendous variety weren't enough, they offer to personalize these sets with your name and address, which are incorporated into the cards' visual style, ensuring that your note card set is perfect inside and out.

·CARDS			

888-808-3463 · FineStationery.com

FineStationery.com

Don't let the word *fine* deter the fun-loving stationery customer. While the bulk of this site surely qualifies as elegant, sophisticated and/or refined, there's just enough whimsy here to keep the shop from having the atmosphere of a mausoleum. Similarly, there's no reason to fear exorbitant pricing, especially if you steer clear of those selections marked by the $$$ symbol (look familiar?). What you can look forward to is a thorough selection including personalized stationery, note card sets, invitations for myriad occasions, business cards and a few products even children would like. In other words, just fine.

·STATIONERY ·CARDS

208-484-4822 · FireFly

FireFly.bz

Encouraging a child to read can be incredibly difficult; encouraging him or her to write can seem downright impossible. This children's stationer might be able to help; with a variety of personalized letterheads and note cards, a youngster will feel a sense of ownership over any correspondence without even writing a line, and will enthusiastically respond by putting pen to page, at least for a minute between cartoons. But hey, even the shortest of notes from a kid is going to be well-received by a grandparent, aunt or uncle.

·STATIONERY ·CARDS

800-281-6068 · The Flour Pot

FlourPotDesign.com

You'll bestow a great gift upon any party when you shop from this homegrown business out of Philadelphia. Among the site's superfun assortments of iced cookies you'll find lovingly decorated Easter eggs, martini glasses, guitars, butterflies, smiley faces and dozens of other styles suitable to just about any personality. The cookies make great party favors, and you may even custom order your own designs by calling the mother-daughter team behind the scenes, but for a quick online purchase they come packaged in beautiful gift boxes to satisfy any sweet tooth.

·CONFECTIONS

800-366-3024 · Flower.com

Flower.com

When you don't want to order a bouquet of flowers until you've viewed at least a thousand options first, take a look at this incredibly well-stocked floral and gift basket site that lets you look at hundreds and hundreds of options in a single visit, and even lets you know how soon they can be delivered. Balloons and fruit baskets add to the selection, which may be viewed by Occasion or Price, and even using a regional locator to help you find something that will show up quick where your recipient lives. Like its name, there's nothing terribly extravagant about this shop, but there's no question it gets the job done.

·FLOWERS ·GIFT BASKETS

ForYourParty.com

Throwing a party can be a simple as calling some friends and putting a bowl of peanuts on your coffee table. But when you really want to go all out, this is the site to visit. Personalized napkins, coasters, matchbooks and favors will turn your fete into a festive event whether you have a reason to celebrate (wedding, graduation, birthday) or just wish to up the ante on hanging out with the gang. Okay, so you'll probably want a good reason to tender personalized matchbooks, but it's nice to know they're available.

·STATIONERY	·TCHOTCHKES		

FraicheGifts.com

Most gift basket retailers focus so much on what goes into the basket that they never stop to consider the quality of the basket it-self. This site actually offers baskets that are lovely and useful, but somehow manage to keep the big picture in mind, filling these beautiful baskets with delicious fruits, mouthwatering chocolates, fine coffee and gourmet meats. Due to the perishable nature of most of these items, shipping must be rushed, and so it can be expensive. But it's an excellent resource if you want to please a finicky gourmand, and quickly.

·GIFT BASKETS			

FredFlare.com

You may need shades to view this bright and colorful site that offers equally bright and colorful paper products for the girl on the go (read: teenagers, and adult women who're funky enough to inspire teenagers). Wild stationery, disposable coasters and outrageous iron-on patches pretty much sum up the thematic concept of this stuff, which originated "off the back of a bike in SoHo." You may not find a whole lot of items here, but the visit should leave you with a goofy grin, and should maybe not be attempted from the office.

·STATIONERY ·CARDS	·WRAP & MAIL ·ALBUMS/DIARIES	·TCHOTCHKES ·UNIQUE GIFTS	·CREATIVE GIFTS

FrenchGeneral.com

This pleasant-looking site has the potential to lead you headlong into a frustrating shopping experience, so how nice of you to use to it find a great gift for somebody else. In particular, the shop offers products and kits that should appeal to women and girls who revel in creative projects and hobbies. The diverse selection included jewelry-making kits, button sets, journals and a kit that lets you make a customized French postcard. You may also notice a few decorative home items and accessories, but only if you're exceedingly patient.

·CREATIVE GIFTS	·ALBUMS/DIARIES		

714-901-3400 · Funantics Toy Group

GagWorks.com

Tasteless, raunchy, startling, disgusting and flat out hilarious, a gag gift is something an entire party can appreciate. This one's stocked with all the classics, and a few no one would ever expect. We spotted such priceless practical joke gifts as fake (winning) lottery tickets, a beautifully gift wrapped rat (toy) and exploding candy. You'll also find the sort of novelty gifts adolescents of any age would love, such as the arrow-through-the-head gag, baldhead wig and the unforgettable, inimitable Whoopee cushion. Clearly, this is a site for the true sophisticate.

·TCHOTCHKES	·UNIQUE GIFTS			

800-670-7441 · Galison

Galison.com

Jot your thoughts and ideas down on scraps of paper and people will think you're crazy; write them down in colorful and decorative journals, and they'll think you're creative. Which is not to say these are mutually exclusive traits, we only intend to point out the colorfully appealing journals and organizers available from this site. You'll find journals with colorful patterns, silk covers and in pocket sizes, all attractive and reasonably priced; characteristics that only rarely go together.

·CREATIVE GIFTS	·CARDS	·ALBUMS/DIARIES		

616-774-2448 · gallery19

Gallery19.us

When this site refers to its selection of "hip modern and edgy items," you'd probably never guess they were talking about greeting cards and wrapping paper. Then again, you may not expect cards and paper to come in such distinct varieties as this. Products for seasonal and everyday occasions may be browsed at your leisure, although the wrapping paper doesn't get so thoroughly categorized so you may be sifting through wedding, baby and kids' birthday designs and you hunt for, say, your favorite kitty theme. If you're lucky enough to find what you like right away, take a moment to look at the shop's Tableware section to see how paper plates can be cool.

·WRAP & MAIL	·CARDS			

888-544-2662 · Gianna Rose Atelier

GiannaRose.com

Gift soaps aren't for everybody, but this site's sure to find a few converts. Featuring a dazzling array of novelty soaps you'll be afraid to get wet, some of these are molded so delicately that they nearly qualify as works of art. Animal and flower shapes seem to be pretty common, but we won't mention everything, as the surprise is half the fun. Truth is, even the rectangular and elliptical bar soaps here are better than average, especially coupled with this shop's fantastic packaging. By any other name, this would indeed smell as sweet.

·HOUSEWARMING				

Gift-World-Collection.com

Gift-World-Collection.com · 704-573-0462

Nothing says "nonrefundable" more than a gift that has the recipient's name engraved upon it. Fortunately, this personalized gift specialist features a great selection of quality goods that nobody will want to return. Custom engraved pocketknives, flasks, pens and beer steins are just some of the many options men will enjoy, while lockets, charm bracelets, compacts and jewelry boxes should please most women. The site also proves a brilliant resource for baby keepsakes and wedding party gifts, but we've found that a personalized gift can work wonders for any occasion.

·TCHOTCHKES	·ALBUMS/DIARIES	·UNIQUE GIFTS	·EXECUTIVE GIFTS

GiftSongs.com

P.S. I Love You! · 800-725-7664

This site offers an unusual and not in the slightest bit cheesy service: personalized songs for your loved ones. By personalized, we mean you can type in traits like the recipient's name (phonetically, so there are no snafus) and eye color (blue, bedroom or shimmering?), and one of the site's dozens of original songs can be altered and recorded to suit a variety of people and occasions. This might work better as a gag gift than one in earnest, but let us tell you, gag gifts do not get any better.

·ROMANTIC GIFTS	·UNIQUE GIFTS		

GlobalExchangeStore.org

Fair Trade Online Store · 800-505-4410

Whether you are an advocate of "socially and economically responsible business" practices, or someone you wish to buy a gift for is, this globally conscious gift shop makes practicing fair trade easier than ever. Tasty items from abroad include coffee, chocolate and gift baskets, while a tidy variety of jewelry, handbags and decorative trinkets represent nations as far reaching as Afghanistan, El Salvador, Colombia, Kenya and Tibet. These are beautiful items regardless of their humanitarian associations; the fact that these products endorse international justice just goes to make some great gifts even better.

·CONFECTIONS ·HOUSEWARMING	·GIFT BASKETS ·UNIQUE GIFTS	·TCHOTCHKES	·ROMANTIC GIFTS

GreatArrow.com

Great Arrow Graphics · 800-835-0490

Setting up shop in what used to be car factories, including that of the original assembly-line product, the Model T, this company puts the spaces to decidedly more creative use. They've developed a slick collection of silk-screened greeting cards, featuring a wide variety for any major holiday or special occasion. But these aren't like your typical greeting cards that feature some silly sort of joke or an even funnier, hackneyed sentiment. Rather, these cards focus on artistically rendered graphic designs, meaning that they may actually be appreciated for more than a momentary viewing instead of barely noticed and cast aside.

·CARDS			

800-840-3660 · Hawaiian Tropicals Direct

There are certain types of flowers that people expect to receive: roses, tulips, dandelions, sunflowers, violets and the dreaded carnations. This is a surefire way to deliver flowers that will surprise and delight whoever is on the receiving end, with arrangements featuring beautiful tropical flowers from the Aloha State. Orchids and birds of paradise can be found in most of these bouquets, and in every case the colors are magnificent. A good means of escaping the doghouse, or getting into someone's good graces; either way, the recipient will undoubtedly say "Mahalo."

·FLOWERS	·ROMANTIC GIFTS			

800-742-6800 · Hillary's

While many gift shops will just sort of scatter their products about and leave it to you to pick something out, this site recognizes the needs of confounded gift hunters—it organizes a host of perfect gifts for any occasion or individual, whether in a brilliantly contrived assortment of gift baskets or some specifically elegant single items. As a nice touch, you'll find personalization services for many of these home and office trinkets, games, stationery and photo albums, and all with no mention to the recipient of just how easy it was for you.

·STATIONERY ·ALBUMS/DIARIES	·GIFT BASKETS ·EXECUTIVE GIFTS	·TCHOTCHKES	·OFFICE SUPPLIES	

800-621-2998 · Illuminations

With the power to light up anybody's life, it's hard to beat candles when you want to set a romantic tone, and this site can lead you to some of the most beautiful, sweetest smelling candles available online. With floating candles, scented candles, unscented candles, tealights and a few aromatherapeutic varieties, you'll be up to your earwax in options. Viewing them all is quite easy, so whether you're planning against the next electrical outage, setting up an intimate evening or searching for a lovely housewarming gift, your day will be brighter for having visited this fine retailer.

·ROMANTIC GIFTS	·CANDLES/SCENTS	·HOUSEWARMING		

800-804-1960 · Impressions In Print

It'll be hard to get people to the party if you don't send them a good invitation. At least so goes the reasoning behind this site, which offers a tremendous number of invitations, each pertaining to very specific events. How many Clambake invites can there be? Not as many as there are for Lingerie Showers. Browsing can take a while, but animated menus and fairly thorough organization should help you get through the hundreds of available designs without too much trouble, because it's hard to send a good invitation if you can't find one.

·CARDS				

Ink-Well.net

Inkwell · 877-945-3083

This well-stocked online gift shop offers a wide enough assortment of small objects, unusual gifts, cute gestures and funky trinkets that you may just find a little bit of everything on any given day. For sure you'll find some fun personalized stationery, including great selections of note cards, letter paper, party napkins and matching paper plates. It's a good place to visit if you've got an upcoming special event, or even just if you know somebody who does and wish to help that person celebrate in a unique and interesting way.

·STATIONERY	·TCHOTCHKES	·UNIQUE GIFTS	

InvitationBox.com

InvitationBox.com · 866-814-4269

Adjust your monitor's brightness and contrast settings before viewing this online stationer, as its extraordinarily pastel veneer can make it difficult to spot the gems of the wide selection of invitations and announcements populating these pages, and you'll need every advantage as you try. Though very well organized, browsing proves a frustrating yet ultimately rewarding process right up until you enter up to a dozen lines of personalized text into the perfect paper product for your event.

·CARDS			

Iomoi.com

iomoi · 925-820-6488

Like many paperies, this site offers classic or fun monogrammed letterheads to suit all of your letter-writing needs, as well as the most functional of gifts: the paperweight. However, this particular stationery specialist also goes the exact opposite direction, having concocted what they call "e-stationery." Essentially, this is an email service that allows you to write notes on artistically rendered pages, rather than simply send blocky text on a white background. Subscription to this service allows you to constantly change your e-letterhead to reflect your mood, and astound your recipients, presuming their email service can recognize such things. The shop's quirky paper goods are more universally accepted.

·STATIONERY	·CARDS		

JamPaper.com

Jam Paper · 800-801-0526

A deep selection of office supplies can be found here, whether you need something to write on, print on, wrap with or mail in. Materials range from recycled paper to plastic, and products include wrapping paper, mail packages, presentation supplies (folders, folios, etc.), print paper, stationery, envelopes and file storage. Primarily, the paper products will grab your attention, but if you have a long afternoon free, you'll find plenty more.

·STATIONERY	·WRAP & MAIL	·OFFICE SUPPLIES	

877-226-4387 · Japanese Style

JapaneseGifts.com

It's one fantastic find after another when you visit this small but excellent purveyor of traditional Japanese styles. Though based in Minnesota of all places, this shop offers beautiful imported household accents like shoji screens, tatami mats, paper lanterns and decorative fans. You'll also find excellent sushi servingware, gongs and of course kimonos. Great prices add to the value of this amazing selection, meaning you can pick up the perfect housewarming gift for a friend and still treat yourself to something special.

| ·STATIONERY ·CANDLES/SCENTS | ·TCHOTCHKES ·HOUSEWARMING | ·ROMANTIC GIFTS ·UNIQUE GIFTS | ·CREATIVE GIFTS | |

800-640-8758 · Jenni Bick Bookbinding

JenniBick.com

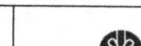

A tremendous source of handmade photo albums, wedding guest books and journals, this Massachusetts bookbinding company makes and sells fantastic products worthy of preserving the most prestigious moments, outstanding ideas and fondest memories. There may be little difference between categories like Brag Books, Keepsake Books, Scrapbooks and Photo Albums other than style, but browsing through them all will easily be worth the time of anyone who appreciates fine craftsmanship and elegant design.

| ·ALBUMS/DIARIES | | | | |

800-782-5666 · Joon New York

Joon.com

For more than three decades, this New York City retailer has been "providing the largest selection of fine writing instruments in the world" to distinguished customers from all walks of civilized life. This site offers you a truly remarkable assortment of the best pens on the planet as created by noted manufacturers like Cartier, Cross and Montblanc. How majestic is it to sweep a beautiful fountain pen across the page when writing a letter? How classy to produce a gold-plated ballpoint to sign a contract or a check? As pens are made more of a novelty in our increasingly digital age, fine writing tools such as these only increase in sentimental value, and always make an elegant gift.

| ·OFFICE SUPPLIES | ·EXECUTIVE GIFTS | | | |

866-237-0152 · Joseph Schmidt Confections

JosephSchmidtConfections.com

Most of the boxed chocolates offered by this confectioner come with a clear top, and with good reason: these are about the best-looking candies we've ever laid eyes on. There may not be a lot to sort through, but the decorated tops of these truffle, caramel, nut and/or fruit candies are beautiful and distinctive enough that you'll probably spend a good deal of time perusing the site anyway. They almost look too good to eat, and the decadent feeling of biting into one makes it taste all the better.

| ·CONFECTIONS | | | | |

KaleidoVisions.com

Kaleidovisions · 512-280-0120

Most of us associate kaleidoscopes with children and toy stores... unless we've taken a look at this site. Not your run-of-the-mill cardboard and plastic scopes, these beautifully rendered creations are sumptuous visual feasts, and that's just looking at their polished wood exteriors. A glimpse of the inner chambers shows just how intricately gorgeous kaleidoscopes can be, with gemstones, feathers, shells and oils reflecting and refracting into brilliant, colorful patterns that will prove timeless and well received to a child of any age.

·UNIQUE GIFTS

KatesPaperie.com

Kate's Paperie · 888-941-9169

Here is the rare stationery shop that offers a great variety, a lot of gift ideas and plenty of charm, and yet still manages to provide an enjoyable shopping experience. The Categories and Gift Ideas animated menus that run across the top of the page will find you journals, pens, blank paper, stationery sets, note cards, invitations, wrapping paper and photo albums. Just remember to use any View All links to get a glimpse of everything in all its charismatic glory.

·STATIONERY ·WRAP & MAIL ·OFFICE SUPPLIES ·CARDS
·ALBUMS/DIARIES

LaughingElephant.com

Laughing Elephant · 800-354-0400

Featuring a classier, often retro-inspired selection of greeting and note cards, this relatively small collection offers a terrific alternative to the big greeting card companies, which are known to churn out cheesy and sappy products by the hundred. Here, you may easily accomplish a year's worth of card shopping, whether you need a boxful of thank-you cards or individual greetings for special occasions. Styles range from art deco to folksy nostalgic with plenty of humor, and yes, a slight bit of cheese, to round out a fine catalog.

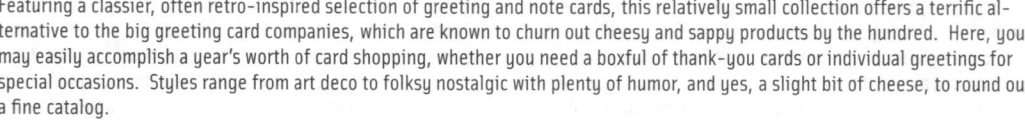

·CARDS

LavaHut.com

Lavahut · 808-356-0972

The spirit of Aloha is alive and well in e-commerce form on this all-things-Hawaiian lifestyle shop. From grass skirts and dashboard hula girls to silk and seashell leis, the site has all the classic covered, including the ubiquitous floral print Hawaiian shirt. Viewing the whole site is easy and worthwhile, as there's not enough here to bog you down, and most of the colorful beach, flower and surf-related fare is amusing, if not lovely. Taking a trip to the Aloha State is still the best way to buy such stuff, but this comes a close second.

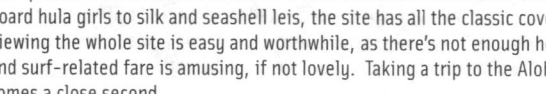

·FLOWERS ·TCHOTCHKES ·ROMANTIC GIFTS ·UNIQUE GIFTS

800-667-8034 · Levenger

Levenger.com

Finding the right gift for that literary loved one has never been easier than with this specialty site, which is dedicated to the appreciation of language. The shop takes reading and writing very seriously, offering a wide range of tools and accessories meant to increase the ease and comfort of settling in to dig deep into a great book, or sitting down to write a long letter. You'll find excellent reading lights, bed trays, lapdesks, desk accessories and one of the better selection of pens online. Chances are you'll find something better than another gift certificate to the local bookstore.

·STATIONERY ·EXECUTIVE GIFTS	·OFFICE SUPPLIES	·CREATIVE GIFTS	·ALBUMS/DIARIES

800-635-4321 · Lincoln Stationers

LincolnStationers.com

This Manhattan stationer spent nearly a quarter of a century developing its inventory as a brick-and-mortar store before going online, and the experience shows. The catalog they've assembled leans heavily toward the executive, but they do this as well as anybody, offering leather organizers, elegant journals and some standout presentation materials. For gift purposes, we admire their selection of pens, though we wish they could be viewed side by side rather than by manufacturer. This should come with another twenty-five years of online experience.

·STATIONERY ·EXECUTIVE GIFTS	·OFFICE SUPPLIES	·CARDS	·ALBUMS/DIARIES

888-370-5775 · Lula Belle

LulaBelleToffee.com

Your dentist doesn't want you to know about this site. See, it's harder than one might think to find great toffee, a fact that your teeth surely appreciate. But this site changes everything, offering a tiny but extraordinarily tasty assortment of toffee, bathed in milk, dark or white chocolate and covered in crunchy bits of pecan. These are served in simple but elegant gift tins, and are sure to please, but will never be enough. If you have children, you might want to keep this decadent treat high up and out of reach.

·CONFECTIONS			

800-586-2729 · Lunar Embassy

LunarEmbassy.com

They say real estate is the wisest investment a person can make, but this site offers land purchases that really work better as a gift than as sound financial planning. In short, this site allows you to buy an acre on the moon. Could such a property ever pan out? Well, there are certainly no guarantees, but since demand is so low, now is the cheapest time to grab an acre or two of "prime view lunar property." What do you get in addition to this unreal estate? A deed to the property of course, which is prime for framing if nothing else.

·ROMANTIC GIFTS	·UNIQUE GIFTS		

LuxePaperie.com

With a lovely selection of boutique stationery brands, this little online paper goods retailer offers a unique assortment of note cards, greeting cards, invitations and wrapping paper. Light colors and simple designs prevent these designs from standing out too much, but the nice-looking cards and paper prove simple to browse, and a shop by Occasion feature ensures you may quickly find the appropriate messages and illustrations, even if the terrific featured brands turn out to be so obscure you've never heard of them.

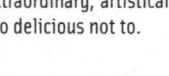

| | ·STATIONERY | ·WRAP & MAIL | ·CARDS | ·ALBUMS/DIARIES |

MarieBelle.com

There's not normally that much to see when you're looking at chocolate, and it's not typically around long enough to observe anyway. This selection is different, though, in an extraordinary way. In some cases here, the candy wrappers, hot chocolate boxes and gift sets simply have beautiful packaging. In other cases, the chocolates themselves have been turned into canvases for some extraordinary, artistically rendered decorations. These elegant edibles literally look too good to eat. On the other hand, they look too delicious not to.

| | ·CONFECTIONS | | | |

MasterStrokeCanada.com

If you think ribbons only come in shiny and metallic primary colors, you haven't seen anything yet. This site covers a range of ribbon materials we never imagined, including Satin, Velvet and Taffeta, in colors and patterns we've never seen. You'll certainly find any standard ribbon styles you remember, but the brilliance of this site is in its ability to help you find something great and out of the ordinary. You'll be surprised how excited you can get about something as simple as a ribbon.

| | ·WRAP & MAIL | | | |

MichaelCFina.com

There are gifts, and then there are gifts. This site specializes in the latter, with presents you don't just haphazardly dole out to friends—at least, not unless your bank balance is written in stanzas. Very high-end merchandise—starting with picture frames and ending somewhere in the stratosphere with items we don't even want to tempt you with—fills these pages, with categories like For Him, For Her and Entertaining to guide you. This site is a must-see for people who're about to attend a cocktail party thrown by, say, the Queen of England. The rest of us may want to skip it.

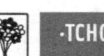

| | ·TCHOTCHKES | ·ROMANTIC GIFTS | ·HOUSEWARMING | ·EXECUTIVE GIFTS |

800-797-6269 · Mountaincow

MountainCow.com

Some people like to make their own stationery and invitations in an arts-and-crafts kind of way, using glue, scissors, sparkles, construction paper and whatnot. But for those of us who're computer savvy, this site offers a distinctly less messy way to design our own cards and letterheads. Specifically, you'll find proprietary software that should make it easy for you to create and incorporate good-looking patterns and backgrounds, without any special artistic talent. Different software packages are available, depending on your computer skills and design intentions, but you'll still need to buy your own paper (see our product index!).

·STATIONERY   **·CREATIVE GIFTS**   **·CARDS**

877-222-2097 · Enhance Marketing

MrGiftWrap.com

Though technically a wholesaler, this very well stocked shop does make a few smaller rolls of terrific wrapping paper available. By smaller, we actually mean one hundred feet in length, these are definitely not your typical retail store rolls of paper, which tend to only wrap two or three moderately sized gifts before petering out. Some savvy ordering here should have no trouble keeping all of your gifts wrapped beautifully for the year to come, even if your family is huge and very demanding during the holidays.

·WRAP & MAIL

818-252-0801 · Music Box Attic

MusicBoxAttic.com

Here's a music box shop so good it may take you a week to decide which product you want to buy. First of all, there are hundreds of different boxes here, ranging from jewelry boxes to dolls and designer boxes. Once you've finally settled on the perfect box, it's time to select the perfect tune, of which there are hundreds, including classical favorites, show tunes and modern pop songs. You'll probably want to use the site's Heavenly Listening Station to check each tune out for yourself, because then you'll know for certain the music box you order will be absolutely perfect.

·ROMANTIC GIFTS

888-997-7899 · MyGatsby.com

MyGatsby.com

One problem that's always been inherent in shopping for the perfect invitation is that, although you might find the perfect invitation card, the matching envelope may not be to your liking. This site solves the problem, not with an endless supply of invitation sets for you to peruse for hours on end, but with a lovely, easy-to-view selection of mix-and-match cards, envelopes and inserts. Simply select the available designs, colors and printing options for all components, enter your personalized text and sit back to await an order sample. It's not always easy to use the interface, but with a little patience this could prove the fastest way to get just what you want for a reasonable price.

·CARDS

NonniesTraditional.com

Nonnie Waller's Traditional Southern · 800-664-0919

The home page will tell you this site is about "the best damn pound cake on earth," but however delicious it may be, we're here to tell you this one's really all about the gift boxes. The original or chocolate espresso pound cakes are offered up in the most impressive beaded and embroidered silk hat boxes; dozens of designs featuring exotic designs and bright colors. If cake is really not your thing, the most gorgeous truffles, molded chocolates and coconut balls come in similarly extravagant packaging, with the option to include flowers. Easy, elegant and delicious.

·FLOWERS	·CONFECTIONS	·UNIQUE GIFTS

NostalgicImpressions.com

Nostalgic Impressions · 877-645-5325

Even as we write this, cell phone text messaging is beginning to eclipse email as the quickest, easiest way to send a note. But traditionalists should not fret! Letter writing still exists, and although the price of postage may increase at an alarming rate, your handwritten missives may still possess a satisfying touch of class. It starts with a fine set of personalized stationery, but to truly elevate your letters to the status of historical keepsake, pick out one of the wax stamp and seal sets offered by this truly old-school specialty retailer. Particularly valuable on wedding invitations, we think you'll find such flourishes will further inspire the very retro activity of sitting down to communicate via the written word.

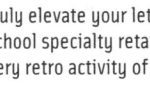

·STATIONERY ·UNIQUE GIFTS	·WRAP & MAIL ·EXECUTIVE GIFTS	·ROMANTIC GIFTS	·CREATIVE GIFTS

ObjectsOfEnvy.com

Objects of Envy · 866-866-3689

To some, fuel for the argument that our nation owns excessive wealth. To others, a lovely way to drop a dime. We're talking about crystal, glass, porcelain and enamel boxes and figurines, which can be found here in abundance. Shop the categories Murano Glass, Fine Crystal, Extraordinary Glass Creations, Extraordinary Pottery Creations or Limoges ("only porcelain made in the west-central Limoges region of France can be honored with the name Limoges") and find a wealth of trinkets made exclusively for people who like trinkets.

·TCHOTCHKES	·HOUSEWARMING		

OneShare.com

OneShare.com · 888-777-6919

They say our nation was built on dreams, and as you'll see on this site, some dreams start small. The unique gift offered here is a single share of stock, mounted and framed for display purposes. Sure, the enticement of a gift that could grow in net worth is enticing, but you should realize that in addition to stock price, you are purchasing the frame, plus giving a hefty donation to the proprietors of this site, meaning that in many cases you could technically buy two, three or as many as twenty-five shares elsewhere for the cost of one purchased here. Still, it's a nice, highbrow alternative to lottery tickets.

·UNIQUE GIFTS	·EXECUTIVE GIFTS		

877-899-2468 · Organic Bouquet

OrganicBouquet.com

There are dozens of great places online to shop for floral arrangements and boxes of chocolates, so how can you choose? Well, if you like to encourage organic and other ecologically sustainable growing practices, this shop wins hands down. With fine bouquets of roses, lilies, tulips and more, this proves a satisfying and easy way to promote your environmental agenda without sacrifice. The flowers look absolutely gorgeous, of course, and while we can't vouch for the flavor of the chocolates, they are also beautifully presented and will surely taste delicious to the green sweet tooth.

| ·FLOWERS | ·CONFECTIONS | | |  |

888-518-2327 · PajamaGram

PajamaGram.com

Of course, the immediate question this site's name brings to mind is: what's a Pajamagram? Simply put, it's sort of a gift basket built around sleeping attire. To that end, there's enough variety here that it could even fit into any of **thepurplebook's** attire sections (including Maternity). In keeping with the spirit of the retailer, however, we've placed it here, knowing that there may indeed be some occasions when pajamas, a robe and slippers or a nightgown might just make the perfect gift... especially used in conjunction with overnight shipping.

| ·GIFT BASKETS | ·CANDLES/SCENTS | ·UNIQUE GIFTS | | |

323-935-9140 · Pamela Barsky

PamelaBarsky.com

If you like books that aren't already filled with words, check out this LA designer's assortment of diaries and journals. Some of these feature note pages, some are blank and others have been set up to record recipes, restaurant reviews, wine tasting recollections, birthday memories, golf outings, travel memoirs and other thematic events. However, the real attraction as you browse these simple pages will be the colorful, funny and/or textured looks of the journals themselves. Truly, these are books to be judged by their covers.

| ·ALBUMS/DIARIES | | | | |

888-727-3711 · Paper Source

Paper-Source.com

Maybe the myriad store-bought stationery designs available online felt lacking, or maybe you're an ardent do-it-yourselfer who would rather cancel the party than send out invitations designed by another. Either way, you'll appreciate the incredible selection of papers and crafts products available here to help you make your own invitations and stationery sets. Imploring you to "Do something creative every day," the site backs up its encouragement with some incredible, high-quality printed pages that almost outdoes the competition even without any work on your part.

| ·STATIONERY | ·CREATIVE GIFTS | ·CARDS | ·ALBUMS/DIARIES | |

PaperHaus.com

Paperhaus · 206-374-8566

A distinctly modern look imbues the office products found on this site; we'd say "futuristic" if this wasn't the 21st century, and the industrial look wasn't practically retro. Penholders, binders, clipboards and briefcases all pretty much adhere to a metallic aesthetic, with the occasional translucent plastic or leather thrown in for effect. Browsing is simple, given that there's not a lot here, but if there's such a thing as corporate nontraditionalists, this is the site for them.

 ·OFFICE SUPPLIES   ·ALBUMS/DIARIES

PaperMart.com

Paper Mart Packaging Store · 800-745-8800

Whether or not you want to send something with love is up to you; if you want to send it in a way that it won't break en route, or be subject to the exploring hands of a corrupt postman, check out this site. Boxes, packaging tape, cushioning (like Styrofoam peanuts) and wrappings are in high supply here, alongside labels, envelopes and gift wrapping that'll enable you to mail stuff with better care than some of the stores featured in this book. Scroll to the bottom of the home page for a more complete menu, or you'll miss out on a lot they have to offer.

 ·WRAP & MAIL

PaperMojo.com

Paper Mojo · 800-420-3818

There's more to the paper world than 8-1/2x11 white pages, and all the proof you'll ever need may be found with this comprehensive web stationer. Pages of many weights, sizes and colors may be found, whether you prefer iridescent stock, flower infused, embossed, tissue or all-natural paper. Better yet, an incredible array of patterned pages may be found, many evoking the diverse cultural traditions of such countries as Italy, Japan, India and Nepal. You wouldn't use any of this stuff for a resume or school paper, but if your paper needs are creative in nature you're not likely to find such a variety elsewhere.

 ·STATIONERY

PaperPresentation.com

Paperpresentation.com · 800-727-3701

If you prefer to work with raw materials when it comes to stationery and paper, this site ought to be of great help. To begin with, they offer a terrific selection of paper, in multiple weights, colors and textures. Then there are the card and invitation options, which vary in shape and design, whether you prefer square cards or those that open from the middle, and a selection of envelopes that ranges from the mundane to the sublime. Best of all, many of these products are available on recycled paper, so you can get the word out to everyone you know without suffering any pangs of conscience.

 ·STATIONERY   ·WRAP & MAIL   ·OFFICE SUPPLIES   ·CARDS

888-670-5300 · PaperStyle.com

PaperStyle.com

Whether you're planning a beach party, barbecue, wine tasting, cocktail party or clambake, you'll be able to find the appropriate set of invitations on this slow but well-put-together site. Even if you're looking for some regular stationery, you will find a great big selection of elegant and/or campy stuff, in most cases easily personalized for no extra cost. But most of these resources are devoted to announcements and invites, and it shows (with options like RSVP envelopes included). In fact, browsing might just inspire you to throw more parties.

·STATIONERY

415-444-0784 · Parapluie

ParapluieDesigns.com

We're not about to attempt pronouncing the name of this site, but we can say that it offers some of the most remarkable gift boxes we've seen anywhere, in real life or online. Here, even the squarish boxes aren't what they seem, as every one unfolds to reveal a masterful gift box design that may put its own contents to shame. Product lines such as Grand Mimsy, Fleurish, Untamed and Züm may not tell you what to expect while browsing, but there aren't too many designs here to view, and since they're all worth seeing, we'll just let the site's heavy use of gibberish slide.

 ·WRAP & MAIL   ·UNIQUE GIFTS

310-482-5800 · Stamps.com

Photo.Stamps.com

Back in 1992 the US Postal Service ran a consumer election to determine whether America wanted a commemorative Elvis Presley stamp to feature the young Elvis or a more mature King. The young Elvis won, leaving many dissatisfied. Thank goodness the technology now exists to make everybody happy. Whether you want to order a book of stamps featuring the older Elvis, or wish to commemorate yourself or a loved one, this innovative postal site allows you to design your own valid stamps featuring any image you desire (within a published set of content restrictions). This almost makes personalized address labels seem silly.

 ·WRAP & MAIL

800-453-9333 · Photowow

PhotoWow.com

Wow is definitely a word you might use in response to this site's specialty: turning your photographs into custom prints and other merchandise. Simply upload or email your picture and select from a list of products including greeting cards, mousepads, coaster sets and puzzles as well as canvas prints. In-house designers will then work to artistically render or restore your image into one of striking quality and memorable style. Gifts are rarely so personalized or fun; just remember to order a couple weeks ahead of time whether it's for a loved one or a vanity project for yourself.

·TCHOTCHKES   ·CARDS   ·UNIQUE GIFTS

PlumParty.com

Plum Party · 800-227-0314

  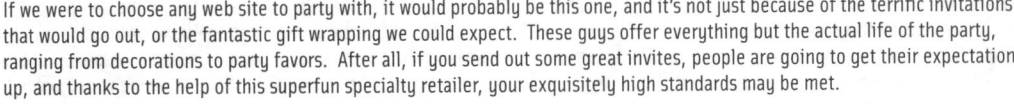

If we were to choose any web site to party with, it would probably be this one, and it's not just because of the terrific invitations that would go out, or the fantastic gift wrapping we could expect. These guys offer everything but the actual life of the party, ranging from decorations to party favors. After all, if you send out some great invites, people are going to get their expectations up, and thanks to the help of this superfun specialty retailer, your exquisitely high standards may be met.

·WRAP & MAIL ·TCHOTCHKES ·CARDS

PulpFactory.com

PulpFactory · 949-675-6404

If you've got a color printer, a color or style in mind and want to mail out your invitations right away, this site offers customizable invitation, note card, greeting card and label designs that allow you to print from your own computer, ultimately saving you a great amount of time, effort and money. If you don't have a color printer, you can still play, going through the same automated selection and layout process, and simply asking the site to do the work for you. Basically, their job is to make it run smoother and easier for the customer; the way it should be.

·WRAP & MAIL ·CARDS

Pylones-USA.com

Pylones · 800-345-6404

With the incredibly diverse assortment of kitschy trinkets available from this site, you'd expect it to be deeply rooted in American culture. Well, in a way it is, but in a more specific way the store has its origins in France. Yes, it's true; the land of fine wine and haute cuisine is responsible for what may be the goofiest selection of bric-a-brac ever sold in one place. Highlights include mermaid bottle openers, cricket-shaped nail clippers, dolls that double as brooms and dustpans and a toaster with a pig face on it. They all add up to the most memorable housewarming presents your friends will ever receive.

·TCHOTCHKES ·HOUSEWARMING ·UNIQUE GIFTS

QuincyShop.com

Quincy · 800-299-4242

With categories like Unique Gifts, Creative Toys and Cool Stuff, you can tell right away that this gift site's offering something intriguing and out of the norm. While you may not find any truly amazing, extravagant gifts, you will almost certainly find something fun and inexpensive for the young at heart, whether it's a silly toy, craft kit, keepsake-quality board game or writing journal. When you visit this site, even boring things like office products and photo albums turn out to be out of the ordinary.

·STATIONERY ·TCHOTCHKES ·CREATIVE GIFTS ·ALBUMS/DIARIES
·UNIQUE GIFTS ·EXECUTIVE GIFTS

800-465-7367 · Rebecca Moss

RebeccaMoss.com

If you want a pen, a bic ball point will cost you about a quarter. If, however, you're after a Writing Instrument, take a gander at the "offbeat and artistic designs" offered by this Madison Avenue boutique. These lofty pens exceed mere function to achieve the level of personal accessory, and if you bandy one of this shop's fine limited-edition fountain pens or rollerballs, your enviable taste and classiness will not be mistaken. Don't worry though, if you don't have five hundred or a thousand dollars lying around to spend on writing instruments, you can still achieve the same effect with one of the less pricey regular-edition pens, or at least one of the eight dollar pencils.

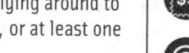

·OFFICE SUPPLIES	·EXECUTIVE GIFTS			

800-459-1897 · Red Ambrosia

RedAmbrosia.com

Welcome to the exotic adult gift site where euphemisms abound, including words like *romantic*, *sensuous*, *sumptuous* and *arousing*. If we had to pick a winner, though, it would be *Functional Erotic Glass Art*, which we won't describe in great detail, but which is a must-see for the ladies. Most of the products here aren't so wild, though, and stuff like silk sheets, cashmere bathrobes, massage oils and scented candles provide a nice balance against the body paint, fur cuffs and "love balm." The biggest surprise? None of this stuff is the slightest bit trashy, and a lot of it is actually fairly classy… which may be disappointing to some.

·ROMANTIC GIFTS			

877-733-3683 · Red Envelope

RedEnvelope.com

Whether they be celebratory, obligatory, romantic or condolent, this popular gifting catalog serves up selections appropriate for any conceivable occasion. Even if the event you have in mind doesn't show up in the animated menu, you may simply browse the different categories to find everything from spa baskets to shoeshine kits, without hassle. If you're still not satisfied, you can shop for particular recipients, either by their relation to you or by their interest in gadgets, gourmet food or travel. This is an excellent and easy place to find useful, thoughtful and entertaining gifts.

·GIFT BASKETS ·HOUSEWARMING	·TCHOTCHKES ·UNIQUE GIFTS	·ROMANTIC GIFTS ·EXECUTIVE GIFTS	·CANDLES/SCENTS	

877-742-5142 · RibbonShop.com

RibbonShop.com

One perk of internet retail is the opportunity to specialize in a product so specific, only a global market could really justify your store's existence. This Illinois web shop has been successful for years, strictly selling "bolts of beautiful, high-quality American-made ribbons." Just when you think it's hard to get excited about ribbons, a glance at these pages shows you just how exhaustive a selection you can put together if you really try. Whether you want ribbons to wrap, scrapbook or show your cultural awareness, this one-stop ribbon shop is all you'll ever need.

·WRAP & MAIL				

Richart-Chocolates.com

In most cases, when you give a box of chocolates as a gift, it's devoured within a day or two and then all but forgotten. However, if you'd like to bestow some truly memorable confections, visit this site, which represents an artisan chocolatier out of Paris. For more than eight decades, this family-founded shop has been "dedicated to producing fine chocolates for chocolate lovers around the world," and it shows, with richly flavored candy that has been crafted to be noticed, and even personalized. These all-around rich confections will still be eaten within hours of receipt, but not a single bite will go unremembered.

  ·CONFECTIONS

RobbSteck.com

Shop here if you're a fan of brilliant, beautiful and funky candles, the likes of which you've probably never seen before. That is, shop here if you think you would like be a fan of such things, and at least visit if you think you might appreciate them. They're quite simply dazzling, and if you're going to have candles at all in your contemporary home, it should be these. Better yet, you should share them with your friends, whether as a housewarming gift or just to let them know that you've got an eye for style, even when it takes waxen form.

 ·CANDLES/SCENTS   ·HOUSEWARMING   ·UNIQUE GIFTS

RockScissorPaper.com

Offering throwback styles in personalized letterheads, invitations, journals and note cards "so cool, you'll find reasons to write," this distinctive stationer's products "can be found in cool stores, museums and now on the world wide web." The funky retro designs work particularly well with a "modern and playful" selection of greeting—or as the site calls them "greeted"—cards, which puts most others to shame. It's a must-shop for those who aren't too cool for paper products, but are way too cool for most paper products.

  ·STATIONERY   ·CARDS   ·ALBUMS/DIARIES

RomanzaGifts.com

Though not pretty look at, and not terribly fun to use, this site does promise to smell good, either through its extensive selection of high-end scented candles, or the many scattered fragrant soaps and lotions. Each brand name is split into subcategories, so you'll want to ignore the same set of featured items that keep turning up and hunt deeper for different ranges of sensuous, stylish and illuminating candles. The bath-and-body products are tougher to pinpoint, but if you look hard enough you should be rewarded with some rather indulgent bubble bath.

 ·ROMANTIC GIFTS   ·CANDLES/SCENTS

877-353-9099 · Ruby et Violette

RubyEtViolette.com

If the thought of soft, chewy cookies loaded with chocolate chunks makes your mouth water, wait until you get a load of this homegrown cookie specialist's site. The cookies here are just as we've described, only they also include additional items such as dried fruit, gingerbread, pistachios, marshmallows, toffee and caramel. You could gain thirty pounds just imagining the fifty-two possibilities, but we're recommending the site anyway, as we're secretly hoping these cookies will be sent to us in any of the lovely gift packaging options.

·CONFECTIONS				

877-400-5263 · See Jane Work

SeeJaneWork.com

There's no reason a career-minded girl can't be stylish, and this site has the desk sets, accessories and other office wares to prove it. Some of it's probably not appropriate for your stodgier corporate environments, but then, some of those environments aren't appropriate for the working girl of exquisite contemporary tastes. Most of this stuff would make a great gift for young college and high school girls, and it just goes to show that executive toys aren't only for the boys.

·STATIONERY	·OFFICE SUPPLIES	·ALBUMS/DIARIES	·EXECUTIVE GIFTS	

866-736-3237 · Send A Frame, Inc.

SendAFrame.com

Finding a picture frame, photo album or document display has never been easier than with this site devoted to archival and presentation products. Begin by selecting the size of the picture in question, then choose from a list of materials including Wood, Crystal, Glass, Leather, Ceramic, Gold and a variety of other metals. Surprisingly, the Easy Search link offers even other search options, including Style and Occasion. In no time you'll be viewing all the options suiting your vision, whether you're trying to match existing products or just have something in particular in mind.

·ALBUMS/DIARIES				

404-387-1754 · Heidi

ShopHeidi.com

After failing to find gift wrapping items that "that captured her style and love of fashion," the founder of this eponymous stationery company turned her attention to design, and if the wrapping paper, note cards and journals she's come up prove anything, it's that doing so was a great idea. Though quite limited in variety, the cool, modern looks of these items are appealing enough to justify the entire business on their own merits. Here's hoping Heidi has plenty more up her sleeve in the years to come.

·WRAP & MAIL	·CARDS	·ALBUMS/DIARIES		

ShopLoveMe.com

Love, Me · 818-707-3003

This site is brought us by the combined efforts of an event planner and invitation/decor designer from good old Los Angeles, California. Popular with celebrities and fashion magazines alike, the two have conspired to deliver a thoughtful assortment of luxe gifts and hip party accoutrements, granting us all access to the graceful backdrops of a Beverly Hills wedding or Hollywood cocktail party; and given that the scenery is often the most important and enduring part of such events, this makes it among the best available in the world.

·TCHOTCHKES	·ROMANTIC GIFTS	·UNIQUE GIFTS	

SignatureByCrayon.com

Crayon, Inc. · 617-395-8455

Probably the best way to make your gift stand out among a stack of wrapped rectangular boxes will be found on this site, which offers a small but artfully created collection of gift boxes. Having gained its expertise "designing and developing custom packaging and containers for gourmet food and specialty gift retailers," this company's exclusive assortment of creatively shaped and patterned boxes literally is small, each one usually no bigger than six or seven inches in dimension. On the other hand, these beautiful boxes require zero skill in wrapping, and we all know what they say about small packages.

·WRAP & MAIL		

Smythson.com

Smythson of Bond Street · 877-769-8476

Originating in London's famous Bond Street, these guys count themselves "the world's foremost stationers, renowned as producers of the highest quality stationery, leather books, accessories and diaries for more than a century." Well, they've left little for us to add, but they actually don't have all that much to offer. See, it's the quality of the stuff that's important here, and while in short supply, it's as fine as this sort of thing is going to get…though they may take exception to our calling it "stuff" and "things."

·STATIONERY	·CARDS	·ALBUMS/DIARIES	

SoleBerry.com

Soleberry Modern Stationers · 917-843-4696

If you find big, faceless stationery shops and manufacturers too cold and impersonal for your business, give this great specialty shop a glance. Founded by a group of friends, and carrying stationery sets, greeting cards, journals, wrapping paper, picture frames and photo albums designed by individuals, this is a shop that's proud of what it sells, rather than how much it sells. The results speak for themselves, and each item possesses that personal touch we sometimes crave in this mass-produced warehouse store world of ours.

·STATIONERY	·WRAP & MAIL	·CARDS	·ALBUMS/DIARIES

212-532-1899 · The Spoon Sisters

SpoonSisters.com

Here's a gift shop that offers a bizarre and eclectic assortment of goods for a variety of people or occasions. Since most of these products don't fit neatly into any particular category, they're organized here by recipient or event, whether you seek a gift for Men, Women, or suitable to an upcoming holiday (from Halloween to St. Patrick's Day). There are also gifts geared toward college students, professionals, party people and pets. However, many of these gifts ride that fine line between funky and tacky, so at this point it's up to you to decide which sort of gift is appropriate.

| ·TCHOTCHKES | ·UNIQUE GIFTS | | | |

312-226-5950 · Sprout Home

SproutHome.com

This home shop offers too sporadic a selection to help most home shoppers fulfill their decorative aspirations, but it does have a lot of individual items that will work perfectly as housewarming gifts. Mostly modern, the home accents, garden accessories and errant serviceware here ranges from funky to sophisticated, with items like shower curtains, salt'n'pepper shakers, clocks, pottery and candlesticks available to give the eclectic new homeowner or apartment dweller something fresh and fun to work with.

| ·TCHOTCHKES | ·CANDLES/SCENTS | ·HOUSEWARMING | | |

800-282-3333 · International Star Registry

StarRegistry.com

While enthusiastic young Casanovas have long been known to promise their loves the stars, it wasn't until fairly recently that they could deliver. Thanks to this site, you can actually name one of the millions of stars visible in the Earth's sky. Sure, most of the big ones already have names like Polaris and Ursa Major, but many of those stars are merely numbered in astronomical records. Here, you may actually pay to name a distant star after yourself or a loved one, and have that name entered into the international star registry. You'll also receive a certificate proclaiming the fact, and a star chart that pinpoints the location of your celestial body, somewhere out there.

| ·ROMANTIC GIFTS | ·UNIQUE GIFTS | | | |

800-444-9059 · Star Treatment Gift Services

StarTreatment.com

All right, so you've decided to bestow upon someone the effortless joy of a gift basket. Want to make it the best, most exclusive, highest-priced gift basket around? Here you go—this site specializes in the sort of gift collections that people will actually be astounded and extremely happy to receive. Not to disparage the creative efforts put forth on your average basket, but these really do raise the bar. Take, for example, a kid's basket that's packaged in a little red wagon. Then there's the tantalizing Spa Relaxation package For Her and an Exectutive Toy Chest For Him. Simply put: you can't do better.

| ·CONFECTIONS | ·GIFT BASKETS | ·EXECUTIVE GIFTS | | |

SugarPaper.com

Sugar Paper · 310-277-7804

We've seen many sites that offer personalized stationery sets, and some of them are hard to tell apart. This site, however, stands out. That is to say, it's rather impressive. While you'll find the same options to add your name and address to these fine stationery selections, the difference here is that the paper isn't printed in the modern laser and ink jet sense. Instead, these folks use antique machinery and inks to press your mark "into soft, cotton paper leaving an impression that you can see and feel." This process, along with the upscale paper designs to choose from, drives up the price considerably, but if you can swing the extra costs, the results will be memorable.

  ·STATIONERY ·CARDS

SurroundingsFlowers.com

Surroundings Flowers · 800-567-7007

For floral arrangements that are at once simple, elegant and extraordinary in their beauty, trust the slim selection offered by this site to win you over quickly and often. Whereas many florists will offer more variety, they'll usually overcomplicate things. On the flipside, these bouquets are content to minimalize, showing utter confidence that tightly bundled calla lilies, or a single orchid spike can express more beauty and sentiment than the most elaborate arrangement. When Surrounding Flowers does add an element of variety, they tend toward understated combinations that blend similar colors that will take your baby's breath away.

 ·FLOWERS ·GIFT BASKETS ·ROMANTIC GIFTS

TeleFlora.com

Teleflora · 800-898-7484

Flowers make a great standard gift to send somebody, because they're pretty, they smell good and, most of all, they're easy to pick out. This site understands this, and makes it pretty simple to view a variety of arrangements, select one and send the order to a florist who will deliver it, anywhere in the nation. There's nothing terribly extravagant about these flowers, but this is a neatly put together site with good photographs and high marks for user friendliness.

 ·FLOWERS

TheMonogramShops.com

The Monogram Shop · 800-401-0806

You won't find many gift items on this shop based in East Hampton, New York, but of course the items involved are almost a secondary consideration. The important thing is that these robes, bags, towels and matchbooks are monogrammed, so you may convey that the gifts were truly intended for their recipient, even if the items themselves were selected mostly out of convenience. Thus, the magic and ease of the Hamptons is preserved, right here, on the internet.

 ·UNIQUE GIFTS

800-530-1988 · Therapy In a Box

TherapyInABox.com

This site's goal "is to create thought-provoking and visually stimulating gifts that will leave many positive and lasting memories." They do so with gift baskets. Now gift baskets have been called many things, but "memorable" isn't generally one of them. But these are actually gift boxes. Aside from being easier to ship, these boxes contain some fine items for men, women or babies, including spa products, cocktail mixing sets and organic foods. At the very least these gift items will give you something to think about.

·GIFT BASKETS				

847-541-5800 · The Stationery Studio

TheStationeryStudio.com

This popular online stationer has got all the goods to make your party, gifting and correspondence beautiful, with a personal touch. A huge assortment of invitations, note cards, business cards, stationery, announcements, napkins, notepads, address labels and wrapping paper will keep you browsing for hours, and as most of it may include personalized text or even photos, you'll probably like most of what you see. A variety of browsing options will help you see everything, eventually, but in the end nothing will help you choose.

·STATIONERY	·WRAP & MAIL	·CARDS		

866-846-0333 · The Welcomed Guest

TheWelcomedGuest.com

"Brimming over with an impressive array of caring amenities, little luxuries and elegant essentials all designed to dazzle and delight," the gift baskets assembled by this specialist incorporate some of the world's most popular spa products into the perfect welcoming gesture to a houseguest. Robes, gift soaps, cushy towels and eye pillows are among the products gathered in each basket, and the option to pick and choose from the many small items available For Him, For Her, For Baby or For Them give you a sense that you've participated in the gift's construction without actually having to put in a lot of time or effort.

·GIFT BASKETS				

866-902-4438 · Things Remembered

ThingsRemembered.com

What began as a small key-making shop in Ohio has transformed over the course of several decades to become "the nation's leading and most experienced retailer of personalized gifts." A surprisingly huge assortment of products are available for personalized embroidering, engraving or embossing. The site's set up to shop by occasion or recipient, but if you use the Advanced Search you should easily find specific products such as pens, flasks, watches, barware, lighters, jewelry and blankets.

·TCHOTCHKES	·ROMANTIC GIFTS	·UNIQUE GIFTS	·EXECUTIVE GIFTS	

Trimorphos.com

Trimorphos · 609-924-8716

If you're offering up an intriguing or peculiar gift, a bland wrapping paper will probably not suffice. And if your gift does happen to be somewhat boring itself, wrapping it in some snazzy paper is the least you can do. In either case, this bizarre web creation offers a tidy assortment of funky paper for holiday and everyday occasions, including some mild optical illusions and Tiki-style patterns. But you should probably put a little more effort into selecting a cool gift.

·WRAP & MAIL

TShipley.com

T. Shipley · 877-874-4753

Elegant office accessories can make the difference between a classy executive and just another schmuck sitting behind a desk. You'll find a tremendous assortment here, ranging from mahogany or ostrich desk accessories to platinum pens and leather laptop cases. The only thing that could make these executive gifts better would be the option to personalize them, and as it happens you may add a monogram or full name to most of these products for a small fee, so at least everybody will know exactly who that schmuck is.

·OFFICE SUPPLIES   ·EXECUTIVE GIFTS

VansGifts.com

Van's Gourmet Gifts · 800-822-7538

Searching for the perfect gift basket? This twenty-year-old company out of Long Beach, California, will at least get you close to your goal. Specializing in gourmet food and drink gifts, the company incorporates fine consumables by such favored brands as Dean & Deluca and Godiva, and spa gifts utilizing L'Occitane. But it's the creative basket options that caught our attention, with elegantly presented gifts packaged in functional items like CD holders, picnic baskets, travel cases, ice buckets and planters.

·GIFT BASKETS

WingardHome.com

Wingard Home · 415-345-1999

A small but lovely supply of housewarming gifts may be had from this well regarded home accents company. Highlights include leather photo albums and picture frames, along with a few distinctive vases, lamps and candlesticks. Most striking, however, may be the MO-BI-LE-O's, which are constructed similarly to mobiles, but may be linked together to form intriguing wall art, room dividers or entry curtains. There's really very little to the site, but in the end this just makes it all quite easy to browse.

·CANDLES/SCENTS   ·HOUSEWARMING   ·ALBUMS/DIARIES

877-785-3914 · Wishingfish.com

WishingFish.com

It's easy to associate gift shops with boring porcelain figurines and other deliberately "charming" products. Make no mistake, though, this site manages to escape the stale trappings of your typical gift store to become a breath of fresh air for the tchotchke fan. Between gift ideas like a crème brulée kit and monogrammed toilet paper, this site's editorial selection of merchandise ranges from fanciful to funky, and from functional to fun. Generally, it's all interesting, to say the least, and you'll usually be able to find something great to match your recipient's personality.

·TCHOTCHKES	·CREATIVE GIFTS	·UNIQUE GIFTS

800-980-9890 · Zazzle.com

Zazzle.com

When it comes to things like t-shirts, posters, note cards and postage stamps, our choices have always been limited by the visions of those people who go into such businesses. Thanks to this site, we no longer have to wear shirts advertising another designer, send the thank-you cards bearing another's pleasing illustration or mail a stamp commemorating somebody else's hero. Here you may custom design your own products, uploading image files from your computer to take control of your products, or create gifts for your friends. Or, you can simply browse other nonprofessionals' creations—either way, it's an egalitarian dream come true on the web.

·WRAP & MAIL	·CARDS	·UNIQUE GIFTS

800-529-9512 · zChocolat

zChocolat.com

What could make for a better candy gift box than these handmade French confections? How about if you could add a personalized engraving to the box? That's the service offered by this online shop that heavily researched French chocolate makers, and then selected the tastiest, relatively low-fat offerings from the best chocolatiers. The result makes for a fantastic personalized gift of beautiful, high-quality, fabulous and none-too-fattening sweets.

·CONFECTIONS	·ROMANTIC GIFTS		

323-951-9190 · Zipper Gifts

ZipperGifts.com

The credo of this gift shop is: "Objects are imbued with art and history—make that connection and the objects you choose will enrich your life." While we don't know exactly how such lofty thoughts apply to items such as a fish-shaped lighter, we can tell you that a site that can sell you stylish nail clippers is worth a look. Certainly, these products are eclectic and uncommon, whether it be a clock that allows you to record your own alarm, or dice cufflinks. You can shop by categories such as Sensuous Home or Personal Accessories, but such names only offer a glimmer of what you can expect to find inside.

·TCHOTCHKES ·EXECUTIVE GIFTS	·OFFICE SUPPLIES	·HOUSEWARMING	·UNIQUE GIFTS

NOTES:

Travel

Technology has done a lot to make this world smaller, but with a long list of terrific travel sites in business today, we're thrilled to point out just how much of this planet is still out there to explore. When travel bookings first became available online, there was fierce competition and daily incentives to attract customers to cheap airfares and hotel reservations. Sadly, things have settled down quite a bit in the past few years, and the difference in price offered by the major travel aggregators is negligible at most, especially when it comes to flights. With this in mind, we've shifted our focus a bit, instead populating most of this section with sites devoted to unique lodging opportunities, international travel, vacation packages, tours, resorts, cruises, on-site activities and adventure travel. You may still find a list of major hotel chains within these introductory pages, but by and large this chapter will guide you to some fabulous global destinations that would otherwise be easy to miss.

Of course, getting there is only half the story, so we've also been sure to include luggage dealers and travel accessory specialists, as well as retailers offering guidebooks, trail maps, translation devices and games. But as we see it, every site included in these pages can help you plan and execute an outstanding journey, whether for business, family or pleasure; by plane, train, car or boat; replete with the greatest luxuries or on the strictest budget. The internet is in the midst of creating the savviest population of travelers in history; where in the world will you go?

TIPS ON BOOKING TRAVEL ONLINE

These suggestions may help keep your vacation from turning into a nightmare.

• **BARGAIN FLIGHTS** • If you're browsing for airline tickets and come across a deal that looks too good to be true, don't take too long making a decision. The best online deals sell out quickly, and in many cases the price you see will be gone within the hour. However, these fares may be restricted and nonrefundable, so read the fine print (the same goes with travel package bookings). Some flight booking agents offer to email you notification of lower fares and seasonal package deals, which can be worthwhile if you have free time or a frequent destination in mind.

• **ONLINE HOTEL BOOKINGS** • Sometimes the same hotel will block off a section of rooms specifically for online reservations, while another group will be set aside for phone reservations. Occasionally different prices will be offered as well, so if you're looking for a specific lodging, it might pay to check offline as well as on, especially if there doesn't seem to be a vacancy. If you've requested certain amenities, bring printed records of your reservation when you check in.

• **ADVANCE BOOKINGS & LAST-MINUTE DEALS** • When all is said and done, travel works best when you don't plan at the last minute. However, very occasionally an airline or hotel may run a promotion offering the same ticket class or room size at cheaper rates. If you book early, avoid getting tickets with too many restrictions, so you can get the better price if they offer it later; call if you're unsure. Also, until your signature is on a bill, hotel prices are often negotiable—you may be able to upgrade your lodgings when you arrive, or reduce the cost of your room. You'll never know if you don't ask.

• **MAILING YOUR LUGGAGE** • Recently, it's become more common for travelers to send their luggage through shipping services like UPS, FedEx, Airborne Express or the US Postal Service. It may cost a little more, but what it saves you in time, effort and frustration might be worth it. Say what you will about the various delivery services, they're less likely to lose your baggage than are most major airlines.

• **TRAVEL INSURANCE** • Particularly if you're planning your vacation far in advance, travel/trip insurance is never a bad idea, as it enables you to recoup your expenses for vacations you can't take due to illness, injury, political unrest, weather or many of life's other unforeseeable disruptions.

• **DISCOUNT TRAVELERS** • Seniors, students and military personnel usually qualify for discounted travel and lodging, but oftentimes online booking agents won't explicitly notify you of these options. If you qualify, keep this in mind, keep your eyes peeled and don't hesitate to call.

INTERNATIONAL HOTEL & RESORT CHAINS

The following sites offer online bookings for well-known lodging groups.

ClubMed.com
Concorde-Hotels.com
Disney.com
Fairmont.com
FiestaAmericana.com
FourSeasons.com

ICHotelsGroup.com
KimptonGroup.com
MandarinOriental.com
RitzCarlton.com
Starwood.com

DIRECT TRAVEL BOOKINGS

You may find special deals directly through these transportation companies' eponymous sites.

AeroMexico.com
AirFrance.com
AlItalia.com
AlaskaAir.com
AmericanAirlines.com
AmericaWest.com
Amtrak.com
BritishAirways.com
CathayPacific.com
China-Airlines.com
ContinentalAirlines.com
Delta.com

ElAl.com
Greyhound.com
HawaiianAir.com
JAL.com
JetBlue.com
Lufthansa.com
NorthwestAirlines.com
Qantas.com.au
SingaporeAir.com
Southwest.com
TWA.com
United.com

TRAVEL BOOKS, GUIDES & REVIEWS

The following sites offer helpful advice and reviews regarding your travel plans.

Fodors.com
Frommers.com
IGoUGo.com
InfoHub.com
Johansens.com
LetsGo.com
LonelyPlanet.com

Moon.com
NBReview.com
RoughGuides.com
TravelZoo.com
TripAdvisor.com
ViaMichelin.com
WikiTravel.com

FAMILY TRAVEL RESOURCES

You'll find these sites useful when you're planning to travel with children.

BabiesAway.com
BabyGoes2.com
FamilyTravel.com

FlyingWithKids.com
KidsClubHolidays.com
TravelWithYourKids.com

SITES THAT MAY COME IN HANDY

The following URLs may be useful when you plan a trip.

AAA.com	Road trip planning
Acuweather.com	Global weather forecasts
BedAndBreakfast.com	Locate a bed and breakfast
BNM.com	Car rental rate comparison
BTOnline.com	Business traveler resources
CountryCallingCodes.com	International calling codes
CruiseMates.com	Cruise ratings and reviews
DogFriendly.com	Pet-friendly travel resource
EarthWatch.com	Global weather center
GoCampingAmerica.com	Locate campgrounds in the US
Gorp.com	Adventure travel resource
Intellicast.com	Global weather forecasts
JoeSentMe.com	Business traveler resources
LetsGoSafari.com	Safari resources
MultiMap.com	World maps online
NationalParkReservations.com	National parks resource
NPS.gov	National parks service site
OAndA.com	Currency converter
PassportHealthUSA.com	Immunizations and health-related travel services
PassportHelp.com	Passport expedition
PCSupport.com	Remote computer help desk
SeeAmerica.com	National parks resource and information
ShawGuides.com	Adventure and interest-related travel resource
Travel.State.gov	Passport/visa services and traveler advisories
TravelDish.com	Cultural and educational vacation resource
VacationHomes.com	Vacation home resource
VocationVacations.com	Plan a vacation to work your dream job

AIR TRAVEL RESOURCES

These sites will help you get the most out of your flight.

AirlineAndAirportLinks.com	Directory of airline and airport sites
AirportBags.com	Luggage delivery service
AirTreks.com	Multiple-leg air travel service
BaggageDirect.com	Baggage check-in service
CheapFlights.com	Airfare comparison site
FlightArrivals.com	Real-time flight arrival and departure times
FrequentFlier.com	Frequent-flier resources
LuggageFree.com	Luggage delivery service
MaxMiles.com	Frequent-flier resources
MilageManager.com	Frequent-flier resources
MileDoner.com	Donate frequent-flier miles
SeatGuru.com	Airline seat location guide
SportsExpress.com	Luggage/sports equipment shipping service
WebFlyer.com	Frequent-flier resources

REGIONAL RESOURCES

The following sites locate regional activities and amenities.

CitySearch.com	Local nightlife and restaurant resource
CultureGrams.com	Country-specific information and resources
Festivals.com	Regional festival resource
FoliageNetwork.com	Fall foliage resource
Foodline.com	Local restaurants and reservations
MuseumNetwork.com	Locate a museum
NYCE.net/atm_locator.asp	ATM locator
OneDayHikes.com	International hiking guide
Pollen.com	Local pollen forecasts
RoadSideAmerica.com	Offbeat tourist attractions
SwimmingHoles.org	Locate swimming holes
TrailLink.com	Locate international outdoor recreation trails
WineCountry.com	California wine tours

*For in-depth reviews of these sites and more, check out www.thepurplebook.com.

SECTION ICON LEGEND

Use the following guide to understand the rectangular icons that appear throughout this section.

LODGING

Aside from camping and couch-surfing, this icon covers the full range of lodging options, from seedy motels to five-star luxury resorts. Along the way you'll encounter plenty of property rentals, hostels and some bed-and-breakfasts as well.

TRANSPORTATION

This catchall icon includes travel by air, land and sea, beginning with flight bookings and continuing on through car rentals and train tickets. Check out the associated key words to figure out if a particular site can serve your needs.

TRAVEL GEAR

Many items can contribute to your travel experience—the most common consisting of luggage (from backpacks to trunks), and some of the most useful being travel-size appliances and foreign outlet adaptors. This icon covers anything that you take with you to make the trip run smoother.

VACATION PACKAGES & ACTIVITIES

Booking transportation and lodging is easy enough to accomplish, especially online. But vacation packages can make it all the easier, setting up your trip from start to finish in one fell swoop. Some package deals will save you money, others will merely coordinate all of your plans. Some of the best will keep you occupied and entertained for the duration of your stay. That's where cruises come in....

>> LIST OF KEY WORDS

The following words represent the types of items typically found on the sites listed in this section. You will find them listed in the orange strip at the bottom of each entry, as appropriate.

ACCESSORIES	Comfort items like pillows and blankets, functional items like electronics devices and power adaptors, as well as travel games, toiletries and apparel.
ADVENTURE	Bicycle tours, safaris, camping trips, water sports, climbing and other "roughing it" type vacations.
AIR TRAVEL	Sites that book air travel for multiple airlines (a list of major airlines can be found on page 521).
AUTO TRAVEL	Don't miss this key word if you're planning a road trip; you'll find maps and comfort items.
BUS & RAIL	Sites that book bus and train trips, whether as a means of travel or as part of a tour.
CRUISES	A great number of cruise types and destinations can be booked through these sites.
FOREIGN TRAVEL	Foreign travel opportunities, including hotel bookings, airfares, tours, adventure travel, cruises, resorts, property rentals, car rentals, bus and rail travel or luxury vacations.
HOTELS	Extensive lodging opportunities, including discount hotels, luxury hotels, boutique hotels, lodges, bed-and-breakfasts and more.
LUGGAGE	Sites that offer great luggage selections, across all price ranges.
LUXURY	The best of the best in all our travel booking sites.
MAPS & GUIDES	Sites offering maps and vacation guides that will help with road trips, adventure travel, tours and simply finding great places to visit on your journeys.
MONEY/SECURITY	Travel insurance, money belts, hotel security and other options to help your vacation be safe and secure.
PETS	Any travel sites that offer pet-specific travel opportunities and equipment. More can be found in our Pets section.
PROPERTY RENTALS	Property rentals around the world, including condos, apartments, bungalows, cabins, houses and villas.
RESORTS	Resort bookings to cover a wide range of interests, including spas, ski lodges, golf courses, adult resorts, beach resorts and plenty of other athletic and/or indulgent activities.
SPECIAL DEALS	Special last-minute or package deals that cover vacation travel, bookings and/or activities.

KEY WORD INDEX

Use the followings lists to locate online retailers that offer the travel services you seek.

ACCESSORIES

AJPrindle.com
CampingWorld.com
ExOfficio.com
FamilyOnBoard.com
Flight001.com
FreshTracksMaps.com
GoingInStyle.com
GPhone.com
InMotionPictures.com
Irvs.com
LuggageOnline.com
Magellans.com
Pakha.com
TeleAdaptUSA.com
TravelSmith.com
WorldCell.com
WorldLanguage.com
WorldTraveler.com

ADVENTURE

AbercrombieKent.com
BackRoads.com
BetterWorldClub.com
Butterfield.com
CountryWalkers.com
EntreeCanada.com
ExOfficio.com
GAPAdventures.com
GlobalVolunteer.org
Hawaii-Activities.com
Hostels.com
iCruise.com
NatHab.com
Trails.com
TravelSmith.com
TrekAmerica.com
Xanterra.com
YosemitePark.com

AIR TRAVEL

EuroVacations.com
Expedia.com
Go-Today.com
LastMinuteTravel.com
MontroseTravel.com
OneTravel.com
Orbitz.com
Priceline.com
Site59.com
SkyAuction.com
SmithsonianJourneys.org
Travelocity.com
Vegas.com

AUTO TRAVEL

AJPrindle.com
EntreeCanada.com
EuroVacations.com
Expedia.com
FamilyOnBoard.com
France.com
Go-Today.com
LastMinuteTravel.com
MontroseTravel.com
OneTravel.com
Orbitz.com
Priceline.com
Site59.com
Travelocity.com
Vegas.com

BUS & RAIL

EntreeCanada.com
EuroStar.com
EuroVacations.com
France.com
Orient-Express.com
SmithsonianJourneys.org
Travelocity.com
TrekAmerica.com
ViaRail.ca

CRUISES

AbercrombieKent.com
Butterfield.com
Cruise411.com
EasyCruise.com
Expedia.com
GAPAdventures.com
Hawaii-Activities.com
iCruise.com
LastMinuteTravel.com
MontroseTravel.com
OneTravel.com
Orbitz.com
Orient-Express.com
Priceline.com
ShoreTrips.com
SkyAuction.com
SmithsonianJourneys.org
SunSail.com
Travelocity.com

FOREIGN TRAVEL

AbercrombieKent.com
AndrewHarper.com
AsiaHotels.com
BackRoads.com
BarclayWeb.com
Butterfield.com
DesignHotels.com
Ectaco.com
EntreeCanada.com
Epiculinary.com
EuroStar.com
EuroVacations.com
Expedia.com
France.com
GAPAdventures.com
GetLostBooks.com
GlobalVolunteer.org
Go-Today.com
GPhone.com
Hostels.com
Hotels-London.co.uk
iCruise.com
Indo.com
LHW.com
Logis-De-France.fr
LuxuryDownUnder.com.au
LuxuryLink.com
MexicoBoutiqueHotels.com
MonasteriesOfItaly.com
NatHab.com
OberoiHotels.com
OctopusTravel.com
Orbitz.com
Orient-Express.com
RentVillas.com
Shangri-La.com
Site59.com
SkyAuction.com
SmithsonianJourneys.org
TabletHotels.com
TheCharmingHotels.com
Travelocity.com
ViaRail.ca
VillasOfTheWorld.com
WorldCell.com
WorldLanguage.com

HOTELS

1800USAHotels.com
AsiaHotels.com
DesignHotels.com
DestinationHotels.com
EntreeCanada.com
EuroVacations.com
Expedia.com
Express-Res.com
FiveStarAlliance.com
France.com
GHOTW.com
Go-Today.com
HistoricHotels.org
Hostels.com
Hotels-London.co.uk
HotelsNearCampus.com
Indo.com
LastMinuteTravel.com
LHW.com
Logis-De-France.fr
LuxuryDownUnder.com.au
LuxuryLink.com
MexicoBoutiqueHotels.com
MontroseTravel.com
OberoiHotels.com
OctopusTravel.com
OneTravel.com
Orbitz.com
Orient-Express.com
Pet-Friendly-Hotels.net
PreferredHotels.com
Priceline.com
QuickBook.com
Shangri-La.com
Site59.com
SkyAuction.com
SLH.com
TabletHotels.com
TheCharmingHotels.com
Travelocity.com
Vegas.com
Wotif.com
YosemitePark.com

LUGGAGE

1800Luggage.com
BaggageForLess.com
Cases2Go.com
Flight001.com
GoingInStyle.com
Irvs.com
LuggageOnline.com
Magellans.com
TravelSmith.com
WorldTraveler.com

LUXURY

AbercrombieKent.com
AndrewHarper.com
AsiaHotels.com
DesignHotels.com
FiveStarAlliance.com
GHOTW.com
iCruise.com
LHW.com
LuxuryDownUnder.com.au
LuxuryLink.com
MontroseTravel.com
OberoiHotels.com
Orient-Express.com
PreferredHotels.com
RentVillas.com
Shangri-La.com
SkyAuction.com
SLH.com
SpaFinder.com
SunSail.com
TheCharmingHotels.com
Vegas.com
VillasOfTheWorld.com

MAPS & GUIDES

AndrewHarper.com
Ectaco.com
France.com
FreshTracksMaps.com
GetLostBooks.com
GoingInStyle.com
ILoveInns.com
Maps.com
MonasteriesOfItaly.com
RandMcNally.com
TopographicalMaps.com
Trails.com

MONEY/SECURITY

AJPrindle.com
BetterWorldClub.com
FamilyOnBoard.com
GoingInStyle.com
Hostels.com
InsureMyTrip.com
Magellans.com
WorldTravelCenter.com

PETS

AJPrindle.com
Pet-Friendly-Hotels.net
Vegas.com

PROPERTY RENTAL

AsiaHotels.com
BarclayWeb.com
DestinationHotels.com
Expedia.com
France.com
Indo.com
LuxuryLink.com
OctopusTravel.com
OneTravel.com
RentVillas.com
ResortQuest.com
SkyAuction.com
VillasOfTheWorld.com

RESORTS

AsiaHotels.com
CountryWalkers.com
DestinationHotels.com
EntreeCanada.com
Indo.com
LuxuryDownUnder.com.au
LuxuryLink.com
MontroseTravel.com
ResortQuest.com
Shangri-La.com
Site59.com
SkyAuction.com
SpaFinder.com
SuperClubs.com
Travelocity.com
Vegas.com
Xanterra.com

SPECIAL DEALS

1800USAHotels.com
Cruise411.com
EntreeCanada.com
EuroVacations.com
Expedia.com
Express-Res.com
GlobalVolunteer.org
Go-Today.com
HotelsNearCampus.com
iCruise.com
LastMinuteTravel.com
LuxuryLink.com
MontroseTravel.com
OctopusTravel.com
OneTravel.com
Orbitz.com
Priceline.com
RoadTrips.com
Site59.com
SkyAuction.com
TennisTours.com
Travelocity.com
VacationTogether.com
Vegas.com
Wotif.com

TOURS

AbercrombieKent.com
BackRoads.com
Butterfield.com
CountryWalkers.com
EntreeCanada.com
Epiculinary.com
France.com
Go-Today.com
Hawaii-Activities.com
Hostels.com
Hotels-London.co.uk
LuxuryLink.com
NatHab.com
OctopusTravel.com
Orient-Express.com
RoadTrips.com
ShoreTrips.com
SmithsonianJourneys.org
TennisTours.com
TrekAmerica.com
VacationTogether.com
YosemitePark.com

1800Luggage.com

1-800-luggage.com · 800-548-4243

Suitcases and travel bags are like Christmas decorations: useless most of the year, but if they're not sitting in the garage or attic when you need them, your holidays won't be very merry. Here's a web retailer that can prepare you for any season, whether you intend to travel light, for business or need to drag half of your possessions around the planet. Easy navigation will guide you through all the hard-sided luggage, trunks, laptop cases, backpacks, duffels, garment bags and briefcases, and with prices as low as these, you might want to make a trip through every section before you check out.

·LUGGAGE			

1800USAHotels.com

1800USAHotels.com · 800-872-4683

If you're looking to quickly ascertain the standard rates of hotels around the world, this site asks little going in and comes back with results, fast. If you're looking for a bargain, it may be able to help you with that as well, usually offering cheaper rates on budget hotels than you'll find with most booking sites. Altogether, it's at least worthy of a bookmark.

·HOTELS	·SPECIAL DEALS		

AbercrombieKent.com

Abercrombie & Kent · 800-554-7016

Somewhere at the crossroads between adventure travel and luxurious holidays sits this vacation packager with a penchant for tours and cruises. Exotic destinations worldwide provide a backdrop for safaris, river rafting and no shortage of pampering, should you desire it. Essentially, these packages cater to those affluent enough to enjoy the fineries of life, yet still keen enough on the essence of living itself to enjoy mixing it up in a foreign land (or sea). Follow one of their professionally staffed programs, or mix and match their services into a voyage of your own design, and remember to forget about the day-to-day.

·CRUISES ·LUXURY	·ADVENTURE	·TOURS	·FOREIGN TRAVEL

AJPrindle.com

AJ Prindle & Co. · 866-774-8278

Interstate freeways aren't just for truckers, and if you like to head out on the highway for some long-distance driving, this road travel specialist has a great assortment of tools and accessories that will make your trip all the more comfortable and satisfying. A wide range of products includes mobile eating utensils, emergency car repair devices, pet safety gear, car seat back supports and portable electronics designed to keep your kids entertained. The point is that the shop has not only the destination in mind, but the journey as well; and that's half the fun of a road trip.

·AUTO TRAVEL	·ACCESSORIES	·MONEY/SECURITY	·PETS

800-235-9622 · Andrew Harper Travel

AndrewHarper.com

"Circling the globe incognito for over two decades," professional traveler Andrew Harper has visited and written about countless lodging establishments around the planet, offering "valuable inside information on the best luxury hotels and secret hideaways." His insights may be read in one of his annual publications, *The Hideaway Report* or *The Harper Collection*. Access to this work is available here online via subscription, or you may just want to enter a bid on one of the luxury Hotel eAuctions and hope for a good deal on a fabulous luxury hotel.

·MAPS & GUIDES	·FOREIGN TRAVEL	·LUXURY	

011-852-2810-0505 · Asia-Hotels.com

AsiaHotels.com

Asia is a huge, complicated place, so it's a good thing there's this massive hotel specialist that makes it fairly easy to sort through the continent's lodging options. With thousands of properties represented, it can help you locate and secure a place to stay in Cambodia, Brunei, Macau, Myanmar, Maldives, Sri Lanka, Indonesia, Nepal and more than a dozen other countries, including Australia and New Zealand. All of the star-rated hotels are broken down by city and region, complete with amenities and priced per night in US dollars. If you're going to the other side of the planet it pays to plan ahead.

·HOTELS ·LUXURY	·RESORTS	·PROPERTY RENTAL	·FOREIGN TRAVEL

800-462-2848 · Backroads

BackRoads.com

If you're looking for a vacation that makes your heart race and body sweat as you lay eyes upon the splendor of a foreign land, this site could be for you. An "Active Travel Company," these guys will send you on tours to walk, bicycle, kayak and even ride camels through Africa, Asia, Europe or the Americas, with much of the equipment often included (don't bring your own camel). Mixed in among these activities you may occasionally find golf and cooking classes available (so you may also relax and eat well, respectively), and truly eager travelers can combine activities with which to test their vigor.

·ADVENTURE	·TOURS	·FOREIGN TRAVEL	

877-422-4243 · BaggageForLess Luggage Outlet

BaggageForLess.com

With a whopping low price guarantee and a long list of reputable brands, finding this virtual luggage shop could actually lower the cost of your next real-world vacation. Briefcases, backpacks, laptop cases, carry-ons and every style of suitcase are ultimately arranged by brand, or as a nearly never-ending set of product pages, and browsing can reproduce the effect of watching luggage drift by at the airport baggage claim carousel. Look at it this way and spotting the bag you would like to spot later doesn't have to seem very hard at all.

·LUGGAGE			

BarclayWeb.com Barclay International Group · 800-845-6636

Hotels and resorts can be great, but on a trip to Europe a cottage, apartment or villa can be something a little more special. Book your own short-term home abroad through this site, which harbors a collection of properties scattered across Europe. These vacation rentals can be as romantic as a villa on Italy's Amalfi coast, an apartment on Paris's Champs-Elysées or a country cottage on the Isle of Wight. You'll still be in an amazing place, but rather than deal with other tourists and a hotel staff you'll get your own kitchen, home entertainment system and possibly laundry. It'll be the closest thing to actually living there.

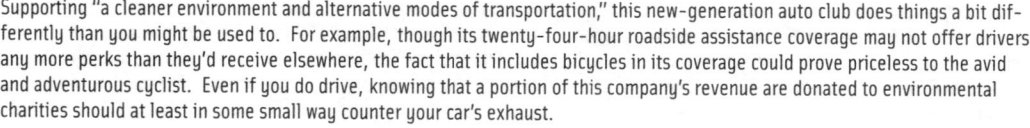

·PROPERTY RENTAL	·FOREIGN TRAVEL		

BetterWorldClub.com Better World Club · 503-546-1137

Supporting "a cleaner environment and alternative modes of transportation," this new-generation auto club does things a bit differently than you might be used to. For example, though its twenty-four-hour roadside assistance coverage may not offer drivers any more perks than they'd receive elsewhere, the fact that it includes bicycles in its coverage could prove priceless to the avid and adventurous cyclist. Even if you do drive, knowing that a portion of this company's revenue are donated to environmental charities should at least in some small way counter your car's exhaust.

·ADVENTURE	·MONEY/SECURITY		

Butterfield.com Butterfield & Robinson · 800-678-1147

If you're not one to travel across the globe just to sit on a bus or take a walking tour of an old museum or cathedral, maybe you'll want to consider one of these Butterfield & Robinson packages. Offering hiking, biking, rafting and kayaking expeditions in exotic locations around the globe, these guys won't let you sit on your haunches, unless perhaps your haunches happen to be on a camel in the Sahara. Or, maybe snorkeling in Bali is your first choice, or mountaineering in Nepal? Meals and lodging are mostly included in these packages that allow you to scour the world with excursions that may ultimately prove more exhausting than your job.

·CRUISES	·ADVENTURE	·TOURS	·FOREIGN TRAVEL

CampingWorld.com Camping World · 866-601-2323

This site doesn't cater to the sort of camping that involves tents, sleeping bags and campfires. Instead, it offers everything you'll need to turn your recreational vehicle into a roaming dream home. Portable comforts, functional accessories and any tools necessary for maintenance and upkeep may be easily found here, along with a bevy of useful RV resources like the Technical Library, a Trip Routing feature and a Campground Search, which will tell you all the best places in the country to plug in and live like a wandering king.

·ACCESSORIES		

800-636-1690 · Cases2Go

Cases2Go.com

Your clothes can withstand a beating from even the burliest of baggage handlers, but any valuable items you might wish to travel with are a different story. You needn't worry about fragile objects being smashed in the tumble and crush of the cargo hold when you shop from this specialty luggage site. Hardside suitcases, briefcases, laptop cases and trunks will protect your delicate possessions from outside forces, and if you discover an easy way to navigate the shop's inventory you'll find plenty of foam that should protect them inside.

·LUGGAGE

800-464-9255 · Country Walkers

CountryWalkers.com

Prepare to "explore the world one step at a time," with the help of this site, which specializes in walking tours of destinations in every corner of the planet. The walking is emphasized, but depending on the tour you choose, you may be spending time in boats—ranging from yachts to kayaks—and lodging in fine hotels, remote lodges, or elegant resorts, either high in the mountains, on beautiful coastlines, or deep in the jungle. Adventurous types with a penchant for high living will have a tough time choosing between brilliant excursions to the Galapagos, the Himalayas and the painted deserts of the American Southwest. Better get yourself some comfortable shoes.

·RESORTS ·ADVENTURE ·TOURS

800-553-7090 · Cruise411.com

Cruise411.com

All the information you really need to know about this site is written large across the home page: "Every Cruise Line Every Ship Every Cabin at a discount… guaranteed!" Simply enter some destinations and departure dates and you can score a great deal on the fine cruising vacation of your choice. However, the site offers plenty more great information, including ship pictures, deck plans, cruise reviews and even photos of your prospective cabin. Got some time to kill in the next couple of weeks? Check out the Last Minute Deals section, and wonder why you'd book a cruise anywhere else.

·CRUISES ·SPECIAL DEALS

011-49-30-62-90-1330 · design hotels AG

DesignHotels.com

For global hotels "synonymous with distinctive architecture and interior design, balanced with functionality and service," check out this site, which is a pain to use, and can only help you if you happen to be staying in one of the select major cities, but which gives you direct access to some of the cooler lodging opportunities on the planet. Ironic that a hotel booking site so obsessed with design would turn in such a terribly designed web site, but we can't hold that against the rooms you'll be staying in; they're exquisite.

·HOTELS ·FOREIGN TRAVEL ·LUXURY

DestinationHotels.com

Lowe Enterprises · 877-347-0347

An impressive and high-quality assortment of spas, resorts and vacation properties can be explored via this site, which offers to let you plan an upscale vacation based on your preferred lifestyle and/or destination. Thus, you can plan a golf trip, ski trip or family excursion at some of the finer domestic lodgings that Lowe's hotel group has to offer, with only a little bit of clicking around. These condominium-oriented getaways may take you to the beach, desert or mountains, but you'll always go in comfort.

  ·HOTELS   ·RESORTS   ·PROPERTY RENTAL

EasyCruise.com

easyCruise · 011-44-1895-651191

Taking exception to the rule that cruises are for families or older couples, this very young cruise line caters to "independently minded people in their 20s, 30s & 40s." Though at this writing the new venture only sets sail with one ship, seasonal journeys through the Caribbean and Mediterranean promise to hold port through the evening so that passengers may enjoy the nightlife of destinations such as Cannes, Monaco, St. Tropez, Martinique and Barbados, as well as the many diverse on-boat amenities (sun decks and cocktail bars). Keep an eye on this one, as it might very well redefine ocean travel.

  ·CRUISES

Ectaco.com

Ectaco · 347-728-1354

The largest single impediment to world travel isn't government restrictions, the high cost of airfare or even finding the time to get away: it's language. If you don't know the language, getting around in a foreign nation can be difficult, and shopping even tougher. Unless you come prepared. This manufacturer and retail site embraces the use of technology for travel by offering a broad range of electronic dictionaries and translation software for dozen of common, and a few not so common, foreign tongues. Including gizmos wired to recognize and translate foreign speech and handy software for your handheld device, you'll be chatting your way to a memorable vacation in no time.

 ·MAPS & GUIDES   ·FOREIGN TRAVEL

EntreeCanada.com

Entree Canada · 888-999-6556

If you intend to make the most of a visit to Canada, this will probably be a good place to start. Between quality hotels, resorts, train trips, tours, family adventures, city excursions, wilderness explorations, ski holidays and perfectly designed road trip itineraries, the site does a terrific job elucidating just how much the mighty neighbor to our north has to offer the itinerant vacationer, and an even better job helping you plan your visit with style. If the people are as polite as their reputation suggests, you might not want to come back.

   ·HOTELS ·TOURS   ·AUTO TRAVEL ·FOREIGN TRAVEL   ·RESORTS ·BUS & RAIL   ·ADVENTURE ·SPECIAL DEALS

888-380-9010 · Epiculinary **Epiculinary.com**

France and Italy hold many allures to the modern traveler, and millions of people flock to these countries every year to see the beautiful architecture, explore the serene countryside and view timeless art. But let's be honest: it's the food we're really after. The unique vacations offered by this unique purveyor are built around the local cuisine of these and other nations. Not only will you sample some of the finest cuisines known to man, but with hands-on instruction included in the tour packages, you'll come home possessing new knowledge of the world's greatest culinary traditions, so the vacation will live on forever in your palate.

| ·TOURS | ·FOREIGN TRAVEL | | |  |

011-44-1777-77-78-79 · Eurostar Group **EuroStar.com**

Travel across the English Channel has taken many forms over the years, and most of them have involved boating and/or swimming. However, a little more than a decade ago, construction of an underground tunnel connecting the United Kingdom and France was completed, and each year since more and more passengers have been enjoying high-speed Eurostar train rides from the British Isles to the Continent. You may now purchase tickets to more than a hundred Western European destinations through this site, and a continent never seemed so small.

| ·FOREIGN TRAVEL | ·BUS & RAIL | | | |

877-471-3876 · EuroVacations.com **EuroVacations.com**

Book a European vacation with ease and convenience thanks to this all-encompassing specialist. You can begin by finding decent midrange hotels in a long list of cities, both popular and off the beaten path, or opt for an airfare-inclusive travel package. If you're a bit more adventurous, you can also rent a car or purchase one of many invaluable rail passes, which are great for getting around in specific nations, regions or the entirety of central Europe. Between hotels and transportation, this site has you covered in a single sitting.

| ·AIR TRAVEL ·BUS & RAIL | ·HOTELS ·SPECIAL DEALS | ·AUTO TRAVEL | ·FOREIGN TRAVEL | |

800-644-7303 · Ex Officio **ExOfficio.com**

When this site refers to "travel and adventure clothing," they're not talking about the Hawaiian shirts and Bermuda shorts that comprise the stereotypical uniform of the American tourist. On the contrary, these are simple, durable clothes that prove ideal for active travel because they are "lightweight, quick-dry, anti-microbial, breathable and low maintenance." Even if you're not impressed with the wrinkle-resistant styles, sun-protective materials and crushable hats, you're certain to appreciate the socks and underwear; maybe not now, but someday, and soon....

| ·ACCESSORIES | ·ADVENTURE | | | |

Expedia.com

Perhaps to guard against being just another web site that wants to book your flights, lodging, car rentals and cruises, Expedia goes a step further by offering different ways of doing so. For example, when it comes to discount air travel, you can either book the standard, available-everywhere fares, or arrange a multistop itinerary that makes a round trip seem relatively square. Your lodging options, on the other hand, may include hotels, B&Bs, condos or even villas. Though if the expensive luxury options prove too painful to look at, you may sort the results to show the bargains first.

·AIR TRAVEL ·PROPERTY RENTAL	·HOTELS ·FOREIGN TRAVEL	·AUTO TRAVEL ·SPECIAL DEALS	·CRUISES

Express-Res.com

It may be true that this hotel booking specialist only covers lodgings in New York, Los Angeles and Chicago, the fact is it's uniquely equipped to get you good rates whether you're traveling for business or pleasure, and whether you want to stay someplace cool, luxurious or just plain convenient. Frequent travelers in particular will appreciate the limited but top-notch properties featured by the agency, which was originally created to assist the fashion industry. This doesn't necessarily imply that models will be staying at these hotels, but it's worth the discounted rates to find out.

·HOTELS	·SPECIAL DEALS		

FamilyOnBoard.com

When traveling with children, you typically deal with three primary concerns: 1) keeping them safe, 2) keeping them comfortable and 3) keeping them quiet. This site addresses all of these needs for both road and air travel, with a brief array of products designed to secure, coddle and/or entertain the kids during the boring travel parts in between the fun on a vacation. From the simplicity of a harness that stabilizes a baby on your lap during airplane turbulence, to the extravagance of an in-car DVD player, there's not much here, and it's not all easy to shop for, but sometime midvoyage you'll be glad you did.

·AUTO TRAVEL	·ACCESSORIES	·MONEY/SECURITY	

FiveStarAlliance.com

Only the best will do for this luxury booking agent, which has selected the world's best twelve hundred hotels for your perusal. A stay at most of these lodgings is a vacation unto itself, as they all combine elegant presentation with incomparable service and comfort. Extensive detail is provided for each property, including photos of available rooms and locations, written reviews and comprehensive descriptions of the many amenities typically offered by five-star hotels, inns, resorts and auberges. None may be called inexpensive, but in most cases this site offers about the best rates you're likely to find for such indulgence.

·HOTELS	·LUXURY		

877-435-8663 · Flight 001

Flight001.com

Billing itself as "A store that recreates the thrill of an international airport with merchandise that addresses every travel need with style and comfort," this travel-gear boutique really isn't as complicated as all that. In fact, it's fairly simple to view all of the site's unique, stylish and/or amazing products. Included in their catalog are some light luggage, travel kits, games and accessories, and while we'd love to make fun of it all, even just a little bit, really everything about this store, from concept to products to execution, is too cool. Damn.

·LUGGAGE	·ACCESSORIES			

800-230-0426 · France.com

France.com

Welcome to one of the most popular travel destinations in the world: cultural apex to the literate, romance capital of lovers, origin of the finest wine to heavy drinkers. Access to France in all its glory (and for good measure, Tahiti) is made simple here, with apartment rentals, car rentals and hotel bookings merely a couple of clicks deep. Additionally, you can book day tours to see museums, fashion shows and, of course, the most popular sights, or opt for night cruises and tours of Paris's famous nightclubs and burlesques; any way you go, you'll be privy to some of the hautest cuisine on the planet, served by the haughtiest waiters.

·HOTELS ·PROPERTY RENTAL	·AUTO TRAVEL ·FOREIGN TRAVEL	·TOURS ·BUS & RAIL	·MAPS & GUIDES	

303-471-5400 · Fresh Tracks Maps Store

FreshTracksMaps.com

Wherever the ultimate destination of your next traveling adventure may be is not as important as whether you make it back in one piece. Hence, this site offers old-school maps and guidebooks, along with the more advanced navigational instruments, GPS devices and mapping software that makes it nearly impossible to lose your way even in the few remote landscapes left on the planet. Speaking of which, the proprietors also endorse and contribute to a couple of interesting environmental concerns, so buying from this no-frills site will help satisfy your moral sensibilities as well as your wanderlust.

·ACCESSORIES	·MAPS & GUIDES			

800-465-5600 · G.A.P Adventures

GAPAdventures.com

This "Great Adventure People" site offers amazing, unique vacations in the form of "sustainable tourism" across the entire globe, east to west, pole to pole. Assembling small groups for each adventure, traveling tour guides lead curious souls through jungles, across snowdrifts, over mountains and on other great explorations. Many packages offer great flexibility in terms of lodging and activities, meaning you can do your own thing here or there as it pleases you. Rarely do you find tour packages so capable of satisfying a heavy case of wanderlust.

·CRUISES	·ADVENTURE	·FOREIGN TRAVEL		

GetLostBooks.com

Get Lost · 415-437-0529

Getting lost doesn't sound like such a bad thing when you're in a beautiful place surrounded by exotic buildings and beautiful landscapes. Ironically, the object of the books offered by this travel specialist is to help you find the best sights and cultural experiences a foreign land has to offer. With travel guides covering locations around the planet, this handy shop might just inspire your next vacation, and with these tools you'll have no trouble finding yourself in exactly the place you want to be.

·MAPS & GUIDES	·FOREIGN TRAVEL		

GHOTW.com

Great Hotels of the World · 888-222-8859

If you demand the best wherever you go, you're going to find a lot of disappointing hotels in the world. Unless, of course, you book through this site, which works exclusively with the finest hotels the planet has to offer, in dozens of countries, from Anguilla to Zimbabwe and anyplace in between that can offer superior service. While all lodgings are luxurious and indulgent, you may find some particularly slated to be Romantic or perfect for Business, while others may offer Golf or Spa amenities. Wherever you're going to be, or anywhere you want to go, the Greatest Hotels of the World are now at your fingertips.

·HOTELS	·LUXURY		

GlobalVolunteer.org

Global Volunteer's International · 800-487-1074

This one deviates a bit from the typical vacation site. On these travels, you won't receive VIP treatment, nor spend your days relaxing poolside, or even take sightseeing tours of the world's great landmarks. No, the money you pay to go to places as far-flung as Ecuador, China, Tanzania and Romania will earn you the right to work on your voyage to a faraway land, either teaching English, building homes, helping the sick and impoverished or preserving natural environments. You may think it's crazy to spend your valuable money and time volunteering, but to many it's not only a satisfying way to get away, but also fulfilling and even rewarding. Hence, entering your credit card info here is only part of the application process; there's no guarantee you'll be accepted.

·ADVENTURE	·FOREIGN TRAVEL	·SPECIAL DEALS	

Go-Today.com

Go-Today.com · 425-487-9632

If you've suddenly found yourself facing some free time in the near future, and feel the urge to visit another country, this site is for you. Whereas spontaneous travel usually entails obscene prices and endless scheduling headaches, here you can find reasonably priced packages to destinations across the planet, airfare inclusive with hotel options at various price ranges. The best way to ensure your vacation's perfection is to plan ahead by as much or more than six months, but in lieu of that, this site helps pick up the slack.

·AIR TRAVEL ·FOREIGN TRAVEL	·HOTELS ·SPECIAL DEALS	·AUTO TRAVEL	·TOURS

800-637-8953 · GoingInStyle.com

GoingInStyle.com

Can one shop prepare you for a lifetime of travel around the planet? If so, this is it. An impressively wide selection begins with an extensive variety of travel appliances and never looks back, offering every necessary piece of luggage, travel books, maps, clothing, comfort aids, personal-care implements, gadgets, hiking equipment and first-aid kits. You're certain to find things you would never think of otherwise, and will probably wind up buying better versions of things you already have, whether you're planning a vacation soon or not.

·LUGGAGE   ·ACCESSORIES   ·MONEY/SECURITY   ·MAPS & GUIDES

703-533-2122 · GlobalPhone Corp.

GPhone.com

Keeping in touch from another country is easier nowadays than ever before, but that doesn't mean it's cheap. At least, not usually. This international communications specialist offers a bevy of solutions for global travelers looking for affordable ways to maintain contact from abroad. Prepaid international calling cards, internet access in more than 150 countries and global cell phone service are just a few from a growing list of options for consumers and businesses, any of which will prove less expensive than traditional means.

·ACCESSORIES   ·FOREIGN TRAVEL

877-877-1222 · Hawaii Activities

Hawaii-Activities.com

If you're planning a trip to one of the United States' most popular travel destinations, Hawaii, take advantage of this site, which allows you to make online reservations for a variety of exciting local activities on any of the state's major islands. On the more adventuresome of these tours, you can encounter dolphins, learn to surf, go sport fishing or take scuba diving excursions. Other tours include day trips between islands, eco-tours, sunset cruises and, of course, luaus. If you weren't already planning a trip to Hawaii, maybe you will be after seeing this site.

·CRUISES   ·ADVENTURE   ·TOURS

866-684-6835 · National Trust Historic Hotels America

HistoricHotels.org

Created a quarter-century ago to "identify quality hotels that have faithfully maintained their historic integrity, architecture and ambience," this arm of the National Trust has selected more than 200 establishments across the United States that preserve an interesting aspect of our culture. When you book a stay in one of these hotels, you may expect to find a building at least fifty years old bearing some degree of regional significance. In other words, you'll find the sort of character and charm that even the locals are proud of.

·HOTELS

Hostels.com

Wouldn't it be great if there was a global network of cheap places to stay for the young, ardent traveler who wants to explore the world but can't afford to travel in style? Wait a second, there is, and the places are called hostels. This site lists some six thousand hostels located in the far corners of every hospitable continent on the planet, and if any ever open in Antarctica, this site will probably add them to its database. While online booking may not yet be available for every location, you'd be surprised just how far you can go through this network, which can also set you up with travel insurance and some fantastic adventure tours.

·HOTELS ·FOREIGN TRAVEL	·ADVENTURE	·TOURS	·MONEY/SECURITY

Hotels-London.co.uk

If every city in the world had a web site as helpful as this London hotel booking specialist, people might just get around more. Aside from tons of very useful information (found under Resources), the site can help you find local tours and get you tickets to the theater. Primarily, though, the beauty here is not found in the page design, but the site's ability to zero in on budget hotels, apartment-style rooms, hip hotels, five-stars, boutiques and B&Bs. These hotels are not computer aggregated, but handpicked to cover the travel needs of any new and, eventually, return visitors.

·HOTELS	·TOURS	·FOREIGN TRAVEL	

HotelsNearCampus.com

Going to college provides kids with an opportunity to get away from home and explore a world free of parental supervision. Of course, as a parent, there are going to be occasions that you want to go make sure they're not getting into too much trouble. For those occasions, this terrific hotel booking specialist offers discount rates on lodging near most US colleges and universities. Simply find the campus in question to track down conveniently located rooms at guaranteed lowest prices. With luck, you'll be close enough to your kids, but still a safe distance from the dorms. Book early for graduation weekends.

·HOTELS	·SPECIAL DEALS		

iCruise.com

Throughout the ages, when man has heard the call to adventure, he's gone to sea. Sure, nowadays such an adventure usually involved upper-deck swimming pools, shuffleboard and all-you-can-eat buffets, but they still qualify as romantic excursions into the ocean blue. Pick your destination, price range, port of departure and/or travel dates and you'll find booking options for cruises around the planet (airfare optional). If you have something more in mind, go to the Advanced Search link, where you may select your cruise based on sports, entertainment or other on-board amenities. Thar'll be no scallywaggin'.

·CRUISES ·SPECIAL DEALS	·ADVENTURE	·FOREIGN TRAVEL	·LUXURY

800-397-4667 · ILoveInns.com

ILoveInns.com

This site's not quite like the others. Devoted to bed-and-breakfasts, it's got a very comprehensive listing of information about B&Bs in US states and territories as well as in Canada. However, here you cannot generally book reservations online (and really, part of the charm of these inns is an almost antitechnological quaintness). Instead, what you can buy here is membership to the Bed & Breakfast and Country Inn Travel Club, or a gift certificate accepted at some locations. It sounds a bit silly, and it is only worthwhile if you're a constant traveler in need of a homey place to stay, but in that case you'll receive discounts and the occasional coupon for a free overnight stay.

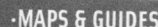

011-62-21-766-6364 · Indo.com

Indo.com

Few lands are more remote to us, in distance as well as culture, than the thousands of Southeast Asian islands known collectively as Indonesia. Here's your chance to get to know them a little better. This site specializes in hotel and resort bookings all over the archipelago: Java, Jakarta and especially Bali, which is alternately referred to as "Island of the Gods," and "Dawn of the World" (depending on whom you want to believe). Beaches, jungles and volcanoes make up most of the geography in this faraway place, and though the region's recently been shaken by natural disasters and political upheaval, the scenery remains some of the best on the planet.

877-383-8646 · In Motion Pictures

InMotionPictures.com

As if a long flight wasn't uncomfortable enough, airlines have to go and make it worse by showing the most terrible movies ever produced (forcing captive audiences to watch what no one else would). This site wants to free you from that slow form of torture by allowing you to reserve portable DVD players and movie rentals for pick up at the airport. You can rent one-way, dropping them off at your destination, or rent round-trip, taking them back to your hotel room (hotel movie offerings are little better than the airlines'). Though a great idea, it is not yet implemented in all airports; for those out of the loop, the site offers to mail both player and movies to your home prior to travel, if you plan ahead.

·ACCESSORIES

800-487-4722 · InsureMyTrip.com

InsureMyTrip.com

Yes, it's true, in this world you can insure against almost anything: theft, car accidents, poor health, even death itself. Well, you can also insure that vacation you're planning. Why? Because if you're doing it right you're devoting a lot of cash and/or vacation time to a once-in-a-lifetime holiday. Should something come up—say, a family emergency, or a government coup in the country you plan to visit—chances are, you may be forced to cancel or postpone your trip. With travel insurance you can recoup your investment, enabling you to travel well another day. This site acts as a broker to many different companies and plans, making it an excellent place to find the right premium for you.

·MONEY/SECURITY

Irvs.com

Irv's Luggage Warehouse · 888-300-4787

Recognizing the "lug" in "luggage," this Chicago-area retailer offers a very extensive catalog of suitcases, garment bags, computer cases, tote bags, cosmetic cases, backpacks and even trunks with which to haul your respective load. But this is barely half the story, as pretty much any of these items can be found here with wheels attached as well (which makes the lugging considerably easier). Browsing may be a little cruder than ideal, but a side-by-side Compare Products feature salvages any doubts that good deals are easy to come by with this family-owned operation.

	·LUGGAGE	·ACCESSORIES		

LastMinuteTravel.com

lastminutetravel.com · 866-210-3290

Low rates on select hotel bookings and "zero booking fees on all flights" make this full-feature travel aggregator one worth visiting when you're getting out of town on a whim. Of course, it works best if you don't have a specific destination in mind and can take advantage of one of the site's few true last-minute deals, in particular some of the late-booking cruise offers. However, even if you are planning ahead, the online agent might save you a couple of bucks, and maybe even as many as five or six over the competition.

·AIR TRAVEL ·SPECIAL DEALS	·HOTELS	·AUTO TRAVEL	·CRUISES

LHW.com

Leading Hotels of the World · 800-223-6800

When you've got only a few moments to find the best possible hotel located in any particular corner of the world, check this site first. Rather than fill up on all of the possible hotels that can be booked in any old place, this group refuses to include any facility that doesn't meet a very high set of standards. Consequently, if you can find a listing here for the place you would like to visit, you can be fairly certain it's among the best in the entire region. From the Caribbean to the Middle East, South America and Africa, there are great hotels to be had all over, right here.

·HOTELS	·FOREIGN TRAVEL	·LUXURY	

Logis-De-France.fr

Logis de France · 011-33-1-45-84-83-84

What's the advantage of using a site specific to the hotels of France? For starters, you may browse for lodging via an interactive map, which allows you to pinpoint specific regions, departments and towns. Alternately, you may search for hotels offering specific facilities, or close-by particular activities. The results are often quaint lodging opportunities that would be tough if not impossible to find by other means. The final advantage, of course, and perhaps the most important, is that when you book a room from this site, it means you're planning a trip to France. Good for you.

·HOTELS	·FOREIGN TRAVEL	

888-958-4424 · Luggage Online

LuggageOnline.com

It doesn't take a full paragraph to explain this web retailer's specialty. "Packed with over 80 brands," the site jokes, its broad selection of luggage is "Priced to move," which we have to say is definitely the case. Finding good deals is remarkably easy, as the suitcases, backpacks, briefcases, duffles, laptop cases, carry-ons, trunks and wheeled luggage are extremely well organized, laid out and elegantly presented, with complete product details and customer ratings. You'll come away with plenty of baggage, but no regrets.

·LUGGAGE	·ACCESSORIES		

011-61-7-3100-7929 · Luxury Down Under

LuxuryDownUnder.com.au

Many g'days are to be had if you check out this site, which boasts "Australia's Finest Travel Experiences." Hotels and resorts can easily be found using an interactive map of the world's smallest continent, but more satisfying might be the Experiences menu, which includes Beaches and The Outback excursions along with Golf Resorts, Spas and Casinos. There are many fantastic things to see and do down there on the other side of the planet, so you'll want to take your time with this one.

·HOTELS	·RESORTS	·FOREIGN TRAVEL	·LUXURY

888-297-3299 · Luxury Link Traveler

LuxuryLink.com

Freely bandying about terms like "the best of the best," this site has been set up to make it easy for you to spend lots of money on decadent and luxurious vacation packages that can put you on a yacht cruising past the French Riviera or in a villa on coastal Italy. If you aren't looking to spend vast amounts of cash but still want to experience such a lavish vacation, they can help with that, too, offering packages for auction and special (often off-season) deals for relatively low prices. Either way, if traveling in style and comfort is your objective, check it out.

·HOTELS ·FOREIGN TRAVEL	·RESORTS ·LUXURY	·TOURS ·SPECIAL DEALS	·PROPERTY RENTAL

800-962-4943 · Magellan's

Magellans.com

Given the relaxed, not at all pushy look of this site, we were surprised to find just how thorough its selection happens to be. Prepared to equip your travels whether you're going to the outback or to the park, you can find a great supply of travel accessories, appliances, comfort aids and clothing, in addition to a fairly standard assortment of luggage. Tops, though, is the Health & Hygiene section, which offers things like dental first-aid kits, water purifiers, insect repellent and emergency blankets. Browsing may also be accomplished by Destination (from Afghanistan to Zimbabwe) or Activity (a Cruise to a Peace Corps mission), as this is a site not to be missed.

·LUGGAGE	·ACCESSORIES	·MONEY/SECURITY	

Maps.com

How well do you know your way around? Sure, getting lost is one of the most exciting parts of spontaneous travel, but let's face it, however often you hear reference to the world being a "global village," this planet is huge. If you don't have a map, you just might not be making it back anytime soon. Scare tactics aside, these guys can hook you up with maps of cities all over the place, whether for driving or sightseeing—or, if you're a purist, you can find a big world map to throw darts at to decide where to get lost next.

·MAPS & GUIDES

MexicoBoutiqueHotels.com

Offering "Mexico at its finest," this specialty hotel site offers you quick and easy access to some of the finest accommodations provided by our neighbor to our south. Affordable luxury might be the biggest reason you have to plan a visit the land of the peso, but once you get a look at the amazing destinations found in the huge and diverse country, you'll find it difficult to choose between the fresh air of mountain villages, the cultural attractions of ancient civilizations or the lush relaxation of tropical beaches.

·HOTELS   ·FOREIGN TRAVEL

MonasteriesOfItaly.com

Imagine staying in some of the most beautiful centuries-old buildings in Italy, rich with history and culture and built-in stunning locations. Now imagine the price for such lodging is well below typical hotel rates. Sound impossible? It might be, but this site boasts a book that offers to guide you on how to board in over 400 of the gorgeous monasteries and convents that adorn Italian cities and countryside. It's a simple purchase, a one-time procurement that could make your stay less expensive and more a vibrant adventure, or you could find yourself sleeping on a wooden cot in a drafty room surrounded by silent Italian monks. It's yours to find out.

·MAPS & GUIDES   ·FOREIGN TRAVEL

MontroseTravel.com

"Helping people travel... one at a time," Montrose Travel has been operating for more than half a century, and if you do your math you'll see that means they preexisted the web. But this hasn't stopped them from doing a good job with this web site. Flights, hotels, rental cars, cruises, vacation packages and luxury travel options are all simply and conveniently arranged, in some cases offering special considerations not always available from most travel aggregators. "One at a time" may no longer seem appropriate now that they're doing it online, but it's sure worth a try.

| ·AIR TRAVEL | ·HOTELS | ·AUTO TRAVEL | ·CRUISES |
| ·RESORTS | ·LUXURY | ·SPECIAL DEALS | |

877-745-4648 · Natural Habitat Adventures

NatHab.com

This site offers vacation packages that take the original concept of an African safari and applies it to all corners of the globe. You can, for example, find a trip to the Amazon jungle, a voyage to the Galapagos Islands and journeys to both North and South Poles. Designed with nature enthusiasts in mind, these packages take you to many of this planet's rich and diverse ecosystems, with a focus on the native animals and vegetation. Climates may vary, and conditions can be rough at points, but as incongruous as it sounds, you can apparently count on one thing: luxurious dining. Go figure.

| ·ADVENTURE | ·TOURS | ·FOREIGN TRAVEL | |  |

800-562-3764 · Oberoi Hotels & Resorts

OberoiHotels.com

If you're the sort to be cavalier about spending for a single night's board what an average person might spend for a whole month's rent, take a look at these hotels and resorts that "are synonymous the world over for providing the right blend of service, luxury and quiet efficiency." What are you paying for? A host of traditional and high-tech amenities (some suites include butler service as well as broadband connections), opulent settings and stellar accommodation in places such as the Middle East, Sri Lanka, Indonesia, India and Australia.

| ·HOTELS | ·FOREIGN TRAVEL | ·LUXURY | |  |

866-462-8678 · OctopusTravel.com

OctopusTravel.com

This latest lodging supersite works hard to offer a lot of information and amenities to its services, which include hotel bookings, property rentals, tour bookings and car services. With hundreds of countries and thousands of options, pinpointing the right hotel, apartment or tour is easy, with price and location sorting of your search results in addition to independent reviews that prove incredibly valuable in the decision-making process. It's no stretch to say this booking specialist can give you eight legs up.

| ·HOTELS
·SPECIAL DEALS | ·TOURS | ·PROPERTY RENTAL | ·FOREIGN TRAVEL | |

800-929-2523 · OneTravel.com

OneTravel.com

All this technology is supposed to save us time, right? Well, this site does its best, offering quick and easy bookings of rooms, flights, car rentals, cruises, condos and vacation packages. In fact, you can set up everything you need for a standard trip in less than ten minutes, and this includes time you may waste looking around for a mid-booking snack. You may find better prices elsewhere, but the big secret of online travel bookers is that most of them access the same databases to find the same rates and fares. Basically, this site incorporates the attractive features of other travel sites and makes them available on one page, now even competing in the "name your own price" arena. This is a great benchmark for comparison shopping, at the very least.

| ·AIR TRAVEL
·PROPERTY RENTAL | ·HOTELS
·SPECIAL DEALS | ·AUTO TRAVEL | ·CRUISES |  |

Orbitz.com

This site searches through the fares of over 450 airlines to find you the best, most convenient itineraries in a very short amount of time. That being said, you should be aware that this site was designed collaboratively for Northwest, Delta, Continental, United and American Airlines, so the "unbiased" distinction may be dubious. Surely, though, the site functions smoothly, and does offer you a range of options to keep the results close to your specifications, especially, of course, if you enjoy flying on these major carriers.

·AIR TRAVEL ·FOREIGN TRAVEL	·HOTELS ·SPECIAL DEALS	·AUTO TRAVEL	·CRUISES

Orient-Express.com

It's not often that a work of fiction begets luxurious traveling opportunities, especially when the book in question is a murder mystery. But with this site literary fans can get a taste of the journey Agatha Christie so famously depicted in her novel *Murder on the Orient Express*. While it doesn't offer passage from Cairo to Calais, you can do something Hercule Poirot never could: take a single train from London all the way to Istanbul. Also offered are train journeys through Thailand and Malaysia, and a riverboat trip through Myanmar. Each trip here makes day stops in different cities, like Venice, Paris or Budapest, with different itineraries to suit personal preferences. Although sometimes, it can be more effective when everyone's in on it....

·HOTELS ·LUXURY	·CRUISES ·BUS & RAIL	·TOURS	·FOREIGN TRAVEL

Pakha.com

Even first-class air travel has its limitations in terms of comfort, and while frequent martinis and made-to-order sundaes can get you through a long flight, if you would like your own little personal upgrade, take a look at the luxurious wares offered by this unique travel comfort specialist. Lightweight sets include cashmere pashminas, silk eye shades and crisp linens. Pack it all in a mink, satin or pony-skin pouch and you'll be the envy of your fellow passengers, the pilot and the entire crew.

·ACCESSORIES			

Pet-Friendly-Hotels.net

While many of the lodging reservations sites listed in this book could book you in pet-friendly hotels, this is the only one that specifically weeds out all the animal prohibitive establishments, making it much easier for pet owners to locate suitable accommodations for your vacation with your favorite animals. It simply operates like any other site, requesting your destination date and the length of your stay, and then responds with available pet-friendly lodging in the specified location. From your pet's point of view, at least, it beats a kennel.

·HOTELS	·PETS		

312-913-0400 · Preferred Hotels & Resorts

PreferredHotels.com

Large luxury hotel chains have all the resources they'll ever need to offer the finest indulgences available, but even they will sometimes miss when it comes to high standards of personal service. This specialty travel firm has assembled a group of the finest independently owned luxury hotels on the planet and made them available to online booking. With around 120 properties represented, you may not find one of these unique and highly rated hotels in exactly the place you want to visit, but if you do, consider yourself incredibly lucky.

·HOTELS	·LUXURY			

800-774-2354 · Priceline.com

Priceline.com

"Name your own price" travel put this multifaceted booking specialist on the internet map, and though the site doesn't play it up so much anymore, you may still opt to seek out your own deals if you look hard enough. A better bet might be the continuously updated PriceBreakers section, which offers deals on flights, hotels and full vacation packages. Or, just follow through the flight, lodging, cruise, tours, car rentals and packages engines to find the latest standard prices for travel via the web.

·AIR TRAVEL ·SPECIAL DEALS	·HOTELS	·AUTO TRAVEL	·CRUISES	

800-789-9887 · Quikbook

QuikBook.com

Some hotel sites have it all; some boast only the finest. These guys focus on making it simple for you to find the best, whether you're into memorable, bargain or luxury lodging. Like most booking sites, you are asked to enter a destination, date and length of stay; here, you're also offered a Price Range filter. However, understanding that this isn't always the way you want to shop, the site sorts hotels by type, including Hip Hotels, Family Fun, Seaside Favorites and the Premier Collection. You won't wind up looking through pages upon pages of options, and you may not find mints on your pillow, but you might just find the perfect place to stay.

·HOTELS				

800-275-7263 · Rand McNally

RandMcNally.com

One of the world leaders in commercial mapping, this company has been getting people to their destinations and back for more than a century. No surprise, then, that its online shop offers a wealth of domestic and international road atlases, city guide, national park maps, wall maps and globes for the avid traveler. Downloadable maps, mapping software and an online Road Trip Planner add to the value of the site, and a section devoted to kids will help get your children on board for that next family adventure.

·MAPS & GUIDES				

RentVillas.com

Rentvillas.com · 800-726-6702

On certain European vacations, you opt to make the most of your time and money by hustling about from city to city, country to country, taking in the important popular sites at light speed, leaving out the ones that just get in the way. Other European vacations are a bit more leisurely. All arguments of quality versus quantity aside, this site makes it simple to find a grand short-term property rental by region in Greece, Italy, France, Spain, Portugal and Great Britain, where you can relax and take in the atmosphere, culture and/or climate that makes the area worth visiting to begin with.

	·PROPERTY RENTAL	·FOREIGN TRAVEL	·LUXURY	

ResortQuest.com

Resort Quest · 877-588-5800

The very notion of North American travel may pale in comparison to that of a voyage to Europe, Africa or Asia, but the truth is that proximity to home doesn't make a resort vacation any less enjoyable. On the contrary, given the benefits of price and language, spending a little time in a home not so far away from home may be just the ticket, or so says this proprietor of (it just so happens) North American vacation rentals. Especially worthwhile to beach, skiing, golf and tennis enthusiasts, this site has a way of making domestic travel an enviable proposition.

	·RESORTS	·PROPERTY RENTAL		

RoadTrips.com

Roadtrips · 800-465-1765

Sports fans who want to get a feel for life on the road can do just that with this site that offers prepackaged tours of events and venues in the realms of professional baseball, football, basketball, hockey, racing and golf. Traveling city to city in style, you're promised good seats and first-class accommodations, whether taking an extended road trip or simply catching an all-star game. If you want to root root root for your home team on the go, they'll also allow you to set up a custom itinerary, even if you intend to follow the US National Soccer Team to points abroad.

	·TOURS	·SPECIAL DEALS		

Shangri-La.com

Shangri-La Hotels & Resorts · 011-852-2599-3000

Not just a mythical haven in the Tibetan mountainside, Shangri-La now refers to this collection of luxurious hotels and resorts scattered across the Asian continent and archipelagoes. Promising serenity and lavish accommodations, every individual hotel is richly detailed, with many colorful images depicting properties in locations as diverse as Beijing and the Fiji Islands, all with so much allure that it will be near-impossible to stay away, let alone leave.

	·HOTELS	·RESORTS	·FOREIGN TRAVEL	·LUXURY

888-355-0220 · ShoreTrips

ShoreTrips.com

Cruise ships may offer a lot of entertaining amusement, but when your boat docks in an exotic land, the last thing you want to do is stay aboard. With the help of this peculiar niche travel site you may see as much as you can of the local action and scenery before leaving port for the next stop. With tours and activity packages for a long list of popular cruise destinations, you may easily set up hikes, driving tours, dolphin encounters, bike rides, snorkeling trips, helicopter rides, jungle treks and many other thrilling, engaging or fascinating experiences that allow you to sit back and enjoy the ride.

| ·CRUISES | ·TOURS | | | |

800-845-0192 · Site 59

Site59.com

That last-minute trip out of town used to be a luxury of the well-to-do but, thanks to internet travel agents like this one, you no longer need to have a private jet fueling on the runway to enjoy spontaneous weekend travel. Although most of the deals on this site actually book about a week in advance, it still promises you'll "save up to 70%" over comparable travel plans arranged through your typical travel supersite. The fun begins when you select your city of departure, and the site offers a great Two Departing Cities option so you may find the best common meeting ground for you and that friend or loved one living elsewhere. This should be your first stop for that romantic getaway.

 ★

| ·AIR TRAVEL ·FOREIGN TRAVEL | ·HOTELS ·SPECIAL DEALS | ·AUTO TRAVEL | ·RESORTS | |

212-486-1250 · skyauction.com

SkyAuction.com

If you're exhausting all possible avenues to find a great deal on your next vacation, don't forget to check out this unique online travel agent. Using an auction system, this site regularly offers intriguing options on luxury lodging, first-class travel, property rentals, cruises and resorts. We'd recommend comparing the minimum bids against deals offered by other web agents before committing to any dollar amount, but if you're feeling open minded, the Auctions Ending Soon section exposes the best deals available worldwide on any given date.

| ·AIR TRAVEL ·PROPERTY RENTAL | ·HOTELS ·FOREIGN TRAVEL | ·CRUISES ·LUXURY | ·RESORTS ·SPECIAL DEALS | |

800-525-4800 · Small Luxury Hotels of the World

SLH.com

Sometimes you want to live large in a very small way. That's what makes this Small Luxury Hotels of the World site valuable to the affluent traveler who wants to keep it simple. The leading small hotels of the world are held to the strictest criteria, subject to "stringent quality controls and...the very highest standards." The result is some 300 fine hotels that have been known to go above and beyond the call of service, in the spectacular locations of the world's greatest destinations, without drawing a crowd.

| ·HOTELS | ·LUXURY | | | |

SmithsonianJourneys.org

Smithsonian Journeys · 877-338-8687

If you'd like a little bit of tutelage or cultural enrichment with your vacation, check out this Smithsonian site dedicated to educational tours. An easily browsed list of Interests to pursue includes Military History, Archaeology, Astronomy and Philosophy. Or you can search by the type of journey you'd like to take, whether to a festival or seminar, on a cruise, in a private jet or by train. Of course, if you're not too particular as long as you and your family can get some quality time exploring the wonders of the planet and its people, simply search by Destination or Departure Date and see all there is to see.

·AIR TRAVEL ·BUS & RAIL	·CRUISES	·TOURS	·FOREIGN TRAVEL

SpaFinder.com

Spa Finder · 800-255-7727

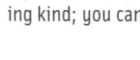

On the far end of the spectrum from adventure vacations is a week at a spa, where relaxation is a disciplined art form, and you are guided from massage to recreation to treatment to dinner, usually in a bathrobe. Spas, of course, range in purpose and location, but this site can guide you to them all, whether you're looking for a golf retreat on the beach or a weight-loss clinic in wine country. Some will pamper you, some accost you with healthy activities and some will just let you cruise. We recommend the pampering kind; you can always work yourself sweaty at home.

·RESORTS	·LUXURY		

SunSail.com

Sunsail USA · 888-350-3568

If you'd like to experience the joy of piloting your own boat, even if just for a week at a time, check out this remarkable site that offers charter yachts from fabulous ports all over the planet. The Caribbean, Mediterranean, Indian Ocean and South Pacific are just some of the bodies of water you can explore as captain of your own ship, which you may select from a variety of vessels ranging from bare-boat to luxury yacht. The experienced seafarer can go it alone, while the novice may hire on a skipper to do the bulk of the work, or even to educate you on the ways of the water. It's not cheap, but the best vacations never are.

·CRUISES	·LUXURY		

SuperClubs.com

Super Clubs · 877-467-8737

When you're ready to take an indulgent vacation away from the mundane aspects of life like preparing your meals, planning your day and handling money, this is the site to check out. Champion of the "super-inclusive vacation," this collection of resorts delivers a wide variety of amenities and activities for its pampered guests, in destinations across the Caribbean and into Brazil. Each resort has its own character, with a variety of sports, recreations and leisure-time activities to keep you busy during the day and at night, whether you opt for a family-oriented location or one of the group's unique adult getaways. All food and drink are included in the package and even tipping is forbidden, so once you're booked you can pretty much leave your wallet and worries at home.

·RESORTS			

212-334-8001 · Tablet, Inc.

TabletHotels.com

Booking a hotel room online gets easier every year, but on most sites it's still not easy to find a great room in a really cool hotel. This slick site keeps tabs on hotels that are either high-class or just plain hip, so you can be sure that the room you book will be as good (or better) looking than your own home, and set in one of the more interesting neighborhoods of your destination city. Opt for Classic or Cutting Edge style, with a Private or Social atmosphere, ensuring you find exactly what you're looking for, whether you're traveling domestically or abroad.

·HOTELS	·FOREIGN TRAVEL			

877-835-3232 · Teleadapt

TeleAdaptUSA.com

Adapting to a foreign environment is tough enough—imagine trying to assimilate if you get there to discover your personal electronics and appliances don't work. With the power converters and telephone adaptors offered by this specialty site you may pack your laptops, hair dryers, fax machines and other business and pleasure travel necessities with impunity. Buy conversion products by particular country or simply purchase kits covering entire regions—the modern world really does get smaller every day.

·ACCESSORIES				

800-468-3664 · Championship Tennis Tours

TennisTours.com

Imagine finishing a morning round of tennis at a luxury hotel, then heading over to the Wimbledon club to watch the best players in the world compete for the cup. If you're a tennis aficionado, the amazing tour packages offered by this unique specialist will let you do just that. Prefer clay? No problem. They'll book you lodging near Roland Garros and secure you tickets to the French Open. In fact, all of the majors are represented, as well as relatively minor championships that are more affordable but no less exciting to watch. Each tour booking is met with a variety of hotel options and special add-on activities, but if you're a die-hard on a budget, you may simply purchase tickets here and sleep on the street if you have to.

·TOURS	·SPECIAL DEALS			

866-425-9090 · The Charming Hotels

TheCharmingHotels.com

Finding lodging "with a unique character" is a cinch with this selective assortment of independent luxury hotels. Any charm is evident within each of the hundred-plus listings, whether you're looking for a posh stay on the Japanese island of Okinawa or Victorian accommodations in downtown Chicago. The only real drawback is that many destinations you may have in mind don't appear to possess any Charming Hotels, at least none recognized by this site, so you might have more success starting here when you seek a vacation destination.

·HOTELS	·FOREIGN TRAVEL	·LUXURY		

TopographicalMaps.com

Though topography is rarely useful to your average tourist, those planning a hiking, bicycling or climbing adventure will certainly want to get an idea of a region's landscape before charting a course. Topographical maps are, of course, the specialty of this niche retailer—in fact you'll find nothing else. Pretty much every parcel of land in the United States and its territories map be found here using an extremely intuitive illustrated browsing system. All you have to do is click to the region you intend to visit, then decide whether you can get away with a 1:250k scale, or if 1:24k would be better.

·MAPS & GUIDES

Trails.com

If your hunger for new hiking, paddling, skiing and biking trails exceeds your local grasp, a subscription to this site will grant you access to more than 30,000 electronic trail descriptions in locations spanning the United States and Canada. Should you forgo a subscription, you can still browse by Region or by activities as explicit as sea kayaking, backcountry skiing, snowshoeing and relaxing in hot springs (which tends to require a bit of hiking first), then peruse a selection of guides, which include topographic maps and trail reviews, available for purchase in print or via download.

·ADVENTURE   ·MAPS & GUIDES

Travelocity.com

With a wide range of booking services available, this travel supersite could easily become a burden of options. Fortunately, this recent rendition of the veteran web shop has streamlined operations with animated menus and handy sorting functions, ensuring that whether you're looking for a flight, lodging, car rentals, cruises or train rides, you may find one or more with ease, and in your desired class or price range. Look a little further and you'll find plenty of global vacation packages, including some last-minute deals that will get you out the door as early as this weekend. It almost is too much to bear, but if you're planning your next vacation, you'll be glad.

·AIR TRAVEL   ·AUTO TRAVEL   ·BUS & RAIL

TravelSmith.com

If you can see through the clutter of special offers on the home page, you will ultimately realize that this convoluted site earnestly intends to give you all the travel options you're looking for. Really, there's only a problem if you get easily frustrated answering lots of questions or doing any amount of actual thinking. Otherwise, for the patient folk among us, we can eventually book flights, hotel rooms, car rentals, rail travel, vacation packages and cruises with satisfactory results. And, if one of the deals does happen to catch your eye...well, maybe clutter ain't always bad.

·LUGGAGE   ·ACCESSORIES   ·ADVENTURE   ·CRUISES
·HOTELS   ·FOREIGN TRAVEL ·RESORTS   ·SPECIAL DEALS

800-221 0596 · TrekAmerica

TrekAmerica.com

For a truly adventurous exploration of the American continents, this tour group offers small (twelve-person) expeditions by van or bus, wherein vast amounts of land may be covered in short amounts of time, exposing tourists to incredible scenery and overnight stays in culturally or naturally significant locations. From cities to remote areas, from Canada to South America, the dozens of tour options usually attract young adults from Europe and elsewhere abroad, promising flexible and rugged itineraries, often involving camping and/or rustic lodgings. It's sure to be fun, but is only luxurious compared to hitchhiking.

| ·ADVENTURE | ·TOURS | ·BUS & RAIL | | 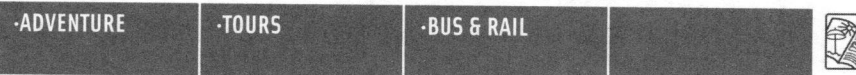 |

877-444-4547 · Trisept Solutions

VacationTogether.com

The number of companies offering bundled vacation packages can be staggering, and trying to put one together a long, arduous affair. However, thanks to this vacation-package aggregator, the deals offered by a dozen different groups may be accessed and booked on a single site. You simply enter your desired starting point, destination and date, and multiple options will be presented, delivering a remarkable flexibility for your travel plans. In most cases, you'll be offered various flight schedules and hotel options, and given the option to prebook regional tours and activities, as well as to add car rentals to the package. This is vacation planning accomplished in minutes.

| ·TOURS | ·SPECIAL DEALS | | |  |

800-851-1703 · Vegas.com

Vegas.com

An unlikely mélange of dry heat, gambling, spectacle and lavish water usage, there's no city on the planet quite like Las Vegas, and whether you're going for a bachelor party, a girl's night out, a gambling weekend or to get married on a whim, you'll want to at least check out this site before you go. While special flight and lodging deals will always be here to help give the illusion that your stay in the city of sin will be affordable, this site might be even more valuable for its event tickets and guides to local attractions and nightlife; the type you'll remember forever, and that which you'll never speak of again.

| ·AIR TRAVEL ·PETS | ·HOTELS ·LUXURY | ·AUTO TRAVEL ·SPECIAL DEALS | ·RESORTS | |

888-842-7245 · VIA Rail Canada

ViaRail.ca

The Canadian rail system may seem as foreign to you as a maple leaf flag, but it makes a little more sense. It may take you some time to understand regional geographies, to tinker with the various routes and schedules and, ultimately, even to decide where you want to go, but the ultimately helpful site can not only book your rail travel, but offers plenty of useful information and other resources to bring it all a little closer to home. If you enjoy traveling by train in the US, you'll definitely like touring Canada this way, you'll just maybe need to dress warmer.

| ·FOREIGN TRAVEL | ·BUS & RAIL | | | |

VillasOfTheWorld.com

This site can connect you with a selection of more than 2000 villas located on coastlines and in countrysides the world over. And when we say "villa," we don't mean glorified shacks either; these short-term rentals have been rated either First Class, Deluxe or Luxurious, though we could scarcely hazard a guess as to what marks such distinctions. Actually, we did find a villa or two with thatched roofs, but as they were located on a private island in the Pacific, we're assuming them to be high-end regardless.

	·PROPERTY RENTAL	·FOREIGN TRAVEL	·LUXURY	

WorldCell.com

When traveling to the end of the Earth, you might feel the urge to call your loved ones back home to tell them about it. A cell phone might suffice, and if you're in need of a mobile phone with international capabilities, you may rent one here for short periods. Of course, you never know when you're going to boat, ride or hike out of signal, so it may prove handier to rent one of this communications company's satellite phones. Allowing you to stay connected virtually everywhere you can still see sky.

	·ACCESSORIES	·FOREIGN TRAVEL		

WorldLanguage.com

If someone were to approach you outside the airport of a foreign land and loudly utter the words "Oensk velkommen til mitt land!" you might have reason to worry. However, with a few key purchases from this site, you'd recognize it as a Norwegian greeting, and be able to respond, "Mange Takk. Hvor er det nærmeste stedet å kjøpe en hamburger?" See, these guys focus on learning and translating foreign languages, whether with dictionaries, instructional materials or electronic devices (very cool). With a little help from such tools, you can seek out a hamburger in any of hundreds of languages (even Estonian, Farsi and Papiamento) spoken around the world. No guarantee you'll find one, though.

	·ACCESSORIES	·FOREIGN TRAVEL		

WorldTravelCenter.com

When all is said and done, most likely you won't have needed insurance for the big vacation. But where some might see a waste of funds, others will discover peace of mind. Offered by this site are quotes for a variety of vacation insurance policies, foreign and domestic, that cover such things as lost baggage, canceled flights, unused hotel deposits, rental car damage and emergency medical expenses. You can rate policies against each other from a variety of brokers featured on the site (with a bit of creative web viewing), to find the one that best suits your vision of a dream voyage.

	·MONEY/SECURITY			

800-314-2247 · World Traveler

Nothing in particular stands out about this site, other than its ease of use. In most cases, if you need luggage, you can find a wide selection here, both in terms of quality and price. Shopping by brand is available, although there are enough different brands here that you'll probably want to stick to browsing by Type in order to comparison shop. If you're fond of the idea of no-frills shopping through an unextraordinary variety of products, this site should be just what you're looking for, and may even be worth remembering.

·LUGGAGE	·ACCESSORIES		

866-514-3281 · Wotif

This uniquely designed site works best when you're looking for late bookings on rooms in Europe, Southeast Asia or Australia (and vicinity). Select the country and city of your destination, and a grid turns up depicting the price and availability of various local hotels over the next two weeks. Rolling over a particular date will reveal a pop-up box describing any relevant amenities, inclusions and terms, or even just terse descriptors like "hip neighborhood," or "wireless internet." The end result may be the easiest-to-use hotel comparisons online.

·HOTELS	·FOREIGN TRAVEL	·SPECIAL DEALS	

888-297-2757 · Xanterra Parks & Resorts

The National Parks system protects nearly 400 of our country's precious native ecosystems, both for environmental preservation and so Americans may visit and enjoy the wonderment of nature. You may purchase a single pass that grants you entry to all parks here, but the true purpose of this site is to offer resort bookings adjacent to many of these popular locations. The advantage is proximity to nature by day, lush accommodations by night, so that even the most urban of folk can appreciate these parts of the world in comfort. In most cases, you'll need to book far in advance for these great lodgings.

·RESORTS	·ADVENTURE		

559-253-5635 · DNC Parks & Resorts at Yosemite, Inc

One of the most popular natural destinations in the world may be found in California, at this site's namesake. The crown jewel of the national parks system, this 1,170-square-mile portion of the Sierra Nevada mountains is roughly the size of Rhode Island, featuring forest, waterfalls, rivers, lakes and a host of geographical marvels. Despite its massive size, seasonal crowds quickly fill up the registered campgrounds and especially the local accommodations, so booking is required well in advance, even planning a year ahead can run you a bit behind. This site becomes all but essential for the nature-loving traveler, so visit here before you make it there, even if you simply wish to plan a several-day hike through its many wonders.

·HOTELS	·ADVENTURE	·TOURS	

NOTES:

Women's Apparel

Women are generally known to be the most experienced and discriminating shoppers on the planet, so we knew we had to take special care assembling this section. Fortunately, the women's apparel industry is one of the biggest on the planet, so we had no shortage of fantastic shopping opportunities to work with. So many, in fact, that we had to leave out a lot of the well-known national retailers to make room for more distinctive boutiques that have figured out the internet is a terrific way to offer unique styles and emerging labels to a broader spectrum of shoppers. The resulting collection of sites will guide you to internationally known designers, stylish professional attire, formal gowns, ethnic-influenced garb, fur coats, hip jeans and activewear for every occasion. You'll also find cute pajamas, sexy lingerie and a massive assortment of swimwear, regardless of your budget considerations or sizing needs.

With the assistance of e-commerce, every clothing taste is made available for every age group, regardless of whether you're a hipster chick in a rural town or an elegant lady living in the suburbs. As hard as it may be to believe, even the woman who lives in a bustling metropolis stands to find a better array of options with a web browser than in her favorite neighborhood shopping district. Online boutiques may never replace trying on outfits in front of a three-way mirror, but they can give new meaning to the term *window shopping*.

 **TIPS ON BUYING WOMEN'S APPAREL ONLINE**

These suggestions may help prevent your online shopping from being a bad fit.

• **RETURN POLICIES** • Of course, the biggest concern when buying apparel online is whether it will actually fit you well. Before purchase, take note of the site's return policy. When you receive the goods, leave the tags on and don't throw away the packaging until you are sure you want to keep the garment. (Note: most lingerie and swimsuits are nonreturnable, for reasons that are obvious. Take special care with the purchase of these items.) As always, when all else fails, use the customer service number; it's there for a reason.

• **SIZING ISSUES** • Trying to determine the proper fit of any given garment can be tricky, especially for those of us who typically fall between sizes. Each clothing line has a different idea of just what constitutes a standard size. Whenever you are uncertain about a fit, take a look, as the site or line itself may offer some hints as to achieving perfect fit. Note, for example, that European sizes tend to run smaller, whereas "generous" sizes run larger than standard.

• **IF YOU LIKE A GOOD SALE** • On most of these sites, you'll find a Sale or Clearance section—don't miss it. Browsing these discount sections is far easier than hunting through sales racks, and often more rewarding to the bargain-hunter. Opt in to a site's newsletters to receive special notice of closeouts and other sales.

• **COLOR COORDINATION** • As always, the colors represented on the screen may differ from the actual color of the object you're purchasing, due to discrepancies between the site's color settings and those of your computer monitor. Whenever possible, it may behoove you to request fabric swatches.

• **e-NEWSLETTERS** • Adding yourself to the mailing list of a web shop allows them to send you special offers and notfications of new stock. If you do it often, however, it can really fill up your email inbox; we'd suggest dedicating a separate email account.

>> SITES THAT MAY COME IN HANDY

The following URLs may be useful when you shop for women's apparel.

ClearwaterKnits.com/info/misses.html	Misses size chart
DressForSuccess.org	Donate business attire
FashionWireDaily.com	Fashion news
FiberGypsy.com/common/women.shtml	Women's size chart
FirstView.com	Fashion news
FittingTips.com/classes/class-brasize.htm	Bra fitting guide
Lingerie-Glossary.com	Glossary of lingerie terms
Narts.com	Locate a thrift store
OnlineConversion.com/clothing.htm	Clothing size conversions
Style.com	Style news and fashion show video/pictures
TopButton.com	Find online sales
WardrobeSupplies.com	Wardrobe care products

>> NATIONAL CHAINS & CATALOGS

The following sites offer online sales for familiar retailers.

AbercrombieFitch.com	Gap.com
ABSStyle.com	Guess.com
AnnTaylor.com	Hollister.com
Anthropologie.com	JCrew.com
ArmaniExchange.com	JJill.com
BetseyJohnson.com	LandsEnd.com
BananaRepublic.com	LLBean.com
Bloomingdales.com	LuckyBrandJeans.com
BostonProper.com	MaxStudio.com
BrooksBrothers.com	MichaelStars.com
Buckle.com	Newport-News.com
Cache.com	Nordstrom.com
CherryTee.com	ScoopNYC.com
Chicos.com	Spiegel.com
EddieBauer.com	Talbots.com
Esprit.com	VictoriasSecret.com
Fitigues.com	WindsorFashions.com
Forever21.com	Yoox.com
Fredericks.com	

*For in-depth reviews of these sites and more, check out **www.thepurplebook.com**.

SECTION ICON LEGEND

Use the following guide to understand the rectangular icons that appear throughout this section.

CUSTOM TAILORING
Look for this icon when you want to make sure the clothes fit you better than they do a mannequin. Custom tailoring is available from several sites, but you'll need to take accurate measurements first.

INTIMATE APPAREL
Whether basic bras and panties, swimwear, hosiery, pajamas or the knockout designs of sexy lingerie, watch out for this icon when you're shopping for undergarments.

SPECIALTY SIZES
At virtually no shop you visit will the selection include clothes for all sizes. Consequently, this icon is here to point out stores that offer clothing in a wider range of sizes, including petite, tall, plus size and more.

STAPLES & ESSENTIALS
We used to use the term *casual* to describe the sort of comfortable, everyday attire women wear when nobody's looking; but with so many high-fashion casual designs available, it's easier to say that this is just the stuff you don't want to do without.

UPSCALE FASHIONS
If you're a stickler for top labels and seasonal trends, you'll want to shop using this icon, which will guide you to high-end designers, upscale activewear and the hippest in casual and club attire.

>> LIST OF KEY WORDS

The following words represent the types of items typically found on the sites listed in this section. You will find them listed in the orange strip at the bottom of each entry, as appropriate.

ACTIVEWEAR	This refers to sportswear, not to be confused with athletic apparel. This stuff is for socially active women.
ATHLETIC	From yoga attire to sports bras and bicycle shorts, this is stuff you won't mind wearing if you get sweaty, including some tracksuits that look good regardless.
CAREER	For the professional, this key word will point out a lot of stylish—or at least acceptable—business attire.
CASUAL	Some of these jeans, t-shirts, skirts and shorts are as casual as it gets, others are the designer and chic label versions.
CHIC LABELS	The hip contemporary brands often featured in fashion magazines and sold in boutiques; not as exclusive as designer apparel, but noteworthy.
DENIM	Whether jeans, jackets, vests or skirts, if it's made of denim you can find it here.
DESIGNER	The top names in fashion should be easier to find if you look for this key word.
FORMAL	Evening gowns and other special-occasion apparel.
FUR & LEATHER	Some of our favorite materials can be located on these sites; check out our Product Index to find some silk.
LINGERIE/HOSIERY	From comfortable bras and panties to the extraordinarily sexy lingerie that men adore.
OUTERWEAR	Whether to protect you from the cold or to add a third piece to your outfit, there's plenty of outerwear, including blazers, hoodies, parkas, raincoats, denim and leather jackets.
SLEEPWEAR	Strictly speaking, you may sleep in lingerie, t-shirts or athletic apparel, but this key word will point out some extremely cute pajamas and robes.
SWIMWEAR	Whether bikinis, one-pieces, cover-ups or separates, these garments are great for tanning or swimming, and occasionally both.
VINTAGE	Gone but not forgotten—we've found some amazing vintage fashions online, and definitely recommend a look at these sites.

>> KEY WORD INDEX

Use the followings lists to locate online retailers that sell the type of apparel you seek.

ACTIVEWEAR

Aarons.com
ActiveEndeavors.com
Alight.com
AvitaStyle.com
BarriePace.com
BluePolly.com
Brora.co.uk
Elisabeth.com
FashionDig.com
Isda-And-Co.com
IShopBlush.com
KiitosMarimekko.com
Kiyonna.com
LaRedoute.com
LisaKline.com
LongTallSally.com
Marciano.com
MarkShale.com
Net-A-Porter.com
Roamans.com
RonHerman.com
ShopBop.com
ShopTwigs.com
Silhouettes.com
SizeAppeal.com
SunWalters.com
Tarsian.com
Teski.com
ToastByPost.co.uk
Torrid.com
ToryLtd.com
VibeTheBoutique.com
WhiteAndWarren.com

ATHLETIC

Alight.com
AnahataClothes.com
Athleta.com
BareNecessities.com
BraSmyth.com
DaisySports.com
Elisabeth.com
Lucy.com
SeeJaneRunSports.com

ATHLETIC (cont.)

ShopIntuition.com
Title9Sports.com
Triple5Soul.com
YellowRatBastard.com
Zodee.com

CAREER

Alight.com
BarriePace.com
Chelsea-Girl.com
ClothesHeaven.com
ElieTahari.com
Elisabeth.com
EnokiWorld.com
FashionDig.com
Kiyonna.com
Lafayette148.com
LaRedoute.com
LongTallSally.com
Marciano.com
MarkShale.com
PaperBagPrincess.com
PieceUnique.com
Roamans.com
Silhouettes.com

CASUAL

ActiveEndeavors.com
Alight.com
AlohaRag.com
AmericanApparel.net
BenShermanUSA.com
BlueBeeOnline.com
BluePolly.com
CustomizedGirl.com
DaisySports.com
Daszign.com
ElectricLadyland.com
Elisabeth.com
GirlShop.com
GoClothing.com
IntermixOnline.com
InThePinkOnline.com

CASUAL (cont.)

Isda-And-Co.com
IShopBlush.com
KarmaLoop.com
KiitosMarimekko.com
LaRedoute.com
LisaKline.com
LongTallSally.com
Lucy.com
MattaNY.com
MichaelStars.com
OnlyHearts.com
PaperBagPrincess.com
ParkVogel.com
RevolveClothing.com
SeeJaneRunSports.com
ShopBlueGenes.com
ShopBop.com
ShopLAStyle.com
SouthMoonUnder.com
SunWalters.com
SwayAndCake.com
Tee-Zone.com
ToastByPost.co.uk
Torrid.com
Triple5Soul.com
YellowRatBastard.com

CHIC LABELS

ActiveEndeavors.com
AllThingsBeneath.com
AntoineEtLili.com
AvitaStyle.com
BareNecessities.com
BarriePace.com
BenShermanUSA.com
Blaec.com
BleuClothing.com
BlueBeeOnline.com
BraSmyth.com
Brora.co.uk
CanyonBeachwear.com
DaisySports.com
Daszign.com
eDressMe.com

CHIC LABELS (cont.)

ElectricLadyland.com
EverythingButWater.com
FaireFrouFrou.com
GirlShop.com
GoClothing.com
GrahamKandiah.com
InStyleSwimwear.com
IntermixOnline.com
InThePinkOnline.com
IShopBlush.com
KarmaLoop.com
LisaKline.com
MaJolie.com
Marciano.com
Overland.com
ParkVogel.com
PolkaDotsAndMoonbeams.com
RevolveClothing.com
RonHerman.com
ShopBlueGenes.com
ShopBop.com
ShopIntuition.com
SouthMoonUnder.com
SunWalters.com
SwayAndCake.com
TheFashionPulse.com
ToryLtd.com
VibeTheBoutique.com
YellowRatBastard.com

DENIM

ActiveEndeavors.com
AlohaRag.com
BenShermanUSA.com
Blaec.com
BleuClothing.com
BlueBeeOnline.com
Daszign.com
ElectricLadyland.com
GoClothing.com
IntermixOnline.com
Isda-And-Co.com
IShopBlush.com

DENIM (cont.)

KarmaLoop.com
LisaKline.com
LongTallSally.com
MaJolie.com
Marciano.com
MyCatwalk.com.au
Net-A-Porter.com
PolkaDotsAndMoonbeams.com
RevolveClothing.com
Roamans.com
RonHerman.com
RustyZipper.com
SatineBoutique.com
ShopBlueGenes.com
ShopBop.com
ShopIntuition.com
ShopLAStyle.com
SouthMoonUnder.com
Tee-Zone.com
TheFashionPulse.com
Torrid.com
VibeTheBoutique.com
YellowRatBastard.com

DESIGNER

BleuClothing.com
BlueBeeOnline.com
BluePolly.com
BrownsFashion.com
Chelsea-Girl.com
ClothesHeaven.com
Custo-Barcelona-Shop.com
Daszign.com
DvF.com
ElectricLadyland.com
ElieTahari.com
EnokiWorld.com
EstiloNet.com
FashionDig.com
IntermixOnline.com
IShopBlush.com
KiitosMarimekko.com
Lafayette148.com
LaRedoute.com
LetrainBleu.com
MaJolie.com
MyCatwalk.com.au
MylaLingerie.com
Net-A-Porter.com
PaperBagPrincess.com
PieceUnique.com
PoshVintage.com

DESIGNER (cont.)

RonHerman.com
SatineBoutique.com
ShopBlueGenes.com
ShopBop.com
ShopLAStyle.com
ShopTwigs.com
TheFashionPulse.com
TraceyRoss.com
Unique-Vintage.com

FORMAL

BarriePace.com
Chelsea-Girl.com
Dresses.com
DvF.com
eDressMe.com
ElectricLadyland.com
ElieTahari.com
FashionDig.com
Lafayette148.com
LongTallSally.com
MyCatwalk.com.au
PaperBagPrincess.com
PieceUnique.com
PoshVintage.com
Roamans.com
ShopTwigs.com
SizeAppeal.com
Torrid.com
Unique-Vintage.com

FUR & LEATHER

FabulousFurs.com
Lafayette148.com
MinkCenter.com
MyCatwalk.com.au
Overland.com
Roamans.com
SearleNYC.com
ShopTwigs.com
Teski.com

LINGERIE/HOSIERY

AgentProvocateur.com
Alectra.com
AlexBlake.com
Alight.com
AllThingsBeneath.com
AmericanApparel.net
Athleta.com
BareNecessities.com
BleuClothing.com
BluePolly.com
BraSmyth.com
Bravissimo.com
CelebrityOnAir.com
CustomizedGirl.com
EnokiWorld.com
EstiloNet.com
FaireFrouFrou.com
GirlShop.com
HeatherBloom.com
HerRoom.com
HipsAndCurves.com
JuliannaRae.com
KarmaLoop.com
Kiyonna.com
LaRedoute.com
Lingerie-Direct.com
LingerieAtLarge.com
MaryGreen.com
MylaLingerie.com
Net-A-Porter.com
OnlyHearts.com
ParkVogel.com
PoshVintage.com
RigbyAndPeller.com
Roamans.com
SeeJaneRunSports.com
Silhouettes.com
StaplesOnline.com
StockinGirl.com
Title9Sports.com

OUTERWEAR

Aarons.com
ActiveEndeavors.com
Alight.com
AlohaRag.com
BenShermanUSA.com
BleuClothing.com
BlueBeeOnline.com
BluePolly.com
Chelsea-Girl.com
Custo-Barcelona-Shop.com
Daszign.com

OUTERWEAR (cont.)

ElieTahari.com
EnokiWorld.com
FabulousFurs.com
FashionDig.com
GirlShop.com
GoClothing.com
InThePinkOnline.com
KiitosMarimekko.com
Lafayette148.com
LaRedoute.com
LetrainBleu.com
LisaKline.com
LongTallSally.com
Marciano.com
MinkCenter.com
MyCatwalk.com.au
Net-A-Porter.com
Overland.com
PolkaDotsAndMoonbeams.com
PoshVintage.com
RevolveClothing.com
Roamans.com
RonHerman.com
RustyZipper.com
SearleNYC.com
SeeJaneRunSports.com
ShopBop.com
ShopIntuition.com
ShopLAStyle.com
ShopTwigs.com
Teski.com
TheFashionPulse.com
ToastByPost.co.uk
Torrid.com
ToryLtd.com
TraceyRoss.com
Triple5Soul.com
VibeTheBoutique.com
YellowRatBastard.com

SLEEPWEAR

Alectra.com
BareNecessities.com
BedHeadPJs.com
BraSmyth.com
EnokiWorld.com
HeatherBloom.com
HipsAndCurves.com
JuliannaRae.com
LaRedoute.com
LingerieAtLarge.com
LisaKline.com
LongTallSally.com
MaryGreen.com
MattaNY.com
Net-A-Porter.com
Roamans.com
RustyZipper.com
Silhouettes.com
SleepyHeads.com
SweetDreamsPJs.com

SWIMWEAR

Alight.com
Athleta.com
BleuClothing.com
BraSmyth.com
Bravissimo.com
CanyonBeachwear.com
CelebrityOnAir.com
CyberSwim.com
Elisabeth.com
EnokiWorld.com
EverythingButWater.com
GingersIslandWear.com
GoClothing.com
GrahamKandiah.com
InStyleSwimwear.com
InThePinkOnline.com
Kiyonna.com
LaRedoute.com
LongTallSally.com
MattaNY.com
MayaSwimwear.com
MermaidsBoutique.com
Net-A-Porter.com
SatineBoutique.com
SouthMoonUnder.com
SwimwearExpress.com
Teski.com
Zodee.com

VINTAGE

BluePolly.com
Chelsea-Girl.com
ClothesHeaven.com
EnokiWorld.com
FashionDig.com
PaperBagPrincess.com
PieceUnique.com
PolkaDotsAndMoonbeams.com
PoshVintage.com
RustyZipper.com
Unique-Vintage.com

NOTES:

_____

_____

_____

_____

_____

_____

_____

_____

_____

_____

_____

_____

_____

_____

_____

_____

_____

_____

Aarons.com

Aaron's Fifth Avenue · 888-768-5400

If you tend to think that contemporary fashions have gotten a bit too risqué, this might be a site you'll appreciate. With stylish but understated fare, it proves a good source of activewear for women of all ages, with garb appropriate for pretty much any social situation that doesn't involve a disco ball or a dart board. Thanks to a deep selection, the Shop By Product categories will lead you into pages upon pages of options, in which case you may want to check down the page to the Shop By Brand menu, which offers a list of labels you'll probably recognize from your last trip to a department store.

	·ACTIVEWEAR	·OUTERWEAR		

ActiveEndeavors.com

Active Endeavors · 800-525-9555

With a list of labels so long it must be split into alphabetical sections, there's a good chance the young women's brand you're looking for is featured on this site dedicated to the "urban active lifestyle enthusiast." The cute, sexy and comfortable brands blend so seamlessly together that you're probably better off just browsing the Women section by garment, where a View All link allows you to scour categories like Pants, Hoodies, Outerwear or Dresses on a single page. These are clothes you can wear out on a Saturday running errands, out on a date and, if you choose wisely, both.

	·ACTIVEWEAR ·CHIC LABELS	·OUTERWEAR	·DENIM	·CASUAL

AgentProvocateur.com

Agent Provocateur · 011-44-87-0600-0229

You have plenty of options when it comes to spicing up the bedroom with sexy lingerie, but this British brand may provide your best one. Elegant and classic, the line incorporates corsets and garters, along with a gorgeous selection of bras, demi-bras, quarter bras and a half dozen varieties of lace panties. You'll find yourself browsing sets named Kabaret, Bunny and Calamity, and even such saucy names don't do justice to the romantic and fantasy-inspired undergarments contained within these pages. Do yourself a favor and view them all.

		·LINGERIE/HOSIERY			

Alectra.com

Alectra · 888-549-6662

Thongs and *plus-size* aren't two terms traditionally known to go together, but this shop is here to change that, offering a wide range of elegant intimate apparel designed specifically for fuller figures. Camisoles and chemises, along with teddies, boy-cut panties and garter belts round out a terrific selection that is well equipped to overcome any tendencies you may have toward modesty. Simple shopping and appealing imagery make this a must-see shop, while the better-than-reasonable prices make it must-buy.

		·SLEEPWEAR	·LINGERIE/HOSIERY		

866-469-3338 · AlexBlake.com

For those of you who know that legs are for more than just walking, here's a store that specializes in fine hosiery, whether sheers, tights or socks, be they knee high, thigh high or go, as they say, all the way up. You can shop through a dozen or so brands or browse by style; either way it's set up conveniently for quick shopping. They also offer reviews for each item (though good luck finding a single critical remark) and a glossary so you can better get to know terms like *control top*, *run guard* and *gusset*—quite useful.

| ·LINGERIE/HOSIERY | | | |  |

516-367-1095 · Alight.com

Giving a stylish boost to wardrobes in the 12-to-32 size range, this impressive e-tailer offers several different ways to shop, each of which will lead you to a better selection of plus-size apparel than you may ever have seen in one place. Jeans, Swimwear, Outerwear and Intimates make up only a few of the product categories, whereas the number of available designers proves too long to list. When all else fails, though, simply shop By Size, and you'll get to look at everything you want to get into.

| ·CAREER ·ATHLETIC | ·SWIMWEAR ·OUTERWEAR | ·LINGERIE/HOSIERY ·CASUAL | ·ACTIVEWEAR |  |

800-717-4243 · AllThingsBeneath.com

As it turns out, most of the things beneath on this site are panties—a lot of panties. With dozens of upscale brands, ranging from Anna Sui to Zazi, you probably won't find a better selection of thongs, hot pants, lace boxers, boy shorts and g-strings anywhere, online or off. You are virtually assured of finding underthings in any color you desire, including many cute and/or sexy patterns, and lots of frilly lace. Look hard and you may even find some matching camisoles.

| ·LINGERIE/HOSIERY | ·CHIC LABELS | | |  |

808-589-2050 · Aloha Rag

You can save time on the site of this Hawaii-based retailer by finding the Store link located near the bottom right corner of the home page. This way you can shop through the slim selections of dresses, pants, jackets, skirts and accessories, which is important because hip labels like Junya Watanabe, Chloe, Martin Margiela are tough, if not impossible, to find elsewhere online. The alternative is to book a trip to Oahu, which isn't such a bad option, but either way you may be surprised to discover they don't sell any bathing suits.

| ·OUTERWEAR | ·DENIM | ·CASUAL | |  |

AmericanApparel.net

American Apparel · 213-488-0226

Growing faster than a Chia Pet, this Loa Angeles–based line of simple tees, tops and underwear is expanding at such a rate that it may well be a household name by the end of the decade. Its selection has widened as well, with skirts, swimsuits and even a few dresses to be found, always using simple colors and classic patterns to create a casual, mix-and-match wardrobe that proves surprisingly versatile. The best part? The skyrocketing brand has taken a strong stance against sweatshop labor, meaning these are some domestically crafted threads we can be proud to wear.

·LINGERIE/HOSIERY	·CASUAL		

AnahataClothes.com

Anahata Clothes · 612-396-0568

This distinctly feminine athletic apparel retailer has assembled a variety of clothing options for the active woman, ranging from the funky to the form fitting. Each section delivers a slightly different sensibility, and at least one is bound to suit you, whether your interest is yoga, Pilates, aerobics or general fitness. Truth be known, there's an element of fashion afoot here as well, so when you wear these Nuala, Marika or Box Apparel designs, you'll be both functionally attired and well dressed. How rare is that?

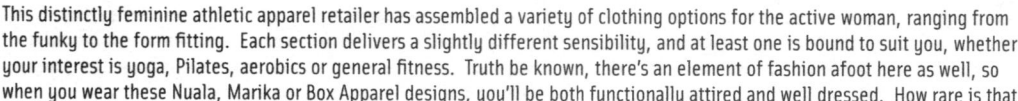

·ATHLETIC			

AntoineEtLili.com

Antoine et Lili · 011-01-53-38-5555

A look at this site begins with one of those rare flash animations that's actually worth watching; a cartoonish little song and dance so bizarre and hysterical you may watch it again. The Online Boutique seems no less peculiar, as the various lines of this Parisian clothier are divided into different "universes," which are connected by a look of fashionable bohemian appeal; simple, chic designs distinguished by colorful tops, rumpled skits and vibrant colors. "One thing's for sure… it's lively."

·CHIC LABELS			

Athleta.com

Athleta · 888-322-5515

Here's a well-designed site for the activity prone, "Where women gear up." With categories like Running/Walking, Fitness Training and Yoga, you know you can find gear for the type of workout you're about to endure, while subcategories like Sports Bras remind you that, yes, this store is conscientious about the female body, even in greater measurements. Garments like hoodies, sweatpants and sports tops are in high supply, and while you may have to click between categories to uncover the entire selection of them, doing so is a relatively easy exercise.

·SWIMWEAR	·LINGERIE/HOSIERY	·ATHLETIC	

213-670-0000 · Avita

AvitaStyle.com

Fans of cashmere will surely love the limited number of clothes by this flirty and colorful line of apparel, which ranges from "casual day wear to sexy, sultry night apparel." Even more interesting may be the label's exclusive Bamboo Collection. Of course, these antibacterial and biodegradable knit tops aren't woody in the least; rather, the spun fiber provides a cool, sensual feel comparable to a silk blend. You may one day find bamboo garments everywhere, but for now you'll definitely want to check out this one-of-a-kind shop.

· ACTIVEWEAR   · CHIC LABELS

877-728-9272 · BareNecessities.com

BareNecessities.com

With so many shops to browse and constantly-changing fashion trends to keep up with, you probably don't want to spend a whole lot of your precious shopping time hunting down essentials like bras, panties and hosiery. This aptly named retailer can take care of all your needs in a single user-friendly shopping session. Whether you're after undergarments that are low budget, especially comfortable, fitness functional or purely indulgent, you'll find an outstanding variety that is thoroughly organized and easily filtered to account for your size, brand preference or design feature. You'll finish shopping with enough spare time to explore the site's sleepwear selection....

· SLEEPWEAR   · LINGERIE/HOSIERY   · ATHLETIC   · CHIC LABELS

800-441-6011 · Barrie Pace

BarriePace.com

Professional attire doesn't have to be fashion death, and this site proves it, with a stylish selection of fine women's suits and career separates for regular, plus and petite sizes. Moreover, a lovely range of sophisticated activewear includes jackets, sweaters, skirts and some killer cocktail dresses that straddle the line between sexy and refined. You may shop by Occasion, Category, Size or in the Outlet, which boasts the sort of tremendous savings you could go broke embracing.

· CAREER   · FORMAL   · ACTIVEWEAR   · CHIC LABELS

310-280-1080 · Bed Head

BedHeadPJs.com

An entire world of intrigue and excitement exists just outside your front door, waiting to be explored. But once you find the Shop link on the home page of this site, you'll be exposed to these incredibly cute and funky pajamas and just want to stay at home. Featuring varied patterns and classic designs in flannel and cotton, as well as some camisole/capri sets, it's a good thing viewing the entire selection of sleepwear is easy, because deciding on your favorites will definitely not be.

· SLEEPWEAR

BenShermanUSA.com

Ben Sherman · 212-840-8000

A very fashionable and successful UK menswear line that's slowly but surely taking over the American market, Ben Sherman has now finally expanded into women's wear, and done so with aplomb. You'll find some very hip and sassy skirts, jeans and tops, along with some particularly appealing jackets and coats. While many of the designs bear a marked similarity to their male counterparts, there's no question that a lot of the garments here hold their own from a feminine standpoint, at least until men start wearing dresses.

·OUTERWEAR	·DENIM	·CASUAL	·CHIC LABELS

Blaec.com

blaec · 800-886-1923

Blaec is right. Time spent on this site is enough to convince you that the designers of this site would just as happily stretch you out on a rack as have you browse these wares. Problem is, these are tremendous, difficult-to-find clothes, including some of the most highly sought-after design brands, the sort carried by fancy stores like Barney's and Fred Segal. Scroll sideways and get a good look at everything while you're here, because if you're going to go through the trouble, you may as well get a glimpse of everything this online boutique is offering.

·DENIM	·CHIC LABELS		

BleuClothing.com

Bleu Clothing · 323-939-2228

This boutique's penchant for strong customer service and its sterling selection of designer fashions has made it one of the most popular upscale stores in Los Angeles, where it caters to celebrities, costume designers and ardent fashionistas, and just about any tasteful shopper with a healthy clothing budget. The customer service may not entirely translate to the web site, but the quality and quantity of fine garments on any given day is the same if not better here. Particularly awesome is the assortment of dresses and skirts, split into Casual and Dressy sections, although if you have the patience to browse them all, the sheer number of jeans, pants, jackets and tops will give you enough great shopping options that you'll never need to go anywhere else.

·SWIMWEAR ·DENIM	·DESIGNER ·CHIC LABELS	·LINGERIE/HOSIERY	·OUTERWEAR

BlueBeeOnline.com

Blue Bee · 866-258-3233

With as many shopping opportunities as you'll find within the vast borders of Los Angeles, you wouldn't think any store would be stylish enough to lure its residents out of the city. However, this Santa Barbara boutique did just that, enticing LA fashionistas to make that two-and-a-half-hour drive north to browse a terrific selection of hip designer wares, including high-end denim, saucy shoes, delicious jackets and enough fine apparel to fill a season, including the garb of hard to find designers such as Nili Lotan and Trovata. Given the state of gas prices and the availability of this supremely user-friendly web site, we'd recommend skipping the long drive next time you want to shop here.

·DESIGNER ·CHIC LABELS	·OUTERWEAR	·DENIM	·CASUAL

603-642-9526 · Blue Polly Boutique

BluePolly.com

If you get the feeling everybody's pretty much wearing the same thing this season, you definitely need to see these clothes—they're not your typical designer apparel. Whereas most contemporary couture threads hug a slender, feminine form, Krista Larson's designs make one size fit all, usually meant to be worn loosely, for a relaxed, sort of old-timey look. Actually it's pretty clear these handmade garments were inspired by vintage styles, and from time to time they even feature antique buttons. Particularly enchanting are the slips, richly textured jackets and outstanding skirts, any of which may be easily found by following the Catalog link.

·DESIGNER ·VINTAGE	·LINGERIE/HOSIERY ·CASUAL	·ACTIVEWEAR	·OUTERWEAR

800-272-9466 · Bra Smyth

BraSmyth.com

Offering "AA-H cup and everything in between," we're going to be presumptuous and say that this bra specialist offers something in your size. You may not find anything particularly fancy here, but so far as your basic set of bra options goes, you'll rarely find so thorough a collection, with just about every conceivable support and exposure option. Although the same can't be said for the shop's assortments of panties, swimwear and sleepwear, the modest selections are worth a look, especially if you're facing size issues elsewhere. Bottom line: if they do it here, they do it right.

·SWIMWEAR ·CHIC LABELS	·SLEEPWEAR	·LINGERIE/HOSIERY	·ATHLETIC

011-44-19-2645-9859 · Bravissimo

Bravissimo.com

Welcome to "the company that is committed to celebrating your curves!" Namely, in terms of "a great choice of pretty lingerie in D-JJ cup." Not every bra, cami, bustier, basque, bikini top or halter is represented in this full range of sizes, however, so you may find it helpful to use the Search For A Style feature, which allows filtering by back size and color, as well as by cup size. If you search right, the toughest part of shopping here should be converting the prices from British pounds into dollars.

·SWIMWEAR	·LINGERIE/HOSIERY		

011-44-207-736-9944 · Brora Scottish Cashmere

Brora.co.uk

If you like sweaters, you'll find a sweater you'll like here—which wouldn't be all that remarkable if the site had hundreds of garments for you to choose from, but these guys only offer a dozen or so different designs, in only a handful of colors. However, these items are constructed from two-ply Scottish cashmere, and cover just enough of your basic design elements (V-neck, round neck and hooded) to win you over at least once or twice. Better yet, even when you incorporate transatlantic shipping costs, this is about as inexpensive as quality cashmere gets.

·ACTIVEWEAR	·CHIC LABELS		

BrownsFashion.com

Shopping across the pond was once an option left only to the jet set, but now the wares of a small but bold cadre of British designers are made available to anyone with a solid internet connection. Thanks to this site, which represents "one of London's most important fashion destinations," you may browse these striking designer garments in just a few moments' time. Though transatlantic shipping may take a while, and the already high prices go up when you convert them from pounds into dollars, the anglophile fashionista won't want to miss this.

 ·DESIGNER

CanyonBeachwear.com

If anyone's going to know about great swimsuits, it's going to be somebody in California. This Santa Monica retailer does nothing to dispel this notion, offering a rotating sampling of bikinis from a lengthy list of the world's top swimsuit designers, as well as some of the sexiest one-pieces you're likely to find. The site's layout is overly simple, and consequently you'll have to scan through a lot of pages to see the entire selection. As it turns out, though, every page is worth viewing, whether or not you've already seen some of these suits in the *Sports Illustrated* Swimsuit Issue.

  ·SWIMWEAR | ·CHIC LABELS

CelebrityOnAir.com

Here's where you'll find the swimsuits of Carol Wior, aka "Slimsuits." These slimming and supportive suits help promote hourglass shapes with compression and underwires. As one of their mottoes says, "Shape & Slim, Forget the Gym!" as these suits promise to reduce waistlines by at least an inch and "lift the buttocks at least 1/2 inch," which is probably more gratifying than comfortable. On the other hand, you'll also find support garments for the active woman (in case you do hit the gym), including support for large bust sizes. If these don't interest you, the pareos and cover-ups might.

 ·SWIMWEAR | ·LINGERIE/HOSIERY

Chelsea-Girl.com

A New York City boutique that specializes in high-end vintage designer apparel, Chelsea Girl boasts a clientele of fashion-forward celebrities like Kirsten Dunst, Cameron Diaz and Julia Roberts. More impressive is the list of top-tier designers who apparently swing by the shop to examine its wares for inspiration: Kate Spade, Betsey Johnson, Donna Karan and John Galliano, among others. Lest you think the entirety of this catalog is superexpensive out-of-reach dresses, suits and separates (most of it is), this shop encourages "cheap chic," which means they offer vintage garments "in every price range." Go ahead, try to prove them wrong.

 ·CAREER ·VINTAGE | ·FORMAL | ·DESIGNER | ·OUTERWEAR

626-440-0929 · Clothes Heaven

ClothesHeaven.com

This site's clever "where good clothes go when they're passed on" slogan illustrates how a good tag line can go a long way. However, the site's vintage designer garments prove that a good tag will take you further. Topping the list of products for this independent Pasadena, California, retailer are prim and exquisite suits by the likes of Chanel and Prada, which of course are the standard-bearers for such items. If you browse deep into their page-by-page selection, you'll find a few dresses and other sundry items from both recent and bygone couturiers, all some of the most valuable "gently worn" apparel available anywhere.

| ·CAREER | ·DESIGNER | ·VINTAGE | | |

866-236-9170 · Custo Barcelona

Custo-Barcelona-Shop.com

"Proud to be the exclusive distributor of Custo-Barcelona on-line," this site that used to simply sell designer shirts now offers a fine sampling of the designer line's dresses, skirts, sweaters, pants and jackets. These print-heavy fashions are not for the conservative dresser, and even the funky at heart will want to choose wisely. That being said, each item exists in limited supply, and is therefore likely to sell out in most sizes. So if you see something you like, and it fits, don't hesitate to nab it, especially if it's in the better-than-average Clearance section.

| ·DESIGNER | ·OUTERWEAR | | | |

800-361-8811 · CustomizedGirl.com

CustomizedGirl.com

Cute and sexy meet with a personalized flair on this make-your-own-message site. Beginning with some sassy t-shirt options, you may add text of your choosing to the garment of your choice, the list of which also includes camisoles, skirts, shorts, yoga pants, hoodies and panties. Examples on the site consist of personal nicknames, clever phrases or telling the world that you love your boyfriend, and deciding what your top or bottom will say is the only hard part. Any limitations of space, color and placement just serve to make sure it looks good when you're through.

| ·LINGERIE/HOSIERY | ·CASUAL | | |  |

800-291-2943 · CyberSwim.com

CyberSwim.com

It's frustrating enough to shop for swimwear without having to hunt through endless shops filled with bikinis designed to look good on teenagers. Here you'll find a deep and more modest assortment of suits created for fuller figures and bigger bustlines, including tankinis, athletic cuts and one of the web's most comprehensive selection of one-pieces. Look deeper and you'll discover most of these are Miraclesuits, a line designed to contour and support your body, whether yours is a girlish or decidedly womanly shape.

| ·SWIMWEAR | | | | |

DaisySports.com

Fitness and fashion go increasingly well together, so it stands to reason the active woman would want "workout gear that's functional enough to perform in the gym yet stylish enough to wear whenever you're taking it easy." This site offers just that, with breezy and sensual pants and tops, and even a few pairs of comfortable designer denim (if that's not an oxymoron)! It's sexy, colorful yoga apparel you can either wear while you work up a sweat or enjoy as you flirt over a fruit smoothie. This stuff could easily become your everyday wear.

·ATHLETIC	·CASUAL	·CHIC LABELS	

Daszign.com

Whether your idea of fashion features casual, sexy or bohemian looks, this hip boutique offers a great deal of fresh attire where infinite appeal is the only common thread. With stores based in New York and Miami, you'll find climate-appropriate garb ranging from flashy short skirts and funky sandals to designer denim and cozy, adorable jackets. As far as the list of available designers and labels go, if the likes of Cathrine Malandrino, Alice & Trixie, lisli and Kasil don't draw you in, there are about three dozen other well-known names that should do the trick.

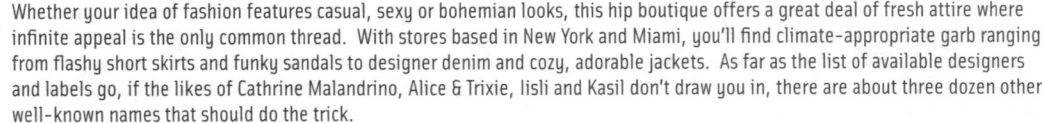

·DESIGNER ·CHIC LABELS	·OUTERWEAR	·DENIM	·CASUAL

Dresses.com

You won't be shocked to discover a lot of dresses available on this site, but you might be surprised to see how fancy they are. Categories named Wedding, Evening, Cocktail and Prom make the case that these aren't your everyday occasion dresses, and a look at the garments themselves proves it. The showy and sexy gowns virtually beg for flashbulbs, and though a slightly annoying item-by-item browsing function may cause you to quit the site with impatience, if you stick with it some of the more classic designs will make you long for a social occasion fancy enough to bring you back to this shop with the easy-to-remember name.

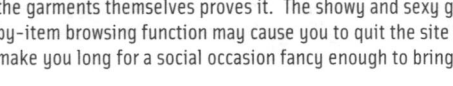

·FORMAL			

DvF.com

This is one messy site that can be quite easily forgiven; after all, it is selling Diane von Furstenberg designs. Between her progressive use of colors and her streamlined tailoring, von Furstenberg is simply one of the best designers working today. Her ultra-chic wrap dresses are the crux of this collection, which changes seasonally and never fails to impress. Shop DvF and then Shop DvF Online to finally start scrolling horizontally through these original designs. Why go through the hassle? Because some of these offerings are exclusive to the web site.

·FORMAL	·DESIGNER		

212-239-6505 · eDressMe.com

eDressMe.com

Dresses for special occasions and other nights out comprise the bulk of this site's catalog. Split into categories like Evening Dresses, Cocktail Dresses, Little Black Dresses, Plus Size and Tango Dresses, the selection includes fashion labels like BCBG and Nicole Miller, as well as some trendy, relatively anonymous alternatives. While the very cluttered menu may seem daunting at first, if you look close you'll see it can lead you quickly to terrific sale items, as well as specialty gowns for bridal parties or proms.

·FORMAL	·CHIC LABELS			

866-948-9341 · Electric Ladyland

ElectricLadyland.com

You would never expect the web's best upscale rocker boutique to be based in the desert, but judging by the funky, sexy selection we found on this Arizona retailer, it might just be the case. While finding anything in particular is impossible without browsing through a long list of brands, lines by Inwga Melero, Miguelina, Jenny Packham, ONG and a host of other favorites make it worth the hassle, while a page of Brand Bios may help you uncover the rest. Search right and you'll find everything from embroidered denim to extravagant gowns, and a bevy of sassy tops no rock star could ignore.

·FORMAL ·CHIC LABELS	·DESIGNER	·DENIM	·CASUAL	

800-736-3821 · Elie Tahari

ElieTahari.com

Elie Tahari is credited with inventing the tube top, but three decades later his collection features far more sophisticated garb, even incorporating sleeves, buttons and contemporary classic designs for the upscale urban woman. Fit for the office or the cocktail hour, most of the blouses, dresses, sweaters, pants and skirts that abound on this site forgo flashy patterns for simple solids, relying instead upon fine design and threadwork to forge lasting impressions. This carries over into an outstanding selection of jackets as well, which demonstrate a richer understanding of the feminine form than a tube would indicate.

·CAREER	·FORMAL	·DESIGNER	·OUTERWEAR	

866-620-8400 · Elisabeth

Elisabeth.com

From fashion mainstay Liz Claiborne comes the Elisabeth line of elegant plus-size office attire, casual clothes and activewear. This site is a boon to any full-figured lady, whether you're shopping for dresses, skirts, jackets or full outfits. You may also come across some lovely swimwear and fitness apparel, and other assorted garb, seasonally. Most of these clothes are made from beautiful fabrics and will decidedly add splendor to any wardrobe—with a sex appeal that's off the chart. It's just hard to go wrong with Liz, whatever form her name takes.

·CAREER ·CASUAL	·SWIMWEAR	·ACTIVEWEAR	·ATHLETIC	

EnokiWorld.com

enokiworld · 314-725-0735

Created in 1999 to offer women in small towns access to designer vintage fashion, this Midwest retailer offers an amazing collection of works by the best designers in history. Beginning with outerwear, and followed by suits, separates, dresses, lingerie and sleepwear (ever heard of a bed jacket?), this one will easily invigorate those who miss the classic fashions of the past, as well as those young enough to have missed out the first time around. How wonderfully ironic is it that the technology of the future has made it easier for us to embrace the past?

	·CAREER ·LINGERIE/HOSIERY	·SWIMWEAR ·OUTERWEAR	·SLEEPWEAR ·VINTAGE	·DESIGNER

EstiloNet.com

Estilonet · 866-378-4566

For a comprehensive selection of Cosabella lingerie, you need only to check out this site, which offers a wide range of the upscale intimates brand. You can browse by one of the many Cosabella lines—such as Francesca, Lissette, Infinity and Soire—or, if these names mean nothing to you, browse by Bras, Chemises, Shapers and Thongs. Whichever way you shop, these exquisite and sensual European designs are sure to make a woman feel sexy and coquettish, while transforming a normal bedroom into a romantic and exciting boudoir.

		·DESIGNER	·LINGERIE/HOSIERY	

EverythingButWater.com

Everything But Water · 888-796-6661

If you're a fan of the *Sports Illustrated* Swimsuit Issue (a fan of the suits, we mean), you may enjoy a feature on this site that shows select pictures from the magazine and lets you purchase the suit in question. Other menu options (Junior, Missy) will help key you in on choosing a suit best suited to your own body style, while others help you avoid ones that may not be. One way or another, you'll find a gorgeous selection of top-end swimsuit designs that are pretty much guaranteed to be the best on the beach in the coming season.

		·SWIMWEAR	·CHIC LABELS	

FabulousFurs.com

Fabulous-Furs · 800-848-4650

The first thing to note about this shop is that its furs are all fake, or faux, as they like to be known. This sure doesn't make a difference in how they look on the site, at least until you get to the price; it turns out that faux fur in nowhere near as expensive as the real thing. The coats here encompass a variety of classic and trendy styles, made to emulate the look and feel of fox, sable, lamb shearling and mink, and realizing that none of these adorable animals contributed to the garments will make you doubly glad you shopped here.

	·OUTERWEAR	·FUR & LEATHER		

818-981-3727 · Faire Frou Frou

FaireFrouFrou.com

The Fashion Bras, Panties/Thongs, Chemises, Hosiery and Bustiers/Corsets pages of this site offer just what their names might suggest: upscale undergarments with beautifully sexy appeal. The Ready-to-Wear sections are a little tougher to explain, wherein they offer "lingerie-inspired" apparel that may be used creatively for a drop-dead gorgeous night on the town. The flip side to the sultry looks of this attire is the occasional panty, bra or ensemble that combines sensuality with flat out adorability—as the home page says: "This jewel box of a store is the place for ladies who appreciate high fashion as well as those who love just being girly girls!"

| ·LINGERIE/HOSIERY | ·CHIC LABELS | | | |

866-327-4344 · FashionDig

FashionDig.com

This clothing site devoted to "exploring 20th century style" aims to satisfy those with vintage cravings. You can browse through the Mod Shop, the Fabulous Fifties or the always intriguing Couture, and you'll easily be met with some truly fashionable attire that is just outdated enough to appear fresh and new. The one big problem: most of the stuff, cool as it is, exists here in a quantity of one and probably won't fit you. However, the site at least warrants a bookmark, as frequent return visits will potentially turn up a perfect fit.

| ·CAREER ·OUTERWEAR | ·FORMAL ·VINTAGE | ·DESIGNER | ·ACTIVEWEAR | |

877-462-1186 · Ginger's Island

GingersIslandWear.com

Break out the tape measure and visit this site next time you want a bathing suit that fits, because all the bikinis and one-pieces here are made to order, including your own measurements and choice of color. Choose from more than five dozen styles of top, and only slightly fewer bottom designs to match your level of modesty and then enter your measurements for an easy fit. If you're still not sure, you may even request samples in your size to try on in the comfort of your home before committing to a purchase. Even Gilligan couldn't screw this one up.

| ·SWIMWEAR | | | | |

888-450-7467 · Girlshop.com

GirlShop.com

Girl Shop brings together a number of chic designer boutiques and makes their exclusive offerings available online, which is no uncomplicated task. You may want to go straight to the Shop by Category link at the bottom of the page, where you can sort particular products by price range and/or brand name. This will be important, as otherwise you'll have to browse indefinitely through products in no discernable order. If you can conquer the layout, though, this is the next best thing to a day of shopping in a hip neighborhood.

| ·LINGERIE/HOSIERY | ·OUTERWEAR | ·CASUAL | ·CHIC LABELS | |

GoClothing.com

GoClothing.com · 877-467-4673

A list of fashionable labels too long to even start can be found stretching deep down the lefthand side of this sunny site. Better to look below this list and follow one of the simple Bottoms, Tops or Swimwear links, which allow you to view the entirety of these selections on one page (with a surprisingly fast page-load). You'll find plenty of wardrobe essentials in the form of jeans and t-shirts, alongside dozens of skirts, playful tops, bikinis and a few scattered garment gems. Look under Jeans Trader to find previously worn jeans with retro cuts, and before you buy too much, remember that you can only wear so many pairs of jeans in a year.

·SWIMWEAR ·CHIC LABELS	·OUTERWEAR	·DENIM	·CASUAL

GrahamKandiah.com

Graham Kandiah · 212-840-7308

It's easy to get wrapped up in this site, which sells extravagant fabrics for use as saris/sarongs. Printed and embroidered by hand in India, the entire collection incorporates spectacular patterns and brilliant colors inspired by its South Asian origins. Follow the Shop link to browse the fantastic selections of bikinis, cover-ups, pants, kurtas (tops) and shifts (pullover dresses), or View By Pattern to view all selections available in your favorite funky print. These clothes look amazing, even the ones that lack characteristics like stitching or shape.

·SWIMWEAR	·CHIC LABELS		

HeatherBloom.com

HeatherBloom.com · 626-403-2144

The online representation of an intimates store located in Old Town Pasadena, California, the products here aren't as steamy or sultry as some of the lingerie we've seen on other sites. This selection tends to promote the comfort of the woman wearing it, both physically and in terms of exhibition. Don't think the stuff isn't sexy, though—it's simply intended to compliment the natural state of a woman's body rather than snap or truss it into shape. The pages are a bit clumsy, but after a bit of browsing you should get the hang of it.

·SLEEPWEAR	·LINGERIE/HOSIERY		

HerRoom.com

Her Room · 800-558-6779

A lot of intimate-apparel sites will try to win you over by showing lots of sexy images of models cavorting in the lingerie… which works great if your husband or boyfriend is buying it. This one goes a step further to ensure that women appreciate the buying experience, as well as the products themselves. While exhaustive categorization can drag out the browsing process, once you make it to the product page it's easily worth the search. There you'll find an incredible amount of detailed information accompanies each listed item, including fabric content and "Fitter's Comments," which describe the garments' texture, construction and other things you can't necessarily get from the pictures.

·LINGERIE/HOSIERY			

800-220-8878 · Hips And Curves

HipsAndCurves.com

Welcome to the web site where fuller figures take an erotic turn. Offering sexy fare constructed of lace, mesh, vinyl and patent leather, these intimates accommodate a variety of sensuous tastes, whether they include costuming, garter belts, body stockings or more romantic inclinations. Tasteful yet exotic displays make this one of the steamier sites online, while the presence of wigs and leather chokers suggest that a healthy appreciation of curves may not be the only thing going on here.

·SLEEPWEAR	·LINGERIE/HOSIERY		

888-954-6789 · InStyleSwimwear.com

InStyleSwimwear.com

Don't adjust your computer monitor, this site has managed to blur the line between steamy and adorable swimwear, with a terrific and incredibly easy-to-browse selection of bikinis, cover-ups and even a few one-pieces. While *sexy* actually rules these pages, these designs are by no means tacky or degrading, rather featuring stylish patterns and cutesy cuts that give you a chance to put your good taste on display without having to resort to any false modesty. If you're planning to flaunt it this swimwear season, you might want to do your shopping here.

·SWIMWEAR	·CHIC LABELS		

212-741-5075 · Intermix

IntermixOnline.com

"Blending hand-selected designers and trendy basics," this incredibly hip web shop was created to serve "a young, savvy shopper, enabling her to look like a trendsetter without forcing her to spend a fortune." It succeeds admirably, offering beautiful, if expensive, accessories and apparel, including to-die-for tunics, relaxed but elegant evening dresses, pants and skirts that prove sexy without being suggestive and plenty of other well-made, colorful garb. Every woman should take a look, even if most of us will simply browse and drool over this top-tier selection.

·DESIGNER	·DENIM	·CASUAL	·CHIC LABELS

888-695-4559 · Lilly Pulitzer

InThePinkOnline.com

If you like Lilly Pulitzer, you like pastels, and possibly vice versa. Here you'll find a comprehensive selection of Lilly Pulitzer designs, in all their breezy, colorful glory. While you might long for primary colors or earth tones after just a few minutes on the site, you shouldn't take it out on the clothes, which are finely represented, including enlarged pattern details. This stuff is perfect for summer beach trips, but these seasonal offerings will work to convince you that soft pink, yellow and turquoise works year round.

·SWIMWEAR	·OUTERWEAR	·CASUAL	·CHIC LABELS

Isda-And-Co.com

Isda & Co. • 877-647-4732

Isda Funari has put together a clean and simple collection of lovely sweaters, tops, skirts, jackets and pants, all of it available here, available via the Shop Online link, then within the Women's Collection and Red Label categories. These are wardrobe basics with a touch of quality, including the occasional cashmere and silk. You'll find plenty of color and style variations here to mix and match, and thanks to fairly simple navigation and prices that never exceed human reason, you'll be tempted to do just that.

	·ACTIVEWEAR	·DENIM	·CASUAL	

IShopBlush.com

Blush • 301-340-2084

Philosophies like "All women should embrace their own personal style" will greet you on the web pages of this Maryland boutique, but that's not all. Once you've been thoroughly impressed by a long menu of designers that includes Fins Denim, Lotta Stensson, White & Warren and Bordeaux, try browsing by the Category menu for a beautiful collection of chic, designer Dresses, Ponchos & Shawls, Outerwear, Cashmere and more. Chances are the exquisite tastes on display here will turn you on to something new.

	·DESIGNER ·CHIC LABELS	·ACTIVEWEAR	·DENIM	·CASUAL

JuliannaRae.com

Julianna Rae • 800-662-5723

For lovely, luxurious intimates built more for comfort than fantasy, visit this specialty retailer that offers sleepwear and lingerie that doesn't forsake function for form. This stuff is effortlessly pretty and sexy without being lewd, meaning a woman will appreciate it every bit as much as a man. Add a soft, often silky touch and you have a line of bedroom attire that you'll want to put on as much as you want to take off. These items make for an indulgent gift, whether you're bestowing it upon a loved one or treating yourself.

		·SLEEPWEAR	·LINGERIE/HOSIERY		

KarmaLoop.com

Karmaloop • 877-465-2762

Before you see it on the high runways of Paris or Venice, or it shows up in the Gap's new season of clothes, you oftentimes see it wandering the streets of the city, worn by the young people who're daring enough to explore the edges of fresh fashion. That's the appeal of this site, which brings together budding and established designer labels from an urban dance culture that extends to all corners of the earth. Most of this gear is made to accommodate dancing into the night, or at least to facilitate movement from sidewalk to sidewalk, and all of it represents a young culture that is entirely aware of the limitless appeal of ever-changing styles.

		·LINGERIE/HOSIERY	·DENIM	·CASUAL	·CHIC LABELS

800-527-0624 · Kittos Marimekko

KiitosMarimekko.com

Even on the web, it's difficult to find clothes hailing from that most mysterious and distant of Scandinavian nations, Finland. How unusual, then, that with this site you can actually find Finnish designer apparel—specifically, that of the Marimekko line. Seasonal and perennial collections of this hard-to-find activewear fill the pages of this site, so you may want to look at everything in order to find the best it has to offer, which happens to be as terrific as it is rare.

·DESIGNER	·ACTIVEWEAR	·OUTERWEAR	·CASUAL

888-549-6662 · Kiyonna

Kiyonna.com

Designed for women above a size 10, this line of sophisticated plus-size apparel could sure stand to be bigger. These fine, full figure fashions will dress you well for a casual lunch or an elegant cocktail party, without breaking your bank, and if there were more items you might fill half your closet with this cute and sassy garb. Sadly, you may view the entire collection in minutes, even with the recent addition of swimsuits. One day, this brand of clothing might be all you need; until then, this can at least be the first place you shop.

·CAREER	·SWIMWEAR	·LINGERIE/HOSIERY	·ACTIVEWEAR

877-324-5148 · Lafayette 148

Lafayette148.com

This upscale, Manhattan-based line of garments "offers the modern, intelligent woman sophisticated, chic designs in the most luxurious fabrics and a wonderfully consistent fit," which may really be summed up in a single word: *elegance*. With materials like cashmere and leather and finely cut patterns covering social, professional and formal occasions, wearing these clothes makes a clear statement about your cultured refinement and cosmopolitan tastes—a statement often echoed by the price tag.

·CAREER ·FUR & LEATHER	·FORMAL	·DESIGNER	·OUTERWEAR

800-781-9170 · Redcats S.A.

LaRedoute.com

If you're interested to see a catalog that French women shop from, take a look at this comprehensive designer, active- and casual wear site. Not interested in what the french are wearing? Maybe you should be. While designer labels that were previously tough to find in the US may be located in the Designer Studio department, the real value of this site may be found in the regular categories, where extremely affordable and decidedly stylish clothes for the active weekend and career woman may be viewed and ordered with ease. Domestic department stores and catalogs should take note....

·CAREER ·LINGERIE/HOSIERY	·SWIMWEAR ·ACTIVEWEAR	·SLEEPWEAR ·OUTERWEAR	·DESIGNER ·CASUAL

LetrainBleu.com

Le Train Bleu · 503-343-5140

Inspired by the carefree attitudes of the circa 1920s French Riviera, this marriage of art and shopping provides at least an online version of that "secret, sumptuous alleyway boutique that you've searched for all your life." The Portland, Oregon–based web shop offers a surprisingly out-of-the-ordinary array of fine designer garments, selected as much for their uniqueness as for their unparalleled charm. The exquisite upscale garb is unlikely to be found elsewhere, whether online, at a local boutique or on anyone you know, so if you like your fashion sense to be the subject of every passing conversation, don't miss the opportunity to shop here.

 ·DESIGNER ·OUTERWEAR

Lingerie-Direct.com

Lingerie-Direct · 800-447-1082

Some lingerie is not meant to be seen, and that's the kind that's readily visible here. Offering panties, bras and shapewear, none of it's built to be particularly exciting, rather it's meant to offer support, comfort and/or contour to a woman's body. This site features a long list of brands, with favorites such as Playtex, Barely There and Wonderbra barely scratching the surface. Consequently, you might want to take advantage of the Personal Shopping menu at the bottom of the page, which allows you to shop for bras and shapewear specifically in your size. Panties, on the other hand, could take a while.

   ·LINGERIE/HOSIERY

LingerieAtLarge.com

LingerieAtLarge · 866-285-2743

So far as plus-size lingerie stores go, this one doesn't offer the greatest variety, nor the sexiest, or even the most elegant, though certainly, nothing here is in any way lacking (aside from material). No, its most memorable offering is a section replete with kinky costumes for the full-figured fetishist, whether you prefer a vinyl-clad nun, bar maid or police officer. No less playful but decidedly more dangerous is the enigmatic The Wild Side category, which at this time is better left unexplained, in deference to minors.

  ·SLEEPWEAR ·LINGERIE/HOSIERY

LisaKline.com

Lisa Kline · 888-547-2554

As incredibly slow to load as this site is, it still manages to beat most others to the punch when it comes to stocking the hippest labels and up-to-the-minute styles. Based in Los Angeles, the store caters to a clientele of young, sexy trendsetters, whether it's serving up blue jeans, warm-weather tops or sassy pajamas. You may shop by product or a list of brand names including Earnest Sewn, Ella Moss, Catherine Brule, Moshi Moshi, Juicy Couture and Autumn Cashmere. Check back often, because this shop is keeping track.

  ·SLEEPWEAR ·ACTIVEWEAR ·OUTERWEAR ·DENIM
·CASUAL ·CHIC LABELS

011-44-87-0990-6885 · Long Tall Sally

LongTallSally.com

Given that most fashion models hover near the six-foot range, most of us take it for granted that the fashion industry caters to tall sizes. Any woman with long legs, long arms, a long torso or all three knows different. This site focuses on women of height, offering all manner of apparel, including swimwear, suits, sleepwear, outerwear, formal attire and, yes, jeans. The best part is that the women who shop here actually stand a good chance of wearing these clothes as well as the models do.

·CAREER ·ACTIVEWEAR	·FORMAL ·OUTERWEAR	·SWIMWEAR ·DENIM	·SLEEPWEAR ·CASUAL		

877-999-5829 · Lucy

Lucy.com

Women who are sporty, casual or stylish are bound to like this site, and if you're a little bit of all three you're going to love it. Proving that hip fashions aren't just for dates and parties, the sweatshirts, lotus pants and athletic tops here combine bohemian style with athletic performance to create fun looks to wear to the gym, breakfast with friends or for lazy evenings in front of some video rentals. A Favorite Looks section of the shop gives you a ideas for a few comfortable outfits, but mostly serves as an apt demonstration of how well these colorful components mix and match to make you look great even when you don't feel like trying.

·ATHLETIC	·CASUAL			

310-471-9545 · ma jolie

MaJolie.com

Intended to be a "showcase for emerging designer talent," this boutique, based in the upscale Brentwood neighborhood of Los Angeles, offers an early look at fresh trends with a fine selection of chic and designer labels. We spotted Joie, Catherine Malandrino and Lotta among a list of labels too long to fit onto a single page, but if you stick to the Category pull-down menu you may discover something new you might otherwise miss. After all, why should the women of Brentwood have all the fun?

·DESIGNER	·DENIM	·CHIC LABELS			

866-446-2724 · Marciano

Marciano.com

You might recognize the name Marciano as belonging to the founders of the popular Guess? brand, and indeed this site does come from the same group. The difference is that this distinctive, high-end collection of clothes is just a bit hipper, and also a bit more refined. Including the sexiest selection of women's suits you'll find anywhere, this catalog features fine trendy tops, beautiful skirts, even-better-than-expected jeans, gorgeous jackets and killer cocktail dresses. We get the impression this is a good place for a devoted Guess? Girl to graduate into something of a more adult femininity without sacrificing the charm that attracted her to the brand to begin with.

·CAREER ·CHIC LABELS	·ACTIVEWEAR	·OUTERWEAR	·DENIM	

MarkShale.com

Mark Shale · 888-333-6964

Keeping it clean and simple, this chic line of apparel ranges from quiet to colorful, all of it finely cut from quality fabrics. Now, if they could only make their web site equally clean and simple. You can narrow down the selection to Women's Clothing, but beyond that, the categories are unevenly dispersed, some with explicit contents, some a little more difficult to fathom. Fortunately there's not too much to sort through, so you can view most of the catalog without too many frustrating side effects.

·CAREER ·ACTIVEWEAR

MaryGreen.com

Mary Green · 800-359-7455

When it comes to lingerie, men and women often find themselves in disagreement. Walking the line of compromise is this proprietary line of bedroom attire. She will like most of this stuff because it is "cute." He will dig it because it's "sexy." Both will like it because it's generally quite affordable. Many combinations of silk, satin, lace and ribbon conspire for a plethora of playful dressing options in several colors and cuts, including robes as well as some delightful underthings. All is conveniently modeled by mannequins and pictured on a single page. Everybody wins.

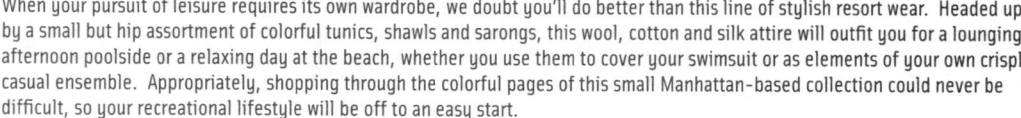

·SLEEPWEAR ·LINGERIE/HOSIERY

MattaNY.com

Matta · 212-343-9399

When your pursuit of leisure requires its own wardrobe, we doubt you'll do better than this line of stylish resort wear. Headed up by a small but hip assortment of colorful tunics, shawls and sarongs, this wool, cotton and silk attire will outfit you for a lounging afternoon poolside or a relaxing day at the beach, whether you use them to cover your swimsuit or as elements of your own crisply casual ensemble. Appropriately, shopping through the colorful pages of this small Manhattan-based collection could never be difficult, so your recreational lifestyle will be off to an easy start.

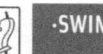

·SWIMWEAR ·SLEEPWEAR ·CASUAL

MayaSwimwear.com

Maya Swimwear · 800-913-8133

If you're prepared to kill them at the beach this summer, one of these exquisitely sexy bikinis is here to help you. Not for the shy, these suits are daring and colorful without being too outlandish or revealing, but the effect will be the same—a widespread tan and lots of attention. A variety of seasonal patterns include some reversible looks, plus some deceptively simple solids that really use sophisticated cuts to define and compliment your shape. These may be the best suits you'll find this year to flatter the physique you've worked hard to maintain.

·SWIMWEAR

305-662-8621 · Mermaids Boutique

MermaidsBoutique.com

You might find that cute and sexy bikini you've been looking for on this site, but even if you've already found your perfect swimsuit somewhere else, check out this Miami-based shop for its fabulous selection of cover-ups. The advantage of shopping this boutique isn't that you'll find a lot of products to choose from—in fact there were only four brands available last we checked—but that what they have is enough to make choosing tough, whether you favor a tunic look, sarong, caftan or pareo.

·SWIMWEAR

877-782-7833 · Michael Stars

MichaelStars.com

If you've got a flirting relationship with fashion but are still just a t-shirt-loving gal at heart, you may never feel complete until there's a good stock of this brand's simple tops in your wardrobe. Tanks, Long Sleeves, Camisoles and Cap Sleeves are just some of the great categories here, each of which features just enough differences in design and color to make a big purchase worthwhile. The clean, classic looks afforded by these sassy garments will make dressing for your everyday life easier, and you'll feel comfortable knowing you look good.

·CASUAL

310-360-0466 · Mink Center

MinkCenter.com

Mink is only one type of fur you'll find at this deceptively small outerwear specialist. You'll also find chinchilla, fox, lynx, rabbit shearling and sable. If you're unlucky, you'll come across muskrat, nutria or raccoon. This should be easy to avoid, though, as browsing begins with a detailed search function. Once you've narrowed down the selection between furs and leather, coat length, designer and/or price range, you'll get good looks at luxurious coat designs that range in both quality and price.

·OUTERWEAR · ·FUR & LEATHER

011-612-9387-4506 · MYCATWALK.com.au

MyCatwalk.com.au

Do they have a healthy appreciation for designer fashions down under? If this site's any indication, they do. While Australia may seem a long way to go for upscale apparel, this will probably be your only shot at seeing how the world of contemporary fashion looks from the Southern Hemisphere. Aside from Aussie designers, you're likely to see a few familiar names interspersed, as the site incorporates some popular European looks into its catalog, but it turns out to be the local talent that shines, and why not? It all looks original from this side of the Pacific.

·FORMAL ·DESIGNER ·OUTERWEAR ·DENIM
·FUR & LEATHER

MylaLingerie.com

Myla · 212-327-2676

Billed as "Sex Life Accessories," this upscale line of lingerie and adult toys endeavors to "create the world's first luxury sex brand for women." We doubt they're hearing any complaints. The ultrasultry collections of silk, lace and mesh unmentionables are often garnished with feathers, pearls and embroidery, meaning these are not simply sumptuous underthings, but something more akin to bedroom artwork. Lest you think the brand entirely built on fantasy, a quick look in the My By Myla section turns up some un-questionably sexy bras and panties that are actually designed to look better underneath your clothes.

·DESIGNER	·LINGERIE/HOSIERY		

Net-A-Porter.com

Net-A-Porter.com · 011-44-14-7332-3032

There are always those designers who are just on the fringe; hard to find and only known in tight circles, but who are making in-credible clothes. That's what makes this site so great. Here, you are given access to the catalogs of dozens of hip, young design-ers—people whose work you just won't see anywhere else…along with a few you already adore. What's more, you can read about all of them to get an idea of who they are and what they're all about. Then follow any seasonal or sale item links to go shopping for clothes by Diane von Furstenberg, Narciso Rodriguez and one of next year's favorites.

·SWIMWEAR ·ACTIVEWEAR	·SLEEPWEAR ·OUTERWEAR	·DESIGNER ·DENIM	·LINGERIE/HOSIERY

OnlyHearts.com

Only Hearts · 212-268-0886

Straddling the line between sensual and functional, this lingerie hails from the mind of designer Helena Stuart, noted to have engendered and even trademarked the notion of wearing bras and camisoles as stand-alone tops. A few of these items might sub for t-shirts in warmer seasons, but for the most part these wares best serve the woman who wants her undergarb to be comfortable enough for everyday use, yet lovely enough to keep her feeling sexy should any chance encounters arise. Browsing generally highlights fabric over styles, but a streamlined selection and great pictures keep it from becoming a hassle.

·LINGERIE/HOSIERY	·CASUAL		

Overland.com

Overland · 800-683-7526

Cold weather becomes a fashion opportunity thanks to this sheepskin, leather and fur specialist that provides a variety of smartly tailored coats and jackets for the style savvy. It's surprising how many colors and styles they can squeeze out of one material or another, especially when they incorporate mink trim and denim. You'll notice floor-length coats and waist-cut jackets, but the prices are determined more by the type of animal rather than amount of material. Either way, just about every garment will keep you feeling warm and looking cool.

·OUTERWEAR	·FUR & LEATHER	·CHIC LABELS	

310-358-1985 · The Paper Bag Princess

PaperBagPrincess.com

If you get excited by names like Prada, Chanel, Galliano, Gaultier, Pucci, Versace and Dior, this site will excite you. Vintage dresses and gowns get the most notice, as do some suits that might just be too good for any office. Shopping on this busy site turns out to be slow-loading, but otherwise easy, even if you want to shop secondhand designer fashions that have been consigned by some popular celebrities. We'll let the celebrities in question remain a mystery. Suffice it to say that poor taste has nothing to do with their contributions to this fascinating shop.

| ·CAREER ·CASUAL | ·FORMAL | ·DESIGNER | ·VINTAGE | |

213-624-9966 · Park Vogel

ParkVogel.com

You'd think it would be hard to create a unique and memorable line of such classic garments as t-shirts and cashmere sweaters, yet somehow the design duo behind this small but unforgettable line of women's apparel have more than succeeded in their quest to create "the perfect T-shirt." Instead, we find sexy, flirty tops and even a few intimate pieces that are delicate, beautiful and original. None of these clothes are likely to keep you warm on a cold night, but they will definitely keep you looking hot.

| ·LINGERIE/HOSIERY | ·CASUAL | ·CHIC LABELS | | |

310-444-0452 · Piece Unique

PieceUnique.com

It's easy to get excited by the haute couture styles to be found on this designer vintage site. Reading like a Who's Who of fashion, high-end designers such as Chanel, Gucci and Versace dominate the list of consignments here, though from time to time you'll spot something by the likes of Sonia Rykiel, Giorgio Armani and Narciso Rodriguez. Clothes are split between Recent Garments and Vintage (usually from the 60s through the 80s), with tiny thumbnail images that make it easy to notice something beautiful on this otherwise convoluted site.

| ·CAREER | ·FORMAL | ·DESIGNER | ·VINTAGE | |

800-210-8051 · Polkadots And Moonbeams

PolkaDotsAndMoonbeams.com

For a touch of vintage style without all the size-availability issues, don't miss the pages of this Los Angeles boutique. With hip modern labels that embrace retro styles, this unique assortment of jeans, dresses, skirts, jackets and tops make funky feel classic, and will definitely leave you feeling feminine and beautiful. Better yet, the menu option to View All Clothing allows you a quick peek of almost all the terrific garments; the only exceptions being the actual Vintage garb that is sometimes available, and which may even occasionally fit.

| ·OUTERWEAR | ·VINTAGE | ·DENIM | ·CHIC LABELS | |

PoshVintage.com

POSH Vintage · 305-609-6398

If you have a taste for vintage styles and nurture a healthy appreciation for high fashion, this may quickly become your favorite site. Browsing here is done on a one-product-per-page basis and though each garment is beautifully presented from multiple angles, if you try to click through the entire selection, you may wear yourself out. However, all is not as difficult as it seems. Select the Start Show link within each category, and you can sit back and watch the vintage designer dresses, jackets, lingerie or tops and bottoms flash by like a slide show, which actually works beautifully, and turns out to be quite an enjoyable experience.

·FORMAL ·VINTAGE	·DESIGNER	·LINGERIE/HOSIERY	·OUTERWEAR

RevolveClothing.com

Revolve Clothing · 888-442-5830

We can think of dozens of reasons to shop from this generously stocked purveyor of urban hipdom, three of them being: free shipping, free returns and a price-match guarantee. But most of the reasons have to do with selection, and how many chic clothing labels it presents for easy inspection and optimum allure of jeans, tops, skirts and jackets. In other words, shop here and you'll find nothing less than a weekly updated collection of highly fashionable items you may freely return if they don't fit. One day, all web shops will treat us this well.

·OUTERWEAR	·DENIM	·CASUAL	·CHIC LABELS

RigbyAndPeller.com

Rigby & Peller · 011-44-20-7491-2200

If we were to offer any advice on shopping from this London lingerie specialist it would be this: buy a lot. Not just because the uncommonly beautiful collection of bras and panties offers elegance, sex appeal and quality, but also because a flat rate for transatlantic shipping means you can add to your order but pay the same for delivery. So take some time, browse through the dozen or so desirable brands like Aubade, Lejaby, Felina and La Perla and feel free to be impressed. We were.

·LINGERIE/HOSIERY			

Roamans.com

Redcats USA · 800-459-1025

Having spent the last sixty years outfitting the plus-size woman, this store's claim to offer "fashion, fit and value" has some merit. Aside from the advertised sizes 12W-44W, the site also offers petite and tall sizes, with a selection covering everything from denim and leather apparel to outerwear, sleepwear, swimwear, formal wear, career attire and lingerie. Follow the Departments link to see a complete set of subcategories, and don't be surprised to find that each section offers a lot to choose from.

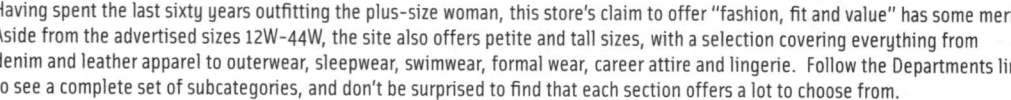   

·CAREER ·ACTIVEWEAR	·FORMAL ·OUTERWEAR	·SLEEPWEAR ·DENIM	·LINGERIE/HOSIERY ·FUR & LEATHER

866-654-4577 · Ron Herman

RonHerman.com

Ron Herman has long been known as a fashion Mecca for the extraordinarily style-conscious shoppers of Beverly Hills, and at last its must-have collection of happening upscale apparel has been made available to the web-savvy as well. An incredibly long list of brands stays impressively current, featuring names like Common Thread, Joy Ann, Miss Davenporte, Stella McCartney and Robert Rodriguez. If you're not caught up on some of the hot new designers, you can still enjoy shopping here, but you'll want to find the clothing categories menu (you might have to look at the bottom of the page).

·DESIGNER ·CHIC LABELS	·ACTIVEWEAR	·OUTERWEAR	·DENIM

503-233-2259 · Rusty Zipper Vintage Clothing

RustyZipper.com

There aren't many stores where you can find disco-style bell-bottoms, mod blouses, swing-era skirts and hippie dresses. This is just such a store. Featuring one of the best vintage apparel selections available anywhere, this site takes it a step further, offering a quick-and-easy search function that allows you to peck through thousands of items by decade, clothing article, size and price range without even a second thought. Individual items are displayed well, both in text and pictures, with special note given to the garment's condition. One word of caution: with so many styles available, try not to mix and match too much.

·SLEEPWEAR	·OUTERWEAR	·VINTAGE	·DENIM

323-655-2142 · Satine Boutique

SatineBoutique.com

Imagine the sort of shop a pair of style-savvy women might put together if they had the time and resources to scour the world for the best in new fashions. That's pretty much what you get from this west side Los Angeles boutique, which keeps a small but expressly hip selection of designer apparel for the fashion-forward young woman. At any given time you may find clothes by Jill Stuart, Catherine Fulmer and Stella McCartney, as well as a fresh list of designers you may or may not yet have heard of.

·SWIMWEAR	·DESIGNER	·DENIM	

212-753-9021 · Searle

SearleNYC.com

NYC, of course, stands for New York City, the irrefutable style center of the United States and, thanks to this site, its vantage point for fashion can now be shared with places like Omaha, Portland and Pittsburgh. We mention these cold locales in particular as they will especially appreciate the wonderful garments found here: shearling, faux shearling, down-filled and raincoats. Not only can this outerwear keep you warm, but hip as well, and a woman wearing these coats will feel confident and sexy wherever she lives, just like New York intended.

·OUTERWEAR	·FUR & LEATHER		

SeeJaneRunSports.com

See Jane Run Sports · 415-401-8338

This fitness apparel specialist might be at home in our Sports & Outdoors section, but seeing as its focus is so decidedly feminine we felt it belonged here. After all, just because a girl can find the perfect yoga outfit, great running shorts and comfortable sports bras here doesn't mean she can't also track down an easy casual top or sporty jacket. A great assortment of recognized brands may be browsed by product category, type of exercise and even by fiber, whether you wish to use these clothes for their intended purposes or for kick-around fashion's sake.

·LINGERIE/HOSIERY	·ATHLETIC	·OUTERWEAR	·CASUAL

ShopBlueGenes.com

Blue Genes · 877-469-3400

The not-so-subtle wordplay behind this shop's name refers to the three sisters who own and operate the Atlanta boutique, as well as to its deep well of designer denim. However, it's not just blue jeans you'll find here, as their selection has expanded in just a few short years to include a wide variety of beautiful and sexy designer tops, along with the occasional pants and dresses. Of course, denim is still the main attraction, and though you may want to browse by designer if you're knowledgeable about such things, simply viewing the entire terrific collection of jeans is easily worth your time.

·DESIGNER	·DENIM	·CASUAL	·CHIC LABELS

ShopBop.com

ShopBop.com · 877-746-7267

We love a shop like this one, which reminds us that fashion isn't merely glamorous, but also fun. As you browse through a long list of designers seemingly plucked from the pages of your favorite fashion magazines or wade through categories as explicit as Casual Capris, Cocktail Dresses, Cashmere, Chunky Knits, Sexy Tops and Dressy Skirts, you might suddenly look at the time to realize you've spent hours gazing rapturously upon the site's endless pages. With a lot of shopping experiences, this can be a bad thing; here, it's beautiful. In fact, you'll probably just go back for more.

·DESIGNER ·CASUAL	·ACTIVEWEAR ·CHIC LABELS	·OUTERWEAR	·DENIM

ShopIntuition.com

Intuition · 877-310-8442

This "hottest boutique in Hollywood" promises "before a trend hits the street, you can find it first at Intuition." Of course, when these clothes hit the streets, they do so on the bodies of those setting the trends: the beautiful young starlets and celebrity wives who frequent the shop. A wealth of hip-label garb and of-the-moment accessories may be found on these regularly updated pages, and in many cases you'll be told who's wearing what, and which fashion magazines flipped out as a result.

·ATHLETIC	·OUTERWEAR	·DENIM	·CHIC LABELS

888-804-0006 · Shop LA Style

ShopLAStyle.com

When this shop refers to Los Angeles style, it's not kidding. Its wealth of established and emerging designers all call LA home, and while New York City may be more commonly associated with upscale fashion, a colorful site proves that the West Coast is impossible to ignore. C&C California, True Religion and Louis Verdad are only some of the hot labels filling the comprehensive assortment of sassy tees, tops, jackets, jeans, dresses and jewelry, and though browsing by designer or category is easy enough, you'll want to wade through the dozens of pages to see all of these fantastic creations before you're through.

| ·DESIGNER | ·OUTERWEAR | ·DENIM | ·CASUAL | |

888-409-9100 · ShopTwigs

ShopTwigs.com

This Madison, Wisconsin, boutique was created to bring New York City fashion sensibilities to the Midwest, and now that it's a website it's bringing them worldwide. A very carefully selected collection includes sophisticated women's apparel by the likes of Milly, Lilly Pulitzer and Tocca, and the fine variety of clothing might even be outdone by the designer handbags and jewelry. It's the sort of shop that can cater to your casual and dressier moments, and if this sense of style appeals to you, we're betting you'll be back.

| ·FORMAL
·FUR & LEATHER | ·DESIGNER | ·ACTIVEWEAR | ·OUTERWEAR | |

888-651-8337 · Silhouettes

Silhouettes.com

For the full-figured lady of slightly conservative tastes, this thorough and well-designed site offers easy browsing through a selection of clothes ranging from underwear to outerwear. Don't get the wrong idea—it's not that this stuff isn't sexy. As the name would suggest, most of these items are quite shapely and flattering. However, the catalog does tend to opt for simplicity over extravagance, making it a valuable source for professional attire, as well as stuff like sundresses or nice slacks. If you like the clothes, you will love the prices.

| ·CAREER | ·SLEEPWEAR | ·LINGERIE/HOSIERY | ·ACTIVEWEAR | |

866-627-7325 · SizeAppeal.com

SizeAppeal.com

The term *Size Appeal* here is complemented by sections named Sex Appeal and Chic Appeal, which should start to give you an idea of this apparel catalog's range. Seeming to understand better than anyone that confidence is the most alluring aspect of style, the founder of this site offers esteem in the form of fashionably cut fabrics, with often titillating results. Railing against the overzealous modesty of other plus-size lines of clothing, funky and sexy attitudes combine here for one hell of a sassy selection.

| ·FORMAL | ·ACTIVEWEAR | | | |

SleepyHeads.com

On its own, sleeping is nothing to be very excited about. With the help of this loungewear specialty site, you'll be eager to nap at all points of the day, if only to show off your bed attire. With a great variety of styles ranging from classic looks to funky patterns, the pajamas, nightgowns and robes found here can keep you warm on a cold night or cozy on a cool one, but always looking good. Touchable fabrics like flannel, terrycloth and silk add to the allure of this sleepwear, so don't be surprised if you wind up buying several pairs.

·SLEEPWEAR

SouthMoonUnder.com

About as colorful a selection of apparel as you're likely to find anywhere, this casually chic retailer happens to come from Maryland. Regardless of its origins, the sunny boutique features affordable, style-savvy tops, dresses and jeans you might more closely associate with the summery tastes of Florida or California. Easy browsing makes the scattered corresponding selection of jewelry, accessories, bikinis and shoes worth a look, but if you stick to the clothes you'll be more likely to come away happy.

·SWIMWEAR ·DENIM ·CASUAL ·CHIC LABELS

StaplesOnline.com

When a selection of underwear is this small and this simple, it better be good. Well, these silk undergarments for men and women promise to be just that, ranging from supremely comfortable long underwear to exceedingly smooth thongs and a few products involving more or less of the luxurious fabric. Many sizes are represented, and most items are available in a variety of colors, but we'd have to say the best part is that nothing here is overpriced; in fact, you'll rarely find such a bargain for something that feels so indulgent.

  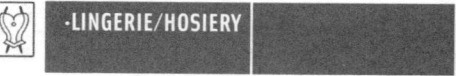 

·LINGERIE/HOSIERY

StockinGirl.com

As slow and difficult as this site can be, the web would be a lesser place without it. That's because the selection of tights, stockings and hosiery here is big enough to satisfy any of your legging needs. To give you an idea, the stockings come in fishnet, printed, with seams, thigh high, with lace tops and in a variety of colors, and on occasion you may even find some sparkles to be had. Once you've dressed your legs, you can undress the rest of you with an assortment of lingerie including garter belts, bustiers and corsets. Once these products are delivered, romance will not be far behind.

·LINGERIE/HOSIERY

800-726-8344 · **Sun Walters**

SunWalters.com

"Aimed at fashion forward shoppers looking for a chic alternative to the larger shopping venues," this Los Angeles–based online boutique endeavors to serve up "an uncommon assortment of labels and designers," handpicked for quality and value. Insofar as these tops, dresses, pants and skirts never fail to be sassy, funky and original, we'd have to say they've succeeded. And while you may not yet readily know chic labels like Beau Bois, Jenny Han and Tulle, spend just a little bit of time here, and you won't forget them.

·ACTIVEWEAR	·CASUAL	·CHIC LABELS	

   WISH

866-900-7929 · **Sway & Cake**

SwayAndCake.com

Cute and *sassy* are probably the best words to describe the selection of youthful, hip apparel available from this online boutique. Boasting some of the best-loved chic labels out there, this one also sees fit to include a few we're not used to seeing, such as Mackage, Min Chan, Issa London, Rachel Pally and L.A.M.B. It's a great source of sexy dresses and tops for day or night, and also features flirty jackets, adorable bottoms, trendy denim and a T-Shirt Shop that proves indispensable to the cool, casual chick.

·CASUAL	·CHIC LABELS		

  WISH

912-786-0522 · **Sweet Dreams**

SweetDreamsPJs.com

Nobody wants to spend a lot of time shopping for loungewear, and thanks to this site no woman has to. The choices are so simple, you could make them in your sleep. Start by choosing from the four basic designs: robe, chemise, drawstring pants or pajamas. Then, select from a variety of colors and patterns, nearly all of which include cute patterns and lovely color combinations, and are very well depicted and quite easy to view and compare. All that's left is to choose your size, and just like that, you're finished.

·SLEEPWEAR			

866-794-6123 · **SwimwearExpress**

SwimwearExpress.com

The proprietors of this online bikini specialist "know that swimwear is fashion," which is why they're proud to feature designer swimsuits you might have seen in magazines such as "*Glamour, Lucky, Marie Claire, Vogue, Elle Girl, Seventeen, Cosmopolitan* and *Sports Illustrated's* Swimsuit Issue." The site's design requires you to view this sexy beachwear by brand, which means you'll have to click back and forth between pages, but browsing is otherwise easy, with colorful images of gorgeous models proving once and for all that bikinis will never go out of style.

·SWIMWEAR			

Tarsian.com

Forget about the fact that these garments are hand stitched by Afghani women, and ask yourself whether these clothes look good. The answer will probably be a resounding *Yes*. Inspired by traditional Central Asian sewing techniques and styles, these exotic yet contemporary and accessible dresses, blouses, pants and skirts are gorgeous, and sure to be unique wherever you might wear them. That supporting this label means helping to revitalize a long-brutalized culture in a time of flux is just a bonus, a concept the proprietors of this site refer to as "conscientiously chic."

 ·ACTIVEWEAR

Tee-Zone.com

Offering shirts of short sleeve, long sleeve, three-quarter sleeve, shrunken sleeve, crew neck, V-neck, scoop neck, roll neck, turtleneck, boat neck, camisole, tank and surplice, this site can make the simple jeans-and-a-t-shirt look a little more complicated in the morning. It will be worth it, though, when you get a look at the assortment of high-quality casual garments offered by this niche retailer that features a lengthy list of chic labels. Pretty soon, this simple look is going to be your most versatile.

 ·DENIM ·CASUAL

Teski.com

While you won't find a lot to look at on this leather specialist's site, you will find a lot to consider. Take, for example, a red-and-black kimono-style leather coat, some sleek low-rise lambskin pants or a suede string-bikini top. Of course, most of the products are jackets, both long and short, feisty and elegant, and each is priced within reason. The label describes "diverse cultures and lifestyles" as the primary inspiration for this collection, and if the products we've described don't show it, just wait until the next batch of seasonal offerings comes along.

 ·SWIMWEAR ·ACTIVEWEAR ·OUTERWEAR ·FUR & LEATHER

TheFashionPulse.com

Are you serious about staying on the cutting edge of fashion? This site is, and its earnest attempt to keep customers informed as well as looking fabulous makes it a great candidate for a bookmark in your browser, even if you choose not to buy anything. Offering a great mix of young established and on-the-horizon designers, along with brief biographies for each, the boutique includes ever-changing selections of dresses, jeans, tops and jackets, complemented nicely by designer shoes and handbags. Ultimately, it proves a valuable window into emerging, avant-garde trends and previews next season's looks for all to see, even those in the suburbs.

 ·DESIGNER ·OUTERWEAR ·DENIM ·CHIC LABELS

800-342-4448 · Title 9 Sports

Title9Sports.com

Frustrated by sports gear that didn't fit right because it had been designed for men, the founder of Title 9 Sports wanted to establish a place where a woman could find athletic apparel that suited the needs of her body's shape and size. The result is a perfect match for active women. A great selection of workout shorts, shoes, tanks and pullovers are easy to find here, all designed for women, to suit a variety of sports. This also may be the best place anywhere to buy a sports bra, as they're split based on size and circumstance, with a barbell ratings system to let you know how well other women have enjoyed a particular model.

·LINGERIE/HOSIERY	·ATHLETIC			

011-44-870-220-0460 · Toast

ToastByPost.co.uk

A deeply ingrained understanding of how to dress well despite the elements give the British an edge on cold, wet days, but thanks to the online selection of this distinctively English clothier we can all enjoy a fashionable rainy day wardrobe. Muted earth tones and warm fabrics prevail here, with classically styled dresses, coats and sweaters—you'll even find a nice variety of Wellington boots to keep your feet dry in the cutest way possible. Transatlantic shipping costs may give you pause, but if your weather forecast calls for ugly days ahead, it might be better to order sooner than later.

·ACTIVEWEAR	·OUTERWEAR	·CASUAL		

866-867-7431 · Torrid Plus Sizes

Torrid.com

The name of this plus-size specialty shop might refer to its selection of flirty tops, sexy dresses and sizzling lingerie for the full-figured woman. While we're no longer surprised to find such elegantly lurid plus-size garb online, we are a bit taken aback by how affordably this shop manages to do it. With only a small investment, you can put together an entire wardrobe of cute and sassy outfits, whether you're casually kicking around town, out for a wild night or attending a more sophisticated affair. Torrid or not, this one's got fun written all over it.

·FORMAL ·OUTERWEAR	·SLEEPWEAR ·DENIM	·LINGERIE/HOSIERY ·CASUAL	·ACTIVEWEAR	

212-334-3000 · Tory by TRB

ToryLtd.com

For chic and clean sportswear that won't show up on everyone you know, check the wares of designer Tory Burch, available exclusively in her New York City flagship store and on this, her web site. The small but riveting selection favors clean lines, sensual fabrics and subdued colors, comprising a trim and ultimately stylish appeal that speaks volumes about self-confidence and femininity, with only a whisper of sexuality. With luck, Burch will find time to expand her smart collection someday soon.

·ACTIVEWEAR	·OUTERWEAR	·CHIC LABELS		

TraceyRoss.com

Tracey Ross · 877-887-2239

One of the top draws of West Hollywood's ultra upscale Sunset Plaza shopping district, this hot boutique is no stranger to a celebrity clientele, which can only be attributed to the fabulous collection of designer garb it offers. Names such as Blue Blood, Daslu, Chloe, Hazel Brown and Nicholas K are just some of the recent labels to catch the attention of tabloid mainstays like Lindsay Lohan, Jessica Simpson and Mandy Moore. With this equally well-stocked web site (complete with designer jewelry and shoes), we may not all be able to spend money like a Hollywood starlet, but with a little bit of good credit we can still shop like one.

	·DESIGNER	·OUTERWEAR		

Trashy.com

Trashy Lingerie · 310-659-4550

With a name like Trashy Lingerie, there's not a whole lot we can really say that you haven't already figured out for yourself; and there are certainly few surprises here. One that may interest you is the lavish selection of robes and pajamas, in materials like satin and silk. But if that's not your idea of trashy apparel, maybe sections devoted to Leather, Lace and Vinyl will be more to your liking. And fellas, thanks to a Shop With Our Models feature, you may find a girl resembling your lady's shape and coloring and get a very general idea of what the garment will look like on her. Just don't let on that you did.

	·SLEEPWEAR	·LINGERIE/HOSIERY		

Triple5Soul.com

Triple 5 Soul · 718-218-9066

The fifteen-year history of this Brooklyn-grown brand/retailer may be plotted by the list of hip hop luminaries that have passed through its doors (from Fab 5 Freddy to Mos Def). Street cred aside, the smooth layout and stylish apparel exhibited by this site is enough to warrant a glance from anyone looking to enhance her wardrobe without any second-guesswork. Hoodies, sweaters and jackets offer the best sampling of styles available here, while backpacks and record bags highlight the accessories section. This site works.

	·ATHLETIC	·OUTERWEAR	·CASUAL	

Unique-Vintage.com

Unique Vintage · 626-437-4626

Though not without its difficulties, this site clearly does offer a unique selection of dresses to fans of retro chic. Although we can't always tell by browsing which items are vintage reproductions and which are the real thing, the designs are always genuine enough to suit the look you're after, whether your partial to 1920s style flapper frocks, 1950s A-line dresses, 1960s chiffon gowns or any other memorable and iconic fashion statements of the past. Unfortunately, browsing requires sifting through the full collection of outfits ten at a time, and sizing is very specific for each garment. You might have an easier time in the sites Shoes & Accessories section.

	·FORMAL	·DESIGNER	·VINTAGE	

866-940-4402 · Vibe the boutique

VibeTheBoutique.com

This style-savvy web boutique wants to know if you are "sick of looking through those tired department store fashions?" If the answer is yes, you can waste almost no time at all here browsing quickly through a deep selection of trendy apparel featuring dozens of popular, of-the-moment labels. We're particularly smitten with the dozens of adorable, sassy and outright sexy dresses, but you'll find great tops, denim jackets and no shortage of designer jeans. Visit this site often and looking around becomes even easier as you may simply view the latest additions to the regularly updated wares. Staying hip should really require more effort than this.

| ·ACTIVEWEAR | ·OUTERWEAR | ·DENIM | ·CHIC LABELS | |

877-887-7707 · White + Warren

WhiteAndWarren.com

If you love cashmere—even if you just kind of like it—you will love the clothes offered by this modern luxury line. Even when they stick to the most basic sweater design it looks good, but it's when the company cofounders add some personality to the items that these cardigans, tunics, crew necks and V-necks become irresistible. Where the limited number of designs end your choice of colors begins, and though you'll be more likely to find what you like in a pastel range, the occasional flash of purple certainly captured our attention.

| ·ACTIVEWEAR | | | | |

877-935-5728 · Yellow Rat Bastard

YellowRatBastard.com

Its name may not inspire a lot of confidence, but this urban-trends site offers a deep selection of hip and underground design brands, as well as a few global giants like Adidas, Puma and Levi's. Primarily, though, category browsing calls up a hefty number of pants, jeans, skirts, tops, tees and sweaters, as well as a solid selection of jackets, hoodies and vests. Its design is a bit clunky, and its intentions questionable, but this store that grew out of an alternative-lifestyles magazine easily has something for somebody, if not everything for anybody.

| ·ATHLETIC
·CHIC LABELS | ·OUTERWEAR | ·DENIM | ·CASUAL | |

011-612-9986-3188 · Zodee

Zodee.com

Almost certainly the most comprehensive online lingerie, hosiery, swimsuit and athletic apparel web shop ever to come out of Australia, this site has two things going for it that will help overcome any anxiety you may have about ordering intimate apparel from such a long distance. First, and quite simply, the prices are great. Second, the selection is huge, and every time you find one great product your eyes might easily catch another. The convenience of this selection may not be what you'd expect from the land that brought us Yahoo Serious, but you'll love it nonetheless.

| ·SWIMWEAR | ·SLEEPWEAR | ·LINGERIE/HOSIERY | ·ATHLETIC | |

NOTES:

Charity

While the number of sites listed in this section makes up only a small fraction of the entire book, it's our sincere hope that 10 percent of your time and disposable income will be spent while browsing these pages. While our primary purpose is to highlight the outstanding shopping opportunities afforded us by the internet, we can't help noting that charitable organizations stand the most to gain from e-commerce.

Aside from making it extraordinarily easy for us to give, the web makes it possible for us to track down those charities that work closest to our hearts, however specific the cause may be. Whether your fight is to stamp out hunger, sustain the environment, protect children, fight disease, defend animals from extinction or promote life and liberty, altruism has never been so ready at hand. To the battle against apathy we contribute the following pages and a simple plea: do your part. Committing your time, energy and cash won't just improve your karma, it feels good. Find new ways to contribute, discover new causes that could use your efforts, include your children. After all, it now takes only a couple of moments to save the world if you do it one small piece at a time.

A TIP ON DONATING ONLINE

• **RESEARCH BEFORE YOU DONATE** • If you're in any doubt about the veracity of a charity, online or otherwise, use some of the helpful sites below to determine how active the charity is, how it uses contributions, whether donations are tax deductible and generally whether the organization is legitimate.

SITES THAT MAY COME IN HANDY

The following URLs may be useful before making online donations.

CharityNavigator.org	Charity evaluations
GuideStar.org	Reports on nonprofit organizations' activities and finances
Idealist.org	Volunteer resources
independentCharities.org	Charity evaluator
IRS.gov/charities	Tax exemptions and deductions information

SECTION ICON LEGEND

Use the following guide to understand the rectangular icons that appear throughout this section.

ANIMAL CHARITIES
One kind of animal-related charity aims to protect endangered species from extinction; another tries to protect a populous species from abuse. There are plenty of organizations focusing on different animal issues found here.

CHILDREN'S CHARITIES
This icon indicates that a charity focuses on the needs of children in particular, whether relating to health, poverty, domestic abuse or educational concerns, national or international.

CHARITY NETWORKS
These sites offer donation collection services for hundreds, sometimes thousands, of different charitable organizations, spanning dozens of general and specific causes. Granting a place for those organizations that might not otherwise afford an online presence, these sites can guide you quickly to the charity that matters most to you.

ENVIRONMENTAL CHARITIES
The bulk of these charities attempt to preserve the natural resources of the planet from pollution, industrialization and other ecological threats, through public policy influence and/or grassroots mobilization.

DOMESTIC ISSUES
The US Constitution provides a system of checks and balances within our federal government, but the price of influence has gone up over the past 200 years, and charitable organizations have sprung up to provide a voice strong enough for government officials to hear, tackling a range of domestic civil and legal issues.

HEALTH CHARITIES
Despite the advancements of modern medicine, countless health issues remain a great cause for concern. Activities of these organizations raise funds for research into cures, focus on public policy/awareness and/or attempt to increase the quality of life of those afflicted.

PEOPLE IN NEED
If we're shopping online we pretty much by definition have it good. Realizing, however, that others in the world, even in our own communities, sometimes need a little assistance, these charities work to combat poverty, end famine, provide disaster relief and much more.

AAH-USA.org

Action Against Hunger · 877-777-1420

With programs active in more than forty countries, this organization works to end famine, with the objective "to help vulnerable populations regain their self-sufficiency for long-term sustainability."

AchievementCenters.org

Achievement Centers for Children · 216-292-9700

Recognizing that early development is of particular importance to children with disabilities, this Cleveland, Ohio–based center works with families and provides education and therapies to "tap into each child's unique potential."

ACLU.org

American Civil Liberties Union · 888-567-2258

For more than eight decades this organization has worked through public advocacy and legal activism to protect every American's civil rights, as outlined in the Bill of Rights.

AIDSResearch.org

AIDS Research Alliance · 310-358-2423

The charitable organization behind this site accepts donations to support its continued research toward "identifying more effective treatments and a cure for HIV/AIDS."

AidToArtisans.org

Aid To Artisans · 860-947-3344

In response to market demand for cultural artifacts, this organization fosters "artistic traditions and cultural vitality" in developing nations. In particular, its outreach programs target women and help direct their craftsmanship into economic independence.

ALZ.org

Alzheimer's Association · 800-272-3900

This site collects donations to support continued research into a cure for Alzheimer's disease, and to offer support to those afflicted and their families.

800-242-8721 · American Heart Association
AmericanHeart.org

This longstanding organization supports research, prevention and education in efforts "to reduce disability and death from cardio-vascular diseases and stroke."

800-392-6327 · American Foundation for AIDS Research
AmfAR.org

This site offers information and accepts donations to support AIDS research, prevention, education and public policy awareness.

212-807-8400 · Amnesty International
Amnesty.org

This site gathers support for the agency's international efforts to uncover and prevent human rights abuses, by offering information and collecting donations.

406=585-3527 · Architecture for Humanity
ArchitectureForHumanity.org

When tsunamis, hurricanes or other infrastructure-damaging events take place, this organization is there to help rebuild, connecting affected people with volunteers, architects and designers, and engaging in public advocacy to promote intelligent urban planning.

212-876-7700 · ASPCA
ASPCA.org

The American Society for the Prevention of Cruelty to Animals is one of the nation's foremost organizations devoted to promoting and protecting the needs of animals big and small.

212-979-3000 · National Audubon Society
Audubon.org

This site supports conservation and restoration of nature (particularly in relation to wildlife) through gifts, membership and merchandise sales.

AvonCrusade.com

Avon · 800-367-2866

This charitable branch of the cosmetics company focuses on raising money for breast cancer research, as well as care and support for its victims, by taking online donations.

BBBSA.org

Big Brothers Big Sisters of America · 215-567-7000

Collecting donations to support its volunteer mentor program, this group has been connecting children of single parents with adult role models for a century.

Cancer.org

American Cancer Society · 800-227-2345

One of the leading supporters of cancer research and prevention, this organization uses donations to fund educational outreach programs as well as the search for better treatments.

CareUSA.org

CARE · 800-422-7385

This international humanitarian effort works to stem the tide of famine and disease in developing nations by combining "immediate food aid with programs that create long-term solutions."

CharityGift.com

Charity Gifts · 877-972-4438

Turning charity into a gifting venture, this site essentially offers gift certificates that your recipient can spend on his or her charity of choice, choosing among thousands in every conceivable field and locality.

CityOfHope.org

City of Hope · 626-256-4673

Donations to this site help operate a medical research center dedicated to discovering cures for cancer, AIDS, diabetes and other dire illnesses.

703-525-6300 · The Conservation Fund

ConservationFund.org

This is a large and efficient organization that has had success in converting financial contributions into protection for wildlife habitat and watersheds.

800-999-9999 · Covenant House

CovenantHouse.com

This group provides shelter and services to homeless and runaway youths in cities domestically and internationally, in part with the help of donations to this site.

800-458-6223 · National Childhood Cancer Foundation

CureSearch.org

Devoted to public awareness, prevention and research into a cure, this cancer-fighting organization pays special attention to the needs of sick children.

859-441-7300 · Disabled American Veterans

DAV.org

Offering you a chance to give back to those fighting men and women who gave so much for our country, this organization collects donations to support family assistance and public advocacy for disabled vets.

800-342-2383 · American Diabetes Organization

Diabetes.org

It's this group's mission "to prevent and cure diabetes and to improve the lives of all people affected by diabetes" by funding research, education and public advocacy.

541-826-9220 · Dogs for the Deaf

DogsForTheDeaf.org

Rescuing "healthy, friendly, intelligent, and energetic" stray dogs from animal shelters, this group trains them to assist the hearing impaired.

DWB.org

Doctors Without Borders · 212-679-6800

This organization sends volunteer doctors worldwide to provide urgent medical relief to victims of natural or man-made catastrophes; donations fund supplies and transportation.

EarthWatch.org

Earthwatch Institute · 800-776-0188

Accepting volunteers and donations, this global organization pursues environmental field studies to collect scientific data used to advocate sustainable practices as well as ecological awareness and conservancy.

EdReform.com

The Center for Education Reform · 202-822-9000

Supporting a variety of teachers' unions and advocacy groups, this organization is committed to educational reform in America, promoting a diverse array of progressive educational techniques and initiatives.

FreshAir.org

Fresh Air Fund · 800-367-0003

Donations to the Fresh Air Fund sponsor nature excursions for inner-city children who would otherwise have limited access to the beauty of the outdoors.

GildasClub.com

Gilda's Club Worldwide · 888-445-3248

Inspired by and named for comedienne Gilda Radner, this organization accepts donations to help provide places for cancer sufferers and their families to find emotional support.

GlobalChild.org

Global Children's Organization · 310-581-2234

This international organization "nurtures children traumatized by intolerance, terrorism, or war" by providing summer programs to promote peace, optimism and emotional healing.

888-811-5271 · The Hunger Site Network

GreaterGood.com

This site links you to many online retailers, wherein a commission on your purchases will go to your choice of charities, including the Humane Society and the March of Dimes.

202-462-1177 · Greenpeace International

Greenpeace.org

"With a presence in 40 countries," this global organization has been pursuing nonviolent, creative activism to promote environmental protection and preservation.

800-295-4050 · Guide Dogs for the Blind

GuideDogs.com

Accepting donations and volunteers, this organization raises and trains guide dogs to assist the visually impaired throughout the US and Canada.

888-483-8180 · Hugs for Homeless Animals

H4HA.org

Donations to this organization assist them in their work to find homes for unplaced pets, including support of shelters and humane societies.

229-924-6935 · Habitat for Humanity

Habitat.org

Donations to this international activism group purchases materials and supports volunteer efforts to build homes for people in need.

800-422-0474 · Heifer International

Heifer.org

Contributions to this organization allow the procurement of farm animals and assistance to impoverished agricultural families world-wide, to help promote self-sufficiency.

HSUS.org

The Humane Society of the U.S. · 202-452-1100

This longstanding national organization accepts donations so that it can continue its work rescuing animals and protecting their environments.

JustGive.org

JustGive.org · 866-587-8448

Making it easy to locate a cause you favor, this online network of over 800,000 charities aims to make the donation process efficient and satisfying.

Komen.org

Susan G. Komen Foundation · 800-462-9273

For more than two decades, this organization has aided the fight against breast cancer "through its support of innovative research and community-based outreach programs."

Landmines.org

Adopt-A-Minefield · 212-907-1300

This site accepts donations and sells merchandise to raise money toward clearing deadly landmines from war-ravaged countries.

LiveStrong.org

Lance Armstrong Foundaton · 866-235-7205

Lance Armstrong isn't just a symbol of hope against cancer; with this organization dedicated to education, advocacy and research, the legendary cyclist uses his global stature to pursue better options for those "living with, through or beyond" the disease.

MDAUSA.org

Muscular Dystrophy Association · 800-572-1717

A "dedicated partnership between scientists and concerned citizens," this organization funds research to stop the effects of neuro-muscular diseases, notably through Jerry Lewis's telethons.

800-292-3355 · Mercy Corps   **MercyCorps.org**

This global nonprofit accepts donations to help provide emergency relief, social justice and humanitarian support to troubled communities at home and abroad, including the development of sustainable agriculture and economies.

800-708-7644 · Michael J Fox Parkinson's Foundation   **MichaelJFox.org**

This foundation, started by the television star, funds aggressive research into Parkinson's Disease, with the objective of finding a cure within the next ten years.

888-989-6667 · Million Mom March   **MillionMomMarch.org**

With product purchase or donation you can support this grassroots movement to prevent gun violence, through advocacy of gun control laws and large public demonstrations.

914-428-7100 · March of Dimes   **MODimes.org**

Founded by FDR during the Great Depression to combat polio, the March of Dimes today works to prevent birth defects, and accepts donations in all denominations.

212-379-6348 · MOUSE   **Mouse.org**

Contributions to Making Opportunities for Upgrading Schools and Education go toward helping the New York City public school system keep abreast of technological advancements in the classroom.

410-521-4939 · NAACP   **NAACP.org**

In addition to news and information about the organization, the National Association for the Advancement of Colored People site takes member dues to support civil rights efforts.

NationalMSSociety.org

National Multiple Sclerosis Society · 800-344-4867

This organization seeks volunteers and donations to help support advocacy and research for the treatment of multiple sclerosis, as well as support programs designed to aid new and long-term sufferers of the disease.

Nature.org

The Nature Conservancy · 800-628-6860

This international organization "dedicated to preserving the diversity of life on Earth" works to protect natural ecosystems from development and pollution.

NDVH.org

National Domestic Violence Hotline · 800-799-7233

This group raises funds to support a telephone hotline that exists to counsel and assist victims of domestic violence.

NESsTorg

NESsT · 209-988-9604

Standing for Nonprofit Enterprise and Self-sustainability Team, this organization should appeal to those who want struggling or developing nations to receive assistance in the form of economic and entrepreneurial training, so future aid may be unnecessary.

NetworkForGood.org

Network for Good · 703-242-9200

This site was established to increase the awareness and funds for hundreds of thousands of charities that might not otherwise have a web presence, including local organizations.

NMFA.org

National Military Family Association · 800-260-0218

Military folk face a unique set of problems, and this group helps protect the interests of military personnel and their families, through education, support and public advocacy, during peace or in wartime.

877-762-3262 · Oceana

Oceana.org

This organization was created "with the sole purpose of protecting the world's oceans," both from pollution and environmentally destructive fishing practices.

888-677-6453 · Operation Smile

OperationSmile.org

Sending volunteers around the globe to perform reconstructive surgeries, this group endeavors to improve the lives of children by repairing facial deformities.

800-678-7255 · Operation USA

OpUSA.org

This "small but growing international relief and development charity" has provided disaster relief around the world for almost thirty years, and donations support continuing efforts to assist those affected by tsunamis, earthquakes, hurricanes and pandemics.

571-203-0270 · The Orphan Foundation of America

Orphan.org

Parentless teens face a difficult road into adulthood, so this very important organization tried to alleviate the pressures through public advocacy for foster youth, and particularly by helping children achieve a postsecondary education.

877-727-7467 · Public Broadcasting System

PBS.org

This nationwide nonprofit media organization increasingly relies on private donations to produce much of its public programming.

888-499-4673 · Glaser Pediatric AIDS Foundation

PedAIDS.org

Although particularly devoted to stopping the spread of HIV and AIDS to babies and young children, this organization actually works to treat and eradicate all pediatric diseases.

Ploughshares.org

Ploughshares Fund · 415-775-2244

This organization administers grants with the objective to support "initiatives for stopping the spread of weapons of war, from nuclear arms to land mines."

POFSEA.org

Prosthetics Outreach Foundation · 206-726-1636

Donations to this organization's site are applied toward outfitting people in impoverished and/or war-torn nations, including children, with prosthetic limbs.

ReachOutandRead.org

Reach Out and Read · 617-629-8842

This organization promotes literacy in children by supplying books to impoverished children aged six months to five years through pediatric offices.

RedCross.org

The Red Cross · 202-303-4498

The site for this trusted international charity accepts donations to support its constant human and natural disaster relief efforts and offers information on giving blood.

RI.org

Relief International · 310-478-1200

Responding to all manner of disasters internationally, this relief organization supports "long-term developmental needs of its beneficiaries even while in the emergency phase."

RIF.org

Reading Is Fundamental · 877-743-7323

Designed to promote children's interest in reading, This program focuses on at-risk communities, accepting donations to buy and distribute books and calling for volunteers to help encourage literacy.

800-728-3843 · Save the Children USA

SaveTheChildren.org

Working to help impoverished, neglected and undereducated children in forty-five countries (including our own), this site seeks assistance in the form of donations and child sponsorship.

888-426-7979 · Shelter For Life International

Shelter.org

Whether due to tsunami, earthquake, fire, flooding, war or other catastrophe, people the world over are displaced from their homes year after year. This organization seeks to provide relief in the form of temporary shelter and placement.

415-977-5500 · Sierra Club

SierraClub.org

"America's oldest, largest and most influential grassroots environmental organization," it is the Sierra Club's mission to "explore, enjoy and protect the planet." It does so through public advocacy, volunteership and with the help of its members' donation.

334-956-8200 · Southern Poverty Law Center

SPLCenter.org

This civil rights organization applies donations to its work toward educating people about tolerance, as well as toward promoting justice and equality in the legal system.

800-822-6344 · St. Jude Children's Research Hospital

StJude.org

This world-class pediatric treatment-and-research facility helps cover the cost of medical treatments for children whose families cannot afford to pay alone.

800-969-4767 · Share Our Strength

Strength.org

With your donations, this group (also known as SOS) "mobilizes individuals and industries" to use their resources to curtail hunger and poverty at home and abroad.

TeachForAmerica.org

Teach For America · 800-832-1230

The political demand for better and more equitable public education has been longstanding and controversial, but rather than over-haul the system this organization simply matches educated, altruistic young teachers with poverty-stricken schools.

UNCF.org

United Negro College Fund · 800-331-2244

Probably best known for its slogan, "A mind is a terrible thing to waste," this organization has more importantly been supporting the postsecondary education of minority youth for more than sixty years, including at doctoral and postdoctoral levels.

UNHCR.org

UN Refugee Agency · 011-41-22-739-8111

This organization assists refugees worldwide by providing living assistance and lobbying governments on refugee-related issues.

UNICEFUSA.org

United Nations Children's Fund · 800-486-4233

Through donations and gift card sales, this US arm of UNICEF helps support the global organization's efforts to save children's lives.

UpwardlyGlobal.com

Upwardly Global · 415-834-9901

This nonprofit helps match qualified immigrant professionals with employers here in the United States. Ways to help include volun-teering and offering employment opportunities.

USVariety.org

Variety — The Children's Charity · 888-852-1300

This organization helps provide medical resources and funds health care for children in need all over the world.

888-841-4687 · VH1 Save The Music

VH1.com

Look to the bottom left of this music channel's site to find the Save the Music link, which explains how you can contribute to a program to buy instruments for the music programs of low-budget schools nationwide.

415-241-6855 · Volunteer Match

VolunteerMatch.org

Linked to more than 20,000 nonprofit organizations nationwide, this site offers searches for local volunteer opportunities in fields from public broadcasting to homeless aid.

718-220-5100 · Wildlife Conservation Society

WCS.org

This global group protects wildlife and their habitats "through careful science, international conservation, education, and the management of the world's largest system of urban wildlife parks."

800-722-9474 · Make a Wish Foundation

Wish.org

"Granting the heartfelt wishes of children" who face life-threatening medical conditions, donations help this group fund activities that raise their spirits and put smiles on their faces.

646-424-9594 · World Monuments Fund

WorldMonuments.org

"Dedicated to the preservation of historic art and architecture worldwide," this organization strives to sustain our cultural landscape through fieldwork, advocacy and education.

800-225-5993 · World Wildlife Fund

WorldWildlife.org

Spearheading "international efforts to protect endangered species and their habitats," this fifty-year-old organization has operations in more than a hundred countries, dedicated to preserving wildlife diversity on our planet.

NOTES:

_____
_____
_____
_____
_____
_____
_____
_____
_____
_____
_____
_____
_____
_____
_____
_____
_____
_____

thepurplebook product index

gadgets

• Product Index •

NOTES:

NOTES:

thepurplebook company index

J

k

K&L Wine Merchants	KAndL.com, 137
k_bee Leotards	K-BeeLeos.com, 464
Kaleidovisions	KaleidoVisions.com, 500
Kalustyan's	Kalustyans.com, 137
Karaoke Warehouse	KaraokeWH.com, 101
KarateDepot.com	KarateDepot.com, 464
Karmaloop	KarmaLoop.com, 314
Kate's Paperie	KatesPaperie.com, 500
Kenmore Stamp Co.	KenmoreStamps.com, 41
Kid's Decor	KidsDecor.net, 346
KidRobot	KidRobot.com, 41
Kids First Internet	KidsFirstInternet.org, 347
Killer Dana	KillerDana.com, 314
King Size	KingSizeDirect.com, 314
Kitazawa Seed Company	KitazawaSeed.com, 238
Kitchen Krafts	KitchenKrafts.com, 68
Kitson	ShopKitson.com, 275
Kittos Marimekko	KiitosMarimekko.com, 579
Kiyonna	Kiyonna.com, 579
Kmart	KMart.com, 271
Knit Witts Yarns & Patterns	KnitWitts.com, 69
Kokopelli's Green Market	KokoGM.com, 271
Kolobags	KoloBags.com, 426
Korin Japanese Trading Corp.	Korin.com, 238
Koshermeal.com	KosherMeal.com, 137
Kultic	Kultic.com, 315

l

L'Atelier Vert	FrenchGardening.com, 230
L'avenue des Bébés	Avenue-Des-Bebes.com, 288
L'épicerie	Lepicerie.com, 138
L.P. Thur Fabrics	FabricsAndHome.com, 228
La Alpargateria de Aigües	EspadrillesEtc.com, 417
La La Ling	LaLaLing.com, 347
Lacrosse Unlimited	LacrosseUnltd.com, 464
Lady Primrose's	LadyPrimrose.com, 192
Lafayette 148	Lafayette148.com, 579
Lafco	LafcoNY.com, 192
Lafeber Company	Lafeber.com, 379
Lake City Craft Co.	Quilling.com, 75
Lakeland Limited	LakelandLimited.com, 239
Lakeshore Learning	LakeshoreLearning.com, 347
LampStore.com	LampStore.com, 239
Lance Armstrong Foundaton	LiveStrong.org, 606
Land of Nod	LandOfNod.com, 347
Lane Four	LaneFour.com, 465
Last Gasp	LastGasp.com, 101
lastminutetravel.com	LastMinuteTravel.com, 540
Laughing Elephant	LaughingElephant.com, 500
Laura Mady's Boucher Jewelry	BoucherJewelry.com, 414
Lavahut	LavaHut.com, 500
Lavender Fields	LavenderFieldsOnline.com, 239
Layla Grace	LaylaGrayce.com, 271
Le Train Bleu	LetrainBleu.com, 580
Le Village	LeVillage.com, 138
Leading Hotels of the World	LHW.com, 540
Lederer de Paris	LedererDeParis.com, 426
Lee Allison	LeeAllison.com, 315
Lee Valley & Veritas	LeeValley.com, 239
Leland Fly Fishing Outfitters	FlyFishingOutfitters.com, 461

Les Poochs	LesPoochs.com, 379
Let's Automate	LetsAutomate.com, 166
Let's Go Clothing & Footwear	HouseOfStyle.com, 313
Let-It-Rain.com	UmbrellaStand.com, 438
LetsTalk.com	LetsTalk.com, 166
Levenger	Levenger.com, 501
Lewis & Sheron Textile Company	LSFabrics.com, 240
Life Extension Foundation	LEF.org, 192
Life Size	LifeSizeKids.com, 348
LifeSolutionsPlus	LifeSolutionsPlus.com, 399
Light Impressions	LightImpressionsDirect.com, 69
Lightology	Lightology.com, 240
Lillian Vernon	LillianVernon.com, 348
Lilliput	LilliputMotorCompany.com, 42
Lilliput Soho Kids	LilliputSoho.com, 348
Lilly Pulitzer	InThePinkOnline.com, 577
Limited Too	LimitedToo.com, 348
Lincoln Stationers	LincolnStationers.com, 501
Linenplace.com	LinenPlace.com, 240
Lingerie-Direct	Lingerie-Direct.com, 580
LingerieAtLarge	LingerieAtLarge.com, 580
Lion Brand Yarn Company	LionBrand.com, 69
Lipmedic	LipMedic.com, 192
Lisa Kline	LisaKline.com, 580
Little Girl Dresses	LittleGirlDresses.com, 349
Liz Lange Maternity	LizLange.com, 294
Liz's Antique Hardware	LAHardware.com, 238
Lobel's of New York	Lobels.com, 138
Logis de France	Logis-De-France.fr, 540
Lomographic Society International	Lomography.com, 167
London Hotels Reservations	Hotels-London.co.uk, 538
Long Tall Sally	LongTallSally.com, 581
Longmire	Longmire.co.uk, 427
Loompanics Unlimited Online Store	Loompanics.com, 102
LorAnn Oils	LorAnnOils.com, 69
Love, Me	ShopLoveMe.com, 512
Lowe Enterprises	DestinationHotels.com, 532
Lucy	Lucy.com, 581
Luggage Online	LuggageOnline.com, 541
Lula Belle	LulaBelleToffee.com, 501
Luna Boston	LunaBoston.com, 427
Lunar Embassy	LunarEmbassy.com, 501
Lunchboxes.com	LunchBoxes.com, 349
Luscious	LusciousCargo.com, 193
Luxe Paperie	LuxePaperie.com, 502
Luxury Down Under	LuxuryDownUnder.com.au, 541
Luxury Link Traveler	LuxuryLink.com, 541
Lyn Gaylord Accessories	LynGaylord.com, 427

m

M&J Trimming	MJTrim.com, 71
m-dc	MD-Canvas.com, 42
M.S. Rau Antiques	RauAntiques.com, 46
ma jolie	MaJolie.com, 581
Mad Imports	MadImports.net, 428
Madison and Friends of Chicago	MadisonAndFriends.com, 349
Magazines.com	Magazines.com, 102
Magellan's	Magellans.com, 541
Maggs Bros Rare Books	Maggs.com, 102
Maine Cottage	MaineCottage.com, 241
Make a Wish Foundation	Wish.org, 613
Make Me Heal	MakeMeHeal.com, 193

P

S

wxyz

NOTES:

thepurplebook url index

wxyz

NOTES:

thepurplebook

submissions & feedback

Submission Guidelines:

Here at **thepurplebook**, we've viewed over 50,000 online retailers, and we're just getting warmed up. If you know of a site you think we haven't seen, or that may have been upgraded since our last visit, please visit our web site at www.thepurplebook.com and follow the submissions link. Otherwise, you may email us at submissions@thepurplebook.com, or fill out and fax this page to 0-385-8022. Please be sure to include the site URL in the email subject line. (NOTE: We will only consider sites operating with secure, functional online ordering capabilities. If a site has been recently updated or redesigned, please indicate the launch date of its current incarnation, so that we may be sure to re-evaluate it.)

Company Name: _____

Site URL:_____

Categories:

___ Art & Collectibles	___ Minors (0-18)
___ Crafts & Hobbies	___ Pets
___ Entertainment	___ Seniors
___ Eco-Friendly Shops	___ Shoes & Accessories
___ Epicurean	___ Sports & Outdoors
___ Gadgets & Electronics	___ Stationery & Gifts
___ Health & Beauty	___ Travel
___ Home & Garden	___ Weddings
___ Lifestyles & Megastores	___ Women's Apparel
___ Maternity	___ Charity
___ Men's Apparel	___ Other/Misc._____

Comments:

_____
_____
_____

Feedback:

If you have any additional comments, questions or suggestions, please send an email to: feedback@thepurplebook.com, or visit our site. Thanks in advance for your input!

www.thepurplebook.com

To learn how to use **thepurplebook** as corporate gifts or promotions, email us at: editor@thepurplebook.com